# Handbook on Sexual Violence

This book contextualises the complexity of sexual violence within its broader context – from war to the resolution of interpersonal disputes – and covers a wide span including sexual harassment, bullying, rape and murder as well as domestic violence. Written by leading academics from a variety of disciplines, contributions also include commentaries that relate the research to the work of practitioners.

Despite advances made in the investigation of sexual offences, evidence still points to a continued belief in the culpability of victims in their own victimisation and a gap between the estimated incidence of sexual violence and the conviction of perpetrators. Adopting an implicitly and explicitly critical stance to contemporary policy responses that continue to fail in addressing this problem, this book focuses on attitudes and behaviour towards sexual violence from the point of view of the individual experiencing the violence – perpetrator and victim – and situates them within a broader societal frame. It is through an understanding of social processes and psychological mechanisms that underpin sexual violence that violence can be combated and harm reduced, and at this individual level that evidence-based interventions can be designed to change policy and practice.

The Handbook is split into four sections:

1. *Legacies: Setting the Scene* offers a critical overview of historical, legal and cultural processes which help to explain the origins of current thinking and offer steers for future developments.
2. *Theoretical Perspectives on Sexual Violence* examines contemporary thinking on sexual violence and reviews explanatory frameworks from a number of perspectives.
3. *Acts of Sexual Violence* reviews a number of specific types of sexual violence, elaborating the range of circumstances, victims and perpetrators with a view to addressing the general and pervasive nature of such violence, thus contradicting narrow cultural stereotyping.
4. *Responding to Sexual Violence* overviews and evaluates current policies and practices and offers new ideas to develop different types of interventions.

The editors' conclusion not only draws out the key themes and ideas from contributions to the Handbook, but also considers the nature and the extent of the progress which has been made in understanding and responding to sexual violence.

This will be a key text for students and academics studying sexual violence and an essential reference tool for professionals working in the field including police officers, probation staff, lawyers and judges.

**Jennifer M. Brown** is the Deputy Director of the Mannheim Centre for Criminology at the London School of Economics. She previously co-edited *Rape: challenging contemporary thinking* with Miranda Horvath and the *Handbook of Forensic Psychology* with Elizabeth Campbell.

**Sandra L. Walklate** holds the Eleanor Rathbone Chair of Sociology at the University of Liverpool. She has written numerous books including *Criminology: the basics*, *Understanding Criminology: current theoretical debates* and *Imagining the Victim of Crime*.

# Handbook on Sexual Violence

Edited by

**Jennifer M. Brown and Sandra L. Walklate**

Routledge
Taylor & Francis Group

LONDON AND NEW YORK

First published 2012 by Routledge
2 Park Square, Milton Park, Abingdon, Oxon, OX14 4RN
Simultaneously published in the USA and Canada
by Routledge
711 Third Avenue, New York, NY 10017

*Routledge is an imprint of the Taylor & Francis Group, an informa business*

2012 Jennifer M. Brown and Sandra L. Walklate; individual chapters, the contributors

*British Library Cataloguing in Publication Data*
A catalogue record for this book is available from the British Library

*Library of Congress Cataloging in Publication Data*
Handbook on sexual violence / edited by Jennifer M. Brown and Sandra L. Walklate.
p. cm.
1. Sex crimes. 2. Sexual abuse victims. 3. Women–Violence against. I. Brown, Jennifer, 1948- II. Walklate, Sandra.
HV6556.H38 2012
364.15'3–dc22
2011013950

ISBN: 978-0-415-67071-5 (hbk)
ISBN: 978-0-415-67072-2 (pbk)
ISBN: 978-0-203-80243-4 (ebk)

Typeset in Palatino by PDQ Typesetting Ltd

MIX
Paper from
responsible sources
FSC® C004839
www.fsc.org

Printed and bound in Great Britain by
TJ International Ltd, Padstow, Cornwall

To Amanda Hart of Counsel
Carla Machado: an inspiration to all who knew her
and to the inspirational life and work of Corinna Seith

# Contents

# Figures and tables

## Figures

## Tables

# Abbreviations

| | |
|---|---|
| Acas | Advisory, Conciliation and Arbitration Service |
| ACPO | Association of Chief Police Officers |
| BCS | British Crime Survey |
| CA | Children Act 1989 |
| CBT | Cognitive behavioural therapy |
| CDVP | Community Domestic Violence Programme |
| CEDAW | United Nations Committee on the Elimination of all forms of Discrimination Against Women |
| CER | Campaign to End Rape |
| CJS | Criminal justice system |
| CLAA | Criminal Law Amendment Act 1885 |
| COSA | Circles of Support and Accountability |
| CPAG | Child Poverty Action Group |
| CPS | Crown Prosecution Service |
| CRB | Criminal Records Bureau |
| CWASU | Child and Woman Abuse Studies Unit |
| DASH | Domestic Abuse, Stalking and Harassment and Honour based Violence Risk Identification Assessment and Management Model |
| DSPD | Dangerous and severe personality disorder |
| EHRC | Equalities and Human Rights Commission |
| EVAW | End Violence Against Women |
| FGM | Female genital mutilation |
| FME | Forensic medical examiner |
| FMU | Forced Marriage Unit |
| FSS | Forensic Science Service |
| GEO | Government Equalities Office |
| GLM | Good Lives Model |
| GUM | Genito-urinary medicine clinic |
| IDAP | Integrated Domestic Abuse Programme |
| IDVA | Independent domestic violence adviser |
| IO | Investigating officer |

| | |
|---|---|
| IPPC | Independent Police Complaints Commission |
| ISVA | Independent sexual violence adviser |
| JCHR | Joint Committee on Human Rights |
| LGBT | Lesbian, gay, bisexual and transsexual |
| MAPPA | Multi-agency public protection arrangements |
| MARAC | Multi-agency risk assessment conference |
| MPFSL | Metropolitan Police Forensic Science Laboratory |
| MPS | Metropolitan Police Service |
| NGO | Non-governmental organisation |
| NPIA | National Policing Improvement Agency |
| NPS | National Probation Service (England and Wales) |
| OECD | Organisation for Economic Co-operation and Development |
| PACE | Police and Criminal Evidence Act 1984 |
| PCL-R | Psychopathy Checklist Revised |
| PHA | Public health approach |
| PIP | Professionalising Investigation Programme |
| PTSD | Post-traumatic stress disorder |
| SANE | Sexual assault nurse examiner programme (USA) |
| SARA | Spousal Assault Risk Assessment |
| SARC | Sexual assault referral centre |
| SARN | Structured Assessment of Risk and Need |
| SART | Sexual assault response team |
| SDVC | Specialist domestic violence court |
| SIO | Senior investigating officer |
| SOA | Sexual Offences Act |
| SOE | Sexual offences examiner |
| SOIT | Sexual offences investigative techniques |
| SOLO | Sexual office liaison officer |
| STD | Sexually transmitted disease |
| STI | Sexually transmitted infection |
| STO | Specially trained officer |
| TDI | The Derwent Initiative |
| UKHTC | United Kingdom Human Trafficking Centre |
| VAW | Violence against women |
| VES | Victim examination suite |
| WNC | Women's National Commission |
| YJCEA | Youth Justice and Criminal Evidence Act 1999 |

# Acknowledgements

This Handbook is the product of the research and scholarship of our contributors. We are grateful to them for sharing their enthusiasm for this project and for addressing their very considerable intellectual talents to the problems arising from sexual violence. Our practitioner commentators rose magnificently to the task we set them in looking at the practice implications of chapters in the various sections of the book. We very much wanted this to be an interdisciplinary text with a unifying thread connecting the chapters. We chose the continuum of violence conceived by Liz Kelly as the common element. Liz has worked tirelessly in the area of women and children's sexual victimisation and her research achievements go well beyond the boundaries of these pages. Scholars and those affected by sexual violence have much to appreciate from her endeavours. We wish too to thank Julia Willan for her assistance in preparing the book. We hope that the chapters will interest, provoke and contribute to more understanding, better policies, and full implementation of recommendations concerning interventions to prevent, investigate, prosecute and support those involved in sexual violence.

# Standing the test of time? Reflections on the concept of the continuum of sexual violence[1]

*Liz Kelly*

## Meet Liz Kelly

Liz Kelly holds the Roddick Chair on violence against women at London Metropolitan University, where she has been Director of the Child and Woman Abuse Studies Unit (*www.cwasu.org*) for almost 20 years. The Unit is recognised as a 'world leader' for its policy-relevant research and also runs the only MA in Women and Child Abuse in Europe. The concept of the 'continuum of violence' was developed during Liz's PhD research, and has been used – sometimes in ways not intended – by many around the globe since. It is perhaps the most satisfying contribution one can make as an academic to bring something into language which stands the test of time.

It seems appropriate in this preface to locate the concept of the continuum of sexual violence[2] (Kelly 1987) in my own and wider feminist thinking. In the 1980s the knowledge base and theoretical frameworks available were considerably less developed than today, and for much of the twentieth century violence against women was considered rare, committed by deviant men and/or in dysfunctional families, with a focus in theorising – academic and populist – on how the victims contributed to their own fate. Much of what we knew as feminists, therefore, originated not in research, but consciousness-raising (CR) groups and/or working in women's services, especially refuges and rape crisis centres. Both were spaces in which women told stories about their lives, and in the process questioned clinical and research constructions, which in turn led to making links between what in traditional discourses were considered disconnected events/experiences. There was not at this point, however, a strong sense of just how common violence was in women's lives, and many key feminist texts continued to differentiate men who used violence from the majority of 'normal' men (see, for example, Brownmiller 1975).

This was the context in which I began my PhD, within which the continuum concept emerged. The impetus to explore the range of forms of violence in women's lives was twofold: my own encounters with 'minor' intimate intrusions as an adolescent and listening to women in CR groups and workshops tell similar stories, including how they changed their behaviour as a consequence; and a young Finnish au pair who sought out the refuge I worked in as a place to 'be' on her day off. She was the first to recount to me a story of sexual abuse by her father, and saw connections between her story and those of the women living in the refuge, which in turn raised new questions for me. The first issue raised the fundamental question of who decides what is abusive, what matters, what should be counted; the second, what is it that connects violations that take place in different relationships/ contexts/points in the life course? The concept of the continuum, and the thinking that informed it, was an engagement with both, and extended existing feminist analysis of particular forms of violence. Judith Herman (1981) had defined incest as an exaggeration of patriarchal family norms rather than a departure from them and Scully and Marolla (1985) argued that rape was the end point of a 'socially sanctioned continuum of male sexual aggression'. Both located sexual violence within the structures of patriarchy, and what would later be theorised as heteronormativity (Jackson 1999) and constructions of masculinity (Connell 1995).

## The continuum concept

In the original formulation two dictionary definitions of continuum were drawn on (Kelly 1987): 'a basic common character that underlies many different events' – that the many forms of intimate intrusion, coercion, abuse and assault were connected. This is the meaning that has been most commonly used since. The second dictionary definition was 'a continuous series of elements or events that pass into one another and cannot be readily distinguished' – that the categories used to name and distinguish forms of violence, whether in research, law or policy, shade into and out of one another. This meaning has been less understood and/or used, but remains a challenge at both the level of women's experience – that they may name the similar experiences differently – and with respect to legal reform. The strongest example used in *Surviving Sexual Violence* (SSV) was the way in which women named unwanted sex, with many unwilling to use the concept of rape. Given that this was a qualitative study, seeking to explore the ways in which women made sense of their own experiences, this led to the concepts of 'pressurised sex' and 'coercive sex' being used for non-consensual sex which women did not name rape. This issue continues to trouble us in research and practice, as many chapters in this book illustrate. It is central to a debate in quantitative prevalence research – whether incidents which fit the legal definition of rape should be coded as such when the respondent does not themselves define it this way (Koss 2005) – and more recently in how non-consensual heterosex should be conceptualised (Gavey 2005). In my more recent work on trafficking (Kelly 2005) this meaning of the continuum has been explored in terms of the ways in which migration, smuggling and trafficking shade into and out of one another in complex ways in the lived experiences of women and men, while being constructed in law and policy discourses as mutually exclusive categories.

There was in the original formulation no implication of linearity or seriousness, with the crucial – and sometimes forgotten exception – of violence that results in death. The only 'more or less' referred to prevalence: that most women recalled encounters with harassment while sexual and physical assaults were less common. It is here that I think that much has been lost in the intervening years, as a focus on crime has meant that research, policy and practice has concentrated on intimate partner violence and, to a lesser extent, sexual assault. The everyday, routine intimate intrusions which were so key to the continuum have dropped off many agendas – leading to the oft-quoted cliché that domestic violence is the most common form of violence against women. It is without question the most researched and counted, but where prevalence surveys include a series of questions on harassment, as recent French and German studies did (European Commission 2010), it emerges as considerably more common in women's lives. A further example of this loss involves a current Child and Woman Abuse Studies Unit (CWASU) PhD student who is revisiting the continuum through the lens of street harassment: in the first draft of her questionnaire neither she nor I noticed that key questions which might illuminate ambiguous experiences were missing.

There are further consequences for the extent to which the continuum within forms of violence is attended to, and understood in terms not only of behaviours, but also their consequences. Here one of the original interviews stands out, of a woman whose father was a lawyer and never did anything that would constitute a crime (at the time), but sexualised his relationship with his daughter throughout her adolescence, including requiring her to dance with him so that his erection pressed against her body. The consequences of this for her, including understanding as an adult the deliberateness through which he orchestrated his own safety while endangering hers, were so similar to those other women talked about where their experiences included repeated rape that it led me to question simplistic notions of seriousness. I still stand by this, but the evidence base on sexual abuse in childhood and its links with subsequent elevated risks of revictimisation (Messman-Moore and Long 2000) does suggest that repeated penetrative assaults are especially harmful. That said, the consequences of the extent of violence and everyday intrusions mean that women, far more than men as a social group, have to factor personal safety into their routine decision-making (Stanko 1990), limiting their 'space for action' (Kelly 2006). We have yet to adequately document the continuum of impacts and consequences[3] – physical, psychological, financial, social and cultural – of violence against women (VAW) in the lives of individuals and with respect to gender equality (see the final section of this preface), although some chapters take up this challenge.

### Limits and potentials

Subsequent critiques of the concept have raised a number of issues, some of which are valid, others are a matter of ongoing contention. Sexual exploitation in the sex industry and forms of VAW often referred to as 'harmful traditional practices' (female genital multilation/cutting, forced marriage and honour-based violence) were not included in SSV, but there is no reason in principle why the continuum concept cannot accommodate them and, arguably, recent discussion of the overlapping of arranged and forced marriage with respect to consent and coercion (Anitha and Gill 2009) does precisely this. It could also be used to explore women's accounts of prostitution: that women within, and having exited, define and understand similar experiences differently along the continua of choice and coercion, agency and exploitation. Current debates on the sex industry tend to work with these concepts and contexts as binaries, and in the process do a disservice to the complexity and ambiguity in many women's accounts (see also Coy 2009). Using the continuum in diverse national and regional contexts would undoubtedly require adjustments in which forms of violence were more or less common.

It is undoubtedly the case that there is little exploration of intersectional issues in women's experiences – especially the ways in which ethnicity inflects with experience and meaning – in part because the sample in SSV was drawn from an area of England which had a homogeneous population, and because of my uncertainty, at that time, about interviewing minority women and interpreting their experiences. Again, there is in principle no reason why the concept could not be developed to embrace intersectionality, but doing so would require a sophisticated layering of data and analysis.

In a strong critique Lynne Segal in *Slow Motion* (1990) argues that the continuum blurs boundaries so much that all heterosexuality is problematised, all men are deemed guilty, and violence is presented as inherent within masculinity.[4] The latter two points are clichéd, while endlessly recycled, responses to any radical feminist perspective, which invariably misrepresent the position of the author and deny that feminists of many hues share a social constructionist epistemology (see also Cameron and Scanlon 2010). I make no apology for questioning 'heterosexuality as usual', of having played a minor part in developing a critical gaze which was deepened subsequently (see, for example, Richardson 1996; Jackson and Scott 2010), theorising the intersections between the construction of gender and sexuality. Lynne Segal revealingly develops her argument for a differentiation of men and violences, stating explicitly that 'violent rape' and those in relationships (p.248) should be separated. Here she reveals limited knowledge of the evidence base on rape – that those by ex/partners are among the most likely to involve weapons and result in additional levels of injury – and reproduces the 'real rape' stereotype which, as several chapters demonstrate, has proved so difficult to shift in policy and practice (see Kelly 2002 for a review of the research and discussion of stereotypes of rape and Munro and Kelly 2009 for how they are implicated in the attrition process). Much of the sound and fury surrounding the Julian Assange case,[5] which continues as I write, turns on precisely these issues – what counts as rape/sexual assault in law and life, and whether it has to be 'violent' in order to qualify. Few commentators have used the ideas underpinning the continuum, nor registered that it was one element in the reforms of recent sexual offences law in Sweden, where violation of women's bodily integrity, rather than force, became the underlying principle.

**What counts and what we are measuring**

One of the implications of the continuum, which was only clear in retrospect, was the potential to move beyond the drama and trauma constructions of violence which suffuse media representations, and are at times reproduced in some feminist discourse. To borrow a phrase from Dorothy Smith (1990), it was the everyday and everynightness of violence that was foregrounded, that these more mundane encounters with gendered power relations were connected to the extremes which are deemed worthy of legal regulation and media attention. The loss of this interest in the fabric of women's everyday lives has already been noted. In this section some of the consequences for research and measuring violence are explored.

Prevalence research requires the creation of a methodology which can measure and analyse events in ways which make clear distinctions between what is included and excluded from analytic categories, and in crime victimisation surveys this has always been organised around documenting 'incidents'. In terms of VAW this has been most strongly developed with respect to domestic violence (European Union 2010), which is arguably the least amenable to this approach. Domestic violence tends to be repeated and most definitions of it emphasise the combination of physical, sexual and psychological abuse. Measuring it as 'incidents' of crime fails to capture this reality, which is more accurately defined as a 'pattern of coercive control' (Stark 2007), not least because from a policy and practice perspective, it is those subjected to 'abusive household gender regimes' (Morris 2009) who need – and seek – protection and support.

It is possible to analyse data in ways which are closer to lived experience – combining, for example, frequency, injury and fearfulness[6] – but even here the questions currently used in surveys are rarely sufficiently nuanced since they tend to be constructed to reflect existing crime categories. Psychological abuse is the clearest example here, since it does not constitute a crime in the nations of the UK,[7] although it does in other EU member states (European Commission 2010). Yet in qualitative studies women invariably speak of it as not only commonplace but undermining and more difficult to move on from: as one of the women interviewed for SSV commented, 'bruises heal but a broken spirit is another thing.' Again the questions arise of who decides what counts, what is 'serious' enough to be worthy of measurement, not to mention protection and justice. Similarly, few surveys, even when they are cast as on VAW and/or health, ask about the everyday intrusions in which women's personal space and being with their self is intruded upon: what is measured counts, and not counting means the everydayness of violence is again hidden, minimised and trivialised. This 'normalisation' has been a strong theme in Nordic theorisation of violence against women (see, for example, Lundgren 2004).

There are profound challenges here for prevalence research, if it is to have a better fit with what we know from qualitative studies and from practice, with respect to questions which ask about a wider range of behaviour, its meanings and consequences, and developing more sophisticated analysis. This is not an argument for collapsing the distinction between quantitative and qualitative research; they are different approaches to knowledge creation and there are philosophical and practical defences of each. Rather, in recognising that the underlying argumentation of the continuum is more difficult to integrate into prevalence research, without more reflection on how it could be better accommodated, measurement will be skewed in ways that move further and further away from lived experience.

## Law, crime and harm

Just as there is tension between the continuum concept with measurement, so there is with the concepts of law and crime. The structure of law has been rooted in strict demarcations between what is and is not permissible, and in the case of criminal law, therefore, what constitutes a crime. Law with respect to violence, throughout most of Europe, is built through gradations of seriousness framed in terms of behaviour (and in some instances levels of injury) applied to discrete incidents. These fundamental building blocks of law and crime sit uneasily with those underpinning the continuum concept, not to mention that wider concepts of harm and how repetition contributes to this are difficult to accommodate. That said, however, there are legal reforms which are more attuned, with the most obvious being the 'course of conduct' offences which have developed to address stalking and/or harassment (see European Commission 2010 for a discussion of legal responses across the EU). Here there is recognition of an accumulation of intrusions, some of which, in and of themselves, may appear innocuous and would certainly not constitute a 'crime'. Sending someone a red rose is normatively viewed as an act of affection; it becomes an act infused by malice only when its meaning can be discerned through prior threats or unwanted interactions.

Sweden has gone a step further through the 'gross violation of integrity' offences, which have some direct connection to how the continuum concept was understood and adapted by feminists lobbying for legal reform, and more accurately reflected the realities of both domestic violence and child sexual abuse. Here the repetition and compounding nature of experiences of violence was linked to human rights concepts of harm and physical integrity, with explicit recognition that this progressively erodes the agency and fundamental freedoms of the victim. The charges can be made separately, or alongside more traditional offences linked to specific incidents.

## Gendered realities

One of the conundrums addressed in this volume is whether anything has really changed in the three decades in which attention has been paid by states to the issue of sexual violence, with a number of chapters documenting contradictory processes. The greater willingness of women to report is one theme here, but we need to reflect more on the complexity of speaking out. It is not simply a question of whether responses are effective and appropriate, which all too often they are not, but what it means to make private troubles public. In much of Europe violence and abuse is no longer 'unspeakable',[8] yet to speak in some contexts can create further danger/vulnerabilities. Where women come from families in which 'honour' is a strong cultural value, to reveal sexual violence risks more than reputation or social exclusion; it can place the woman herself at risk of further, potentially lethal, violence (Hossain and Welchman 2005). Being 'dishonoured' could be considered a continuum, with its meanings more or less explicit depending on cultural contexts. Here the example of women who give public testimony, including to human rights campaigners, about rape in conflict is instructive. Rather than being viewed as heroines in their own communities, the all too frequent response is rejection and exclusion, resulting in many finding the only livelihood option is selling sex (Stiglmayer *et al.* 1994). These are more extreme examples of the potential negative consequences of telling; as some chapters in this volume note, women continue to weigh the benefits and losses, including being seen and treated differently by friends and family, in deciding whether and who to tell. 'To be a victim', for a woman, continues to carry stigma and reputational risks, which persist despite feminist efforts and agency engagement.

Gender inequality is a durable inequality (Tilly 1998) with efforts to address it stalling across Europe, and potentially deepened by aspects of globalisation (Walby 2009). The barriers to progress are many, but include a failure to locate violence as one of the core 'pillars' of gender regimes/orders (Walby 1990). Exploring sexual violence in this way is revealing. There is no simple link between women having more financial autonomy/economic resources and decreasing violence – in fact the reverse appears to be the case in the short term across a range of societies. The Nordic countries, for example, are consistently rated at the top of all conventional measures of gender equality (equal pay, paid employment, political representation), yet the levels of violence against women are as high, and on some measurements higher, than in countries where less progress has been made. Similarly, development programmes are increasingly aware that channelling economic resources through women, while more effective in promoting income generation, often has the unintended consequence of heightening tension and violence in interpersonal relations. These examples raise the troubling policy issue that violence might actually increase in response to efforts to create more gender equality, at least in the short/medium term. These disturbing examples illustrate that neither recognition nor redistribution (Fraser 2003) provide an adequate framework for understanding the persistence of gender inequality, VAW and the intersections involved. Nor are they sufficient to explain why decades of reform, new policy and practices have made such little difference in the overall picture, albeit that for many individuals having access to safety and support, and being treated with respect, makes a considerable difference in their lives.

To analyse these tensions and contradictions, we need new theoretical framings which place the continuum of violence at the core of gender inequality, while allowing for change, retrenchment and unintended consequences at multiple levels. In the MA on Women and Child Abuse at London Metropolitan University we encourage students to draw on and develop Connell's (2009) theoretical framework which distinguishes between the overarching 'gender order', 'gender regimes' (more localised within institutions, including the family) and 'gender relations' between individual women and men. While the levels are connected, convergences and divergences between them are not only possible, but to be expected and explored. This is just one potential framework; we undoubtedly need more, if we are to create conceptual maps which enable us to make sense of the paradoxes of violence against women in the twenty-first century.

## Notes

1  I wrote this in the weeks after the death of my life partner, Dr Corinna Seith. It was remembering her insistence and desire that I should return to theory and conceptualisation that gave me the strength to complete what on many days seemed an impossible task.

2  In *Surviving Sexual Violence* (SSV) (Kelly 1987) the concept of 'sexual violence' is used, within a gender analysis, to mean all forms of violence against women, albeit that not all forms were researched explicitly: subsequently in the Nordic countries the term 'sexualised violence' has been used in a similar way. In the intervening years 'sexual violence' tends to be used more narrowly and 'violence against women' or 'gender-based violence' have become the preferred overarching terms.

3  I continue to use impacts and consequences rather than the more limited concept of 'effects' for reasons that were outlined in *Surviving Sexual Violence*.

4  In some parts of her discussion she vacillates between critique and accepting some core parts of the conceptual analysis – that everyday sexism is connected to more obvious assaults, that flashing and harassment are intrusive and exacerbate women's fear, especially in public space.

5  Julian Assange, founder of Wikileaks, has been charged with sexual offences against two Swedish women – one charge of rape, two of sexual molestation and one of unlawful sexual coercion. While there is no dispute as to whether sex took place, the legal charges turn on refusal to wear a condom and having sex while one woman was asleep. Much of the resistance to the possibility that there might be a case to answer conflates the issue of the US contemplating charges for publishing thousands of classified documents with his sexual behaviour. As with the Bill Clinton case, an either/or position proposes that either there is a case to answer or the accusations are being used solely for political ends – the possibility that both may be the case is seldom contemplated.

6  This is done to an extent in the British Crime Survey (Smith *et al.* 2010), and was done in more depth in an Irish study (Watson and Parsons 2005), and it is these analyses which reveal gendered disproportionality in victimisation and perpetration. The headline figures, however, which are those that enter popular and media discourse, continue to be based on those reporting any incident – which can be limited to a push – producing similar prevalence findings for women and men. The one in four headline prevalence finding is rarely accurately qualified, meaning it is widely misunderstood as referring to repetition and multiple forms of violence.

7  In *Yemshaw (Appellant)* v. *London Borough of Hounslow (Respondent)* [2011] UKSC 3, the Supreme Court ruled that 'domestic violence' in section 177(1) of the Housing Act 1996 includes physical violence, threatening or intimidating behaviour and any other form of abuse which, directly or indirectly, may give rise to the risk of harm. This has yet to be extended to criminal law.

8  Swati Pande (2009) has shown that in Hindi there are literally no words with which to name sexual violation.

# References

Anitha, S. and Gill, A. (2009) 'Coercion, consent and the forced marriage debate in the UK', *Feminist Legal Studies*, 17(2): 165–84.

Brownmiller, S. (1975) *Against Our Will: Men, Women and Rape*. New York: Simon and Schuster.

Cameron, D., and Scanlon, J. (2010) 'Talking about gender'. http://www.troubleand strife.org/?page_id=527 [accessed 22 January 2010]

Connell, R.W. (1995) *Masculinities*. Berkeley: University of California Press.

Connell, R.W. (2009) *Gender* (2nd edition). Cambridge: Polity Press.

Coy, M. (2009) 'This body which is not mine: the notion of the habit body, prostitution and (dis)embodiment', *Feminist Theory*, 10: 61–75.

European Commission (2010) *Feasibility Study to Assess the Possibilities, Opportunities and Needs to Standardize National Legislation on Violence Against Women, Violence Against Children and Sexual Orientation Violence*. Luxembourg: Publications Office of the European Union.

Fraser, N. (2003) *The Radical Imagination: Between Redistribution and Recognition*. New York: New York University Press.

Gavey, N. (2005) *Just Sex?: The Cultural Scaffolding of Rape*. Hove: Routledge.

Herman, J. (1981) *Father–Daughter Incest*. Boston: Harvard University Press.

Hossain, S. and Welchman, L. (eds) (2005) *'Honour': Crimes, Paradigms, and Violence Against Women*. London: Zed Books.

Jackson, S. (1999) 'Heterosexuality, heteronormativity and gender hierarchy: some reflections on recent debates', in S. Jackson, *Heterosexuality in Question*, pp. 159–85. London: Sage.

Jackson, S. and Scott, S. (2010) *Theorizing Sexuality*. Buckingham: Open University Press.

Kelly, L. (1987) *Surviving Sexual Violence*. Cambridge: Polity.

Kelly, L. (2002) *A Research Review on the Reporting, Investigation and Prosecution of Rape Cases*. London: HMCPSI.

Kelly, L. (2005) *Fertile Fields: Trafficking in Persons in Central Asia*. Geneva: IOM.

Kelly, L. (2006) 'A conducive context: Trafficking of persons in Central Asia', in M. Lee (ed.) *Human Trafficking*. London, Willan Publishing.

Koss, M. (2005) 'Empirically enhanced reflections on 20 years of rape research', *Journal of Interpersonal Violence*, 20(1): 100–107.

Lundgren, E. (2004) *The Process of Normalising Violence*. Stockholm: Riksorganisationen för kvinno-och tjejjourer i Sverige (ROKS).

Messman-Moore, T.L. and Long, P.J. (2000) 'Child sexual abuse and revictimization in the form of adult sexual abuse, adult physical abuse, and adult psychological maltreatment', *Journal of Interpersonal Violence*, 15(5): 489–502.

Morris, A. (2009) 'Gendered dynamics of abuse and violence in families: considering the abusive household gender regime', *Child Abuse Review*, 18: 414–27.

Munro, V. and Kelly, L. (2009) 'A vicious cycle? Attrition and conviction patterns in contemporary rape cases in England and Wales', in M. Horvath and J. Brown (eds) *Rape: Challenging Contemporary Thinking*, pp. 281–300, Cullompton: Willan Publishing.

Pande, S. (2009) 'Name and Shame: An exploratory study into the relationships between availability of sexual vocabulary in Hindi and its impact in disclosure of sexual violence'. Unpublished MA dissertation, London Metropolitan University.

Richardson, D. (ed.) (1996) *Theorising Heterosexuality: Telling It Straight*. Buckingham: Open University Press.

Scully, D. and Marolla, J. (1985) '"Riding the bull at Gilley's": Convicted rapists describe the rewards of rape', *Social Problems*, 32(3): 251–63.

Segal, L. (1990) *Slow Motion: Changing Masculinities, Changing Men*. London, Virago.

Smith, D. (1990) *Texts, Facts and Femininity: Exploring the Relations of Ruling*. London: Routledge.

Smith, K. (ed.), Flatley, J. (ed), Coleman, K., Osborne, S., Kaiza, P. and Roe, S. (2010) *Homicides, Firearm Offences and Intimate Violence 2008/09*. Supplementary Volume 2 for Crime in England and Wales 2008/09. Home Office Statistical Bulletin 01/10. London: Home Office. Available at http://www.homoffice.gov.uk/rds/pdfs10/hosb0110.pdf

Stanko, E. (1990) *Everyday Violence: How Men and Women Experience Sexual and Physical Danger*. London: Pandora.

Stark, E. (2007) *Coercive Control: How Men Entrap Women in Personal Life*. Oxford: Oxford University Press.

Stiglmayer, A., Faber, M., Enloe, C., and Gutman, R. (1994) *Mass Rape: The War Against Women in Bosnia–Herzegovina*. Lincoln: University of Nebraska Press.

Tilly, C. (1998) *Durable Inequality*. Berkeley, CA: University of California Press.

Walby, S. (2009) *Globalization and Inequalities: Complexity and Contested Modernities*. London: Sage.

Walby, S. (1990) *Theorising Patriarchy*. Oxford: Blackwell.

Watson, D. and Parsons, S. (2005) *Domestic Abuse of Women and Men in Ireland*. Dublin: Stationery Office.

# Introduction

*Jennifer Brown and Sandra Walklate*

**Meet Jennifer Brown**

Jennifer Brown is a visiting professor at the London School of Economics where she is the Deputy Director of the Mannheim Centre for Criminology. She is enjoying what might be considered an extended sabbatical, catching up on writing and publishing, having spent the last several years as head of Surrey University's Department of Psychology. Her earlier work looked at sexual harassment, which was stimulated by observations of the experiences of policewomen when she was the research manager for Hampshire Constabulary. More recently Jennifer has been involved in research projects looking at rape, and has supervised several PhDs including one on police decision-making and another on drug-assisted rape. In 2010 she helped put together the literature review for Baroness Stern who, at the last government's invitation, examined the investigation and prosecution of rape in England and Wales.

**Meet Sandra Walklate**

Sandra Walklate holds the Eleanor Rathbone Chair of Sociology, a title she holds with particular pride, not just because it is a Chair but also because of the name it honours. Eleanor Rathbone was an active campaigner for social justice that included campaigning on issues relating to women. While sexual violence is not exclusively experienced by women, it is the commitment to social justice that links the work Sandra has been involved with in relation to victims of crime to her involvement with sexual violence. Having spent a good number of years working with a range of victim-oriented organisations as a volunteer, trainer and adviser and having also worked with a number of police forces on training officers responding to sexual violence, Sandra's concerns on these issues are not purely academic. They also stem from trying to understand and help individuals deal with the real problems they may face in their working lives in the best interests of those with whom they are working.

## Central themes

When Liz Kelly published *Surviving Sexual Violence* she gave voice to women against the backdrop of an environment in which society was at best reluctant to admit the extent of the violence and the harm it wreaked on its victims and was at worst victim blaming (Kelly 1988). The book's central themes were that sexual violence is part of many women's lives, that a wide range of male behaviour is abusive to women, and that the social context of sexual violence is men's power and women's resistance. In the two decades since that book was written, important reforms and advances have been made in reforming ways of dealing with complaints of sexual violence. In England and Wales, the Sexual Offences Act of 2003 was a major overhaul and consolidation of legislation. The Youth Justice and Criminal Evidence Act of 1999 introduced special measures to protect vulnerable witnesses including video links and screens in court. Police training has been updated as described in Horvath and Yexley's Chapter 5 and Sharon Stratton's practitioner commentary in Chapter 6. They refer to the introduction of sexual assault referral centres (SARCs) and independent sexual violence advisers (ISVA) where victims of sexual violence can receive medical care, counselling and support throughout the criminal justice process (see Westmarland's Chapter 13 for a discussion of these initiatives). Rape shield legislation designed to curtail the use of questioning about the past sexual history or character of complainants has been introduced in the UK, Australia, New Zealand and the United States of America (see for example Jordan 2008 about developments in New Zealand). So, is the battle won in recognising and reducing sexual violence and processing its perpetrators through the criminal justice system? Or, as Jan Jordan opines in Chapter 12, this volume, do women's voices remain muted? The story of John Worboys is instructive when considering the answer to these questions.

Worboys was the driver of a London black cab. London cabbies are licensed and enjoy something of an institutional reputation as trusted commentators on London life. A number of women made complaints of an assault that took place in a black cab in different parts of London. It appears that the women passengers were invited to share in the cabbie's windfall by drinking a glass of champagne that, unbeknownst to them, was spiked. Once the woman was insensible, Worboys sexually assaulted them. Not only were these complaints not collated so that a pattern could be seen to be emerging, but also as the subsequent Independent Police Complaints Commission's investigation revealed, the detective constable in charge early on in the enquiry was of the opinion that, given the victim could not remember anything past getting into the cab, it would seem unlikely that a cab driver would have alcohol in his vehicle, let alone drug substances (IPCC 2010: 10). The IPCC was of the view that a mindset had been formed 'that a black cab driver would not commit such an offence. This mindset would have meant that the cab driver, rather than the victim, had been believed, and it would have damaged the victim's confidence in the police handling of her allegation.' In another instance, case papers relating to a complaint were lost. Worboys was first identified as a suspect in July 2007 but it was not until February 2008 that he was charged with a large number of sexual assaults dating back to October

2006. He was found guilty and sentenced in April 2009. Some 80 victims contacted the police after Worboys' arrest, many not previously having reported their assault to the police.

The Independent Police Complaints Commission (IPCC) charted the progression of the Worboys enquiry. After the July 2007 arrest it was decided there was insufficient evidence to take the case to the Crown Prosecution Service (CPS). The IPCC noted that there were not only failures to comply with standard operating procedures for the investigation of rape but also systemic failures to identify and link offences. The IPCC concluded that there had been a poor initial investigative response, a failure to trust victims, failures in front line supervision, and a lack of facility to cross-check systems to link similar offences. They did not substantiate a complaint that a particular complainant had been dealt with in an insensitive manner, or that she had been given misleading information by the sexual offences investigative techniques officer, but they did find that the detective sergeant missed crucial investigative opportunities. Such a story is not peculiar to the UK. Jordan (2008) relates a similar catalogue of disbelief and premature closure of a rape investigation that led to a Commission of Enquiry into the conduct of the New Zealand Police which revealed major flaws within the police and the wider criminal justice system. Her chapter invokes the concept of 'silencing' to argue the case for systemic failures of the criminal justice system, and indeed the academic community for failing to hear the voices of those suffering sexual violence.

This is not a singular failure because embedded in the Worboys case are patterns of the bigger picture relating to sexual violence: underreporting, attrition of cases as they drop out at key stages of the criminal justice process, disbelieving of complaints and giving men's explanations greater credence than those of the women complainants. In England and Wales the British Crime Survey reveals that a significant number of victims tell no one about their assaults with only 11 per cent making a report to the police (Povey *et al.* 2009). The voices heard in Liz Kelly's book seemed to have been muted again and the chapters in this Handbook revisit the issues raised by Kelly's text.

## Scale of sexual violence

Statistics on sexual violence demonstrate the universal finding that more cases occur than are dealt with by the courts (see for example Kelly and Lovett's 2009 analysis of European data). By way of illustration of this point, it can be shown that the UK Home Office rules for recording sexual crime counted 43,579 serious sexual offences in 2009/10 (Flatley *et al.* 2010). This represents a 7 per cent increase compared with the 40,748 recorded in 2008/09. Previously there had been a decrease in reporting.

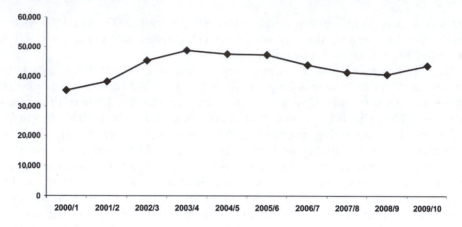

**Figure I.1** Recorded crime in England and Wales of the most serious sexual offences 2000–2010

Within this 2009/10 total, police-recorded rapes of a female increased by 15 per cent to 13,991 offences, and sexual assaults on a female increased by 1 per cent to 19,873 offences. Rapes of a male increased by 22 per cent to 1,174 offences and sexual assaults on a male decreased by 2 per cent to 2,270 offences. This trend also reverses a previous downturn.

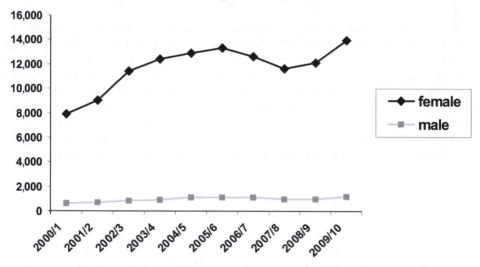

**Figure I.2** Recorded crime of rape of males and females in England and Wales 2000–2010

But if the Crown Prosecution Service's statistics for the number of domestic violence and rape allegations reported to the police that are actually charged and for which a guilty verdict is recorded are examined then the attrition rate is clearly visible (see Table I.1).

**Table I.1** Police and CPS data on numbers of domestic violence incidences and rapes 2006-2009

|  | 2006/7 | 2007/8 | 2008/9 |
| --- | --- | --- | --- |
| **Domestic violence** | | | |
| Reported to police | 336,600 | 376,550 | 337,450 |
| All dealt with by CPS | 66,639 | 74,065 | 80,423 |
| Charged | 36,957 | 47,115 | 52,412 |
| Convicted | 19,978 | 19,842 | 18,629 |
| **Rape** | | | |
| Recorded by police | 12,624 | 11,629 | 12,140 |
| All dealt with by CPS | 6,590 | 5,722 | 6,597 |
| Charged | 1,963 | 2,220 | 2,565 |
| Convicted | 1,778 | 2,021 | 2,018 |

The number of suspects charged for domestic violence and rape is a fraction of the number of reported or recorded cases. The rates of convictions for domestic violence as a function of those reported to the police are about 6% and about 17% of all recorded rapes (this figure is about 6% of all reported rapes).

Walby, Armstrong and Strid discuss at length in Chapter 4 the meaning and implications of measuring sexual violence. In England and Wales the British Crime Survey measures self-reported victimisation across a range of different crime types on an annual basis. Rape is part of a special self-completion module on intimate violence. Myhill and Allen (2002) calculated prevalence for sexual victimisation and estimated 0.4 per cent for rape and 0.9 per cent for sexual assault, i.e. one in 250 for rape. More recent data from the 2007/08 British Crime Survey (Povey *et al.* 2009) showed that nearly one in four women (23.3 per cent) and one in 33 men (3 per cent) had experienced some form of sexual assault (including attempts) since the age of 16. For rape (including attempts) the prevalence was nearly one in 20 women (4.6 per cent) and one in 200 men (0.5 per cent) since the age of 16. Rand (2007) calculated a sexual victimisation rate for rape and sexual assault in the United States as one per 1,000 persons in the United States. Worldwide estimates suggest one in three women have experienced rape or sexual assault, and in some countries up to a third of adolescent girls reported forced sexual initiation (George Mason University Sexual Assault Services 2005).

Notwithstanding the scale of sexual violence, there is still evidence of the public holding victim-blaming attitudes. For example, a Home Office survey reported that a large proportion of respondents thought a woman was at least partially responsible for being raped or sexually assaulted, especially if alcohol or drugs were implicated (Home Office 2009). All the evidence points to the continued presence of sexual violence within a society which retains beliefs in victims' culpability in their own victimisation. These issues are looked at in some detail in the first section of the Handbook.

## Policy changes

Despite the many enquiries and recommendations (the latest in the UK is Baroness Stern's report) there has been a failure of implementation and a preservation of what has been termed 'the justice gap' (Temkin and Krahé 2008) whereby many complaints of sexual violence are dropped out of the criminal justice process.

In an overview of the impact of legislative and policy changes within England and Wales, Brown *et al.* (2010) concluded:

- There is as yet little evidence to show that the 2003 Sexual Offences Act has helped to secure a greater number of convictions against sex offenders;

- Rape shield provisions have not stopped the practice of attempting to discredit complainants because of their sexual histories;

- Only a small number of vulnerable witnesses who might benefit from the application of special measures in court are identified by the CPS;

- Victims were more likely to complete the initial investigation process in SARC areas compared to non-SARC areas and the conviction rate was higher in SARC areas.

This implementation failure is frustrating and is an issue discussed in the final chapter of the Handbook.

## Outline of the book

This Handbook speaks to the complexity of sexual violence, situating that complexity within a broad arena from war to the resolution of interpersonal disputes. Liz Kelly in her preface sets scholars the challenge of finding more comprehensive frameworks for understanding these complexities. The focus of the Handbook's chapters is attitudes and behaviour of individuals placed within a broader societal frame. The reason for this is because both individual perspectives and societal levels of analysis are required if evidence based interventions are to be designed to change policy and practice. It is through an understanding of social processes and the individual's psychological mechanisms that underpin sexual violence that it can be combated and harm reduced.

There are four parts to the Handbook.

**Part One: Legacies: Setting the Scene** provides a critical overview of past practices and policies which help to explain the origins of current thinking and offer steers for future developments.

**Part Two: Theories and Concepts** examines contemporary thinking and explanatory frameworks from a number of perspectives.

**Part Three: Acts of Sexual Violence** reviews a number of specific types of sexual violence, elaborating the range of circumstances, victims and perpetrators with a view to addressing the general and pervasive nature of such violence and contradicting narrow cultural stereotyping.

**Part Four: Responding to Sexual Violence** evaluates current policies and practices and offers some new ideas to develop different types of interventions.

The distinctive aspect of the contributions will be to try and draw out the range of manifestations of sexual violence from the mundane and everyday to the death of a victim. We also want to try and signal the range of victims within each chapter rather than have specific chapters categorised by gender, race or age of victim, or adult women or men, and where possible to identify cross-cultural dimensions to the research. We wanted a multidisciplinary exposition with an underpinning unifying theme to give a sense of coherence to the chapters but without impeding individual styles of writing and emphasis that the contributors wish to take. We thought that Liz Kelly's idea of a continuum of sexual violence, articulated in her book *Surviving Sexual Violence*, is a helpful common reference point. Kelly notes the difficulties of defining sexual violence and she opts for the following definition (Kelly 1988: 41):

> Any physical, visual, verbal or sexual act that is experienced by the woman or girl at the time or later as a threat, invasion or assault that has the effect of hurting her or degrading her and/or takes away her ability to control intimate contact.

Clearly her focus is on women as victim of sexual violence. So, as a starting point, this definition is helpful, but part of the project of this Handbook is to extend the definition to incorporate other victims and potential perpetrators.

Kelly makes it clear in her book that there are ranges of behaviour defined by those experiencing sexual violence that are not reflected in legal codes nor in analytic categories defined by research. She conceptualises sexual violence as a continuum. Continuum is used in two senses: generic and specific. There are many different behaviours, for example abuse, intimidation, coercion, intrusion, threat and force, and Liz identifies the following:

- threats of violence;
- sexual harassment;
- pressure to have sex;
- sexual assault;
- obscene phone calls;
- coercive sex;
- domestic violence;
- flashing;
- rape;
- incest.

She makes the point that these specific forms of sexual violence do not have strict boundaries between categories and that the continuum does not imply either a linear progression or progressive seriousness. It is a continuum of prevalence. The contributors were invited to use the concept of the continuum of violence to extend, critique or propose an alternative when developing their particular approaches.

We also wanted the Handbook to offer some practical guidance. Arlene Vetere's Chapter 9 is a description of the programme she and her colleague, Jan Cooper, pioneered working with offenders, victims and families subjected to violence. In Chapter 21 Rebecca Campbell presents an evaluation of the sexual assault nurse examiner (SANE) programme running in the United States which sees a shift from a solely criminal justice response to a partnership between health and justice personnel.

In Part One, Chapter 1, Shani D'Cruze lays out the historical heritage, showing that the idea of sexual violation implying the loss of a woman's reputation is located in Anglo-Saxon times but still has resonance today. D'Cruze's view is that the continuum of violence provides a powerful critique of the insidious presence of sexual violence in contemporary society. Joan McGregor (Chapter 3) adds a legal dimension to this understanding. In perhaps an unusual contribution to a social science text, Bell, Finelli and Wynne-Davies in Chapter 2 provide insights from literature to deconstruct victimhood and pose the question of whether, in order to restore power balances between men and women, the latter themselves have to become violent. Their analysis resonates with but also offers an intriguing take on individual and societal attitudes towards sexual violence.

Walby, Armstrong and Strid take us in Chapter 4 through the various ways in which sexual violence is measured, i.e. victimisation surveys, official police records and academic studies. In trying to disaggregate data, they make the point that, depending on what is the basis of the calculation, different rates of success or improvement are reported. This is not simply a semantic discussion, but is important if we are to track the results of policy changes. In Chapter 5 Miranda Horvath and Mark Yexley analyse the reforms in police practice and show huge improvements since the 1980s. There can be little doubt that much has been accomplished in instituting more humane approaches to victims of sexual violence. There are some grounds for optimism insofar as more women are reporting greater satisfaction in the manner with which they are being treated by the police (Temkin 1999) although it was still the case that women attacked by a stranger seemed to be treated more sympathetically than those who knew their attacker. Felson and Pare (2008) report satisfaction levels from a secondary analysis of the US National Violence Against Women (and Men) Survey in which 35 per cent of men and 41 per cent of women victims were dissatisfied with police and 23 per cent of men and 39 per cent of women were dissatisfied with the way the courts dealt with their cases. The main issues of contention were perceived leniency of punishment, scepticism, insufficiency of the investigation and insensitivity. This study too found that, if the perpetrator of the violence was known to the victim, the complainant was less satisfied with their treatment.

In Part Two of the Handbook, a number of theoretical perspectives are described and discussed. Thus in Chapter 8 Helen Jones examines sexual violence from a sociological perspective by looking at the functions it serves and its structural foundations. She also looks specifically at sexual violence in war, adding a dimension of analysis to Kelly's continuum. Jennifer Brown also adds a further dimension to the Kelly conceptualisations by asking us in Chapter 7 to think about different forms of sexually violent behaviour from a psychological perspective. She argues that there is a common core of behaviour, physical threat, linking all forms of sexual violence; thereafter, more specific behaviours are associated with its different manifestations. Jo Phoenix's Chapter 10 is perhaps most challenging to Kelly's continuum by arguing it is disassociated both historically and socially. Her analysis of the economics associated with selling sex requires a greater degree of specificity in situating sexual violence. In Chapter 9 Arlene Vetere offers a clinical psychological perspective in which she and her colleague, Jan Cooper, have pioneered a working model within which the victim and violator can meet in the same space and work through the reasons for and consequences of violence.

In their way each of these contributions grapples with the problems of definition and measurement. Walby, Armstrong and Strid suggest that Kelly's definition does not help us disaggregate the different kinds of sexual violence, while Brown attempts to show common and distinctive behaviours within its varied forms. How sexual violence is defined dictates how it is measured and the accuracy of that measurement. The continuum idea is subjected to scrutiny and contributors offer an extension in both breadth and depth to increase its explanatory and predictive power.

Part Three of the Handbook changes the focus of attention to acts of sexual violence. In Chapter 12 Jan Jordan takes on the challenge of examining the assumptions implicit in 'having done rape' meaning that, as reforms are now in place, might we expect to see a diminution of instances and better criminal justice response? Jordan uses the concept of silencing to review, somewhat pessimistically, how victims themselves, criminal justice professionals, the courts, and indeed researchers, mute women's voices, which is in stark contrast to Kelly's project of placing women's voices at the centre of discourses about sexual violence.

Nicole Westmarland in Chapter 13 traces the changing policy context in respect of domestic violence. Like Jordan, Westmarland notes that domestic violence appears to be occupying a more central position in policy terms, having moved from the margins. She details various initiatives and the increases in funding and innovative practices. Along with Vetere in Part Two, Westmarland also examines the role of the perpetrator in sexual violence, along with programmes that incorporate them into the solution to this intractable problem. One noteworthy shift of emphasis is the idea of information sharing, rather than preservation of strict boundaries of confidentiality, between involved agencies. It is often these communication failures that give rise to the problematic instances as described earlier and lead to formal enquiries. This is a theme we pick up in our concluding thoughts.

Anette Ballinger takes a case study approach in Chapter 14 when examining sexual murder comparing the investigation of the Peter Sutcliffe series in the 1980s with that of the more recent Steve Wright murders of prostitutes in Suffolk. At the heart of her analysis is Kelly's notion of the ordinary, i.e. sexual violence arises out of the routines of everyday life, and its perpetrators, rather than being monsters, are themselves often 'ordinary'. These killers are at the extreme end of sexual violence – they fatally silence their victims – but they are also the proverbial man next door, your neighbour, or someone you say good morning to in the supermarket. Steph Petrie, in Chapter 15, continues the silencing theme by looking at whose voices are heard and listened to in the case of child sexual abuse. She too examines the normalisation of violence and gives a voice to children, as does David Shannon in Chapter 16 on Internet offending. Shannon looks at the kinds of sexually abusive behaviour children are exposed to on the Internet where the continuum notion is a helpful analytic device.

Part Four of the Handbook addresses responses to sexual violence. In Chapter 18 Helge Hoel and Duncan Lewis draw on their research on bullying at work to review how organisations cope, especially focusing on the lesbian, gay, bisexual or transsexual worker. In Chapter 20 Hazel Kemshall compares public and voluntary sector responses to offenders, while Kate Cook's focus in Chapter 19 is on supporting victims, as is Becki Campbell's in Chapter 21. Campbell summaries her extensive series of studies evaluating the Sexual Assault Nurse Examiner (SANE) programme in the United States, offering a reciprocal continuum of violation of survivors of sexual violence. A recurrent theme through these chapters is ideas about risk and how this is defined and managed.

Given our commitment to bridging the gap between the hallowed groves of academe and the messy world of the practitioners, we invited four people actively working in the area of sexual violence to comment on how the work reported by academics has helped or may help them. Sharon Stratton is a serving Metropolitan Police officer, specialising in the areas of domestic and sexual violence. In Part One, Chapter 6 she notes that notwithstanding changes in procedures, policies and practices, 'traditionally police training has had little input from external sources'. It is her view that specialist training should include an understanding of rape myths, typologies of rapists, and an appreciation of the impacts of sexual violence on victims and family members, particularly children. She was of the view that the chapters contextualising sexual violence from historical and legal points of view were helpful resources for police officers to develop their appreciation of the origins and persistence of social attitudes. Ruth Mann works for Her Majesty's Prison Service and in Part Two, Chapter 11 she asks challenging questions of academics: how can practitioners be helped to distinguish good practice from quackery, and does research extend knowledge in relation to risks, need and responsivity principles in intervening with offenders? Mann finds the discussion of individual and societal responsibility helpful in thinking about working with offenders as is the discussion of differentiating motives into different manifestations of sexual violence.

In Part Three, Chapter 17 Stephanie Kewley offers a perspective from the Probation Service and describes divergent pathways for interventions with sex offenders and domestic violence perpetrators. She is not entirely convinced that this divide is particularly helpful, especially as the research and academic analysis show much in common between the offences and the offenders. She is asking for a deeper analysis of treatment needs and for the challenging of men's propensity to distance themselves from their use of violence as a way of coping. Vetere's clinical approach in Chapter 9 is premised on the notion that perpetrators have to take responsibility for and 'own' their violence and its consequences. Both Kewley and Mann find this chapter especially appealing, informing practitioners as it does about means to access the issue of responsibility.

Sheila Coates is Director of South Essex Rape and Incest Centre. It is fitting that her practice commentary in Chapter 22 gives voice to survivors. These are raw and difficult testimonies to read and they do tell of both positive as well as negative experiences. When professionals are good, the experience is enormously supporting but when they are impatient, indifferent or sceptical it can be very damaging, and as Rebecca Campbell vividly describes, is felt to be a second violation. Coates is asking for consistency in service provisions and a multilevel attack on prevention, and makes some key recommendations.

Our concluding chapter discusses the challenge laid down by Jordan and by Westmarland, in respect of rape and domestic violence, that these have been 'done' and are no longer at the margins of policy. We note that there have indeed been reforms in police training and in service provision to help and support both victims and perpetrators of sexual violence. In particular there have been attitudinal shifts in terms of a decline in complicity in the violence, with more victims reporting what happened to them. There has been an explosion of research since Liz Kelly undertook her pioneering research in the 1980s. However, the justice gap – the estimated number of cases of sexual violence compared with the number of convictions of perpetrators – persists. One of the reasons we postulate for this in our conclusions is the other gap, i.e. of implementation. We suggest that failure to define what improved communication is for, and between whom, leads to a lack of clarity of purpose. We also argue that risk assessment has become a policy mantra and its presence can represent a device for managers to deflect organisational responsibility for systemic failures rather than necessarily to provide a means to improve service provision. We offer a new definition of sexual violence, because definition is critical to what is measured, and in the present climate, measurement is inextricably linked to resourcing.

We end, we hope, on a constructive note, offering an analysis that identifies some key ideas for both better and more informed communication between all the constituencies who have an interest in reducing sexual violence and supporting those whose lives are caught up in the havoc caused. We were inspired by the crucial work of Liz Kelly, whose research has proved both enduring and capable of expansion and refinement.

### References

Brown, J., Horvath, M., Kelly, L. and Westmarland, N. (2010) Connections and disconnections; assessing evidence, knowledge and practice in responses to rape. http://www.equalities.gov.uk/search.aspx?terms=Brown+Horvath+kelly+Westmarland

Crown Prosecution Service (2010) *Violence Against Women Crime; key findings*. London: CPS.

Felson, R.B. and Pare, P.-P. (2008) 'Gender and the victim's experience with the criminal justice system', *Social Science Research*, 37: 202–19.

Flatley, J. *et al.* (2010) *Crime in England and Wales 2009/10*. London: Home Office Statistical Bulletin 12/10.

George Mason University Sexual Assault Services (2005) Worldwide sexual assault statistics. http://www.woar.org/resources/sexual-assault-statistics.html (accessed 30 October 2010).

Home Office (2009) *Results from the Ipsos Mori poll of telephone interviews with people in England and Wales regarding their opinions on violence against women.* London: Home Office.

Independent Police Complaints Commission (2010) IPCC independent investigation into the Metropolitan Police Service's enquiry into allegations against John Worboys. http://www.ipcc.gov.uk/worboys_commissioners_report.pdf (accessed 1 December 2010).

Jordan, J. (2008) 'Perfect victims, perfect policing? Improving rape complainants' experiences of police investigations', *Public Administration*, 86(3): 699–719.

Kelly, L. (1988) *Surviving Sexual Violence*. Minneapolis: University of Minnesota Press.

Kelly, L. and Lovett, J. (2009) *Different Systems, Different Outcome? Tracking attrition in Europe*. London: Child and Women Abuse Studies Unit.

Kelly, L., Lovett, J. and Regan, L. (2005) A *Gap or a Chasm? Attrition in reported rape cases*. London: Home Office.

Kershaw, C., Nicholas, S., Walker, A. (2008) *Crime in England and Wales 2007/8*. London: Home Office Statistical Bulletin 07/08.

Myhill, A. and Allen, J. (2002) Rape and sexual assault of women; the extent and nature of the problem; findings from the British Crime Survey. Home Office Research Study 237. London: Home Office.

Povey, D., Coleman, K., Kaiza, P. and Roe, S. (2009) *Homicides, firearm offences and intimate violence; supplementary volume 2 to Crime in England and Wales 2007/8*. London: Home Office Statistical Bulletin.

Rand, M. (2007) *Criminal Victimization, 2007*. Washington: US Department of Justice, Office of Justice Programs.

Stern, V. (2010) The Stern Review http://www.equalities.gov.uk/PDF/Stern_Review _acc_FINAL.pdf (accessed 13 November 2010).

Temkin, J. (1999) 'Reporting rape in London: A qualitative study', *The Howard Journal of Criminal Justice*, 38: 17–41.

Temkin, J. and Krahé, B. (2008) *Sexual Assault and the Justice Gap: A Question of Attitude*. Oxford: Hart Publishing.

**Part One**

# Legacies: Setting the Scene

# Introduction

*Jennifer Brown and Sandra Walklate*

## Context

In this first section of the Handbook there are five essays providing a context for thinking about sexual violence, especially in understanding the attitudes which help to shape the modern criminal justice system's responses. The first three chapters – Shani D'Cruze on the historical heritage; Liam Bell, Amanda Finelli and Marion Wynne-Davies, who give us a critical literary analysis; and Joan McGregor's legal legacy work – provide a temporal frame, not often used as an analytic dimension when considering sexual violence. Halford *et al.* (1997: 19) argue that 'historically established modes [of behaviour] are vitally important in shaping current activities'. It is their position, and one we share, that present practices do not exist in a time warp, but rather are derived from past forms of agency which are stored, retrieved, reworked and reactivated in the present. By salvaging the origins of thinking about sexual violence, how this is sedimented in literature, enmeshed in culture and reflected in law, we can see the durability of past prejudice.

Notwithstanding the advances made in the investigation of sexual offences, documented in Horvath and Yexley's Chapter 5, there is a preservation of myths about rape, and the maintenance of a belief that there is a greater harm rendered to men wrongly called rapists than to women wrongly called liars when making complaints of sexual assault or rape. But they are rather more optimistic that changes in policing practice have wrought changes in attitude and improved police and medical procedures for victims of violence which in turn encouarge more to come forward. Bell and colleagues offer a more sanguine analysis of the preservation of myth through the medium of fiction. Walby and colleagues' Chapter 4 though reminds us of the starkness of the numbers of those suffering sexual violence and the relatively few whose aggressors are brought to book. Solutions that these authors offer come with a price and certainly imply a more radical shift in thinking in order to close what has been termed the 'justice gap' (Temkin and Krahe 2008), i.e. the failure of the Criminal Justice System to protect victims of sexual violence and bring its perpetrators to justice.

Sharon Stratton's practitioner commentary in Chapter 6 provides further details of the improving practice by police officers when investigating sexual violence. She discusses the professionalising of the police sexual violence investigator and a shift in the ethos of policy, which has become one where the victim's fundamental right is to be believed.

## The 'deserving' victim

Shani D' Cruze's chapter presents an historical overview and locates the idea that rape was a loss to a woman's reputation in Anglo-Saxon times. She notes that the notion of more deserving victims also emerges very early, whereby the rape of a virgin heiress exacted higher penalties than that of poorer, lower status women and bondswomen (servants), who were excluded from the protection of the law altogether. Prosecuting a case of rape has always been arduous and early legal requirements included prompt and 'rational' action after a rape, displaying of the violated body to appropriate (male) authority figures, and the need to make repeated visits to court to demonstrate causation of the violation. D'Cruze points out that the chance of a successful prosecution was rare, partly because the law gave husbands unfettered rights of access to their wives' bodies and partly because of issues of credibility for younger, lower status women. She argues that husbands' entitlement to their wives' bodies generalised to men's sexual access to women, with women being held responsible for remaining chaste and faithful. So these ideas of prompt reporting to appropriate authorities, and having to demonstrate that the violation occurred, has resonances for modern-day beliefs and practices. This almost mirrors Susan Estrich's 'real rape' scenario where she identifies differences in treatment for those who have experienced an 'aggravated' rape, i.e. one in which a stranger waylays an unsuspecting and unknown woman, compared to the majority of rapes that take place between people who know each other, often in social situations (Estrich 1987). Estrich also points out that failure to report in the immediate aftermath of rape can give rise to serious doubts about the credibility of the complaint. D'Cruze historically locates Estrich's evocation of the notion that rape resides in women's failure to avoid the rape, put up a fight or report promptly.

There is also a modern version of the 'deserving' victim. In a review of rape and rape prosecutions in contemporary London, Stanko and Williams (2009) presented an analysis of rape complaints made to the Metropolitan Police Service. They found that of 697 rape allegations made (i.e. during April and May 2005) only 5 per cent resulted in a prosecution, a statistic more broadly supported for the successful prosecution rate achieved in England and Wales (Stern 2010). Thus achieving successful prosecutions still remains difficult. Secondly, Stanko and Williams developed the idea of the vulnerable victim, who, in terms of their criteria, may be thought of as especially deserving of support and protection. The factors Stanko and Williams identified were comparative youthfulness i.e. under 18 years of age at the time of the attack; having some kind of mental health issue; consumption of alcohol or a drug immediately prior to the attack; and a previous intimate relationship with the attacker. They found that the more these vulnerabilities were present, the more likely it was that the allegation would not be formally classified as a crime and so progressed through the criminal justice system. Stanko and Williams (2009: 218) conclude that 'most reports of rape are experienced as a "private" encounter, in situations that are not too dissimilar to consensual sex.' Thus, where women find it difficult to articulate 'non' consent, men are given the benefit of the doubt. This benefit is conferred by jurors both in mock jury studies and in real trials (Finch and Munro 2008). Page (2008) reports the results of a study of police attitudes in the United States and found that if a prostitute reported rape 14 per cent of officers were very unlikely and 30 per cent unlikely to believe her.

Joan McGregor in Chapter 3 discusses some of the reasons why the law still fails to protect women and appears to protect men's sexual autonomy at the expense of the former. She too argues that men [still] have privileged access to women's bodies; that assumptions are made about the manner and nature of consent to sexual intercourse; that women still face the test of the amount and kind of resistance they put up to avoid being subjected to sexual violence, and the presumptions by men that they had a reasonable belief that the woman had consented to sex. In addition, McGregor notes the maintenance of victim-blaming attitudes by the public and the 'when does "no" mean "yes" problem'.

**Mad or bad**

McGregor suggests that rape laws were designed to protect men's interest in their daughters or wives but not so much as to constrain male sexuality. D'Cruze adds to this analysis by proposing that women's autonomous sexual pleasure was tainted by ideas of wantonness, being a whore, or indeed witchcraft. Women who failed to preserve their chastity until marriage or their faithfulness within marriage were considered fallen. The Faustian bargain was that women relied on men for protection but it was their responsibility to reserve sexual access to their bodies to those who had entitlement. If they failed they could no longer rely on male protection. There are several consequences of this chivalric heritage. First, sexual attractiveness is seen as provoking, with the potential of unleashing uncontrolled desire in men. Thus women are seen as the causal agents in their own victimisation. Second, there was a demonisation of rapists whereby men who raped and thus fell below the chivalric ideal were brutish. Third, there was a societal expectation that women would preserve their honour to the death. D'Cruze charts a shift by the nineteenth century towards marginalising men who fall short of chivalric standards as being morally degenerate monsters, which leads to the pathologising of perpetrators. She cites the work of the Italian criminologist Cesar Lombroso who thought criminal types could be identified by their physiology. Thus rapists, he thought, have sparkling eyes, delicate features, and swollen lips and eyelids. D'Cruze sees the pathologising of violence based on these nineteenth-century ideas as society's protection against the notion that sexual violence can and is indeed perpetrated by the ordinary, not the monstrous; a position outlined by Liz Kelly in her continuum of violence conceptualisation, which D'Cruze comments is a powerful critique of the insidious presence of violence in contemporary society that does not necessarily work in the same way in every historical epoch.

This psychological process of inferring characteristics of the individual from facial features has been termed 'metaphysical generalisation' by Paul Secord. Secord *et al.* (1960) describe how impressions can be formed of people based on relatively little information. Thus coarse skin may be associated with coarse behaviour, thin lips with meanness, eyes that are close together with deviousness. Cultural associations provide the link between the feature and the attribute. There is also a tendency for the perceiver to maximise congruency; in other words to make the impression fit the attribute even if this means some adjustment in the interests of creating a unified impression. One example of this is the so-called halo effect, whereby a positive feature of an individual is generalised and other attributes are made to fit this overall impression. The opposite is also observable when a negative feature generalises to attributions of behaviour to fit the negative impression. So, as Joan McGregor describes in the rape allegation made against William Kennedy Smith, the discussion of his accuser's underwear cast her as a woman in search of sex, undermining the credibility of her complaint. Advice to defendants by their counsel is still likely to be 'turn up to court looking presentable in a suit', to give the impression that a good-looking and smart young man would have no need to force a sexual encounter.

## Blaming the victim

The idea of blaming the victim can be found in Victorian ideals which suggested that to have unsanctioned sex outside marriage was such a blow to respectability that it was a fate worth fighting literally to the death to preserve. The belief that chastity should be protected at all costs meant that failure to do so implied consent. The victim is blamed both for precipitating her own victimisation through her sexual attractiveness and also through her failure to resist when attacked. As Horvath and Brown (2010) point out, this places the victim between a rock and a hard place: greater believability is attached to notions of 'real' rape – the stereotype stranger attacks in the dark alley with a knife, which is actually relatively rare – whereas the more frequent, contested consent cases involving allegations against someone the woman knows tend to be more often disbelieved. In that latter instance, successful prosecution relies on scrutiny of the consent rather than the behaviour of the attacker (Stanko and Williams 2009). Blaming the victim and exonerating the perpetrator is a prevailing rape myth which experimental social psychological studies by, for example, Bieneck and Krahé (in press) show to be attributable to schematic information processing, i.e. when people judge social information on the basis of their generalised beliefs and knowledge that are stored in their memories. They found that this tendency was more pronounced in cases of rape rather than other crimes such as robbery, when the issue of prior relationship and being drunk seemed significantly less related to the attribution of blame. Rape, they concluded, represents a special case. Brown and Horvath (2009) then argue that the operation of such culturally embedded myths acts to attenuate the perceived harm experienced by women and actually creates a reversal whereby men become the victims of sick, vindictive or vengeful women by virtue of belief in the number of false allegations that are thought to be made.

There is a commonly held belief that many women offer only token resistance to sex and that when they say no they actually mean yes (Muehlenhard and Hollabaugh 1988). Young college women (N=610) completed a questionnaire designed to measure their explicit verbal behaviour and behavioural intentions whether to engage in sex. Muehlenhard and Hollabaugh report that 40 per cent of women indicated saying no to sex when actually they meant yes. The reasons for this were: fear of appearing promiscuous; feeling inhibited about sex; or more game playing. The conclusion drawn from this study was that although there was a substantial minority who did say no when they meant yes, this could be attributable to perceptions of the attitudes embedded in cultural expectations about sex. Most women did not engage in token resistance, thus 'when a woman says no, chances are that she means it regardless of the incidence of token resistance; if the woman means no and the man persists, it is rape' (Muehlenhard and Hollabaugh 1988: 878). Brown and Horvath (2009: 333) argue that culturally embedded sexual scripts, which dominate the negotiation of sexual encounters, make it difficult for women to change their minds. Such scripts tend to cast men as the sexual pursuer and initiator of sex while women are the gatekeepers whose role is to grant permission for sex to take place. Reliance on such scripts can lead to some confusion because if women fail to signal no clearly, or men fail to understand, there is a perception by men that the confusion is the result of miscommunication. This represents blame shifting, whereby the woman becomes responsible for the apparent communication problem.

Communicating is at the heart of Liam Bell, Amanda Finelli and Marion Wynne-Davies's Chapter 2. Their starting point is the notion of the commonality of sexual violence, a point which resonates with Kelly's continuum of violence concept. Their point of departure is Brownmiller's notion of women 'fighting back' and the idea that rather than violence being an act of self-defence, women may actually initiate it, a point the Kelly continuum does not concede. Their gripping analysis deconstructs the victim–perpetrator relationship through the medium of the novel. Using Angela Carter's *The Passion of New Eve* they challenge the concept of the self-defending woman by examining the violating woman. They also discuss the idea of responsibility for violence and the excuse given by a male character in the novel, Zero, that the notion of repressed sexual dissatisfaction gives rise to sexual violation. Interestingly David Canter, in his exposition of the rapes and murders committed by John Francis Duffy, notes that Duffy blamed his wife for his escalating levels of violence perpetrated on his victims. Canter writes: 'John Duffy had found out that he was infertile and some of his most violent assaults took place after he discovered that his ex-wife had become pregnant by another man after she had left Duffy' (Canter 1994: 51). In court, Duffy's former wife explained that 'he [Duffy] said he raped a girl and said it was my fault.'

**Are things getting better?**

All this sounds pessimistic and rather bleak. So has there been any progress? In Chapter 4 Sylvia Walby and her colleagues map the occurrence of sexual violence over time through a self-report victimisation survey (the British Crime Survey), police-recorded crime and academic research results. They discuss the problems of accurate measurement of the extent of sexual violence and the continued problem of attrition, in other words the pinch points at which cases drop out of the justice process. A major pinch point is the failure to report sexual violence to the police in the first instance and the high percentage of cases in which the police decide to take no further action.

Miranda Horvath and Mark Yexley's Chapter 5 charts the development of police training in sexual offences investigations. They start with the 'bad old days'. In the 1970s the attitude of police towards sexual offences was one of suspicion and disbelief of the victim. This was epitomised by a comment by Detective Sergeant Alan Firth of the West Midlands Police, who wrote in the *Police Review* of 28 November 1975 (page 1507):

> Women and children complainants in sexual matters are notorious for embroidery or complete fabrication of complaints ... It should be borne in mind that except in the case of a very young child, the offence of rape is extremely unlikely to have been committed against a woman who does not immediately show signs of extreme violence ... If a woman walks into a police station and complains of rape with no such signs of violence, she must be closely interrogated. Allow her to make her statement to a policewoman and then drive a horse and cart through it ... call her an outright liar. It is very difficult for a person to put on genuine indignation who has been called a liar to her face ... Do not give her sympathy. If she is not lying, after the interrogator has upset her by accusing her of it, then at least the truth is verified.

Horvath and Yexley move on ten years to 1985 and the now notorious scenes from the Thames Valley Police fly-on-the-wall documentary by Roger Graef which showed the oppressive interviewing of a rape complainant. This sequence emphatically illustrates the points being made by both D'Cruze and McGregor as, in the documentary, it was the woman's reputation as a prostitute which minimised both her credibility and the harm she was believed to have suffered. The ensuing outrage resulted in women's groups, The Women's National Commission and the Home Office working to create new principles of good practice when dealing with sexual crime. Specialist training had begun in the Metropolitan Police Service in 1984 with officers being made more aware of the criticality of forensic evidence and the need to support the complainant through the courts process. By 2008, the approach had become a co-ordinated response with officers being familiarised with the special measures that can be undertaken to support or protect vulnerable witnesses.

Sharon Stratton, herself a serving police officer specialising in sexual violence investigation, argues in Chapter 6 that training and guidance have improved dramatically in police forces in England and Wales. She suggests that the establishment of specialist teams, known as Sapphire units, illustrates the importance attached to police investigations into rape allegations. Certainly in England and Wales there has been a steady increase in the numbers of reported rape cases. Notwithstanding these developments, the Metropolitan Police Service was severely criticised by the Independent Police Complaints Commission (2010) over two specific serial rape investigations involving John Worboys and Kirk Reed. The IPCC concluded that the investigative shortcomings were not just of individuals but were also systemic failures of supervision and cross-referencing of reports. The Commission stated (p. 16): 'there is a widely held perception that women reporting rape and other sexual offences have not been taken seriously, either because of the nature of the offence or because priority has been given to other offences such as burglary.'

Reforms in police investigations may have had some limited successes but because of the adversarial nature of the prosecution system complainants are also witnesses and often face hostile cross-examination designed to destroy their moral character; a strategy which, as D'Cruze and McGregor show in their chapters, was at the heart of men's and society's upholding of the established social order.

## Conclusions

The first five chapters in the Handbook offer some historical and cultural grounding to ideas about the perpetration, perpetuation and victimisation associated with sexual violence. Contemporary issues around complainants' credibility as a victim, the need to have resisted and to have made an early report of the assault have resonances with historical precedent outlined by D'Cruze and with their embedded nature in popular culture as discussed by Bell *et al.*. Ideas such as that of the more deserving victim have their modern-day counterpart in victim vulnerabilities. Modern medical technologies have been something of a double-edged sword. The contraceptive pill liberated women from the risk of pregnancy following sex, but that very freedom signalled her sexual availability without the previously almost inevitable consequences of conception. DNA analysis has shifted the contested grounds of an allegation from whether or not sex took place, and with whom, to whether or not what took place was consensual. Sylvia Walby and her colleagues suggest that it is crucial that accurate measurement of the extent of sexual violence is undertaken if effective monitoring of policy changes is to be undertaken. They suggest a standard definition of conviction rates in order that there is both a clear and commonly used metric whereby agencies and the public understand what is being measured.

Joan McGregor's suggestions of more radical reform, such as relabelling sexual assault to conform to the rules of physical rather than sexual assault, might at least see more defendants in the dock but risk obscuring the unique harm of rape. Differential penalties for unaggravated assaults could imply some rapes are worse than others. Liz Kelly's pioneering work in the 1980s argued against such comparisons. The essays presented in the chapters here find her continuum of sexual violence helpful in so far as it shows its emergence out of the routines of everyday life, and its ubiquitousness, but that level of generality limits its explanatory power.

## References

Bieneck, S. and Krahé, B. (in press) 'Blaming the victim and exonerating the perpetrator in cases of rape and robbery: Is there a double standard?', *Journal of Interpersonal Violence*.

Brown, J. and Horvath, H. (2009) 'Do you believe her and is it real rape?', in M. Horvath J. and Brown (eds) *Rape; challenging contemporary thinking*, pp. 325–42. Cullompton: Willan Publishing.

Canter, D. (1994) *Criminal Shadows; inside the mind of the serial killer*. London: Harper Collins.

Estrich, S. (1987) *Real Rape; how the legal system victimises women who say no*. Boston: Harvard University Press.

Finch, E. and Munro, V. (2008) 'Breaking boundaries? Sexual consent in the jury room', *Legal Studies*, 26: 303–20.

Halford, S., Savage, M. and Witz, A. (1997) *Gender Careers and Organisations*. London: Macmillan.

Horvath, M. and Brown, J. (eds) (2009) *Rape; challenging contemporary thinking*. Cullompton: Willan Publishing.

Horvath, M. and Brown, J. (2010) 'Between a rock and a hard place', *The Psychologist*, 23: 556–9.

Independent Police Complaints Commission (2010) Independent investigation into the Metropolitan Police Service's inquiry into allegations against John Worboys. London: IPCC.

Muehlenhard, C. and Hollabaugh, L.C. (1988) 'Do women sometimes say no when they mean yes? The prevalence and correlates of women's token resistance to sex', *Journal of Personality and Social Psychology*, 54: 872–9.

Page, A. Dellinger (2008) 'Judging women and defining crime: police officer attitudes towards women and rape', *Sociological Spectrum* 28: 389–411.

Secord, P., Stritch, T. and Johnson, L. (1960) 'The role of metaphorical generalization and congruency in the perception of facial characteristics', *Journal of Social Psychology*, 52: 329–37.

Stanko, B. and Williams, E. (2009) 'Reviewing rape and rape allegations in London: What are the vulnerabilities of the victims who report to the police?', in M. Horvath and J. Brown (eds) *Rape; challenging contemporary thinking*, pp. 207–28 Cullompton: Willan Publishing.

Stern, V. (2010) *The Stern Review*. London: Government Equalities Office.

Temkin, J. and Krahé, B. (2008) *Sexual Assault and the Justice Gap; a question of attitude*. Oxford: Hart.

## Chapter 1

# Sexual violence in history: a contemporary heritage?

*Shani D'Cruze*

### Meet Shani D'Cruze

Shani D'Cruze first found herself researching the history of sexual violence when the 99 per cent male academic department where she was a junior researcher proposed a project on that topic. The department soon gave up the idea, but she went on eventually to publish a monograph, *Crimes of Outrage: Sex, Violence and Victorian Working Women* (UCL Press 1998). Most of her academic publications are on gender and the history of violence. After a career based in English universities she has run away to Greece where she combines academic research and writing with Cretan rural living. She is currently Honorary Reader in the Research Institute for Law, Politics and Justice at Keele University. Recent publications include: *Murder: Social and Historical Approaches to Understanding Murder and Murderers* (with Sandra Walklate and Samantha Pegg, Cullompton: Willan Publishing 2006) and *Women, Crime and Justice since 1660* (with Louise Jackson, Basingstoke: Palgrave 2009).

### Introduction

This chapter reviews the social and cultural history of sexual violence between the medieval period and the new interpretations of Second Wave Feminism in the late twentieth century. Many of the sources historians use come from the law, the courts and the police. Therefore, much of what can be known about sexual violence in the past becomes visible when it became a matter of criminality; something that occurred only rarely. Historically, there were very few rape, attempted rape or indecent assault cases (around 1 per cent of known felonies in the Early Modern period) and much sexual violence has remained socially and criminologically opaque (Walker 1998: 1). This is perhaps especially true for sexual violence experienced by men and boys; until very recently a different legal framework was applied and the constraints on speaking publicly were often even heavier.

Recorded interpersonal violence in Western Europe declined significantly between the medieval period and the mid-twentieth century (Gurr 1981; Eisner 2003). This has been explained by increasing control through legal sanctions and a growing criminal justice system to enforce them combined with the shaping of modern social identities which privileged restraint over all kinds of bodily excesses. Consequently this 'civilising process' reduced interpersonal violence, mostly public violence between males intended to resolve disputes and preserve personal honour (Elias 1978; Carroll 2007). Sexual violence qualifies the 'civilising process' concept. Although there is a 'dark figure' of undisclosed and unprosecuted criminal activity of all kinds, the extremely low levels recorded since medieval times make sexual violence a special case.

In the UK in the early twenty-first century a range of studies indicate that only something like 5 per cent of rapes reported to the police end in conviction. Furthermore fewer than half of rapes are ever reported – in some studies the non-reporting figure is between 80 and 90 per cent (Bourke 2007: 390–94). While we do not have comprehensive crime figures for earlier historical periods, the very low numbers tried, together with the appearances of sexual violence in the records of different offences, suggest persuasively that there has been a consistent historical continuity in non-reporting. For this reason alone, it cannot be assumed that sexual violence has followed the long-term downward trend of other kinds of interpersonal violence. Furthermore, crime statistics have numerous shortcomings in documenting the incidence of sexual violence, and shifting perceptions and categories of sexual violence over time mean that we cannot know how much of what would now be thought of as sexual violence took place at any historical period. In fact, recent historical investigation is demonstrating that sexual violence has long been an opaque matter for criminal justice systems; both symbolically highly transgressive but difficult to read in particular instances. We cannot assume that behaviours which would now count as sexual violence were always considered as such. The injuries that laws on sexual violence were intended to punish have also changed over time. The sexed body, and violence directed towards it, are therefore produced historically at the intersections of discourse, power and pain (Scarry 1985; Bourke 2007).

The chapters in this volume each engage in different ways with Liz Kelly's feminist concept of sexual violence as a continuum of behaviours that are threatening, degrading, or humiliating within the context of intimate contact (Kelly 1987, 1988). Historically, the criminal justice process since the medieval period, the Early Modern church courts which policed sexual matters as sin rather than as violence, and the medico-legal constitution of offenders and victims especially since the nineteenth century, have all tended to define sexual violence both narrowly and imprecisely. Those who have experienced sexual violence have frequently been held as at least in part culpable. Of course, it was central to the feminist politics of Liz Kelly's research to demonstrate the limitations of pre-existing definitions and to place the blame for sexual violence emphatically with the perpetrator. However, the idea of a continuum of violence does have some limitations in historical analysis. It is a concept that emerges out of feminist readings of modern sexual identities and as such mounts a powerful critique of the insidious presence of violence in contemporary sexual culture. Superficially, the same kinds of things seem to have happened through history. As a feminist researcher one recognises and empathises with the stories of those who have experienced sexual violence, even in the far distant past. However, it is also important to distinguish this emotional and political reaction from historical analysis. Historians are now sensitive to the histories of superficially timeless aspects of human existence. The body, sexuality, reproduction, intimacy and emotion are physiological and psychological 'facts of life' but they are also culturally produced and reproduced and shift over time in meaning and how they are experienced. It is therefore questionable how far we can read back modern formulations of sexual violence into past societies in which both violence and sexuality figured rather differently than they do today.

This is not to say that modern feminist theory, such as the idea of the continuum of violence, has been ignored in historical analysis. Recently, gender historians have read the historical material against the grain, looking outside of the criminal justice system's own definitions and boundaries. The historical record is inevitably incomplete and these interpretations are always contingent and often tentative, though they are expanding knowledge about the intersections of violence and sexuality over time. Furthermore, the changing nature of the sources means that different questions can be asked and answered for different periods and also the varying concerns of historians researching specific eras means that sexual violence crops up rather differently in their writing. Nevertheless, it is possible to detect changing perceptions of sexual violence in the law, medicine, psychiatry and later psychology from the nineteenth century which, by the twentieth century, coincided with recognisably modern sexualities. In the later twentieth century, a new generation of feminists challenged the blind spots about power and gender in these dominant perceptions both theoretically and politically, not least by developing concepts such as the continuum of sexual violence.

## Rape law and medieval society

Research on the medieval period has explored the origins of the laws on sexual violence. These differed from current formulations, but established principles and assumptions which proved historically enduring, despite the changes in the social contexts of sexual violence which were brought about by centuries of historical change. Social experience of sexual violence and people's uses of the medieval courts are harder to recover, but there are indications of tensions between the written law, legal practice and individuals' sense of injury (Carter 1982, 1985).

There were few cases of sexual violence in the medieval legal system and the conviction rate was significantly lower than for other crimes (Jones 2006: 78). This period saw the growth of written law and the development of criminal justice. The individual harm to women and girls was de-emphasised in new statute law on rape (Gourlay 1996). The trend was to conflate laws against rape (bodily sexual assault) with the punishment of *raptus* or ravishment (the abduction of women, in particular of virgins). *Raptus/ravishment* was a crime against property, and as such it attracted severe punishment (Bashar 1987). It was also sometimes used to prosecute the abduction of male servants, or to discipline clergy who had reneged on celibacy (Hawkes 2007: 126; Jones 2006: 77; Bullough 1982). These laws were a complex and uncertain amalgam of two evolving legal traditions. Roman law, as adopted in continental Europe, also underpinned the ecclesiastical law enforced in the English church courts. This gave greater emphasis to the element of abduction. A more oral Germanic tradition, originating in Anglo-Saxon England, distinguished rape from abduction and treated rape as personal injury and the loss of a woman's sexual reputation – something vital for her social worth. In post-Conquest England the formal (rarely applied) penalty was castration and blinding (Saunders 2001: 73–6). The law on *raptus* did not address sexual violence against men and boys. Sodomy, a moral crime for which both parties were triable, was a matter dealt with, if at all, by the ecclesiastical courts (Bray 1990).

Two key statutes known as Westminster I and II of 1275 and 1285 first codified the shift in the law on rape (Post 1978). Following the Westminster statutes ravishment was a capital felony defined as the abduction of a woman without her consent or, if she was under 14, irrespective of consent. Even if a woman subsequently consented, the crime was still to be tried and she was to be barred from any inheritance, thus dealing with situations where an abduction was the cover for (voluntary) elopement (Jones 2006: 77). Furthermore, the King was given the right to prosecute the crime if a woman had not lodged the case within 40 days. A statute of 1382 extended the right to prosecute to a woman's male kin or guardians (Saunders 2001: 37; Baines 1998: 70).

The growth of the law and legal process in the medieval period was a consequence of monarchs' attempts to establish a countrywide system of justice which would ensure the 'king's peace' over and above the authority of local, manorial courts (Harding 1973). Punishment for all kinds of offences was generally more severe for those of lower social status (Hanawalt 1975). The law aimed to maintain social inequalities, including but by no means exclusively those of gender. The rape of virgin heiresses or nuns attracted higher penalties than that of poorer, lower-status women. An Act of 1487 specifically excluded bond women (servants) from the protection of the law on rape (Hawkes 2007: 127).

Following the Norman Conquest, primogeniture, the inheritance of property by the eldest legitimate (male) heir, became more common. Questions of family, legitimacy, the regulation of reproduction (and hence the control of women's sexuality) were important to property transfer. There was therefore an overlap in the law's intention to punish both sexual violence and the encroachment on the rights of fathers, husbands or other male kin to control a woman's sexuality and reproductive capacity (Saunders 2001: 48). The laws on ravishment served the interests of the wealthy, and some cases amounted to dynastic power struggles fought out over the bodies of elite women. However, many cases were originated by women of more moderate social status.

In Emma Hawkes's study of 132 later fourteenth-century indictments, around two thirds of cases involved married women and where the violence was against single women, the loss of virginity was not emphasised. However, indictments for the *raptus* or ravishment of wives also often mentioned the theft of their husbands' property. On marriage women's material possessions became legally owned by their husbands; the abduction of a wife meant the theft of the husband's property in her clothing and personal items. Although medieval women were not chattels, women, reputation and family or household property were closely associated. Hawkes finds that indictments were careful to use different words to distinguish property theft from sexual violence. The prosecutions focused on personal injury, but in the legal instrument which defined the crime, elements of property, theft and the wrongs to male kin remained closely associated (Hawkes 2007).

Prosecuting a case was arduous for the woman or girl involved. It required prompt and rational action following the attack, the humiliating display of her violated body to male authority figures, repeated visits to court and having to remember and repeat her charge word for word (Saunders 2001: 63; Hanawalt 1978: 34, 61). The legal formulae required were precise; any error or deviation could lose the case. Declaring rape in public jeopardised sexual chastity and the possibility of future marriage. There was a requirement to show resistance, but this in itself could indicate a lack of feminine respectability. The problems of proof were exacerbated since pregnancy was widely taken as evidence of sexual consent, the theory being that conception required the sexual pleasure of women as well as men. Many cases were settled out of court or abandoned, sometimes with a cash settlement and sometimes by marriage. Where the woman or girl who brought the original complaint used the older legal process of appeal she was subject to imprisonment if the case was abandoned. Women bringing unsuccessful charges of rape might also face charges of defamation or fornication (Jones 2006: 78). Even if a verdict was obtained punishment was often light (Kittel 1982; Orr 1994; Walker 1987). However, Barbara Hanawalt has suggested that even when a rape prosecution resulted in acquittal, the opportunity to relate the events and name the accused might have proved sufficiently satisfying to 'outweigh the danger to women's own reputation' (Hanawalt 1998: 133; Klerman 2002: 312).

The medieval laws established the legislative framework for the criminal prosecution of sexual violence against women and girls until the nineteenth century. Statutes of 1555 and 1597 indirectly established abduction and rape as separate offences. In 1576 rape became a capital felony. However, there is no sign that greater clarity in the law led either to larger numbers of charges or to a higher conviction rate (Baines 1998: 72).

## Interpreting Early Modern cases

The greater production and survival of court records for the Early Modern period (the fifteenth to eighteenth centuries) has meant that by examining cases of fornication, adultery, defamation, sodomy and assault as well as those for rape and attempted rape, historians have been able to ask more detailed questions about narrative construction and cultural meanings of sexual violence than has generally been possible for the medieval period. Both rape and sodomy were widely written about as heinous offences which destabilised social order. However, as specific criminal offences they were extremely difficult for the law to 'see' (Herrup 1999: 27, 29). Cases often pitted younger or lower-status complainants against adult men in a society where credibility depended on social status and where unequal social status frequently legitimated the use of force (Walker 1998: 29; Gowing 2003: 90).

As an offence, sodomy was differently positioned than rape since the 'property' element did not apply. Sodomy first became a secular offence in the 1530s as part of the legislative programme which accompanied Henry VIII's break with the legal authority of the Catholic Church in England. It was defined as penetrative sex between male partners, between human and animal, or anal sex between men and women, and was an offence for both parties irrespective of consent, unless one of them was either a boy below the age of criminal responsibility (14) or a girl below the age of sexual consent (effectively 10). Male homosociality, clientage and patronage underpinned much of Early Modern public life. The idea that homosexual practice defined a distinct sexual identity emerged (arguably) only much later in the Early Modern period. Sodomy was seen as unfettered desire, and this disturbed social rather than sexual order. Sodomy was dangerous not primarily because it involved unauthorised sexual choices, nor because it might involve coercion, rather because it manifested a lack of the self-control that was becoming increasingly necessary to ideals of manhood. Because of this, 'sodomy "existed" only when someone chose to see it' (Herrup 1999: 35); that is, where a man's conduct disturbed the prevailing social order, usually on a local or sometimes on a wider scale. King James I and Francis Bacon, Earl of Verulam were two of several examples of high-status men accused of sodomy together with other allegations of misconduct in public life (Herrup 1996, 1999: 33–4; Shepard 2003; Breitenberg 1996: 59–61).

Probably the most widely publicised case of rape and sodomy was that of the Earl of Castlehaven (1631). Castlehaven was a rare example of a high-status man found guilty and executed for sexual offences, which included abetting the rape of both his wife and daughter-in-law and sodomy with his servants. Although analyses of the case since the eighteenth century emphasise the Earl's sexual transgression, at the time the case seemed most disturbing because of his failure to maintain proper decorum in his own household. The (orderly) Early Modern household was the microcosm of hierarchical society and the kingdom itself. During the 1630s, as King Charles I's relations with his parliaments worsened, such disruption within an elite household had particular political resonance and mirrored what seemed rotten in the Stuart state (Herrup 1996, 1999).

Sexual violence in warfare has been a recurrent event across centuries of history and can be located at the most extreme reaches of a continuum of violence since it is about inflicting pain and humiliation on communities and nations over and above that which it causes to specific individuals. I shall take up these issues in more detail when reviewing the modern period. However, the historical nuances were equally complex at earlier periods and, as Herzog comments, sexual violence in war has figured in the spectrum of torture, killing and mutilation visited on defeated and often civilian populations 'in quite distinct historically and geographically specific ways' (Herzog 2009: 4). The 1641 Irish rebellion arose from native (Catholic) Irish indignation at what they saw as the illegitimacy of the rule of the English king and the threats to their own independence and culture. Narratives of the ordeal of Protestant settlers in Ireland, seeking recognition of losses in the rebellion, included stories of rape in which the degree of wrong, blame and dishonour was adjudicated from a community perspective. Rape underlined the atrocity but only when a woman's existing reputation was good, or the circumstances rendered blame impossible to attribute to her. Even in wartime, sexual violence was in the eye of the commentator (Hall and Malcolm 2010).

In the Early Modern period there was a cultural acceptance of women's sexual pleasure. However, outside marriage the sexually desiring woman very often appeared tainted by 'whorishness, witchcraft ... [or] ... sin' (Gowing 2003: 85). Sexual violence is rare in Early Modern records, but some women and girls did come to court to protest against the personal injury of sexual violence even though the odds were stacked against them and they could articulate their wrongs only in muted form. This was an era that often understood emotional states through their social effects and consequences, through religion and the workings of providence, or even through the action of the supernatural, not as in modern society through interiority and the psyche. Although there are examples of women suffering emotional hurt following sexual assaults (Macdonald 1981: 87, 106), the chief injury of sexual violence was considered to be to reputation, rather than the modern view which prioritises psychological damage. Women's reputations were crucial in shaping their social position and depended on sexual chastity even more than on their work and household duties (Walker 1996). Loss of virginity was not the only concern. Married women, who arguably had greater access to the range of metaphor and allusion with which rape could be described in court, made up the majority of the complainants in Laura Gowing's research, which uses ecclesiastical court records (Gowing 1996, 2003). Given the cultural complexities of sexual violence and the power dynamics in the legal institutions that tried it, courtroom narratives need to be appreciated as multilayered and allusive texts which, with careful reading, can shed some light, however tangential, on sexual identities and cultures as well as on legal process.

Anthropologist Mary Douglas argued that rituals or talk about dirt and pollution sign social and cultural disruptions and things out of place (Douglas 1991). Miranda Chaytor has used a psychological approach to read the silences and metaphors in women's court depositions, which, she proposes, were a narrative means of skirting around the shame and dishonour implicit in a woman's description of the injury done to her. Although there was no pattern of 'honour killing' as can, for example, be identified in mid-twentieth century Greece (Avdela 2010), metaphors of pollution, of disruption, or assertions of honour founded in non-sexual matters provided a way of signalling the sexual violence which, Chaytor argues, might be sufficiently shameful to be repressed in direct memory (Chaytor 1995). However, as Garthine Walker points out, such an approach tends to read modern perceptions of sexual violence back in time (Walker 1998: 1). In fact the legal definition of rape shaped seventeenth-century narratives in a variety of contexts.

Such accounts navigated understandings of sex grounded in men's activity and women's passivity (Walker 1998: 3–4, 2003: 53–60; Gowing 2003: 86). Husbands' long-established rights of ongoing sexual access to their wives meant that inequalities were easily generalised to other sexual relationships. Gender was one of several intersecting axes of subordination which together meant that women's rights over their own bodies were constrained. Women 'submitted' to intercourse and submission implied consent even when forced. Women testified that they had been 'thrown down' when they were describing both consensual and forced intercourse (Gowing 2003: 100) and courtroom stories emphasised fear, powerlessness and silence. Other cases explained sexual violence as the perpetrator's overweening passion and so mirrored the understanding of sodomy as excessive desire. Men's counter-stories suggested entrapment or seduction and Capp has argued that, alongside insults alleging sexual impotence or cuckoldry, accusations of sexual violence were feared by Early Modern men and could be damaging to male reputation (Walker 1998: 9–11; Shepard 2003; Capp 1999). In general rape was described in terms of men's violence, not of sex. One woman told how a man

> tooke my horse by the bridle beateing me on the face with his fist till I was bloddy and forced me to alight telling me I should stay till morneing, and being downe he fell upon me, strugling with me, almost stranglinge me with my hood and there forceably ravished me and had the Carnall use of my bodye against my will, I cryeing out but none came to helpe me.... All which being done... [he left her].
>
> (Walker 1998: 7)

The sexual intercourse is neither described nor elaborated by adjectival emphasis. The woman stressed her physical struggle against strangulation but when raped she called for the help of (absent) others. Few women who escaped sexual violence through their own physical force underlined the fact. Crying out, being rescued or running away were narratively more successful strategies, which could hope to distinguish a rape from the kind of forced submission which, in the dominant understanding, amounted to consent. Early-nineteenth century texts on the emerging discourse of medical jurisprudence, which inherited and documented this formulation of consent, argued that 'contusions on various parts of the extremities and body... are compatible with final consent on the part of the female' and also 'it is to be recollected that many women will not consent without some force' (Farr 1815: 45; Beck 1825: 55–7; cited by Clark 1987b: 17).

Because the courts aimed to police sexual morality, seventeenth-century records also include plenty of stories of consensual and enthusiastic sexual activity (particularly heterosexual). However, rape narratives which emphasised female passivity were culturally dominant. Forced intercourse outside marriage was understood as causing personal and social injury which, where it could be articulated, demanded severe punishment, but at the same time it remained always on the map of (authorised) sexual behaviour. Within marriage, sexual violence was perhaps even harder to articulate, though by the eighteenth century at least, nervous illness was one indirect means for genteel women to signal the injuries of an abusive marriage (Foyster 2002). There was therefore a very complex relationship between such stories and sexual culture, which some historical analyses of sexual violence miss (Gowing 2003: 108–10).

For example Edward Shorter argued that the rape of adult women declined by the late nineteenth century because of the greater opportunities for consensual sex in industrial society (including earlier marriage and contraception) (Shorter 1977). Shorter was correct that the social conditions of sexuality had changed over time. However, his theory means projecting a twentieth-century model of male heterosexuality as an innate drive requiring libidinous release, back into the sixteenth and seventeenth centuries. He did not perceive how sexual cultures and sexual practices might change historically and was also overly confident in the extent to which criminal statistics might reflect the social incidence of sexual violence.

## Sexual violence, sexual culture and the transition to modernity

Shorter's work (Shorter 1975, 1982) can be positioned with other research that aims to construct metanarratives about modernisation and cultures of sexuality, family and procreation and which directly or indirectly raises questions about violence in sexual culture. Lawrence Stone argued that modern society gave greater priority to companionate sexual intimacy (Stone 1977). The egalitarian nuclear family, affective intimate relations and (by implication) consensual, romantic sex between married couples was the eventual outcome of social historical changes that originated in the middle classes from the later eighteenth century. By this token, violence should arguably have been displaced from intimate relations, including sexual ones, in parallel with the decline of public violence suggested by the 'civilising process'.

More recent work (inspired in part by Foucault) also suggests that with the approach of modernity, sexuality became more central to identity and, by extension, that sexual violence became increasingly an aspect of sexuality. Randolph Trumbach detects cultural changes whereby a specifically homosexual identity (the third sex) took shape around sexual subcultures centred on certain inns known as 'molly houses' which became centres of same-sex encounter in eighteenth-century London (Trumbach 1988). Nevertheless, homosexual sexual practices did not in general shape an individual's social value in the same way as loss of chastity did for women and girls. Sexual violence and coercion in all-male locations (in the Navy or the universities) was hardly unknown though rarely became a matter for the courts. A conviction for sodomy required evidence of penetration and ejaculation, to be confirmed by two witnesses. Unsurprisingly, few acts of sodomy came to court, and even fewer where the sex was consensual. Most cases involving homosexual sex were tried as indecent assault. The evidential requirements were less exacting and the penalties imprisonment or the pillory (Hitchcock 1997: 60–4).

Both Trumbach and Hitchcock argue that the cultural priority was for eighteenth-century heterosexual men to demonstrate their difference from 'sodomites'. Heterosexual masculinity had to be demonstrated aggressively by penetrative sex with women and avoiding masturbation and same-sex practices. Hitchcock sees masculine phallocentrism and penetrative sex replacing a pattern of premarital intimate relations that included a wide range of sexual play and avoided intercourse. This cultural change can explain the increasing numbers of illegitimate births by the early 1800s, something earlier accounted for (for example by Shorter) by the early development of industrial society, population increase and the growth of towns (Hitchcock 1997).

For women and men of the middle and upper classes, the cultures of 'sensibility', which historian Lawrence Stone saw as evidence of more modern emotionality in his history of the modern family (Stone 1977), are in this model more divisive. In literature (and arguably in culture), sensibility prioritised narratives of seduction, which matched a predatory male heterosexuality with a subservient female response, gilding the earlier narratives of male activity/ female passivity with (a kind of) romance and further sexualising the inevitability of female submission. Nevertheless, as with all such cultural narratives, it cannot be assumed that all 'fallen' women necessarily internalised it. Tanya Evans argues that single women who petitioned London's Foundling Hospital to look after their illegitimate children preferred to speak of misfortune and bad luck rather than seduction (Evans 2005).

While sensibility and romance enabled more affluent women to indulge in some pleasurable if illicit sex, for the most part this merely added a certain gloss to the brutish tendencies of heterosexual masculinities. Among working people, where increasing numbers of young women were domestic servants, subjected to intersecting grids of authority and highly vulnerable to sexual predation, sexual violence was just the nastier end of a continuum of courtship (Trumbach 1998).

If eighteenth-century rape could lead to marriage, this was not historically unprecedented, as research on the medieval period has shown. Seventeenth-century rape narratives also recount this kind of sexual behaviour. It seems likely that this model describes a shift in emphasis across more heterogeneous sexual cultures, rather than signalling entirely new behaviours. These models of changing (hetero)sexualities may or may not indicate that heterosex acquired an increasing potential for male on female sexual violence as the modern era dawned (Porter 1989). If they do, this qualifies and limits substantially the behaviour change argued to be a civilising process. Either way it is clear that even more effective neutralisations of sexual violence were becoming available, embedded in cultures of sexuality that thought about seduction and romance. The modern founding statement of the marital rape exemption is commonly attributed to jurist Matthew Hale in 1736 (Bourke 2007: 307).

Anna Clark argues that between 1770 and 1845 there was indeed an alteration in how sexual violence articulated gender and class relations (Clark 1987a). The idea of sexual 'fallenness' heightened the emphasis on women's responsibility to preserve their own chastity, now assumed to be even more vulnerable to predatory male sexuality. Clark suggests a shift from an earlier 'libertine' to a 'chivalric' model. Earlier, as we have seen, male sexual irregularities (including both violence and sex with other men) were decried as an uncontrolled (libertine) excess of desire. Those subjected to sexual violence were unlikely to see their attacker punished. However, they were not necessarily morally responsible for his violence. The succeeding 'chivalric' mode addressed sexual violence to women and girls in particular. Under this framework, women were increasingly taught to rely on the protection of men (particularly husbands and fathers) to preserve their chastity (though they themselves remained responsible for its loss). A stronger investment in domestic life and companionate if strictly unequal marital relations became an attribute of respectable mid-Victorian masculinities (Tosh 2007). Away from the protection of husbands and fathers, feminine sexual attractiveness was seen as provoking potentially uncontrolled male desire, and hence, in effect, female victims were assumed to have caused the violence they experienced. The rapist became represented as monstrous and therefore different from respectable men; by the later nineteenth century he was a marginal, working-class deviant. His gender opposite was the prostitute, the symbolic embodiment of social marginality and dangerously excessive female sexuality (Walkowitz 1992: 20).

The Victorian family, on the model of middle-class, gendered domesticity, had become an important symbol of social order. Rape of women and girls therefore acquired heightened significance; it had the potential for great social harm – a 'fate worse than death'. This bolstered male authority in the home and made it increasingly difficult for women to make full use of the criminal justice process, which was itself taking a greater interest in interpersonal violence as crime. So much of Victorian women's 'deviance', from illegitimate pregnancy to promiscuity, from prostitution to public discussion of sexual violence, was explained by feminine sexuality, that these overlaps seem to suggest another application of Kelly's continuum concept. However, though these connections had powerful effects on nineteenth-century gender relations, the notion of a continuum does not really work. The debilities and dangers attributed to female sexuality were ubiquitous. If this misogyny was a continuum of (cultural) violence then the concept is so far broadened that it loses interpretive momentum. In fact, such sexually-rooted frailties were re-examined, reinterpreted and redeployed in terms of the circumstances of individual cases. As a result, some women did get justice for the sexual violence done to them. Those perpetrators were punished in the interests of maintaining hegemonic masculinity, a move that rendered so much other sexual violence invisible, scaffolded the inequalities of the gender order, and thus underwrote dominant (hetero)sexual cultures and the potential for violence within them.

## Sexual violence and the law, eighteenth–nineteenth century

Many new capital statutes were introduced in the later eighteenth century, but trials and convictions for sexual violence remained rare. The Old Bailey Sessions Papers show an average of 29 defendants tried for rape per decade between the 1750s and 1810s. Other assize circuits show even lower totals (Simpson 1984: 811–13). The legal definition had tightened over the eighteenth century until courts required proof of emission and physical force as well as penetration. Over half of eighteenth-century complainants at the Old Bailey were below the age of consent; adult women's chances of seeing a rapist convicted (then as now) were remote. Simpson suggests that the sexual abuse of girls was encouraged by the belief that intercourse with a virgin cured venereal disease (Simpson 1987). The acquittal rate was also extremely high. At the Old Bailey between the 1750s and 1810s, an average of 4.5 men per decade were found guilty of rape (calculated from data at http://www.oldbaileyonli-ne.org). On the Norfolk Assize circuit there were a mere 15 convictions and 11 executions for rape between 1768 and 1818 and a further four convictions and three executions for buggery and sodomy. On the Home circuit between 1755 and 1814, 38 rape convictions led to 18 executions, and 14 buggery convictions produced 12 executions (Emsley 2005: 262).

In the early nineteenth century, prison sentences replaced hanging for many property and subsequently violence offences. Prison seemed a more rational measure since capital punishment had done nothing to deter rising crime rates (Gatrell 1994). There was also a progressive codification of the laws against violence. Given its class bias and the fact that far more violent crime was (and is) committed by men than women, these laws took greatest effect against working-class men. Wiener argues that this 'civilising offensive' meant more sexual violence cases in the higher courts from the 1820s. However, conviction rates increased only after capital punishment for rape was first discontinued (1836) and then repealed (1841) (Wiener 2004). The Old Bailey Sessions Papers show seven defendants found guilty of rape in the 1820s, 12 in the 1830s, 85 in the 1840s and as many as 196 in the 1880s (http//:www.oldbaileyonline.org). By 1860 the offences of indecent assault, assault with intent and assault with sodomitical intent had been written into black letter law and secondary charges could be brought together with rape or sodomy (Wiener 2004: 91). Sodomy, by this time used to prosecute a range of male–male sexual practices, formally became a non-capital offence in 1861 though hanging had been discontinued in 1836 (Weeks 1977: 14).

The 1861 Offences Against the Person Act was a major consolidating statute. This named rape as a felony subject to at least three years penal servitude, but left the precise definition of the offence unclear (Stevenson 2000: 96, 2005). In a remark which says more about dominant models of manliness than it does about sexual violence, indecent assault was specified as 'what all right-minded men, men of sound and wholesome feelings would say was indecent' (Justice Brett, *The Times*, 3 August 1875: 10). Although conviction rates for rape improved, the imprecise definitions meant many cases were dropped or tried as a lesser offence before they reached the higher courts. There are instances of judges simply refusing to hear evidence where they thought the defendant too respectable to have committed the crime (Wiener 2004: 90; D'Cruze 1998; Conley 1986: 24).

Criminal justice had developed since the eighteenth century and many of the institutional and professional characteristics of modern criminal justice were being forged in this period, including the stereotypes that distinguished 'deserving' from 'undeserving' complaints of sexual violence. Defence counsel were generally retained (Prisoners Counsel Act 1836). Trials took longer and, although the same situation did not apply in Ireland (Conley 1995), English complainants regularly faced hostile cross-examination designed to destroy their moral character. Less respectable women rarely obtained a verdict – it was assumed that they were little harmed by sexual violence since their characters were already lost. Judges were required to warn juries about the dangers of convicting on a complainant's uncorroborated testimony in trials for sexual offences until 1994 (Stevenson 1999). An accusation of rape was less damaging to the reputation of an otherwise respectable, 'manly' man or boy than the experience of having been raped could be for a woman who could not demonstrate the highest standards of sexual probity. Nevertheless, chivalrous masculinities on the bench and the fact that feminine weakness was taken for granted also meant gestures towards the protection of demonstrably respectable women. Associations such as the Society for the Protection of Women and Children funded some particularly 'deserving' complainants (Conley 1986: 526).

Summary courts, where magistrates tried minor offences without a jury and referred serious cases to the higher courts, became an important site for the filtering of sexual violence cases (D'Cruze 1998; Stevenson 1999, 2000). However, even a conviction for a lesser offence meant a kind of limited justice, when pursuing a case into the higher court would be expensive and with a good chance of an acquittal. Indeed, courts' agendas of punishing disorderly (working-class) masculinities meant they could be realistic about what kind of sexual chastity constituted appropriate victimhood (Jones 2000). Magistrates also heard paternity cases where an illegitimate child was liable to be charged to the poor rate. As in earlier centuries, these cases might enable at least some kind of public hearing of a complaint of rape. In fact, the criminal justice process stood alongside other informal means of settlement, usually by the payment of money. Louise Jackson notes Victorian child sexual abuse cases that came to court only when informal negotiations failed. The lower courts were also where most of the comparatively few sexual abuse cases involving boys (7 per cent in Jackson's research sample) were dealt with (Jackson 2000: 38, 100).

In Victorian times sexual chastity came nearer to encompassing women's moral integrity and sense of self. If Early Modern witnesses often emphasised violence to avoid describing sex, in the nineteenth century a melodramatic narrative of violent seduction became a common discursive terrain on which courts, the fast-growing press and other print culture discussed sexual violence. This language indicated a shift in legal and cultural perceptions of the harm of sexual violence, from damaging a woman's social reputation to what Vigarello refers to as its 'moral violence' (Vigarello 2001). Frequently complainants used this discourse, taking up appropriately feminine, vulnerable and sexually passive subject positions (Clark 1987a; Conley 1991; Stevenson 2000: 240; Bourke 2007: 398). Witnesses argued that 'he did what he should not do', or that 'he effected his purpose'. The euphemism and allusion made it difficult to specify the precise details about sexual acts which were necessary evidence (Stevenson 2005). There were class (and race) as well as gender interests at work. These were 'crimes of outrage' and chivalric courts and juries might well punish the attackers, provided they appeared unmanly, brutal and uncivilised. Hegemonic manly masculinities needed some 'real' rapists to punish. 'Real' rape was physically very violent, non-consensual intercourse, perpetrated by a (probably) lower-class man who failed to live up to masculine ideals on other fronts, and which was accomplished against a chaste woman who was robbed of her moral probity and thus of her social worth. However, if the case could be made to look like seduction – or even boyish high spirits – punishment could be slight. The nineteenth-century 'civilising offensive' not only increased the discipline of (working-class) male violence through the criminal justice system, it also had lessons for women and girls. If it taught (some) men restraint, the burden of the feminist scholarship would also be that it taught women the demeanour of femininity with all its powerlessness and need for protection.

As in the Early Modern period, the nineteenth century also saw moments when sexual violence became very visible and apparently socially destabilising. Victorian ideologies meant that above all violated young girls embodied this sense of threat. The symbolic importance of the (middle-class) family also involved the idealisation of the innocent (girl) child. However, assumed feminine weakness meant fears about the potential (sexual) corruption of girls. The sexual abuse of young girls was located as an urban problem of the social and sexual depravity of the labouring classes. Medical opinion was slow to recognise the physical evidence of sexual abuse and sexually transmitted diseases (gonorrhoea was identified only in 1879) and much readier to attribute such bodily signs to dirt, poor childcare or masturbation. The sexually precocious and knowing girl herself became a source of danger, a perspective reproduced in early criminological studies on female delinquency (Jackson 2000).

Middle-class campaigners on moral (social purity) issues bundled sexual violence against children together with the issue of child prostitution. Their lobbying achieved a rise in the age of consent for girls to 13 in 1875. In the 1880s there were scares over 'white slavery' and the trafficking of English teenagers to Belgian brothels (Mort 2000: 102–6; Bland 1995: ch. 3). A big public campaign included a series of articles in the popular press, for which the editor of the *Pall Mall Gazette* actually procured a girl, ostensibly for prostitution (Gorham 1978; Walkowitz 1992: ch. 3). The 1885 Criminal Law Amendment Act (CLAA) raised the age of consent for girls to 16 and, as an afterthought, also criminalised 'gross indecency' (other than sodomy) between men. The 1885 CLAA also recognised other kinds of moral violence as rape. It confirmed the existing tendency in case law that intercourse obtained by fraud, against a drunk or drugged victim or with 'imbeciles' was also rape, and thus moved further towards a model of consent as rational and contractual while criminal justice practice continued to reflect dominant assumptions of femininity as non-rational. These statutes framed the law on sexual violence – and the philosophy behind it – until late in the twentieth century. The Victorian legal positioning of sexual violence as something that did not impinge on authority relations or intimacies within families meant that vaginal rape within marriage remained excluded from the criminal law until 1991

(1989 in Scotland). Nor was there a law against incest until 1908 (Temkin 1986: 59).

During the First World War legal and criminal justice attention to sexual disorder focused on the potential damage to fighting men. Some of the earliest official and unofficial policewomen were recruited to police the sexual behaviour of women in garrison towns. There were of course concerns about the disorderliness of the 'licentious soldiery' but even greater anxieties were focused on so-called 'amateur prostitutes', teenage girls driven by 'khaki fever' to undermine fighting fitness and spread venereal disease among the troops. The Defence of the Realm Act (albeit later rescinded) ordered the detention of a woman infected with venereal disease who had intercourse with members of the armed forces. On the home front in both World Wars questions of violence and coercion were largely subsumed to matters of morale and national defence (D'Cruze and Jackson 2009: 150–51).

There was a sustained increase in cases of sexual violence reported after the Second World War. In 1947 there were 240 rape cases in England and Wales. There were 1,090 in 1976, 2,471 in 1987 and 6,281 by 1997. The British Crime Survey, which records data by interview rather than police records, estimated in the 1980s that only around a quarter of cases were reported to the police, and women's organisations which assist rape victims suggested even higher levels of non-reporting. As in earlier centuries, many cases were filtered out of the criminal justice process and failed to reach a verdict, let alone a conviction (Gregory and Lees 1999). From the late nineteenth century the police prosecuted criminal offences and became an important institutional site where sexual violence cases were filtered out of the criminal justice process. A Scottish study in the 1970s found that a quarter of cases reported as rape, or attempt to ravish, were marked as 'no crime' by the police. The Scottish Procurator Fiscal decided not to initiate proceedings in 30 per cent of the cases referred to him by the police (a much higher rate than for other kinds of crime) (Temkin 1986, 2002; Rumney 2001).

The 1956 Sexual Offences Act (SOA) consolidated but did not change the Victorian law. It specifically excluded the possibility of male rape. Homosexual acts between adult men in private were decriminalised only in 1967 (SOA 1967). As regards rape, complainants were if anything further disadvantaged by the SOA of 1976 which codified the decision in *DPP* v. *Morgan* the previous year and stated that a defendant could not be guilty of rape if he believed the complainant had consented, however unreasonable his belief was. This same Act turned a deaf ear to the Heilbron Report of 1975 which argued for a clearer statement that evidence of physical resistance should not be required. Case law of 1981 (Olugboja 1981 3 All ER 1382) reserved the matter of consent to the jury; juries might be even more influenced by victim-blaming rape myths than were judges and the police (Temkin 2002: 92).

Women complaining of sexual violence were still regularly disbelieved and treated harshly by police and criminal justice. The myths that it was impossible to rape a resisting woman, that women and girls lie about rape or that they say 'no' when they mean 'yes', were widely accepted. Post-war generations of (especially white, middle-class) Western women had greater access to education, paid work and, from the 1960s, to oral contraception.

37

Reliable contraception loosened the connection between sexuality and reproduction, though this could prove an ambiguous benefit. While it liberated some women from anxieties about pregnancy it also reinforced masculine assumptions about women's sexual availability. Being 'on the pill' could be taken to imply ongoing consent. Jobs and careers meant the risk of sexual harassment in the workplace (Gregory and Lees 1999). The greater autonomy that Western women obtained in the post-war era ironically could be held to increase their complicity. In 1982 in Britain a man was merely fined for raping a young woman hitchhiker. A judge commented that 'it is the height of imprudence for any girl to hitchhike at night. ... She is in the true sense asking for it.' The following year another judge said of the statutory rape of a seven-year-old girl by her father's friend that it was 'one of the kind of accidents that could almost happen to anyone.' In 1982 an episode of a documentary TV series on police work showed hostile treatment of a rape complainant by Thames Valley Police and caused a marked public reaction (Adler 1987: 2–3; Temkin 2002: 3).

As late as 1984/5, a Royal Commission refused the opportunity to rethink or expand the legal definition of rape and other sexual offences, except in setting aside the marital rape exemption where couples were legally separated (Temkin 2002: 83–4). Britain lagged behind other countries in seriously reviewing its laws on sexual violence (Temkin 1986: 26, 36). Male rape was recognised only in 1994 (Criminal Justice and Public Order Act 1994) and a comprehensive overhaul in the law was delayed until the SOA 2003 (Stevenson *et al.* 2004).

### Sexual violence, penality and medical science

Although the Victorian law on sexual violence had become focused on the harm of moral violence, by the early twentieth century, the identification of sexual violence with deviance and marginality had become authorised by the emergent discourses of criminology, psychiatry and subsequently psychology.

Between 1860 and 1914, progressively less indictable crime including fewer violence offences came to court; key evidence for the 'civilising process' (Gurr 1981: Eisner 2003). However, sexual offences increased in number. This has been explained as reduced tolerance for sexual violence and rather greater gender equality (Fuchs 2005: 67); even so, it qualifies the nature and extent of any 'civilising process'. Furthermore, many of these cases involved the sexual assault of children, and less than a third resulted in conviction (Jackson 2000: 23-4). From a different perspective, these trends indicate new and intensified disciplinary regimes directed at poor families. A wider complex of combined penal and welfare measures in the first half of the twentieth century enabled a role for social workers, psychologists, probation officers and police, many of them women. What Garland has termed the 'penal-welfare' complex (Garland 1985) confronted sexual violence in a number of ways. Growing numbers of sexually abused girls were placed in children's homes alongside both young offenders and girls needing care for other reasons, despite concerns that they would morally corrupt the other children (Children's Acts 1908, 1933).

Notwithstanding emergent criminological and psychological knowledges, their treatment continued to combine moralistic and therapeutic approaches well into the twentieth century. To adopt Garland's terminology, Victorian and modern cultures of penality persistently remained combined (Garland 1991: 127). Both of these perspectives targeted sexual promiscuity and knowingness as the key danger, thus obscuring issues of sexual violence and coercion (Jackson 2000: 68, 71, 150; Cox 2003: ch. 6).

This was contested professional territory. In Scotland medical and legal professionals explained child sexual abuse by citing an unsubstantiated popular belief in the 'virgin cure' for sexually transmitted disease. This countered the moral arguments of feminists and social purists and allowed professionals to focus on the physical rather than the emotional damage caused (Davidson 2001). Differences of opinion among psychologists, following Freud's change of mind over whether adult neuroses were rooted in child abuse or were the outcome of hysteria, helped submerge the violence of child abuse in diagnoses of family dysfunction and adolescent girls' sexual waywardness. The incidence of child sexual abuse is extremely hard to determine. There is some evidence of a reduction during the two World Wars but an increase thereafter (Jackson 2000: 25-6). The issue resurfaced in the 1970s. The identification of numbers of children as sexually abused in Cleveland turned on medical diagnoses of abuse and marked something of the limits of professional interventionism. Children were taken into care, some apparently mistakenly. Later moral panics about the 'satanic' abuse of children have proved more indicative of cultural anxiety than actual practices (Itzin 2000).

By the late twentieth century fears about the sexual danger to children had multiplied. Child sexual abuse was reconfirmed as a problem of families and neighbourhoods, but the potential this offered for insights into how sexual violence might be embedded into 'normal' intimate relationships was blunted by the more terrifying 'stranger danger' of the paedophile and the psychopathic murderer of children. The paedophile and the psychopath are psychiatric identity constructions that located sexual violence in specific, pathological individuals and superseded definitions of nineteenth-century sexual offenders as socially deviant, marginal and impoverished. Until extremely recently, these identities have been exclusively male (Bourke 2007: 127–9, ch. 10).

Nineteenth-century doctors were increasingly authoritative adjudicators of the bodily signs of sexual violence and physical resistance to it, though they were often reluctant to detect rape. From the 1880s there was closer medical and psychiatric scrutiny of the offender. By 1900 the science of criminal identification accompanied explorations of criminal physiognomies and other bodily identifiers. The Italian criminologist Lombroso worked to an evolutionary model which positioned sexual offenders as atavistic throw-backs. Criminological attention then moved from the body to the mind as Krafft-Ebing and other criminal psychiatrists elaborated taxonomies of sexual perversion and interpreted the harm of sexual assault as victims' psychological trauma (Davidson 2001; Cole 2002: ch. 2; Garvey 2005: ch. 1; Bourke 2007: 92–7).

For decades, convicted sexual offenders, from rapists to homosexuals, were subjected to medicalised regimes intended to cure them of their deviancy. Moreover, whereas some sexual offenders, including homosexuals, were considered as inadequate masculinities, rapists and other heterosexual violent offenders were thought of as displaying exaggerated masculine behaviour, positioning them as deviant but at the same time validating the potential for violence in 'normal' sex. From the early twentieth century sex offenders were 'treated' by sterilisation or castration intended to calm their sexual desire. Results were ambiguous, but there was some evidence that castrated offenders reoffended less frequently and became more socially conformist. Nazism and its genocidal programmes reduced the public credibility of surgical castration as a treatment for sexually violent offenders following the Second World War and there was contrary evidence that it did not necessarily destroy sexual function. From the 1940s chemical castration using synthetic oestrogens and other drugs was (and is) also used on both male and female offenders. This technique, directed mostly at male paedophiles, persisted despite psychological and physiological side effects, including in some cases the development of breasts. Attempts to cure violent sex offenders by lobotomy or leucotomy (surgically destroying particular neural pathways in the brain) also had variable outcomes. Psychological analysis was too protracted and expensive a procedure to be considered on any scale, though from the 1920s behaviouralist and conditioning techniques were used to reorientate rapists' patterns of sexual arousal. Group therapy and psychodrama were employed in prisons in the late 1940s. Better educated offenders appeared to be more suited to softer 'talking cures'. More forceful interventions were applied to resistant prisoners. Punishment and control have been disproportionately directed towards men who were already disadvantaged, often by race or class (Bourke 2007: chs 6, 7, 10). At the same time, the sexual violence intrinsic in many prison subcultures (a part of inmate power hierarchies rather than an expression of homosexuality) was dismissed as inevitable among a deviant offender population (Bourke 2007: ch. 12).

As Joanna Bourke argues, rape discourses produce the subjects they claim to describe. For example, indecent exposure had been classified under nineteenth century laws against vagrancy as a minor breach of order. By the mid-twentieth century it was defined as a sexual offence produced by a psychiatric condition. Such identifications enabled compliant sex offenders to occupy legitimated if deviant subject positions. Such constructions became sufficiently entrenched to take on other, less scientific meanings. The psychopath and the paedophile eventually became late-twentieth century hate figures in popular retributive moralism. By this time the penal-welfare complex had been substantially dismantled, and the influences of medicine and psychiatry in knowledges about and the treatment of sexual offenders were retained only insofar as they had become harnessed to more punitive strategies (Bourke 2007: 398, ch. 9).

## Sexual violence and modern warfare

Britain escaped invasion during the two World Wars and so was spared the epidemic outbreaks of rape perpetrated by victorious troops, including British and Allied forces, against defeated civilian populations across Europe and the Far East. Nevertheless there was an increase in sexual crime in Britain during the war, by both the military and civilian men. Some children were placed in sexual danger when they were evacuated (Bourke 2007: 363).

Sexual violence in warfare is frequently a technique aimed at increasing the pain and humiliation of defeat. The rape and murder of women is also an insult directed at the masculinities of the vanquished, manifestly unable to defend their homes, families and society. Despite the fact that rape was a serious contravention of most modern Western military codes, it has been very frequently condoned by military authorities. Since until very recently combatant military forces have been composed almost entirely of men, the gender dimensions of wartime rape have been stark. Rape provided a key sexual component to military masculinities and emphasised the feminised vulnerabilities of the defeated. Very often the victims of sexual violence were then murdered and there are many examples of associated mutilation and torture. (Herzog 2009; Harris 1993; Horne and Kramer 2001; Lilly 2007; Seifert 1994, 1996).

During the Second World War American GIs in Europe raped around 14,000 civilian women, in England, France and Germany. There were around 3,500 rapes by American servicemen in France between June 1944 and the end of the war. Robert Lilly's analysis explores the diversity of contexts of these rapes. In some situations rape was a cultural weapon or a matter of strategy. In others, it was part of masculine militarism or revenge against the enemy. Practices such as gang rape acted as recreation and social bonding among combatants, or were treated as a necessary libidinous release following combat. Between 110,000 and 900,000 women were raped by Russian soldiers in and around Berlin in 1945. The violence was indiscriminate. As well as Nazi supporters the victims included Jewish women and forced labourers. French soldiers committed rape on a large scale in Southern Baden Wittenberg. Moroccan mercenaries fighting with the remnants of the Free French Army in Italy were explicitly given licence to rape and plunder and British soldiers also raped women in France and Italy (Askin 1997: 59; Seifert 1996: 64; Bourke 2007: 360–1, 368–9; Lilly 2007).

Coerced sex was also part of a more general appropriation of female bodies which included forced prostitution and domestic labour. Many women chose prostitution rather than starvation or death, though many were killed anyway and others preferred suicide to the humiliation of rape (Askin 1997: 72, n. 238). Nazi attempts at genocide included forced sterilisations (of both women and men), abortions and other medicalised violence in the concentration camps. Following conflict, mixed-race children and their mothers have often faced hostility and discrimination since women's sexual and reproductive capacities were seen as national resources. Some births arose out of consensual sexual relations, but others were the result of rape. Other women had had very constrained choices. The children in Europe fathered by black American soldiers were especially visible. An estimated 5 per cent of all children born in Berlin between winter 1945 and summer 1946 had a Russian father (Ericsson and Simonsen 2005: 232–3). Although societies differed in the way that they addressed the issue, the original damage done by sexual violence was extended by the subsequent social stigma of miscegenation. The most recent large-scale example on European territory was the use of rape as a weapon of systematic genocide by Serbian forces in Bosnia–Herzegovina in 1992-3 (Stiglemayer 1994).

Following conflict the war crimes of the defeated attract punishment more readily than those of the victors, though some Allied troops were punished for sexual violence, including the execution of 70 American soldiers (Bourke 2007: 361). In 1945 tribunals at Nuremberg and Tokyo investigated major war crimes committed by the Axis Powers. However, unlike in Tokyo, Nuremberg paid little attention to crimes of sexual violence (including forced sterilisation and prostitution) (Askin 1997: 73, 88; Brouwer 2005: 6–7). It was a further half century before international law on sexual violence in warfare was substantially readdressed in a European tribunal. Meanwhile, prevailing international law had not prevented the genocide and sexual violence in Rwanda in 1994 (Melvern 2004: 251–4). The International Crime Tribunal for the former Yugoslavia argued for the explicit inclusion of wartime rape as a form of torture as well as a crime against humanity, and prosecuted rape in several trials (Hansen 2001). The Statute of the International Criminal Court (1998, applied from 2002) has expanded the specification of crimes against humanity to include a range of sexual offences, including sexual slavery, enforced prostitution, forced pregnancy, enforced sterilisation or other grave sexual violence (Brouwer 2005: 85). As with all changes in black-letter law, however, the direct effect on the violences in war and conflict cannot be expected to be great. In fact, on a global scale, if anything, in recent conflicts the distinction between combatants and non-combatants seems to have collapsed ever further, increasing people's vulnerabilities to all the violences of conflict.

**Modern sexual identities and sexual violence**

Alongside the medicalisation of sexual deviancy, sex itself was retheorised. Early in the twentieth century, sexology was an innovative, secular, scientific explanation which acknowledged the importance of sexual pleasure for both women and men. However, because it privileged and naturalised a model of sexual practice based on sharp gender dichotomies it provided a new rationale for the well-established premise that masculinity was the active, aggressive principle and femininity involved submission. Plenty of men, now charged with the responsibility of delivering female sexual fulfilment, found new levels of anxiety about their sexual performance (Hall 1991). If women could be blamed for 'frigidity' men could also be held accountable for causing it (Bourke 2007: 307ff). At the same time many women found sexology's insistence on female sexual pleasure liberating. However, the interwar popularisation of (Freudian) psychological models of human subjectivity and the idea of female masochism meshed with sexology to naturalise violent intercourse. Psychologist Helene Deutsch argued that women desired and fantasised rape (Garvey 2005: 19–20, 22). As Havelock Ellis argued, 'Rooted in the sexual instinct ... we find a delight in roughness, violence, pain and danger' (Ellis 1948: 95). Ordinary heterosexual practice seems to have concealed what would now be thought of as sexual violence or coercion, although at the time sexual violence was identified by its pathological nature, most clearly where it focused on an inappropriate sexual choice, especially children, or where it was accompanied by extreme physical violence. By the 1970s theories of victim precipitation elaborated a psychological framework for victim blaming (Garvey 2005: 29).

## Feminism and changing analyses of sexual violence

In her 1913 pamphlet *The Great Scourge* Christabel Pankhurst advocated 'Votes for Women and Chastity for Men'. The slogan sums up the position of first wave feminists; sexuality was a site of women's oppression but this could be remedied by giving women the vote. The Victorian women's movement had campaigned on prostitution and domestic violence and recognised the transmission of sexually transmitted diseases (STDs) as a form of sexual violence (Mort 2000: Part 3). Into the interwar period feminists recognised the injustices in the way women and child victims of sexual abuse were treated by police and criminal justice. They took up first voluntary and later professional work as advocates and statement takers and became part of emergent penal welfare approaches. Between the wars, some feminists campaigned for birth control or to change the law to allow abortion (Hall 2000; chs 6, 7; Hall 2005), but overall feminist attention to sexuality decreased. The predominance of sexology and scientific legitimation of patriarchal models of sex constrained feminist analyses until the 1970s saw a 'sea change' (Garvey 2005: 17) in attitudes to sexual violence, prompted in no small measure by new wave feminism and encouraged by a climate of post-war liberalisation of culture and in a number of areas of law, though as we have seen it took decades before there was meaningful revision of sexual violence law.

Out of this post-war generation for whom better access to paid work, education, public institutions and contraception increased both their exposure to sexual violence and their articulateness about it, emerged the breakthroughs in gender theory which prioritised the violent potential in dominant heterosex. Kate Millet introduced the then startling idea that sexuality and intimacy had a politics and were infused by power (Millet 1970). Susan Brownmiller made the radical feminist argument that:

> From prehistoric times to the present, I believe, rape has played a critical function. It is nothing more or less than a conscious process of intimidation in which *all* men keep *all* women in a state of fear.
>
> (Brownmiller 1975: 14–15, emphasis in the original)

Brownmiller's polemic was deliberately ahistoric. Her insistence that *all* men

43

were rapists meant that date, acquaintance and marital rape, and sexual harassment became more visible. However, *Against Our Will* located sexual violence as an issue for white women, ignoring how race doubled with gender in constituting sexual vulnerabilities. It veiled both the (far smaller amount of) sexual violence committed by women and victimisation of men as well as the inequalities in the punishment of sexual offenders. Nevertheless, this and other key second wave feminist texts mobilised a body of work which by the 1990s was to become a full and systematic engagement with gender oppression in dominant modes of sexuality in fields as diverse as pornography, media representation, criminal justice and the law. It is to no small extent due to feminist theorising and activism that the reactionary climate of 1970s and 1980s criminal justice has been eroded to the extent of changing the statute law, though, as the following chapters of this volume make clear, those who experience sexual violence (women, men and children) are still not necessarily assured of justice.

## Conclusion

In the Early Modern era the use of force was a prerogative of social status, and although both rape and sodomy were decried as serious crimes, in practice sexual violence and coercion was often hidden or unreadable, not least because dominant models of sexuality read submission as consent even when obtained by force. The medieval legal legacy conceptualised rape or *raptus* at least in part as a crime against the property men held in women's bodies and reproductive capacity. The transition to modernity was marked by changes from the later eighteenth century which gave greater value to masculinities that were aggressively heterosexual, although the potential for violence in these sexual cultures was glossed by romance and narratives of seduction. Although changes in sexual practices cannot necessarily be directly substantiated from cultural change, if valorised masculinities aimed to distance themselves from those whose same-sex practices branded them as 'sodomites' the outcome was to provide an increasingly sexualised rationale for male sexual predation. By the middle of the nineteenth century, dominant masculinities were committed to the chivalrous protection of female chastity but this also had the effect of containing and policing female sexuality in the name of family, respectability and social order. The nineteenth-century law and criminal justice system pursued social order through a civilising offensive against visible (male) violence. Its treatment of sexual violence was more contradictory. Because female sexuality was thought to be inherently unstable, dangerous and often threatening to respectable masculinities, women and girls complaining of sexual violence were frequently disbelieved and treated harshly. However, the project to police 'uncivilised' men meant there could also be chivalric gestures to 'protect' demonstrably chaste female victims. The location of the injury caused by sexual violence had shifted over time, from the social reputation of the Early Modern victim to the violence done to the victim's moral status by the late nineteenth century; moral status was heavily predicated on sexual chastity and the victim was gendered feminine.

As well as the law, other professions developed in the nineteenth century. In particular medicine, psychiatry and subsequently psychology claimed authority to speak out (not least as expert witnesses in court) on criminality, on sexuality and the signs of both sexual violence and sexual deviance on bodies and minds. One fairly early outcome was that by the 1880s homosexuality was established as a deviant social identity (rather than a sexual practice) and further criminalised, making sexual violence against men even more opaque before the law. By the interwar period homosexuality had been bundled into a wide range of sexually violent offences which were held to be in some measure amenable to medical or psychiatric interventions. At the same time, sexology was finding new, scientific ways to normalise violence in heterosex while victims of same-sex violence were manifestly culpable through their own deviance.

There were, of course, broader effects of the development of modern subjectivities which valued individuality and the centrality of the psyche. This view of subjectivity idealised constructions of sexuality associated with intimacy, equality and trust, hence sexual violence could be understood to inflict psychological damage and violate key aspects of the self irrespective of physical injury or social reputation. As Joanna Bourke argues, 'sexual practices have changed dramatically – boundaries between normal sex and abuse have also shifted' (Bourke 2007: 413). Part of this process has involved the (belated) recognition of sexual violence against men and the few women perpetrators. Modern subjectivities were also the prerequisite for second wave feminist theory on sexual violence. The concept of a continuum of sexual violence in its fullest sense is therefore most strongly applicable to modern society. Politically this concept challenged the prevailing assumptions of criminal justice, the police and sections of public opinion. These remained shaped by the nineteenth-century idea of moral violence which in the later twentieth century still dealt in outdated notions of sexual chastity as a measure of personal and social worth. In their most reductive forms such ideas continue to inform the popular myths which neutralise violence in sexual relations, and which some juries, police, criminal justice and medical professionals still believe.

The history of sexual violence therefore involves some key continuities. Sexual violence works across power differentials including but not exclusively those of gender. Many of those victimised by sexual violence have, across centuries, been disadvantaged by the criminal justice system, however much statute law and dominant discourse decried these as heinous crimes. Nevertheless, sexual cultures have shifted over time and consequently sexual violence has been differently understood, not only by criminal justice but arguably by those who have experienced and perpetrated it. Medicine and psychiatry came to shape knowledges about sexual deviance which became embedded in criminal justice, penal and eventually popular cultures and produced deviant sexual identities, not least violent ones.

The development of modernity saw a slow transition in sexual violence law which eliminated the residue of rape as a property offence and named it as individual psychological and physical injury. Eventually this enabled the recognition of sexual violence against men and boys on similar terms to that against women and girls, and the limited amount of sexual violence perpetrated by women. The historical invisibility of much sexual violence contrasted with moments of high visibility when specific kinds of sexual assault or coercion (most often against females) have become bound up with questions of gender, society and nation. Ultimately, sexual violence disturbs metanarratives which talk about civilising processes or the growth of the modern and affective in intimate relations.

## Further reading

Joanna Bourke's *Rape: A History from 1860 to the Present* (2007) is a powerful and wide-ranging analysis for the modern period, though for earlier periods much of the best recent work on sexual violence is contained in studies of gender, violence and sexuality or gender, crime and law. For the medieval period, C. J. Saunders's *Rape and Ravishment in the Literature of Medieval England* (2001) has a thorough discussion of the law as well as other literature and Barbara Hanawalt's *'Of Good and Ill Repute': Gender and Social Control in Medieval England* (1998) includes a close study of a medieval rape case in the context of other kinds of gendered social control. Karen Jones's *Gender and Petty Crime in Late Medieval England: The Local Courts in Kent, 1460–1560* (2006) places sexual violence in the context of gender and crime more generally. For the sixteenth and seventeenth centuries, Cynthia Herrup's *A House in Gross Disorder: Sex, Law, and the 2nd Earl of Castlehaven* (1999) prefaces an examination of one notorious case with a discussion of rape and sexual violence at that period. Both Garthine Walker (in particular, *Crime, Gender and Social Order in Early Modern England* (2003)) and Laura Gowing (for example, *Common Bodies: Women, Touch and Power in Seventeenth-Century England* (2003)) have much insightful analysis of how violence and sexuality intersected in Early Modern England. Randolf Trumbach's *Sex and the Gender Revolution*, volume 1, *Heterosexuality and the Third Gender in Enlightenment London* (1998) and Tim Hitchcock's *English Sexualities, 1700–1800* (1997) argue for changing cultures of masculinity in the eighteenth century, with a heightened potential for sexual aggression. For the nineteenth century, Martin Wiener's *Men of Blood: Violence, Manliness and Criminal Justice in Victorian England* (2004) finds that English higher courts were tougher on violent men, including rapists, in contrast to studies which emphasise how women and girls who had experienced sexual violence and abuse were disadvantaged in court. See for example Anna Clark, *Women's Silence, Men's Violence: Sexual Assault in England, 1770–1845* (1987), Carolyn Conley's *The Unwritten Law; Crime and Justice in Victorian Kent* (1991), Louise A. Jackson's *Child Sexual Abuse in Victorian England* (2000) and S. D'Cruze, *Crimes of Outrage: Sex, Violence and Victorian Working Women* (1998). The highly searchable online Old Bailey Sessions Papers at http://www.oldbaileyonline.org give direct access to sexual violence cases between the seventeenth and nineteenth centuries. On the modern history of sex, violence and warfare, *Brutality and Desire: War and Sexuality in Europe's Twentieth Century* (2009), edited by Dana Herzog, is a powerful collection of articles.

## References

Adler, Z. (1987) *Rape on Trial*. London: Kegan Paul.
Askin, K. (1997) *War Crimes Against Women: Prosecution in International War Crimes Tribunals*. The Hague: Martinus Nijhoff.
Avdela, E. (2010) 'Making sense of 'hideous crimes': homicide and the cultural

reordering of gendered sociality in post-civil-War Greece' in E. Avdela, S. D'Cruze and J. Rowbotham (eds) *Problems of Crime and Violence in Europe, 1780–2000*. Lewiston, Queenston, Lampeter: Edwin Mellen Press: pp. 281–310.

Baines, B. J. (1998) 'Effacing rape in Early Modern representation', *ELH*, 65(1): 69–98.

Bashar, N. (1987) 'Rape in England between 1550 and 1700', in London Feminist History Group (eds) *The Sexual Dynamics of History*. London: Pluto.

Bland, L. (1995) *Banishing the Beast, English Feminism and Sexual Morality, 1885–1914*. London: Penguin.

Bourke, J. (2007) *Rape: A History from 1860 to the Present*. London: Virago.

Bracton, Henry de (1968) *On the Laws and Customs of England* (trans. Samuel Edmund). Cambridge: Selden Society, Belknap Press of Harvard University Press.

Bray, A. (1990) 'Homosexuality and the signs of male friendship in Elizabethan England', *History Workshop Journal*, 29(1):1–19.

Breitenberg, M. (1996) *Anxious Masculinity in Early Modern England*. Cambridge: Cambridge University Press.

Brouwer, A.-M. (2005) *Supra-National Criminal Prosecution of Sexual Violence: the ICC and the Practice of the ICTY and ICTR*. Antwerp: Intersentia.

Brownmiller, S. (1975) *Against Our Will: Men, Women and Rape*. New York: Martin Secker and Warburg.

Bullough, Vern L. (1982) 'The sin against nature and homosexuality', in Vern L. Bullough and James A. Brundage (eds) *Sexual Practices and the Medieval Church*. Buffalo, NY: Prometheus Books.

Capp, B. (1999) 'The double standard revisited: plebeian women and male sexual reputation in Early Modern England', *Past and Present*, 162: 70–100.

Carroll S. (2007) 'Introduction', in S. Carroll (ed.) *Cultures of Violence: Interpersonal Violence in Historical Perspective*. Basingstoke: Macmillan.

Carter, J.M. (1982) 'Rape and medieval English society: the evidence of Yorkshire, Wiltshire and London, 1218–76', *Comitatus*, 13(1): 33–63.

Carter, J.M. (1985) *Rape and Medieval England: An Historical and Sociological Study*. London: University Press of America.

Chaytor, M. (1995) 'Husband(ry): narratives of rape in the seventeenth century', *Gender and History*, 7(2): 378–407.

Clark, A. (1987a) *Women's Silence, Men's Violence: Sexual Assault in England, 1770–1845*. London: Pandora.

Clark, A. (1987b) 'Rape or seduction? A controversy over sexual violence in the nineteenth century', in London Feminist History Group (eds) *The Sexual Dynamics of History*. London: Pluto.

Cole, S.A. (2002) *Suspect Identities: a History of Fingerprinting and Criminal Identities*. Cambridge, MA: Harvard University Press.

Conley, C. (1986) 'Rape and justice in Victorian England', *Victorian Studies*, 29: 519–36.

Conley, C. (1991) *The Unwritten Law; Crime and Justice in Victorian Kent*. New York: Oxford University Press.

Conley, C. (1995) 'No pedestals – women and violence in late-nineteenth-century Ireland', *Journal of Social History*, 28: 801–18.

Cox, P. (2003) *Gender, Justice and Welfare: Bad Girls in Britain, 1900–1959*. Basingstoke: Palgrave.

Davidson, R. (2001) ' "This pernicious delusion": law, medicine, and child sexual abuse in early-twentieth-century Scotland', *Journal of the History of Sexuality*, 10: 62–77.

D'Cruze, S. (1998) *Crimes of Outrage: Sex, Violence and Victorian Working Women*. London: UCL Press.

D'Cruze, S. (2006) 'Protection, harm and social evil: the age of consent, c.1885–c.1940', in J. Parry (ed.) *Evil, Law and the State*. Amsterdam: Rodopi.

D'Cruze, S. and Jackson, L.A. (2009) *Women, Crime and Justice in England since 1660*. Basingstoke: Palgrave Macmillan.

Douglas, M. (1991) *Purity and Danger: An Analysis of the Concepts of Pollution and Taboo*. London: Routledge.

Eisner, M. (2003) 'Long-term trends in violent crime', *Crime and Justice: a Review of Research*, 30: 83–142.

Elias, N. (1978, 1982) *The Civilizing Process: the History of Manners and State Formation and Civilization* (trans. E. Jephcott) (2 vols). Oxford: Oxford University Press.

Ellis, H. (1948) *On Life and Sex*. London: Heineman.

Emsley, C. (2005) *Crime and Society in England, 1750–1900* (3rd edn). Harlow: Longman.

Ericsson, D.K. and Simonsen, E. (eds) (2005) *Children of World War Two*. Oxford: Berg.

Evans, T. (2005) '"Unfortunate objects": London's unmarried mothers in the eighteenth century', *Gender and History*, 17(1): 127–53.

Foyster, E. (2002) 'Creating a veil of silence? Politeness and marital violence in the English household', *Transactions of the Royal Historical Society*, 12: 395–415.

Fuchs, R. (2005) *Gender and Poverty in Nineteenth-Century Europe*. Cambridge: Cambridge University Press.

Garland, D. (1985) *Punishment and Welfare: a History of Penal Strategies*. Aldershot: Gower.

Garland, D. (1991) *Punishment and Modern Society: a Study in Social Theory*. Oxford: Clarendon.

Garvey, N. (2005) *Just Sex? The Cultural Scaffolding of Rape*. London: Routledge.

Gatrell, V.A.C. (1994) *The Hanging Tree: Execution and the English People 1770–1868*. Oxford: Oxford University Press.

Gorham, D. (1978) '"The maiden tribute of modern Babylon" revisited', *Victorian Studies*, 21: 353–79.

Gourlay, K. (1996) 'Roses and thorns: the prosecution of rape in the Middle Ages', *Medieval Life*, 5: 29–31.

Gowing, L. (1996) *Domestic Dangers: Women, Words and Sex in Early Modern London*. Oxford: Clarendon.

Gowing, L. (2003) *Common Bodies: Women, Touch and Power in Seventeenth-Century England*. New Haven and London: Yale University Press.

Gregory, J. and Lees, S. (1999) *Policing Sexual Assault*. London: Routledge.

Gurr, T.R. (1981) 'Historical trends in violent crime: a critical review of the evidence', *Crime and Justice: an Annual Review of Research*, 3: 295–353.

Hall, D. and Malcolm, E. (2010) 'The rebels Turkish tyranny: understanding sexual violence in Ireland during the 1640s', *Gender and History*, 22(1): 55–74.

Hall, L. (1991) *Hidden Anxieties: Male Sexuality 1900–1950*. Cambridge: Polity.

Hall, L. (2000) *Sex, Gender and Social Change in Britain since 1880*. Basingstoke: Macmillan.

Hall, L. (ed.) (2005) *Outspoken Women; an Anthology of Women's Writing on Sex, 1870–1969*. London: Routledge.

Hanawalt, B. (1975) '"Fur-collar crime": criminal activity among the nobility of fourteenth-century England', *Journal of Social History*, 8: 1–17.

Hanawalt, B.A. (1978) *Crime and Conflict in English Communities, 1300–1348*. Cambridge, Massachusetts: Harvard University Press.

Hanawalt, B.A. (1998) *'Of Good and Ill Repute': Gender and Social Control in Medieval England*. Oxford: Oxford University Press.

Hansen, L. (2001) 'Gender, nation, rape: Bosnia and the construction of security', *International Feminist Journal of Politics*, 3: 55–75.

Harding, A. (1973) *The Law Courts of Medieval England*. London: George Allen and Unwin.

Harris, R. (1993) 'The "child of the barbarian": rape, race and nationalism in France during the First World War', *Past and Present*, 141: 170–206.

Hawkes, E. (2007) 'Preliminary notes on consent in the 1382 rape and ravishment laws of Richard II', *Legal History*, 11: 117–132.

Herrup, C. (1996) 'The patriarch at home: the trial of the 2nd Earl of Castlehaven for rape and sodomy', *History Workshop Journal*, 41: 1–18.

Herrup, C. B. (1999) *A House in Gross Disorder: Sex, Law, and the 2nd Earl of Castlehaven*. New York: Oxford University Press.

Herzog, D. (ed.) (2009) *Brutality and Desire: War and Sexuality in Europe's Twentieth Century*. Basingstoke: Palgrave.

Hitchcock, T. (1997) *English Sexualities, 1700–1800*. Basingstoke: Macmillan.

Horne, J. and Kramer, A. (1994) 'German "atrocities" and Franco-German opinion, 1914: the evidence of German soldiers' diaries', *Journal of Modern History*, 66: 1–33.

Horne, J. and A. Kramer (2001) *German Atrocities 1914: a History of Denial*. New Haven: Yale University Press, 2001.

Itzin, C. (2000) *Home Truths about Child Abuse: a Reader*. London: CRC Press.

Jackson, L.A. (2000) *Child Sexual Abuse in Victorian England*. London: UCL Press.

Jones, J. (2000) '"She resisted with all her might": sexual violence against women in late-nineteenth-century Manchester and the local press, in S. D'Cruze (ed.) *Everyday Violence in Britain, 1850–1950: Gender and Class*. Harlow: Longman.

Jones, K. (2006) *Gender and Petty Crime in Late Medieval England: The Local Courts in Kent, 1460–1560*. Rochester, NY: Boydell Press.

Kelly, L. (1987) 'The continuum of sexual violence', in Jalna Holmes and Mary Maynard (eds) *Women, Violence and Social Control*. London: Macmillan.

Kelly, L. (1988) *Surviving Sexual Violence*. Cambridge: Polity.

Kittel, R. (1982) 'Rape in thirteenth-century England: a study of the common-law courts', in D. Kelly Weisberg (ed.) *Women and the Law: the Social Historical Perspective*. Cambridge, MA.: Schenkman.

Klerman, D. (2002) 'Women prosecutors in thirteenth-century England', *Yale Journal of Law and the Humanities*, 14(27): 271–319.

Lilly, R. (2007) *Taken by Force: Rape and American GIs during World War II*. Basingstoke: Palgrave.

Macdonald, M. (1981) *Mystical Bedlams: Madness, Anxiety and Healing in Seventeenth-Century England*. Cambridge: Cambridge University Press.

Melvern, L. (2004) *Conspiracy to Murder: the Rwandan Genocide*. London: Verso.

Millet, K. (1970) *Sexual Politics*. New York: Doubleday.

Mort, F. (2000) *Dangerous Sexualities: Medico-Moral Politics in England since 1850* (2nd edn). London: Routledge.

Old Bailey Sessions Papers, available at http://www.oldbaileyonline.org

Orr, P. (1994) 'Men's theory and women's reality: rape prosecutions in the English Royal Courts of Justice, 1194–1222', in L.O. Purdon and C.L. Vitto (eds) *The Rusted Hauberk: Feudal Ideals of Order and their Decline*. Gainesville: University Press of Florida.

Porter, R. (1989) 'Does rape have a historical meaning?', in S. Tomaselli and R. Porter (eds) *Rape: an Historical and Social Enquiry*. Oxford: Blackwell.

Post, J. B. (1978) 'Ravishment of women: the Statutes of Westminster', in J.H. Baker (ed.) *Legal Records and the Historian*. London: Royal Historical Society, pp. 150–64.

Rumney, P.N.S. (2001) 'The review of sex offences and rape law reform: another false dawn?', *Modern Law Review*, 64(6): 890–910.

Saunders, C.J. (2001) *Rape and Ravishment in the Literature of Medieval England*. Suffolk, UK: D.S. Brewer.

Scarry, E. (1985) *The Body in Pain: the Making and Unmaking of the World*. Oxford: Oxford

University Press.

Seifert, R. (1994) 'War and rape; a preliminary analysis', in A. Stiglmayer (ed.) *Mass Rape; the War against Women in Bosnia–Herzegovina*. Lincoln: University of Nebraska Press: 54–69.

Seifert, R. (1996) 'The second front: the logic of sexual violence in wars', *Women's Studies International Forum*, 19(1–2): 35–43.

Shepard, A. (2003) *Meanings of Manhood in Early Modern England*. Oxford: Oxford University Press.

Shorter, E. (1975) *The Making of the Modern Family*. New York: Basic Books.

Shorter, E. (1977) 'On writing the history of rape', *Signs*, 3: 471–82.

Shorter, E. (1982) *A History of Women's Bodies*. New York: Basic Books.

Simpson, A.E. (1984) *Masculinity and Control: the Prosecution of Sex Offenses in Eighteenth-Century London*. PhD., New York University.

Simpson, A.E. (1987) 'Vulnerability and the age of female consent: legal innovation and its effect on prosecutions for rape in eighteenth-century London', in G.S. Rousseau and R. Porter (eds) *Sexual Underworlds of the Enlightenment*. Manchester: Manchester University Press.

Stevenson, K. (1999) 'Observations on the law relating to sexual offences: the historic scandal of women's silence', *Web Journal of Current Legal Issues*, 4. Available at http://webjcli.ncl.ac.uk/1999/issue4/stevenson4.html

Stevenson, K. (2000) ' "Ingenuities of the female mind": legal and public perceptions of sexual violence in Victorian England, 1850–1890', in S. D'Cruze (ed.) *Everyday Violence in Britain, 1850–1950: Gender and Class*. Harlow: Longman.

Stevenson, K. (2005) 'Crimes of moral outrage: Victorian encryptions of sexual violence', in J. Rowbotham and K. Stevenson (eds) *Criminal Conversations: Victorian Crimes, Social Panic and Moral Outrage*. Illinois: University of Illinois Press.

Stevenson, K., Davies, A. and Gunn, M. (2004) *Blackstone's Guide to the Sexual Offences Act 2003*. London: Blackstone Press.

Stiglemayer, A. (1994) (ed.) *Mass Rape: The War Against Women in Bosnia–Herzegovina*. Lincoln: University of Nebraska Press.

Stone, L. (1977) *Family, Sex and Marriage in England, 1500–1800*. London: Weidenfeld and Nicholson.

Temkin, J. (1986) 'Women, rape and law reform', in S. Tomaselli and R. Porter (eds) *Rape: an Historical and Cultural Enquiry*. London: Basil Blackwell.

Temkin, J. (2002) *Rape and the Legal Process* (2nd edn). Oxford: Oxford University Press.

Tosh, J. (2007) *A Man's Place: Masculinity and the Middle-Class Home in Victorian England*. Yale: Yale University Press.

Trumbach, R. (1988) 'Sodomitical assaults, gender role and sexual development in eighteenth-century London', *Journal of Homosexuality*, 16(1–2): 407–29.

Trumbach, R. (1990) 'Is there a modern sexual culture in the West; or, did England never change between 1500 and 1900?', *Journal of the History of Sexuality*, 1(2): 296–309.

Trumbach, R. (1998) Sex and the Gender Revolution (vol. 1), *Heterosexuality and the Third Gender in Enlightenment London*. Chicago: University of Chicago Press.

Vigarello, G. (2001) *A History of Rape: Sexual Violence in France from the Sixteenth to the Twentieth Century* (trans. J. Birell). Cambridge: Polity.

Walker, G. (1996) 'Expanding the boundaries of female honour in Early Modern England', *Transactions of the Royal Historical Society* (6th ser.), 6: 235–45.

Walker, G. (1998) 'Re-reading rape and sexual violence in Early Modern England', *Gender and History*, 10(1): 1–25.

Walker, G. (2003) *Crime, Gender and Social Order in Early Modern England*. Cambridge: Cambridge University Press.

Walker, S. Sheridan (1987) 'Punishing convicted ravishers: statutory strictures and actual practice in thirteenth- and fourteenth-century England', *Journal of Medieval History*, 13(3): 237–50.

Walkowitz, J. (1992) *City of Dreadful Delight. Narratives of Sexual Danger in Late-Victorian London*. London: Virago.

Weeks, J. (1977) *Coming Out: Homosexual Politics in Britain from the Nineteenth Century to the Present*. London: Quartet.

Wiener, M. (2004) *Men of Blood: Violence, Manliness and Criminal Justice in Victorian England*. Cambridge: Cambridge University Press.

## Chapter 2

# Sexual violence in literature: a cultural heritage?

*Liam Murray Bell, Amanda Finelli and Marion Wynne-Davies*

### Meet Liam Murray Bell

Liam currently combines research towards a PhD in Creative Writing with a position as Graduate Teaching Assistant within the English Department of the University of Surrey. His writing, both critical and creative, concerns discourses of violence and the role of women in the Northern Irish Troubles (1969 to the present) and he has published creative work in *Wordriver*, the literary journal of the University of Nevada, Las Vegas, as well as in *New Writing Scotland*, issues 21 and 26. Critical work will appear shortly in *Writing Urban Space*, from Zero Books, and the journal *New Writing: The International Journal for the Practice and Theory of Creative Writing* (Routledge).

### Meet Amanda Finelli

Amanda Finelli received her undergraduate degree from the Ohio State University in the United States, before undertaking Masters Studies at Royal Holloway University of London in modernist and postmodern literature. Currently, she is pursuing a PhD in Creative Writing at the University of Surrey where she is working on her first novel, which explores modern-day mental health culture in the United States through the lens of psychoanalytic theory on hysteria, in conjunction with French anti-essentialist feminist theory of language and narrative.

### Meet Marion Wynne-Davies

Marion Wynne-Davies holds the Chair of English Literature in the Department of English at the University of Surrey. Her main areas of interest are Early Modern literature and women's writing and she has published two editions of primary material, *Renaissance Drama by Women: Texts and Documents* (with S.P. Cerasano) and *Women Poets of the Renaissance*, as well as several collections of essays in the same field. Her interest in women's writing has also led her to publish five monographs: *Women and Arthurian Literature*; *Sidney to Milton*; *Women Writers of the English Renaissance*; *Familial Discourse*; and *Margaret Atwood*. The interest in sexual violence began when Marion was a witness in a rape trial on behalf of a woman she counselled. This led indirectly to her work on Shakespeare's *Titus Andronicus* which she uses in the essay for this book.

## Introduction

There is an urban legend that circulates in Belfast – one among many explicit tales to emerge from Northern Ireland during the Troubles – of a female prostitute who, tired of performing sexual acts and passively accepting the violence that often accompanied them, turned the tables by secreting shards of broken glass within her vagina in order to inflict serious injury on her male customers as they penetrated her. This woman set out to blindly maim and mutilate, without compunction, using the only tool she had – her sexuality – thereby perpetuating a discourse of sexual violence within Northern Ireland that includes the IRA's use of a 'honeytrap', a practice whereby paramilitaries recruited women to lure unsuspecting soldiers not to bed but to the tomb (Coogan 1996: 302). Through use of her body, so the story goes, the prostitute sought to remove herself from the role of victim and, in so doing, became perpetrator. It is this interface – this dialectic – that the chapter will examine, seeking to chart representations of sexual violence in literature and examine whether the female, in laying claim to subjectivity, can challenge patriarchal discourses. It is perhaps fitting that in discussing sexual violence within literature we begin with an urban legend – a story that may be a fictional or at least an embellished cautionary tale but that, like many of the fictional representations discussed, may well hold a grain of truth with regard to the social circumstance of women within the narrative. The subsequent sections of this chapter focus upon: theoretical perspectives; literary history; textual analysis (Angela Carter's *The Passion of New Eve*); and textual creativity (Liam Murray Bell's *rubber bullet, broken glass*).

## Theoretical perspectives

American feminist Susan Brownmiller's seminal work *Against Our Will: Men, Women and Rape* (1975) shattered earlier conceptions of rape and sexual violence, embarking upon a dialogue that would dispel the fallacies of how women were located in and trapped by discourses of assault. Images and accounts of rape and violence have existed for centuries, whether in ancient mythology, literature, or multiple varieties of popular culture. However, the proliferation of these representations did not serve to challenge rape, but rather to normalise it, and it was precisely this tacit acceptance that Brownmiller found problematic. She identified the fascination with rape as a quest for achieving victory; when a man 'conquers the world, so too he conquers the woman' (Brownmiller 1975: 289). Moreover, this rendering of an idealised and omnipotent masculinity ultimately allowed for the 'myth of the heroic rapist' (Brownmiller 1975: 289) to flourish, a view that for Brownmiller was made worse by the fact that popular culture as well as scholarly discourse refused to dismantle the myth.

At a time when female rape accusations were regarded as dubious, Brownmiller engaged in an intensive sociological experiment to unearth the statistical evidence that revealed rape was more common than civilians and government officials cared to believe and, in turn, she legitimated the use of the female voice against violence. However, Brownmiller tended to construct women as habitual victims. Although she used statistical evidence to reveal the indiscriminate nature of violent sexual crimes with regard to race, age and socio-economic status, she tended to ignore the possibility of sex as a variable factor in the rape equation. Within this context rape exists in purely heterosexual terms, as it is only 'within the heterosexual world that most of us inhabit by choice, sexual violence is exalted by men to the level of ideology only when the victims are female and the victimizers are male' (Brownmiller 1975: 293). For a text that strives to deconstruct the universalising assumptions about rape, it is surprising that the idea of a token victim is imagined and that the author argues for a 'uniform response to a rape, or a uniform time for recovery' (Brownmiller 1975: 361). Thus, when Brownmiller begins to examine the actual motivation of rape, she appears to express these in purely dichotomous terms.

The last chapter of Brownmiller's book is titled 'Women Fight Back', which would superficially seem to suggest the possibility of female violence. In actuality it is a discussion of self-defence as a mode of protection in pre-emptive preparation for a worst-case scenario. As such, the chapter excludes the idea of women initiating violence and how this might function within a dialogic engagement with the passive construct of the victimised woman. While Brownmiller's path-breaking feminist agenda provided a necessary exposé of rape 'myths', the question that must be considered today is: how do we move on from a statistical or sociological study of rape and violence that constructs women as victims, in order to develop a more complex theoretical contextualisation that does not undermine the severity and injustice of the crime? Specifically in this essay, it is important to understand how we evaluate writing violence that is performed both against and by women, and ask: can illustrations of female-generated violence ever serve as a means of reclaiming the female experience?

One way of interpreting the physical realities of rape and sexual assault in literature is to compare the narrative framework with the literary form. In order to understand how form may be implicated in the wider discourse of sexual violence, it is useful to consider the work of Monique Wittig, a French Materialist feminist, who saw contemporary linguistic forms as an inadequate means of expression for women, and especially a problematic discourse for lesbians. She argues that the only way to manoeuvre a language saturated in heterosexist and patriarchal tenets is to dismantle it. Violently. In 'For a Women's Liberation Movement' (1970) Wittig, along with other French feminists, emphasised the need for violent struggle in order to dismantle the inferior status of women in capitalist society, in particular their role as culturally constructed sexual objects. Radically, they state:

We don't want to waste our energy and strength struggling against male chauvinism inside the already existing organizations. The time is past when we asked men...for permission to revolt. No one can liberate another, one must liberate oneself.

(Wittig *et al.* 2005: 32–3)

Building upon her work in *Les Guérillères* (1969), where female revolutionaries carry out acts of violence metaphorically to represent their immediate social plight, Wittig assumes a mentality of violence in order to manipulate, and exist in, patriarchal society. More recently, in *Gender Trouble* (1990), Judith Butler argues that Wittig's use of violence is not intended to 'turn the tables' or seek revenge against men, but rather to complicate the way violence is viewed. Furthermore, Butler explains how violence can be used in order to reveal suppressed truths: '[t]he violence of the text has the identity and coherence of the category of sex as its target, a lifeless construct, a construct out to deaden the body' (Butler 1990: 172). By transferring the physicalities of violence onto the literary form, texts are able to highlight the complexities of rape and violence, and provide reclamation through narrative. The body of the text thus becomes analogous with the body of both victim and perpetrator, engendering and submitting to violence within an inescapable and self-perpetuating dialectic. In the subsequent section on literary history this more complex understanding will be explored and texts that have previously been read as representing women as victims of sexual violence re-excavated in order to destabilise the cultural conventions that have served to represent women as passive objects.

## Literary history

There are a number of histories on literary representations of women and sexual violence, including those that are period specific, as well as works that address particular areas, such as post-colonialist surveys. The purpose of this section is, however, not to reproduce such scholarship, but to challenge earlier literary approaches in order to understand how female subjectivity is embedded in the dialectic of victim/perpetrator. Traditionally, literary criticism has focused on the role of women as victims – of assault, domestic violence, abuse and rape – yet by excavating key textual moments, it becomes apparent that these manifestations of violence are more complex. The following examples have been organised into thematic categories – violent revenge and social circumstance – in order to develop an understanding of how women may be simultaneously victims and perpetrators of violence.

One of the most horrific rapes in literature occurs in Shakespeare's *Titus Andronicus* where Lavinia, a young and innocent woman, is raped by the Empress's two sons, Demetrius and Chiron. While the sexual assault happens offstage, its consequences are manifest as Lavinia emerges with her tongue cut out and her hands sliced off:

Dem. So, now go tell, and if thy tongue can speak,
    Who 'twas that cut thy tongue and ravish'd thee.

55

> Chi. Write down thy mind, bewray thy meaning so,
>      And if thy stumps will let thee play the scribe.
>
> (Shakespeare 1954: 54)

The mocking tone adopted by the young men suggests a vicious pleasure, not only from sexual gratification but also from the erasure of female agency. Unexpectedly, this negation of independent subjectivity is countered in the play with powerful revenge, as Lavinia evades the constraints of silence by taking a staff – replete with the metaphor of sexual transference – into her mouth and, using her 'stumps' as a guide, writes the names of her rapists. A bloody revenge ensues as Lavinia's father, Titus, feeds the Empress a pie made with the flesh of her murdered sons. Rather than being passive victim, Lavinia helps engender a horrific retribution against another woman that matches rape and dismemberment with murder and enforced cannibalism.

In constructing this bloody narrative, Shakespeare drew upon Ovid's tale of how Tereus rapes his sister-in-law Philomela and cuts out her tongue to conceal his identity from his wife, Progne. Philomela, however, weaves a tapestry depicting the assault and the two sisters revenge themselves by murdering Tereus's son and serving him as a dish of meat to his father. The metamorphosis of the characters into birds does little to undermine the graphic violence and, as in *Titus Andronicus*, the women turn from being victims into perpetrators of violence, uniting against their male kin.

Not all texts represent female violence as a vengeful response to an immediate and bloody assault; some represent women as perpetrators of violence because of social circumstance. These accounts need to be located within the dominant patriarchal discourses of the periods in which the works were written; for example, the lack of female independence experienced by medieval women may be evidenced by their lack of legal rights, in particular, rape that was interpreted by the law as an act of theft against the senior male within a woman's family and not a crime of assault against the female victim (see also Chapters 1 and 3 by D'Cruze and McGregor respectively, who discuss this idea). Chaucer refers to this legal practice in *The Tale of the Wife of Bath* where a knight rapes a maiden but is redeemed when he agrees to marry a hag, the magic 'other' of the ravished woman. The sexual consummation of the marriage is often read as revealing the desire of the narrator – the middle-aged Wife – to bed a handsome and virile young man. However, the initial rape is paralleled by the Wife's experience, in that she is first married when she 'twelf yeer was of age', was 'bet on every bon' by her fourth husband, and hit so violently by her fifth spouse that her ear 'weex al deef' (Chaucer 1992: 27, 46 and 49). In these circumstances, perhaps her final retaliation, when she floors her husband with a punch on the 'cheke' (Chaucer 1992: 54), should not be read as the stereotypical action of a hardened and aggressive older woman, but as the final breaking point of someone who has suffered years of legally condoned abuse. Chaucer offers us no conclusive judgement on the Wife, but the text illuminates how women suffered injustice and sometimes had the strength of character to fight back.

A more tragic figure may be found in Wordsworth's poem 'The Thorn', which focuses on the plight of a pregnant young woman who has been jilted by her betrothed and, after the baby's death, descends into depression, sitting beneath the thorn tree 'by day and night, in rain, in tempest, and in snow' (Wordsworth 1988: 72). The poem's narrator offers no sympathy, under-standing or evidence, instead recounting local gossip:

> ... but some will say
> She hanged her baby on the tree,
> Some say she drowned it in the pond ...
> I've heard the scarlet moss is red
> With drops of that poor infant's blood;
> But kill a new-born infant thus!
>
> (Wordsworth 1988: 77)

The plight of an unmarried mother and the abusive nature of the rumours are ignored by the narrator, whose judgement is harsh and moralistic, yet the poem offers a more complex understanding of her situation, giving the last lines to the woman:

> Oh misery! Oh misery!
> 'O woe is me! Oh misery!'
>
> (Wordsworth 1988: 78)

It is impossible to determine whether or not the woman has committed infanticide rather than continue to suffer the censure and denunciation of society, or whether the baby simply died. At the same time, her voice evinces an overwhelming grief and the title of the poem, 'The Thorn', rather than 'the thorn tree', suggests both continued pain and the image of Christ as he is made to wear a crown of thorns. Wordsworth constructs the woman as both ultimate victim (Christ) and definitive perpetrator (a mother who murders her child), trapped within the dialectic of society's opinion of unmarried mothers.

When exploring how women and violence are represented in literature, it is essential to recognise that while female characters are shown as victims (of rape, physical and verbal abuse, as well as social values that privilege men), at the same time, they are also depicted as perpetrators of violence. In the four examples drawn from canonical authors the crimes committed by, enabled by, or attributed to, women range from murder, cannibalism and physical abuse, to infanticide. Contemporary recognition of how brutality against women is often paralleled by female violence needs to be located firmly within a literary tradition of ambiguity. In the next two sections of the chapter, this dialectic of victim/perpetrator will be investigated in relation to more recent writing: Angela Carter's *The Passion of New Eve* and an extract from Liam Murray Bell's new novel, *rubber bullet, broken glass*.

## Textual analysis: Angela Carter, *The Passion Of New Eve* (1977)

In Angela Carter's *The Passion of New Eve* the roles of perpetrator and victim are both complicated and conflated by the novel's numerous acts of sexualised violence performed and received by both men and women. As such, the novel offers a complex representation of gender identity that is further problematised by the novel's setting – a dystopia in which unrestrained violence occurs at the hands of sexually and racially marginalised insurgents. The importance of social circumstance and place is thereby embedded in the conflict between victim/perpetrator and women/men.

The importance of dialectical representation may be identified in the novel's locational contrasts: between East and West Coast America; between the city and the desert; and between the grotesque and the bare. For Carter, place and social circumstance are fundamental to understanding sexualised violence. As Peggy Reeves Sanday argues in 'Rape and the silencing of the feminine', the cultural consequences of rape vary according to the society in which it is committed, so that some areas are 'classified as rape-free, others as rape-prone' (Sanday 1986: 84). Sanday provides an example of a man committing rape in West Sumatra, with the possible consequence not only of having his 'masculinity ridiculed' but also having to 'face...assault, perhaps death.... be[ing] driven from his village, never to return' (Sanday 1986: 84). In examining the sociocultural implications of this rape she locates a trend that typically identifies rape-*prone* societies as imbuing women with less personal autonomy and government involvement (Sanday 1986: 85).

Cartographic discourse complicates the way we read the violence depicted in Carter's novel, since it is enacted and endured in Western society where women, arguably, experience greater independence. In using the United States, Carter subverts the idea that rape is a primitive model of abuse only to be used by those existing outside of highly 'civilised' nations, demanding that sexualised violence is acknowledged to be as likely in Western culture as anywhere else. This covert embedding of sexualised violence in the West had been foregrounded by Brownmiller in 1975 two years prior to the publication of *The Passion of New Eve* and Carter engages with 1970s feminist discourse. Subsequently, Roy Porter focused more specifically on how the West straddles a fine line between using violence as a tool of gendered subordination while at the same time appearing to promote equality among the sexes:

> the rise of the West – its institutions, attitudes and destiny – has been deeply bound up with sexual violence, threat and reality...coexisting, uneasily, unstably, with a polity officially dedicated to equality between the sexes... [so that rape has become] the objects and effects of Western militarism and imperialism.
>
> (Porter 1986: 232 and 231)

Carter's use of a North American setting negotiates these covert practices, showing that, while sexual violence might be packaged differently in terms of the United States and the Western psyche, rape and sexualised violence remain part of a complex manipulation of sexual identity where the individual is both repressed and liberated.

This dialectic is realised through the narrative progression of the novel's protagonist, Evelyn (later transformed into Eve), who begins his sojourn in the grotesque landscape of New York City where 'roaches swarmed on the floor and the worm-eaten night-light of the city flooded in through a curtainless window' (Carter 1977: 25). Unexpectedly, the landscape of the grotesque does not repulse Evelyn's delicate English sensibilities, instead he finds it invigorating; it leads him to feel a 'savage desire' (Carter 1977: 25) that juxtaposes his tranquil English upbringing as a '[c]hild of a moist, green, gentle island' with the 'violence, fear [and] madness' of New York (Carter 1977: 15). Finally, however, Evelyn's lust for the danger that New York promises becomes misinterpreted as a promise of freedom that, in turn, renders him both a perpetrator and victim of rape.

It is in New York that Evelyn meets Leilah, the 'blythe, callous, ghetto nymph' (Carter, 1977:21); she is a visual representation of the dark and corrupt sensuality that he lusts after and his treatment of her – raping, impregnating, and leaving her to a Haitian abortionist who performs an irreparable procedure – leaves her as a despoiled victim. Leilah is 'infected' and forced 'to go to hospital at the cost of all the rest of her furs, at the price of her womb' (Carter 1977: 34). Evelyn's initial objectification of women as sexual victims is, however, undercut later in the novel through the character of 'Mother', who depicts his act as abuse: 'And you've abused women, Evelyn, with this delicate instrument that should have been used for nothing but pleasure. You made a weapon of it!' (Carter 1977: 65–6). Even when Evelyn meets Leilah after he has been transformed into Eve, he still tries to rationalise his former assault, interpreting his own transformation as an act of vengeance on the part of women, asking 'had [Leilah] really suffered when I'd fathered a child on her, was it real blood that spilled on the floor of the taxi when she came back to me, torn, mutilated, from the Haitian abortionist? And was my body her revenge?' (Carter 1977: 172). Although Eve recognises that Evelyn left Leilah 'torn' and 'mutilated' he still seeks to justify male aggression by claiming this as a quest for justice, women's desire to turn the tables against men.

The revenge performed upon Evelyn is analogous to Wittig's determination to 'revolt... [and] to liberate oneself' (Wittig *et al.* 1970: 32–3), as the protagonist is violently transformed into Eve. Again Carter uses material space as a way of foregrounding sexual difference and the novel shifts in location from the furore of New York to the starkness of the desert: the East is replaced by 'the abode of enforced sterility, the dehydrated sea of infertility, the post-menopausal part of the earth' (Carter 1977: 40). The site of rebirth is called Beulah: 'a profane place. It is a crucible. It is the home of the woman who calls herself the Great Parricide, also glories in the title of Grand Emasculator... but her daughters call her Mother' (Carter 1977: 49). After the operation, an operation performed by Mother, Eve resides in a cell that is a 'simulacrum of the womb' (Carter 1977: 52). Sanday claims that 'women are victims of phallic sadism because men are victims of uterine dependency... [I]t is male dependency on the feminine reproductive model for their masculine sense of self, power and control' (Sanday 1986: 87). As a result of Evelyn's violence against women, he is forced to rely on the womb he rejects in sexual assault and is recreated and fitted with a womb of his own, carried out by the ultimate symbol of matriarchal power, Mother.

This transformation is befittingly violent in response to the sexualised violence committed by Evelyn. In order to become woman, an instance of rape must occur, an act which the female renegades under Mother's control associate with being reborn, an act to '[r]eintegrate the primal form!' (Carter 1977: 64). In the scene where Mother rapes Evelyn, stereotypical gender roles are reversed, especially in considering traditional narratives of rape, as Evelyn is the passive, submissive victim, who feels no sexual pleasure from the act, but instead performs the role of object:

> [Mother's] Virginia-smoked ham of a fist grasped my shrinking sex; when it went all the way in, Mother howled and so did I. So I was unceremoniously raped; and it was the last time I performed the sexual act as a man, whatever that means, though I took very little pleasure from it. None at all, in fact, for her thighs grasped me with the vigour of the female mantis and I felt only engulfment.

> (Carter 1977: 64–5)

Mother is analogised to the female praying mantis known to tear the heads off her male mantis counterparts, metaphorically illustrating her role in the dismembering castration of Evelyn. The novel appears to create a binary division located in social circumstance: the patriarchal city of New York where men are predators and women passive victims, and the matriarchy of Beulah where women revenge themselves against male violence by making men suffer rape and physical assault.

The superficiality of this binary relationship is, however, complicated by the house of the poet Zero, a blatant misogynist who lives on a ranch in the desert with seven wives. After Eve escapes from Mother she is captured by Zero and brought to his ranch where she experiences a more violent and polarised form of assault, since the poet does not know of Eve/lyn's past as a man. All women on Zero's ranch are treated as subhuman; the wives are deprived of civilised modes of living as the poet believes women to be composed of 'more primitive, animal stuff, and so did not need the paraphernalia of civilised society such as cutlery, meat, soap, shoes, etc' (Carter 1977: 87). The subservient roles adopted by the women are, however, problematised by the fact that the wives fulfil this status complacently. Eve observes that Zero's 'wives ... who so innocently consented to be less than human, filled me with an angry pity. When I saw their skins were often greenish due to the beatings [Zero] inflicted on them, I was moved by an anger they were too much in love with him to feel' (Carter 1977: 108). Zero, in fulfilling the 'myth of the heroic rapist' (Brownmiller 1975: 289) manages to convince the women that they deserve his violent acts, indeed they actually desire and deify him: the wives 'dedicated themselves, body, heart and soul to the Church of Zero' (Carter 1977: 99). Indeed, the other women turn upon Eve, who has been manufactured by Mother as an ultimate sex symbol, because she receives the greatest attention from Zero. This envy leads the women to inflict violence upon Eve, enacting female against female violence, cutting Eve's face: the foremost sign of her beauty.

The sexual violence Eve experiences as the eighth wife of Zero causes her to conflate her identity with his. After the first instance of rape, Eve remarks, 'I was in no way prepared for the pain, his body was an anonymous instrument of torture' (Carter 1977: 86), then increasingly she feels a 'sense of grateful detachment from this degradation' (Carter 1977: 91), until finally she relinquishes her identity completely, saying, 'I felt myself to be, not myself but he; and the experience of this crucial lack of self always brought with it a shock of introspection, forced me to know myself as a former violator at the moment of my own violation' (Carter 1977: 102). Zero, unaware of Eve's previous sex, reveals to her Evelyn's identity as a male perpetrator of violence. Seemingly, however, what should be an epiphanic moment for Eve fails, as she still sees Evelyn as superior to Zero, and fails to acknowledge Evelyn's past abusive acts.

The overarching point of location lies in Tristessa, the idealised Hollywood actress, with whom both Evelyn and Zero are infatuated. In considering media and popular culture representations of rape in the United States, Sanday argues that 'the images...teach men to silence the vulnerable in themselves by objectifying and possessing the bodies of women' (Sanday 1986: 99). This notion of repressed sexual dissatisfaction spiralling into sexualised violence is apposite when considering Zero's relationship with Tristessa, who Zero claims through her own sexualised image left him impotent. As Eve learns, '[Zero] believed the movie actress had performed a spiritual vasectomy on him' (Carter 1977: 92), a situation which can only be rectified through Zero's usurpation of Tristessa's sexuality, ultimately resulting in the 'Witch, bitch, and typhoid Mary of [sterility's]'death, who according to Zero, only spurns him because he is 'Masculinity incarnate' (Carter 1977: 104). Zero's infatuation with Tristessa turns into obsession, as it is easier to locate his own inadequacies in an idealised starlet than in his own faulty masculinity. In contrast, Evelyn/Eve's infatuation with Tristessa is part of a fantasised idea of femininity. At the start of the novel, Evelyn imagines Tristessa as a feminine ideal, even though in his dreams of her she becomes the object of violent fantasy, 'stark naked, tied, perhaps to a tree in a midnight forest under the wheeling stars' (Carter 1977: 7). Towards the end of the book, when Tristessa is revealed as a biological male, Eve notes that the movie star's perfection could only be born from a man's imago, exclaiming: '*That* was why [Tristessa] had been the perfect man's woman! He had made himself the shrine of his own desires, had made of himself the only woman he could have loved!' (Carter 1977: 128–9, emphasis Carter's). Whereas this fact repulses Zero, Eve is drawn to Tristessa more; for Eve this masculine identity makes Tristessa superior, implying that for Eve biologically female 'women' are inferior. Zero's anger and repulsion culminates when he forces Tristessa, the biological male who wishes to be a woman, to have sex with Eve, who has been constructed as biologically female. Tristessa notes that he thought 'I was immune to rape' (Carter 1977: 137), but the sexualizsd violence of the novel cannot be contained either by biological sex or gender identity.

At the end of the novel Carter returns to the question of a justified violence as a pregnant Eve is reunited with Leilah who reveals that her real name is 'Lilith...Adam's first wife...Rape only refreshes my virginity' and with Mother who has become 'gentle' and old (Carter 1977: 174). Even though Leilah seems to acknowledge that she has committed sexual violence against Evelyn, at the same time she merges with Eve and Mother and Tristessa to form a compound femininity that suffers rape even as it enacts it. As such, Carter's narrative contemplates whether or not female violence as a validated response might reclaim the female experience, utilising rape as a means of revenge or a way to alert society to the damage caused in abuse. As we will see, the authority of violence is often questionable and multitudinous, as different historical and social contexts construct violence as a vehicle of either redemption or destruction.

### Textual creativity: Liam Murray Bell, *rubber bullet, broken glass* (2011)

My current work-in-progress is a novel entitled *rubber bullet, broken glass* that examines Northern Ireland during the Troubles. Specifically, the narrative focuses on the character of Aoife, a protagonist who moves from being a victim of the conflict to being a perpetrator of (sexualised) violence. This transition – following on from Wittig – is made in order to afford the character the ability to challenge both (male) discourses of violence and the constructs of gender itself, which as we explored earlier is categorised within Wittig's work as 'a lifeless construct, a construct out to deaden the body' (Butler 1990: 172). The rationale for portraying this (female) character as engaging in acts of sexualised violence within the narrative – as this section will explore – lies in the inherent inability of women to complicate the patriarchy inherent in Northern Irish society without also complicating their own sexuality and the status of their gender within existing discourses. As Robin Morgan argues, in her discussion of Palestinian women fighters, 'The woman who rebels via the male mode can only do so up until the point where her own rebellion might begin' (Morgan 1990: 211). That is, the female characters of the novel can only register their protest at perceived injustices via the existing (male) structures and, following on from this, can only do so until their gender begins to impact upon their ability to protest, at which point they must decide whether they wish to undergo a double rebellion against the constructs of gender itself. It is this contention that this case study will examine: the idea that if a woman wishes to subvert the discourses of violence in a conflict such as the Troubles – which has the subjugation of women inherent within it – then she is required to do so in a way that not only makes her voice heard as a participator in the violence – as a perpetrator – but also lays claim to a subjectivity for herself as a woman – as a female perpetrator.

The female characters of *rubber bullet, broken glass*, then, need to respond to and challenge the 'male dominated, patriarchal relations that permeate' (Little 2002) the Northern Ireland contemporary to the narrative. There are certain expectations of women within this patriarchal structure, involving a subjugation of women into the domestic sphere, with duties limited to the kitchen and the bedroom. This is borne out by the representation of the character of Josie in Edna O'Brien's novel *House of Splendid Isolation*, in which her husband speaks of Josie by equating her to a horse: 'Feed. Shovel. Ride. Woman and horse.' (O'Brien 1995: 137) This presents women, within the literature of Northern Ireland, as often oppressed, and this also manifests in historical examples of degradation such as the ritualistic tarring and feathering of Nationalist women who were seen consorting with British soldiers (see Aretxaga 1997: 152) or in the implicit tolerance of sexual violence evidenced by the domestic violence legislation which was amended by the Northern Ireland Assembly to specify 'that it should be applied to married couples only and not to cohabitees, since the latter "chose to live in sin they would have to face the consequences"' (McWilliams 1991: 83). Women, in these discourses, are marginalised and categorised as being somehow lesser to men and answerable to (male) rule of law, whether that be through institutions of state, as in the latter example, or through the imposed laws of the paramilitaries, as in the former.

One method of rebelling against this assigned role is characterised, within my novel, by Aoife's mother, Cathy, who responds to witnessing the death of her neighbour, Eamonn, at the hands of the British Security Services by withdrawing into silence. This form of protest, Myriam Diaz-Diocaretz argues, is necessary due to the essential maleness of the language itself, which 'is inherently saturated by the male view of the world, and molded according to men's experiences', and in the face of this overwhelming inability to express their viewpoint with the language tools available, women find themselves lapsing into 'mutedness' (Diaz-Diocaretz 1989: 124). So, Cathy witnesses the death of her neighbour and finds that she is unable to speak of what she has seen:

> Aoife's mammy started to have problems with her mouth in the weeks after Eamonn Kelly was shot by the Brits. It started as a tingle, she told the doctor, like a cold sore forming at the corner of her lip, then it began to scour at her gums like she was teething. It was when it started to burn, though, like taking a gulp of scalding tea and swilling it around; it was when it began to feel like it had left the inside of her mouth and throat as nothing more than a raw and bleeding flesh wound; when every morsel of food or sip of water felt like swallowing a razor blade, this writhing agony that only got worse when she stretched it into a scream; it was only then that Cathy Brennan phoned for the doctor.
>
> (*rubber bullet, broken glass*)

As a direct result of this psychosomatic pain, Cathy is medicated and becomes prone to long spells of silence. This can be seen as her response to what happens around her: an inability to articulate what she has seen leads her to withdraw.

The character of Aoife, by contrast, seeks to confront those responsible for the maiming of her brother, Damien, through a protest that – while often being repellent and, indeed, misdirected – is a more active response to the perceived injustice than her mother's actions or the actions of the character of Josie in the O'Brien novel mentioned earlier, who outrages the paradigm of a housewife only insofar as cutting her hair short and trying to 'mediate between' (O'Brien 1995: 204) an escaped Republican gunman, McGreevy, and the police. The actions of Cathy and Josie do little to challenge the prevalent attitude which sees women as 'passive and peace-loving' (Pelan 2005: 82), but Aoife is able to assert herself more definitively against this demarcation of gender roles by assuming the alter ego of Cassie, who performs sexualised violence in the same way as the prostitute in the urban legend that began this chapter. This central premise for the narrative, of Aoife/Cassie actively pursuing a role as perpetrator, allows the character to follow in the footsteps of the Armagh women involved in the Dirty Protest[1], who 'demanded to be full militants of the IRA' and in so doing were seen to be 'criticizing a genderized system that held [women] as political subsidiaries' (Aretxaga 1997: 143). Further to this, Aoife/Cassie seeks to cast gender to one side in her approach to violence, engaging with the existing discourses of violence without reference to her femininity. She challenges the traditional depiction of women as being synonymous with a 'mothering nature that was contrary to violence' (Aretxaga 1995) through her relentless pursuit of her victims. It would be difficult, I would argue, to categorise a passage such as this one as being inherently 'female':

> My heartbeat quickens to the sound of his breathing on the other side of the door. As the door opens, I swing. You'd expect the bottle to shatter against his skull. It doesn't. It thuds against his forehead and collapses him to his knees.
>
> *(rubber bullet, broken glass)*

The objective, almost practical, tone of this narration does not conform to the idea of women as being, in some way, removed from violence. It doesn't hold any gender signifiers, just as I would contend that the passage below from V.S. Naipaul's *Magic Seeds* – which is narrated from the point of view of a male fighter – is not impacted upon by the gender of the character:

> And the figure who had been trembling in and out of the gun-sight half spun to one side, as though he had been dealt a heavy blow, and then fell on the path on the slope.
>
> (Naipaul 2004: 145)

The violence in both passages still performs as aggressive action regardless of the gender of the assailant; the purpose of the character to injure or even kill is clear in both extracts. Indeed, the sense of nervous energy present in 'trembling in and out of the gun-sight' in Naipaul's narrative directly corresponds with 'My heartbeat quickens to the sound of his breathing' in my own. These are human reactions to violence, rather than male or female reactions. By engaging in the conflict in this way, Aoife/Cassie attempts to dismiss her status as a woman within male-dominated discourses of violence as irrelevant.

However, to repeat the Morgan quotation, 'The woman who rebels via the male mode can only do so up until the point where her own rebellion might begin.' This is important because, however much Aoife/Cassie may wish to discount her gender in participating in the conflict, her sex impacts upon her ability to be perpetrator due to the physical differences between male and female. That is, the body itself calls into question her participation in implicitly male – or ungendered – discourses of violence.

Within the context of the Troubles, the body is the currency of the conflict, as Allen Feldman argues in writing that 'the practice of political violence entails the production, exchange and ideological consumption of bodies' (Feldman 1991: 9). Yet this manifests – conventionally – in different ways across the gender divide, with women typically being heavily involved in the 'production' and 'ideological consumption' of bodies, through childbirth and the subsequent rearing of their children: 'Women are idealised as the emotional guardians of hearth, home and for children's upbringing and morality' (Baillie 2002: 124). Women are often portrayed as being passive, however, when it comes to the 'exchange' of bodies, with the bodies utilised as the hard currency of the violence more often being male; those of their sons or husbands rather than their own. Aretxaga categorises this dichotomy succinctly by noting:

> In republican culture men's suffering is inscribed in their own bodies through their fighting; women's is inscribed in the bodies of others: fathers, sons, brothers, husbands or friends.
>
> (Aretxaga, 1997: 50)

This is not to say that practices associated with degradation of women and sexualised violence towards women – such as the strip-searching of women carried out by the security services – do not operate as violations against women's bodies, but rather that women are rarely presented as actively utilising their own bodies for the purpose of engaging in the conflict. They are not involved in the 'exchange'. Instead, they watch passively as the men are maimed or killed, their pain derived from association and felt as emotional pain, at a remove from the actual physical pain inflicted upon the body. This is represented, within the narrative of *rubber bullet, broken glass*, by Aoife's suffering at the sight of her brother struggling with his injuries:

> The bullet had struck and everything had been crushed and squeezed backwards into his beautiful face, beneath the skin everything was crumpled and disfigured, whilst on the outside it only showed whenever he tried to smile, or laugh, or frown, or sleep, or cry. Or look up.
>
> (*rubber bullet, broken glass*)

Later in the novel, however, Aoife dispenses with this passive suffering and assumes the guise of Cassie in order to actively utilise her body in order to gain revenge against those she views as responsible for Damien's pain. As Cassie, she puts her body forward as a battleground, by way of the broken glass hidden within her vagina. That this causes her physical pain – the glass 'shifts and stabs, stings and slits, scrapes and scours' (*rubber bullet, broken glass*) – is of little consequence when compared with the benefit of being able now to engage in the 'exchange' of bodies, being able to use this weapon of her body to inflict damage on those she deems responsible for having inflicted damage, as in this passage:

A sudden, high-pitched screech of pain. He's scurrying and scuttling beneath me. I'm not for letting him go, though, not yet. Clamping my thighs, keeping him in. My own teeth set together with the agony of it. I close my eyes, grind down, and listen as the screams grow louder and sharper. I listen as the hurt and sorrow of it all penetrates through his whisky-addled confusion. Opening my eyes. I'm for waiting until his cries crack, until the tears stream, until he's ready to plead. Until enough blood has been spilt.

*(rubber bullet, broken glass)*

In a modern rendering of the biblical 'An eye for an eye, a tooth for a tooth', Aoife/Cassie rationalises that as Damien was harmed by a member of the British Security Forces, she will retaliate by harming policemen and soldiers – thereby transitioning from victim to perpetrator.

Thus, following on from Wittig, the character of Cassie can be seen to be challenging the gender demarcations imposed upon her by a patriarchal society. In other words, Aoife/Cassie is undergoing the second part of her double rebellion. She rejects the role of mother and aligns herself, instead, with the idea of a woman freedom fighter/terrorist – distinct from a male of the same ilk – in a way that echoes one of the Palestinian women Morgan discusses in *The Demon Lover: On the Sexuality of Terrorism*, who asserts: 'My body is not a weapons factory. I am done with being the mother of martyrs' (Morgan 1990: 287).

By presenting her body as a weapon, Aoife/Cassie is laying claim to agency and identifying herself as a participant in, rather than a spectator to, the violence. She is doing so – explicitly – as a woman. It is her sexuality and her (female) body, and her use of both, that allows her to lure her victims away from safety with the promise of sex, in a way that mirrors the IRA practice of the 'honeytrap'. Such actions may, of course, strike the reader as abhorrent, but they are necessary in order for Aoife/Cassie to operate as a female paramilitary, not subservient to either (male) power structures or to her gender.

To conclude, the narrative of *rubber bullet, broken glass* should not be seen as an attempt to portray women as perpetrators of sexualised violence any more than it should be seen as a furtherance of existing discourses that see women as victim. Instead, it proposes a transition that allows the female protagonist of the novel to lay claim to agency, to follow the example of the Armagh women prisoners, whom Aretxaga sees as 'stepping out of their assigned allegorical value as suffering mothers and victimised girls and [laying] a claim to subjecthood' (Aretxaga 1995). The character of Aoife/Cassie does so through sexualised violence, furthering and complicating an existing (male) discourse by imposing her own (female) body onto the conflict. The question inherent in this transition, however, remains whether this movement from victim to perpetrator, through the course of the narrative, is successful in achieving the subjectivity that the character desires.

## Conclusion

As Carol Vance contends, 'It is not enough to move women away from danger and oppression; it is necessary to move toward something: toward pleasure, agency, self-definition' (Vance 1989: 29). The texts discussed in this chapter, from canonical male authors (Chaucer, Shakespeare and Wordsworth), through the late twentieth-century feminist work of theorists (Butler and Wittig) and novelist (Angela Carter), to contemporary writing (Liam Murray Bell) all query the ways in which women move 'away from danger' and the role of victim in order to gain 'agency'. At times that attempt to attain independent subjectivity leads to women becoming perpetrators of sexualised violence themselves. At the same time, it is debatable, in the end, whether women are able to assert their independence through becoming perpetrators, just as it is arguable whether Wittig advances a response to (male) sexualised violence by responding with female militancy. In posing this problem, however, and charting the transition from (female) victim to (female) perpetrator of sexualised violence, it is hoped that this essay will challenge the literary precedents that often stigmatise women as passive and powerless victims of sexualised violence and instead explore the ability of women to transgress and subvert (male) discourses of patriarchy and seek a subjectivity of their own, and add a dimension to the Kelly continuum of violence that she does not address.

## Further reading

For a nuanced perspective on various narratological techniques employed in writing of and about rape in literature, see Sorcha Gunne and Zoe Brigley Thompson's *Feminism, Literature and Rape Narratives: Violence and Violation* (2009). For a further discussion of authors and literary texts mentioned throughout this chapter, L.E. Tanner's *Intimate Violence: Reading Rape and Torture in Twentieth Century Fiction* (1994) provides an interesting account of violence in Hubert Selby Jr's *Last Exit to Brooklyn* (1964), as well as Brett Easton Ellis's psychological journey into unmitigated violence, *American Psycho* (1991).

## References

Aretxaga, Begoña (1995) 'Ruffling a few patriarchal hairs: Women's experiences of war in Northern Ireland', *Women and War*, 19(1). Available at: http://www.culturalsurvival.org/ourpublications/csq/article/ruffling-a-few-patriarchal-hairs-womens-experiences-war-northern-ireland (accessed 22 September 2010).

Aretxaga, Begoña, (1997) *Shattering Silence: Women, Nationalism and Political Subjectivity in Northern Ireland*. Chichester: Princeton University Press.

Baillie, Sandra M (2002) *Evangelical Women in Belfast: Imprisoned or Empowered?* London: Palgrave MacMillan.

Brownmiller, S. (1975) *Against Our Will: Men, Women and Rape*. New York: Martin Secker and Warburg.

Butler, Judith (1990) *Gender Trouble*. New York/London: Routledge.

Carter, Angela (1977) *The Passion of New Eve*. London: Virago.

Chaucer, Geoffrey (1992) *The Tales of the Clerk and the Wife of Bath*, Marion Wynne-Davies (ed.). London: Routledge.

Coogan, Tim Pat (1996) *The Troubles: Ireland's Ordeal 1966–1996 and the Search for Peace*.

London: Arrow Books.

Diaz-Diocaretz, Myriam (1989) 'Bakhtin, discourse and feminist theories', *Critical Studies*, 1(2): 121–39.

Easton Ellis, Brett (1991) *American Psycho*. New York: Vintage Books.

Feldman, Allen (1991) *Formations of Violence: The Narrative of the Body and Political Terror in Northern Ireland*. Chicago: University of Chicago Press.

Frayling, Christopher (1986) 'The house that Jack built: some stereotypes of the rapist in the history of popular culture', in Sylvana Tomaselli and Roy Porter (eds) *Rape: An Historial and Social Enquiry*. Oxford: Basil Blackwell, pp. 174–215.

Giles, James Richard (ed.) (1998) *Understanding Hubert Selby, Jr.* Columbia: University of South Carolina Press.

Gunne, Sorcha and Brigley Thompson, Zoe (eds) (2009) *Feminism, Literature and Rape Narratives: Violence and Violation*. London: Routledge.

Irigaray, Luce (1985) *Speculum of the Other Woman*. Ithaca: Cornell University Press.

Little, Adrian (2002) 'Feminism and the politics of difference in Northern Ireland', *Journal of Political Ideologies*, 7(2): 163–77.

Maguire, Tom (2006) *Making Theatre in Northern Ireland: Through and Beyond the Troubles*. Exeter: University of Exeter Press.

Morgan, Robin (1990) *The Demon Lover: On the Sexuality of Terrorism*. London: Mandarin.

Naipaul, V.S. (2004) *Magic Seeds*. London: Picador.

O'Brien, Edna (1995) *House of Splendid Isolation*. London: Orion Books.

Pelan, Rebecca (2005) *Two Irelands: Literary Feminisms North and South*. New York: Syracuse University Press.

Porter, Ray (1986) 'Rape – Does it have a historical meaning?', in Sylvana Tomaselli and Roy Porter (eds) *Rape: An Historical and Social Enquiry*. Oxford: Basil Blackwell, pp. 216–36.

Rose, Christine, M. and Robertson, Elizabeth (eds) (2001) *Representing Rape in Medieval and Early Modern Literature*. London: Palgrave.

Sanday, Peggy Reeves (1986) 'Rape and the silencing of the feminine', in Sylvana Tomaselli and Roy Porter (eds) *Rape: An Historial and Social Enquiry*. Oxford: Basil Blackwell, pp. 84–101.

Selby, Jr., Hubert (2004) *Last Exit to Brooklyn*. London: Bloomsbury.

Shakespeare, William (1954) *Titus Andronicus*, J.C. Maxwell (ed.). London: Routledge.

Sielke, Sabine (2002) *Reading Rape: The Rhetoric of Sexual Violence in American Literature and Culture, 1790–1990*. Princeton: Princeton University Press.

Stockton, Sharon (2006) *The Economics of Fantasy: Rape in Twentieth Century Literature*. Columbus: Ohio State University Press.

Vance, Carol S. (ed.) (1989) *Pleasure and Danger: Exploring Female Sexuality*. London: Pandora.

Tanner, L.E. (1994) *Intimate Violence: Reading Rape and Torture in Twentieth-Century Fiction*. Bloomington: Indiana University Press.

Wittig, Monique (1969) *Les Guérillères*. Boston: Beacon Press.

Wittig, Monique *et al.* (2005) 'For a Women's Liberation Movement', in Namascar Shaktini (ed.). *On Monique Wittig*. Chicago: University of Illinois Press, pp. 22–34.

Wordsworth, William (1988) *Lyrical Ballads*, R.L. Brett and A.R. Jones (eds). London: Routledge.

Zerilli, Linda M.G. (2005) 'A new grammar of difference: Monique Wittig's poetic revolution', in *On Monique Wittig*, Namascar Shaktini (ed.). Chicago: University of Illinois Press, pp. 87–114.

# Chapter 3

# The legal heritage of the crime of rape

*Joan McGregor*

## Meet Joan McGregor

Joan McGregor is a professor of philosophy and adjunct professor of law at Arizona State University in Tempe, Arizona. Her interest in rape grew out of her earlier work on coercion and exploitation where she argued that given the unequal bargaining positions of individuals, those with more bargaining power (power can come in various forms) can use that power to exploit or coerce the vulnerability of the weaker party. That framework for coercion was not premised on the notion of explicit threats of violence. Most rapes, particularly acquaintance rapes, don't involve explicit threats of violence. In acquaintance rape cases, the nonconsensual sexual interactions are a result of the unequal bargaining positions of men and women. The power that is used is not necessarily physical power but may be economic, social, political, or even exploiting the coercive environment where many women find themselves. McGregor subsequently wrote a book entitled, *Is it Rape?: On Acquaintance Rape and Taking Women's Consent Seriously*, morally criticising the criminal laws of rape, arguing that the criminal justice system is supposed to protect individuals from harm from others but that it is not adequately protecting women's sexual autonomy from harm.

## Introduction

Current rape laws around the world continue in failing to protect women's interests in their sexual autonomy. For instance, last year Afghanistan's government tried to enact legislation that would permit men to force their wives into sex (Abawl 2009). Other countries still exclude rape charges, including India, Malaysia, Tonga, Ethiopia, Lebanon, and Guatemala and Uruguay if the perpetrator marries the victim (Neuwirth 2004). Mali, Sudan and Yemen have laws mandating 'wife obedience' in marital relations (Neuwirth 2004). A Saudi judge recently sentenced the *victim* of a gang rape to

90 lashes (CNN.com 2007). Lest the problem is viewed only as one in non-Western nations, notice the recent findings that judges in England are 'getting around' the new sexual assault law that was supposed to shield the sexual history of victims during trials for rape (Dyer 2008). Shield rules were designed to prevent defence lawyers from routinely cross-examining victims about their sexual history as a method of undermining the victim's credibility and playing into myths about women and sexuality (Kelly *et al.* 2006). Compounding the problem in Britain is the treatment by police of rape. The following story is indicative: 'After Linda Davies reported to police that her 15-year-old daughter had been raped, it took three months – plus two dozen phone calls and a threat of legal action – before police questioned the suspect, a 28-year-old neighbour' (Jordan 2008). In that case, the defendant was later acquitted after the police lost the cellphone records that would have contradicted the defendant's account and the judge told the jury to disregard the victim's age and that the defendant was 'in a way a man of good character' because his earlier criminal convictions did not involve violence. The result was another acquittal for rape in Britain, not unusual given the fact that based on the government's statistics of officially recorded rapes, only 5.7 per cent of rapes end in conviction (Stern Report 2010). In a study conducted by Kelly and colleagues (2005) about rape investigations in London's Metropolitan Police, in about one third of the reported rapes, the accused offenders had histories of other accusations of rape, targeting young women who were intoxicated or high on drugs, many of whom suffered from mental illness, and yet many of those same cases were labelled 'not-crimed', i.e., not treated as crimes by the police (Kelly *et al.* 2005). And finally it is suspected that the rapes that are reported to police in Britain represent only 10 per cent of the rapes that occur annually. Dismal statistics tell a tale of a system that even with thoroughgoing and progressive revisions to its criminal sexual assault laws is failing to protect women from serious harms.

Criminal laws are supposed to protect people from harms perpetrated by others. Why are the criminal laws that address sexual violence around the world not protecting women from the harms to their sexual autonomy and physical integrity? Before answering that question, it is important to remember that the area of sexual violence recognised by criminal laws is only a small subset of the much wider range of sexual violence. Sexual violence falls on a continuum and the range of sexual violence that is recognised and ostensibly protected by the criminal law is narrow. In Liz Kelly's *Surviving Sexual Violence* (Kelly 1988), she defines sexual violence as 'any physical, visual, verbal or sexual act that is experienced by the woman or girl at the time or later as a threat or assault that has the effect of hurting her or degrading her and/or takes away her ability to control intimate contact'. Some of the different behaviours she identifies include abuse, intimidation, coercion, intrusion, threat and force. Her definition picks out a more expansive range of behaviour than is identified by any country's criminal code. Once we acknowledge Kelly's more expansive range of sexual violence, the fact that the criminal laws are doing a dismal job at protecting women from the narrower subset of instances is even more disturbing.

This chapter will consider just the area of sexual violence that the criminal law addresses. The chapter will give a brief history of the theoretical underpinning of rape law, particularly focusing on laws of the twentieth century and the Anglo-American system, and then examine the reforms that were supposed to solve certain problems and consider how and why many of the reforms failed.

## The legal heritage of the crime of rape

How did the system of criminal laws addressing sexual violence get to its current state? The history of rape in the Anglo-American legal system illustrates treatment of women that is shocking and indefensible in its blatant unfairness and this is still true with an increasingly progressive legislation. An increasing chorus of theorists has been raising objections and advocating changes in rape law since the 1970s and 1980s. Some changes have come, but even with the revisions in the 1970s and 1980s, extensive ones in Canada in 1992 (Criminal Code of Sexual Assault) and in Britain again in 2003 (Sexual Offences Act 2003), the statutes and the criminal justice system continue to reflect a legacy of patriarchy and a disappointing lack of respect for women's sexual autonomy and physical integrity (McGregor 2005). The assumptions and standards of rape law and the procedures to enforce them have been biased against women since the beginning. This begs the question of the law's objectivity and fairness. The Anglo-American criminal justice system has a morally significant procedural safeguard of the presumption of innocence of the defendant until proven guilty which, of course, needs to be preserved. Here it is argued that statutes, procedures and assumptions in rape prosecutions go far beyond the interests of this procedural protection.

There are numerous dimensions to the problems with the prosecution of rape:

- First, there is the fact that rape laws and the enforcement of them protect men's interests in sexual access to women and against prosecution.

- Second, the statutes and the criminal justice system, the police, prosecutors and judges employ assumptions and standards about rape, consent, force, reasonable belief, resistance, 'proper behaviour for women' that fail to account for the perspective and interests of women.

- Third, attitudes of the public (who make up juries) about proper and improper behaviour for women and, consequently, who can be a 'victim' of sexual violence – what one theorist called 'good victimhood' – reinforce and entrench sexist attitudes about women and sexuality.

Feminist legal theorists have criticised standard doctrines in rape law, pointing out that 'utmost resistance', i.e. the requirement of strong physical resistance, the corroboration requirement, marital exception, and routine introduction at trial of past sexual histories in rape cases, do not advance the legitimate ends of criminal law and are blatantly unfair to women. The legal rules and the implementation of them are either not designed to protect women's interest in the physical integrity and security, or the rules are implemented in a fashion that does not secure women's autonomy. Feminist theorists and others have also been critical of the procedures and attitudes of police, prosecutors, judges and the public who have perpetuated the injustices of rape enforcement against the interests of women. For instance, police and prosecutors who persist in believing that many rape allegations are false and don't believe women's account of their victimisation because they were drinking and knew their attackers, judges who are dismissive of women's stories of sexual abuse due to their previous consensual sexual history, and the public's attitude that victims are responsible for their own victimisation when they drink or engage in other 'risky' behaviours are all contributing to the injustices against women (see for example http://www.equalities.gov.uk/pdf/ConnectionsFinal_acc.pdf).

The 2009 British case involving John Worboys is a recent example of women's complaints of rape not initially being taken seriously or being believed. Worboys was arrested but held only briefly, allowing him to go on to rape a number of other women until he was finally arrested again and convicted on a number of other rape charges. The police incredulity was based on among other reasons, the fact that the female victims had been drinking prior to the assault, there was no 'physical injury' to the victims, and the assaults involved the 'trusted black cab' company in London. Even after all the reforms and attention to the issues of sexual violence in Britain, including the 2003 reforms, the problems of addressing rape in the criminal justice system continue (IPCC 2010).

The twentieth-century definition of rape in Anglo-American systems can be directly traced to the eighteenth-century definition of rape in William Blackstone's 1765 *Commentaries on the Laws of England*. Blackstone's definition of rape was 'carnal knowledge [by a man not her husband] of a woman forcibly and against her will'. That definition of rape statutorily exempted husbands and it required a finding of force *and* absence of consent. A wife could not be raped by her husband, even if she were estranged from him and there was extreme force. In 1736 Lord Matthew Hale said of the exclusion of husbands: 'the husband cannot be guilty of a rape committed by himself upon his lawful wife, for by their mutual matrimonial consent and contract the wife hath given up herself in this kind unto her husband, which she cannot retract' (Hale 1736). 'Carnal knowledge' meant penetration of a vagina by a penis; other sexual violations were excluded. Amazingly, the eighteenth-century definition would not be changed in the United States, England and Wales, and Canada until the late 1970s and early 1980s when the American Law Institute attempted reform of the entire criminal code. In 1976 England and Wales began rape reform by passing the Sexual Offences (Amendment) Act and Canada's Federal Government made substantive rape reforms in the early 1980s. Acknowledging that husbands can rape their wives would not be statutorily changed in most Anglo-American systems until the 1990s.

## The requirement of resistance

Rape historically was viewed as a threat to male interests since it: 'devalued wives and daughters and jeopardized patrilineal systems of inheritance' (Rhode 1989: 245). Rape laws were designed to protect men's interest in their women, which included their daughters and their wives. On the other hand, policy-makers perceived 'too stringent constraints on male sexuality ... equally threatening ...' (Rhode 1989: 245). The 'utmost resistance' requirement is a prime example of protecting male interests in their own women and in male interest in sexual access. The requirement was used to determine whether the sexual interaction was 'against her will' and reflected the belief that a woman should protect her chastity with her life. Women's chastity was worth a lot to men interested in marrying off their daughters and ensuring that children conceived during their marriage were biologically their progeny. Without chastity, women lost their value and were often ostracised by family and community. The assumption of these laws was that women too held chastity to be of the highest value and would protect theirs with their own life. Given this assumption, failure to protect one's chastity with 'utmost resistance' was seen as giving consent to the sexual interaction. Rather than protecting women's sexual autonomy or even their physical well-being, these rules were designed to protect the interests of men. Even in contexts where resistance would have been extremely dangerous, women were held to this standard. Moreover, victims were often humiliated when their resistance or lack of it resulted in judgment that they must have really desired the sexual interaction and 'consented' to it. For example, in an American case, *Brown* v. *State* (1906), the perpetrator tripped his 16-year-old victim to the ground and physically forced himself on her. The Supreme Court of Wisconsin found that *the victim had not adequately demonstrated* her non-consent, even though she tried screaming and he was physically restraining her. 'Not only must there be entire absence of mental consent or assent, but there must be the most vehement exercise of every physical means or faculty within the woman's power to resist the penetration of her person, and this must be shown to persist until the offence is consummated.'

'Utmost resistance', on the other hand, protected men's interest in sexual access, thus making it difficult to obtain a criminal charge and conviction for rape. The result was that to prove 'forcibly' and 'against her will', courts (and some statutes) required victim resistance as 'utmost resistance'. This meant that unless the victim used 'utmost' physical resistance, a physical fight to near death, the sexual interaction was not against her will. Utmost resistance was claimed to be the natural response of a woman of virtue, therefore not an imposition on any woman. In another American case in the 1800s, *People* v. *Dohring* (1874), where the appeals court reversed the conviction of a man found guilty of raping a servant in his house, the court said:

> Can the mind conceive of a woman, in the possession of her faculties and powers, revoltingly unwilling that this deed should be done upon her, who would not resist so hard and so long as she was able? And if a woman, aware that it will be done unless she does resist, does not resist to the extent of her abilities on the occasion, must it not be that she is not entirely reluctant?

Women's resistance was judged, put 'on trial', even with evidence of extreme force or weapons. There have been instances where the victim was beaten to the edge of death and it was determined that she was not raped because she didn't resist with enough vehemence. A Texas court said in *Perez* v. *State* (1906) that 'although some force be used, yet if she does not put forth all power of resistance which she was capable of exerting under the circumstances, it will not be rape.' This requirement reflected the view that it was better for a woman to die than be 'dishonoured'. And the assumption was that if a woman did not put up such a fight she probably was consenting and just wouldn't admit to it.

In another case from the 1880s, *Whittaker* v. *State* (1880), where even though the assailant had the woman's hands and feet so tight that she couldn't move, and when she screamed for help, Whittaker threatened her with his revolver, the Supreme Court of Wisconsin reversed his conviction, saying, 'this is not a case where the prosecutrix was overcome by threats of person violence.' Then the court continued that Whittaker's threat to use his gun was merely 'conditional upon her attempting again to cry out...The testimony does not show that the threat of personal violence overpowered her will, or...that she was incapable of voluntary action.'

These historical court decisions illustrate that consent was understood as equivalent to submission, and submission no matter how reluctantly given. With the element of consent present, an essential element of the crime of rape is missing. The 'utmost resistance' requirement, as Stephen Schulhofer argued, 'became impossibly difficult to satisfy and dangerous to any victim who tried' (Schulhofer 1998: 19). These were malicious standards and got support from medical writers who insisted that women have the physical means to stop rape if they so desire, by using hands, limbs and pelvic muscles. They claimed that any woman who wasn't willing to have sex could stop any man regardless of size from penetrating her. The implication was that successful penetration meant that the woman was a willing sexual partner (*Brown* v. *State* (1909)).

## Suspicion of female victims

Add to the utmost resistance requirement, the criminal justice system and societies' belief that women make up rape complaints. There has been and continues to be an entrenched suspicion and distrust towards female victims (Kelly *et al.* 2005). The persistence of the belief that women 'cry rape' is illustrated by the lengthy discussion in the recent Stern Report of how rape is investigated and prosecuted in England and Wales. The report recommended, because of the prevalence of the belief that many charges of rape are false charges, that the Ministry of Justice carry out research on the frequency of false allegations of rape (Stern Report 2010). The assumption was that unless the victim could prove that she physically resisted, what reason would the investigation and prosecuting authorities have to suppose that she is not lying about the rape? Two other requirements, which reinforced the belief in the unreliability of female victims, were the requirements for *corroboration* of the woman's testimony and the requirement that the *complaint is promptly filed*. Currently, elaborating on the suspicion of female victims, countries like Pakistan and Sudan have required four male (not female) witnesses to corroborate a claim of rape. If the victim's complaint was not quickly made, it was assumed that she was having second thoughts about her consensual sexual activity.

Distrust of female victims has found its way into jury instructions too. The practice was to instruct the jury that it was unsafe to convict for rape on the uncorroborated evidence of the alleged victim. No other crime requires the victim to have corroboration. The legacy of this suspicion is epitomised by the warning given three centuries ago by the English Lord Chief Justice Matthew Hale, who said that rape is a charge 'easily to be made and hard to be proved, and harder to be defended by the party accused, tho' never so innocent' (Hale 1736: 635). This quote was for many years, and up until very recently, recited to juries before their deliberations. Glanville Williams, a leading twentieth century jurist, supporting the distrust of female victims of rape, said, 'There is a sound reason for it [the instruction to the jury], because these cases are particularly subject to the danger of deliberately false charges, resulting from sexual neurosis, phantasy, jealousy, spite or simply a girl's refusal to admit that she consented to an act of which she is now ashamed' (Williams 1962: 159). Williams worries that those psychological approaches – namely, having a physician question the complainant, to determine whether she is having fantasies, is neurotic, and so forth – may not be able to pick out all falsehoods and suggests that all female complainants take polygraph tests. Furthermore, it was the opinion of John Wigmore, author of the United States's most influential treatise on evidence, that 'No judge should ever let a sex-offence charge go to the jury unless the female complainant's social history and mental make-up have been examined and testified to by a qualified physician' (Wigmore 1970: vol. 3A, sec. 924a).

The nexus between rape as a dishonour, expectations of a woman's behaviour when confronting a rape attempt, and distrust of female victims still presents itself in modern rape prosecutions. In 1998, the Italian Supreme Court overturned a rape conviction in part on the grounds that the victim was wearing jeans. The court's opinion stated that since it is difficult to remove jeans worn by another, the victim must have assisted the defendant with the removal of her jeans, and hence she could not have been raped by the defendant (Van Cleave 2005). The court's argument reflected the idea that any woman of virtue would have fought hard to protect herself from sexual assault.

### The consent standard

The consent standard in rape law was like no other standard for consent in law. Consent in rape was inferred from submission, no matter how long it took or whatever it took to get that submission. Even when threatened or assaulted, if the victim submitted, consent has often been inferred. The consent standard in rape is unique since it requires victims of rape, unlike victims of any other crime, to demonstrate their 'wishes', that is, demonstrate their *non-consent* through physical resistance. Moreover, in some cases, even resistance has not been sufficient to establish non-consent since, as was expressed in Glanville Williams's classic textbook on criminal law, women often welcome a 'masterly advance' and 'present a token of resistance'. An article published in the *Stanford Law Review* in the 1960s argues that although a woman may desire sexual intercourse, it is customary for her to say 'no, no, no' while meaning 'yes, yes, yes'. In a *Yale Law Journal* article it further suggested that women do not know what they want, or mean what they say, and often require *force* to have a 'pleasurable' experience (Note 1952). Rather than requiring an explicit sign of consent and worrying about the circumstances in which the alleged consent was given (for example, were the circumstances threatening? Was the victim intimidated? Were implicit threats made?), the courts have interpreted silence and non-resistance as signs of consent. This approach to consent effectively assumes the default position that women are consenting to sex, that there is a presumption of consent which could only be defeated by the most extreme circumstances. In other areas of law, consent is not assumed but must be affirmatively sought.

Overwhelming force has not been sufficient to have courts put aside their attempts to find some semblance of consent. In *People* v. *Burnham* (1986) a woman was severely beaten and then forced to engage in intercourse with her husband and a dog and the court held out the possibility of consent or at least that the defendant might reasonably believe that she was consenting. So-called 'submission', no matter how 'reluctantly given', negated the element 'without consent' which was an element of the crime of rape. These interpretations of consent eviscerate the normative force of consent. In other words, the reason for requiring consent in the law in the first place is to ensure the moral autonomy of the person is respected. By assuming that women are consenting in all but the most egregious circumstances, the law is not permitting consent to protect women's sovereignty over their bodies.

**Race and sexual assault**

Many of these rules and standards that made rape prosecution so difficult have lasted well into the present day. The exception to the difficulty of prosecuting rape was in the case of white women charging black men with rape, particularly in the United States, during the period of slavery and the era of systematic legal discrimination and segregation known as the Jim Crow era. In those cases, the law did not require 'utmost resistance' since it was assumed that a white woman wouldn't consent to sexual intercourse with a black man. White women's testimony was taken as truth and not requiring corroboration. For instance, in Virginia in 1921 a black man was sentenced to the death penalty for a rape of a white, 'simple, good, unsophisticated country girl' (*Hart* v. *Commonwealth*). The court never looked for her 'utmost resistance' nor scrutinised the case. The horrific history of the use of rape charges against black men, many in southern United States resulting in the death penalty, on very little evidence, illustrates another way in which the law has treated groups unequally. Black women who were victims of rape did not, however, get similar treatment; in fact their claims of rape, particularly against white men, got very little attention.

## Reforming the law

In the 1950s the American Law Institute proposed reforms to the criminal codes of the states including reforms to rape laws. The writers were worried about the extremely low conviction rate for rape. The Model Penal Code, however, keeps the requirements of corroboration of the woman's testimony, the special cautionary instructions to the jury, the marital exception, and extends the exemption to cases where the man and woman are living together. The Code suggested eliminating the victim's consent altogether and focusing on the man's illegitimate behaviour. Changing the focus from the woman to the man's conduct sounded like a step in the right direction; until then, the woman's conduct was put on trial, judged, and often found wanting. The status of the victim then becomes a factor in the trial; was she a virgin, was she married, was she a 'party girl' or prostitute? Nevertheless, the reasons for not including consent in the Model Penal Code rules rested on sexist notions about women and consent too. The writers assumed that women say 'no' and don't mean it, that women are ambivalent about consent to sex, and that women have conflicting emotions and are unable to directly express their sexual desires. Model Penal Code contributors delineate between forcible rapes, on the one hand, and on the other, reluctant submission. Only the former, forcible rape, was a serious crime. The focus then was on 'forcible compulsion' as a trustworthy guide to when women had not consented. But gaining submission without overwhelming violence, through intimidation, threats, deception is recognised as legitimate sexual conduct.

Force continues to this day to play a major part in the understanding of rape. Without physical force, and even extreme physical force, the assumption is that the sexual activity was consensual. As mentioned earlier, Kelly identified a much wider range of sexual violence than what the criminal law recognises as criminal behaviour. The reforms were meant to bring more of the continuum of sexual violence, including non-consensual behaviour without explicit physical force, under the purview of the criminal law. For example, including non-consensual sex without physical force is to expand what the criminal law addresses, so is recognising that 'rape' can occur in a marriage. Nevertheless the criminal law has not been very successful in its attempts to secure prosecutions of that wider range of sexual violence.

In the United States, individual states reformed their statutes in the 1960s but didn't adopt the Model Penal Code's suggestions wholesale, deciding instead to adopt parts of it, particularly focusing on 'forcible compulsion'. Most states kept the resistance requirement, the marital exception, the special rules about prompt complaint, corroboration, and the cautionary jury instruction. They reduced the utmost resistance requirement to 'earnest resistance' and later 'reasonable resistance', keeping to this day the requirement of the woman's physical resistance (Williams 1963: 162). Current rules and practices still rely upon a woman's resistance as necessary evidence that it is a rape. When the victim is intoxicated, or afraid, or for other reasons does not resist, the legal system is unlikely to consider it an instance of rape. The laws continued to see rape as only a violent attack and then only if the woman resists. Non-consensual sex outside of that paradigm was not protected.

### Reforms again

In the 1970s feminists such as Susan Brownmiller and Susan Griffin exposed many of the problems with the Anglo-American laws and the criminal justice system's treatment of rape victims (Griffin 1971). The baseline assumption of consent, the corroboration rule, the routine introduction of a victim's sexual history, the force and resistance requirement, and the marital exception continued to support the protection of men's interests in sexual access and not the protection of women's sexual choice (MacKinnon 1989: 179). Feminists argued that the rules themselves, particularly the force and resistance requirements, embody typical male perceptions, attitudes and reactions rather than female ones. Moreover, some feminists argued that far from protecting women, the rape laws, through their expectations of proper female behaviour and their high expectations of impermissible force, actually served to enhance male opportunities for sexual access. What women wore or did, 'she wore a tight sweater', 'she went to the man's apartment', 'she drank alcohol', led police and prosecutors to assume that she consented or had only got what she deserved given her dress and behaviour. Feminists argued that the rape laws actually increase a woman's dependence on a male protector and reinforce social relations of male dominance.

Rape cases that went to trial resulted in the victim being subjected to brutal and humiliating cross-examination of her life, particularly her prior sex life. The object of these cross-examinations was to make her out, no matter how violent or outrageous the alleged rape was, to be a 'bad girl' who either consented to the events or got what she deserved given her 'loose' lifestyle. Susan Griffin's article in *Ramparts* magazine in the 1970s was one of the first to document the rape trial ordeal. She described a rape trial where a man, along with three other men, forced a woman at gunpoint to go to his apartment where the four men sexually assaulted her. At trial, other women testified that this man had sexually assaulted them as well. The defence attorney characterised the events as consensual, suggesting that the victim was a 'loose woman'. The attorney asked her if she had been fired from a job because she'd had sex on the office couch, if she'd had an affair with a married man, and if her 'two children have a sex game in which one got on top of the other and they...'(Griffin 1971: 971). All of these allegations she vehemently denied; however, the attorney had successfully created in the jurors' minds a distrust of the victim and a picture of her as a 'loose woman'. This resulted in the defendant being acquitted. A standard trial tactic was for defence attorneys to 'put the woman' on trial, asking questions about her previous sexual experiences, whether she used birth control, whether she went to bars, what she wore, either suggesting that she consented to the sexual events or that she 'got what she deserved'. Recall the 1990s rape trial of Kennedy-Smith (nephew of the late Senator Edward Kennedy), where it was recounted that among other things, the victim's Victoria's Secret underwear suggested that anyone who wears such underwear is looking for sex. This played into jurors' ideas about 'proper' female behaviour. Even victims who admitted to having consented to sex with their boyfriends were consequently portrayed as likely to consent to the stranger who was on trial for raping them. In the USA, at the preliminary hearing of the Kobe Bryant rape case, Bryant's lawyer asked if the victim's injuries were consistent with her having sexual intercourse with three partners, putting the idea to the media that she had been promiscuous. Bryant, a National Basketball Association superstar, claimed that he had consensual sex with the 19-year-old resort employee. Between Bryant's scorched earth lawyering and the media's hounding, the sites all over the Internet about her, and the death threats to her, she eventually withdrew her rape charge.

In the 1970s and the 1980s, response to feminists' objections resulted in reforms such as dropping the corroboration requirement, the special instruction to juries and eventually presumptive 'rape shield' rules to bar defence attorneys from routinely introducing past sexual experiences as a way of undermining the credibility of the victim. How well, for example, the rape shield rules are used is debatable. For instance, Kobe Bryant's lawyer was able early on to get into play the victim's sexual history (or even her possible sexual history). And the judges in England, as mentioned earlier, are also subverting the objective of the shield rules.

Concern for equality led some feminists to design gender-neutral statutes, replacing traditional statutes which punished the rape of a woman by a man with gender-neutral ones (Estrich 1987: 81 onwards). Support for gender-neutral statutes also arises from the following concern: 'Men who are sexually assaulted should have the same protection as female victims, and women who sexually assault men or other women should be as liable for conviction as conventional rapists.' Gender neutrality is seen as a way 'to eliminate the traditional attitude that the victim is supposed to resist earnestly to protect virginity, her female "virtue" or her marital fidelity' (Bienen, 1980: 74–175). Problems, however, arise from making rape statutes gender neutral. Indeed, gender-neutral statutes may address one set of problems but create others. Because women do not necessarily react in the same way as men do, and if gender-neutral statutes mean retaining male norms and reactions to rape scenarios, then women will continue to be disadvantaged by such statutes. So, for example, physical resistance might be a typical male reaction to attack, but not necessarily a typical female reaction. Men are socialised to fight, to respond physically. Women are not and may respond by crying or just being silent.

Consider the results of the attitude survey to the question: 'What would you do if a man tried to rape you?' (see Figure 3.1).

Subjecting women to the resistance requirement disadvantages them. Further, rape is typically something that is perpetrated on women by men. Rape is not generally a gender-neutral crime; men rape, not women. Women are overwhelmingly the victims of rape. Making rape gender neutral obscures this fact. Gender-neutral statutes are, however, the norm today.

If a man attempted to rape you, do you think you would be most likely to ...(%)

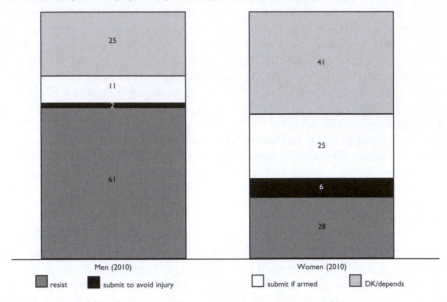

*Source*: http://www.equalities.gov.uk/pdf/ConnectionsFinal_acc.pdf

**Figure 3.1** Self-reported behavioural intentions if raped

Another reform was to relabel 'rape' as a form of assault. The purpose of the change was to eradicate from the offence the baggage from the common law, to place it more centrally within the criminal rules of assault that focus attention on the defendant and away from the victim. Relabelling rape 'sexual assault' may, however, assume a position in the debate as to whether rape should be considered a crime of sexual desire or violence. Some theorists argue that rape is motivated by desire to dominate, to have power, and is a crime of violence; not, as was long assumed, by uncontrollable sexual desire. Focusing on the violent aspects of rape makes it clear that the law is not trying to prohibit all sex and that those violent men must be incapacitated as dangerous criminals, not treated as only sexually aberrant. Moreover, to see rape as violence is to recognise that sex should be inconsistent with violence. Reconceptualising rape as assault, however, has prompted some to question the seriousness of rape, particularly non-aggravated rape (Davis 1984: 984). How serious an assault is rape if the victim isn't cut up, bruised and broken? In 1989 the Manhattan Supreme Court of Justice justified a light sentence for a rapist, even though he had an extensive criminal history, because the victim was not being 'tortured or chopped up' (Arce 1989). Assaults are normally graduated in terms of level of bodily injuries. Supporters of the change recognised that equating rape with assaultive conduct may obscure the unique meaning and understanding of the indignity and harm of rape. The harm of rape is different from other assaults. The meaning and significance of sexual touching is different from other kinds of touching (McGregor 2005: 219–48).

Another problem with conceptualising rape as a form of assault or an act of violence is that a man can force sex against a woman's will without physical violence. Having power over the victim will do. The definition of force, still a major component in many statutes or in the prosecution of rape, needs to be clearly articulated and not confused with exclusively physical force. Think of coercive force that can be exerted upon your will – for example, when three bullies in an alley ask for your wallet. We should distinguish two senses of force: first, overwhelming physical force – the perpetrator lying on top of the victim so that she cannot resist, for example; and, second, coercive force, explicit or implicit threats to do harm that put pressure on the victim's will.

Feminists who argue for rape as *sexual* assault want to reinforce its violent character *and* its sexual nature. Some argue that the so-called power rapists' and anger rapists' 'choice of the vagina or anus as the object of aggression is not accidental, but essential...the rapist seeks to spoil, corrupt, or even destroy those aspects of a woman's person that should be a source of pride, joy, and power for her rather than a source of shame, depression, and humiliation' (Tong 1984: 17). On the other hand, rape as sexual assault focuses on women's sexuality as being particularly susceptible to attack and hence in need of special protection. This view may reinforce the myth of rape 'according to which the invasion of sexual integrity is so traumatic that the victim's psychic wounds never heal' (Tong 1984: 65). The sexual assault approach may unwittingly cast women back into the position of victim, a role which many feminists would like to move beyond.

Making prosecutions easier and attempting to address the interests of victims lead to various approaches. One of the ways thought to increase prosecution and convictions was to argue that penalties for rape be reduced, recognising that juries are unlikely to convict for unaggravated rape when the defendant faces a long sentence. Not all rapes are the same (the same can be said about assaults); some rapes involve aggravated assault too, and consequently some rapes are 'worse' than others. So-called 'simple rapes', often they are acquaintance rapes, don't have other assaults along with the rape. Saying that some rapes are worse than others is not to suggest that 'simple rapes' or unaggravated rapes are not serious offences and worthy of some punishment. Moving beyond the adversarial criminal trial to a restorative justice model has been proposed by Mary Koss, Kathleen Daly and J. Stubbs as a method of achieving some of the aims of victims (Koss 2006; Daly and Stubbs 2006). These scholars, who have been researching rape for decades, have recently argued for 'expanded justice alternatives', including a restorative justice model in conjunction with criminal prosecution. Their approach has not been met with unequivocal support. One concern of the restorative justice approach is the possible danger of losing sight of the fact that all rapes are serious crimes, involving serious harms to their victims.

In the United Kingdom there were reforms in the 1980s triggered by a television documentary in 1982 showing the police's sexist attitudes towards women who claimed to be raped and their role in the attrition rate for the crime of rape (Lea *et al.* 2003). Even with those changes in the sexual assault law, the police still tended to pursue cases that fitted the 'stranger violent rapist' profile and designate as 'no crime' the more common acquaintance rapes (Lea *et al.* 2003). Then, in 2003, the Sexual Offences Act attempted to modernise the consent rule and overhaul the law. With all these attempts at reforms, results are still not as good as was hoped.

## Physical force, resistance and consent

Many contemporary criminal justice systems, even when the changes include explicitly getting rid of the force requirement, still search for victim resistance. The following case in the United States is representative. In *State* v. *Rusk* the victim gave the defendant a ride home from a bar where they had met through a mutual friend. The defendant invited the victim up to his apartment but she declined. After he took her car keys, she reluctantly accompanied him to his apartment. The defendant started to undress the victim, and before intercourse the victim said to the defendant, 'If I do what you want, will you let me go without killing me?' The victim started to cry and then the defendant, according to the victim, started lightly choking her. The appellant court argued that she had not been raped as she had not been *forced* since she had not resisted.

The standards used in *Rusk* exemplify what feminists label 'the male orientation to the law'. 'Prohibited force' is defined in terms of physical force and the victim's response to the situation. The victim's response must be physical resistance and not merely verbal protests – or crying! If the law were interested in protecting the autonomy rights of women, then it should consider verbal protests as resistance. Beyond that, if the law were interested in protecting the autonomy rights of women, it would drop altogether the resistance requirement and see verbal protests as sufficient for non-consent and beyond that ask for affirmative assent. The 'physical force' and 'physical resistance' requirements in rape law embody what Susan Estrich called 'a male perception of threatening situations' and a male way of responding to a threatening situation (Estrich 1987). Physical force is seen as threatening, and one responds to the threat with physical resistance. Force translates into 'physical force' rather than into the various power relationships to which women might feel vulnerable. Being isolated, without transportation, with someone you hardly know, who is physically more powerful than you are, possibly someone who is in a role of authority, all could contribute to feeling threatened and thereby being 'forced' into sex. The law's standard, however, of the 'reasonable person' is one who fights back, not cries. As Estrich says: 'The reasonable woman, it seems, is not a schoolboy "sissy"; she is a real man' (Estrich 1987: 65). Also worth noticing is that the woman's behaviour, and not the defendant's, is the one that is subject to evaluation. The law is judging what the alleged victim did or didn't do to make an assessment of whether she was truly a victim or not.

When the 'physical' resistance requirement is applied to women, the results have been disastrous because many women do not respond with physical force to a threatening situation. Women, as illustrated in Figure 3.1, don't respond with force but often will respond by crying. One reason for the failure to use force may merely be a result of the normal differentials in strength between men and women. Other reasons for women's lack of physical and sometimes even lack of verbal response are probably related to social conditioning. Women are socialised not to fight or respond physically; they are also trained to be passive, especially around men, particularly men they know (Warshaw 1994: 52–4). For a rape conviction, a victim may only fail to resist, the courts have argued, when based on a *reasonable* fear that if she (the victim) resists, she will be seriously harmed. In *Rusk*, the victim's fear was based upon being isolated, in an unknown part of town, late at night, without her car keys, with a man she didn't know. The court claimed that her *fear was not reasonable*. 'She may not simply say, "I was really scared", and thereby transform consent or mere unwillingness [sic] into submission by force. These words do not transform a seducer into a rapist.' Again the courts have enshrined a standard of *reasonable fear* that is *not* based upon the experiences of women. To whom is the fear reasonable? For some (many?) women, being isolated with a man, who is larger and who has made some intimidating remarks or gestures, may be a frightening and unpredictable situation. Just as a man might be afraid of three big men in an alley and comply with their wishes without resistance, for many women one man may be enough.

Force is defined in terms of the victim's resistance; if she did not resist, there was no force – therefore, no rape. And, if the reason for not resisting is fear, then the situation must be one which is objectively threatening, i.e. one which men would find threatening. Consider *State* v. *Alston*, in which Alston and the victim had a 'consensual' relationship over a period of months. During that relationship, Alston had behaved violently towards the victim on many occasions. A month after their relationship had ended, Alston came to the school where the victim was a student and attempted to block her path, demanded to know where she was living, and when she refused to tell him, grabbed her arm and stated that she was coming with him. At one point the defendant told the victim he was going to 'fix her face'. The defendant told her that he had a 'right' to have intercourse with her again. The two went to the house of a friend of the defendant. The defendant asked her if she was 'ready' and the victim told him she did not want to have sexual relations. The defendant pulled her up from the chair, undressed her, pushed her legs apart, and penetrated her. She cried. The court agreed that she had not consented but since there was no 'force' it was not rape. The definition of force is extremely narrow and does not acknowledge the range of power relationships that don't neatly map onto this standard definition of force.

Consider the Wyoming Supreme Court's reversal of a conviction in *Gonzales* v. *State*. Like *Rusk*, the defendant and victim met in a bar and the defendant requested a ride home. The victim refused, but the defendant got into her car anyway. The victim repeated her refusal to drive him, but after unsuccessfully trying to get him out of her car she started to drive. He asked her to turn down a road and stop so that he could urinate. Before getting out of the car he removed her keys from the ignition. When he returned he told her he was going to rape her; she tried to talk him out of it. 'He told her he was getting mad at her and then put his fist against her face and said, "I'm going to do it. You can have it one way or the other."' The Wyoming Supreme Court argued that the trial court's standard of reasonable fear was in error; it should not place the determination 'solely in the judgment of the victim and omit the necessary element of a reasonable apprehension and reasonable ground for such fear; and the reasonableness must rest with the fact finder.' Surprisingly the court didn't find that it was a 'harmless error' since a fact finder should (if asking whether the reasonable woman would have been afraid) have found that the fear was reasonable. The court seemed to suggest that a trier of fact might not find the fear in this case reasonable. What is the standard of reasonable?

Again, looking for physical force and physical resistance in *Commonwealth* v. *Minarich*, where Minarich threatened a 14-year-old girl living in his custody with return to the detention home if she refused sex with him. The court found no forcible compulsion, hence no rape. The court said the legislature 'did not intend to equate seduction, whether benign or sinister, with rape...' Here is an obvious power relationship where no physical force was required, but the courts still look for them. And in 1994 in *Commonwealth* v. *Berkowitz*, a 19-year-old sophomore at a Pennsylvania college one afternoon went to the dorm where her boyfriend lived. While waiting for him to return she entered the room of an acquaintance, Robert Berkowitz. She sat on the floor and talked with him for a while. He sat next to her and began kissing and fondling her. She protested at his advances and said that she had to go. Berkowitz disregarded her protests, got up and locked the door, came back and pushed her on the bed, lay on top of her, removed her clothes, and penetrated her. Throughout she was saying 'no'. Berkowitz said that he took the 'nos' to be passionate moaning. He was found not guilty of rape since the court could not find force.

England, Wales and Canada have explicitly dropped the force requirement, in the UK requiring consent and, in Canada, going even beyond that in what appears a very progressive reform requiring affirmative consent. The Sexual Offences Act of 2003 in England and Wales says that rape occurs when someone 'intentionally penetrates the vagina, anus or mouth of another person with his penis' and that the other person does not consent to the penetration.' How consent is defined was a major revision in the sexual assault laws of the UK. The act requires 'free agreement' to take place for a sexual relationship to be consensual and there is no requirement for force. Nevertheless, even with what appear to be radical progressive reforms to the law of sexual offences, results such as the ones in *R*. v. *Dougal* ((2005) Swansea Crown Court) and *R* v. *Bree* ((2007) EWCA 256) occur where there were no findings of rape because of the intoxication of the victims. The victims were unable to remember all the details of the occurrences (in both of these cases the victims were in and out of consciousness) and the judges held that 'drunken consent is still consent' (Dougal 2005: 176). In the Crown's closing remarks, it argued that the reason the victim hadn't resisted (and thereby shown that she hadn't consented) was due to the effects of alcohol (Bree 2007). As Sharon Cowan argues about these cases:

[H]ow do we know when a woman is too drunk to consent? How do we know whether or not she has consented to sex if she herself does not know, because she cannot remember the event? *R v. Bree* alongside *R v. Dougal* ... seems to suggest that if she cannot remember a refusal, or indeed if she cannot remember anything at all, providing that she was conscious, then she will be presumed to have consented, or at least, the man's belief in her consent will stand, and it is not rape

(Cowan 2005: 914)

Presumed to have consented because the victim was too incapacitated to remember what happened. In no other area of the law would that type of circumstance result in a finding of consent.

Canada's new legislation, which requires affirmative consent, would appear to circumvent the problem of smuggling in the resistance requirement and having a baseline presumption that the woman is consenting. Positive and affirmative consent has resulted in Canadian courts increasing conviction rates in many cases where the victim is intoxicated or passed out, and therefore incapable of consent. Still, there are many instances, as Lise Gotell argues, where women are viewed as 'risk takers', they are drug addicts, runaways, or homeless, and thereby perceived as not exercising appropriate caution as 'good' women should, their behaviours are scrutinised and criticised and found to come up wanting (Gotell 2008). For example, consider the case of a Saskatchewan 12-year-old aboriginal girl who was running away from home and was picked up outside a bar by three white men. After giving her numerous beers in less than an hour, the men proceeded to have sex with the girl even as she went in and out of consciousness. The judge portrayed her behaviour in running away and willingly getting into the truck with the men and drinking the alcohol as behaviour signalling that she was, in his words, the 'sexual aggressor' and not the victim. The appropriateness of women's behaviour and whether they can thereby be a victim of sexual violence is still being judged by the criminal justice system of Canada.

### Mens rea for rape: honest or reasonable beliefs

Guilt for the crime of rape, along with most serious crimes, requires the defendant to have a specific mental state, or *mens rea*. The defendant's mental state refers to what he actually believed or understood at the time of the crime. For rape, the defendant must have believed that his victim was not consenting or believed that she might not be consenting. Defendants may claim 'mistake' about the consent of the victim, that is, claim as a defence for rape that they believed their victims were consenting in the situation, and thus fail to have the mental state necessary for the crime.

The UK House of Lords held in the famous (or infamous) *Morgan* decision that unreasonable but honestly held beliefs should exculpate or excuse from liability for rape. The details of the 1975 case are as follows: Morgan was a senior non-commissioned officer in the RAF and invited his three drinking partners, who were his subordinates, to have sex with his wife, claiming that she liked 'kinky' sex and would feign refusal but in fact welcomed the intercourse. The four men dragged Mrs Morgan from the room where she was sleeping to a room with a double bed. They held her down while each of them took turns having intercourse with her. Throughout, she vigorously physically and verbally protested, including screaming to her children to call the police. Morgan, because he was her husband, could not be charged with rape, but was charged with aiding and abetting rape. The other three men were charged with rape. Relying upon the story that Morgan had told them, they said that they believed that she was consenting. They argued at trial that they thought she had consented, and consequently, could not be convicted of rape since they did not have the *mens rea* for rape. The trial judge in his instruction to the jury added that the belief about consent to exculpate had to be reasonable, that is, 'such a belief as a reasonable man would entertain if he applied his mind and thought about the matter'. The defendants were subsequently convicted. They appealed, claiming that the judge erred in giving that instruction to the jury. Any belief in consent, they argued, as long as it was honestly held, would be incompatible with the intention to commit rape. The House of Lords accepted the argument that unreasonable but honestly held beliefs would exculpate. In other words, any belief about the woman's consent, no matter how objectively unreasonable, would establish that the defendant was without fault and, hence, could not be convicted of the crime of rape.

Many people saw serious problems with *Morgan*. It permits a defendant to be acquitted of rape if he believes that a woman is consenting, no matter what his reasons are for believing it. In favour of *Morgan* were theorists like Glanville Williams, who argued that not permitting unreasonable mistakes to exculpate is to convict a man for being stupid. 'To convict the stupid man would be to convict him for ... honest conduct which may be the best that this man can do but that does not come up to the standard of the so-called reasonable man' (Williams 1975).

The Sexual Offences Act of 2003 explicitly addressed this issue and requires that the belief be reasonable; an unreasonable belief that is honestly held will no longer exculpate the accused. What, however, constitutes a 'reasonable belief' and who defines it are still important questions. As long as men, police, prosecutors, judges and juries continue to believe myths and stereotypes about women – for instance, that 'no' means 'yes', that women require some force, that women desire to live out rape fantasies, and so on – then it may be true in many cases, particularly the so-called acquaintance rape cases, that the defendants will lack the *mens rea* for the crime. In *Dougal*, the defendant claimed that he believed that the victim had consented to sex with him even though she was intoxicated. She claimed that there was no way that she would have consented to sex with the man since he was a complete stranger to her. Was it a reasonable belief for this security guard at the university where the victim was a student to believe that an intoxicated student whom he didn't know would consent to have sex with him? *Rusk*, an American case discussed earlier, illustrates the problem with the 'reasonable belief' standard for consent based on what men in a sexist society would believe reasonable in the circumstances; namely, that since he did not use 'excessive' force and she did not strenuously resist, then she was consenting. Unless the standard of 'reasonable belief' includes what women would consider reasonable in those circumstances, the standard may continue to fail to protect women from sexual assault.

## Conclusions

Criminal rape laws have come some distance from the days of Blackstone's *Commentaries*. At least in some places, husbands can be liable for raping their wives, force and resistance are not explicitly required as independent elements for rape, independent corroboration is not always necessary, shields against regular introduction of sexual history are in place, prompt complaint is not a requirement, and consent is required. Nevertheless, not only are there many places globally where these rules are not in place but even in nations appearing to have progressive legal reforms, such as Britain and Canada, the old standards and myths get smuggled into the process through entrenched attitudes by agents in the system, namely, police, judges and even the public. After considering the problems that arise out of the historical treatment of rape, the question becomes, can laws and policies be changed enough to protect women's sexual autonomy? Educating the public, changing views about women and sexuality, including recognising the continuum of violence that many women experience, may ultimately be needed to address the problems of sexual violence. Nevertheless, the legal system should demand more from men's behaviour in regards to sexual interactions. When seeking a sexual interaction, men should proceed with caution, ensuring consent is obtained, that the person has the prerequisites for consent – namely that they are not incapacitated in various ways – and that the circumstances are not coercive or exploitative, and they should recognise the risks involved for the failure to behave cautiously. The legal system itself should be held to a higher standard to protect women from sexual violence and not perpetuate gender stereotypes which seriously diminish the status of women and undermine women's sexual autonomy.

## Further reading

Starting with Brownmiller's seminal text (Brownmiller, S. (1975) *Against Our Will: Men, Women, and Rape.* New York: Simon and Schuster) the following are a selection of classic works addressing philosophical issues pertaining to rape: Archard, D. (1998) *Sexual Consent.* Boulder: Westview Press; Brison, S. (2002) *Aftermath: Violence and the Remaking of a Self.* Princeton: Princeton University Press; Burgess-Jackson, K. (1996) *Rape: A Philosophical Investigation.* Brookfield, VT: Dartmouth Publishing Company; Burgess-Jackson, K. (ed.) (1999) *A Most Detestable Crime: New Philosophical Essays on Rape.* New York: Oxford University Press; Cahill, A. (2001) *Rethinking Rape.* Ithaca NY: Cornell University Press; Card, C. (1991) 'Rape as a Terrorist Institution', in R. Frey and C. Morris (eds) *Violence, Terrorism, and Justice.* Cambridge: Cambridge University Press, pp. 296–319; Davis, A. (1981) 'Rape, racism, and the myth of the black rapist', in *Women, Race, and Class.* New York: Vintage Books; Estrich, S. (1987) *Real Rape.* Cambridge MA: Harvard University Press; Frye, M. and Shafer, C. (1977) 'Rape and respect', in M. Vetterling-Braggin, F. Elliston and J. English (eds) *Feminism and Philosophy.* Savage, MD: Rowman and Littlefield, pp. 333–46; Husak, D. and Thomas, G. (1992) 'Date rape, social convention, and reasonable mistakes', *Law and Philosophy*, 11: 95–126; MacKinnon, C. (1987) *Feminism Unmodified: Discourses on Life and Law.* Cambridge MA: Harvard University Press; MacKinnon, C. (1989) *Toward a Feminist Theory of the State.* Cambridge MA: Harvard University Press.

Looking more particularly at the issue of consent, the following are helpful reading: McGregor, J. (1996) 'Why when she says no she doesn't mean maybe and doesn't mean yes: A critical reconstruction of consent, sex, and the law', *Legal Theory*, 2: 175–208; McGregor, J. (2005) *Is It Rape?: On Acquaintance Rape and Taking Women's Consent Seriously*. Hampshire: Ashgate Publishing; Pineau, L. (1989) 'Date rape: A feminist analysis', *Law and Philosophy*, 8(2): 217–43; Scheppele, K. (1991) 'The reasonable woman', *The Responsive Community*, 1(4): 36–47; Schulhofer, S. (1998) *Unwanted Sex: The Culture of Intimidation and the Failure of Law*. Cambridge MA: Harvard University Press.

## References

Abawl, Atia, (2009) 'Afghanistan "rape" law puts women's rights front and center' *CNN.com*, 7 April 2009 http://edition.cnn.com/2009/WORLD/asiapcf/04/06/afghan istan.law/

Arce, Rose Marie (1989) 'Women rap rape judge', *New York Daily News*, 8 February: 12.

Archard, David (1998) *Sexual Consent*. Boulder: Westview Press.

Bienen, Leigh (1980) 'Rape III – national developments in rape reform legislation', *Women's Rights Law Reporter*, 6: 74–175.

Blackstone, William (1765) *Commentaries on the Laws of England*. The Fifth Edition. Oxford at the Clarendon Press, MDCCLXXIII, printed for William Strahan, Thomas Cadell and Daniel Price, 8vo, 4 vols.

CNN.com (2007) 'Saudi court ups punishment for gang-rape victim' available at http://edition.cnn.com/2007/WORLD/meast/11/17/saudi.rape.victim/

Cowan, Sharon (2005) 'The trouble with drink: Intoxication, (in)capacity and the evaporation of consent to sex', *Akron Law Review*, 41 (4): 899–922.

Daly, K. and Stubbs, J. (2006) 'Feminist engagement with restorative justice', *Theoretical Criminology*, 10(1): 9–28.

Davis, Michael (1984) 'Setting penalties: What does rape deserve?' *Law and Philosophy*, 3: 984.

Dyer, Clare (2008) 'Judges admit they get round law designed to protect women in rape trials: Sexual history is still being introduced at hearing: New book reveals judicial attitudes to legislation', *The Guardian*, 1 April.

Estrich, Susan (1987) *Real Rape*. Cambridge: Harvard University Press.

Gotell, Lisa (2008) 'Rethinking affirmative consent in Canadian sexual assault law: Neoliberal sexual subjects and risky women', 41 *Akron Law Review* 865.

Griffin, Susan (1971) 'Rape: The all-American crime', *Ramparts*, 971.

Hale, Sir Matthew (1971) *The History of the Plea of the Crown*. 635 London Professional Books (first published in 1736).

Independent Police Complaints Commission (2010) *Commissioner's Report: IPCC independent investigation into the Metropolitan Police Service's Inquiry into allegations against John Worboys*. Available at www.ipcc.gov.uk/worboys_commissioners_report.pdf

Jordan, Mary (2008) 'In Britain rape cases seldom result in conviction', *Washington Post*. Available at http://www.washingtonpost.com/wp-dyn/content/article/2008/05/28/AR2008052803583.html

Kelly, Liz (1988) *Surviving Sexual Violence*. Minneapolis: University of Minnesota Press.

Kelly, Liz, Lovett, Jo and Regan, Linda (2005) *A gap or a chasm? Attrition in reported rape cases*. Home Office Research Study 293. London: Home Office.

Kelly, L., Temkin, J. and Griffiths, S. (2006) *Section 41: an evaluation of new legislation limiting sexual history evidence in rape trials.* Home Office Online Report 20/06. London: Home Office Research, Development and Statistics Directorate.

Koss, M.P. (2006) 'Restoring rape survivors: justice, advocacy and a call to action', in F. Denmark, H. Krass, E. Halpern and J. Sechzer (eds). *Violence and exploitation against women and girls. Annals of the New York Academy of Sciences,* 1087, 206–34. Boston, MA: Blackwell Publishing on behalf of the New York Academy of Sciences.

Lea, Susan J., Lanvers, Ursula and Shaw, Steve (2003) 'Attrition in rape cases. Developing a profile and identifying relevant factors', *The British Journal of Criminology,* 43: 583–99.

MacKinnon, Catherine (1989) *Towards a Feminist Theory of the State.* Cambridge: Harvard University Press.

McGregor, Joan, (2005) I*s it Rape: On Acquaintance Rape and Taking Women's Consent Seriously.* Hampshire: Ashgate Publishing.

Neuwirth, Jessica (2004) 'Unequal: a global perspective on women under the law', MS. Available at http://www.msmagazine.com/summer2004/globalwomen/law.asp

Note: 'Forcible and statutory rape: An exploration of the operation and objectives of the consent standard,' 62 (1952). This note is recited many times, most recently in comments to the influential edited *Model Penal Code* published in 1980.

Rhode, Deborah (1989) *Justice and Gender.* Cambridge, Mass.: Harvard University Press, pp. 245.

Schulhofer, Stephen (1992) 'Taking sexual autonomy seriously: Rape law and beyond', *Law and Philosophy,* 11: 1 and 2.

Schulhofer, Stephen (1998) *Unwanted Sex: The Culture of Intimidation and the Failure of the Law.* Cambridge, Mass.: Harvard University Press.

Stern Report (2010) Available at http://www.equalities.gov.uk/pdf.SternReviewof RapeReporting1FINAL.pdf

Tong, Rosemary (1984) *Women, Sex and the Law.* Totowa, NJ: Rowman and Allanheld.

Van Cleave, Rachel A. (2005) 'Beyond prosecution: Sexual assault victims' rights in theory and practice symposium: Sex, lies, and honor in Italian rape law', *Suffolk University Law Review,* 38(2).

Warshaw, Robin (1994) *I Never Called it Rape.* New York: Harper Collins.

Wigmore, John Henry (1970) *Evidence in Trials at Common Law* (revised edition, James Chadbourn). Boston: Little, Brown, Vol. 3A, sec. 924a.

Williams, Glanville (1962) 'Corroboration – Sexual cases', *Criminal Law Review,* 662.

Williams, Glanville (1963) *The Proof of Guilt.* London: Stevens and Sons, p. 159.

Williams, Glanville (1975) Letter to *The Times,* London.

# Chapter 4

# Developing measures of multiple forms of sexual violence and their contested treatment in the criminal justice system

*Sylvia Walby, Jo Armstrong and Sofia Strid*

## Meet Sylvia Walby

Sylvia Walby is Professor of Sociology and holds the UNESCO Chair in Gender Research at Lancaster University UK. She has worked with Jo Armstrong and Sofia Strid in the Gender Research Group on several projects including gender-based violence against women, the measurement of equality, the comparison of gender equality policies in the EU in the context of intersecting inequalities, and the gendering of the financial crisis, with funding from the EU, the Equality and Human Rights Commission and UNESCO. She has worked with the Home Office in the development of the measurement of domestic violence, sexual assault and stalking in the British Crime Survey, with the Women and Equality Unit in the measurement of the cost of domestic violence, and with the UN in the development of indicators of violence against women. In her book, *Globalization and Inequalities: Complexity and Contested Modernities* (Sage 2009), she argues that it is important that social science theorises violence as a fourth institutional domain alongside the economy, polity and civil society, in recognition of its importance in structuring inequalities and social relations.

## Meet Jo Armstrong

Jo Armstrong is currently a researcher in the Sociology department at Lancaster University and a member of the UNESCO Chair in Gender Research group. She has worked on equalities issues for several years, particularly gender equality, and has been involved in a variety of projects which have examined the measurement of and policies to tackle violence against women. These projects include two reviews of data and indicators for the Equality and Human Rights Commission in Britain, as well as comparative work at the EU level on gender equality policies. Having previously researched the classed and gendered dimensions of women's work, she is now working on bringing together the fields of employment and violence to explore the impact of the economic climate on levels of violence against women.

## Meet Sofia Strid

Sofia Strid is a researcher in the Sociology department at Lancaster University, a lecturer in Gender Studies at Orebro University, Sweden, and a member of the UNESCO Chair in Gender Research Group. Sofia's research interests and projects include gender equality and the intersection of multiple inequalities, in particular in the policy field of violence against women; the quality of gender-based violence policy; comparative (gender) equality policy; and the institutionalised relation between political authorities and feminist civil society. Her most recent project examined the criminal and legal justice system in Britain with a special focus on violence and was carried out for the Equality and Human Rights Commission.

## Introduction

What is sexual violence and how is it measured? What are the implications of using and taking different definitions and different approaches to its measurement? This chapter addresses the measurement of a wide variety of forms of sexual violence. The breadth of definition and the nature of the procedures to measure sexual violence have changed very considerably since Kelly (1988) wrote her book on the 'continuum' of sexual violence. The chapter focuses on the UK criminal justice system, while recognising that many forms of sexual violence have only recently been named and recognised as important within the criminal justice system, and others are still treated as if they were marginal to it.

There are three main forms of measurement of sexual violence. The first and most reliable is that of a nationally representative population survey, such as the British Crime Survey, though this addresses only the most common forms of sexual violence. The second is that of administrative data: offences recorded by the police as 'recorded crime' and data on cases where a criminal conviction has been obtained. The third form of measurement is found in small-scale studies, often by academics and non-governmental organisations (NGOs), using a diverse range of methods and sources. In addition to these, there are important derivative statistics for public policy purposes: the 'attrition' or 'conviction' rate that identifies the proportion of cases that are brought to justice.

There have been significant changes in the measurement of sexual violence, which take place in the context of a dynamic policy environment, in which government is responding to pressure from NGOs and other experts (Walklate 2008). The law on sexual offences in Britain has undergone review and revision (Sexual Offences Act 2003). An action plan on tackling sexual violence and abuse was developed by the British government in 2007 (HM Government 2007), the government launched a strategy and an action plan to end violence against women and girls in November 2009 and in March 2010 respectively (HM Government 2009a, 2010), following a wide-ranging consultation (HM Government 2009b). The Crown Prosecution Service since around 2005 has embarked on a major programme of reform in practice and data collection including: domestic violence and sexual offences policies (e.g. CPS 2008a, 2009a, 2009b, 2009d); and a consultation on the single equality duty for 2010–11 (CPS 2009c). There have been a number of reviews and reforms especially the Stern Review (Stern 2010) into the way rape complaints are handled. In addition, there have been developments in the way police respond to sexual violence, as well as the emergence of specific services such as Rape Crisis Centre phone lines and Sexual Assault Referral Centres (Lovett *et al.* 2004).

The aims of the chapter are to provide both an outline of the forms of data available and an illustration of the ways in which this data can be used to develop indicators to assess change. It also intends to convey the importance of properly understanding matters of definition and methods in measuring sexual violence.

### Defining sexual violence

There are different ways of defining sexual violence. While rape and sexual assault have long been recognised as forms of sexual violence, indeed legally identified as 'sexual offences' (Home Office 2008a), though with changing definitions (Home Office 2000a, 2000b), the potential inclusion of sexual harassment, stalking, female genital mutilation, forced marriage, and trafficking are more recent developments.

Kelly (1988: 41) defines sexual violence as 'any physical, visual, verbal or sexual act that is experienced by the woman or girl, at the time or later, as a threat, invasion or assault, that has the effect of hurting her or degrading her and/or takes away her ability to control intimate contact'. This definition has the advantage of conceptual breadth and naming the interconnections between different forms of sexual violence, but it is not helpful in distinguishing between its different forms. There is also a problem in the restriction of the victim/survivor only to women. While most sexual violence is against women and girls, not all of it is, so it is inappropriate to build this restriction to women and girls into a definition of sexual violence. The chapter here tries to distinguish between different forms of sexual violence, even while recognising that they may be part of a continuum. It does not restrict victims/survivors to women and girls, even though most of them are. It addresses the issue of different points of view in the definition of the act of sexual violence, by including not only reports by victims/survivors to surveys, but also the judgement of the criminal justice system at different stages in the processing of allegations. The chapter focuses primarily on data relating to violence against women. While the data in this chapter primarily concern England and Wales, the methods of measurement have wider application.

Three types of data are reported here: first, data from the British Crime Survey; second, police-recorded crime and criminal statistics; and third, data from small studies. The crime surveys, which ask a random sample of the population about their experiences of crime, provide the most robust data on the extent to which certain forms of violence against women are committed. Data from police records are used with caution, and only in the absence of other data, as they are likely to be a serious underestimate of the actual number of crimes committed since substantial numbers of people do not report such violence to the police. Data from small studies are used where these are the only data source, but here too there must be caution about any claim to representativeness or accurate knowledge about the national extent of any issue.

**Measurement of sexual violence by national surveys**

In recognition that recorded crime statistics do not include all crimes committed, there has been the development of population surveys commissioned by the government, in particular the Home Office. The British Crime Survey (England and Wales) asks a nationally representative sample of the population whether they have suffered a crime in the last year. The BCS include both crime code definitions and other definitions of violence. These surveys are in two parts: the first uses face-to-face interviewing and crime codes; the second is a self-completion section comprising different modules that vary from year to year, including a module on interpersonal violence. Self-completion encourages a higher rate of disclosure of domestic and sexual violence, and the module uses a wider range of definitions. The level of domestic violence disclosed in the self-completion module is five times higher than that in the face-to-face part of the survey (Walby and Allen 2004). A self-completion module on domestic violence was included in 1996, 2001, 2004/05, 2005/06, 2006/07 and 2007/08, and in some years there have been questions on sexual victimisation, which include asking about the relationship of the offender to the victim.

Thus the source of the most reliable data on the extent of sexual violence is the British Crime Survey (BCS), in particular the sections of the self-completion module that address sexual assault. These surveys are more reliable than recorded crime data because of the low rate of reporting such crimes to the police, although even survey data may still underestimate the extent of crime. Since this is a sample survey, forms of sexual violence that are less common cannot be accurately identified using this method, so remain invisible.

According to the British Crime Survey, approximately 10,000 women are sexually assaulted every week (BCS self-completion 2007/2008). There have been small fluctuations in the percentage of women who suffer sexual assault, but no substantial change in any one direction, as shown in Table 4.1. According to the BCS self-completion, this varies between 2.1 per cent in 2000/

01, 2.7 per cent in 2004/05, 3 per cent in 2007/08 and 2.5 per cent in 2008/09. While percentages for men are included in the table, they are too small to be reliable, and are included merely to indicate that there were a few such reports.

**Table 4.1** Prevalence of sexual violence among adults aged 16–59 in the last year, England and Wales, % (British Crime Survey)

|  | Sex | 2001 | 2004/05 | 2007/08 | 2008/09 |
|---|---|---|---|---|---|
| Sexual assault (any assault including attempts) % | M | 0.2 | 0.6 | 0.4 | 0.4 |
|  | F | 2.1 | 2.8 | 2.9 | 2.5 |
| By type: |  |  |  |  |  |
| Serious sexual assault including attempts | M | 0.1 | 0.1 | 0.1 | 0.1 |
|  | F | 0.5 | 0.5 | 0.6 | 0.5 |
| Serious sexual assault excluding attempts | M | <0.1 | 0.1 | 0.1 | 0 |
|  | F | 0.3 | 0.3 | 0.4 | 0.3 |
| Rape including attempts | M | <0.1 | 0.1 | 0.1 | 0.1 |
|  | F | 0.3 | 0.4 | 0.5 | 0.4 |
| Rape excluding attempts | M | <0.1 | 0.1 | 0.1 | 0 |
|  | F | 0.2 | 0.2 | 0.3 | 0.3 |
| Assault by penetration including attempts | M | <0.1 | 0.1 | 0 | 0 |
|  | F | 0.3 | 0.2 | 0.3 | 0.3 |
| Assault by penetration excluding attempts | M | <0.1 | 0 | 0 | 0 |
|  | F | 0.2 | 0.2 | 0.2 | 0.1 |
| Less serious sexual assault | M | 0.2 | 0.5 | 0.3 | 0.4 |
|  | F | 1.9 | 2.6 | 2.7 | 2.3 |

*Sources*: 2004/05-2008/09: Walker *et al.* (2009); 2001: Finney (2006)

Data are available on the amount of intimate partner abuse that is sexual, as shown in Table 4.2.

**Table 4.2** Prevalence of intimate violence in the last year (partner abuse, non-sexual; sexual assault), % England and Wales (British Crime Survey)

|  | Sex | 2001 | 2004/05 | 2008/09 |
|---|---|---|---|---|
| Partner abuse (non-sexual) |  |  |  |  |
| – any abuse, threat or force | M | 4.5 | 3.6 | 2.7 |
|  | F | 6 | 4.7 | 4.4 |
| – threat or force | M | 2.3 | 2 | 1.2 |
|  | F | 4.2 | 3.2 | 2.7 |
| Sexual assault |  |  |  |  |
| – any including attempts | M | 0.2 | 0.6 | 0.4 |
|  | F | 2.1 | 2.7 | 2.5 |
| – serious including attempts | M | 0.1 | 0.1 | 0.1 |
|  | F | 0.5 | 0.5 | 0.5 |
| – serious excluding attempts | M | <0.1 | 0.1 | 0 |
|  | F | 0.3 | 0.3 | 0.3 |

| | | | | |
|---|---|---|---|---|
| – rape 2003 including attempts | M | <0.1 | 0.1 | 0.1 |
| | F | 0.3 | 0.3 | 0.4 |
| – rape 2003 excluding attempts | M | <0.1 | 0.1 | 0 |
| | F | 0.2 | 0.2 | 0.3 |
| – assault by penetration 2003 including attempts | M | <0.1 | 0.1 | 0 |
| | F | 0.3 | 0.2 | 0.3 |
| – assault by penetration 2003 excluding attempts | M | <0.1 | <0.1 | 0 |
| | F | 0.2 | 0.1 | 0.1 |
| – Less serious sexual assault | M | 0.2 | 3.6 | 0.4 |
| | F | 1.9 | 4.7 | 2.3 |

*Sources*: 2008/09: Walker *et al.* (2009); 2001 and 2004/05: Finney (2006)

## Recorded crime statistics

Data on the extent of violent crime offences, that are defined by crime codes and recorded by police, are reported on by the Home Office and placed in the public domain as 'recorded crime'. Recorded crime is a source of data only on those offences that are reported to and subsequently recorded by the police. Many instances of violence are not reported to the police (Walby and Allen 2004). Events that are reported are variously recorded: as incidents, crime-related incidents, or crimes. In some instances, events that may be considered crimes are recorded as incidents. This means that these data do not constitute a reliable estimate of the full extent of violence, but rather an underestimate.

In order to measure the extent of violent crime and access to justice, the criminal justice system collects data using units that are defined predominantly in crime codes. These are embedded in law and institutional practice, with manuals specifying the definitions together with instructions as to coding practice. Changes to both the Crime Code (for example the creation of new offences in law) and to the rules used in counting crime impact upon crime recording practices and, by implication, the availability of data and whether it is possible to conduct analyses over time. Recording practices changed with the introduction of the National Crime Recording Standard in 2002 (England and Wales) (Home Office 2009a). The recording of sexual offences was modified by the Sexual Offences Act 2003, slightly widening the definition of rape (Home Office 2008a).

Table 4.3 shows the number of sexual offences recorded by the police 1997–2009. The category 'most serious sexual crime' includes rape of female/male; sexual assault on male/female; gross indecency; unlawful sexual activity with child; and trafficking for sexual exploitation. 'Other sexual offences' includes incest; abduction of female; exposure or voyeurism; and exploitation of prostitution. Police-recorded crime statistics (Table 4.3) show an increase in the number of most serious sexual crime and sexual offences reported and recorded by the police over the past 11 years. The number of recorded rapes has more than doubled. However, changes in reporting and recording practices mean that this is not necessarily indicative of an increase in rape; rather it is an increase in the official recording of rape.

**Table 4.3** Police-recorded crime statistics on sexual offences, England and Wales

| Year | 1997 | 1998/99 | 2000/01 | 2002/03 | 2004/05 | 2006/07 | 2008/09 |
|---|---|---|---|---|---|---|---|
| Rape of a female | 6,281 | 7,132 | 7,929 | 11,445 | 12,869 | 12,624 | 12,165 |
| Rape of a male | 347 | 504 | 664 | 850 | 1,144 | 1,150 | 968 |
| Total most serious sexual crime | 31,334 | 33,424 | 35,152 | 45,317 | 47,542 | 43,738 | 40,787 |
| Other sexual offences | 1,756 | 12,948 | 10,726 | 13,573 | 15,320 | 13,784 | 10,701 |
| Total sexual offences | 33,090 | 46,372 | 45,878 | 58,890 | 62,862 | 57,522 | 51,488 |

*Source*: Walker *et al.* (2009)

Table 4.4 shows the police-recorded crime statistics for exploitation of prostitution, abduction of a female (includes forced marriage), trafficking for sexual exploitation and female genital mutilation (FGM) (unfortunately the category of FGM and poisoning is not disaggregated).

**Table 4.4** Police-recorded crime statistics on specific forms of violence 2002/03–2008/09, England and Wales

| Year | Exploitation of prostitution | Abduction of female | Trafficking for sexual exploitation | FGM (or poisoning) |
|---|---|---|---|---|
| 2002/03 | 127 | 291 | – | – |
| 2003/04 | 186 | 403 | – | – |
| 2004/05 | 117 | 86 | 21 | – |
| 2005/06 | 153 | 36 | 33 | – |
| 2006/07 | 190 | 21 | 43 | – |
| 2007/08 | 184 | 4 | 57 | – |
| 2008/09 | 174 | 4 | 54 | 159 |

*Source*: Home Office Recorded Crime Statistics 2002/03–2008/09

**Reports on the extent of sexual violence by smaller studies**

Data on specific forms of sexual violence, such as forced marriage and trafficking, draw on research estimates; there is no national survey data or full administrative data to collect or assess (HM Government 2009a). Instead, qualitative evidence and reports published by the voluntary sector, national and international governmental reports, and academic research are the main sources of evidence in this area. In general, there is an agreement among academics and within the Home Office that there is no reliable or commonly accepted data on the number of incidents of forced marriage, female genital mutilation (FGM) or trafficking (HM Government 2009a; Kelly and Regan 2000).

The majority of cases of forced marriage reported to date in the UK involve South Asian families (HM Government 2008; Force Marriage Unit no year). However, forced marriage is not solely a South Asian problem. There have been cases involving families from East Asia, the Middle East, Europe and

Africa. In 2008, over 1,600 incidents of suspected forced marriage were reported to the Forced Marriage Unit (FMU) (see Table 4.7). In 2009, the FMU gave advice or support on 1,682 cases. More women than men seek support or advice from the FMU: 86 per cent of the cases involved females and 14 per cent involved males (FCO 2010). The number of annual forced marriage cases dealt with by the FMU ranges from 250 to 300. In total, 1,600 annual cases are reported to the FMU (see Table 4.7). Research shows that this number does not reflect the number of actual annual cases of forced marriage; an estimated 5,000 to 8,000 cases are reported by Kazimirski *et al.* (2009) and DCSF (2009). An estimate of the national prevalence by civil society organisation Karma Nirvana and the Forced Marriage Unit also suggests that there are between 5,000 and 8,000 cases of forced marriages in England and Wales each year (see Table 4.7). The estimate is based on the number of forced marriage cases encountered by local organisations within ten local authorities (FMU no year; HM Government 2009c). Civil society organisation Women's Aid reported 194 phone calls regarding forced marriage in 2007 (Women's Aid website 2007).

Data on the actual number of women refugees fleeing from forced marriage are not available from any official survey, although Women's Aid reports 870 refugee women fleeing from forced marriage annually (Women's Aid 2007). Thirty five cases of forced marriage were prosecuted over a nine-month period in four CPS areas (CPS 2008). All defendants were male and Asian, most were spouse or ex-spouse (all were spouse or ex-spouse when there was only one defendant). Victims were equally likely to be male as female (CPS 2008).

Estimates on female genital mutilation (FGM) are equally varied (see Table 4.7). For example, estimates of the total prevalence of FGM in England and Wales range from 66,000 (Home Office 2009c) to 273,500 (Dorkenoo *et al.* 2007). The estimated number of girls under 15 at risk of FGM ranges from 16,000 (End Violence Against Women (EVAW) 2007) to 240,000 (Government Equalities Office (GEO) no date). In between those numbers, Dorkenoo *et al.* (2007) estimate that 22,000 girls under the age of 15 are at risk of becoming victims of FGM. The data are thus very variable. Some suggestions as to why this is the case, and why the estimates differ, include: the use of different sample sizes; the inclusion of more countries practising FGM in some studies; and whether or not second generation immigrants are included in the sample. Dorkenoo *et al.* apply a method where they: 1) identify countries in which FGM is practised and from which there is considerable migration to England and Wales; 2) identify published data on the prevalence of FGM in those countries; 3) apply that data to the Census and birth registration data for England and Wales to estimate the number of FGM cases. Kwateng-Kluvitse (2004), whose estimation of the total prevalence of FGM is similar to Dorkenoo *et al.*, derives the numbers by applying the World Health Organisation's estimates of the prevalence of FGM figures in FGM practising countries to estimates of numbers of women reporting FGM from six of these countries of origin. Studies are, according to Dorkenoo *et al.*, producing underestimates of the prevalence of FGM as they omit the second generation of women; women who were born in the UK but who may have undergone FGM. Secondly, Dorkenoo *et al.* suggest that the UK Labour Force Survey, which has previously been used to derive the estimates of females affected by FGM, was not large enough to produce relevant estimates; previous estimates were subject to sampling variability.

There is a lack of reliable data on the number of women (and men) trafficked for the purpose of sexual exploitation in the UK; the range of estimates is shown in Table 4.7. In 1998, research carried out by Kelly and Regan (2000) identified 71 women victims being trafficked into prostitution in the UK but they describe the estimation as problematic. Key problems in estimating the number of victims include, first, defining what counts as trafficking since there is no commonly agreed definition and, second, that there is a vast number of 'hidden' cases of trafficking for sexual exploitation. The average annual number of trafficking cases between 2005 and 2009, according to recorded crime statistics, is 42 (see Table 4.7). Kelly and Regan (2000) identify 71 cases. Estimations of the extent of trafficking cases vary from 1,450 (Kelly and Regan 2000) to 4,000 (Zimmerman *et al.* 2006a, 2006b; Home Office 2007; HM Government 2009c). There is reason to believe that trafficking for sexual exploitation is increasing in the UK (Kelly and Regan 2000; HM Government 2009c; Joint Committee on Human Rights (JCHR) 2006; Zimmerman *et al.* 2006a, 2006b).

In addition to the governmental departments, the United Kingdom Human Trafficking Centre (UKHTC), End Violence Against Woman (EVAW), (formerly) the Women's National Commission, and the Poppy project are main actors in the field. The Poppy project offers accommodation and services to victims. Between March 2003 and May 2006, 489 referrals were made to the Poppy project, 99 women were accepted for accommodation and support, and 25 women were provided with outreach services. The scheme operates mainly in London, has tightly focused criteria, and depends upon self- or official referral. As a result, there is reason to suspect that the number of victims nationwide will be considerably higher, and indeed may well be higher than the estimated 4,000 provided by the Home Office. The suggestion that the number of women being trafficked for prostitution into the UK is on the increase seems to be corroborated by the fact that 'whereas 10 years ago 85% of women in brothels were UK citizens, now 85% were from outside UK' (JCHR 2006: Q14).

Further estimates of these forms of sexual violence, drawn from academic research, the voluntary sector, government reports and specialised governmental units, are shown in Table 4.7. The Forced Marriage Unit presents data but only on the number of reported cases per year. For estimations of the prevalence, Kazimirski *et al.* (2009) is one of the key sources referred to by academia, NGOs and governmental departments, as are reports by the NGO Karma Nirvana. Dorkenoo *et al.* (2007) appears to be one of the most widely cited sources on the number of victims of FGM, referred to in both governmental and civil society publications, including the Home Office, the (formerly) GEO and EVAW, as well as by other researchers. The UK Human Trafficking Centre (2009) provides information on the number of defendants and victims in trafficking cases. In terms of estimating the number of actual trafficked women, Kelly and Regan (2000) and Zimmerman (2006a, 2006b) seem to be the most reliable sources and are widely cited within academia, by NGOs and used by the Home Office.

**Table 4.5** Forced marriage protection order applications made since implementation in November 2008 to end of October 2009

| Location | Total applications | Adult victims | Child victims | Third party applicants | Other applicants | Outside jurisdiction |
|---|---|---|---|---|---|---|
| England and Wales | 83 | 18 | 39 | 15 | 11 | 13 |

*Source*: Ministry of Justice (2009)

**Table 4.6** Forced marriage protection orders made since implementation in November 2008 to end of October 2009

| Location | Total disposals | Withdrawn | Refused | Undertaking made | Order made | Dealt with ex-parte | Orders with power of arrest |
|---|---|---|---|---|---|---|---|
| England and Wales | 94 | 4 | 1 | 1 | 86 | 55 | 71 |

*Source*: Ministry of Justice (2009)

**Table 4.7** Estimates for forced marriage, FGM and trafficking

| Form of violence | Highest estimate | Lowest estimate |
|---|---|---|
| Forced marriage | 5,000–8,000[1] | 1,600[2] |
| | | 159[3] |
| <15 FGM risk | 24,000[4] | 16,000[5] |
| FGM annual cases | 3,000–4,000[6] | 3,000–4,000[6] |
| FGM total | 279,500[7] | 66,000[8] |
| | 273,500[9] | |
| Honour crimes | 18[11] | 18[11] |
| Incidents/offences | 256[10] | 132[10] |
| Honour murders | 12[12] | 10[13] |
| Trafficking | 4,000[14] | 164[16] |
| | 1,450[15] | 71[17] |
| | | 42[18] |

*Sources*:
1. DCSF (2009). Numbers refer to estimated prevalence.
2. FMU (no year); HM Government (2009d). Number refers to annual number of cases reported to the Forced Marriage Unit.
3. Home Office recorded crime statistics 2008/2009.
4. Dorkenoo *et al*. 2007. Number refers to girls under 15 at risk of FGM in the UK.
5. EVAW (2007).
6. Sleator (2003).
7. Kwateng-Kluvitse (2004).
8. HM Government (2009c); HM Government (2009a).
9. Dorkenoo *et al*. (2007).
10. HM Government (2009a).

11. CPS (2008). Prosecuted cases over a nine-month period in four CPS areas.
12. HM Government (2009a).
13 Meetoo and Mirza (2007).
14. HM Government (2009c); Zimmerman *et al.* (2006a); Zimmerman *et al.* (2006b). Estimated number of trafficked women in the UK 2003.
15. Kelly and Regan (2000); HM Government (2009c). Estimated numbers in 1998.
16. UKHTC (2009).
17. Kelly and Regan (2000).
18. Home Office (2009b) Recorded crime statistics. Annual average 2005–2009.

## Developing indicators of justice: attrition in rape cases

Using sources of data such as those discussed above, indicators can be derived which enable monitoring of changes in the justice system. One example is rates of attrition, used in examining the concept of a 'justice gap'. The 'justice gap' is defined by the House of Commons Justice Committee (2009: 11, note 28) as: 'the difference between the number of crimes which are recorded and the number which result in their perpetrator being brought to justice'. However, it could be argued that the 'true' starting point of the gap is possibly 'earlier' in the process, i.e. the number of crimes committed, as estimated by surveys, as opposed to the number recorded. These statistics on the number of crimes committed relative to those brought to justice are used to calculate the extent of attrition, which can be used as a measure of the 'justice gap'. Attrition refers to those cases dropping out of the criminal justice process. Cases may 'drop out' for a number of reasons at various stages, including the decision of the victim not to report a crime and discontinuance by the prosecutors (Kelly *et al.* 2005).

The terms 'attrition' and 'conviction' are sometimes used interchangeably, or at least confused, in debates over 'attrition rates' and 'conviction rates'. The conviction rate refers to the proportion of crimes committed that result in conviction. Following this definition, a higher or increased rate of conviction implies improvement (i.e. a greater proportion of cases are resulting in conviction) while a lower rate implies deterioration (i.e. a lower proportion of cases are resulting in conviction). If the meaning of 'attrition' is the fall out or the extent to which cases are lost before being brought to justice then, strictly speaking, the attrition rate refers to the proportion of cases that 'fall out' over the course of the criminal justice process. Using this definition, then we would refer to say a '70 per cent attrition rate' where we mean that 70 per cent of crimes are not brought to justice. A decline in the attrition rate to 60 per cent would imply an improvement, in that a lower proportion of cases were dropping out; an increase in the attrition rate to 80 per cent would imply deterioration, in that a higher proportion of cases were dropping out. Following this definition, we can use 'points of attrition' to refer to those stages at which cases are lost, for example, between reporting and prosecution for reasons such as insufficient evidence. However, in some studies (e.g. Lovett and Kelly 2009), the figure attached to the term attrition is the same as the figure that others call 'conviction'. This is a little confusing, so we adopt the practice outlined here.

Conviction rates can be defined differently depending on the start and end points of their measurement, and there is currently no agreement on how they should be calculated. This leads to various figures being used as 'conviction rates'. There are at least three potential starting points for measuring conviction rates. The most commonly practised method is to start with the number of crimes that are recorded by the police. A second method, and one recommended by most of those consulted by Alkire *et al.* (2009) for the Equality Measurement Framework, is the number of crimes reported in the British Crime Survey. The third is the number of crimes prosecuted by the Crown Prosecution Service, a method used by the CPS (2009b) and recommended by the Stern Review (2010). There are also different potential end points of the process. These include: 'conviction' as charged (e.g. conviction for rape following a charge for rape), which is the most commonly understood meaning (and used by, for example, Lovett and Kelly 2009); and conviction which includes convictions for a related offence, for example where someone charged with rape is convicted for the lesser crime of sexual assault. This end point is used by the CPS (e.g. CPS 2009b). In addition there is the category of 'sanction/detection' which is a police category for when offences are 'cleared up', and includes, in addition to the formal charging of a suspect, police cautions and offences that have been taken into consideration (Walker *et al.* 2009). The CPS is responsible for the prosecution of criminal cases in England and Wales and, in all but minor cases, determines the charge.

The most comprehensive way to calculate the conviction rate would be to use the earliest possible point at which the numbers of crimes are measured: the national surveys of crime victims. The next most comprehensive would be to use the number of crimes recorded by the police. A narrower way is to measure it from the point of prosecution. The first produces the worst (or lowest) conviction rate, the last the best (or highest). There are a number of issues that are relevant to the selection of the starting point. These include: the relatively small number of some of the specific crimes against women and minority groups so that the numbers in the BCS do not always constitute a statistically reliable base; differences between the concepts and categories that are used to measure crime at different points within the criminal justice system (CJS) and BCS; whether data is collected and disaggregated by equality groups; and the different responsibilities of different agencies in the CJS.

In selecting the end point, the strictest (and probably the most popularly understood) way to calculate the conviction rate is to limit it to convictions as charged. This produces the lowest conviction rate. The inclusion of conviction for lesser offences loosens the meaning, and 'improves' the conviction rate. The category of 'sanction detection' is a much wider one. Including convictions for lesser offences in the conviction rate is common practice across the CJS, and not only for equality issues; the differences in the way conviction rates are calculated often reflect the different priorities of different CJS agencies. Feist *et al.* (2007: 91) note that 'the oft-reported conviction rate for rape offences of approximately 6% is, in itself, accurate in that it correctly compares convictions for *rape* against offences *for rape'*. They also note that 'There is, of course, a debate to be had about whether it is more or less appropriate to include convictions for lesser offences in the calculation of a conviction rate for rape.' They conclude by recommending moving to 'report on both figures to give the public as informed a picture as possible'.

Several different figures have been offered as the conviction rate for rape.

**Table 4.8** Reports, prosecutions and convictions for rape, England and Wales

|  | 1997 | 2000 | 2003 | 2006 |
|---|---|---|---|---|
| Reports | 6,281 | 8,593 | 12,760 | 14,047 |
| Prosecutions | 1,880 | 2,046 | 2,790 | 2,567 |
| % of cases leading to prosecution | 30 | 24 | 22 | 18 |
| Convictions | 599 | 598 | 673 | 863 |
| % of prosecutions leading to conviction | 32 | 29 | 24 | 34 |
| Conviction rate (convictions as % of reports) | 10 | 7 | 5 | 6 |

*Source*: Table calculations based on Lovett and Kelly (2009)

Table 4.8 shows that the conviction rate for rape, calculated by Lovett and Kelly (2009) as the percentage of recorded crimes of rape that end with a conviction for rape, was 6 per cent in 2006 in England and Wales (although Lovett and Kelly prefer to call this attrition).

Our own calculations, drawing on data published by the Home Office on the number of recorded crimes (Walker *et al.* 2009) and by the Ministry of Justice (2010a) on the number of offenders found guilty or cautioned, show that the percentage of rapes recorded as crimes that led to a conviction for rape in 2007 was 7.0 per cent and in 2008 was 7.6 per cent (see Table 4.9).

**Table 4.9** Rape of a female: number of offences, sanction detections and number of offenders found guilty or cautioned for rape of a female, England and Wales

|  | 2007/08 | |
|---|---|---|
| Number of offences | 11,631 | |
| Number of sanction detections | 2,899 | |
|  | 2007 | 2008 |
| Offenders found guilty or cautioned for rape of a female | 818 | 880 |
| Offenders found guilty or cautioned for rape of a female as % of total offences | 7.0 | 7.6 |

*Sources*: Walker *et al.* (2009); Ministry of Justice (2010a)

When the 'conviction' rate includes convictions for a lesser offence (e.g. for sexual assault following a charge of rape) the figure is higher, as shown by the rate of 12 per cent calculated by Feist *et al.* (2007) for 2003/04.

Conviction rates calculated using the wider concept of 'sanction detection', which includes processes that conclude a case within the CJS but without a formal conviction (e.g. caution), are higher again, as shown by the figures in Table 4.10.

**Table 4.10** Sanction detection rates by offence group and selected offence types, percentages and percentage point change between 2002/03 and 2008/09

| Offence | 2002 /03 | 2003 /04 | 2004 /05 | 2005 /06 | 2006 /07 | 2007 /08 | 2008 /09 | % change |
|---|---|---|---|---|---|---|---|---|
| Violence against the person – with injury | 34 | 32 | 32 | 38 | 39 | 41 | 41 | 7 |
| Violence against the person – without injury | 37 | 34 | 40 | 47 | 53 | 55 | 53 | 16 |
| **Total violence against the person** | **36** | **33** | **36** | **42** | **46** | **49** | **47** | **11** |
| Most serious sexual crime | 31 | 29 | 27 | 29 | 28 | 28 | 30 | −2 |
| *of which*: | | | | | | | | |
| Sexual assault on a female | 30 | 28 | 27 | 29 | 28 | 28 | 30 | 0 |
| Rape of a female | 30 | 26 | 25 | 25 | 25 | 25 | 26 | −4 |
| Other sexual offences | 34 | 33 | 32 | 35 | 35 | 38 | 38 | 4 |
| **Total sexual offences** | **32** | **30** | **28** | **31** | **30** | **30** | **31** | **−1** |

*Source*: Walker *et al.* (2009)

The highest conviction rates for rape are calculated by the Crown Prosecution Service (2009b), using the percentage of rape cases that were prosecuted as a starting point, and the percentage that led to a conviction for rape or a related and lesser offence as an end point. In 2008–9 this figure was 58 per cent for England and Wales (see Tables 4.11 and 4.12 for sexual offences excluding rape).

**Table 4.11** Rape crime: pre-charge decisions and completed convictions by outcome, England and Wales

| Pre-charge decisions | 2006–07 | | 2007–08 | | 2008–09 | |
|---|---|---|---|---|---|---|
| All defendants | Volume | % | Volume | % | Volume | % |
| Charged | 1,963 | 29.8 | 2,220 | 38.8 | 2,565 | 38.9 |
| Request for further evidence | 110 | 1.7 | 55 | 1 | 43 | 0.7 |
| No prosecution | 3,559 | 54 | 3,025 | 52.9 | 3,511 | 53.2 |
| All other decisions | 958 | 14.5 | 422 | 7.4 | 478 | 7.2 |
| Total | 6,590 | 100 | 5,722 | 100 | 6,597 | 100 |

| Completed convictions by outcome | 2006–07 | | 2007–08 | | 2008–09 | |
|---|---|---|---|---|---|---|
| | Volume | % | Volume | % | Volume | % |
| Convictions | 1,778 | 54.5 | 2,021 | 57.7 | 2,018 | 57.7 |
| Unsuccessful | 1,486 | 45.5 | 1,482 | 42.3 | 1,477 | 42.3 |
| Total | 3,264 | 100 | 3,503 | 100 | 3,495 | 100 |

*Source*: CPS (2009b)

**Table 4.12** Sexual offences excluding rape: completed convictions by outcome, England and Wales

| Completed convictions by outcome | 2006–07 | | 2007–08 | | 2008–09 | |
|---|---|---|---|---|---|---|
| | Volume | % | Volume | % | Volume | % |
| Convictions | 5,675 | 68.3 | 5,976 | 73.5 | 5,955 | 75.1 |
| Unsuccessful | 2,630 | 31.7 | 2,154 | 26.5 | 1,976 | 24.9 |
| Total | 8,305 | 100 | 8,130 | 100 | 7,931 | 100 |

*Source*: CPS (2009b)

### Changes in rape attrition/conviction rates

In the period 1997 to 2006, the rate of convictions for rape, as a percentage of police-recorded rapes, declined from 10 per cent in 1997 to 6 per cent in 2006 in England and Wales, according to Lovett and Kelly (2009) (Table 4.8) and from 9 per cent to 8 per cent according to Feist *et al.* (2007). If convictions for lesser offences are also counted, then the conviction rate fell from 18 per cent to 12 per cent between the same years (Feist *et al.* 2007).

In the more recent period, 2006/7 to 2008/9, the rate of charging of alleged rapists and the rate of convictions of those prosecuted have risen slightly in England and Wales. The rate of charging rose from 30 per cent to 39 per cent; while the rate of conviction (including for lesser offences) of those prosecuted rose slightly from 55 per cent to 58 per cent (see Table 4.11; CPS 2009b).

For the period 2002/3 to 2008/9, the sanction detection rate for 'rape of a female' fell from 30 per cent to 26 per cent, the lowest point being 25 per cent between 2004/5 and 2007/8 (Table 4.10; Walker *et al.* 2009).

In order to understand these changes, several cross-cutting processes need to be separated, together with a distinction between the pre- and post- 2003/6 periods.

Throughout the period 1997 to 2009 (and stretching further back in time) there has been an increase in the willingness of women to come forward to report rape to the police. The number of rapes recorded by the police more than doubled, increasing from 6,281 in 1997 to 14,047 in 2006 (Table 4.8; Lovett and Kelly 2009). Women appear to have demonstrated an increased confidence in the police and CJS to address the crime of rape; however, the increased reporting has not been matched by an increased rate of convictions (for discussion of the potential reasons for attrition in the criminal justice process, see Feist *et al.* 2007).

Between 1997 and 2006, there was a decline in the percentage of cases that led to prosecution, from 30 per cent to 18 per cent. Between 1997 and 2003, there was a decline in the percentage of prosecutions that led to conviction, from 32 per cent to 24 per cent (Table 4.8; Lovett and Kelly 2009).

When looking at conviction rates from the point of prosecution, the pattern is reversed from 2003. Lovett and Kelly's (2009) data set (Table 4.8), shows an increase in the percentage of prosecutions that led to conviction for rape from 24 per cent in 2003 to 34 per cent in 2006. Another data set (Table 4.11; CPS

2009b) shows an increase in the percentage of prosecutions that led to conviction for rape or some related lesser offence from 55 per cent in 2006/7 to 58 per cent in 2008/9. In addition, between 2006/7 and 2008/9, there is an improvement in the percentage of recorded rape cases which resulted in defendants being formally charged, increasing from 30 per cent in 2006/7 to 39 per cent in 2008/9 (Table 4.11). There have been many changes in policy by the CPS since around 2003, and these appear to have had effects. In particular, the CPS took over the decision-making on prosecution. Without specialised in-depth study the specific impacts of these changes cannot be identified.

It would be useful to be able to investigate whether attrition (or the proportion of cases falling out) from the point of police recording to conviction had declined (implying improvement) during the recent period, 2006/7 to 2008/9. Unfortunately, the way the CPS (2009b) presents data for the public domain does not allow an attrition rate to be calculated for the CJS as a whole since there is a major discontinuity in the data provided by the CPS for the pre-charge and prosecution parts of the CJS process. There are many possible reasons for this, for example one set of data may refer to defendants and the other to offences, but these do not appear to be noted by the CPS in their report. So, while separate stages in the process can be investigated, it is not possible from the CPS data to produce a summary attrition rate for the CJS overall.

In summary, it would appear that the attrition rate for rape appears to have got worse (i.e. a higher proportion of cases being lost before being brought to justice) in the period 2002/3 to 2008/9, with a very small improvement (a higher proportion of cases resulting in conviction for rape) since around 2006.

### Comparative attrition/conviction rates

While the rates of charging and rate of conviction after the start of the prosecution no longer give rise to the same level of concern as was noted in the past (Stern 2010), there is still serious concern about other points of attrition. A high proportion of cases are being lost between reporting to the police and charging (Feist et al. 2007), and from the point of recording by the police (Baird 2010). In order to make an assessment of the extent to which these attrition rates from the point of police recording are worse for equality groups than for non-equality groups it is necessary to make comparisons.

Table 4.10 shows that the sanction detection rate for 'rape of a female' was 26 per cent in 2008/9 compared with 47 per cent for 'violence against the person' and 41 per cent for 'violence against the person with injury' (Walker et al. 2009). The attrition rate is thus considerably worse for rape than for other violent crimes.

Similarly, of the offenders proceeded against, guilty verdicts were handed down in 38 per cent of the cases involving 'rape of a female', and 69 per cent of the cases involving 'violence against the person' (Table 4.13). This again shows that the attrition rate is considerably worse for rape than for other violent crimes, whether violence against the person or other sexual offences.

**Table 4.13** Total offenders proceeded against and total found guilty, all courts, England and Wales

|  | 2008 |
| --- | --- |
| *Violence against the person* |  |
| Total proceeded against | 59,943 |
| Total found guilty | 41,519 |
| % of proceeded against found guilty | 69% |
|  |  |
| *Sexual offences* |  |
| Total proceeded against | 8,440 |
| Total found guilty | 5,135 |
| % of proceeded against found guilty | 61% |
|  |  |
| *Rape of a female* |  |
| Total proceeded against | 2,233 |
| Total found guilty | 855 |
| % of proceeded against found guilty | 38% |

*Source*: Ministry of Justice (2010b)

### Developing the measurement of attrition rates

There is controversy over the reasons for this greater attrition. The CPS (2009a: 31) notes the high number of unsuccessful outcomes in rape prosecutions due to jury acquittals. However, a report commissioned by the Ministry of Justice (Thomas 2010) found that juries convicted more often than they acquitted in rape cases and concluded that juries are not the primary source of the low conviction rate on rape. There are a number of studies that look at the various steps, including Kelly *et al.* (2005) and Feist *et al.* (2007), which identify several points rather than a single point at which attrition takes place. The scale of the attrition has become subject to some controversy, following the Stern Review's (2010) comments on the use of the 6 per cent figure, which were in turn met with critical comments (Baird 2010; Fawcett Society 2010). So the identification of the best procedure by which to measure it is of some importance.

It may be argued that the 6 per cent figure for rape convictions is actually a high estimate; a fully comprehensive attrition rate would use as its starting point the number of crimes committed as opposed to those recorded by the police, resulting in a much lower rate of conviction. This is particularly the case for rape, and indeed for cases of intimate partner and domestic violence, for which the rates of reporting are low relative to other crimes.

Conviction rates are measures of the extent to which the perpetrators of crimes are held to account by the CJS through criminal convictions. One method, developed for rape (Kelly *et al.* 2005), includes attrition across the whole of the CJS process in one statistic. Another method, developed by the CPS (2009b), addresses only the attrition that occurs after the point at which cases are prosecuted. There are further issues: the CPS regularly includes convictions for lesser offences than the one charged as if they constituted convictions for the offence, doubling the success rate; a practice that some have called into question and consider inappropriate (Baird 2010; Fawcett Society 2010; House of Commons Home Affairs Select Committee 2008).

In consultations on indicators for legal security, the measure for attrition proposed by Alkire *et al*. (2009) for domestic violence, rape and hate crime was based on successful prosecutions of cases as a proportion of the total number of victims (as estimated by survey data). This received widespread support except from the Home Office, which considered the proposed measures to be statistically unsound because the use of data from more than one source introduced methodological inconsistencies. The revised proposal by Alkire *et al*., following the consultation, is to report three sets of figures in raw form: number of cases (estimated from surveys); cases reported and recorded by police; cases successfully prosecuted. While this provides the raw data needed to calculate an attrition rate (expressed as proportion or ratio), such raw data is not itself an attrition rate, thus it would be difficult to use this indicator in estimating the direction of shifts over time.

A narrower way of calculating the attrition is that used by the CPS. Here, the conviction rate is the proportion of total prosecutions that lead to convictions. However, this omits the attrition of cases in all the CJS procedures prior to the decision to prosecute (reporting, recording, detecting, arresting and charging). In relation to domestic violence, the House of Commons Home Affairs Committee (2008: 89) have criticised this method of calculation:

> Although some progress has been made by the Crown Prosecution Service over the last few years in increasing conviction rates for domestic violence offences, it is sobering to note that, in areas in which the attrition process has been tracked, the conviction rate for domestic violence, at around 5%, is even lower than that for rape, which is 5.7%. Without linking CPS data on successful prosecutions to data on incidence, arrest, charge and caution, the increase in successful prosecutions tells us little about the criminal justice response to domestic violence.

There is a range of possible solutions here. One may be to calculate the attrition rate for different parts of the CJS separately, for example providing specific rates for the police (from the cases recorded to the number of cases referred to the CPS) and the CPS (from prosecution to conviction). Another solution might be to bring the statistical systems into sufficient alignment such that concerns about different methodology become insignificant and a figure for the system as a whole can be produced. A further approach would be to track individual cases throughout the criminal justice system to monitor attrition more accurately at the different stages in the process and subsequently develop measures to prevent these cases being lost. But whether the procedure is to split the attrition into parts or to produce it as one for the whole system, the concept of attrition is best understood as the proportion of rape cases that do not lead to conviction.

## Conclusions

The quantitative measurement of the extent of sexual assault has contributed to the process of making the issue one of public debate. The tension between the different measurements of sexual violence is significant. The difference between the extent of sexual violence reported to national surveys, that reported to and recorded by the police and that of convictions in court is vivid testimony to the social processes that allow only some limited numbers of cases to be made visible to the public and be brought to justice. The concepts of 'attrition rate' and 'conviction rate' are important in measuring this 'justice gap'. Given the importance of this justice gap for both gender justice and justice in general, it is not surprising that the way it is conceptualised and measured is subject to critical commentary and public debate. While official reports have recommended a narrow focus on conviction rates after cases enter the court system, most experts have recommended that the concept encompasses the proportion of actual cases of rape that lead to criminal convictions for rape. This latter statistic captures the attrition or 'fall out' of cases across the criminal justice process and the points at which improvements are necessary in order to increase the proportion of cases that are brought to justice.

The source of the most reliable data on the extent of sexual violence is the British Crime Survey and in particular the self-completion module. The crime surveys are more reliable than other forms of data, for example recorded crime data, because of the notorious under-reporting of sexual violence crimes. Although survey data may still underestimate the extent of sexual violence crimes, they are nonetheless more reliable than other data. However, less common forms of sexual violence cannot be accurately identified using this method and remain invisible. This is particularly a problem for measuring sexual violence against social groups found at the intersection of two or more inequalities, here examined as forced marriage, trafficking for sexual exploitation and FGM. There are no national survey data or administrative data for these forms of violence. Indeed, there is agreement among academics, civil society actors and policy-makers that there is no reliable data or, at present, way of measuring incidents of forced marriage, trafficking or FGM, let alone agreed definitions of these forms of sexual violence. Agreeing on a definition to enable measurement is a necessary first step. Where quantitative measurements of the extent of sexual assault have contributed to making sexual assault visible and to the process of making the issue one of public debate, other forms of sexual violence remain less visible.

Kelly's early work on the definition of sexual violence was important in broadening the understanding of sexual violence by drawing attention to issues in addition to rape and highlighting the centrality of gendered power to its analysis. Building on the subsequent 20 years of research on sexual violence, we can now develop beyond the initial concept of the continuum of sexual violence. During this period several further forms of sexual violence have been identified and named, along with the development of specific laws and policies to address them. While they are doubtless all connected, it is important to recognise the distinctions between them, the better to measure and address them, hence we have provided data on the measurement of multiple forms of sexual violence.

The quality of the measurement of the nature and extent of sexual violence has been improving substantially over recent years, but much further improvement is still needed.

## Further reading

For a further account of measurement issues in sexual assault (as well as domestic violence and stalking) see Sylvia Walby and Jonathan Allen (2004) *Domestic Violence, Sexual Assault and Stalking: Findings from the British Crime Survey*. HORS 276. London: Home Office. For an account of how rape cases fall out of the criminal justice system see Liz Kelly, Jo Lovett and Linda Regan (2005) *A Gap or a Chasm? Attrition in Reported Rape Cases*. Home Office Research Study 293. London: Home Office. For an account of the 'complexities and pitfalls' in measuring trafficking, see Ernesto Savona and Sonia Stefanizzi (eds) *Measuring Human Trafficking*. New York: Springer. The forthcoming book by Sylvia Walby (2012) *Gender Violence* (Cambridge: Polity) situates the identification and counting of sexual violence in a wider context.

## References

Alkire, S., Bastagli, F., Burchardt, T., Clark, D., Holder, H., Ibrahim, S., Munoz, M., Tsang, P. and Vizard, P. (2009) *Developing the Equality Measurement Framework: selecting the indicators*. Manchester: EHRC. Available from: http://www.equalityhu-manrights.com/fairer-britain/equality-measurement-framework/ (accessed 15 November 2010).

Baird, V. (2010) 'Stern review published – Rape reporting in England and Wales', *Women's National Commission*. Available from: http://www.thewnc.org.uk/work-of-the-wnc/violence-against-women/sexual-violence/307-stern-review-published-rape-reporting-in-england-and-wales.html (accessed 15 November 2010).

Burman, M., Lovett, J. and Kelly, L. (2009) *Different systems, similar outcomes? Tracking attrition in reported rape cases in eleven countries. Country briefing: Scotland*. Child and Woman Abuse Studies Unit: London Metropolitan University.

CPS (2008) *Pilot on forced marriage and so-called 'honour' crime – findings*. Available from: http://www.cps.gov.uk/publications/docs/findings_from_cps_pilot_on_forced_marriage.pdf (accessed 15th November 2010).

CPS (2009a) *Violence Against Women: Guidance*. Available from: http://www.cps. gov.uk/legal/v_to_z/violence_against_women/#content (accessed 15 November 2010).

CPS (2009b) *Violence Against Women Crime Report 2008–09*. London: CPS. Available from: http://www.cps.gov.uk/publications/docs/CPS_VAW_report_2009.pdf (accessed 15 November 2010).

CPS Equality and Diversity Unit (2009c) *Proposals for our next Single Equality Scheme 2010–2011: Public Consultation Document*. London: CPS. Available from: http://www.cps.gov.uk/consultations/ses_consultation.pdf (accessed 15 November 2010).

CPS (2009d) *CPS Policy for Prosecuting Case of Rape*. Available from: http://www.cps.gov.uk/publications/docs/prosecuting_rape.pdf (accessed 15 November 2010).

Department for Children, Schools and Families (DCSF) (2009) *Forced Marriage – Prevalence and Service Response*. Available from: http://www.dcsf.gov.uk/pns/

DisplayPN.cgi%3Fpn_id%3D2009_0123 (accessed 15 November 2010).

Dorkenoo, E., Morison, L., and Macfarlane, A. (2007) *A Statistical Study to Estimate the Prevalence of Female Genital Mutilation in England and Wales*. Foundation for Women's Health, Research and Development (FORWARD) in collaboration with The London School of Hygiene and Tropical Medicine and the Department of Midwifery, City University.

End Violence Against Women (2007) *Making the Grade. The third annual independent analysis of UK Government initiatives on violence against women*. London: EVAW. Available from: http://www.endviolenceagainstwomen.org.uk/data/files/evaw_mtg _uk.pdf (accessed 15 November 2010).

Fawcett Society (2010) *Statement on Stern Review Recommendations on the Handling of Rape Complaints*. Available from: http://www.fawcettsociety.org.uk//index.asp?Page ID=1115 (accessed 22 April 2010).

Feist, A., Ashe, J., Lawrence, J., McPhee, D. and Wilson, R. (2007) *Investigating and Detecting Recorded Offences of Rape*. (Home Office Online Report 18/07). Available from: http://rds.homeoffice.gov.uk/rds/pdfs07/rdsolr1807.pdf (accessed 15 November 2010).

Finney, A. (2006) *Domestic Violence, Sexual Assault and Stalking: findings from the 2004/05 British Crime Survey* (Home Office). Available from: http://www.homeoffice.gov.uk/ rds/pdfs06/rdsolr1206.pdf (accessed 15 November 2010).

Forced Marriage Unit (no year) *Forced Marriage Unit*. Available from: http:// www.fco.gov.uk/en/global-issues/human-rights/forced-marriage-unit/ (accessed 15 November 2010).

Government Equalities Office (no year) *Factsheet Female Genital Mutilation*. Available from: http://www.equalities.gov.uk/pdf/Female%20Gential%20MutilationFACT SHEET.pdf (accessed 3 December 2009).

HM Government (2007) *Cross Government Action Plan on Sexual Violence and Abuse*. Available from: http://www.homeoffice.gov.uk/documents/Sexual-violence-action-plan

HM Government (2009a) *Together We Can End Violence Against Women and Girls: a strategy*. London: Home Office. Available from: http://webarchive.nationalarchives.- gov.uk/20100418065544/http://www.homeoffice.gov.uk/documents/vawg-strategy-2009/end-violence-against-women2835.pdf?view=Binary

HM Government (2009b) *Together We Can End Violence Against Women and Girls: a consultation*. London: Home Office. Available from: http://www.homeoffice.gov.uk/ documents/cons-2009-vaw/ (accessed 15 November 2010).

HM Government (2009c) *Mainstreaming the Commissioning of Local Services to Address Violence Against Women and Girls*. London: Home Office. Available from: http:// webarchive.nationalarchives.gov.uk/+/http://www.homeoffice.gov.uk/documents/ cons-2009-mainstreaming/index.html (accessed 15 November 2010).

HM Government (2010) *Call to End Violence against Women and Girls: Action Plan*. London: Home Office. Available from http://www.homeoffice.gov.uk/publications/ crime/call-end-violence-women-girls/vawg-action-plan?view=Binary

HM Government, Foreign and Commonwealth Office, Home Office, Department for Children Schools and Families, Department of Health, Department for Communities and Local Government, Department for Innovation, Universities and Skills, Welsh Assembly Government, Association of Chief Police Officers (2008) *The Right to Choose: Multi-agency statutory guidance for dealing with forced marriage*. Available from: http://www.fco.gov.uk/resources/en/pdf/3849543/forced-marriage-right-to-choose (accessed 156 November 2010).

Home Office (no year) *The National Crime Recording Standard: what you need to know*. Available from: http://www.homeoffice.gov.uk/rds/pdfs08/ncrs.pdf (accessed 15

November 2010).

Home Office (2000a) *Setting the Boundaries: Reforming the Law on Sexual Offences.* (London: Home Office). Available from: http://lawbore.net/articles/setting-the-boundaries.pdf (accessed 15 November 2010).

Home Office (2000b) *Setting the Boundaries: Reforming the Law on Sexual Offences. Volume 2: Supporting Evidence.* London: Home Office. Available from: https://www.wholesm.com/Downloads/SettingTheBoundariesVol2.pdf (aAccessed 15 November 2010).

Home Office (2007) *Control of Immigration: Statistics United Kingdom 2006.* Available from: http://www.official-documents.gov.uk/document/cm71/7197/7197.pdf (accessed 15 November 2010).

Home Office (2008a) *Home Office Counting Rules for Recorded Crime: Sexual Offences.* Available from: http://www.homeoffice.gov.uk/rds/pdfs08/countsexual 08.pdf (accessed 15 November 2010).

Home Office (2009a) *Home Office Counting Rules for Recorded Crime: General Rules.* Available from: http://www.homeoffice.gov.uk/rds/pdfs09/countgeneral09.pdf (accessed 15 November 2010).

Home Office (2009b) *Crime in England and Wales. Volume 1. Findings from the British Crime Survey.* Statistical Bulletin July 2009. Available from: http://rds.homeoffice.gov.uk/rds/pdfs09/hosb1109vol1.pdf (accessed 15 November 2010).

Home Office (2009c) *Together We Can End Violence Against Women and Girls.* London: Home Office. Available from: http://webarchive.nationalarchives.gov.uk/20100418065544/http://www.homeoffice.gov.uk/documents/vawg-strategy-2009.end-violence-against-women2835.pdg?view=Binary (accessed 8 June 2011).

Home Office Recorded Crime Statistics 2002/03–2008/09. Available from: http://www.homeoffice.gov.uk/science-research/research-statistics/crime/crime-statistics/police-recorded-crime/ (accessed 8 June 2011).

House of Commons Home Affairs Select Committee (2008) *Domestic Violence, Forced Marriage and 'Honour'-Based Violence. Sixth Report of Session 2007–08.* London: The Stationery Office. Available from: http://www.publications.parliament.uk/pa/cm200708/cmselect/cmhaff/263/263i.pdf (accessed 15 November 2010).

House of Commons Justice Committee (2009) *The Crown Prosecution Service: Gatekeeper of the Criminal Justice System. Ninth Report of Session 2008–09.* London: The Stationery Office. Available from: http://www.publications.parliament.uk/pa/cm200809/cmselect/cmjust/186/186.pdf (accessed 15 November 2010).

Joint Committee on Human Rights (House of Lords and House of Commons) (2006) *Human Trafficking. Twenty-sixth Report of Session 2005–06.* Volume 1, Report, together with formal minutes. HL paper 245-1, HC 1127-1. London: The Stationery Office. Available from: http://www.publications.parliament.uk/pa/jt200506/jtselect/jtrights/245/245.pdf (accessed 15 November 2010).

Kazimirski, A., Keogh, P., Kumari, V., Smith, R., Gowland, S. and Purdon, S. with Khanum, N. (2009) *Forced Marriage. Prevalence and Service Response.* National Centre for Social Research. Department for Children, Schools and Families Research Report DCSF-RR128.

Kelly, L. (1988) *Surviving Sexual Violence.* Cambridge: Polity.

Kelly, L. and Regan, L. (2000) *Stopping Traffic: exploring the extent of, and responses to, trafficking in women for sexual exploitation in the UK.* Home Office Police Research Series Paper 125. London: Home Office.

Kelly, L., Lovett, J. and Regan, L. (2005) *A Gap or a Chasm? Attrition in reported rape cases.* Home Office Research Study. London: Home Office.

Kwateng-Kluvitse, A. (2004) 'Legislation in Europe regarding female genital mutilation and the implementation of the law in Belgium, France, Spain, Sweden and the UK'. International Centre for Reproductive Health, Ghent University, De Pintelaan 185

P3,9000 Ghent, Belgium.

Lovett, J. and Kelly, L. (2009) *Different Systems, Similar Outcomes? Tracking attrition in reported rape cases in eleven countries. Country briefing: England and Wales.* Child and Woman Abuse Studies Unit: London Metropolitan University. Available from: http://www.cwasu.org/publication_display.asp?pageid=PAPERS&type=1&page key=44&year=2009 (accessed 15 November 2010).

Lovett, J., Regan, L. and Kelly, L. (2004) *Sexual Assault Referral Centres: Developing Good Practice and Maximising Potentials.* London: Home Office. Available at: http://rds.homeoffice.gov.uk/rds/pdfs04/hors285.pdf (accessed 15 November 2010).

MacLeod, P., Kinver, A., Page, L., Iliasov, A. and Williams, R. (2009) *SCJS 2008–09 Sexual Victimisation and Stalking.* Edinburgh: The Scottish Government. Available from: http://www.scotland.gov.uk/Resource/Doc/296164/0092066.pdf (accessed 15 November 2010).

MacLeod, P., Kinver, A., Page, L., Iliasov, A. and Williams, R. (2009) *SCJS 2008-09 Partner Abuse.* Edinburgh: The Scottish Government. Available from: http://www.scotland.gov.uk/Resource/Doc/296149/0092065.pdf

Meetoo, V. and Mirza, H.S. (2007) 'There is nothing "honourable" about honour killings: Gender, violence and the limits of multiculturalism', *Women's Studies International Forum*, 30: 187–200.

Ministry of Justice (2009a) *One Year On: the initial impact of the Forced Marriage (Civil Protection) Act 2007 in its first year of operation.* Available from: http://www.justice.gov.uk/publications/docs/one-year-on-forced-marriage-act.pdf (accessed 15 November 2010).

Ministry of Justice (2010a) *Criminal Statistics Annual Report 2008.* Available from: http://www.justice.gov.uk/publications/criminalannual.htm (accessed 25 May 2010).

Ministry of Justice (2010b) *Supplementary Tables Volume 5 Proceedings at all courts.* Available from: http://www.justice.gov.uk/publications/criminalannual.htm (accessed 15 November 2010).

Sexual Offences Act 2003: http://www.legislation.gov.uk/ukpga/2003/42/contents

Sleator, A. (2003) *The Female Genital Mutilation Bill.* House of Commons Library.

Stern, Baroness Vivien (2010) *The Stern Review.* London: GEO, Home Office. Available from: http://www.equalities.gov.uk/pdf/Stern_Review_of_Rape_Reporting_1FINAL.pdf (accessed 15 November 2010).

Thomas, C. (2010) *Are Juries Fair?* Ministry of Justice Research Series 1/10. London: Ministry of Justice.

United Kingdom Human Trafficking Centre (UKHTC) (2009) *United Kingdom Pentameter 2 Statistics of Victims Recovered and Suspects Arrested during the Operational Phase.* Available from: http://www.ukhtc.org/sites/default/files/UKHTC_UKP2_stats_ not_ protectively_marked.pdf (accessed 15 November 2010)

Walby, S. and Allen, J. (2004) *Domestic Violence, Sexual Assault and Stalking: Findings from the British Crime Survey.* London: Home Office.

Walby, S., Armstrong, J. and Humphreys, L. (2008) *Review of Equality Statistics.* EHRC Research Report No. 1. Manchester: EHRC. Available from: http://www.lancs.ac.uk/fass/doc_library/sociology/Walby_review_of_equality_statistics_241008.pdf (accessed 15 November 2010).

Walker, A., Flatley, J., Kershaw, C. and Moon, D. (2009) *Crime in England and Wales 2008/09.* London: Home Office.

Walklate, S. (2008) 'What is to be done about violence against women? Gender, violence, cosmopolitanism and the law', *British Journal of Criminology*, 48 (1): 39–54.

Women's Aid (2007) *Residents Questionnaire, Annual Survey 2007.* Available from: http://womensaid.org.uk/domestic_violence_topic.asp?section=0001000100220031&section Title=Forced+marriage (accessed 8 June 2011).

Zimmerman, C., Roche Yun, B., Shvab, I., Watts, C., Trappolin, L. and Treppete, M. (2006a) *The Health Risks and Consequences of Trafficking in Women and Adolescents: findings from a European study*. London: The London School of Hygiene and Tropical Medicine.

Zimmerman, C., Hossain, K., Roche Yun, B., Morison L. and Watts, C. (2006b) *Stolen Smiles: The physical and psychological health consequences of women and adolescents trafficked in Europe*. London: The London School of Hygiene and Tropical Medicine.

## Chapter 5

# Developments in investigative approaches to rape: the investigative heritage[1]

*Miranda A.H. Horvath and Mark Yexley*

**Meet Miranda Horvath**

Dr Miranda Horvath is a Senior Lecturer in Forensic Psychology at Middlesex University where she is developing Forensic Psychological Services (www.mdx.ac.uk/FPS). Her PhD (2006) investigated the role of alcohol and drugs in rape. The greater part of her research is focused on sexual violence, working from an applied social psychological perspective using data from the police and sexual assault referral centres. She has both published and presented in a range of arenas including international peer-reviewed journals and national and international conferences. She has recently co-edited a book, *Rape: Challenging Contemporary Thinking* (Willan Publishing 2009), and co-authored a book, *Understanding Criminal Investigation* (Wiley 2009). Her current research interests include multiple perpetrator rape and the links between men's use of 'lad's mags', their attitudes towards women and paying for sex. She is an Associate Editor of the *Journal of Sexual Aggression*.

**Meet Mark Yexley**

Mark Yexley retired from the Metropolitan Police Service in 2011 with the rank of Detective Chief Inspector. He now works as independent consultant on investigation, criminal justice and health partnerships. Mark joined the Metropolitan Police Service (MPS) in 1981 and before retirement led the Sapphire Cold Case Investigation, Partnership and Improvement Teams dealing with rape and serious sexual violence. He was the Chair of the Strategic Board for London's three Haven sexual assault referral centres. During his 30 years of service he worked in central, south and west London and has experience in the investigation of homicide, sexual offences and child abuse. He also worked on the Racial and Violent Crime Task Force, leading a team managing strategic intelligence and innovative responses to tackling men of violence. He has been commended for his work in investigating serial sexual offenders. Mark's teams have won the National Justice Awards for partnership in cold case investigation and the Havens. In 2009 Mark was a commissioner of the Wake Up to Rape Report and the 2010 follow-up *Where is Your Line?* film. These examined public attitudes towards sex and consent. They were released in 2010, receiving international attention.

### Introduction

This chapter will provide an account of the many changes in police investigative approaches to rape since the early 1980s. The Handbook editors' desire to bring together academics and practitioners provided us with the unique opportunity to integrate a police officer's 'on the job' experience investigating rape over the past 30 years alongside the academic literature. In outlining the developments in rape investigation we will focus on innovations that have made the most difference to day-to-day policing including:

- specially trained officers (STOs);
- advances in DNA technology;
- sexual assault referral centres (SARC); and
- cold case work on sexual offences.

We will provide examples from actual cases[2] and we do not seek to be exhaustive: the focus will be on England and Wales and on adult victims (female and male). Further, as we are focusing on police data and procedures we will use the terms they commonly do: victim, i.e. a person reporting a sexual assault to the police; and suspect, i.e. someone who has been arrested and is the subject of police enquiries.

Combining the experiential and academic approaches means it is necessary to give some context for our relationship. We have worked together since 2007 when we met in an advisory group for Project Sapphire (the Metropolitan Police's specialist sexual offences investigation team); subsequently Mark facilitated access to data for research projects Miranda was conducting.

Many of the early changes in responses to rape within the police were brought about by the actions of a handful of officers, in response to the embarrassing publicity resulting from a Roger Graef TV documentary. Among the officers were Thelma Wagstaff and Ian Blair (Rock 1988). Mark was at Hendon Police Training School when the Roger Graef documentary *Police* was screened. It was required viewing for new recruits in the process of being taught textbook ways of managing initial investigations and reporting crime. The series was one of the first 'fly-on-the-wall' programmes showing the workings of the 'real world', in this case the Thames Valley Police Force. None of the young recruits then could have known the impact that the series would have on the investigation of rape. One programme detailed the severe questioning by male detectives of a woman reporting a rape to police, despite the fact that at the time interviewing of women was typically seen as being the preserve of women police constables. The television programme and subsequent public outcry led to acknowledgement within the police service of the need for specialist trained officers investigating serious sexual offences. The reaction from women's interests campaigning groups included a joint publication, authored by Ruth Hall, in 1985 by the Women's Aid Federation and Women Against Rape entitled *Ask Any Woman* which suggested detailed requirements for improving police procedures in the investigation of rape. Additionally there was an influential report from a working party of the Women's National Commission (1986). The Home Office responded by producing a number of circulars on rape investigation and prosecution (1983, 1986), the first of which was couched in somewhat vague terms because the officials had insufficient time to select examples of good practice.

## Specially trained officers

The Metropolitan Police Service (MPS) responded to the Graef documentary by starting the first specialist training courses in October 1984. In the MPS the term sexual offences investigative techniques (SOIT) trained officers is used but most national policy uses the alternative terminology specially trained officers (STO) which will be employed in the remainder of this chapter. The MPS course lasted for five days and concentrated primarily on victim care and the need to obtain a detailed witness statement.

The original SOIT course mainly focused on the taking of extensive notes and completing a comprehensive victim statement. Officers were also trained on forensic packaging, cross-contamination of exhibits and discussing the taking of relevant samples with the forensic medical examiner (FME). Officers were also given guidance on preparation for giving evidence in court.

Over the years, the MPS STO course has been developed and extended. It is a challenging 'pass or fail' course and STOs are recognised by the service as being among the best statement takers. Officers who completed the earliest STO courses report how invaluable the course was throughout a detective career. The course enabled officers to obtain the best information while being mindful of forensic opportunities (Metropolitan Police Service 2009b). In 2002 the course was lengthened to cover the provisions of the Youth Justice and Criminal Evidence Act (YJCEA) 1999 (dealing with special measures and questioning of a witness about previous sexual history). STO officers were also trained on the services of sexual assault referral centres and the work of dedicated rape investigation teams.

In April 2008 the STO course, now run by the Crime Academy at the Hendon Police Training School, was extended to 20 days following the enactment of section 17A YJCEA 1999, allowing visually recorded evidence to be used as evidence in chief (Yexley 2008). The requirement to record an accurate written statement is still an essential element of the course. In addition to the interviewing and technical aspects to the training there is clear focus on victim care and officers are taught about the effects of trauma on victims and families. At a national level the training of STOs is delivered through modular training designed by the National Policing Improvement

Agency (NPIA). The training of investigators within England and Wales is set to the Professionalising Investigation Programme (PIP), which is jointly sponsored by the Association of Chief Police Officers (ACPO) and NPIA. The aim of the programme is to 'improve the professional competence of all police officers and staff who are tasked with conducting investigations' (www.npia.police.uk). PIP ensures that investigators and managers are trained to set standards and maintain those skills throughout police service. It would cover the investigation of volume crime through to the management of major investigations. Box 5.1 provides a brief summary of the programme offered by the NPIA for sexual offences.

The role played by the specialist officer is now recognised as most important to rape investigations. Her Majesty's Crown Prosecution Service Inspectorate (HMCPSI) report highlighted this as pivotal: 'The role of the STO is key – STOs are a vital and integral part of the investigation team' (HMCPSI 2007: 55). Their skills are seen as critical to the investigation of serious sexual offences. In a 2005 review of 677 rape investigations in London the work of STOs was identified as 'best practice' in investigation, specifically: 'a victim-focused ethos must be at the core of each investigation. Repeated close contact is proven to reduce attrition, while meeting victim needs is central to reducing victim withdrawal from investigations' (Stanko et al. 2005: 31).

---

**Box 5.1**. National Policing Improvement Agency (NPIA)
Sexual Offences – Specially Trained Officer Development Programme
(PIP Level 1 Specialist)

This programme sets out the performance-related outcomes
for practitioners selected to:

- provide an initial response in serious sexual offence allegations
- co-ordinate forensic retrieval from the medical examination
- conduct interviews with sexual offences complainants and
- co-ordinate support for sexual offence complainants.

---

*Source*: http://www.npia.police.uk/en/10173.htm

### Rape investigative practice

When a report of serious sexual violence is made, current national police guidance is that an STO should be deployed as soon as possible. Within London, the Sapphire teams aim to deploy an STO to a victim within one hour of the initial report to police (Metropolitan Police Authority 2009). When the STO is called to the initial report of a serious sexual offence their protocol ensures the victim receives any required immediate medical care, provides for their safety, establishes the nature of the incident, takes details of the suspect (including initial description and possible location), finds out where the incident took place and what the victim has done in the time since. Additionally, the STO establishes whether anyone else has been told about the incident and whether there are any witnesses to the events or time leading up to or after (Rights of Women 2008). The STO then arranges medical examinations and secures forensic exhibits such as clothing. The STO is responsible for conducting interviews with the victim, which could be in the form of a written statement or a visually recorded interview. The Crown Prosecution Service (CPS) and ACPO policy states: 'All victims' statements, whether in written form or visually recorded, will be taken by a police officer trained in sexual offence investigative techniques' (CPS 2008a). STOs are the vital link between the investigating officer (IO), senior investigating officer (SIO) and the victim. Figure 5.1 shows the process for victims who report to the police and the role of the STO. As can be seen the STO should remain attached to the case until the conclusion of the investigation or any subsequent court proceedings.

The initial response of all police officers is crucial, but the need for an STO to make early contact is essential. This matters whether the victim reports a case immediately to the police or the attack had taken place some time before. As the recent Stern Review[3] states: 'It is critical that the victim's first encounter with officialdom is sympathetic and professional. Because this encounter is so important, it has been a focus of substantial changes in police practice. Efforts have been made to ensure that the person reporting a rape is dealt with by a police officer with special training, whatever time of day or night the rape is reported' (Stern 2010: 63).

The STO will be responsible for informing the victim about options for forensic medical examination and how a statement will be taken. Often, a victim expresses concern about giving evidence when providing the initial report (both the first time they speak to the police and the first 'official' written report taken by on officer), thus the officer needs to have a good understanding of the legal process. An assessment is needed as to whether it would be preferable to take a written statement from the victim or to visually record the interview. CPS guidance indicates that 'the police will not make an automatic decision to visually record interviews with complainants. Decisions will be taken on a case by case basis following receipt of the witness's views which should be obtained following a full explanation of the available options to include the advantages and disadvantages of pre-recorded evidence' (CPS 2008: 2–3).

In addition to the legal aspects of the case the STO is there primarily to ensure the health and welfare of the victim. STO officers provide support and ensure that medical advice is sought from the outset of an investigation. They will arrange for the forensic medical examination to take place, if this is appropriate to the case.[4] In London the forensic medical examination would take place at a sexual assault referral centre (SARC).[5] The victim is taken to the SARC and responsibility handed over to the sexual offences examiner (SOE) and crisis worker (for more detail about the international variations in treatment see Rebecca Campbell's Chapter 21 in this volume). Generally within the UK the SOE will be a doctor; within London they will always be females who have followed a career in medicine, gynaecology or family

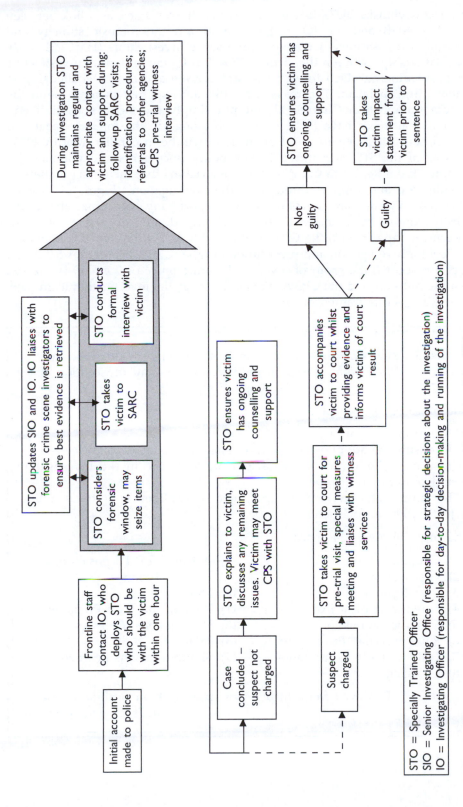

**Figure 5.1** The process for victims who report to the police and the role of the STO

STO = Specially Trained Officer
SIO = Senior Investigating Office (responsible for strategic decisions about the investigation)
IO = Investigating Officer (responsible for day-to-day decision-making and running of the investigation)

Initial account made to police

Frontline staff contact IO, who deploys STO who should be with the victim within one hour

STO considers forensic window, may seize items

STO takes victim to SARC

STO conducts formal interview with victim

STO updates SIO and IO. IO liaises with forensic crime scene investigators to ensure best evidence is retrieved

During investigation STO maintains regular and appropriate contact with victim and support during; follow-up SARC visits; identification procedures; referrals to other agencies; CPS pre-trial witness interview

Case concluded – suspect not charged

STO explains to victim, discusses any remaining issues. Victim may meet CPS with STO

STO ensures victim has ongoing counselling and support

Suspect charged

STO takes victim to court for pre-trial visit, special measures meeting and liaises with witness services

STO accompanies victim to court whilst providing evidence and informs victim of court result

Not guilty

Guilty

STO ensures victim has ongoing counselling and support

STO takes victim impact statement from victim prior to sentence planning (Cybulska 2007). It is important that the STO acts as a link between the SARC staff and the IO as this can inform the forensic strategy and subsequent investigative actions of crime scene investigators (HMCPSI 2007). The relationships between the victim, STOs, SARC staff and other investigators and prosecutors involved in each case are delicate and can be challenging to establish and maintain. The reasons for this are explored in more depth by Rebecca Campbell in Chapter 21 but put simply the victim's medical and psychological needs have to be considered alongside the forensic, legal and public interest requirements and often these will be in conflict (Martin 2005). The role of the STO is featured in key policy documents and manuals, for example, 'From Report to Court' outlines for victims that the officer is there to 'provide care and support throughout the investigation' (Rights of Women 2008: 34). Victims are encouraged to report any concerns about the investigation or their safety to the STO. In addition to their policy for prosecuting rape, in 2008 the CPS together with ACPO developed a new joint protocol for investigation and prosecution of rape (CPS 2008; see Box 5.2 for an overview of areas the protocol covers). The importance of the STO is stressed from the outset where the CPS/ACPO policy states the investigation team 'will' include a specially trained officer.

---

**Box 5.2** Key points covered by the Protocol between the police and Crown Prosecution Service in the investigation and prosecution of allegations of rape

The protocol has four objectives:

- To reflect national ACPO and CPS policy;
- To ensure the adoption of the recommendations of *Without Consent*;
- To achieve improved and consistent performance in the investigation and prosecution of rape;
- To improve the service to, and increase confidence in the Criminal Justice System for, victims of rape.

The protocol covers 14 areas:

| | |
|---|---|
| 1) Communication | 9) Out of Court Disposal or No Further Action |
| 2) First response | |
| 3) Investigation | 10) Disclosure |
| 4) Forensic Medical Examination | 11) Review and Case Preparation |
| 5) Forensic Submissions | 12) Victims and Witnesses |
| 6) Rape Specialist Prosecutors | 13) Trial |
| 7) Full and Early Consultation | 14) Sharing Lessons Learned |
| 8) Charging | |

Retrieved from: http://www.cps.gov.uk/publications/agencies/rape_protocol.html

Communicating developments in the case to the victim is also critical in the investigation and prosecution and is the responsibility of the STO. In a number of studies that have interviewed rape victims one of the most consistent criticisms of the police has been that they have not maintained regular contact and provided information to victims throughout the investigation and in some cases the lack of contact has resulted in many victims not being informed of the outcome of their case (see for example Lees and Gregory 1993; Temkin 1999). Good practice dictates that the STO should inform the victim of news about any arrest, charging or bailing of a suspect.

Even when decisions are made by the prosecution team to drop a case or reduce charges then an explanatory letter should be delivered by the STO to the victim in person.

---

**Box 5.3** Mavis's account of the value of her STO

It was my worst nightmare come true to be raped. The impact not only on me, but also my family, was profound and threw our normal lives into complete turmoil. We were driven by an overwhelming need for justice and put all our faith in the police. From the crucial role of the first response officer, every police contact left a lasting impression, but it was my SOIT officer who really made the difference. Because she was with me, at my most vulnerable, from just after my assault, through the forensic examination and taking my statement, she knew my story and how I would react in certain situations better than anyone else involved. It was invaluable, for me and my family, to have one dedicated police contact, who we all trusted to have my best interests and welfare at heart. She would always take time to explain some, often very bewildering, aspects of the legal process or find answers to very real concerns about what was happening. Above all, I knew she was on my side and understood how important it was for me to have done everything in my power to stop any further assaults. I sat in court with my SOIT when my attacker received a life sentence for rape – I have absolutely no hesitation in saying that I would never have lasted the 18 difficult months to trial without her constant dedication and support.

Account provided by personal communication to the second author

---

There are times where the dedicated STO will not be able to provide direct support to a victim; an example of this would be any involvement of victims in visual identification procedure. The Police and Criminal Evidence (PACE) Act 1984 Code of Practice for the Identification of Persons by Police Officers (2008) specifies: 'No officer or any other person involved with the investigation of the case against the suspect, beyond the extent required by these procedures, may take any part in these procedures' (PACE Act Code D: 151). In such cases a second independent STO would be deployed to support the victim taking part in this process.

Since the justified public concern raised after the Graef programme, there have been significant developments in the investigative response to victim care and STO officers are the frontline police officers in rape investigation. The victim-focused work of STOs has often led to victims of serious sexual violence wanting to give testimony in support of the police service and the high standards of victim care (see Box 5.3). Victims of serious sexual violence will sometimes come forward to promote the work of STOs to those considering applying for training or to promote the service provided to those outside the police service.

In responding to the need to enhance the evidence-gathering and investigation process, while at the same time supporting victims, the role of the STO is now firmly established as the essential police officer role for rape investigation. Only a handful of evaluations of STOs have been conducted but they have consistently found that STOs, when properly resourced and supported, provide an excellent service for victims (this is evidenced by the account in Box 5.3 from a victim about the value of her STO), although some concerns have been raised about the need for better provision for STOs themselves (see for example Jamel et al. 2008; Noble 2007).

## DNA

In the early 1980s, when investigating serious sexual offences, consideration was given to forensic analysis of crime scene stains and intimate swabs. The best result available from a bloodstain was the category from the ABO Blood Grouping system. When dealing with other staining from body fluids, an investigator's best hope would rely on whether the body fluid came from a 'secretor'. A secretor is a person who secretes their blood group type in other body fluids such as saliva or semen. If a blood group for a suspect could be established then this could be compared to the Metropolitan Police Forensic Science Laboratory Blood Group index. The index contained names of suspects who had had blood taken for elimination purposes. The Blood Group Index could then be used to prioritise suspects or create new lines of enquiries, but was only available at best as corroborative evidence.

The mid 1980s saw the development of DNA technology by Sir Alec Jeffreys at Leicester University. Named at the time 'DNA fingerprinting', this is now commonly referred to as 'DNA profiling'. There was no identifiable pressure from the police or government for the development of DNA technology but the techniques that evolved have had a significant impact on rape investigations. Gilbert (2010: 347) summarises how DNA profiling works:

Profiles are drawn from short, repeating sequences of DNA scattered throughout the genome, called short tandem repeats (STRs). Because the number of repeats varies widely from person to person the length of these STRs is also highly variable, meaning that by measuring several STRs – between 10–17 – forensic scientists can declare with calculable probability whether DNA left at a crime scene belongs to a suspect.

---

**Box 5.4** The Colin Pitchfork case

In 1983, a 15-year-old schoolgirl was found raped and murdered. A semen sample taken from Lynda Mann's body was found to belong to a person with type A blood group and an enzyme profile which matched 10 per cent of the adult male population. At that time, with no other leads or forensic evidence, the murder hunt stopped. Three years later, Dawn Ashworth, also 15, was found strangled and sexually assaulted in the same town. Police were convinced the same assailant had committed both murders. Semen samples recovered from Dawn's body revealed her attacker had the same blood type as Lynda's murderer. The prime suspect was a local boy, who after questioning revealed previously unreleased details about Dawn Ashworth's body. Further questioning led to his confession but he denied any involvement in the first murder.

Convinced that he had committed both crimes, officers from Leicestershire Constabulary contacted Professor Sir Alec Jeffreys at Leicester University, who had developed a technique for creating DNA profiles. Using this technique Dr Jeffreys compared semen samples from both murders against a blood sample from the suspect, which conclusively proved that both girls were killed by the same man, but not the suspect. The Forensic Science Service (FSS) confirmed Dr Jeffrey's conclusions.

The police then undertook the world's first DNA intelligence-led screen. All adult males in three villages – a total of 5,000 men – were asked to volunteer and provide blood or saliva samples. Blood grouping was performed and DNA profiling carried out by the FSS on the 10 per cent of men who had the same blood type as the killer. The murderer almost escaped again by getting a friend to give blood in his name. However, this friend was later overheard talking about the switch and that he'd given his sample masquerading as Colin Pitchfork. A local baker, Colin Pitchfork, was arrested and his DNA profile matched with the semen from both murders. In 1988 he was sentenced to life for the two murders.

Retrieved from: http://www.forensic.gov.uk/html/media/case-studies
/f-18.html

---

The first case to be solved through DNA profiling was the two murders committed by Colin Pitchfork (see Box 5.4 for further details) in 1983 and 1986, although it was Pitchfork's efforts to avoid providing an elimination sample in a mass screening that brought him to the attention of the enquiry team (Wambaugh 1989). The first conviction using DNA was at Bristol Crown Court on 13 November 1987. Scientists had calculated that the chances of the sample from the scene of a rape not coming from the accused (Robert Melias) was one in four million of the male population, in the light of which he pleaded guilty.

A key case that demonstrated the innovative application of DNA technology was a homicide that took place in south London in December 1988, and is particularly relevant to this chapter because of the rapes that were linked to it. On 20 December Lorraine Benson was attacked and murdered in Raynes Park, in the London Borough of Merton. Lorraine's body was found in open ground in the early hours of the morning. She was partially clothed and had died as a result of ligature strangulation. She had also been subject to blows and had bite marks on her body. A wider search of the area revealed a second crime scene in an access road behind some shops. At this scene some of Lorraine's belongings and a man's handkerchief were found. Marks in dust on a vehicle at this scene matched the weave on Lorraine Benson's coat. At the same time as this incident, a separate police enquiry was running on a linked series of serious sexual assaults in Kingston upon Thames, a neighbouring area. In this series the police had already released a description of a suspect. The media focused on the description of the suspect and it was decided to run the Kingston enquiry alongside the Lorraine Benson case. There was a great deal of media interest and a television reconstruction generated 400 calls from the public. This enquiry coincided with the first year of the opening of the DNA profiling unit at the Metropolitan Police Forensic Science Laboratory (MPFSL). The use of DNA technology was so new that police had to approach medical practitioners to obtain the appropriate preservatives for detained suspects' blood samples, as this had never been routinely used by police before. At the time most suspect elimination samples were obtained from blood; these are now routinely taken from mouth (buccal cell) swabs.

The breakthrough in the Benson case occurred when a DNA profile from nasal mucus was found on the handkerchief. It was also established that the handkerchief contained a separate DNA profile from a bloodstain that matched Lorraine Benson's DNA. But the mucus sample did not match any suspects from the Kingston enquiry. Enquiries continued and in February 1989 an attempted rape took place in the Raynes Park area. Fingerprints found at the scene matched those of John Dunne, a 19-year-old local man. While in custody dental impressions were taken from Dunne which matched the marks found on Lorraine's body. Dunne was charged with the murder of Lorraine Benson, and his DNA was later found to match the nasal mucus in the handkerchief. Dunne later made an unsolicited confession to the murder of Lorraine Benson, admitting striking Lorraine and then giving her his handkerchief to wipe her face. Dunne pleaded guilty to murder but he was not forensically linked to the Kingston cases, which remain unsolved. This case was the first murder solved by DNA profiling in the MPFSL and the first recorded DNA profile from nasal secretions (Allard 1992).

A recent issue of *Nature* focusing on science in court highlighted how DNA-profiling laboratory techniques have evolved further, while those used in criminal investigations have not (to the same extent at least) (Gilbert 2010). However, in another article in the same issue the authors, who are co-founders and co-directors of the Innocence Project,[6] acknowledge that compared with other forensic methods currently in use, such as bite-mark comparisons and fingerprint analysis, DNA profiling has been proved to reliably and accurately demonstrate a connection between evidence and a specific source (Neufeld and Scheck 2010). While there is clearly a need to develop the DNA profiling techniques used in criminal investigations, it remains the most reliable and efficient tool in the rape investigator's kit.

One consequence of the efficacy of DNA profiling is a shift in the kind of cases investigating officers need to build. If DNA evidence is available then IOs can be confident that they can prove sex took place. The challenge has now become proving that consent was not given. There is always a need to identify the suspect in a rape investigation and before the advent of DNA evidence, the defence case was often based on challenging the identification of the suspect. This identification or links to the crime would invariably be through visual identification, admissions made by the suspect or some other form of forensic evidence, such as fingerprints or trace evidence. All of this evidence is still available and widely used; however, given the prominence of DNA they may become sidelined. As Rook and Ward (2004) emphasise though, in their widely used book on sexual offences law and procedure, 'obviously DNA evidence (and the random occurrence ratio) needs to be put in the context of all the other evidence in the case' (Rook and Ward 2004: 600). The value of fingerprints in interpreting crime scenes and providing corroborative evidence comes under the remit of a specialist Sexual Offences Development Team[7] (MPS 2010). Fingerprint experts can often provide evidence of suspects' or victim movements at a crime scene that can prove compelling.

Although DNA evidence is sometimes challenged this is unusual. Strong identification evidence is more likely to lead to challenges focusing on the victim's account and the issue of consent. This is often a traumatic experience, likened in some research to a 'second rape' (Koss 2000; Orth 2002). However, it is also possible that the provision of clear scientific evidence can lead to a plea of guilty being entered, which means the victim is not required to give evidence. No research has been conducted that allows estimations to be given about the frequency of guilty pleas or challenges to the victim's account but it is worth mentioning here that there are growing concerns about the so-called 'CSI Effect', based on the prevalence of popular television shows where forensic evidence is at the heart of every case (see for example Desmarais et al. 2008; Houck 2006; Lovgren 2004; Tyler 2006). This has led to the public and juries having a distorted view of the value of scientific evidence with the perception of 'near-infallibility' scientific evidence and the availability of instant results (Rincon 2010). In fact in some rape cases the forensic evidence can lead to emphasis being focused back on the behaviour of the victim.

## Sexual assault referral centres

A major challenge for investigators of serious sexual offences has always been the lack of suitably qualified female forensic medical examiners (FME). Research into victims' needs in the aftermath of rape has consistently found that they want to be examined and supported by women practitioners (Schonbucher et al. 2009), and perhaps most fundamentally be seen and treated as whole persons (Kelly et al. 2005).

In the London area, and across most of the UK, in the 1980s and 1990s, when a victim of serious sexual violence reported to the police there was no guarantee that they would be examined by a female doctor. When female police FMEs were available, victims could be asked to wait for long periods of time or travel long distances for the examination. The lack of suitably trained female doctors not only frustrated investigations but also adversely affected care of victims. Examinations took place in victim examination suites (VES) that were on police property. The suites were maintained by police staff and replacement clothing was often obtained by well-motivated police officers securing 'charitable' donations. If a victim required medical treatment such as medication for potential sexually transmitted infections or other infection, then police officers were required to take the victim to an accident and emergency medicine sites or a genito-urinary medicine (GUM) clinic. Emergency contraception had to be obtained through normal health service channels. The medical and legal responses to rape were lacking and a radical change was needed (Lovett *et al.* 2004).

The solution to the problems outlined in the previous paragraph was the adoption and amalgamation of models used in America, Australia and Canada to provide victim care combining crisis intervention, high quality forensic practice and advocacy (Lovett *et al.* 2004). In the UK these are known as sexual assault referral centres and are usually based in hospitals. SARCs are one-stop shops where victims of recent rape and serious sexual assaults can receive medical care, counselling, and support police investigations by, for example, undergoing a forensic medical examination with the option to formally report or provide anonymous intelligence. What seems to be clear, both anecdotally and from research, is that specialist provision such as that provided by SARCs is key to ensuring victims do not experience 'secondary victimisation', diminishes poor practice and increases service use (Brown *et al.* 2010a; Campbell 2008; Sampsel *et al* 2009).

The development of SARCs across the United Kingdom has been slow. The first was opened in Manchester in 1986 (St Mary's) and two further SARCs were established in the 1990s, in Northumbria (Rape Examination Advice, Counselling and Help – REACH) and West Yorkshire (Surviving Trauma After Rape – STAR). In September 2007, there were 18 SARCs operating in England and Wales and a pilot centre in Glasgow (Coy *et al.* 2009). Despite the pledge to establish 40 SARCs in England and Wales by the end of 2008 (made in the Westminster Government's *Action Plan on Sexual Violence and Abuse*, HM Government 2007), Coy *et al.*'s (2009) analysis of service provision identified only 26.

This chapter focuses on the evolution of SARCs in London. By 2000 the lack of provision of essential services in London was developing into a critical issue. A commitment was made at a senior level within the MPS and health services to work in a true 50/50 partnership, and develop a service that offered the highest standards of clinical care combined with forensic evidence gathering. The SARCs in London are known as the Havens (www.the havens.co.uk).

In contrast to the pioneering three SARCs opened in the 1980s and 1990s the establishment of the London Havens was the first where the police and the National Health Service shared the cost equally, thus providing a demonstrable commitment to joint partnership working. In 2000 London opened its first Haven at Kings College Hospital, Camberwell, South London. This was followed in 2004 by two further Havens in Paddington and Whitechapel. The doctors in the new SARCs were specially selected from practitioners with experience mainly in genito-urinary, obstetrics and gynaecological medicine. They were chosen for their people skills and focus on victim care and in addition were provided with forensic training. The doctors work as part of a team and are subject to supervision in the form of peer review and NHS clinical governance. Where police officers would sometimes wait beyond a day to find a female doctor, the Havens aim to offer an appointment within one hour of referral.

There are a number of benefits for investigators when accessing a SARC. All staff are trained and focused on providing the best possible service for victims of serious sexual violence. When a victim arrives at a centre with an STO they are met by a crisis worker. The crisis worker then works with the sexual offences examiner (SOE) to ensure that the victim receives the highest levels of medical treatment and support available. The examinations take place in medical suites that have forensic integrity to ensure that there is no cross contamination of trace evidence. The Havens provide immediate access to emergency contraception and antiretroviral drugs and testing, health advice and counselling for sexually transmitted infections (STIs). In the past this would have entailed untrained police officers visiting emergency pharmacies and then taking victims to emergency medicine units and sexual health clinics. These changes have significantly improved a victim's experience of reporting rape and in turn have improved police investigations (Against Violence and Abuse 2010). Specifically when the care of the victim is handed over to the healthcare professionals the STO can spend time updating the investigating officer, passing on information that may assist with developing a forensic strategy, and also ensuring that any potential risks to the victim are reduced. Furthermore, within London, the Havens are linked to the internal police computer network.

One unique element of the SARC service is the availability of the 'non-police referral' option. This allows victims to report directly to a SARC without first contacting the police. They have the choice of being forensically examined and having swabs taken. They can then choose to have the samples passed to the police anonymously to be analysed and checked against the national DNA database. If analysis results in a match, the SARC client is notified by their crisis worker and they can choose whether to formally report to police. If the client wants to remain anonymous then vital intelligence has still been gathered by the police. Access to this service is quantifiable: in London 'non-police referral' cases account for approximately 10 per cent of Haven clients. During targeted awareness campaigns, the number of 'non-police referrals' has risen to 20 per cent (Yexley 2009a). The advantage of the SARC service is that these cases would never have been reported to the police in the past and many offenders would still have been at large. A significant proportion of these people subsequently go on to report to the police, but even if they choose not to, their medical and psychosocial needs are still addressed through the provision of the SARC.

Earlier in this chapter we mentioned the key role played by STOs. In London the Havens offer an 'STO clinic', where Haven clients can speak in confidence to an STO about reporting to the police and the criminal justice process. The clinics were set up to allow Haven clients to speak to a police officer anonymously about what is likely to happen if they were to report a case to the police. Officers can talk through the process of providing a statement, the case being reviewed by a prosecutor and the possibility of applying for special measures.[8] Seeing a police officer in a caring and supporting role can have a very positive impact on a Haven client. There is no obligation to report to the police but the clinic has had significant successes in increasing reporting rates. The manager of the Haven, Whitechapel, commented on the successes of the scheme: 'We have a weekly STO clinic, when a victim can speak in confidence to a specialist officer about what would happen if they did report...Around 60 per cent of people who do that do go on to make a formal allegation. So that is very encouraging that the approach is working' (Metropolitan Police Service 2009a: 9). The establishment of STO clinics was also identified as good practice in Baroness Stern's review (2010).

SARCs have been identified as good practice in a number of reports because they improve victim care, which in turn can lead to victims continuing to support an investigation, from report to court, and provide a better standard of forensic evidence (HMIC and HMCPSI 2002; HMCPSI 2007). Further, there has been a small number of studies in the UK evaluating SARCs which overwhelmingly find their services to be valued both by victims and the police (Lovett et al. 2004; Payne 2009; Regan et al., 2008; Robinson 2009; Schonbucher et al. 2009). For example, the recent evaluation by Schonbucher et al. (2009) used a multimethodology approach, combining quantitative and qualitative data, and this design ensured that baseline and more in-depth data were collected from diverse perspectives, including: service users; service providers; and stakeholders. Service users were found to be highly satisfied with the SARC and commended the care, sensitivity and respect with which they were treated. The evaluation team concluded that the SARC 'undoubtedly improved immediate response to, and aftercare of, victims of sexual assault and may be making an important contribution to reducing attrition' (Schonbucher et al. 2009: 10). Despite all of these endorsements, more systematic evaluations of SARC services are required and, perhaps more importantly, access to such specialist services is limited by under-resourcing of sexual violence services in the UK (Coy et al. 2009; Women's Resource Centre and Rape Crisis 2008).

The commitment of the police service to funding healthcare beyond the immediate retrieval of forensic evidence demonstrates the most significant steps forward in a victim-focused approach to crime investigation. This recognises that a positive outcome for a victim of sexual violence does not always rest with a criminal justice outcome, but also with positive physical and mental health outcomes. This in turn places responsibility for victim care within the remit of health services as well as police. The most effective and sustainable way of maintaining and developing SARC services for victims of serious sexual violence is promoted in the Stern Review:

> We acknowledge that the existing funding arrangements for Sexual Assault Referral Centres vary across the country, and we would not wish to be prescriptive about how they are set up and run. However, it is clear to us that there is a greater chance of success when there is a strong partnership between the NHS, the police and elements of local

government, and equal commitment in the setting up and operation of a Sexual Assault Referral Centre. We recommend this commitment should be shared equally by the police, the NHS and local government.

(67: 2010)

## Cold cases

The investigation of historic unsolved crimes or 'cold cases' has only developed in the past ten years, as a result of changes in the law and scientific advances that have opened up this new area of criminal investigation. The advances of DNA technology[9] and the development of the national DNA database have enabled the Police Service to apply scientific processes that were not available when the original investigations were undertaken. In England and Wales the investigation of cold cases initially focused on availability of DNA technology, but advances in fingerprint work and the ability to prosecute 'double jeopardy'[10] cases have also proved valuable.

February 2003 saw the establishment of the Cold Case Rape Investigation Team within the Metropolitan Police Service. This unit was originally set up as a pilot and initially focused on linked series offences. The Home Office provided funding to support forensic analysis of potential DNA material held by the Forensic Science Service (FSS). As a result of the pilot work, the Home Office Police Standards Unit commenced Operation Advance on a national basis in January 2004. Operation Advance examined unsolved serious sexual offences from the late 1980s and early 1990s (Home Office 2004). By 2007 Operation Advance had reviewed over 11,000 cases (outside London) and had gained 30 convictions. During a similar period the Metropolitan Police Service Cold Case Team had obtained 40 convictions from reviewing over 900 cases (Yexley 2008).

The MPS cold case teams demonstrate the success of working in partnership with criminal justice agencies to bring to justice men who had long since thought they had evaded capture. It consists of a dedicated team of detectives working with a crime analyst. The key to effective cold case investigation is the establishment of specialist partnership arrangements and protocols. In London this works with specialist detectives, lawyers, forensic practitioners and scientists. The investigative process involves examining evidential material retained in storage in forensic archives and applying new scientific processes to them. The application of new forensic processes to old retained material can result in the development of new DNA profiles to be loaded on to the national DNA database. In the UK that national DNA database is run and maintained by the National Policing Improvement Agency (NPIA). If a match is made on the database, the cold case team work with the Crown Prosecution Service to ensure that there is a strong evidential case before a decision is made to contact a victim. Careful consideration is given to approaching a victim of a historic case: 'each approach to a victim is carefully risk assessed, and will only be made after careful consideration of the likelihood of a conviction by the CPS. In addition to the deployment of a local SOIT officer, the healthcare needs of the victim are considered as a priority' (Yexley 2009b).

Cold case investigations often attract media attention with some cases being widely reported. For example in 2006 Fion Gunn described how officers approached her from the MPS cold case team. They told her they had found the man who seriously sexually assaulted her some 15 years before (Stuart 2006). The original attack involved oral penetration, in Fion's home, in the presence of her young baby. Re-examination of evidence seized at the time allowed investigators to identify Christopher Cleary, a man with convictions for sexual offences, as a suspect. He was subsequently convicted and sentenced to ten years' imprisonment.

Another widely reported case involved a series of sex attacks against teenage girls that commenced in 1989, that were solved some 17 years later. The attacks took place between 1989 and 1996 in recreational areas in south London and north Surrey (Fresco 2006). The victims were all female aged between 13 and 16 years, they were abducted and sexually assaulted with the threat of a knife. The cases were linked by investigators, but remained unsolved. Anthony DeBoise, a local government planning officer, was not known to police but became a suspect for the offences when he was arrested for an unrelated matter. A sample of DNA taken while he was in custody matched crime scene stains from the north Surrey series. Further forensic analysis linked the two series and DeBoise pleaded guilty to a series of counts relating to his attacks. His victims now in their twenties were present at Southwark Crown Court to see DeBoise sentenced to 13 years' imprisonment. These cases demonstrate how scientific developments and the work of specialist teams can deliver justice for the victims of serious crimes.

In May 2010 the London *Evening Standard* reported that the MPS cold case team had reviewed over 1,100 crimes and convicted 58 men of 125 offences. The team have also 'loaded' a further 112 new DNA profiles of unsolved crimes onto the national DNA database (Davenport 2010).

## Conclusions

In this chapter we have presented an overview of key developments in the investigation of rape in England and Wales including: STOs; advances in DNA technology; SARCs and cold case work. In doing so we have reflected the increasing focus on victim care and professionalising the investigative process, both of which, we believe, represent significant steps forward for victims and criminal justice professionals. The developments discussed in this chapter have emerged from a range of origins including police and Crown Prosecution Service initiatives, government (through the auspices of the Home Office) initiatives and on occasion through the determination of a small group of individuals. Progress in rape investigation policy and practice often seems to occur through a process of attention being raised about an issue by feminist campaigning groups, activists or media controversy; changes being made or at least piloted on an operational level by the police and non-governmental organisations; and then when they are proven to work they are adopted by the government. It is questionable whether this could be considered a 'best practice' or 'gold standard' approach to dealing with an offence which affects more than four in ten women and over a quarter of men over their lifetime (McGee *et al.* 2002).

Most of the developments in rape investigation outlined in this chapter ultimately point to forensics evidence being the key. This is supported by Andy Feist and colleagues' 2007 research which included 676 cases from eight police forces across England and Wales. They found five factors best predicted whether a case would get to court or result in a conviction, one of which was that forensic evidence was recovered.

Despite the improvements in case building, investigators and prosecutors are still left with the age-old problem of attitudes towards rape and sexual violence. When discussing attitudes we include their own but also those of the general public. A number of unrelated surveys have explored the general public's attitudes towards rape, including Amnesty International (2005), Scottish Executive (2007) and Home Office (2009) and the most recent the Havens' 'Wake up to rape' report (Opinion Matters 2010). Fairly similar findings emerge across these surveys but due to the different questions asked direct comparisons cannot be drawn. To give the reader a sense of the attitudes the surveys pick up, we outline a few findings from the Havens' report (Opinion Matters 2010), which surveyed a random sample of 1,061 people in London aged 18 to 50 online. Close to one in five respondents agree with the statement, 'most claims of rape are probably not true' (18%). This suggests that the general public are not aware of the existing evidence which suggests that only between 3–8 per cent of rape allegations are false (Kelly *et al.* 2005). Further, there are many situations in which some people feel that a person should take responsibility for being raped. Over half (56 per cent) of those surveyed think that there are some circumstances where a person should accept responsibility. These circumstances are: performing another sexual act on a person (73 per cent); getting into bed with a person (66 per cent); drinking to excess/blackout (64 per cent); going back to theirs for a drink (29 per cent); dressing provocatively (28 per cent); dancing in a sexy way with a man at a night club or bar (22 per cent); acting flirtatiously (21 per cent); kissing them (14 per cent); accepting a drink and engaging in a conversation at a bar (13 per cent).

What these independent surveys do not tell us is whether there have been attitudinal changes over time. Many of the surveys that have been done have asked different questions and used different populations, which inhibits direct comparison consequently scant evidence exists to indicate whether attitudes have changed over time (Brown *et al.* 2010a). One of the only replication studies was conducted in February 2010. This reran the questions from a 1977 survey and conducted a comparative analysis (Brown *et al.* 2010b). The original 1977 poll of opinions on rape was commissioned by the *Daily Mail*, partly in response to a rape case which was widely reported in the press at the time because of a particularly lenient sentence. The poll asked respondents about which offence types they saw as most serious, whether they thought these offences had increased, whether they personally knew someone who had been raped, whether they agreed or disagreed with a range of statements about rape victims and offenders, which factors they thought should be and which actually were taken into consideration when deliberating punishment for those found guilty of rape, and how women should react if they were raped. The results of this poll were reported in the *Daily Mail* on 1 July 1977. The 2010 survey found that opinions on rape remain negative in some ways (for example that the law is unfair on rape victims and that many people would not report rape to the police or were unsure). However, in other ways the findings were optimistic (for example that rape is a serious crime; less support for the opinions that if a woman gets raped it is usually her fault and that the prior sexual experience of the woman should be taken into consideration when punishing those found guilty of rape).

## Further reading

To understand more about the relationship between investigators and prosecutors in England and Wales see *A Protocol Between the Police and Crown Prosecution Service in the Investigation and Prosecution of Allegations of Rape* (Crown Prosecution Service 2008). The most recent guidance on prosecuting rape cases can be found in *CPS Policy for Prosecuting Cases of Rape* (Crown Prosecution Service 2009). The most detailed reports on the investigation and prosecution of rape in England and Wales are *The Report on the Joint Inspection into the Investigation and Prosecution of Cases involving Allegations of Rape* (HM Inspectorate of Constabularies and HM Crown Prosecution Service Inspectorate 2002) and *Without Consent: A Report on the Joint Review of the Investigation and Prosecution of Rape Offences* (HM Crown Prosecution Service Inspectorate 2007). However, for the most up-to-date perspective on what's happening nationally see *The Stern Review* (2010). For more general information on criminal investigations in England and Wales, including sections on sexual offences, see *Understanding Criminal Investigation* (Tong *et al.* 2009).

## Notes

1  The views expressed in this chapter are solely those of the authors. They do not represent those of the Metropolitan Police Service.
2  All details of the cases referred to in this chapter are publicly available. When appropriate some details are anonymised or changed to protect victims/witnesses/suspects or organisations.
3  The Stern Review was an independent review into the treatment of rape complaints by public authorities in England and Wales. It was commissioned by the Government Equalities Office and Home Office in 2009 and conducted by Baroness Vivien Stern. It made 23 recommendations and due to the change in government shortly after the review was published it is unclear at this time whether they will be implemented.
4  The need for a forensic examination would be based on the initial assessment of the case and a discussion between the STO and SOE.
5  SARCs were first developed in England and Wales in the 1980s based on similar models which existed in North America, Canada and Australia. Their primary focus is on providing services for those in the aftermath of a recent rape. SARCs have the dual aim of meeting the needs of both victims and the Criminal Justice System (Lovett *et al.* 2004). They are discussed in more depth later in this chapter.
6  The Innocence Project is a national litigation and public policy organisation in the

USA dedicated to exonerating wrongfully convicted people through DNA testing and reforming the criminal justice system to prevent future injustice (see www.theinnocenceproject.org).

7 The Sexual Offences Development Team aims to respond to sexually motivated crime at the highest possible forensic level. There is a dedicated fingerprint team, which specialises in providing interpretation and corroboration evidence incorporating graphics, which has proved crucial in consent cases. Each borough in London has forensic Sexual Offence Liaison Officers (SOLOs) who are there to forensically support police officers and Haven staff.

8 'Special measures' are available to assist vulnerable and intimidated witnesses to give their best evidence in criminal proceedings. The special measures apply to prosecution and defence witnesses, but not the defendant. Special measures are available to defence witnesses in the youth court. Special measures include: screens; live link; evidence given in private; removal of wigs and gowns; a video-recorded interview; examination of the witness through an intermediary; and aids to communication. For further information see the Crown Prosecution Service legal guidance at http://www.cps.gov.uk/legal/s_to_u/special_measures/

9 The current method of DNA profiling, developed in June 1999, the SGM Plus®, gives an average discrimination potential for one in a billion.

10 Until the Criminal Justice Act of 2003 was passed the criminal law of England and Wales did not permit a person who had been acquitted or convicted of an offence to be retried for that offence. The risk of the retrial is known as double jeopardy.

## References

Against Violence and Abuse (2010) *And still, like dust, we rise: London survivors of domestic and sexual violence*. Unpublished manuscript.

Allard, J.E. (1992) 'Murder in South London: a novel use of DNA profiling', *Journal of the Forensic Science Society*, 32(1): 49–58.

Amnesty International (2005) *Sexual assault research: summary report*. Prepared by ICM.

Brown, J., Horvath, M.A.H., Kelly, L. and Westmarland, N. (2010a) *Connections and Disconnections: Assessing evidence, knowledge and practice in responses to rape*. London: Government Equalities Office.

Brown, J., Horvath, M.A.H., Kelly, L. and Westmarland, N. (2010b) *Has Anything Changed? Results of a comparative study (1977–2010) on opinions on rape*. London: Government Equalities Office.

Campbell, R. (2008) 'The psychological impact of rape victims' experiences with the legal, medical, and mental health systems'. *American Psychologist*, 68: 702–17.

Coy, M., Kelly, L. and Foord, J. (2009) *Map of Gaps 2: The Postcode Lottery of Violence Against Women Support Services*. London: End Violence Against Women Coalition.

Crown Prosecution Service (2008) *A Protocol Between the Police and Crown Prosecution Service in the Investigation and Prosecution of Allegations of Rape*. Retrieved on 16 July 2010 from http://www.cps.gov.uk/legal/p_to_r/rape_manual/annex_f_protocol_between_the_police_and_the_cps/index.html

Crown Prosecution Service (2008b) *Special Measures*. Retrieved on 30 August 2010 from http://www.cps.gov.uk/legal/s_to_u/special_measures/#Specialmeasures/

Crown Prosecution Service (2009) *CPS Policy for Prosecuting Cases of Rape*. Retrieved on 20 July 2010 from http://www.cps.gov.uk/publications/docs/prosecuting_rape.pdf

Cybulska, B. (2007) 'Sexual assault: key issues', *Journal of the Royal Society of Medicine*, 100: 1–4.

Davenport, J. (2010) 'Cold case rape squad finds the DNA of 112 London sex attackers',

*London Evening Standard*, 28 May. Retrieved on 18 July 2010 from http://www.thisislondon.co.uk/standard/article-23839260-cold-case-rape-squad-finds-the-dna-of-112-london-sex-attackers.do

Desmarais, S.L., Price, H.L. and Read, D.J. (2008) 'Objection, your honor! Television is not the relevant authority. Crime drama portrayals of eyewitness issues', *Psychology, Crime and Law*, 14(3): 225–43.

Feist, A., Ashe, J., Lawrence, J., McPhee, D. and Wilson, R. (2007) *Investigating and detecting recorded offences of rape*. Home Office Online Report 18/07. Retrieved on 15 July 2010 from http://rds.homeoffice.gov.uk/rds/pdfs07/rdsolr1807.pdf

Fresco, A. (2006) 'Bogus tramp who attacked young girls is jailed for 13 years', *The Times*, 18 September. Retrieved on 20 July 2010 from http://www.timesonline.co.uk/tol/news/uk/crime/article642611.ece

Gilbert, N. (2010) 'DNA's identity crisis', *Nature*, 464 (7287): 347–8.

Hall, R. (1985) *Ask Any Woman – A London Enquiry into Rape and Sexual Assault*. London: Falling Wall Press.

HM Crown Prosecution Service Inspectorate (2007) *Without Consent: A Report on the Joint Review of the Investigation and Prosecution of Rape Offences*. London: HMCPSI.

HM Government (2007) *Cross Government Action Plan on Sexual Violence and Abuse*. London: HM Government.

HM Inspectorate of Constabularies and HM Crown Prosecution Service Inspectorate (2002) *The Report on the Joint Inspection into the Investigation and Prosecution of Cases involving Allegations of Rape*. London: HMCPSI and HMIC.

Home Office (1983) *Circular 25/1983; Investigation of Offences of Rape*. London: Home Office.

Home Office (1986) *Violence Against Women*. Home Office circular 69/1986. London: Home Office.

Home Office (2004) *Operation Advance – a Joint Initiative with the Home Office Police Standards Unit (PSU)*. Retrieved on 29 July 2010 from http://213.52.171.242/forensic_t/inside/news/news_docs/Op_Advance.doc

Home Office (2009) *Results from the Ipsos Mori poll of telephone interviews with people in England and Wales regarding their opinions on violence against women*. London: Home Office.

Houck, M.M. (2006) 'CSI: Reality', *Scientific American*, 295: 84–9.

Jamel, J., Bull, R. and Sheridan, L. (2008) 'An investigation of the specialist police service provided to male rape survivors', *International Journal of Police Science and Management*, 10(4): 486–507.

Kelly, L., Lovett, J. and Regan, L. (2005) *A Gap or a Chasm? Attrition in reported rape cases*. Home Office Research Study 293. London: Home Office.

Koss, M.P. (2000) 'Blame, shame, and community: Justice responses to violence against women', *American Psychologist*, 55: 1332–43.

Lees, S. and Gregory, J. (1993) *Rape and Sexual Assault: A Study of Attrition*. London: Islington Council.

Lovett, J., Regan, L. and Kelly, L. (2004) *Sexual Assault Referral Centres: developing good practice and maximising potentials*. Home Office Research Study 285. London: Home Office.

Lovgren, S. (2004) '"CSI" effect" is mixed blessing for real crime labs', *National Geographic News*, 23 September. Retrieved 30 July 2010 from http://news.nationalgeographic.com/news/2004/09/0923_040923_csi.html#main

Martin, P.Y. (2005) *Rape Work: victims, gender, and emotions in organisation and community context*. New York: Routledge.

McGee, H., Garavan, R., de Barra, M., Byrne, J. and Conroy, R. (2002) *The SAVI Report. Sexual Abuse and Violence in Ireland. A national study of Irish experiences, beliefs and attitudes concerning sexual violence*. Dublin: Liffey Press.

Metropolitan Police Authority (2009). *Transfer of responsibility for rape investigations*. Strategic and Operational Policing Committee, 15 October. Retrieved on 15 July 2010 from http://www.mpa.gov.uk/committees/sop/2009/091015/09/

Metropolitan Police Service (2009a) 'Home is where the harm is', *The Job*. Retrieved on 15 July 2010 from http://www.met.police.uk/job/job1008/the_job_38.pdf

Metropolitan Police Service (2009b) '25 Years on ... SOIT Officers look back on progress in education', *The Job*. Retrieved on 15 July 2010 from http://www.met.police.uk/job/job1012/the_job_42.pdf

Metropolitan Police Service (2010) *Specialist Crime, Forensic Services, Sexual Offences Development Team*. Retrieved on 29 July 2010 from http://www.met.police.uk/scd/specialist_units/forensic_services.htm

Neufeld, P. and Scheck, B. (2010) 'Making forensic science more scientific', *Nature*, 464(7287): 351.

Noble, T. (2007) *An investigation into the psychological well-being of SOIT officers within the Metropolitan Police Service*. Thesis submitted to the University of Hertfordshire for the degree of Doctor of Clinical Psychology.

Opinion Matters (2010) Wake up to rape research summary report. Prepared by Opinion Matters for The Havens. Retrieved on 15 September 2010 from http://www.thehavens.co.uk/docs/Havens-WakeupToRapeRepoortSummary.pdf

Orth, U. (2002) 'Seconary victimisation of crime victims by criminal proceedings', *Social Justice Research*, 15: 313–25.

Payne, S. (2009) *Rape: The victim experience review*. London: Home Office.

Police and Criminal Evidence Act (1984) 'Code D Codes of Practice for the Identification of Persons by Police Officers'. Retrieved on 29 July 2010 from http://www.homeoffice.gov.uk/publications/police/operational-policing/pace-codes/pace-code-d?view=Binary

Regan, L., Kelly, L. and Ward, K. (2008) *Moving On Up? Evaluation of the Daffodils Sexual Assault Referral Centre*. Unpublished final report for funders (note the name is anonymised).

Rights of Women (2008) From report to court: A Handbook for adult survivors of sexual violence. Retrieved on 12 July 2010 from http://www.rightsofwomen.org.uk/pdfs.report%20to%20court%204%20web.pdf

Rincon, P. (201) *CSI shows give unrealistic view*. BBC News. Retrieved on 29 July 2010 from http:news.bbc.co.uk/1/hi/sci/tech/4284335.stm

Robinson, A. (2009) I*ndependent sexual violence advisors: a process evaluation*. Accessed on 12 June 2010 from 222.cardiff.ac.uk/people/robinson

Rock, P. (1988) 'Governments, victims and policies in two countries', *British Journal of Criminology*, 28(1): 44–66.

Rook, P.E.G. and Ward, K. (2004) *Rook and Ward on Sexual Offences: Law and Procedure* (3rd edn). London: Sweet and Maxwell.

Sampsel, K., Szobota, L., Joyce, D., Graham, K. and Pickett, W. (2009) 'The impact of sexual assault/domestic violence program on ED care', *Journal of Emergency Nursing*, 35(4): 282–9.

Schonbucher, V., Kelly, L. and Horvath, M.A.H. (2009) *Archway: Evaluation of the Pilot Scottish Rape and Sexual Assault Referral Centre*. Final report for Greater Glasgow and Clyde NHS Trust, June.

Scottish Executive/TNS System 3 (2007) *Findings from the Wave 10 Post-campaign Evaluation of the Domestic Abuse Campaign 2006/07*. Edinburgh: Scottish Executive.

Stanko, E., Paddick, B. and Osborn, D. (2005) *A Review of Rape Investigations in the Metropolitan Police Service*. December.

Stern, V. (2010) *The Stern Review*. Government Equalities Office. Retrieved on 10 July

2010 from http://www.equalities.gov.uk/PDF/Stern_Review_acc_FINAL.pdf

Stuart, J. (2006) 'Project Sapphire: Rape victims get justice', *The Independent*, 26 February. Retrieved on 10 July 2010 from http://www.independent.co.uk/news/uk/crime/project-sapphire-rape-victims-get-justice-467406.html

Temkin, J. (1999) 'Reporting rape in London: a qualitative study', *Howard Journal of Criminal Justice*, 38(1), 17-41.

The Justice Awards (2007) *CPS team wins award for historic rape convictions*. Retrieved on 1 July 2010 from http://www.cps.gov.uk/news/press_releases/171_07/

Tong, S., Bryant, R. and Horvath, M.A.H. (2009) *Understanding Criminal Investigation*. West Sussex, UK: Wiley.

Tyler, T.R. (2006) 'Viewing CSI and the threshold of guilt: Managing truth and justice in reality and fiction', *The Yale Law Journal*, 115: 1050–85.

Wambaugh, J. (1989) *The Blooding*. London, Bantam.

Women's National Commission (1986) *Violence against Women: Report of WNC working party*. London: WNC.

Women's Resource Centre and Rape Crisis (2008) *The Crisis in Rape Crisis: A survey of Rape Crisis (England and Wales) Centres*. London: Women's Resource Centre.

Yexley, M. (2008) *Metropolitan Police Authority Rape Update*, 10 April. Retrieved on 5 July from http://www.mpa.gov.uk/committees/x-ppr/2008/080410/08/?qu=soit&sc=2&ht=1

Yexley, M. (2009a) *Metropolitan Police Authority Rape Performance Update*, 12 March. Retrieved on 5 July 2010 from http://www.mpa.gov.uk/committees/cep/2009/090312/09/?qu=haven&sc=2&ht=1

Yexley, M. (2009b) *MPA Domestic and Sexual Violence Board report on the Sexual Abuse of Disabled People*, 28 July. Retrieved on 5 July 2010 from http://www.mpa.gov.uk/dsvb/2009/090728/06/?qu=cold%20case&sc=2&ht=1

*Youth Justice and Criminal Evidence Act* (1999) London: OPSI.

# Chapter 6

# Practitioner commentary: a police perspective[1]

*Sharon Stratton*

## Meet Sharon Stratton

Sharon has been a police officer with the Metropolitan Police Service (MPS) for over 30 years. For the past 13 years she has worked predominantly in the area of domestic violence, honour-related violence and sexual violence, both as an investigator on a specialist team and subsequently on a team developing strategy, policy, training and initiatives to improve service delivery and advising on the police response in relation to these subject areas. She sits on the Home Office and London Domestic Homicide review panels. Sharon assisted in the development of the DASH 2009 domestic violence risk assessment tool (see Richards *et al.* 2008) as a member of the Association of Chief Police Officers (ACPO) risk expert panel and has delivered training for the tool across many agencies in the UK. She is co-author with Laura Richards and Simon Letchford of a book entitled *Policing Domestic Violence* (2008), part of Blackstone's practical policing series, published by Oxford University Press.

## Introduction

I have been asked to provide commentary on the first five chapters of this book from a practitioner perspective and will concentrate specifically on domestic rather than stranger sexual violence, although there are fundamental similarities for the management and investigation of all serious sexual offending.

The chapters on the legacy of sexual violence in history, historical literature and legal heritage I have taken together. Each chapter is extremely emotive and thought-provoking in its own right but nevertheless they prompt similar responses in their usefulness in relation to contemporary policing. The chapters provide context to the journey, along a social, political and legal course, to understanding current attitudes and practices. The chapters also provide an explanation for society's present response to domestic and sexual violence, how some of the earlier attitudes still prevail and what needs to be done for continuous improvement. Bringing together such a wealth of learning and knowledge over time into one read should prove essential to professionals hoping to specialise in these areas of investigative practice. Traditionally, police training has had little input from external sources but the availability of this material as a pre-read to police training for specialist sexual violence investigation will be extremely beneficial.

Improvements in the police response to sexual violence, in partnership with other agencies, including sexual assault referral centres (SARCs),[2] the CPS and other support services, are outlined in Chapter 5 by Miranda Horvath and Mark Yexley and provide a welcome relief after the preceding chapters, which present a particularly daunting and somewhat adverse description of the treatment of victims of sexual violence. Horvath and Yexley explain that now when a victim decides to disclose a sexual assault to police, the response by the criminal justice system is less oppressive and more supportive throughout the process. They discuss the importance of partnership working alongside SARCs and Havens to encourage victims to access support, particularly when they might be at a point where they do not want to report to police. Recent joint working with the Haven in Paddington has involved the training and implementation of the DASH 2009 risk assessment tool for domestic cases to be completed with victims who are present at the service, with referral to an IDVA (independent domestic violence adviser) service in high-risk cases or in other cases where this is requested by the victim. However, their chapter does not emphasise sufficiently that prevention of domestic violence and sexual violence extends beyond the criminal justice system and cannot be the responsibility of any one agency alone; rather several agencies are needed in a co-ordinated community response, with the same key messages of intolerance to violence.

Horvath and Yexley discuss the history of police training and I have distinct memories of dealing with calls in relation to domestic abuse in the early 1980s when our response as police officers was limited to providing details of local solicitors. We rarely recorded allegations and in cases where there had been an assault, if the response to the question 'Are you willing to go to court?' was 'No', then we would do no more than perhaps ask the perpetrator to stay elsewhere for the night. Training in domestic violence was limited to the process of dealing with civil disputes. Early courses established for sexual offences investigative techniques officers (SOITs) for dealing with victims of sexual abuse were confined to victim care and statement taking with little training for officers in relation to investigation. Chapter 5 outlines how the police response has changed since the 1980s with the role of the STO pivotal to the investigation. The STO is now expected to respond to a report of serious sexual offending in London within an hour of the contact and will be expected to remain in contact with that victim throughout the investigation and beyond. They are the conduit between the investigator and the victim, providing a two-way flow of information on the progress of the investigation and the victim's wishes.

In the 1990s, prompted by women's support groups and academic research, the Home Office issued a circular (60/1990)[3] for domestic violence, encouraging police services to:

- take a more interventionist approach in domestic violence cases – with a presumption in favour of arrest;
- ensure that domestic violence crimes are recorded and investigated in the same way as other violent crimes;
- adopt a more sympathetic and understanding attitude towards victims of domestic violence.

Early initiatives included the establishment of units, generally consisting of one or two female officers developing links with partner agencies and providing a support role, with cases being dealt with by response officers or appointed investigation officers. However, there was still an absence of in-depth training for police on this subject.

It was not until 1997 that the MPS introduced Community Safety Units[4] responsible for the investigation of hate crime and domestic abuse. Systems were developed to enable the recording and flagging of cases. Multi-agency forums were developed to ensure that the support of victims was paramount in the local response across stakeholder agencies. The introduction of these units has served to professionalise the police response in the protection of victims of domestic violence and ensure that perpetrators are held to account.

The MPS works to the Association of Chief Police Officers (ACPO) definition of domestic violence as:

> Any incident of threatening behaviour, violence or abuse (psychological, physical, sexual, financial or emotional) between adults who are or who have been intimate partners or family members, regardless of gender.

This definition was updated in 2004 to define adults as over 18, define family members and include any sexual orientation, and remains current.[5]

Early communication strategies with our partners, from both the voluntary and the statutory sector, were aimed at encouraging reporting. They included:

- introducing referral processes;
- launching various media campaigns;
- setting up third party reporting sites;
- holding London conferences (specifically the launch of the MPS domestic violence (DV) strategy 'Enough is Enough' 2001 conference);
- publication of academic research, e.g. *The Day to Count: a snapshot of the impact of domestic violence in the UK on September 28, 2000* (Stanko 2000).

Professor Betsy Stanko, when Director of the Economic and Social Research Council's Programme on Violence at the Royal Holloway, University of London, organised a census of agencies around the United Kingdom to analyse how much of their work was related to domestic violence.

This activity served to build trust and confidence in victims to report to police. Rates of reporting in the MPS increased from 9,000 incidents in 1997 to a little short of 100,000 incidents in 2001. It was established that 25 per cent of homicides in London were as a result of domestic violence.

The demand placed on key service providers by domestic violence cases (one contact every six minutes within the MPS alone (Stanko 2000)) meant that it was important to find ways to respond appropriately to the different typologies of cases, nature of need and levels of risk. A multi-agency review process for domestic homicide in London was developed in 2001 with a view to establishing whether there were lessons to be learnt from the cases about the way in which local professionals and agencies worked together to safeguard victims of domestic violence, identifying clearly what those lessons were, and how they would be acted upon, and what was expected to change as a result and as a consequence to improve inter-agency working and provide better safeguards for victims.

In addition, research and analytical work on domestic serious violence and sexual assaults recorded by the MPS identified recurrent factors that were indicators to serious harm and homicide. This research, *Findings from the Multi-agency Domestic Violence Murder Reviews in London* (Richards 2003), and academic research were the main drivers for the development of the MPS DV risk assessment model (SPECSS+ model) and other strategies for prevention.

The research identified sexual assault as a high-risk factor with the following findings:

- Analysis of four months of domestic sexual assaults (2001) demonstrates that those who are sexually assaulted are subjected to more serious injury.
- Those who report a domestic sexual assault tend to have a history of domestic abuse whether or not it has been reported previously.
- One in 12 of all reported domestic sexual offenders are considered very high risk and potentially dangerous offenders (Richards 2003).
- Men who have sexually assaulted their partners and/or have demonstrated significant sexual jealousy are more at risk for violent recidivism.

(Stuart and Campbell 1989)

Implementation of the SPECSS+ model was underpinned by the publication of standard operating procedures for the investigation of domestic violence and introduction of an investigation booklet for response officers encouraging early evidence gathering, risk assessment and management and victim advice and support. The MPS embraced the need for training for domestic violence, introducing mandatory training for all response officers up to the rank of inspector.

Training and guidance on matters of domestic violence and sexual violence has improved dramatically in the past decade with forces developing training based on academia and learning, reviews of internal working practices, early national guidance for police, and more recently guidance and packages provided by the NPIA (National Police Improvement Agency). This training has now been incorporated into foundation training, specialist and leadership courses. Horvath and Yexley explain that in London, specialist teams were introduced in the late 1990s, known as Sapphire units, dedicated to the investigation of rape cases. These have now developed and been incorporated into the Specialist Crime Directorate alongside murder investigation teams, which gives a sense of how seriously rape is regarded within the MPS. In addition, a dedicated Crown Prosecution Service (CPS) charging unit for serious sexual assault works alongside those investigative teams to encourage early consultation to establish best evidence and appropriate charging decisions.

The ethos of police policy in relation to the domestic and serious sexual assault policies is that victims have a fundamental right to be believed; their safety and protection must remain paramount throughout the investigation; perpetrators must be held to account through the criminal justice system; and where a prosecution is deemed unfeasible then alternative courses of action, in consultation with partner agencies, to support victims aims to stop the violence and keep victims and their children safe. This activity is in addition to ensuring a focus on intelligence in relation to the perpetrator.

Specialist training for sexual violence for officers does not and should not concentrate solely on subjects of legislation, evidence gathering, case preparation, and so forth but, in order to professionalise the role of the investigator should discuss matters such as:

- dispelling urban myths and avoiding assumptions (e.g. rape myths);
- understanding why victims withdraw;
- appreciating the effects of experiencing sexual and domestic violence on victims and children;
- risk identification, assessment and management (specifically the DASH 2009 model, an amalgamation of existing DV 'risk tools');
- partnership working through Havens,[6] independent domestic and sexual violence advisers (IDVAs/ISVAs), multi-agency risk assessment conferences (MARACs)[7] and other specialist DV and SV agencies;
- typology of rapists;
- forensic strategies;
- advanced interviewing skills.

Where teams specialise it is important that there is 'cross-pollination' of training across areas of domestic, sexual and child abuse and other forms of violence against women, as they are intrinsically linked.

In London, local example studies of cases are used to make the training 'real' for officers, particularly when discussing risk assessment and management. Here Kelly's continuum of violence comes to the forefront when looking at high-profile offenders such as Levi Bellfield, Mark Dixie and Karl Taylor, where their violent and sexual offending started at home with their girlfriends and family, went unchallenged and escalated into homicide. (Interestingly it is reported that these three offenders met while remanded in Belmarsh prison and formed a gang called the Ladykillers (*The Sun*, 5 April 2008)). Cases are used to impress the importance of effective early intervention and how that might prevent escalation.

Specialist serious and complex investigative interviewing training is essential for officers to understand what we know of the 'psyche' of offenders. Input on this training is provided by external experts who have worked with or researched offenders to give some understanding on how they might react to certain questioning, how they might try to manipulate professionals, how they might view women based on personal or cultural effects of their upbringing and so on. Most important is the ability for investigating officers to use the detailed victim statement obtained by the STO (discussed at length by Miranda Horvath and Mark Yexley in Chapter 5) and any other corroborative evidence to 'close down' the defence of consent in rape cases. If the victim's statement covers in depth how the victim felt, reacted, what they were thinking, rather than just 'did they say yes or no'; and, similarly, if the behaviour of the offender from the victim's perspective is detailed within that statement, then this can have an extremely beneficial effect on the course of the interview.

The use of 'bad character' evidence (Criminal Justice Act 2003) or similar factual evidence and how to cover this in interview is also taught. This area of training is essential to many cases involving domestic and sexual violence where there may not have been many previous convictions, to ensure that the case is supported and appropriate sentencing is considered.

One case comes to mind whereby an officer discovered that despite just one conviction for harassment, an offender being dealt with for raping his current girlfriend and assaulting her young son had been the subject of civil court non-molestation orders[8] for rape and violence against several previous partners. The affidavits from the civil court formed the basis of a bad character application to the court. The victim in this case was extremely fearful of giving evidence at court and subsequently withdrew her support. Despite this, the case went ahead due to the seriousness and the risk posed by the offender. He was convicted and a pre-sentence report[9] requested. The allocated probation officer commented that had he not had sight of the report regarding the offender's previous unconvicted history, he might have been convinced that the offender was a victim of injustice, was a hard-working man, had many women who were infatuated by him and that this particular one was jealous, which was why she had brought the charge – as the offender would try to make him believe. After the offender was sentenced to four years in prison, his victim informed the officer that while the offender was in custody he had forced one of his ex-girlfriends to write a letter of withdrawal to the police, to visit the victim and force her to sign it and threaten her that if she did not drop the case she and her son would suffer severe consequences.

Advances in forensic technology and application have proved essential in the support of domestic violence and sexual violence cases, again clearly outlined by Horvath and Yexley. References to the historical requirement for corroboration, mentioned on more than one occasion in Chapter 3 by Joan McGregor and regarded as negative, are understandable because that probably related to the corroboration of an eyewitness. However, corroborative evidence can take many forms including the ability to 'match' forensic findings to a victim's statement, in order to refute any defence forthcoming in the perpetrators interview, and to interpret scenes (which includes the victim, offender and venue), CCTV footage, 999 call recordings, medical evidence, photography, statements of attending officers' observations, etc. Such evidence has enabled several cases to continue through the criminal justice system independently of the victim. Victims are more likely to feel supported through the criminal justice system if the case does not rely solely on their evidence, particularly in cases of domestic violence where the parties will be known to each other. The presence of forensic material might be used for 'interpretation' rather than 'identification'.

Routine DNA sampling of offenders on arrest is vital for identification, intelligence and prevention. The MPS cold case review team, discussed by Horvath and Yexley, were involved in an investigation in which a man arrested for assaulting his wife was swabbed for DNA. When the samples were submitted to the DNA database they were found to match samples recovered at the scenes of four stranger rapes some ten years previously. During a subsequent search of the offender's home address a divorce petition from a previous marriage was discovered in which the grounds for divorce were cited as sexual abuse.

Nevertheless, despite the improvement in policing there are still many real and perceived barriers to reporting for victims. For example, media approaches are not always helpful where the focus remains on the behaviour of the victim rather than the offender. The MPS approach to the domestic violence campaigns in more recent years has been to target offenders rather than victims. Campaigns containing straplines such as 'your partner's silence no longer protects you' and 'there are no safe houses for men who commit domestic violence' have been extremely successful in relaying the policing message. (See the example below.)

> **Relax, go ahead and read. No one on this platform can tell you're a wife beater.** You don't look like someone who would hit a woman. But then who does? Domestic violence is a crime committed by men from all walks of life. If you're abusing your partner, you should know that the Police no longer need her statement to make an arrest. If we have reasonable grounds, we will arrest you immediately. And, if you have left the scene, we will track you down. Remember, there are no longer any safe houses for men who commit domestic violence.

© MPA 2005

For many victims the fear of attending court is real. 'Special measures', including video-recorded evidence, live link, screens, private sitting, use of intermediaries and other methods of enabling a victim to give their evidence, are available in accordance with the Youth Justice and Criminal Evidence Act 1999.[10] These must be utilised whenever appropriate. The introduction of specialist domestic violence courts in London. where there is provision of advocacy for the victim, normally through an IDVA, trained district judges, police presence in court, secure seating areas, etc., has seen a significant increase in successful prosecutions.

Cultural matters across many different racial, ethnic and faith backgrounds have a significant part to play in the reluctance to report domestic or sexual violence. There may be mistrust in the police in people who come from countries where there is corruption or sexism within the police service. Victims may be isolated due to language barriers, insecure immigration status, no access to public funding, pressures to conform to patriarchal codes of behaviour, etc. For some, being raped is seen to bring shame on the family and wider community, and there are many examples where victims have reported and asked that no one in their family or community is made aware that they have been a victim of sexual assault because they will be ostracised or otherwise punished for bringing shame onto the family or community. This is concerning. The MPS has experienced significant success in increasing reporting, at the same time reducing seriousness in domestic violence (homicide rate for 2003/4 was 43 and decreased to 25 in 2009/10)[11], of the 25 domestic homicides in 2009/10, the majority of the 15 cases which were not known previously to police, or apparently any other agencies, involved those who were not British nationals. In addition, the practice of forced marriage often results in rape, and this brings to mind the references in Chapter 3 by Joan McGregor in relation to the historical requirement to prove force, which required evidence of physical force. In forced marriage the definition provided in the Government Multi-Agency Practice Guidelines for the Handling of Forced Marriage cases states:

> A forced marriage is a marriage in which one or both spouses do not (or, in the case of some adults with learning or physical disabilities, cannot) consent to the marriage and duress is involved. Duress can include physical, psychological, financial, sexual and emotional pressure.[12]

The use of the word duress and accompanying forms of behaviour is distinctly more appropriate than the word 'force', particularly in cases of rape where fear overcomes the victim's reactions. Agencies must work together to ensure that violence within isolated communities is being recognised and given an effective response. For the police, this responsibility is as much to do with neighbourhood policing to identify isolated victims, as it is with specialist units.

Finally, in Chapter 4, Sylvia Walby, Jo Armstrong and Sofia Strid discuss the various forms of measuring sexual violence and how data are presented in different ways. The recording of data in relation to domestic violence and sexual violence is crucial to inform strategy, intelligence, resourcing, performance, budgeting and many other aspects of policing, and yet this chapter demonstrates how difficult it is to obtain consistent and reliable data. How do we understand where the gaps in our service are and whether our prevention approach is effective, if a common data set for all domestic and sexual crime types, across services, is not available? The MPS has developed their recording practices for domestic violence significantly over the past few years, assisted by the clear definition outlined earlier in this chapter. Strategists and analysts with expertise in the area have worked closely with IT departments to ensure that crime-reporting systems have mandatory fields in areas such as equalities data, risk assessment, outcomes, repeat victimisation, methods and other information that can be easily retrieved using various formatted searches. However, the interface with CPS data remains problematic and there is still difficulty in retrieving the data for measuring 'offender brought to justice'.

When compiling business cases for new initiatives or commissioning services, data and cost benefits are important to the success of the bid, and ready access to this information, whether through academic research or local systems, should be available. Sylvia Walby's previous research on the *Cost of*

*Domestic Violence* (Walby 2004, updated 2009) has been particularly beneficial to the prevention work for domestic violence in the MPS, especially the cost to policing. Further breaking down of the cost of a homicide investigation sends the message to senior officers that the resourcing of the initial response, and further risk management, could make savings, when lives are saved as a result.

## Conclusion

These first five chapters provide us with an exceptional, if not depressing, insight into the historical cultural attitudes towards sexual violence. Change has been slow and there is still much to be done to create a society in which there is a distinct intolerance to all forms of violence against women. The overview in Horvath and Yexley of the improvements within the legal system in response to sexual violence is heartening. Communication among professionals working to prevent and respond to such cases is vital; we can learn so much from each other to advance our work and to ensure a co-ordinated community response when victims come forward. Media and other social networking facilities have an important part to play to ensure that the legacies of the past, as outlined in these chapters, do not continue to be promulgated and that the onus of responsibility for domestic and sexual violence is transferred from the victims of sexual violence to the perpetrators. Educating children from a young age to treat each other with respect and to develop healthy and equal relationships has an important part to play in eliminating such attitudes towards women, and to ensure a future healthy society where women are free from violence from partners, family members and strangers alike.

## Notes

1  The views expressed in this chapter are solely those of the author. They do not represent those of the Metropolitan Police Service.
2  http://www.dh.gov.uk/en/Publicationsandstatistics/Publications/PublicationsPolicy AndGuidance/DH_107570
3  http://ndvf.org.uk/files/document/1032/original.pdf
4  http://www.met.police.uk/csu/
5  http://www.acpo.police.uk/documents/crime/2008/2008004CRIIDA01.pdf
6  http://www.thehavens.co.uk/
7  http://www.caada.org.uk/
8  http://www.womensaid.org.uk/domestic-violence-survivors-handbook.asp?section= 000100010008000100330002
9  http://www.cps.gov.uk/legal/p_to_r/provision_of_pre_sentence_report_information/
10 http://www.cps.gov.uk/legal/s_to_u/special_measures/
11 MPS Performance Information Bureau, April 20101
12 http://www.fco.gov.uk/en/travel-and-living-abroad/when-things-go-wrong/forced-marriage/info-for-professionals

## References

Richards, L. (2003) *Findings from the Multi-agency Domestic Violence Murder Reviews in London*. London: Metropolitan Police.

Richards, L., Letchford, S. and Stratton, S. (2008) *Policing Domestic Violence*, part of Blackstones practical policing series. Oxford: Oxford University Press.

Stanko, E. (2000) 'The Day to Count: a snapshot of the impact of domestic violence in the UK on 28 September 2000', *Criminal Justice*, 1:2.

Stuart, E. and Campbell, J. (1989) 'Assessment of patterns of dangerousness with battered women', *Issues in Mental Health Nursing*, 10: 245–60.

Walby, S. (2004) *The Cost of Domestic Violence*. London: Women and Equality Unit.

Walby, S. (2009) *The Cost of Domestic Violence: Update 2009*. Lancaster: Lancaster University.

# Part Two

# Theoretical Perspectives on Sexual Violence

# Introduction

*Sandra Walklate and Jennifer Brown*

As Joan McGregor has illustrated in Chapter 3, the law has provided a crucial and contested framework that has historically informed how sexual violence has been understood and responded to: hence the significance of feminist informed campaigns of different theoretical persuasions that have focused on the importance of the law as a vehicle for change. However, as Smart (1989) cogently argued, changes in the law have not necessarily yielded the kinds of reforms that feminists were looking for. The contemporary persistence of attrition in cases of rape, even in countries where the law has been changed to make the act less penis- and heterosexual-centred and more accommodating of different weapons, orifices and sexualities, stands as testimony to the resistance of the law in theory to impact upon the law in practice. (See in particular Daly and Bouhours 2009; Lovett and Kelly 2009.) Part of the explanation for that continued resistance lies with the central preoccupation of the law with incidents, and the provision of evidence associated with particular incidents, as opposed to the processes that comprise real life. This preoccupation with incidents not only drives how the law itself makes sense of the cases brought before it, but also informs much criminal justice practice. In cases of sexual violence this classically presents itself as 'her word against his' and the need for corroborative evidence to support 'her words'. Given the seriousness of the likely punishment outcomes for a defendant found guilty of rape, such a concern with evidence 'beyond reasonable doubt' is perhaps understandable but not necessarily in and of itself defensible. In this part of this book we gain an insight into how disciplines outside of the law frame sexual violence, and the implications that these different ways of thinking might have for criminal justice practice.

The emphasis here then is on how different theoretical perspectives define and understand sexual violence. We are primarily concerned with what can be gained from appreciating the commonalities and differences between different disciplinary takes on sexual violence and what can be learned about the nature and extent of sexual violence if we adopt an interdisciplinary position on this topic. Thus by implication this section of the book challenges disciplinary boundaries and pushes at the limits that they have historically imposed upon work in this area. Here we have four different disciplinary contributions. Helen Jones considers the kinds of sociological questions that the problem of sexual violence poses. Jennifer Brown offers an overview of psychological perspectives. Arlene Vetere takes us through an appreciation of how a clinician might approach sexual violence and Jo Phoenix looks to consider the nature of our understandings of sexual violence that occurs when the sexual is conjoined with the economic as in prostitution. Ruth Mann considers the efficacy of these different perspectives for criminal justice practice. Each of these different perspectives poses different questions for Kelly's concept of continuum and, as we shall see, each adds further subtle and nuanced dimensions to our understanding of it.

In Chapter 8, Helen Jones asks a very clear and straightforward question: what can sociological analysis tell us about sexual violence? She offers us a way of thinking about an answer to this question through addressing what kinds of light the classic sociological perspectives might throw on it. In doing this she provides us with three different ways of answering: by considering what function sexual violence performs for society; who benefits from it, and what understandings are attached to it. At the heart of Jones's analysis of each of these answers is the problem of measurement and what is included and excluded when researchers proceed to measure the nature and extent of sexual violence. (This also resonates with some of the issues raised by Jan Jordan in Chapter 12.) For Jones, the historical exclusion of sexual violence in the context of war is particularly problematic in this respect (adding a significant dimension to Kelly's work), but perhaps more significantly for a sociological analysis is that, in her view, violence evades definition at all if it is not recognised as rooted in the structural foundations of societal behaviour. Hence the need to reflect on the myths that surround rape that also support those structural foundations, at the centre of which, she suggests, is the notion of the ideal family. This family is classically formed around a heterosexual (married) partnership and is especially focused on child rearing. It is an image that erases anything problematic associated with such family life and is a concept on which much sociological and policy responses to rape have been built.

In a somewhat different vein, though interestingly posing a similar question to Jones, Jennifer Brown, in Chapter 7, starts by asking us to think about what Kelly's concept of continuum presumes to be 'normal' in the context of sexual violence. Brown takes Kelly's conceptual approach forward by arguing that whilst it is not tenable to say that all sexual violence is committed by those deemed 'mad' or abnormal, by the same token it is not viable to adopt the position that such violence is all routinised and normal. Taking five categories of sexual violence (that resonate with the acts of sexual violence subjected to detailed scrutiny within this book), Brown explores the common features between them (unacknowledged victimisation that echoes the work of Jan Jordan, under-reporting that is also commented on by Helen Jones, and perceptions of false allegations) but proceeds then to analyse these acts in terms of what it is that is known about their perpetrators. In a fascinating analysis of existing knowledge of offenders, Brown offers us a complex but none the less meaningful framework for making sense of the ways in which different types of sexual violence are overlaid with different kinds of offenders and the ways in which these may or may not shade into one another. So, for example, stalking behaviour may relate to murder and rape in a different way to the way in which stalking behaviour relates to domestic violence. Moreover, whilst Brown's analysis is heavily reliant on what is known psychologically about known offenders, she nevertheless makes a convincing case for a more inclusive definition of sexual violence concerning who can do what to whom.

Arlene Vetere, in Chapter 9, is also concerned with known offenders but from a clinical perspective. Interestingly, at the centre of her approach are three concepts: risk, responsibility and collaboration. All of which are worked through as a process with the parties concerned. The focus on process is key to the establishment of a sound working relationship with the people they are concerned with. The aim of this working relationship is to produce a reflective space in which the individuals themselves can come to terms with their responsibility for their violent behaviour. In an interesting example, one man who had hit his daughter in contravention of their 'no violence contract' commented, 'but I didn't hit you like a man'. This distancing from responsibility for violence is also observed by Kewley in Chapter 17 and is also raised by Ruth Mann in Chapter 11. The ability to recognise, embrace and to challenge such distancing practices in such a way that perpetrators recognise their responsibility for their behaviour is considered central to the success of clinical interventionist work. None of this implies making excuses for violence but does involve recognising the processes that result in violence, trying to understand them and what triggers a violent response; whether that be excessive use of alcohol or what Vetere refers to as the 'paradox of power'. This paradox is a way of trying to capture how the use of violence may be born out of fear but results in the victim nevertheless feeling the offender's power. Whilst more relationship-focused than other perspectives so far discussed, this clinical approach nevertheless recognises the gendered nature of sexual violence alongside the perspectives discussed by Jones and Brown. The gendered nature of sexual violence is also the starting point for Jo Phoenix's analysis of the relationship between sexual violence and economics.

In Chapter 10 Phoenix encourages us to think very hard about the ways in which prostitution, as an institution, blurs the boundaries between behaviour regarded as intimate and private and an activity (like paying for a service) usually regarded as public, like economics and associated regulatory activities. In the context of the violence that occurs as part of prostitution as an institution, Phoenix argues that Kelly's concept of a continuum conflates as much as it reveals. This she suggests results from the fact that Kelly's work, whilst hugely impactive in shifting thinking on violence that centred women's experiences, was ahistorical and asocial. Phoenix raises these issues as significant since the tendency with work on prostitution is to prioritise the selling of sex as problematic. This does two things: first it denies the reality of prostitution as an institution that perhaps more accurately needs to be referred to as 'prostitutions'; and, second, it silences questions around the impact of both regulatory activities and economic drivers on those women who choose to sell sex. As a result 'sex worker' becomes the 'master' status that denies other aspects of both women's lives and the institution in which they work. The denial of the structurally specific context in which women make these kinds of choices is problematic since it is this structural specificity that is key to understanding the relationship between sexual violence and economics. It is the lack of structural specificity that Phoenix finds problematic with the concept of a continuum. Such a call for 'analytical specificity' enables us to situate the violence that occurs under these circumstances in the context of wider cultural processes (for example, changes in attitudes about what might be considered 'degrading' in terms of sexuality, suggesting some resonance with the position adopted by Jones) and within the specific context of women's lives: women who (rather like the subjects of Matza's 1964 classic study of young delinquents) may drift in and out of prostitution as their economic needs dictate. Phoenix's analysis in no way suggests that extreme violence does not occur (like that for example documented by Anette Ballinger in Chapter 14) but she is suggesting that it is important not to conflate prostitutions into prostitution, or prostitute into prostitutes. The latter, of course, in particular results in male prostitution being hidden both for men and for women.

Throughout this part of the book evident tensions emerge between the different disciplinary levels of analysis classically articulated, particularly by the inevitable inherently different emphases offered by psychology as opposed to sociology. This tension is particularly captured in Ruth Mann's practitioner commentary around the question of responsibility. If it is accepted that the individual is responsible for their offending behaviour, that carries with it quite different implications than if it is accepted that responsibility lies at the level of societal values. Carefully situating her exploration of this kind of tension within the hotly contested debates as to whether offender treatment for sexual offences in particular is about punishment, rehabilitation, or what she calls 'professional quackery', Mann suggests that there is some value in getting men to challenge their own behaviours without rendering them deviant or abnormal. The is a position that lends some weight to Brown's thoughtful analysis of matching what is known about particular offenders and their propensity for committing particular kinds of sexual crimes.

Taken together these chapters draw our attention to three themes: the problem of definition; the problem of measurement; and the efficacy of Kelly's work. In what follows we shall say a little about each of these themes in turn.

## The problem of definition

All the contributors allude to this in different ways. Vetere addresses this most explicitly. Her clinical and therapeutic approach demands a non-judgemental stance towards behaviour in order to ensure the participation of the family or couple for whom violence is a problem. However, from her approach we get an important message: violence needs to be understood in its context, particularly if the desire is to change the nature of the violence perceived to be problematic. This, of course, is a highly individualistic approach to understanding violence. As Jones also points out, violence is societal. What is considered to be acceptable and/or unacceptable (sexual) violence (as in times of war for example) is structural and political. Thus individual behaviour maybe validated in some politico-structural moments in time and not in others. Moreover, as both Jones and Phoenix comment, what is understood as sexual violence is also cultural. Our contemporary understandings of acceptable and unacceptable sexual violence needs to be set against a backcloth of changing social attitudes towards sex (the cultural drive for more and better sex might be a case in point) in which what might be considered degrading and by implication abusive some time ago may not be the case contemporarily. In a different way, Brown too is concerned with definitional issues, but in this case in the context of offenders. The need to differentiate different kinds of violences (a point that is well developed by Sylvia Walby and colleagues in Chapter 4) that differentiate different types of offenders, whose behaviour may become overlaid in some kinds of crime and not others, adds an important dimension to our understanding of what sexual violence actually means and to whom.

## The problem of measurement

Logically following on from definitional issues, there are clearly problems with measurement: who does what to whom and when. The nature and extent of sexual violence has been historically a moot point between feminist-informed research and more 'official' statistics on this issue. Classically stemming from the outrage caused by the work of Amir (1971), who in analysing police data on rape suggested that in one in five cases the woman precipitated what had happened to her, feminists have worked hard to challenge not only the conceptual basis of such work, but also what it is that police statistics actually record. Adopting survey methodologies that asked women about their lifetime experiences, this work clearly pointed to not only the conceptual shortcomings of the notion of precipitation but also the shortcomings in assuming what is was that police statistics actually captured. Lifetime experiences of sexual violence suggest a picture of its nature and extent that far outweighed the picture presented by the police. More recently, as Jones points out, criminal victimisation surveys, and international violence against women surveys, have become increasingly more sophisticated and sensitive in their capacity to measure the extent of sexual violence and that data illustrates that it is for the most part a behaviour that men direct towards women. What is less clear is the extent to which this constitutes the complete picture. All the contributors here have been careful to point out that whilst there is increased awareness contemporarily of both homosexual as well as heterosexual sexual violence between men, between women, and committed by women on men, with perhaps the exception of some work done with prison inmates and that produced by campaign groups like Stonewall, our vision of this kind of sexual violence is severely distorted by the lens of heterosexuality assumed in much mainstream measurement work. Thus whilst the sexual violence has been sexed, it remains to be truly gendered.

**The value of Kelly's continuum**

What is particularly interesting about each of the contributions to this part of the book is not only the importance that they all attach to the intervention made by Kelly in the 1980s in significantly shifting both the conceptual and empirical debate forwards on the question of sexual violence, but also the way in which each of them adds to and develops this intervention. This is despite the fact that each of these interventions starts from a very different place. Jones, for example, adds to Kelly's continuum by adding breadth of understanding to the way in which societal conditions condone sexual violence ranging from cultural presumptions relating to sexual mutilation through to rape and murder in times of war. These additions remind us of the myriad ways in which sex is used to control both individuals as well as populations. Brown, on the other hand, adds conceptual depth to Kelly's work by thinking through the implications for our understandings of offenders. Her intervention challenges the normalisation of a relationship between men and sexual violence by problematising both types of violences and their link with types of offenders. Thus we are left with the view that neither are all known offenders mad nor are they all potentially capable of the same kinds of offending behaviour. In a very different way Vetere embraces an appreciation of the processes that underpin both the expression of sexual violence and its therapeutic management. This perspective reminds us that even in violent relationships there are other interpersonal dynamics that bind people together. So, whilst one aspect of their behaviour might be problematic, it does not mean that they are totally 'mad' or 'bad' but can be worked with, encouraged to reflect on their behaviour and change. Finally, but by no means least, Phoenix's discussion offers a serious challenge to the conflation of sexual violences found in the way in which the intimate and the economic become bound together within prostitution. Arguing for context specificity in our understandings of the relationship between sexual violence and prostitution, her analysis reminds us that prostitution is quite a complex business in which the image of the prostitute as victim is only one part. All contributions point to the contemporary recognition that the relationship between sex and the recourse to sexual violence is not sex or heterosexual specific, offering further enhancement to the contribution of Kelly. However, where they all agree is in the recognition that gender is one key problem that underpins sexual violence(s).

**Conclusion: gendered inequality**

Each of these contributions in their different ways centre gendered inequality as significant in the production of social relationships that produce sexual violence, whether that inequality is at the level of the interpersonal or at the level of the structural. Whilst Kelly's work was part of a significant shift in attention from a focus on victim blaming to a focus on naming men as not only responsible for but with a vested interest in the sexual control of women, since that time our understandings of the nature and extent of gendered inequality have become both wider and subtler all at the same time. As other chapters in this book illustrate, our appreciation of workplace harassment or the use of cyberspace as sites of violence have emerged, as has our appreciation of the ways in which that has been manifested. At the same time much more work needs to be done on the specific ways in which gender (not sex) is utilised as a resource in the different contexts in which sexual violence manifests itself. How gendered inequality is handled, however, is also cross-cut by other structural variables, whether that be class, ethnicity, or sexuality. Each of these cross-cutting relationships produce visibilities and invisibilities in who is seen to be doing what to whom and when. There is still a long way to go before we fully understand how and when gender, as opposed to any other variable, is the salient one that results in some people (male and female) becoming victims or perpetrators of sexual violence.

## References

Amir, M. (1971) *Patterns of Forcible Rape*. Chicago: Chicago University Press.

Daly, K. and Bouhours, B. (2009) 'Rape and attrition in the legal process: a comparative analysis of five countries'. Forthcoming in *Crime and Justice: An Annual Review of Research*, 39. Downloaded October 2010.

Lovett, J. and Kelly, L. (2009) *Different Systems: Similar Outcomes*. London Metropolitan University: CWASU.

Matza, D. (1964) *Delinquency and Drift*. New York: John Wiley.

Smart, C. (1989) *Feminism and the Power of Law*. London: Routledge.

# Chapter 7

# Psychological perspectives on sexual violence: generating a general theory

*Jennifer Brown*

## Introduction

This chapter takes a psychological perspective on sexual violence. In particular it looks at theoretical levels of analysis against the background provided by Kelly's (1988) conceptualisation of the continuum of violence. The chapter will argue that Kelly's formulation, which is articulated in terms of quantum, i.e. a prevalence continuum, is helpful at the descriptive stage of theorising but is limited in terms of explanation and predictive requirements of theory. The present chapter offers a qualitative addition to Kelly's thinking as a way to develop our understanding of the different types of sexual violence; and, further, challenges Kelly's conceptualisation of sexual violence as being solely normalised rather than pathologised.

Marx (2005) outlines what we know about sexual violence after 20 years of research (see Box 7.1).

This suggests that sexual violence is part of the routine of life and is something that most women experience in some shape or form. Indeed Kelly argues that sexual violence is connected to everyday aspects of male behaviour and cites as an example street sexual harassment where women are subjected to comments about their figures and/or lascivious wolf whistling while walking in public places. Sheridan *et al.* (2003: 150) note that 'stalking is an extraordinary crime, given that it may often consist of no more than the targeted repetition of an ostensibly ordinary or routine behaviour.' Kelly is critical of psychological explanations, which are couched in terms of an underlying pathology, because she suggests that violent behaviour being part of normal life as something to which women adapt or minimise is among the reasons for it remaining such an under-reported crime. She is also critical of research that identifies a plethora of subtypes of rapists together with a failure to link any pattern of personality characteristics causally to rape. This presents

---

**Box 7.1** Summary of findings from sexual violence research (Marx 2005)

1. Sexual violence is a common experience; lifetime prevalence in US suggests 20 per cent of all women will be victims of sexual violence.
2. It is a life-altering experience for those who experience it, effects can be pernicious and long lasting and include psychological, behavioural, and physical consequences (including STD, chronic pain disorders, anxiety, depression, substance misuse, sexual problems and interpersonal difficulties).
3. The validity of reports of sexual violence is often questioned and survivors blamed for their assault.
4. Consequences for survivors often trivialised or ignored by family members, friends, police, legal officials, and mental health professionals.
5. Stigma and shame attach to survivors.
6. Demographic factors are associated with severity of reactions as are previous sexual trauma, pre-existing psychiatric conditions, availability of social support, neurological functioning and peritraumatic variables.
7. Intervening treatments are not always successful (factors such as intense anger, disassociation, substance abuse, personality disorders, inability to emotionally engage associated with failure to respond to treatment).
8. Risk of sexual assault is not evenly distributed: previous childhood sexual abuse is a strong predictor of subsequent sexual victimisation (also maladaptive coping, affect regulation difficulties, maladaptive interpersonal behaviours, and difficulties in recognising threats).
9. Cognitive therapies found to be particularly efficacious.

---

areas for discussion as there clearly are issues relating to the pathologising–normalising dimension underpinning sexual violence to which this chapter addresses itself. Notwithstanding the routinised nature of sexually violent behaviours and the unreported nature of victim experiences, the emphasis in the present chapter will focus on subcategories of crime within the spectrum of sexual violence and demonstrate that there is a range of offenders including those who manifest personality-disordered pathologies.

Another implication of Marx's summary of findings is the often minimalising or ignoring of claims of sexual violence victimisation. Implied but not stated is also the perception that many claims are believed to be false. The chapter will show that assertions of false allegations are common to all forms of sexual violence.

## Definitional framing

Kelly offers the following definition of sexual violence:

> any physical, visual, verbal or sexual act that is experienced by the woman or girl at the time or later as a threat, invasion or assault that has

the effect of hurting her or degrading her and/or takes away her ability
to control intimate contact.

(Kelly 1988: 41)

Clearly her focus is on women and girls as resisters of and copers with the
exertion of male controlling power in the form of sexualised violence.
Moreover, the definition is contextualised by the idea that the sexualised
violence takes away women's sexual autonomy. There are problems with
anchoring the definition in this way. It is certainly the case that there is a
gender disparity in terms of the victims and perpetrators of sexual violence.
Ministry of Justice Statistics for 2008/9 show, on the one hand, the pattern of
victimisation in England and Wales for those between 16 and 59 years of age
(Figure 7.1), where clearly women are the more likely targets both in terms of
lifetime prevalence and current cases. On the other hand in 2007/8 0.3 per cent
(838) of women had been arrested for a sexual offence compared with 2.5 per
cent (31,178) of men.

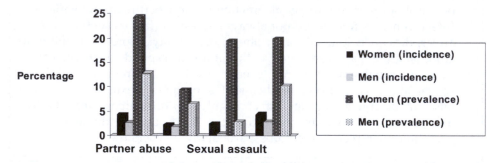

**Figure 7.1** Incidence and prevalence (since 16 years of age) of intimate violence
experienced in 2008/09 in England and Wales

However, there are female perpetrators of sexual violence as shown by
these figures and male victims (Abdullah-Khan 2008: Wijkman *et al.* 2010).
There is also violence within same-sex relationships (Hester *et al.* 2010). Bartol
and Bartol (2008) report rates as high as 44 per cent of gay men and 56 per
cent of gay women suffering some form of physical abuse. They note that prepubescent girls are thought to commit sexual offences at a much higher rate
that commonly supposed. Moreover, there are other consequences of
sexualised violence as well as the threats to choices about what sex to have,
with whom and when, such as damage to personal or community
relationships (Giner-Sorolla and Russell 2009).

Kelly makes it clear that the range of behaviours defined by those
experiencing sexual violence are neither reflected in legal codes nor in
researchers' analytic categories. She conceptualised a continuum of sexual
violence comprising:

• threats of violence;
• sexual harassment;
• pressure to have sex;

- sexual assault;
- obscene phone calls;
- coercive sex;
- domestic violence;
- flashing;
- rape;
- incest.

She argues that these specific forms of sexual violence do not have strict boundaries, rather they 'shade into' one another (pp 75, 132) such that there are no clean, discrete analytic categories or straight lines connecting different experiences of sexual violence. Furthermore, the continuum does not imply either a linear progression or progressive seriousness; rather she presents the continuum as a quantum, i.e. of prevalence to underscore their derivation from normal routines of life. She argues that there are three common underlying dimensions: violence is physical and/or sexual; abuse involves single or multiple events; assaults can be by people known or unknown to the victim. However, given Kelly's conditions and exceptions, it is difficult to extract the explanatory power of the continuum. First there are the problematics of the meaning of the verbal labels and second the meaning attached to the frequencies. Helen Jones, in Chapter 8 of this Handbook, discusses the symbolic importance of language that describes sexual violence and cautions against terminology that may obscure rather than clarify. Kelly's conceptualisation seems to assume a degree of equivalence in the categories that masks subcategories nested within assigned labels. In other words obscene phone calls are a rather specific behaviour whereas sexual harassment is much broader and indeed may include obscene phone calls. Stalking has been conceptualised as a form of domestic violence rather than as a discrete category (Mullen *et al.* 2000). So Kelly's categories are not mutually exclusive and some are higher order categories which can themselves be broken down into more specific behaviours. What do the numbers mean other than rate of reported occurrence if the categories are neither progressively more serious nor linked in some way? That some kinds of sexual violence occur more often than others is not in itself explaining very much. There is research to suggest that previous behaviour can indeed predict escalation in terms of rising levels, increasing episodes and shorter gaps between episodes and was found to predict murder in domestic violent relationships (Campbell *et al.* 2003). Wyre and Swift (1990: 55) suggest that 'men who commit [obscene phone calls] may be at the beginning of a career of sexual offending destined to take them to rape and even murder.' Salfati (2008) proposes, with respect to homicide, that frequency of behaviours related to an underlying dimension of impulsiveness. Thus high-frequency behaviours such as multiple wounds confined to a relatively small area of the body, or the body being found face up and uncovered, suggested a degree of impulsivity rather than planning, with an emotional component rather than being organised. Low frequency behaviours had a more instrumental theme, bringing a weapon to the scene, taking property from the scene. Offenders engaging in these rarer behaviours were also more likely to exhibit a greater degree of forensic awareness and attempted to cover their tracks, implying a level of pre-planning. Thus, for Salfati, the continuum of frequencies is where 'the offender reacts in an impulsive way towards the emotions engendered through the conflictual interpersonal relationship with the victim, to where the offender interacts with the victim much more at a removed level, both physically and emotionally' (p. 509). This then attempts to provide an explanatory level of analysis to the frequency of the behaviours' occurrence.

This chapter will argue that there is a need to conceptually distinguish types of sexual violence and that there are not only common but also category-specific behaviours associated with different types of sexual violence. Moreover, similar behaviours may span the range of broader categories, e.g. threats may appear in sexual harassment, domestic violence and rape. Psychological theorising does provide a way to make such qualitative distinctions between high-frequency behaviours which are common to all manifestations of sexual violence, the more specific manifestations of sexual violation, and rarer idiosyncratic or individualised personal violation (Canter 2000). Psychological analysis also permits distinctions to be made of offender types, including those with specific pathologies, within different kinds of sexual violence. This is helpful both as a basis for treatment interventions and predictions about likely escalation and crossover between classes of violence. While it is recognised that it is not sensible to say that sexual violence is only committed by the mad, neither is it tenable to locate all sexual violence as arising from the routine and the normal.

The chapter then examines psychological theories and concepts against the backdrop of Kelly's continuum formulation. Five specific types of sexualised violence are discussed: sexual harassment, domestic violence, stalking, rape and sexual murder. The stance taken here is to look more closely at offenders and their behaviours as well as motivations and other postulated causal factors. While some support for the idea of a continuum is found, it is argued here that there is a case for a richer conceptual differentiation with offenders/ perpetrators either maintaining strict boundaries that limit their behaviour within a category of offence or overlapping offence categories and escalating in severity.

Finally, it is worth noting that the discussion in this chapter is for the most part limited to criminalised behaviour, not least because of the under-reporting problems and difficulties in obtaining data from the general population about non-reported sexual violence alluded to earlier.

## Explanatory framing

The critical reason for theorising is to answer the 'why' question (Breakwell and Rose 2000: 5). Meloy (2007: 1) sets one question related to sexual violence: 'Why on earth would someone want to pursue another who shows absolutely no interest in his or her attentions?' Ward *et al.* (2006) present other 'why?' questions, such as why would men force a woman to have sex when she is drunk or asleep and ignore her obvious distress? Why are adults sexually interested in young children? They suggest that there are practical implications in gaining the answers to these questions. Clinicians need clear descriptions of the phenomena they are dealing with and an understanding of the aetiological factors if their interventions are to be effective. Arlene Vetere (this volume) discusses the importance of such clarity if parties to intimate violence are to engage in effective conflict reduction and resolution. Thus treatment deliverers should address different motivations for offending and be aware of the different pathways to reoffending. McEwan *et al.* (2009) argue that to facilitate prompt and targeted interventions, in relation to stalking, clinicians need to conduct risk assessments to predict likely duration, escalation and recidivism rates. Proclivities in offending behaviours also have implications for supervisory arrangements. An offender convicted of child molestation may reoffend with an adult or vice versa (Cann *et al.* 2007). Others (e.g. Canter and Heritage 1990; Canter 2000; Canter and Fritzon 1998; Salfati 2008) suggest that understanding the behaviours may aid police investigations by indicating important variations between crimes that relate to differences between the people who commit them and allow inferences to be made about the likely offender. Offenders differ in their actions, intentions and motivations (Canter and Heritage 1990) and behavioural investigative advice requires accurate information regarding patterns to predict both escalation within and serial offending (Cann *et al.* 2007). Macpherson (2003) for example notes the importance of predicting those who escalate from non-contact sexual offences to sexual violence involving physical contact. Post-conviction restrictions need to be conversant with the full array of risk (Oliver *et al.* 2007) and, as Hanson and Bussiére (1998), argue, it is important to assess chronicity in order to target those more likely to reoffend. Meloy (2007) states that 'why?' questions help to set the research agenda.

Before these questions can be addressed, we need to be clear about what phenomena we are talking about, hence the requirement for clear definitions.

## Definitions

Definitions are not unproblematic (Sheridan *et al.* 2003) and there are differences between legal and research codifications and what is psychologically meaningful to victims (which may result in a failure of congruence between the scholarly, legal and personal). Some theorists offer rather global and undifferentiated definitions of 'women abuse' such as DeKeseredy and Kelly (1993) (not Liz Kelly). Liz Kelly herself suggests a range of behaviours across the spectrum of sexual violence. As discussed above, there are some problems about the descriptive status of the labels she uses. The approach that is often taken by psychologists is to look at both internal motivations of offenders/perpetrators and the different behaviours they engage in, in order to differentiate between offence types and within offence, different types of offenders. Early researchers devised taxonomies of assailants, such as Groth *et al.* (1977) who described rapists in terms of anger or power, creating four motivational types: excitation anger, retaliation anger, power reassurance, power dominance, and a fifth opportunistic type. Prentky and Knight (1991) further distinguished the opportunistic into high and low social competency and added a sexual type. Horvath (2010: 546) critiques the typological approach by arguing that they do not take into account the means by which perpetrators effect the violence, they tend to conflate motivation and cognitions, they lack reliability and validity and assume that individuals fall into one type such that there is no scope for hybrid types or crossover from one type to another. Horvath concluded that as yet no taxonomy has been able consistently to discriminate between different groups of offenders. So while motivational taxonomies have helped to confirm some of the underlying reasons for committing sexually violent acts and permitted some further understanding of the role of power and anger, they have been limiting, as Kelly implies. If our focus shifts from internal processes to observable behaviours, then psychological enquiry suggests that underlying actions are themes that have some psychological significance (Salfati 2008). Thus Canter and Heritage (1990) described the themes of intimacy, violence, impersonal, criminality and sexuality underpinning rape which then are associated with a cluster of associated behaviours serving the same underlying psychological purpose. The intimacy theme contains behaviours such as using the confidence trick approach, seeking verbal participation from the victim, even complimenting her and being apologetic. This characterises a type of rapist referred to as pseudo-intimate whereby the perpetrator seeks to engage with the victim as a person. Impersonal on the other hand describes behaviour that is associated with a blitz attack (use of sudden and unexpected violence incapacitating the victim) showing no response to the victim's reactions, tearing her clothing and treating her more as an object.

So the first task in theorising is to define and differentiate subclasses of sexual violence. For present purposes five classes of sexual violence will be considered (see Table 7.1).

**Table 7.1** Definitions of different types of sexual violence

| Type of sexual violence | Definition | Comment |
| --- | --- | --- |
| Sexual harassment | Creation of a hostile workplace that is sexualised in such a way that the general experience of working there is offensive, or where a situation where a person of power implicitly or explicitly creates a situation in which a fellow worker must engage in or endure sexualised behaviour to retain their job status, make career progress or prevent a loss of status (Bowers and O'Donohue 2010) | Approximately 25% of working populations estimated to have experienced sexual harassment, with women more likely to perceive harassment, discrimination and negative health outcomes in terms of gender than men (Marsh *et al.* 2009) |
| Domestic violence | Any incident of threatening behaviour, violence or abuse (psychological, physical, sexual, | Intimate partner violence accounts for 25% of all violent crime in the UK and lifetime prevalence |

| | | |
|---|---|---|
| | financial or emotional) between adults who are or have been intimate partners or family members, regardless of gender or sexuality (Home Office 2005) | estimates suggest 45% of women and 26% of men experience at least one such episode (Gilchrist and Kebbell 2010) |
| Stalking | An intentional pattern of unwanted behaviours over time towards a person or persons that result in their experiencing fear, or behaviours that a reasonable person would view as fearful or threatening (Häkkänen-Nyholm 2010) | Estimates vary depending on definitions (lifetime prevalence range between 3–13% for males and 8–32% for females with average duration of two years) (Häkkänen-Nyholm 2010) |
| Rape | Intentional penetration of vagina, anus or mouth with a penis without consent (Sexual Offences Act 2003) | Large rate of under-reporting (13,093 cases in 2008); lifetime prevalence of rape or attempted rape for those over 16 (and under 59) was 1 in 24 women and 1 in 200 men (Stern Review 2010) |
| Sexual murder | Murder with an apparent or admitted sexual motivation (Oliver *et al.* 2007) | Difficult to assess numbers because typically, if murder committed, albeit with a sexual motive, the offender is charged only with the murder (Milsom *et al.* 2003) |

These broad definitions imply within them a range of either overlapping or distinctive behaviours which can be further broken down into their constituent elements. Table 7.2 presents examples from research reporting the discrete behaviours within the broad categories, together with their frequencies of occurrence.

There is obviously an overlap between sexual harassment and stalking and between stalking and domestic violence as there is between rape and sexual murder. Stealing something from the victim is present in murder, rape and stalking, tearing clothing, use of non-controlling violence and use of weapon characterises both rape and sexual murder. There is also a sexual component to sexual harassment. Berdahl and Aquino (2009) differentiate sexual behaviour from sex-based harassment, i.e. that which is experienced because of one's gender and takes a non-sexual form such as bullying or being undermined. Sexual harassment can also have a sexual component such as being threatened with a promotion failure if the employee does not give in to a demand for sex.

## Commonalities

There are several behaviours within these sexual violence offences that are common: notably threats of and actual use of violence; and the sexual content of threatening behaviours. Other behaviours are specific to the type of sexual

**Table 7.2** Behaviours associated with sub classes of sexual violence

**Sexual harassment[1,2]**

- Screamed or yelled at 54%
- Hostile offensive gestures 49%
- Told offensive jokes 49%
- Made crude offensive sexual remarks 42%
- Whistled, hooted at you 46%
- Drew into sexual conversation 41%
- Treated as though not good enough 41%
- Controlled non-work time 41%
- Stared, leered, ogled at 39%
- Treated you differently because of your gender 39%
- Made offensive remarks about gender 37%
- Sworn at 37%
- Talked down to 37%
- Continued to ask for dates 31%
- Treated unfairly in work assignment 25%
- Unwanted attempts to fondle or kiss you 19.5%
- Touched you in a way that made you feel uncomfortable 19%
- Bribed for sexual favours 14%
- Treating you badly for refusing to have sex 10%
- Attempted to have sex with you against your will 9%
- Afraid treated poorly if not sexually co-operative 9%
- Offered to be sexually co-operative 6%
- Killed 0%
- Raped/sexually assaulted 6%[7]

**Stalking[3]**

- Threats 80%
- Follows 78%
- Telephone calls 76%
- Confronts 52%
- Sends letters 46%
- Gains access to victim's house 46%
- Surveillance 44%
- Invites contact 42%
- Physical violence 42%
- Threatens others linked to victim 40%
- Contacts others 40%
- Explicit sexual content 32%
- Destroys property 32%
- Public defamation 28%
- Sent gifts 28%
- Threatens to commit suicide 18%
- Asking personal details 16%
- Researches victim 16%
- Drives by 14%
- Reveals knowledge about victim 12%
- Abuses victim's family 12%
- Killed between 2–8%
- Raped/sexually assaulted between 1–32%*

**Domestic violence[4]**

- Shouted at 54%
- Criticised 49%
- Put down in front of others 31%
- Restricted socially 28%
- Checked movements 28%
- Punched walls, furniture 25%
- Shouted at, threatened kids 23%
- Pushed grabbed shoved 22%
- Threatened you 19%
- Threw things at you 19%
- Kept short of money 19%
- Threatened with fist 18%
- Slapped you 15.5%
- Demanded sex 14%
- Forced you to do something 13%
- Twisted arm, pulled hair 12%
- Hit/hurt kids 11%
- Punched you in face 10%
- Punched, kicked body 9%
- Threatened to kill you 9%
- Choked you 9%
- Forced you to have sex 9%
- Threatened with weapon 8%
- Used object to hurt you 7%
- Tried to strangle, burn, drown 6%
- Kicked in face 2%
- Killed*
- Raped 9%

**Rape[5]**

- Vaginal penetration 83%
- Impersonal 70%
- Clothing disturbed 70%
- Surprise attack 67%
- Displays weapon 52%
- Steals 44%
- No reaction to V resistance 42%
- Insults 35%
- Fellatio 35%
- Blindfold 35%
- Controlling violence 32%
- Identifies victim 27%
- Non-controlling violence 26%
- Binds 26%
- Demands goods 26%
- Tears clothing 24%
- Gags 23%
- Verbal violence 23%
- Con approach 21%
- Threaten so as not to report 21%
- Implies knowledge of victim 20%
- Uses disguise 14%
- Anal penetration 15%
- Verbal threats 15%
- Compliments 12%
- Apologetic 8%
- Offender deterred 8%
- Killed
- Raped/sexually assaulted 100%

**Sexual murder[6]**

- Found naked 86%
- Non-controlling violence 75%
- Multiple wounds 72%
- Vaginal penetration 59%
- Single wound 57%
- Control with weapon 45%
- Weapon found at scene 35%
- Fellatio/cunnilingus 35%
- Steal something of value 29%
- Forensic awareness 29%
- Steal low-value item 24%
- Anal sex 19%
- Took weapon 13%
- Ripped clothing 10%
- Binds 8%
- Blindfolded 5%
- Killed 100%
- Raped/sexually assaulted 60%

1 Marsh et al. (2009)
2 Street et al. (2007)
3 Canter and Ioannou (2004)
4 Bradley et al. (2002)
5 Canter and Heritage (1990)
6 Salfati and Taylor (2006)
7 Brown et al. (1995)

* This is difficult to calculate; approx two women a week are murdered by partners in England and Wales

violence, thus keeping a partner short of money is particular to domestic violence, treating a person unfairly in a work assignment is particular to sexual harassment, sending unsolicited gifts particular to stalking. Escalation from one category to another in the form of rape or murder is also apparent.

As well as the behaviours, there are also some other common underlying features of sexual violence. These are:

1. unacknowledged victimisation;
2. under-reporting of behaviours;
3. perceptions of false accusations.

## Unacknowledged victimisation

In the first instance, victims may not wish to acknowledge their experiences with a given label. Thus Petersen and Muehlenhard (2004) describe several reasons why, in their survey, respondents did not want to acknowledge coerced sex as rapes: unwilling to see oneself as a victim; not wishing to view the perpetrator as a rapist; not having the emotional reactions they perceived to be consistent with rape. Mary Koss refers to this as unacknowledged rape and means the non-labelling of a sexual assault that constitutes rape by virtue of the legal definition but where victims do not choose to do so (Koss 1985). Similar unwillingness to acknowledge behaviours of sexual harassment have also been reported (e.g. Harris and Firestone 2010). They analysed survey responses from the US military where 21 per cent of women and 13 per cent of men had experiences of sexual harassment which they declined to label as such. Fear of being blamed or unwillingness to name a perpetrator were among the reasons suggested for not acknowledging the behaviour as sexual harassment. Muehlenhard and Kimes (1999) report similar labelling problems associated with domestic violence. Jordan's Chapter 12 (this volume) discusses at more length problems associated with the unacknowlededgment of women's experiences of sexual violence.

## Under-reporting

A recent British Crime Survey (Povey *et al.* 2009) reports that a significant minority of rape victims had not told anyone about their assault and only a minority had told the police. HMCPSI/HMIC (2002) provide estimates that between 75 per cent and 85 per cent of rape complainants never report their assault to the police. Some of the reasons for not reporting include: loyalty because perpetrator is known to the victim, feelings of embarrassment, fear of further attacks or retaliation, worries about own perceived culpability, perceptions of the police's treatment of complainants and fear of court proceedings (Kelly *et al.* 2005, Helen Jones, Chapter 8, this volume).

Harris and Firestone (2010) report from their analysis of sexual harassment in the US military under-reporting of complaints often because of myths surrounding the making of a complaint, such as that the complainer will be fired, demoted or transferred. Being labelled a troublemaker was also another reason for not reporting incidents. They also report that people's beliefs about how seriously a complaint will be taken and the strength of the organisation's response are also factors associated with likelihood of reporting.

### False accusations

Sheridan and Blaaw (2004) report from the literature that perhaps 2 per cent of stalking accusations are false, although in their own study they found 11.5 per cent. Mullen *et al.* (2000) identified five broad classes of false allegation: anger retaliation provoked by the ending of a relationship; delusional associated with severe mental disorder; the previously stalked who misinterpret ordinary behaviours as stalking; factitious victims seeking gratification of dependency needs; and malingerers who intentionally fabricated or exaggerated for external incentives. False accusers' accounts did differ in important details from authentic stalking victims: false claims were less likely to involve receiving unwanted letters or threats of attacks on third parties. In Sheridan and Blaauw's study there were no demographic differences distinguishing false from true accusations. Interestingly, genuine victims were twice as likely to report assault.

The literature, although rather sparse, does support that false allegations of sexual harassment can be made (O'Donohue and Bowers 2006). They report an estimated rate of false allegations of between 2 and 8 per cent. Reasons suggested for false allegations include: confused interpretation of events, coaching to make false reports, mental disorders, hypersensitivity, revenge and financial gain, excusing poor work performance, gaining a desired change in job status, gaining of power within the relationship dynamics of the workplace.

Kanin (1994) determined that 41 per cent of rape allegations made to a midwest police department in the United States were false. The reasons for making these allegations were: revenge, providing an alibi and/or obtaining sympathy and attention. Other commentators suggest that this rate of false reporting is too high and that police scepticism or the victim's exhaustion with the criminal justice process may lead to perceptions of false allegations (Brown *et al.* 2007).

Custody disputes involving children can result in false allegations of domestic or child sexual abuse (Jaffe *et al.* 2008). Again evidence is sparse but rates of between 25 per cent and 50 per cent of allegations have been reported that are difficult to substantiate. That is not to say they are necessarily false, because, for example, after some distance has been achieved in the relationship and/or counselling received, a victim may come to understand the abusive nature of the relationship.

### From description to explanation: general theories of ordinary behaviour

McGuire (2004) argues that there is a role for psychological factors in helping to understand the causes of crime and does so by considering everyday, ordinary or mundane activities which avoid the purely pathologising approach. This relies on the notion that most people's lives are grounded in the routine of getting up, enjoying some form of organised activity such as work interspersed with leisure and recreation built around defined time bands. People form routinised habits which are well established and accustomed patterns of behaviour. As such most behaviours are learnt and are part of a developmental maturation process taking place within a social context. Most of these daily routines involve a level of cognitive processing implicated in decision-making (e.g. whether or not to implement or vary the routines). For the most part these serve functional purposes. However, under some circumstances, routines which have served positive and constructive purposes may become harmful. To take the example of anger, showing this emotion can be a reasonable psychological reaction and illustrate some dissatisfaction in a relationship and serve to deal with the precipitating issues and even strengthen the relationship. Anger can become dysfunctional when it is out of control and is a disproportionate response relative to the issues that provoked it. Canter and Heritage (1990) provide another example. Desire for social contact or intimacy is a normal human reaction and difficulties in achieving this can lead to inappropriate reading of social-sexual cues and may result in rape. The pseudo-intimate rapist often engages subterfuge to make contact with the victim and behaviours include verbal contact, asking questions about her lifestyle and wanting the victim to participate in the sex acts and even asking to see her again. Bennell *et al.* (2001) found that approaches made to children by adult abusers mapped onto conventional adult–child behaviours in terms of control and love.

Canter (1994) argues that human transactions and interactions in any one arena of people's lives reveal something about the way they act and/or interact in other arenas. Canter suggests that if interpersonal violent crime is thought of as a transaction between two people then other transactions conducted by potential offenders may reveal clues about how an offender interacts with people in a violent encounter. Moreover there will be some congruence between the individual's non-criminal and criminal transactions. Canter also observes that criminals exist in the same physical world and social milieu as their potential victims, and as such they are subject to many of the same constraints on their behaviour. Furthermore, criminals are not constantly committing crime; in fact for the majority of their time they are going about their everyday non-criminal lives. Canter supposes that offenders will commit crime in a way that reflects their behaviour in 'everyday' life. For example, Horvath and Brown (2007) suggest that a drug-assisted rapist may regularly go with friends to a club in which there are many women consuming alcohol and drugs. The offender may use this opportunity from their everyday life to look for victims to rape and may even go so far as to target preferred women by buying them drinks in order that they become incapacitated to increase his opportunity to commit a rape. Given the prevalence and social acceptability of drinking alcohol (and, to a lesser extent, drug consumption) in social situations in Western society it is quite likely that everyday life will present opportunities for drug-assisted rape to occur. Scully and Morolla (1985) take the view that rather than suggesting sexual offenders are sick individuals, with underlying pathologies, they propose a learning model, such as the ideas expounded by McGuire (2004) mentioned previously. In this instance sexual violence serves several different purposes such as revenge, a means of access to unwilling or unavailable women or a recreational activity providing sensation and excitement, or even a 'bonus' activity while committing another offence such as burglary.

## Pathological theories

There are clinical approaches to understanding the commission of sexual violence. Beech (2010) describes three sets of intersecting dynamic factors associated with sex offending, i.e. biological determinants including genetic inheritance and brain development; ecological such as social, cultural and personal context; and neuropsychological. Thus genetic predispositions and social learning impact on brain development and three neuropsychological systems: motivation/emotional, perception and memory and action selection and control. These interplaying factors create clinical problems for offenders in terms of deviant arousal, offence-related thinking and sexual fantasies, social difficulties and emotional regulation problems. Sexually abusive behaviour then functions to maintain a positive feedback loop which alleviates the offender's anxieties and serves to maintain or even escalate the deviant actions.

Personality disorders (PD) have been implicated in sexual violent offending. PD is not a mental illness, rather a style of interacting. Lord (2010) draws on the internationally recognised classifications to describe personality disorders as severe disturbances of the individual leading to persistent and problematic behaviour in which there is a low frustration tolerance, disregard for social norms, rules or obligations and low threshold for aggression and violence. Psychopathy in particular has been linked with sex offences (Porter *et al.* 2003; Storey *et al.* 2009). Psychopathy is described as involving impulsivity, remorselessness, lack of empathy, thrill seeking and a callous interpersonal style (Canter and Youngs 2009: 153). Psychopaths are predators who use charm, manipulation and violence to control others. The Hare Psychopathy Checklist Revised (PCL-R) is most frequently used to measure levels of psychopathy, with scores of between 25–30 being used to classify psychopaths. Thus Porter *et al.* (2003) found elevated levels of psychopathy in 125 male homicide offenders where there was sexual content to the murders. They concluded (p. 467) 'not only are psychopathic offenders disproportionately more likely to engage in sexual homicide, but when they do, they use significantly more gratuitous and sadistic violence.' They hypothesised that the psychopath's profound lack of empathy and their desire for thrill seeking are especially pertinent in promoting such behaviours as they seek to optimise their pleasure through the damage they inflict on their victim. Storey *et al.* (2009) found psychopathic symptoms, especially affect deficits, associated with stalking victimisation of casual acquaintances described as 'boldness and coldness'. They note that psychopathic stalkers were rare but where psychopathy was a factor those offenders were more likely than non-psychopathic stalkers to be highly preoccupied with their victims, escalate their stalking behaviours and target highly vulnerable victims. They were unlikely to be the unrequited 'lovesick' type of stalker or romantically inept (the pseudo-intimate types), nor were they motivated by strong emotional attachment to their victim. Psychopathic stalkers are not likely then to be motivated by a need to re-establish close or positive relationships or reflect a separation protest, rather their behaviours reflect interpersonal dominance and control following what they perceive as a 'narcissistic injury' to the victim's rejection of them. Thus stalking is a form of bullying to enhance the stalker's sense of self. Mullen *et al.* (2000) describe erotomanics who meet DSM criteria for delusional (paranoid) disorder. They are convinced they are loved by someone they often have not even met, who are often media figures. Geberth (1992) describes psychopathic personality stalkers who may destroy property, make threats over the phone and engage in some form of harassment to gain control over the victim.

Grubin (1994) compared 21 men who murdered in the course of a sexual attack with 121 rapists. They were found to differ with respect to their personal history, with the murderers reporting much higher levels of social isolation both in childhood and adulthood. Sexual murderers were less sexually experienced than the rapists and fewer had had sexual relationships in their lifetime and they were older than the rapists when committing their index offence. They were more likely to 'bottle' their temper.

The murderers had few intimate relationships with women and those that they did form were emotionally limiting with little sharing and confiding. Grubin speculates that their social isolation may be indicative of underlying personality abnormalities which are a cause of their isolation and allow them to cross over from sexual attack to murder. They may also be a cause of their lack of ability to empathise, and this impoverished internal life weakens the restraint that inhibits excessive sexual violence.

Interestingly there appear to be no differences between murderers and rapists in terms of their relationship to their victims, and sexual fantasy and interest in aggressive pursuits was equally likely (Oliver *et al.* 2007). Their own study of 58 sexual murderers and 112 rapists about to enter a treatment programme within the England and Wales prison system differed in terms of age at index offence (rapists were older), mean IQ (murderers were more intelligent). Rapists had a greater number of prior violent offences (twice as many) and murderers were less likely to be in a relationship at the time of the murder. The rapists and murderers did not differ in terms of juvenile sex offending, or previous sexual offences. Rapists had more self-revealing personalities, both groups had similar degrees of anxiety, avoidance and anxiety personality disorders and alcohol dependency. Rapists had higher scores on paranoid suspicion and resentment and self-esteem thus having a more negative outlook on life compared with the murderers. Rapists committed offences against younger victims and more committed rapes against both adults and children.

## From quantum to qualitative differentiation

Kelly's notion of quantum is found in psychological theorising but in a somewhat different form. As mentioned earlier, Salfati (2008) described a frequency continuum of homicide behaviours. Thus, as she demonstrates in homicides, some behaviours occur more than 50 per cent of the time and were classified as high-frequency common behaviours but which do not differentiate individual offenders. Canter (2000) argues for a hierarchy of distinctions between crime behaviours in which lower-frequency behaviours are differentiated from the higher-frequency, core actions. Canter suggests that at the most general end of the hierarchy these common features are indicative of criminal behaviour but are not especially helpful in differentiating between different types or themes of crime. As actions become more specific to a given crime, Canter hypothesises that behaviours become more indicative of the individuals carrying them out, termed the modus operandi, until at the most detailed level of specificity, signature behaviours characterise a particular individual because they are idiosyncratic. Canter's idea is that crimes can be differentiated along this continuum of generalised typicality to the highly individualised. His classification of qualitative distinctions between the high and low frequencies finesses Kelly's prevalence continuum.

Sexual violence can be thought of in terms of the same hierarchy. Thus core behaviours that are typical of sexual violence (which Kelly (1988) identifies as threats of violence experienced by all the respondents in her study) distinguish this offence from, say, others such as property crime but in and of themselves are an undifferentiating characteristic of all subtypes of sexual violence. So these typical behaviours occurring with high frequency do not help to distinguish the different types of sexual violence or indeed different types of offenders. To do this Canter and Youngs (2009: 144) argue that themes, identifying some underlying psychological purpose, can be used to differentiate different types of crime. Canter (2000) and Canter and Youngs (2009) use the analogy of colour to explain how these themes merge into one another and should not be thought of as independent dimensions or 'pure' differentiated types. This analogy fits well with Kelly's notion of shading. As well as differentiating between crimes, such a model can describe themes that occur within a crime category. As mentioned above, Canter and Heritage (1990) found five themes that accounted for different groupings within rather than between rape behaviours. Canter and Youngs then argue that at the next level of specificity, the offender's behaviour needs to be taken into account. They use the term modus operandi (MO) to describe a pattern of behaviours that typify different types of offender. These patterns enable individuals with similar MOs to be thought of as sharing certain common characteristics but also allow for variations within a sexual violence subcategory. Thus, by way of example, rapists motivated by anger may show a similar degree of gratuitous physical violence in the rapes they commit but which is of a different character from that of rapists motivated by mistaken attempts at intimacy.

Kelly's prevalence continuum of sexual violence, which combines all types of violence, can then be thought of within this formulation.

**Table 7.3** Reconceptualising Kelly's prevalence continuum

| Kelly's identified sexually violent behaviours | % | |
|---|---|---|
| **Threat of violence** | 100 | Core behaviours of sexual violence |
| Sexual harassment | 93 | |
| **Pressure to have sex** | 83 | |
| Sexual assault | 70 | |
| **Obscene phone calls** | 68 | Behaviour patterns associated with different classes of sexual violence |
| **Coerced sex** | 63 | |
| Domestic violence | 58 | |
| **Sexual abuse** | 50 | |
| **Flashing** | 50 | |
| Rape | 50 | |
| Incest | 22 | |

The emboldened behaviours having more than 70 per cent frequency are undifferentiating of a particular manifestation of sexual violence whereas those with lower frequencies begin to look like more specific forms such as obscene phone calling or sexual abuse. There are no behaviours in Kelly's formulation that map onto the Canter MO and signature levels, but these are theoretically possible if looked for as demonstrated in Table 7.2.

To recapitulate the argument thus far, Canter's (2000) theorising proposed a model to distinguish between types of crime (say burglary, robbery, and violence). Youngs (2004) was able to demonstrate this showing clear distinctions between property-based crime and those crimes committed against the person. Thereafter, within a particular crime such as rape, behaviours can be differentiated by general to increasingly particular actions grouped around a number of overarching themes (Canter and Heritage 1990). The present chapter takes these ideas to present a model conceptualising the different subclasses within sexual violence. Thus it should be possible to focus on the broader area of sexual violence and show the within variations of its different manifestations. This is represented in Figure 7.2.

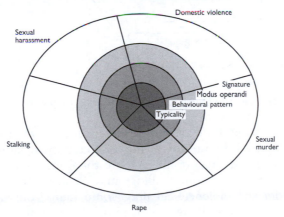

Figure 7.2 A model differentiating subclasses of sexual violence (adapted from Canter 2000)

Such a model hypothesises that each subclass of sexual violence would have behaviours that are typical of all classes of sexual violence, represented by the dense shading at the centre, as indeed is shown by Kelly. Thereafter behaviours reduce in frequency and begin to separate such that there are distinguishable behavioural patterns associated with different types of sexual violence, as implied by Kelly. Then behaviours become less frequent and begin to be associated with different styles of crime typifying offenders. It is at this level that types of offender can be identified and differentiated such as the erotomanic or predator stalker (Mullen *et al*. 2000) or the exploiter, violent and controlling sexual murderer (Salfati and Taylor 2006). Finally, behaviours that are low frequency would identify specific offenders by virtue of singular, signature behaviours, not indicated by Kelly's prevalence continuum. This is exemplified by the particular method of killing, a ligature, used by railway murderer John Duffy (*The Independent*, 3 February 2001).

The position of the subclasses of sexual violence around the model is also significant. Adjacent classes would expect to have more behaviour in common and that there is a more direct connection in terms of escalation across boundary behaviours than with a type of sexual violence further round the circle. As shown previously in Table 7.2, there are overlapping behaviours that feature in more than one subclass of sexual violence. Moreover, there also may be some crossover by a perpetrator, for example the intimidating aspects of sexual harassment at work parallel the intimidation of domestic violence at home. Domestic violence may lead to murder as can rape. The potential escalation and crossover between types of sexual violence can be represented diagrammatically as shown in Figure 7.3.

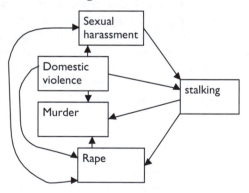

**Figure 7.3** Potential crossover between subclasses of sexual violence

Thus sexual harassment or domestic violence may migrate to stalking, stalking in turn can result in murder, as indeed may rape or domestic violence. Moreover, some behaviour may occur in more than one subclass, for example it is likely that obscene phone calling may feature in stalking, sexual harassment or domestic violence. Stealing some item from the victim may occur in rape, murder or stalking. Demeaning the person by putting them down in front of others may occur in sexual harassment and domestic violence. Adjacent subclasses would be expected to share more behaviours than those further away around the circle. This then adds a qualitative distinctiveness to the Kelly prevalence continuum. There is a relationship between behaviours in their likelihood to occur together. Moreover this suggests different pathways, for example an offender may start by sexually harassing, and then engage in stalking, leading to rape and eventually murder. Alternatively, there may be a measure of domestic violence in a relationship which then escalates to rape and ultimately murder (as appeared in the case of John Duffy). It is also possible that an individual may only engage in one specific form of sexual violence.

Finally, it should be possible to identify themes within each subclass of sexual violence. Canter (2000) employs the term theme to overcome the problem with types or taxonomies in that often there is not a 'pure' type, rather it is more likely there will be some degree of overlap between behaviours. As has been demonstrated above, themes have been used to describe criminality in general and the crime of rape in particular. It is likely then that themes can be found that are associated with other manifestations of sexual violence such as expressive or instrumental themes identifying homicide behaviours (Salfati 2008).

## Empirical support for qualitative differentiation

Salfati and Taylor's (2006) idea of a continuum proposes that crime scene behaviours are associated, to a greater or lesser extent, with the type of crime, and as a function of the association can be placed on the continuum. This in effect suggests there is a stronger relationship of behaviours that are adjacent to each other and a weaker one between those behaviours that are further away on the continuum. They sought to differentiate between the behaviours of rapists and sexual murderers. By using a multivariate statistical analysis they were able to map rapist and murderer behaviour along a continuum as follows.

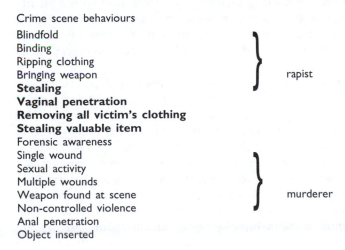

Crime scene behaviours
Blindfold
Binding
Ripping clothing
Bringing weapon                    } rapist
**Stealing**
**Vaginal penetration**
**Removing all victim's clothing**
**Stealing valuable item**
Forensic awareness
Single wound
Sexual activity
Multiple wounds
Weapon found at scene              } murderer
Non-controlled violence
Anal penetration
Object inserted

**Figure 7.4** Continuum of rapists' and murderers' behaviours (after Salfati and Taylor 2006)

The behaviour at the top is typical of a rape and less likely found to typify murderers' behaviour whereas anal penetration and inserting an object were more likely to be associated with sexual murder than rape. The emboldened behaviours were found in both offences. The typical rape behaviours appear to be more instrumental in controlling the victim whereas in the murder part of the continuum, behaviours appear more expressive and hostile acts of violence. The sexual behaviours at the end of the continuum are especially violent and degrading. Salfati and Taylor conclude that this does demonstrate a progression and represents a movement away from planned controlling behaviours to more extreme hostile and expressive acts perpetrated against the victim.

Kocsis *et al.* (2002) looked at 85 Australian sexually motivated murder behaviours, using the same multidimensional scaling procedure as Salfati and Taylor. They found a central core of undifferentiated behaviours that were typical of all sexual murders in the sample and included movement of the body, premeditation and precautions and degree of force used in the sex. Thereafter four subtypes of offence clusters were differentiated which they labelled rape, fury, perversion and predator. These were associated with different degrees of violence and the role of sex in the murders. Moreover they found differences in perpetrators of the different types of murders. The predator pattern was associated with older, mobile offenders, well groomed, living with a partner and highly likely to operate with an accomplice and prone to reoffend. With the fury pattern, where there is an attempt to literally obliterate the victim, offenders are drawn from the violently mentally ill as well as those not suffering from such a disorder. The non-psychotic offender was likened to the anger retaliation rapist whose hatred for women is expressed through violent sexual assault. The taking of souvenirs by this type of perpetrator may act as a reminder of the retributive motivation for the offence.

Canter and Ioannou (2004) undertook a multidimensional scaling analysis of stalking behaviours (listed in Table 7.2). They had hypothesised that there would be four distinct themes reflecting the mode of interaction with a victim: sexuality, intimacy, aggression-destruction, possession. Thus the differentiation between stalkers they suggested includes sexual infatuation, intimacy seeking, a reactive rejection and passion. This last reflects a belief that the object of the stalking remains the stalker's 'property'.

If the proposed general model of sexual violence is presented and schematic representations of the above analyses added, it can be seen that subcrime types do indeed have both overlapping and distinctive themes. In the examples presented in Figure 7.5, stalking and rape have the intimacy theme, reflecting attempts to engage in a relationship albeit in an oppressive way. Interestingly, criminality and possession were distinctive themes in rape and stalking respectively. Within these themes specific behaviours are located that serve similar psychological functions. In stalking the giving of unsolicited gifts mirrors normative affectionate behaviours. The pseudo-intimate rapist attempts to mimic authentic relationships by being solicitous and attempting to engage his victim's active co-operation in the sex acts he is requiring her to perform. The more violent behaviours in rape and murder go beyond compliance and are often an expression of eroticised sexual aggression.

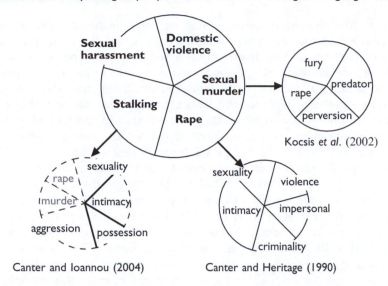

**Figure 7.5** Themes associated with sexual violence

No equivalent multivariate analyses of domestic violence or sexual harassment have been located but it would be predicted that, if undertaken, then they too would show some common as well as distinctive themes.

## Conclusion

This chapter suggests Kelly's continuum of violence has been a helpful conceptual tool to build a more complex model having potential explanatory and predictive powers. A general model of sexual violence was presented suggesting a series of continua as radii forming a circular ordering of subclasses of sexual violence. Frequency of behaviours were argued to vary from core or common feature to those that become progressively more differentiating until they identify a specific individual by virtue of the singularity of the actions. Behaviours are linked to themes which can be identified to serve some psychological purpose such as intimacy seeking or venting anger. This model, it is argued, offers a means to differentiate offenders/perpetrators with a view to assessing risk factors in escalation or crossover, designing programmed interventions with offenders, aiding detection, and assessing and treating them.

Sexually violent behaviours arise from both normative and pathological routes. Dixon *et al.* (2008) found that they could distinguish different types of sexual murder by looking at levels of psychopathology and criminality. Individuals who were medium to high on criminality and high on psychopathology were more likely to have previously stalked their victim, threatened suicide and engaged in substance misuse. Those high on criminality and low to moderate on psychopathology were more often unemployed, and had had previous convictions for violence. A third group who were low on both dimensions had no prior history of violence and more often committed the murder for instrumental gains. This study rather neatly illustrates that sexual violence may be associated with the more normal and mundane motivation of personal gain as well as be a product of psychopathological factors. Bartol and Bartol (2008) note that sex offenders may not be prone to violence or physical cruelty but can be rather timid, shy and socially inhibited. But they also point out that in the United States a class of offender identified as a sexually violent predator was deemed sufficiently dangerous to be subjected to special commitment facilities. Lord (2010) also describes special provisions for offenders classified as having dangerous and severe personality disorders (DSPD). Moreover there is evidence that behaviours associated with different types of sexual violence may indeed escalate and this counters Kelly's idea that there is not a linear progression in the continuum of violence. Indeed Kelly and her colleague Linda Regan (Regan and Kelly 2008) did propose that previous physical violence, sexual abuse, jealous surveillance, coercive control and an actual or potential separation were factors predicting the eventual murder in domestic violence cases.

The model presented in the chapter argues for a qualitative addition to Kelly's continuum of violence to chart the relationship between different manifestations of sexual violence such that types of violence having a greater number of behaviours in common are more likely candidates for crossover offending. This is not to say that offenders progress in a linear fashion through the different types of violence, as it may be that a perpetrator only offends within one category; rather there may be different pathways for offenders to progress through different forms of sexual violence. The model suggests a number of hypotheses such as that sexually motivated murderers are likely to be different if they are single-focus offenders compared with offenders who escalate or cross offence boundaries. Some preliminary empirical evidence is offered to support the model, but confirmation awaits further research data.

## Further reading

This chapter draws on a particular approach to research, Facet Theory devised by Louis Guttman. There are accessible accounts of Facet Theory and Facet Design by Jennifer Brown in the *Cambridge Handbook of Forensic Psychology*. In the same text Darragh O'Neil and Sean Hammond provide a description of the statistical procedures described in the chapter, especially Smallest Space Analysis (SSA).

David Canter and Donna Youngs's book *Investigative Psychology; Offender Profiling and the Analysis of Criminal Action*, published by Wiley, provides a good overview and summaries of much of the research drawn on in this chapter as well as outlining the radex of criminality concept.

Salfati and colleagues have two papers that are particularly helpful in explaining the ideas of frequencies of sexually violent behaviour and the notion of a continuum. These are Salfati, G. (2008) 'Offender profiling; psychological and methodological issues of testing for behavioural consistency', *Issues in Forensic Psychology*, 8: 68–81 and Salfati, G. and Taylor, P. 'Differentiating sexual violence; a comparison of sexual homicide and rape', *Psychology, Crime and Law*, 12: 107–25.

# References

Abdullah-Khan, N. (2008) *Male Rape; the emergence of a social and legal issue*. Basingstoke: Palgrave/Macmillan.

Bartol, C.R. and Bartol, A.M. (2008) *Criminal Behaviour; a psychological approach* (9th edn). Upper Saddler River, NJ: Pearson Educational.

Beech, A.R. (2010) 'Sexual offenders' in J.M. Brown and E.A. Campbell (eds) *Cambridge Handbook of Forensic Psychology*, pp. 102–10. Cambridge: Cambridge University Press.

Bennell, C., Alison, L., Stein, K. *et al.* (2001) 'Sexual offences against children as the abusive exploitation of conventional adult-child relationships', *Journal of Social and Personal Relationships*, 18: 115–71.

Berdahl, J., and Aquino, K. (2009) 'Sexual behaviour at work; fun or folly?', *Journal of Applied Psychology*, 94: 34–47.

Bowers, A. and O'Donohue, W. (2010) 'Sexual harassment', in J.M. Brown and E.A. Campbell (eds) *Cambridge Handbook of Forensic Psychology*, pp. 718–24. Cambridge: Cambridge University Press.

Bradley, F., Smith, M., Long, J. and O'Dowd (2002) 'Reported frequency of domestic violence; cross sectional survey of women attending general practice', *British Medical Journal*, 324: 271–5.

Breakwell, G. and Rose, D. (2000) 'Research; theory and method', in G. Breakwell, S. Hammond and C. Fife-Schaw (eds) *Research Methods in Psychology* (2nd edn), pp. 5–21. London: Sage.

Brown, J.M., Campbell, E.A. and Fife-Schaw, C. (1995) 'Adverse impacts experienced by police officers following exposure to sex discrimination and sexual harassment', *Stress Medicine*, 11: 221–8.

Brown, J.M., Hamilton, C., and O'Neill, D. (2007) Characteristics associated with rape attrition and the role played by skepticism or legal rationality by investigators and prosecutors. *Psychology, Crime and Law*, 13, 355-370.

Campbell, J.C., Webster, D., Kozoil-McLain, J. *et al.* (2003) 'Risk factors for femicide in abusive relationships; results from a multisite case control', *American Journal of Public Health*, 93: 1089–97.

Cann, J., Friendship, C., and Gozna, L. (2007) 'Assessing crossover in a sample of sexual offenders with multiple victims', *Legal and Criminological Psychology*, 12: 149–63.

Canter, D.V. (1994) *Criminal Shadows*. London: Harper Collins.

Canter, D.V. (2000) 'Offender profiling and criminal differentiation', *Legal and Criminological Psychology*, 5: 23–46.

Canter, D. and Fritzon, K. (1998) 'Differentiating arsonists: a model of firesetting actions and characteristics', *Journal of Legal and Criminological Psychology*, 3: 185–212.

Canter, D., and Heritage, R. (1990) 'A multivariate model of sexual offence behaviour: developments in offender profiling', *Journal of Forensic Psychiatry*, 1(1): 185–212.

Canter, D.V. and Ioannou, M. (2004) 'A multivariate model of stalking behaviour', *Behaviormetrika*, 31: 113–30.

Canter, D.V. and Youngs, D. (2009) *Investigative Psychology; Offender Profiling and the Analysis of Criminal Action*. Chichester: Wiley.

DeKeseredy, W. and Kelly, K. (1993) 'The incidence and prevalence of woman abuse in Canadian university and college dating relationships', *The Canadian Journal of Sociology/Cahiers canadiens de sociologie*, 18: 137–59.

Dixon, L., Hamilton-Giachristsis, C. and Browne, K. (2008) 'Classifying partner femicide', *Journal of International Violence*, 23: 74–93.

Geberth, V.J. (1992) 'Stalkers', *Law and Order*, October: 138–43.

Gilchrist, E.A. and Kebbell, M.R. (2010) 'Intimate partner violence: current issues in definitions and interventions with perpetrators in the UK', in J.R. Adler and J.M. Gray (eds) *Forensic Psychology; Concepts, Debates and Practice*, pp 351–77. Cullompton: Willan Publishing.

Giner-Sorolla, R. and Russell, P. (2009) 'Anger, disgust and sexual crime', in M.A.H. Horvath and J.M. Brown (eds) *Rape; Challenging Contemporary Thinking*, pp. 46–73. Cullompton: Willan Publishing.

Groth, A.N., Burgess, A.W. and Holmstrom, L.H. (1977) 'Rape: power, anger and sexuality', *American Journal of Psychiatry*, 134, 1239–43.

Grubin, D. (1994) 'Sexual murder', *British Journal of Psychiatry*, 165: 624–9.

Hanson, B.K. and Bussiére, M.T. (1998) 'Predicting relapse: a meta analysis of offender recidivism studies', *Journal of Consulting and Clinical Psychology*, 66: 348–62.

Harris, R.J. and Firestone, J.M. (2010) 'Victimization in the US military: the impact of labelling events on officially reporting sexual harassment', *Journal of Sociological Research*, 2: 1–20.

Hester, M., Donovan, C. and Fahmy, E. (2010) 'Feminist epistemology and the politics of method: surveying same sex domestic violence', *International Journal of Social Research Methodology*, 13: 251–63.

HMCPSI and HMIC (2002) *A Report on the Joint Inspection into the Investigation and Prosecution of Cases involving Allegations of Rape*. London: HMCPSI and HMIC.

Home Office (2005) *Domestic Violence: a national report*. London: Home Office.

Horvath, M. (2010) 'Sexual assault', in J.M. Brown and E.A. Campbell (eds) *Cambridge Handbook of Forensic Psychology*, pp. 543–51. Cambridge: Cambridge University Press.

Horvath, M.A H. and Brown, J. (2007) 'The role of alcohol and drugs in rape', *Medicine, Science and the Law*, 46(3): 219–28.

Jaffe, P.G., Johnston, J.R., Crooke, C. and Bala, N. (2008) 'Custody disputes involving allegations of domestic violence; towards a differentiated approach to parenting plans', *Family Court Review*, 46: 500–22.

Kanin, E.J. (1994) 'False rape allegations', *Archives of Sexual Behaviour*, 23: 81–92.

Kelly, L. (1988) *Surviving Sexual Violence*. Minneapolis: University of Minnesota Press.

Kelly, L., Lovett, J. and Regan, L. (2005) *A gap or a Chasm? Attrition in reported rape cases*. London: Home Office.

Kocsis, R.N., Cooksey, R.W. and Irwin, H.J. (2002) 'Psychological profiling of sexual murders; an empirical model', *International Journal of Offender Therapy and Comparative Criminology*, 46: 532–54.

Koss, M.P. (1985) 'The hidden rape victim: Personality, attitudinal, and situational characteristics', *Psychology of Women Quarterly*, 9: 193–212.

Lord, A. (2010) 'Treatment of offenders classed as having dangerous and severe personality disorders', in J.R. Adler and J.M. Gray (eds) *Forensic Psychology; Concepts, Debates and Practice*, pp. 285–305. Cullompton: Willan Publishing.

McEwan, T.E., Mullen, P. and Mackenzie, R. (2009) 'A study of the predictors of persistence in stalking situations', *Law and Human Behavior*, 33, 149–58.

McGuire, M. (2004) *Understanding Psychology and Crime; perspectives on theory and action*. Maidenhead: Open University Press.

Macpherson, G. (2003) 'Predicting escalation in sexually violent recidivism: Use of the SVR-20 and PCL:SV to predict outcome with non contact recidivists and contact recidivists', *Journal of Forensic Psychiatry and Psychology*, 14: 615–27.

Marsh, J., Parel, S., Gelaye, B. *et al.* (2009) 'Prevalence of workplace abuse and sexual harassment among female faculty and staff', *Journal of Occupational Health*, 51: 314–22.

Marx, B.P. (2005) 'Lessons learned from the last twenty years of sexual violence research', *Journal of Interpersonal Violence*, 20: 225–30.

Meloy, J. Reid (1998) *The Psychology of Stalking; Clinical and Forensic Perspectives*. San

Diego: Academic Press.

Meloy, J. Reid (2007) 'Stalking; the state of the science criminal', *Behaviour and Mental Health*, 17: 1–7.

Milsom, J., Beech, A.R. and Webster, S.D. (2003) 'Emotional loneliness in sexual murderers; a qualitative analysis', *Sexual Abuse; A Journal of Research and Treatment*, 15: 285–96.

Muehlenhard, C.L., and Kimes, L.A. (1999) 'The social construction of violence: the case of sexual and domestic violence', *Personality and Social Psychology Review*, 3: 234–45.

Mullen, P., Pathé, M. and Purcell, R. (2000) *Stalkers and Their Victims*. Cambridge: Cambridge University Press.

O'Donohue, W., and Bowers, A.H. (2006) 'Pathways to false allegations of sexual harassment', *Journal of Investigative Psychology and Offender Profiling*, 3: 47–74.

Oliver, C.J., Beech, A.R., Fisher, D. and Beckett, R. (2007) 'A comparison of rapists and sexual murderers on demographic and selected psychometric measures', *International Journal of Offender Therapy and Comparative Criminology*, 51: 298–312.

Page, A. Dellinger (2008) 'Judging women and defining crime; police officer attitudes towards women and rape', *Sociological Spectrum*, 28: 389–411.

Peterson, Z.D. and Muehlenhard, C.L. (2004) 'Was it rape? The function of women's rape myth acceptance and definition of sex in labelling their own experiences', *Sex Roles – A Journal of Research*, 51(3/4): 129–44.

Porter, S., Woodworth, M., Earle, J., Drugge, J. and Boer, D. (2003) 'Characteristics of sexual homicide committed by psychopathic and non psychopathic offenders', *Law and Human Behavior*, 27: 459–70.

Povey, D., Coleman, K., Kaiza, P. and Roe, S. (2009) *Homicides, firearm offences and intimate violence; supplementary volume 2 to Crime in England and Wales 2007/9*. Home Office Statistical Bulletin. London: Home Office.

Prentky, R.A. and Knight, R.A. (1991) 'Identifying critical dimensions for discriminating among rapists', *Journal of Consulting and Clinical Psychology*, 59: 643–61.

Regan, L. and Kelly, L. (2008) 'If only we'd known: an exploratory study of seven intimate partner homicides', *SAFE*, 27: 11–13.

Salfati, C.G. (2008) 'Offender profiling: psychological and methodological issues of testing for behavioural consistency', *Issues in Forensic Psychology*, 8: 68–81.

Salfati, C.G. and Taylor, P. (2006) 'Differentiating sexual violence; a comparison of sexual homicide and rape', *Psychology, Crime and Law*, 12: 107–25.

Scully, D. and Marolla, J. (1985) 'Riding the bull at Gilley's: convicted rapists describe the reward of rape', *Social Problems*, 23: 251–63.

Sexual Offences Act (2003) http://www.opsi.gov.uk/acts/acts2003/pdf/ukpga_20030042_en.pdf

Sheridan, L.P. and Blaaw, E. (2004) 'Characteristics of false stalking reports', *Criminal Justice and Behaviour*, 31: 55–72.

Sheridan, L.P., Blaaw, E. and Davies, G.M. (2003) 'Stalking; knowns and unknowns', *Trauma, Violence and Abuse*, 4: 148–62.

Stern, V. (2010) The Stern Review: a report by Baroness Vivien Stern of an independent review into how rape complaints are handled by public authorities in England and Wales. London: Home Office, Government Formalities Office.

Storey, J., Hart, S., Reid Meloy, J. and Reavis, J. ( 2009) 'Psychopathy and stalking', *Law and Human Behavior*, 33: 237–46.

Street, A.E., Gradus, J. and Stafford, J. (2007) 'Gender differences in experiences of sexual harassment; data from a male dominated environment', *Journal of Counselling and Clinical Psychology*, 75: 464-472.

Ward, T., Polaschek, D. and Beech, A.R. (2006) *Theories of Sexual Offending*. Chichester: Wiley.

Wijkman, M., Bijleveld, C., and Hendriks, J. (2010) 'Women don't do such things! Characteristics of female sex offenders and offender type', *Sex Abuse*, 22: 135–56.

Wyre, R. and Swift, A. (1990) *Women, Men and Rape*. London: Headway/Hodder and Stoughton.

Youngs, D. (2004) 'Personality correlates of offence style', *Journal of Investigative Psychology and Offender Profiling*, 1: 99–119.

## Chapter 8

# On sociological perspectives

*Helen Jones*

## Meet Helen Jones

Helen Jones is a Principal Lecturer in Criminology at Manchester Metropolitan University. Helen's research and teaching interests include the politics of gender violence, critical analysis of policy on rape and sexual violence, and educational pedagogy. Her book *Rape Crisis: Responding to Sexual Violence* (with Kate Cook) was published by Russell House in 2008. She has written chapters in a number of books and is a member of the editorial panel of the journal *Enhanced Learning in the Social Sciences*. Helen has been a consultant on a number of government committees, including the Sexual Offences Review, which culminated in the enactment of the Sex Offences Act 2003. She has published work in journals such as *Social Policy and Society*, *Feminist Media Studies* and *Contemporary Issues in Law*. She has contributed to the *Encyclopaedia of Victimology and Crime Prevention* published by Sage in 2010 and has presented papers at numerous academic conferences in the UK, USA, Canada, Portugal, Sweden, Finland and Mongolia. Helen considers herself to be 'so lucky to have worked with so many fine people, from research and writing partners, my students and colleagues, to my local rape crisis group and the women supported there. Yes, the work can be really tough but there is also much laughter and support. Whether we are writing articles or taking part in demonstrations, it all helps to move us forward and speak out.'

## Introduction

Sociology has been defined as 'a science implicated in the policy process' (Walklate 2001: 20) and the 'science of society' (Abbott and Wallace 1990: 3). Sociological analysis operates at the collective level, such as the family, or the community, the city, the organisation, the nation state, and internationally. Of primary importance is how the social structure is maintained or changed through processes that may be beneficial or detrimental to certain social groups. Simply stated, in sociology the emphasis is on society rather than the individual. Certainly, sociological perspectives offer complex theoretical and methodological frameworks through which to understand and explain sexual violence. Theory is informed by methods and by discourses regarding the nature of the social world. Sociology can therefore offer historically and culturally informed discussions from a range of perspectives to open the door on the once secret world of sexual violence. With around 40 years of sociological research on sexual violence since the advent of the second wave of feminism, many characteristics of sexual violence are now well understood, we have some idea of the extent of the problem, the response of the state and the impact on the lives of the women, children and men affected. Although cross-cultural research suggests that some (rape-prone) societies have higher rates of sexual violence than others it is reasonable to claim that many societies contain some level of sexual violence and that all modern Western societies can be considered rape-prone (Sanday 1981; Seifert 1996: Hagemann-White 2001; Lovett and Kelly 2009).

The primary questions addressed within this chapter concern whether sociological analysis can tell us anything about the extent of sexual violence; whether the behaviour of the legal system can tell us anything about societal attitudes to victims of sexual violence; and to what extent sociological analysis can help in understanding the phenomenon of myth acceptance across the continuum of sexual violence. Wilson (1983: 12) discussed women's sexual lives as existing on a pleasure/danger continuum: 'Men whistle and call after us on the street. This is at the other extreme of the pleasure/danger continuum and is a more contradictory experience than the sheer terror of rape and mutilation [...] Yet the daily control of women by sexual innuendo is not trivial.' Radical analyses of the violence perpetrated against women helped to identify a continuum of violence (Kelly 1988), placing 'everyday' violations (Stanko 1990) within a structural context to explore the connections between sexual violation and social control. These theoretical developments from a feminist-informed sociological perspective cast light on the mythology that still exists to support and legitimise sexual violence.

## Taking the sociological imagination into women's lives

*Sociology* focuses on human relationships within social settings, how relationships influence other people, what external forces might be influential and the social institutions and structures of the world around us. In 1959, sociologist C. Wright Mills defined 'the *sociological imagination*' as the ability to see the impact of social forces on individuals' private and public lives. Sociological imagination is a central concept to the sociological perspective and yet, until the 1960s and 1970s, sociology demonstrated little ability to see the impact of social forces on women's private and public lives. The denial of the importance of gender within sociology and other cognate disciplines was 'in part a product of an uncritical acceptance of deeply embedded assumptions about the nature of scientific enterprise and what could count as knowledge' (Walklate 2001: 56). Patriarchal ideologies (male patterns of ideas) explained and legitimated the prevailing social structure and culture through partial knowledge: knowledge that served the interests of men (Abbott and Wallace

1990). During the next sections of this chapter some key issues will be explored:

- Violence against women is an element of society and part of the continuum of sexual violence;
- Violence against women is complex but functions as a symbolic expression of control;
- Statistical data matters because it helps to document the extent of violence;
- Rape has been known about for a long time but has only recently been focused on by sociological research;
- Violence against women has a profound impact on families and communities;
- Women's role within the structure of the community means that violence against them has significance for all within that community;
- Violence against women continues despite changes in legislation.

Patriarchal ideologies have the effect of disguising the reality of male power and although in recent years the flow of ideas and understandings about rape has contributed to academic knowledge (Horvath and Brown 2009) and has had an impact on social and criminal justice policy, it is important to continue to examine theoretical perspectives that remain prominent in explaining social life.

### Violence against women is an element of society: structural-functionalism

Structural-functionalism focuses on the ways social institutions meet social needs. A key example is the concept of the family. All aspects of the family are seen as functional in the sense of working together to achieve a state of solidarity. Through this sociological perspective, important questions to ask include: 'What is the function of this person/institution/system?' Thus, we can ask, 'What is the function of sexual violence for societal stability?' This would yield different answers to those questions posed by psychology, which might instead pose questions of a more personal and individual nature. The sociological answer is complex and necessitates a detailed analysis of gender politics, sex-role theory, sexual relationships and criminal law, but one answer is that sexual violence functions to keep all women in a state of fear because it is impossible for a woman to tell which men are safe and which are not, thereby maintaining the status quo of patriarchy (Brownmiller 1975; Banyard 2010; Walter 2010).

Structural-functionalism has been criticised because it thinks about elements of social life in relation to their present function but gives no analysis of potential futures. It tends to support the status quo and so it is not the best perspective through which to understand why or how something might change. So in returning to our question, 'What is the function of sexual violence for societal stability?', structural-functionalism can tell us about the present but it does not offer a framework for how things might change.

**Violence against women is complex: conflict theory**

Conflict theory differs from structural-functionalism because instead of understanding society as striving for equilibrium, society is seen as in *competition* and subject to *change*. Resources (not merely material resources but also things such as power and influence) are limited and some social structures have more resources than others and so have higher status and greater ability to maintain their position. Where the structural-functionalist approach struggles to explain change in society, conflict theory argues that society is constantly in change and conflict over resources. So competition over resources is at the heart of all social relationships. Inequality is inherent in all social structures and change occurs because of competing interests. Through this sociological perspective, then, important questions to ask include: 'Who benefits?' Thus, we can ask, 'Who benefits from sexual violence within society?' Again, this sociological question has no easy answers but since the 1970s the developing answer has had a gendered analysis at the heart of it. Thinking about sexual violence this way demonstrates why both structural-functionalist and conflict theories are helpful in understanding how society works.

Many early second-wave feminists of the 1970s worked within a conflict-theory approach, analysing gender inequalities and seeking to explain why women experienced discrimination. Of course feminism was not the only social movement to take a conflict-theory approach to the issue of social discrimination. Marxist theories on the exploitation of the working class and critical theorists analysing ethnic discrimination are likely to take such an approach. However, many feminists critiqued the explanatory power of Marxism to explain the subordinate, unequal position of women in modern capitalist society. Hartmann (1981) challenged Marxist economic analysis as sex-blind in its inability to explain women's subordinate position to men inside and outside the family. A combined sociological perspective on capitalism and patriarchy has been described as a 'dual-system theory' (Abbott and Wallace 1990) but Walby (1990) argued that writers often tend to keep the two distinct and separate, assigning economic production to capitalism and reproductive formation to patriarchy. This can result in a failure to account for gender inequality within the public sphere (and capitalism has undoubtedly benefited from the marginalisation of women in the workforce). Towards the end of the twentieth century Walby (1990) confirmed that while liberal feminism made many gains – from the vote, property ownership and rights in marriage – patriarchy was not defeated: a view that is being confirmed again in the early twenty-first century (Horvath and Brown 2009; Wykes and Welsh 2009; Banyard 2010; Walter 2010). Feminist perspectives have branched in many directions but one constant has been the perception of patriarchy as central to understanding gendered roles.

**Violence against women functions as a symbolic expression of control: symbolic interactionism**

Symbolic interactionism understands human action and interaction within society through the exchange of meaningful communication. Therefore *meaning* and *interaction* are key concepts. The symbolic meanings relating to gendered language mean that when we speak of 'a woman' or 'a man' a tidal wave of meanings, assumptions and understandings are brought into play. The meanings we give to these words are bigger than mere biological categories. As Connell argues, 'When an American football coach yells at his losing team that they are a "bunch of women", he does not mean they can now get pregnant' (1987: 65): he is saying something which is contextually and symbolically important. The potential for violation committed by symbolically laden language should not be underestimated. From the wolf whistle in the street, to the example given here by Connell, right through to the death threat, language is an important factor in the continuum of sexual violence (Kelly 1988).

One way of understanding symbolic interactionism is through the concept of the 'looking-glass self' (Cooley 1902), which suggests that one's sense of self develops from one's interactions with others. Certainly MacKinnon (1987: 105) has argued that women understand their own position by measuring themselves 'against every rape case she ever heard about' and Walter makes the point that young women today 'know they are likely to be judged not for their competence and skills, but on how closely they resemble a porn star' (2010: 121). Yeung and Martin (2003) suggest there are three main components of the looking-glass self: first we imagine how we must appear to others, then we imagine the judgement of others of that appearance, and then we develop our sense of self through the judgements of others. Through this focus on micro-level interactions, important questions to ask include: 'Do some people understand certain phenomena differently from others in society?' Thus, one can ask, 'Do men and women have different understandings of sexual violence in society?'

Banyard (2010: 106) suggests that 'sexist violence is the Houdini of modern-day social crises' because it evades definition, and Walter (2010: 33) adds that there is a danger that by 'co-opting the language of choice and liberation' we obscure the realities of sexual violence. It has been argued that it is in 'men's interest, as a class and as the perpetrators of sexual violence, to ensure the definitions of sexual violence are as limited as possible' (Kelly 1988: 130). Feminists have struggled with the limitations imposed by narrow definitions and have campaigned to have different forms of sexual violence acknowledged by the law, including marital rape, oral penetration and 'more "taken for granted" forms such as sexual harassment' (ibid.: 27). These boundaries of definition continue to be pushed as women increasingly enter the realm of cyberspace. In virtual worlds, human-like avatars can be constructed by choosing from a palette of characteristics such as age, gender, physical shape and colour where the female form is human enough to be raped but not human enough for it to be deemed a crime (Jones 2010).

## Can sociological analyses tell us anything about the extent of sexual violence?

Sociological research will employ empirical evidence from a variety of sources.

Two main data sources in the UK are official statistics based on incidents reported to the police (Walker *et al.* 2009) and the British Crime Survey which relies on self-reported experiences (Walby and Allen 2004). The prevalence and incidence rates vary depending on the source, with official rates of sexual violence almost always much lower than data from surveys and victim agencies. In understanding the continuum of sexual violence, a cautious approach needs to be taken to any statistical data on sexual violence due to the unknown level of unreported violence. From a sociological perspective we also need to be wary of focusing on the individual and think critically about how we can unmask wider social forces because the 'collection of data is of course important but only in so far as it can be put to practical use' (Jones 2005: 589).

### The British Crime Survey

The British Crime Survey is a tool for gathering statistical data and defines sexual assault as that part of their intimate violence typology that includes 'indecent exposure, sexual threats and unwanted touching ('less serious'), rape or assault by penetration including attempts ('serious'), by any person including a partner or family member' (Coleman *et al.* 2007). Findings from the 2005/06 British Crime Survey show that almost a quarter (24 per cent) of women reported having experienced sexual assault since age 16. Serious sexual assaults were less prevalent with five per cent of women reporting rape since age 16 and the prevalence rates of sexual assaults were considerably lower among men (Coleman *et al.* 2007).

Survey data provides evidence that sexual violence is strongly gendered and that the majority of perpetrators are male (Powis 2002; Kimmel 2004; Walby and Allen 2004). This does not mean that all perpetrators are male or that all men are sexually violent. Indeed, the majority of men are non-violent and some women are sexually violent. ChildLine's (2009) research showed that calls in 2008 about sexual abuse of children by women had risen and of the 16,094 children who called, 2,142 told of abuse by a woman, up 132 per cent on 2004–5. Of course, it has been long known that a small percentage of all known offenders are women. Vanessa George, who in 2009 stood trial on sexual abuse offences, gained access to the children she abused through her employment in a nursery: 'She sexually assaulted them and used the camera on her mobile phone to record the abuse. She used objects found at the nursery in the assaults, but also smuggled a sex toy in for at least one attack' (Morris and Carter 2009). Research from the 1990s shows that female perpetrators tend to commit fewer and less intrusive acts of sexual abuse compared with males (Saradjian 1996). But while we acknowledge this we also recognise that although some sexual offending by women remains hidden, it is still a very small percentage of the overall total. Any search for equivalence in male and female offending rates runs the risk of detracting from the need to acknowledge fundamental issues of male power in society (McLeod and Saraga 1988; Forbes 1992).

## Official statistics

Serious sexual crime is defined by the police as including 'rape, sexual assault and sexual activity with children' (Walker *et al.* 2009). The Sexual Offences Act 2003, introduced in May 2004, altered the definitions of all three categories and so the comparison of present-day data with previous data is complicated and any patterns in recorded sexual offences should be considered with regard to this. The police recorded 40,787 serious sexual offences in 2008/09 compared with 41,440 similar offences in 2007/08 (Roe *et al.* 2009). Within this 2008/09 total, police recorded 12,165 rapes of a female and 968 rapes of a male.

However, sociological critique suggests that even seemingly hard data requires critical examination. Certainly on the release of the Stern Review into the handling of rape complaints (March 2010), a key focus was on the number of rapes which resulted in a conviction in the courts. This is of course just the most recent of a long line of reviews, reports and evaluations conducted by government over the years, many of which can be found listed on the website of the Child and Woman Abuse Studies Unit (http://www.cwasu.org/). One of the aims of the Stern Review was to 'explore ways in which the attrition rate in criminal cases can be reduced, and how to fairly increase the conviction rate' (Stern 2010: 6). While it is useful that both the attrition rate and the conviction rate are features of the review, the media and other social commentators remain confused about the differences in these two terms. The attrition rate refers to the number of convictions secured compared with the number of rapes reported to the police (Lovett and Kelly 2009). The conviction rate refers to the number of convictions secured against the number of persons brought to trial for rape.

> Of every 100 cases reported, about 15 were eventually not recorded as crimes, were retracted or were withdrawn very quickly by the complainant. Of the remaining 85, about 20 were subsequently withdrawn by the victim, 23 were not proceeded with because the evidence was felt to be not strong enough and about 14 were not proceeded with for other reasons. In about 26 cases a suspect was charged with the offence of rape. That figure was reduced to 19 at the time the decision was made to go ahead with a prosecution. A number of the prosecutions were unsuccessful because the complainant decided not to continue or did not attend, the evidence of the victim did not support the case, or there was a conflict of evidence or an essential legal element missing. Some cases were withdrawn because of fears of the effect on the complainant's mental health. Finally of those taken to court around 12 were found guilty of rape *or a related offence*.
>
> (Stern 2010: 44–5, emphasis added)

This is largely a repetition of what has been known for many years, certainly since the report *A Question of Evidence?* (Home Office 1999) but paradoxically endorses analysis on attrition (Lovett and Kelly 2009; and see the website of the Child and Woman Abuse Studies Unit, http://www.cwasu.org/) while negatively claiming that the attrition figure dominates the public discourse 'without explanation, analysis and context, [and] is extremely unhelpful' (*ibid.*:

45). It is unclear to whom it is unhelpful. The concept of the attrition rate has allowed researchers to unpick the reality of why so few cases of rape are reported, recorded, investigated and prosecuted. Over the past 30 years, the attrition rate had fallen from 33 per cent in 1977 to 5.29 per cent in 2004 (Office for Criminal Justice Reform 2006: 8). Instead of using attrition as a measure, the Stern Review seems to prefer to use the conviction rate of 58 per cent (Stern 2010: 10). Yet it does not make comparable conviction rates available to help the reader make sense of the statistic. If the 58 per cent is compared with that for violence against the person, which is 71 per cent (Kershaw *et al.* 2008), it would seem that the statistical likelihood of securing a conviction in rape is more difficult than in other violent crimes and many offenders walk free. Let me rephrase that: many rapists walk free. There is an intellectual reluctance to confront what else this means in real terms, even though there is a well-known sociological phenomenon that some criminals are serial offenders. Let me rephrase that: each time a man walks free from raping or sexually violating someone, the risk increases that he will offend again. In a society where only around six per cent of rapes reported to the police result in a conviction (Stern 2010), rape still constitutes a low-risk activity for many men.

Within just the Metropolitan Police Authority area, rape has the highest percentage change of all violent crime (Table 8.1) with an increase of 470 cases in a 12-month period. The large increase was an effect of a correction in data after it came to light that the Metropolitan Police failed to record large numbers of rape allegations as criminal offences. Speaking in *The Guardian*, former Deputy Assistant Commissioner of the Metropolitan Police Brian Paddick said, 'It is shocking this has happened for such a serious offence. It could be a reflection of the pressure the police are under from the Home Office to improve the clear-up rate and reduce reported crime. There is not the political will in government and the Home Office to put resources into place, which the offence requires, to bring people to justice' (Dodd 2009). It also marks an almost institutionalised distrust of rape victims whereby the initial report is deemed unworthy of officially recording.

**Table 8.1** Crime in London 2008

|  | Down | Up | Change in number of offences | Percentage change |
|---|---|---|---|---|
| Violence |  |  |  |  |
| Most serious violence and assault with injury |  | ↑ | +147 | +0.2 |
| Gun crime |  | ↑ | +283 | +14.3 |
| Knife crime | ↓ |  | -1319 | −9.9 |
| Youth violence | ↓ |  | -1098 | −5.2 |
| Rape offences |  | ↑ | +470 | +22.0 |
| All other serious sexual offences |  | ↑ | +534 | +8.2 |
| Homicide | ↓ |  | −24 | −15.6 |

*Source*: Metropolitan Police Authority 2010

## Invisible or unrecorded

Sexual violence might also be a feature of other recorded crimes and/or might go completely untold, unreported and unrecorded. Following a Freedom of Information Act request, the BBC reported that many rape claims do not even make it to official crime records (BBC News 2009). Previous criticism of police data on sexual violence includes a report by Fawcett which highlights the differences across England and Wales, with attrition rates from 1.6 per cent in Dorset to 18.1 per cent in Cleveland (Fawcett 2009). At another point on the continuum, sexual violence can culminate in death. Domestic homicide is strongly associated with gender (Stark and Flitcraft 1996) and victims are overwhelmingly women. Women are more likely to be killed by a partner or ex-partner than by any other category of assailant (Lees 1997; Coleman *et al.* 2007) and men form the overwhelming majority of perpetrators of all forms of homicide and in particular for all forms of domestic homicide including child homicide. When women kill it is frequently in order to defend themselves or their children from a male partner who has been abusing them and more than half of all male victims of domestic homicide are killed by a partner they had been abusing (Stark and Flitcraft 1996). Lees (1997) suggested that the discourses used by judges in considering the lethal actions of men legitimise many rape myths and Mason and Monckton-Smith (2008) argue that murders of women are regularly sexualised by journalists. They use discourse analysis of six case studies of rape and/or murder of women by men to show how a conflation of the offences of rape and murder contributes to the acceptance of rape myths by criminal justice professionals, victims and the wider public. One such myth is that rape is always accompanied by physical violence. They argue that Jack the Ripper was defined by the media as the archetypal rapist despite the fact that 'there is no evidence to suggest that any attempts to rape the victims were made, or that the killer ejaculated over the bodies' (2008: 692). It is argued that this type of mythmaking had real consequences in hampering the investigation into the murders committed by Peter Sutcliffe (dubbed the Yorkshire Ripper). The construction of offender profiles reinforces an 'extremely limited and distorted image of what serial murder is, who commits it, who is victimized, how they are victimized and why they are victimized' (Schmid 2005: 79).

Assumptions about roles and entitlements frequently underlie the justifications presented in court for serious sexual violence. Lees (1997) researched how women (and girls) who give evidence in criminal trials as victims were subjected to inquisitions concerning their sexual reputation. Such a reputation was examined by questioning their past sexual experiences. The cross-examination aimed to undermine their credibility and a key question in a rape trial frequently examines the separation between consensual and non-consensual activity. A rape case against five men in 2010 illustrated this issue of credibility when it collapsed after a court heard that the female victim had used an online forum to talk about taking part in group sex (BBC News 2010). The judge ordered the jury to return not guilty verdicts after learning that the woman had shared fantasies with a man over the Internet and then went to visit him. She said her intention was to have sex only with him but when she arrived at his house she was confronted by several men. The judge stated, 'This case depended on the complainant's credibility...Not to put too fine a point on it, her credibility was shot to pieces.' By doing this, the judge suggested that the complainant had, by sharing her fantasies, invited the rape and only had herself to blame. This suggests again an institutionalised distrust of rape victims and how women who have been raped continue to be questioned on their behaviour, underpinned by the assumption that she has somehow provoked the attack (Stanko 1990; Temkin 2000; Horvath and Brown 2009). It has long been recognised that victims of rape are 'put on trial' (Abbott and Wallace 1990: 174) despite changes in the law (see Section 41, Youth Justice and Criminal Justice Act 1999) and that it is women's behaviour (rather than men's) that is scrutinised by the courts and held to be responsible for provoking the violence of men. In the case from 2010, no question was raised of the credibility of men regarding whether they fabricated their belief in her consent. Even if a person initially consents to sex, they have a legal right to change their mind. Regardless of any sexual fantasies, withdrawal of consent is legally permissible and to continue without consent constitutes rape. The issue should have been about consent rather than assumptions about the credibility of someone who has fantasised about a particular form of sex. It is an illusion that sociological understandings of sexual violence have filtered into the hearts and minds of the judiciary or the wider public. A survey was published in 2010 of the views of more than 1,000 people in London to mark the tenth anniversary of the Haven service for rape victims. More than half of those of both sexes questioned said there were some circumstances when a rape victim should accept responsibility (The Havens 2010). Gender-based assumptions may not make certain outcomes inevitable but while they go unchallenged, or even supported, many abusive men will continue to treat such assumptions as adequate justification for their own sexually violent behaviour.

### Falling outside of local statistics: war and oppressive regimes

The horror of sexual violence in wartime can often be obscured by limits of terminology. Although the expression 'rape in war' will be used as a shorthand term throughout this section we need to be alive to the fact that sexual violence in war takes a variety of forms, including 'individual rapes, sexual abuse, gang rapes, genital mutilation, and rape-shooting or rape-stabbing combinations, at times undertaken after family members have been tied up and forced to watch' (Pratt and Werchick 2004: 6). Forced prostitution, sexual slavery and sterilisation are also common forms of wartime sexual violence. This section explores the same issues identified earlier but within the context of war:

* Violence against women is an element of war and part of the continuum of sexual violence;
* Violence against women in war is complex but functions as a symbolic expression of defeat;

- Statistical data matters because it helps to document the extent of violence against humanity;
- Rape in war has been known about for a long time but has only recently been focused on as a ritualised expression of masculinity;
- Violence against women has a profound impact on the cultural heritage of a people;
- Women's role within the structure of the community means that violence against them has significance for all within that community;
- Violence against women continues after formal conflict has ended;
- Rape can be a 'spoil of peace' as well as a 'spoil of war'.

Caution has to be raised about the statistics of sexual violations committed in war because, as with local-level reporting cited earlier, violations against women are rarely fully recorded or documented systematically (Wood 2006; Gray and Marek 2008). Do statistics even matter? What is the difference between one million rapes and two million in the context of war? Why count rapes in war (or in peace for that matter)? It matters to the sociological imagination, however, because each victim is a human being and by acknowledging their experiences and connecting them to others who have suffered, by making even just the best estimate possible, we can acknowledge their value as human beings, connected to the wider humanity of us all and take the first step towards trying to support the survivors (Enloe 2000).

From early feminist demands that sociological analysis take women's lives seriously, 'experts' from a range of different fields have been challenged to construct knowledge based on credible evidence and this includes assessing gender impacts. Pilch (2009) suggests that the concept of rape as genocide began to emerge in the 1990s when the systematic rape of women was used as a strategy of war in the former Yugoslavia. However, Seifert (1996) claims the understanding of rape in war was not new and cites Brownmiller's reporting of mass rapes in Bangladesh: 'The rapes were so systematic and pervasive that they had to be conscious Army policy' (Brownmiller 1975: 85). Seifert documents some of the known cases of rape in war:

> In the Chinese city of Nanking in 1937, an estimated 20,000 women were raped, sexually tortured, and murdered during the first month of the Japanese occupation [...] According to evidence presented at the Nuremberg war-crimes tribunal, the German command had opened a brothel in a hotel in the city of Smolensk into which women were forcibly driven. It also became known that it was the usual practice to tattoo the legend 'Whore for Hitler's troops' on the bodies of captured partisan women and to use them accordingly [...] In Korea during World War II between 100,000 and 200,000 women (the 'comfort women' who are now speaking out) were abducted to camps and raped or sexually tortured by the Japanese [...] 200,000 women were raped in Bangladesh in 1971 [...] in Kuwait, according to official statistics at least 5,000 women are assumed to have become victims of rape during the [1990] Iraqi occupation.
>
> (Seifert 1996: 37)

Geraldine Brooks (1996: 183) discusses how during the 1991 Gulf War, Kurdish women were raped by Iraqi soldiers 'as part of the regime of torture [...] Others had been raped as a means of torturing their imprisoned fathers, brothers or husbands.' Other conflicts in which rape was widespread include civil wars in Bosnia–Herzegovina, the Democratic Republic of the Congo, Liberia, Sierra Leone, Rwanda, Sudan and Somalia (Canning and Tobin 2010). Although it is less common than female sexual assault during conflict, men are also raped or forced to rape or perform other sexual acts and have suffered sexual mutilations (Wood 2006).

Wielding a sociological imagination means that real-life micro-level consequences can be connected to macro-level events. In the case of war, this sociological analysis of taking the lives of women seriously can illuminate how modern-day warfare is conducted and how an examination of socio-economic forces highlights how, for many young men, the only available source of 'employment' is the military or some militarised group which is underpinned by cultures of masculinity toxic to women and children (Enloe 2000). Such cultures of masculinity encourage obedience to authority, dilute individual responsibility and progressively lead to moral disengagement (Wood 2006; Canning and Tobin 2010). Seifert suggests that feminist understandings of rape in war finally made an impact in mainstream understandings due to the escalation of rape in Yugoslavia with the establishment of 'camps explicitly intended for sexual torture' (1996: 35) together with the rise in the number of women in 'politics, academia, science, and the media enabling them to make these incidents a political issue and to question the established, marginalising explanations that have been offered' (*ibid.*).

Using our earlier sociological framework, we can ask certain questions of the issue of rape in war:

1. What is the strategic function of sexual violence within war?
2. Who benefits from sexual violence within war?
3. Do men and women have different understandings of sexual violence within war?

Of course these are just some of the questions that can be raised but in considering the *function*, *benefits* and *understandings* of sexual violence against women in war we can begin to see that an attack on the social cement of families and communities is an effective strategy in conflict and that the 'dehumanisation of the woman through this process is used to persecute the community to which they belong' (Jones 2005: 590). The destruction of social and cultural stability through rape in present-day Sudan has a physical and symbolic impact on the self-image of the whole people (Gray and Marek 2008). Destruction of women has a more profound impact on the cultural heritage of a people than the destruction of buildings, art or other cultural artefacts.

Social stigma has left large numbers of rape victims and children born of rape rejected by their families and communities. Many cases of HIV and other infections remain untested and untreated. Fear of going to fields and markets – sites where rapes often take place – has resulted in spiralling malnutrition and economic loss.

(Pratt and Werchick 2004: 6)

Outside of war, brutal regimes use sexual violence as a tactic in their military control of populations. Under the Taliban, oppressed and terrorised Afghan woman 'suffered massive, systematic, and unrelenting human rights abuses that have permeated every aspect of their lives [...] on the basis of both gender and ethnicity' (Human Rights Watch 2001: 2). Under such a regime women who had sex outside of marriage or were accused of being prostitutes were executed. Married women who were raped were deemed to have been unfaithful and faced being stoned to death. The Ministry for the Promotion of Virtue and Prevention of Vice enforced restrictions against women through public beatings.

It has been argued that 'The Northern Alliance (NA) may be viewed by the West as a great improvement on the Taliban, but Afghan women do not see it that way. In 1992, after the NA entered Kabul and other cities, it embarked on a spree of murder, rape, plunder and torture, attacking men and women from 7 to seventy. They killed more than 50,000 people in Kabul alone between 1992 and 1996' (The Guardian, 7 March 2002). Just imagine, 50,000 people; that would more than fill a football stadium. Indeed, many of the executions took place in sporting stadia, under full public scrutiny.

(Jones 2005: 591)

The Afghanistan Independent Human Rights Commission (AIHRC 2010) recorded 184 cases of self-immolation by Afghani women in 2007: women desperate to escape sexual and domestic violence. This rose from 106 in 2006 and an estimated 90 per cent died from their serious burns. The Revolutionary Association of the Women of Afghanistan (RAWA) says on its website:

The US 'War on terrorism' removed the Taliban regime in October 2001, but it has not removed religious fundamentalism which is the main cause of all our miseries. In fact, by reinstalling the warlords in power in Afghanistan, the US administration is replacing one fundamentalist regime with another.

(RAWA 2009)

The World Health Organisation suggests that 'in many countries that have suffered violent conflict, the rates of interpersonal violence remain high even after the cessation of hostilities – among other reasons because of the way violence has become more socially acceptable' (2002: 15). In December 2009, United Nations peacekeepers in the Democratic Republic of the Congo (DRC) suspended operations due to evidence showing their operations had contributed to human rights violations. Over the first nine months of 2009, the UN recorded over 7,500 cases of sexual violence against women and girls across eastern Congo, probably representing only a fraction of the total. Most of the women and girls were gang raped, some so violently that they later died. Many were raped repeatedly and some were mutilated and then killed by machete or shot in the vagina (Reuters 2009). The power of the military to control the peace extends to controlling violence in the examples of Kosovo where women have been trafficked into the country for forced prostitution by the military, Somalia where a teenage girl was bought as a birthday present for a Belgian paratrooper and reports of sexual violence committed by Italian peacekeeping forces in Mozambique (Amnesty International 2004: 54–5). Mexican women 'pay the price' of rape in exchange for not being deported from the US by border militia (Falcœn 2006: 120), while male prisoners of US detention camps at Abu Ghraib and Guantánamo suffered numerous forms of sexual violations, including being forced to adopt homosexual group sex poses (Wood 2006).

Sexual violence in war, in so-called peacetime under male oppression, such as under the Taliban rule in Afghanistan, and by peacekeepers, demonstrates the widespread nature of such violence. These sexual violations illustrate how rapists in these contexts capitalise on their institutional power over women in similar ways to those by which violence is perpetrated at a local level by men known to women (Canning and Tobin 2010). A more comprehensive understanding of the motivations for sexual violence is critical to the development of effective strategies for prevention and response. Nation states have duties under international law to respect, protect and fulfil women's rights: in other words, to take effective steps to stop violence against women (Stewart 2004: Jones and Wachala 2006). On a local level, justice systems often fail to deliver justice despite the existence of legislation to protect women. Societal tolerance of violence, patriarchal cultural norms and a lack of political will often combine to nullify the law in practice and instead provide a context for the perpetuation of rape myths.

## Challenging myths

Within sociology, theories of sexual violence existed prior to the second wave of feminism; however, few dealt directly with social structures. Instead, theories suggested that individuals learned to behave violently, or that biochemical processes might be the cause of abnormal behaviour. It has been suggested that biological theories of sex differences 'have come and gone like fashions in hem length' (Walter 2010: 203). Some theories took a psychological path in considering how jealousy, fear and blame might result in sexual violence, while social learning theories prioritised learning, differential association and intergenerational transmission of violence (Bourke 2007). Yet in many locations, rape remains an everyday event rather than an out-of-the-ordinary violation (Stanko 1990; Coleman *et al.* 2007; Lovett and Kelly 2009; Banyard 2010). Utilising such theories, men have been able to excuse themselves as victims of their own sex drives, or blame their own upbringing or women themselves for stepping outside of accepted gender roles. If existing theories of violence were too limited (and there is little doubt of that) and if the different expressions of sexual violence are connected (and there is little doubt of that), then what is needed is a coherent approach that goes beyond current provisions. If public and political responses are to change, the change has to come from society as a whole. While society continues to accept the myths surrounding male violence against women, the actuality of violence will not change.

Despite the legislative reforms of the mid 1970s surrounding socio-economic rights (Equal Pay Act 1975; Sex Discrimination Act 1975; Employment Protection Act 1975; Sexual Offences Amendment Act 1976), women were still not equal within the private domain of the home and it was not until 1991 that marital rape became a crime in England and Wales (Jones and Cook 2008). Within mainstream sociological theory the family is a primary social structure and 'remains symbolic of security, stability and the known' (Wykes and Welsh 2009: 105). The family functions as a location for sex-role behaviour within society and rape within marriage disturbs the myth of the family. Utilising the concept of the continuum of violence has helped to reframe individual harms into social problems (Kelly 1988; Banyard 2010). Women in many parts of the world have come to redefine the violence they experience as a crime. Whether they receive justice or not is dependent on institutional responses from the state. This is where the police, prosecutors and legislators still have far to go in translating sociological understandings into social transformation. Any action along the continuum of sexual violence that diminishes autonomy, choice, bodily integrity and equality is more than an individual harm: it is a challenge to justice.

If we ask how well these different models work to explain the statistical data on sexual violence the question cannot be answered adequately as most quantitative surveys have not been designed with explicit reference to theoretical models. Although statistical data fail to account for one in 20 rapes (according to the accounts from victim organisations (Jones and Cook 2008: 71)), it can be argued that sexual violence against women appears to be widespread across history and within different cultures. Sexual violence is not necessarily a universal phenomenon, but where sexual violence is embedded in social systems (in peacetime and in warfare) a key sociological endeavour should aim to understand the function of rape myths, to ask who benefits from rape myths and whether men and women have different understandings of rape myths.

Rape myths function to give people a false perception of the reality of sexual violence. They may operate in providing women with a false sense of security by minimising or denying the extent of sexual violence. Such myths are comforting to believe because individual women can reassure themselves that they are safe from rape: 'I would never walk in the dark, wear those clothes, or drink too much.' Myths often work by blaming the victim and making excuses for the perpetrator. The generally held assumptions and myths that surround sexual violence include Box 8.1 (however, this is not an exhaustive list).

---

**Box 8.1** Assumptions and myths around sexual violence

**Myth – sexual violence is rare**
Reality – around 21 per cent of girls and 11 per cent of boys experience some form of child sexual abuse; 23 per cent of women and 3 per cent of men experience sexual assault as an adult; 5 per cent of women and 0.4 per cent of men experience rape (Rape Crisis 2009).

**Myth – false allegations of rape are common**
Reality – there is no reliable evidence that more false complaints are made in rape cases than in other serious crimes. In fact, 40 per cent of adults who are raped tell no one about it and 31 per cent of children who are abused reach adulthood without having disclosed their abuse (Rape Crisis 2009).

**Myth – rape victims should put up a fight and show signs of struggle and a victim will sustain genital injuries**
Reality – not all rape survivors sustain physical injuries. However, support groups highlight the harms that go beyond immediate physical injuries: 'Direct physical health consequences of sexual violence and child sexual abuse include physical injury, sexually transmitted infections and unwanted pregnancy. Long-term consequences of sexual violence and child sexual abuse include post-traumatic stress disorder, anxiety and panic attacks, depression, social phobia, substance abuse, obesity, eating disorders, self harm and suicide, domestic violence and in some cases, offending behaviour. Child abuse can also impact on educational attainment and school attendance. The overall cost to society of sexual offences in 2003–04 was estimated at £8.5 billion, with each rape costing over £76,000. Much of this cost is made up of lost output and costs to the health service resulting from long-term health issues faced by victims' (Rape Crisis 2009).

**Myth – most rapes are committed by strangers**
Reality – most rapists are known to the victim and are likely to be a partner or former partner, friend, colleague, acquaintance or health professional (Walby and Allen 2004; Wykes and Welsh 2009).

**Myth – stranger rape is more traumatic than rape by a known person**
Reality – sexual assault can be more traumatic if a breach of trust is involved (Stanko 1990; Walby and Allen 2004).

---

Belief in such myths means that women's credibility, if they do speak out against sexual violence, is questioned and their accounts frequently discredited. This may be challenged as rape myths received media attention in March 2009 when revised policy guidance from the Crown Prosecution Service directed prosecutors to challenge ideas that women provoke rape by the way they dress, if they get drunk or if they do not scream: 'Other myths to be challenged are the way a victim acts proves whether she was raped or not, victims cry rape if they regret having sex or want revenge, only gay men are raped and prostitutes cannot be raped' (Whitehead 2009).

However, societal attitudes are hard to shift. Within military cultures there is a code of silence that prevents soldiers reporting on each other (Falcón 2006) and the same is true of men in other contexts (Temkin 2000). There is often a claim that there is too much media and not enough news but in the reporting of sexual violence there is a lack of portrayal of known perpetrator rape. Media reports tend to focus on stranger rapes, which obscures the extent of sexual violence that is perpetrated by men known to the victim (Wykes and Welsh 2009) and encourages the myth that if the perpetrator is someone known (and especially if there are no physical injuries) then there has been no rape. This, together with inefficient reporting systems and lack of proportionate levels of investigation staff across many police areas (Fawcett 2009), means that a failure to report known perpetrator rapes acts to negate their importance and may add to an institutionalised distrust of rape victims (Burt 1980; Grover and Soothill 1996; Temkin 2000; Fitzpatrick 2001). For jurors in court this might mean that 'If they have little or no personal or sociological knowledge of sexual assault and abuse, this may entail referencing media images where rape myths portraying typical victims and offenders flourish' (Bufkin and Eschholz 2000: 1338). The sexual offender is therefore seen as deviant, monstrous even, and above all a 'stranger', abnormal from 'ordinary' men, standing outside of the marital family.

Sociology still conceptually places the family at the heart of Western culture, 'even though the perfect nuclear family is certainly a myth for many of us in the twenty-first century' (Wykes and Welsh 2009: 92). Despite this, politicians adhere to the myth of the ideal family. In January 2010, Secretary of State for Children Ed Balls launched *Support for All – the Families and Relationships Green Paper* and states in the introduction, 'Marriage is an important and well-established institution that plays a fundamental role in family life in our society.' Also in January 2010, in an interview with the *Daily Mail*, Conservative leader David Cameron said he remained committed to tax breaks for married couples, saying, 'I don't care if it's popular or not. I care whether it's right or not. It's important to say that commitment matters, that relationships matter, that marriage is a good institution and we should back it rather than undermine it' (Groves 2010).

## Conclusion

The contribution of sociology to understanding violent behaviour has revealed power inequalities and power abuses, and has resulted in some policy changes. Feminism (in whatever guise it takes) is not 'owned' by sociology or any other cognate discipline but it has helped to inform the discipline and to advance the ways in which sexual violence can be understood. Feminism has highlighted the entitlement of the powerful to sexually violate women in a myriad of different social circumstances. This entitlement is at the heart of a hegemonic web of commonly taken for granted power relations.

To engage in meaningful research into sexual violence, we need to understand the connections between the micro-dynamics (why individual men rape) and the macro patterns (why rape is a global phenomenon). Sexual violence, whether in peace or in war, is functional to patriarchal societies as it creates a sense of fear, restricts women's freedom of movement and economic activity: 'All rape is related as it derives from a system of dominance and subjugation that allows, and in fact often encourages, precisely the violent crime of rape as a way of maintaining the system' (Falcón 2006: 129). Wherever the violation exists on the continuum of violence, it can result in the demoralisation of survivors, family and friends, limiting their ability to respond effectively, and can tear communities apart by breaking family and community bonds.

Sociological perspectives can be useful in understanding the structural context of sexual violence rather than attributing causality to any individual characteristics of victims or offenders. This more structural analysis might give voice to those outside of the ethnic and economic mainstream and also has implications for service responses to the problem of sexual violence. It highlights the importance of gender as an analytical tool, together with class and race as explanatory variables. In war and in peace it is important that the public and private spheres are not viewed as separate worlds but areas of interwoven influence.

The extent of sexual violence is underestimated in all arenas and violence encompasses more than physical assault, extending across the continuum, and includes all behaviour that acts to control and intimidate women (Kelly 1988). Historically women have been reluctant to reveal the extent to which men are violent but some of the hidden crime has become visible and that is important in assessing what needs to be done to support survivors. The development of rape crisis groups, for example, represents an effective response in countering the self-blame and stigma that victims often face. However, effective support systems alone cannot counter the underpinning cultures of violence and belief systems that are highlighted by prevailing rape myths. The Stern Review (2010: 115) made the point that 'policies are not the problem. The failures are in the implementation'; and surveys, even large-scale tools such as the British Crime Survey, have failed to measure key structural factors. Research that focuses on the individuals involved and their characteristics, rather than examining the underlying social structures, may only perpetuate the problem because the issue of sexual violence does not necessarily reduce to a question of individual decisions taken by individual men. More systematic measures of violence normalisation underpinned by belief structures which give power to assumptions about acceptable behaviour are urgent imperatives.

What sociological analysis offers is an understanding that efforts to define and respond to sexual violence are built on shifting sands if the foundational social structures of violence are not examined. Sexual violence has its roots in the structural foundations of societal arrangements and relationships. Although it is widely accepted that violence does not represent an acceptable form of behaviour, violence still evades definition and pervades many aspects of life, from the macro arena of war and genocide to the private domain of the home.

## Further reading

A primary question addressed within this chapter concerned whether sociological analysis can tell us anything about the extent of sexual violence. For a comprehensive guide to researching sexual violence, see Tina Skinner, Marianne Hester and Ellen Malos's *Researching Gender Violence: Feminist Methodology in Action* (2005) Cullompton: Willan Publishing. The website of Rape Crisis (England and Wales) is a useful starting point when researching sexual violence (http://www.rapecrisis.org.uk/) and for an overview of the history of Rape Crisis see *Rape Crisis: Responding to Sexual Violence* (Helen Jones and Kate Cook 2008). Recent changes in legal procedures can be illustrative of how the legal system views societal attitudes to victims of sexual violence. The website 'Rights of Women' provides up-to-date materials on a range of legal issues, including rape and domestic violence (http://www.rightsofwomen.org.uk/). Media and cultural analysis can uncover the phenomenon of rape myth acceptance and Natasha Walter in *Living Dolls: The Return of Sexism* (2010) provides a thorough debate on the connections between gender inequality and the normalisation of sexual violence. Finally, *The Stern Review* (2010) points to future changes in how statutory agencies deal with rape, highlighting the need to tackle misconceptions and join up services.

## References

Abbott, P. and Wallace, C. (1990) *An Introduction to Sociology: Feminist Perspectives*. London: Routledge.

AIHRC (2010) *Evaluation report on General Situation of Women in Afghanistan*. Afghanistan Independent Human Rights Commission. Available at: http://www.aihrc.org.af/Evaluation_Rep_Gen_Sit_Wom.htm (accessed on 19 March 2010).

Amnesty International (2004) *It's In Our Hands: Stop Violence Against Women*. Oxford: Alden Press.

Banyard, K. (2010) *The Equality Illusion: The Truth About Men and Women Today*. London: Faber and Faber.

BBC News (2009) *Records of rape crime 'distorted'*. 21 September. Available at: http://news.bbc.co.uk/1/hi/uk/8266014.stm (accessed on 19 March 2010).

BBC News (2010) *Men cleared as rape woman's group sex fantasy revealed*. 12 January. Available at: http://news.bbc.co.uk/1/hi/england/manchester/8455161.stm (accessed on 19 March 2010).

Bourke, J. (2007) *Rape: A History from 1860 to the Present*. London: Virago.

Brooks, G. (1996) *Nine Parts of Desire: Hidden World of Islamic Women*. London: Bantam Doubleday.

Brownmiller, S. (1975) *Against Our Will: Men, Women and Rape*. Harmondsworth: Penguin.

Bufkin, J. and Eschholz, S. (2000) 'Images of sex and rape', *Violence Against Women*, 6(12): 1317–44.

Burt, M. (1980) 'Cultural myths and support for rape', *Journal of Personality and Social Psychology*, 28: 217–30.

Canning, V. and Tobin, A. (2010) 'Policy, impunity, safety and community: Women, rape and asylum', *Journeys and Justice: Forced Migration, Seeking Asylum and Human Rights*, Amnesty International Conference, University of Leeds, 29 January 2010.

Childline (2009) Childline Casenotes. London: NSPCC. Available at: http://www.nspcc.org.uk/inform/publications/casenotes/clcasenotessexualabuse2_wdf 69493.pdf (accessed on 19 March 2010).

Coleman, K., Jansson, K., Kalza, P. and Reed, E. (2007) *Homicides, Firearms Offences and Intimate Violence 2005/2006 (Supplementary Volume to Crime in England and Wales 2005/ 2006)*. Home Office Research, Development and Statistics Directorate. Available at: http://www.homeoffice.gov.uk/rds/pdfs07/hosb0207.pdf (accessed on 19 March 2010).

Connell, R. (1987) *Gender and Power*. Stanford: Stanford University.

Cooley, C.H. (1902) *Human Nature and the Social Order*. New York: Scribner's.

Dodd, V. (2009) 'Rape complaints were not classified as crimes by police', *The Guardian*, 16 March. Available at: http://www.guardian.co.uk/uk/2009/mar/16/rape-complaints-police-breached-guidelines (accessed on 19 March 2010).

Enloe, C. (2000) *Manoeuvres: The International Politics of Militarizing Women's Lives*. Berkeley: University of California Press.

Falcón, S. (2006) 'National security and the violation of women', in Incite! (eds) *Color of Violence: The Incite! Anthology*. Cambridge, Mass: South End Press.

Fawcett (2009) *Regional Rape Conviction Rates*. Available at: http://www.fawcettsociety. org.uk/index.asp?PageID=244 (accessed on 19 March 2010).

Fitzpatrick, C. (2001) 'Hypothetical rape scenarios as a pedagogical device to facilitate students learning about prosecutorial decision-making and discretion', *Journal of Criminal Justice Education*, 12: 169–91.

Forbes, J. (1992) 'Female sexual abusers: the contemporary search for equivalence', *Practice*, 6: 102–11.

Gray, M.W. and Marek, S. (2008) 'The statistics of genocide,' in J. Asher, D. Banks and F. J. Scheuren (eds) *Statistical Methods for Human Rights*. New York: Springer.

Grover, C. and Soothill, K. (1996) 'A murderous "underclass"? The press reporting of sexually motivated murder', *Sociological Review*, 44: 398–415.

Groves, J. (2010) 'Something deeply wrong in society', *Daily Mail*, 23 January. Available at: http://www.dailymail.co.uk/news/article-1245171/David-Cameron-charges-Brown-social-recession.html#ixzz0fcxDshHC (accessed on 19 March 2010).

Hagemann-White, C. (2001) 'European research on the prevalence of violence against women', *Violence Against Women*, 7: 732–59.

Hartmann, H. (1981) 'The unhappy marriage of Marxism and feminism', in L. Sargent, *Women and Revolution: A Discussion of the Unhappy Marriage of Marxism and Feminism*. Boston: South End Press.

Home Office (1999) *A Question of Evidence? Investigating and Prosecuting Rape in the 1990s*. London: HMSO.

Horvath, M. and Brown, J. (2009) *Rape: Challenging Contemporary Thinking*. Cullompton: Willan Publishing.

Human Rights Watch (2001) 'Afghanistan: Humanity Denied', *Human Rights Watch*. Available at: http://www.hrw.org/en/reports/2001/10/29/humanity-denied (accessed on 19 March 2010).

Jones, H. (2005) 'Visible rights: Watching out for women', *Surveillance and Society*, 2(4): 589–93.

Jones, H. (2010) 'One hand on the keyboard: sexual violence in hyperspace', *Crime and Social Justice Seminar Series*, Manchester Metropolitan University, 1 February.

Jones, H. and Cook, K. (2008) *Rape Crisis: Responding to Sexual Violence*. Lyme Regis: Russell House.

Jones, H. and Wachala, K. (2006) 'Watching over the rights of women', *Social Policy and Society*, 5(1): 127–36.

Kelly, L. (1988) *Surviving Sexual Violence*. Cambridge: Polity Press.

Kershaw, C., Nicholas, S. and Walker, A. (2008) *Crime in England and Wales 2007–08: Findings from the British Crime Survey and police recorded crime*. Home Office Research, Development and Statistics. Available at: http://www.homeoffice.gov.uk/rds/pdfs08/

hosb0708.pdf (accessed on 19 March 2010).

Kimmel, M. (2004) *The Gendered Society*. New York: Oxford University Press.

Lees, S. (1997) *Ruling Passions: Sexual Violence, Reputation and the Law*. Buckingham: Open University Press.

Lovett, J. and Kelly, L. (2009) *Different systems, similar outcomes? Tracking attrition in reported rape cases in eleven countries*. Country briefing: ENGLAND. Available at: http://www.cwasu.org/publication_display.asp?type=1&pageid=PAPERS&pagekey=44 (accessed on 19 March 2010).

MacKinnon, C. (1987) *Feminism Unmodified: Discourses on Life and Law*. Cambridge, MA: Harvard University Press.

Mason, P. and Monckton-Smith, J. (2008) 'Conflation, collocation and confusion: British press coverage of the sexual murder of women', *Journalism*, 9(6): 691–710.

McLeod, M a.nd Saraga, E. (1988) 'Challenging the orthodoxy: towards a feminist theory and practice', *Feminist Review*, 28: 16–55.

Metropolitan Police Authority (2010) *Crime Statistics*. Available at: http://www.mpa.gov.uk/statistics/crime-stats/#h1000 (accessed on 19 March 2010).

Morris, S. and Carter, H. (2009) 'Vanessa George: from angel to paedophile', *The Guardian*, 1 October. Available at: http://www.guardian.co.uk/society/2009/oct/01/vanessa-george-plymouth-abuse-background (accessed on 19 March 2010).

Office for Criminal Justice Reform (2006) *Convicting Rapists and Protecting Victims– Justice for Victims of Rape*. London: HMSO. Available at: http://www.cjsonline.gov.uk/downloads/application/pdf/Rape_consultation.pdf (accessed on 19 March 2010).

Pilch, F.T. (2009) 'Rape as genocide', in S. Totten (ed.) *Plight and Fate of Women During and Following Genocide (Genocide – A Critical Bibliographic Review)*. New Jersey: Transaction Publishers.

Powis, B. (2002) *Offenders' Risk of Serious Harm: a literature review*. Home Office Research, Development and Statistics Directorate. Available at: http://homeoffice.gov.uk/science-research/research-statistics/

Pratt, M. and Werchick, L. (2004) *Sexual Terrorism: Rape as a Weapon of War in Eastern Democratic Republic of Congo: An assessment of programmatic responses to sexual violence in North Kivu, South Kivu, Maniema, and Orientale Provinces*. USAID. Available at: http://www.peacewomen.org/resources/DRC/USAIDDCHADRC.pdf (accessed on 19 March 2010).

Rape Crisis (2009) *Myths and Facts*. Available at: http://www.rapecrisis.org.uk/myths.html (accessed on 19 March 2010).

RAWA (2009) *Not All Feminists Love Escalation in Afghanistan*. Revolutionary Association of the Women of Afghanistan. Available at: http://www.rawa.org/rawa/2009/12/06/not-all-feminists-love-escalation-in-afghanistan.html (accessed on 19 March 2010).

Reuters (2009) *U.N. suspends support to Congo army units in east*. Reuters, 2 November. Available at: http://www.reuters.com/article/idUSL2295018._CH_.2400 (accessed on 19 March 2010).

Roe, S., Coleman, K. and Kaiza, P. (2009) *Crime in England and Wales 2008/09 Volume 1*. Findings from the British Crime Survey and police recorded crime. Available at: http://www.crimestoppers-uk.org/webfiles/stats/2008-09/bcs-violent-and-sexual-crime08-09.pdf (accessed on 19 March 2010).

Sanday, P.R. (1981) *Female Power and Male Dominance: On the Origins of Sexual Inequality*. Cambridge: Cambridge University Press.

Saradjian, J. (1996) *Women Who Sexually Abuse Children*. Chichester: Wiley.

Schmid, D. (2005) *Natural Born Celebrities. Serial Killers in American Culture*. Chicago: University of Chicago Press.

Seifert, R. (1996) 'The logic of sexual violence in wars', *Women's Studies International Forum*, 19(1/2): 35–43.

Stanko, E. (1990) *Everyday Violence*. London: Pandora Press.

Stark, E. and Flitcraft, A. (1996) 'Preventing gendered homicide', in E. Stark and A. Flitcraft (eds), *Women at Risk: Domestic Violence and Women's Health*. London: Sage.

Stern, V. (2010) *The Stern Review*. Available at: http://www.equalities.gov.uk/PDF/Stern_Review_acc_FINAL.pdf (accessed on 19 March 2010).

Stewart, A. (2004) *Aspirations to Action: 25 Years of the Women's Convention (CEDAW)*. London: British Council.

Temkin, J. (2000) 'Prosecuting and defending rape: Perspectives from the Bar', *Journal of Law and Society*, 4(2): 219–48.

The Havens (2010) *Wake Up to Rape Report*. London: Opinion Matters. Available at: http://www.thehavens.co.uk/docs/Havens_Wake_Up_To_Rape_Report_Summary.pdf (accessed on 19 March 2010).

Walby, S. (1990) *Theorising Patriarchy*. Oxford: Blackwell.

Walby, S. and Allen, J. (2004) *Home Office Research Study 276, Domestic violence, sexual assault and stalking: Findings from the British Crime Survey*. Home Office Research, Development and Statistics Directorate. Available at: http://www.homeoffice.gov.uk/rds/pdfs04/hors276.pdf (accessed on 19 March 2010).

Walker, A., Flatley, J., Kershaw, C. and Moon, D. (2009) *Crime in England and Wales 2008/09. Volume 1. Findings from the British Crime Survey and police recorded crime*. Home Office Research, Development and Statistics Directorate. Available at: http://www.homeoffice.gov.uk/rds/pdfs09/hosb1109vol1.pdf (accessed on 19 March 2010).

Walklate, S. (2001) *Gender, Crime and Criminal Justice*. Cullompton: Willan Publishing.

Walter, N. (2010) *Living Dolls: The Return of Sexism*. London: Virago.

Whitehead, T. (2009) Rape myths to be challenged in court by prosecutors, *The Daily Telegraph*, 19 March.

Wilson, E. (1983) *What's to be Done about Violence Against Women?* London: Penguin.

Wood, E. J. (2006) 'Variation in sexual violence during war', *Politics and Society*, 34: 307-42.

World Health Organisation (2002) *World Report on Violence and Health*. Geneva: WHO.

Wykes, M. and Welsh, K. (2009) *Violence, Gender and Justice*. London: Sage.

Yeung, K. and Martin, J. L. (2003) 'The Looking Glass Self: An Empirical Test and Elaboration', *Social Forces*, 81(3): 843–79.

## Chapter 9

# Family violence and family safety: working therapeutically with victims, perpetrators, survivors and their families

*Arlene Vetere*

**Meet Arlene Vetere**

Arlene Vetere and Jan Cooper are both systemic family therapists. Arlene is also a clinical psychologist and Jan is also a social worker. Together they established a domestic violence service in a major city in the south of England. Their safety methodology was developed over 16 years of independent practice, alongside local statutory agencies. They put safety first at all times. Arlene and Jan encourage people to develop a sense of entitlement to their own safety, to take responsibility for their own and others' safety, as much as they challenge any sense of entitlement to treat others with disrespect, and they encourage family members to take responsibility for their behaviours that harm others.

Their moral position is clear – they tell clients that they believe that no one should live in fear of the people they love. In saying this, they recognise that they are subject to the same confusing and contradictory social discourses around the use of violence as their clients and that they experience similar moral dilemmas over the use of violence. They discuss this at their first meeting with families, and similarly that they too struggle to find constructive solutions – hence why they emphasise responsibility and give people credit for trying to make a difference.

Jan has now retired, and Arlene continues with the therapeutic work.

**Introduction**

In this chapter, I shall describe an approach to working therapeutically with family violence, established by Jan Cooper and myself in the Reading Safer

Families project, UK (Cooper and Vetere 2005). Our safety methodology is informed by systemic thinking and practice, and draws on a number of social science theories to understand and explain how violence comes to pass, and gives us a road map for therapeutic change (e.g. family systems theory, social learning theory, attachment theory, feminist theories of power and control in relationships, cognitive behaviour therapy). The three cornerstones of our methodology are risk, responsibility and collaboration. So, in this chapter, I shall describe how we manage the risk of violence, assess for risk of further violence, and attempt to work collaboratively with family members and professional colleagues in an area of practice where legal and moral considerations are paramount. Safety planning and supporting signs of safety in family members' relationships is key.

In our psychotherapeutic work with couples and families, we sometimes know that physical violence and emotional abuse are present, and sometimes, despite asking the question initially, we only find out during the course of therapeutic work. In both circumstances, i.e. knowing of family violence, or knowledge emerging, it is of vital importance to assess the safety of family members and their safety in the therapeutic work. If violence has already been talked about, within the family system, or the professional referring network, establishing a safe platform for practice is our first priority on meeting the couple or family, as we put safety first. If violence is revealed during therapy, we need to stop what work we are doing, and establish safety for family members before proceeding again with therapy as such. Thus safety is our highest priority and our highest context for therapeutic practice, within the framework of the UK law, statutory agency policy on working with family violence, and within our own moral positioning on the use of, and effects of, violence in intimate relationships.

**Definitions**

Violence in the family can involve physical, sexual and psychological abuse, and neglect, in combination, and over time, and sometimes spanning generations. The term interpersonal violence is favoured by some to capture the complexity of both single events of violence and repeated, chronic violence, both predictable and unpredictable (Walby and Allen 2004). The Home Office defines domestic abuse as 'any incident of threatening behaviour, violence or abuse (psychological, physical, sexual, financial or emotional) between adults who are, or have been, intimate partners or family members, regardless of gender or sexuality' (2009). The definition has been widened recently to include practices such as female genital mutilation, forced marriage and so-called honour crimes. The full definition recognises the effects on children of 'witnessing' violence in the family, as much as they might also be direct victims of assault.

Liz Kelly's (1988) idea of a continuum of sexual violence helpfully overlaps with formulations of violence in family members' relationships to amplify complexity, i.e. an evolving and dynamic interaction between different forms of violence, severity, frequency and duration that may involve two or more people once, or continuously. Systemic thinking tries to understand the constant interplay of patterns in behaviour, in relationships, and over time, and the impact of meaning and levels of context in determining outcomes. Within a systemic framework, the notion of a continuum of violence is helpful in pointing out the many shapes and forms of interpersonal violence and perhaps developments in violent behaviour over time, but cannot explain the complex interweave of emotion, thought, entitlement, action and reaction in feedback processes within dyadic, triad and larger family relationships. Systemic thinking is concerned with what goes on both for individuals and between individuals in different family, social and political contexts. Thus a systemic perspective provides a useful meta-theoretical framework for 'continuums of thought' to explore potential linkages and to hypothesise their interconnectedness to other explanatory theories of pattern and process in relationships.

### Incidence and prevalence

Estimates of incidence and prevalence vary, but most demographers suggest that domestic assault is under-reported. It has been estimated that nearly one third of reported violent crime in the UK is domestic assault (British Crime Survey 2000, 2010). Walby and Allen (2004) estimated that one in five women and one in ten men are assaulted by someone they know well. Sexual assault involves physical assault and emotional abuse, and many sexual assaults in adult intimate partnerships occur in the context of wider physical violence in the family. Moffitt and Caspi (1998) estimate that children are present during two-thirds of all family assaults, and that they are four to nine times more likely to be assaulted themselves than are children who live in households without physical violence. Many perpetrators of violence are themselves past or present victims of assault and the short- and long-term adverse effects on development and relationships are well documented (Vetere and Cooper 2005).

### Ways of working

We work in a gender-inclusive way, with men and women who are both victims and perpetrators in opposite-sex relationships and in same-sex relationships; with violence between parents, children and adolescents, of any age and at any point in the family life cycle; with sibling violence; and with violence between older people and their carers. We take equally seriously all forms of physical and psychological violence, however the victims and perpetrators themselves might attribute meaning and seriousness to acts, events and intentions. This means that we use our safety methodology for all levels of risk, duration, frequency and severity when working with interpersonal violence.

Patterns of threat, coercion, intimidation and assault can be unidirectional, bidirectional, and involve three or more people. People can be both victims and bullies/perpetrators. Violence and psychological abuse can be intended as self-defence or both self-defence and payback. For example, when the man partner has physically abused his woman partner, she may continue with strategies of humiliation once the violence has stopped, claiming the moral high ground and her right to pay him back for the years of abuse she endured. Disentangling these patterns takes time, care, and a sustained focus. We describe our approach to this work in the section on safety planning. Patterns of abuse tend to be similar across all nature of family and couple relationships, but always need to be understood in relation to theories of power and control and moral and legal notions of responsibility. Couples in same-sex relationships appear to engage in similar patterns of physical, emotional and sexual violence as do couples in opposite-sex relationships. It is in the intersect between attachment relationships on the one hand, and power and control on the other, that we see the complexity in the mix of passion, love and violence. Arguably, the capacity for violence is held by us all and it is in our developed capacity for empathy that we stay our hand. This chapter is dedicated to thinking about how practitioners can help people develop responsibility for their own and others' safety.

In working towards safety, we use the concepts of risk, responsibility and collaboration (Vetere and Cooper 2001, 2008). We divide risk into the management of risk and the assessment of risk. We look for signs of safety in what people do and try to do, and we hold people responsible for their behaviour. We are clear with our clients about our responsibilities as therapists in the therapeutic work. Finally we try to create an atmosphere of collaborative practice, even though some of our clients are told to meet with us by the family courts, and have little choice but to meet us! At all times, we put our concerns and issues on the table for discussion, alongside those of our clients. If we have anything to say that is difficult, we find a way to say it to them directly. We are able to honour this commitment within our working relationships. Jan and I work together in the therapy room, with one taking the lead therapist/assessment position and the other taking the role of the in-room consultant. We use our reflecting process to raise difficult questions in ways that are less directly challenging to the therapeutic relationship. We write extensively about our use of the reflecting process in Cooper and Vetere (2005).

We pay attention to our own safety in a number of ways: we have an alarm and our colleagues in the building are well briefed in what we do, and what assistance we may require; we do not sit in front of the door inadvertently blocking someone's way out, should they need to leave if they feel unable to manage themselves in a difficult conversation; we do not have objects in the room that could be used as weapons; and so on. This is all as you might expect. It seems to us though, based on our lengthy experience, that it is our approach to safety, our wish to work collaboratively, and our use of our reflecting relationship in the room together, that most contributes to a calm, well managed and secure working environment, for ourselves and for the families who look to us for help.

## Establishing safety

### 1.(a) Risk management

When we know that violence has occurred in a couple or family relationship at the time of referral, we manage the risk of future violence by bringing in a 'stable third' person, and establishing a safety plan with family members, using a no-violence contract. The 'stable third' advises on whether the safety plan can work, and is seen to be working. In our experience, the stable third is crucial, as we now explain.

When violence is known about and/or suspected, it creates anxiety within the family system and within the professional network. It is essential to understand and manage that anxiety within a safety methodology that enables you, the practitioner, to get on with your work with the couple and/or family. If the anxiety about future possible violence is not addressed it will slip around the 'system of concern' (extended family members, the professional network, and other interested parties) and will have a negative impact on your ability to settle down into your work. For example, family members may receive contradictory and ambivalent messages about the safety of working with you, and may miss meetings or be called to attend meetings with other professionals too often to be able to meet with you consistently. Similarly, other professionals, worried about the possibility of further violence, may believe that family members will lie about the cessation of violence and that practitioner therapists will simply believe what they are told. For these reasons it is necessary to manage risk and corroborate what family members tell us about how and when they ended the violence. We do this by including a stable third in both our thinking and our practice. This expands the system and offers more points of view about safety and protection. Who, then, can be the stable third?

The stable third may be the referrer, such as a social worker, but must be a person who is trusted by the family and the professional network. It may be a grandparent, a faith leader, a community worker, a family doctor, and so on – but if children are involved it has to be someone who knows the children and can visit the family home. Thus our minimum sufficient condition for safe practice in our therapeutic work is a triangle, based on the psychodynamic idea that the triangle is the basic human relationship and has the potential for stabilising relationships (Vetere and Dallos 2003). The triangle consists of ourselves, the couple/family, and the stable third. The stable third helps us think about safety and safety planning and helps corroborate what the family members tell us about the cessation of violence. We include the stable third in our first meeting with the family, where possible, or as soon as possible thereafter. Subsequently, we meet with the stable third at the third or fourth meeting, to review safety and the safety plan. Very often, families are involved with other professional practitioners, and they too may be part of safety planning. When we can all begin to have confidence that the safety plan is working, then the stable third can reduce their attendance at safety review meetings as we begin to address other therapeutic issues and concerns with the family members.

We require a minimum of six meetings to establish the safety plan and to see if the no-violence contract can hold. Typically we meet people every week or every two weeks for this safety planning work. If we are working with a couple, we see them separately and together, and similarly with other family relationships, we meet people on their own and in combination. When all three perspectives (us, the couple/family, and the stable third) are satisfied that the safety plan can work, and is working, then we can proceed with other therapeutic tasks.

Safety planning is done within a no-violence contract. We ask perpetrators/ family members to agree to stop the violence by making a no-violence contract. The contract may be spoken or written. If social services are involved, they usually want a written contract. In our experience, our clients use the no-violence contract creatively. For example, we met a divorced father who hit his 16-year-old daughter during an argument on a contact visit. As a result, his daughter refused to see him again. The father contacted us and asked us to help him, so that he did not behave with violence again. He wanted a written no-violence contract so that he could lodge it with his family lawyer, as evidence of his commitment to ending violence, and in the hope his daughter would one day read it.

The no-violence contract is underpinned by the safety plan. The safety plan attempts to predict those interactions and circumstances where an escalation into violence is likely, in an attempt to pre-empt violence and de-escalate unhelpful and distressing interactions. In order to do this, we first identify the last episode of violence or the worst episode of violence. We use behavioural tracking techniques to deconstruct the episode and ascertain what happened, so that we may identify the triggers to violence. Behavioural tracking involves asking:

(i) who was there;
(ii) what happened;
(iii) who said what; and
(iv) what happened next, and so on.

We do this tracking very slowly so that we can be sure we understand what happened as well as is possible. Precursors and immediate triggers to intimate violence in couple relationships are often attachment-related triggers, for example, fear of loss, rejection or abandonment, or actual loss, rejection and abandonment. Thus a partner may threaten to walk out or leave, or a parent may threaten to put a child 'in care' in an angry verbal exchange; or anger might be the response to fearing a partner loves us less. It is the attachment significance that is key to understanding the cycle of behaviour that escalates to violence, and how power and control are used in response to a perceived or actual attachment threat. Similarly other associated emotional responses, such as shame, anger, fear and humiliation, are often present in the moment, including the paradox of power – it is often when a person feels powerless in an interaction (powerless to stop a partner leaving, or powerless to get children to do as they are told) that they strike out, but of course, the victim feels them to be very powerful in that moment. From the attacker's perspective they 'lost it', but from the victim's perspective they 'gained it'.

Attachment theory suggests that anger is the secondary emotion in response to the primary emotions of fear, sadness and shame when we perceive ourselves to be threatened by loss – real or imagined (Bowlby 1988). For example, a man who was humiliated by his own father, watched his father beat his mother, and whose mother was less emotionally available to him as a result, may be prone to shame, and primed to seeing the intent to humiliate him, or demean him, during an argument with an intimate partner, when none was intended.

Many of the couples/family members we work with are prone to shame and oversensitised to interpreting their partner's behaviour as an attempt to humiliate them. Such sensitivity is often the legacy of earlier childhood abuse that included parental shaming, and of witnessing domestic violence. We find that many perpetrators we work with are not so easily able to soothe themselves and calm themselves down when unhelpfully aroused, both emotionally and physiologically. Often people will turn to psychoactive substances to help them avoid painful emotions, to numb themselves and otherwise manage their emotional experience. If a perpetrator has a drugs and alcohol problem, we insist they seek help from the local drugs and alcohol service, with whom we seek permission to liaise, so that we can work alongside them. We do not insist the drugs/alcohol work is finished before we do our safety planning work as, often, the alcohol is used to help manage difficult and unbearable feelings in response to interpersonal distress. So, in understanding the violent episode and its triggers, we coach people in other forms of coping and looking after themselves, to increase their range of responses in difficult, threatening and painful interpersonal encounters, such as seeing others as potentially helpful and talking with others, turning to faith, developing and maintaining reflective abilities, distraction activities, and other methods known to calm and soothe. Sometimes, when a person has been treated badly as a child and they have learned not to trust others as a form of self-protection, the slow development of a trusting therapeutic relationship forms the first bridge back into trusting others, and thus can a therapist work to help rebuild trust more widely in family relationships. Learning to understand and manage our emotional responses is arguably a lifelong task, but for those who protected themselves from danger as children by learning to downplay their emotional reactions, or who never learned to regulate emotional responding or who never developed a sense of entitlement to comfort or to being looked after, trust is necessary. It is the platform from which people are encouraged to take emotional risks that make them feel vulnerable, to learn to see others as a source of comfort, and to seek comfort, and to help process trauma responses, past and present.

At the same time as we slowly deconstruct the episode/s of violence, we want to know about other stressors the family members must cope with, such as debt, poverty, family conflict, work-related stress, community harassment, adverse life events, and so on. Similarly, we seek out resources and sources of strength and inspiration for family members that will support them in their efforts to end the violence. We want to know about family members' aspirations, for themselves and others. Asking future questions often allows people to speak well of what they wish for the future – for their children, their partners, their families, themselves, and so on. Such a future orientation often enables people to soften, to feel less blamed, and thus to engage in responsibility work without feeling the need to be too defensive. So, we might ask, 'John, as a father, what do you want your son/daughter to learn from you about how to keep themselves safe in their future relationships?' 'Mary, as a mother, what do you want your son/daughter to learn from you about how men and women show respect to each other for their future relationships?'

When we think we have sufficient information to understand what fuels unhelpful arousal and distress, and what triggers an escalation into interpersonal violence, so that we can predict where the risk lies for the family members, we agree a safety strategy, such as time out, using mediation, developing self-talk and other calming strategies, predicting and avoiding certain topics for discussion and then bringing them to a meeting with us, and learning to listen. These safety strategies are initially short-term, and designed to de-escalate potentially conflictual, hostile and/or inflammatory interactions. If we are working with a perpetrator who is in an intimate relationship, we seek the partner's involvement as a consultant to the safety plan. If the partner is not in agreement with the safety plan or is not convinced it can work, we need to know this and include their views. For example, at home, during a difficult argument, if the perpetrator uses time out, the partner might fear the perpetrator is using time out to avoid a difficult conversation, and may bar their exit from the room – under those circumstances the victim is not thinking of their own safety. Similarly, the victim may fear the perpetrator will abandon them during time out and not return. In using time out successfully, the perpetrator needs to recognise their own emotional and physiological arousal and make judgements about when to leave a conversation. For example, a person may not be practised in naming their own emotional responses, in reflecting on their emotional responses, or in recognising the build-up of muscle tension, or changes in breathing and heart rate as indicators of unhelpful physiological arousal. In addition, we ask about self-talk, for example, what does the perpetrator say to him or herself during the build-up to violence. Our clients tell us they cannot identify self-talk, but with patience and persistence, we can help people recognise how they 'talk' themselves up into a state of unhelpful physiological and emotional arousal, where they find it harder to exercise self-control. The development and use of constructive self-talk strategies has been pioneered by the cognitive behavioural therapists (Novaco 1993).

Frequent rehearsal of the safety plan is key. If time out is called by either partner, what happens next? Where do they go? If it is three o'clock in the morning and raining outside, what do they do?? What happens to the children, and so on? Rehearsal of the safety plan makes action in the moment more likely. When people are anxious, afraid or otherwise unhelpfully aroused, they are neither able to process information quickly, nor to problem-solve in novel, flexible and creative ways. They are more likely to fall back on old solutions and over-learned responses. Hence rehearsal makes it more likely that both victim and perpetrator observe the safety plan and call time out. It is important to take regular feedback from people about their attempts to calm and soothe themselves – what did they notice? What did it feel like as they calmed down, and so on? Similarly, the safety plan needs to include ways of calming down, and then needs to address what happens next. So, when both are calm, do they return to the topic of conversation, for example, or do they wait until their next meeting with us, or take the issue to the stable third, or a trusted family member, and so on? Healing and making up after an argument need to be addressed so that issues are not left unresolved, or to fester and lead to resentment. Family members may wish to avoid speaking again of the topic that led to a violent escalation between them, for fear of reinvoking the violence. They may think this is protective and the safer option. Hence the need for careful, slow therapeutic work that helps to de-escalate fears and to manage conflict in a safe therapeutic context. It is hoped that these experiences scaffold attempts to heal and avoid misunderstandings for the future.

When it looks as if the safety plan is working, we can agree with the couple/family, and the stable third, that we proceed to other therapeutic matters. If the no-violence contract is broken, we do not abandon people, rather we convene a meeting with the stable third and the couple/family and decide what to do next. We may do individual work with the perpetrator, or recommend group work, or we may continue with safety planning depending on the judged severity of the violence. Severe violence may require a legal response rather than a therapeutic one.

### 1.(b) Risk assessment

We separate the management of risk from the assessment of risk. The management of risk enables us to think about, and respond to, others' anxiety about the possibility of repeat violence, and clearly our safety planning work is therapeutic in intent. Similarly we assess the risk of future violence in order to help promote the safety planning. We look for signs of safety and give people credit for trying to stop the violence. We recognise that past violence predicts future violence and that this knowledge creates uncertainty and anxiety about the future. In assessing for risk, we take account of a number of factors, such as the frequency of episodes of violence, and the contexts within which violence occurs; for example, is the perpetrator of domestic violence also violent at work, in the sports hall, or in the pub? We want to observe, in our meetings, how people manage themselves in the heat of the moment, so to speak, when they are unhelpfully aroused, or discussing a conflict. Can they respond to our efforts to calm a conversation and give a good account of themselves? Do they show signs of empathy – can they suppress their own needs in order to listen to family members talk about upsetting events, and do they have a sense that the 'other' is the same as them, with the same feelings and attachment needs?

The risk assessment process is interwoven with the management of risk and safety planning, in feedback and conversational exchanges with relevant family members, over a minimum of six meetings. The conversation is informed by detailed questioning and exploration of experience as described above. It is not an heuristic, rather it is rooted in clinical judgement and experience, and the outcome of stopping the violence is determined with the family members, the stable third and other involved professionals. The safety plan is designed to help family members take responsibility for their behaviour and for safety.

As part of risk assessment, we want to explore reflective functioning and learn how family members might reflect on past events and learn from experience (Fonagy and Target 1997). For example, at the request of child protection social workers, we met a father who had been accused of physically harming his daughter, to assess his capacity to be a safe parent of his daughters. The father told us that he could remember nothing of his life before the age of 18 years, and that there was no point in us asking him about his experience of being parented. As far as we knew there was no organic reason for his memory loss. Thus we responded by asking him systemic questions about the effects of 'not remembering' on his ideas and practices of fathering, for example, where did he get his ideas from about being a father? Who/what has helped him develop his ideas as a father? If he cannot remember being parented, what helps him stand in the shoes of his children now, and understand their needs? If he cannot remember what he needed from a parent, as a child, what helps him think about his children's needs developmentally? And so on.

We see it as our responsibility to manage the assessment/therapeutic process to help establish a secure base – a reflective space where people can think. When people are traumatised, frightened and/or anxious, they are slower to process negative information, become preoccupied with regulating their own internal states, and find it harder to read relationship cues – hence our responsibilities within the therapeutic alliance are clear, and we expect that people will develop their reflective positioning with our support. In any psychological intervention the development of a safe and trusting therapeutic alliance is considered necessary for change to occur, and in our work, most people have been subject to danger, harm and adversity at some time in their lives that has compromised their willingness and ability to trust. Thus we work hard to build trust in our working relationships with our clients, to support them in thinking about their own behaviour, feelings, thoughts, decisions and actions. Reflective functioning is thought to be essential for the development of empathy.

The capacity for empathic responding is also part of our assessment for safety. The development of empathy is the best protection against the propensity for violence. The ability to put yourself in the emotional shoes of the other, to recognise the other as similar to you, rather than lesser than you, to partly suppress your own needs in order to listen to what the other is saying when they are upset or talking about how we might be implicated in their upset can be described as empathy. This relational capacity is thought to arise out of the experience of attunement in early relationships with care-givers (Stern 1985). Such empathy is most often seen in how people listen and how they feel heard.

## 2. Responsibility

As explained above, safety in relationships is our highest context marker, so we are looking for signs of safety in how people talk and in what they do. We are always prepared to give people credit for trying. Part of this emphasis on safety is an extension of how we are all helped, in our development, to take responsibility for behaviour that causes harm to others alongside the development of a sense of entitlement to one's own safety and the support of others' entitlement to safety – to live without fear of the people we love. We expect perpetrators to acknowledge there is a problem to be solved, and to recognise that their behaviour has a relational impact – that any behaviour that frightens, threatens and intimidates others affects the quality of perpetrators' own relationships with their family members in terms of how safe and trusting others can feel around them. In making the safety plan, we use a minimum of six sessions, as said earlier, and during this time there is an opportunity for people to develop their sense of responsibility and own their behaviour and its effects. This is our responsibility, to help them develop their accountability for their actions, and this is also their main responsibility, to themselves, to their family, and to professional and legal services.

We do not interview the children in front of their parents/carers until we are clear that the parents take responsibility for safety seriously, and have been shown to do this through their actions. We might talk to the children separately or as a sibling group, but we do not ask the children to talk about the effects of living with fear until we know the parents are psychologically able and ready to really listen to what their children are saying. In our experience it is often the children who call for help during an attack, from neighbours, the police, extended family or so on. Many of the children we meet have developed a capacity to take action and to seek safety and for that reason they like to be included in safety planning discussions. In one family we met, the older daughter of 13 years ran to a neighbour's house to phone the police for help when she overheard her father sexually assaulting and trying to kill her mother. Her father was arrested, but in subsequent meetings between her mother and the social services, where her safety was discussed, she was not included in any of the discussions. When we met her she told us she protested at this exclusion by refusing to co-operate with the social worker. A careful exploration and appreciation of her understanding of safety, and how she had tried in the past to keep her mother safe, and took action in the past to call for help, paved the way for her to co-operate with her new social worker.

We do not ask children and young people to make themselves emotionally vulnerable in a conversation until we are reasonably sure that it is safe for them to do so. Similarly we may support a traumatised parent in listening to their child talk about the effects of witnessing a violent attack on the parent. During these early safety planning discussions with the adults we are listening for evidence that the parents understand that violence has the potential to frighten and traumatise their children. This can be poignant; for example, we sometimes meet women who have comforted themselves as mothers by saying, 'I take the violence and the children do not know...' In these moments we talk to the women about the research on the effects of domestic violence on children (Vetere and Cooper 2005). We tell women that research estimates that two-thirds of violent attacks are actually witnessed (Moffitt and Caspi 1998), but that we think the children always know. Even if they are at school or with their grandparents during an attack, they do not believe their mothers (or fathers for that matter!) walk into doors or fall down the stairs. We talk to parents about the development of children, and how children monitor the well-being of their parents and their parents' relationship, as it has profound implications for the safety, well-being and psychological development of the child. We track when and how children might get involved in attacks, by trying to prevent the escalation of an argument, and what the children are learning about relationship safety and how adults get on together.

We listen carefully to the words people use when talking about their violent behaviour towards others, and when talking about safety. It is in the talk that responsibility and explanation meet, where it is possible to minimise and deny our actions or the effects of our actions, where explanation can be used to dilute responsibility, or to slip away from responsibility with excuses and promises. As systemic thinkers we track how people talk and what words they use and we raise questions about how social realities are constructed in the talk about violence. We meet women who tell us they deserve to be hit, so we deconstruct the word 'deserve'. It is as if the woman thinks others are entitled to hit her. Where did that idea come from, we ask, as you were not born thinking like this? Similarly, if language is used to minimise the violence or the effects of violence, we pause in the session, notice the words, and deconstruct their use in the here and now, and the effects of their continued use over time. There are many examples to note. For example, a man may say, 'I only hit her.' We ask about the word 'only' – what does 'only' look like, and if I were there what would I see? Was your fist open or clenched – where did you hit her, and what did that feel like, and so on . . . ? We pause and walk around in the description, thus highlighting the seriousness of the 'hit' and the effects of the 'hit'. This offers an opportunity to reflect and deconstruct the 'taken-for-granted' in people's lives. In another example – a woman might say, 'I just hit him.' Similarly we would be curious about the use of the word 'just' as it too minimises and denies the impact of our actions towards others.

The point to be made here is that we use language to minimise and deny the import of our behaviour and its adverse effects on others, and our task is to track such use of language and help people see where and how they minimise violence. Such linguistic deconstruction can be used with all forms of violence in all intimate and family relationships.

We notice how people describe their experience of anger, as if it builds up or explodes in an instant, with phrases like, 'I go from 0 to 100 in 10 seconds.' We deconstruct this idea of speed of arousal and also ask the partner to comment, who often tells us, 'but I saw the tension building all day.' Similarly people describe anger as 'losing it' – we ask what was gained, not lost, by using violence. Who loses and who gains? Another example comes from our first meeting with a divorced father, who hit his 16-year-old daughter. He told us: 'She knows I love her, the silly cow, she knows I won't hit her again.' We asked him, 'What does she know?' He has put this in the framework of love, but what actually does she know, we ask. The father looked at us in return and began to deconstruct his use of language, thoughtfully, and to acknowledge that his daughter could not know she was safe. In another example, we met a man and woman in a first meeting, where she said to him, 'You hit me.' 'I didn't,' he replied. 'You did,' she said, 'you hit me!' 'I didn't', he said, 'I didn't hit you like a man.' Although we might recognise some control of his violent behaviour in this description, the woman understood this to mean that she was not safe in the relationship and decided to separate from the man. The woman worked with a women's refuge shelter worker and we helped the man, at his request, to understand his behaviour, to take better control and to make sure this could not happen again. They managed a safe separation.

### 3. Collaboration

It is an interesting question as to whether we can work collaboratively in this context, where external motivation to change may be higher in some respects than internal motivation. We strive for transparency in our work by aiming to be clear, at every step of the way, about our thinking and our intentions. This is reflected in our early meetings with the family and stable third, where we try to identify the risks of further violence, from all three perspectives, and the means we have to work towards safety in relationships. We try to be clear about our moral position in this work, namely, that we believe that no one should live in fear of the people they love. This sounds simple to say, and in practice we know that it is often hard to live by. We try not to inhabit the moral high ground in our work by talking about our own ethical dilemmas around violence in relationships; for example, as parents ourselves, we have struggled with the issue of physical bullying against our sons and the dilemma of striving for peaceful resolutions or supporting them in fighting back. Often we do not have solutions, but we hold a commitment to try to help our clients find legal, moral and ethically responsible solutions . . . and we give people credit for trying. As the systems model is a strengths-based model, it enables us to look for success and to build on it (Vetere and Dallos 2003).

We do not offer confidentiality in the work, rather we say we need to negotiate what may be held as confidential. We explain that if the information pertains to safety, we cannot keep it confidential, as we may need to speak about it at a safety planning meeting. And of course in the early stages of our work we do not know whether what we are being told pertains to safety or not. Thus we negotiate confidentiality as we progress in the work. We realise that colleagues in the professional network have to know that we will not keep violence a secret, and that we will take appropriate action for reasons of safety and protection. At first we thought none of our clients would trust us, but we received interesting feedback – they told us that at least they knew where they stood with us! Finally, and in the interests of transparency, we make clear our relationship with social control and the agencies of social control, such as the local police family violence unit, and the social services. For example, if we know the social worker involved with the family, we talk about our relationship with the social worker and how we have worked with them in the past. We tell people that if we are worried about them, or for them, we will not go behind their backs to other professionals, rather we shall talk to them about why we are worried about safety and why we think we need to take action for reasons of safety.

It is essential that families can be seen to work co-operatively within the professional system and that they see professional workers as potentially helpful. This is a tall order for some families. We met a man and his family where, for the past 13 years, their social worker had reviewed their care of the five children, and each time had told them their parental care was just good enough. Then the social worker retired and a new social worker reviewed the family. The new social worker did not think the level of parental care was adequate, and told the family she was going to start child protection proceedings. The father was furious – he did not understand why the social services department had deemed their care adequate for 13 years and then seemed to change their view. The father did a very foolish and dangerous thing – he threatened to kill the social worker and, overnight, he earned a reputation of being a dangerous man. We understood the father's behaviour in the context of living with the effects of constant scrutiny. We helped the father to take responsibility for his behaviour, to apologise for the threat, and to find ways to restore co-operative working – essential if he was to continue to live with his wife and children.

## Conclusion

We review and audit all our work during the safety assessment and safety planning process, with the family members, the stable third and other involved professionals. We do not progress into family therapy and couples therapy as such if the no-violence contract cannot hold. When working with couples, for example, a safe separation would be judged as a good outcome. Since much of our work is done within the child protection system, we cannot always find out what happens to families subsequently. We offer 'top-up' meetings and follow-up meetings to support families in their attempts to live safely. Our door is always open for further work if that seems to be needed. Our own audit processes show that safety planning work has been helpful to more than two-thirds of the couples and families we meet, both within the child protection system and with referrals from other health care professionals. We think this is due in part to the high stakes – the risks of enforced family break-up and the wish to stay connected are highly motivating for people, alongside the high level of selection that has occurred in the family's journey to our door.

In this chapter, I have tried to show how responsibility for violent behaviour can be developed alongside explanations and interventions that try to understand and pre-empt violence, and to understand and predict safety and protection. As systemic practitioners we try to work within a collaborative framework. We use systemic thinking to help us hold the complexity of violent behaviour in mind, while planning and working for safety, and reviewing and monitoring the development of the entitlement to safety.

## Further reading

The main question addressed in this chapter is how to work therapeutically with both victims and perpetrators of family violence with safety as the highest priority. The focus of the chapter therefore is on the development of safe practice and a visible safety methodology. My book with Jan Cooper outlines in much more detail, and with many worked examples, how this can be done in practice, across a range of client groups, and in different health and social care settings: Cooper, J. and Vetere, A. (2005) *Domestic Violence and Family Safety: A systemic approach to working with violence in families.* London: Whurr/Wiley. If readers are interested in understanding the developmental impact of witnessing family violence for children, they might like to look at the work of the Wave Trust, and their 2005 report, *Violence and What to Do about It.* It is available at www.wavetrust.org

## References

Bowlby, J. (1988) *A Secure Base.* New York: Basic Books.

British Crime Survey (2000–2010) See Home Office below.

Cooper, J. and Vetere, A. (2005) *Domestic Violence and Family Safety: Working systemically with violence in families.* London: Whurr/Wiley.

Fonagy, P. and Target, M. (1997) 'Attachment and reflective function: Their role in self organisation', *Development and Psychopathology,* 9: 679–700.

Home Office Research, Development and Statistics Directorate and BMRB (2009) *Social Research, British Crime Survey: 2000–2010.* Colchester, Essex: UK Data Archive.

Kelly, L. (1988) *Surviving Sexual Violence.* Cambridge: Polity Press.

Moffitt, T. and Caspi, A. (1998) 'Annotation: Implications of violence between intimate partners for child psychologists and psychiatrists', *Journal of Child Psychology and Psychiatry,* 39: 137–44.

Novaco, R. (1993) 'Clinicians ought to view anger contextually', *Behaviour Change,* 10: 208–18.

Stern, D. (1985) *The Interpersonal World of the Infant.* New York: Basic Books.

Vetere, A. and Cooper, J. (2001) 'Working systemically with family violence: risk, responsibility and collaboration', *Journal of Family Therapy,* 23: 378–98.

Vetere, A. and Cooper, J. (2005) 'Children who witness violence at home', in A. Vetere and E. Dowling (eds) *Narrative Therapies with Children and Their Families: A Practitioner's Guide to Concepts and Approaches.* London: Routledge.

Vetere, A. and Cooper, J. (2008) 'Supervision and family safety: Working with domestic violence', in J. Hamel (ed.) *Intimate Partner and Family Abuse.* NY: Springer.

Vetere, A. and Dallos, R. (2003) *Working Systemically with Families: Formulation, intervention and evaluation.* London: Karnac.

Walby, S. and Allen, J. (2004) *Domestic Violence, Sexual Assault and Stalking: Findings from the British Crime Survey.* Home Office Research Study 236. London: Home Office Research, Development and Statistics Directorate, March.

# Chapter 10

# Violence and prostitution: beyond the notion of a 'continuum of sexual violence'

*Jo Phoenix*

## Meet Jo Phoenix

Jo Phoenix is Professor of Criminology at Durham University. She has been researching prostitution and the regulation of sex and sexuality since the mid 1990s. Her interest in the area started with involvement in the anti-pornography grass-roots feminist campaigning of the 1980s. Many of her concerns when campaigning were changed as a result of meeting, researching and working with women in the sex industry (and those organisations and agencies working for and on behalf of them). The main driver behind Jo's research now is a deep concern about how to obtain a measure of social justice for marginalised, victimised groups of people (children, women, young people) whose lives have been shattered by their experiences of violence, poverty and so on and for whom government intervention is often experienced as a form of punishment and/or control.

## Introduction

Prostitution, pornography, murder, rape, exploitation, drugs, trafficking and the sexual degradation of women are little more than standard settings and plot devices in the world of straight-to-DVD and B-rate crime dramas. Everyone knows that in these forms of entertainment, women in the sex industry are expendable or more likely 'just' the victims that help push the story along. Doubtless the portrayal of sexual violence in the sex industry is fed partly by stereotype and partly by a selective understanding of the empirical realities experienced by women in the sex industry. For instance, some of the more extreme and shocking forms of sexual violence are intimately associated with the sex industry. The opening decade of the twenty-first century bore witness in the UK to the serial murders of five sex workers in Ipswich and three sex workers in Bradford. To this list of eight women we can add more than a dozen known names of UK sex workers whose murders have gone unsolved in the past two decades as well as the unknown numbers of sex workers who have simply gone missing in that time period. Qualitative academic research generated across North America, Australia, New Zealand, Europe and UK testifies to the regularity with which women in the sex industry experience sexual violence. Hence, it is hardly surprising that crime dramas and thrillers draw on what have become, by now, 'set pieces' connecting the sex industry to sexual violence and constructing the sex industry as some dark hinterland beyond the rule of law and beyond the boundaries of human decency.

The aim of this chapter is not to catalogue sexual violence/s in the sex industry, but rather to prise it open and in so doing pose several critical theoretical questions. What does it mean to claim that, even at a very basic level, there is an interconnection between sexual violence and the sex industry? How can we begin to make sense of it, or to theorise it? In order to address these questions, this chapter focuses on prostitution because it provides an excellent case study that illuminates some of the enduring theoretical difficulties. Sexual violence in prostitution happens at the conjunction of both 'the sexual' and the economic realm. The theoretical difficulties it demonstrates are those connected with trying to understand sexual violence in relation to the specific social, ideological, economic and political conditions of existence for a particular social institution (that is, prostitution). How can the relationship between the intensely personal, the social and the economic be captured and how does that relationship shape, influence and/or structure vulnerability and responses to sexual violence? To clarify, one of the defining features of prostitution *as a social institution* (and thereby not reduced to the level of the activity of selling sex for money) is the blurring of boundaries between the personal, private and intimate world of sex, the public realm of economy, and of work and the political realm of regulation and formal social control. In prostitution, intensely private experiences (such as sex) become commodities to be produced, consumed and exchanged in an impersonal, commercialised setting. As a social institution, prostitution is comprised of a seemingly endless variety of relationships and social activities, that are formally and informally regulated, policed and controlled – which in turn has objective effects on the relationships, activities and individuals within prostitution. Indeed, it may be more accurate to discuss *prostitutions*, as the experiences of those working from, for instance, the streets are substantially different from those working within, for instance, escort services or bondage, discipline and sado-masochism or parlours. Underpinning the sheer diversity of prostitution, though, is that it is one of the few social institutions which directly link the intimate and private realm (and practice) of sex to the public realm of the economic. This, therefore, raises the question of why particular types of theoretical tools are needed that do not collapse the economic into the sexual or vice versa.

As a means of organising the discussion, this chapter asks whether Kelly's (1988) concept of a continuum of sexual violence can be applied to understanding or theorising sexual violence in the context of prostitution. The main argument of the chapter is that no matter how innovative the concept may have been in the 1980s, it obscures and conflates more than it illuminates in relation to prostitution. In order to make this argument, the first section of this chapter briefly reviews Kelly's concept of a continuum of sexual violence. The second section explores some of the difficulties in measuring and naming 'sexual violence' in the context of prostitution. The third part of the chapter works through the implications of applying the concept of a continuum of sexual violence to prostitution.

## A continuum of sexual violence

One of the legacies of 1980s feminist scholarship on sexual violence was the calling into question of the idea that legal or 'common-sense' definitions of sexual violence were sufficient. Instead, early feminist scholars argued that sexual violence is a social phenomenon that takes its meaning from the social and historical context. Critical in establishing this shift in thinking was Liz Kelly's (1988) pioneering analysis of sexual violence and her concept of a continuum of sexual violence.

At the time of its publication, Kelly's (1988) *Surviving Sexual Violence* was groundbreaking. It provided a then much-needed bridge between feminist activism addressing the issue of men's violence against women and academic feminism attempting to theorise the extent and range of women's and children's experiences of sexual violence. As Kelly herself remarked: 'The concept was used in a number of talks given to a variety of women's groups (some were feminist groups involved in work around male violence, some were local community groups). Many of the women present found it helpful in understanding their own experiences and sexual violence generally' (Kelly 1987, 2002: 128–9). It also provided an academic challenge to constructions and definitions of sexual violence in women's lives which treated sexual violence as merely and only about sex, as pathological, abnormal or aberrant forms of sexuality and as rare events. The challenge came from the broad definition that Kelly used. For her sexual violence is

> any physical, visual, verbal or sexual act that is experienced by the woman or girl, at the time or later, as a threat, invasion or assault, that has the effect of hurting her or degrading her and/or takes away her ability to control intimate contact.
>
> (Kelly 1988: 41)

This definition allowed Kelly to move beyond the idea that the sexual violence was an instrumental (if pathological) way of getting sex. Instead, Kelly constituted the 'sex' in sexual violence as a means by which men achieved social power. Her object of inquiry was the extent, range and impact of this newly defined sexual violence on women's and girls' lives and it was in this context that she developed the concept of a continuum of sexual violence. By 'continuum', Kelly meant two things. First she meant that the forms of behaviour identified (that is, obscene phone calls, sexual harassment, rape, incest, coerced or pressurised sex and so on), no matter how seemingly disparate, were part of the same social phenomenon, i.e. that of men's social control of women. Second, she meant that at the level of social experience, these disparate forms of behaviour were not easily distinguished, that they blurred into and out of each other. So, the argument to be distilled from *Surviving Sexual Violence* and the various articles that were published by Kelly shortly afterwards can be summarised as follows: women's and girls' lives are limited and their experiences of freedom and autonomy are constrained by a continuum of sexual violence which functions to ensure men's social power and control.

Before moving on, it is helpful to highlight a few obvious exclusions in the following discussion. This chapter concerns itself with women's involvement in prostitution. This is not for any reason other than a purely pragmatic one – Kelly's concept was never developed to address sexual violence per se but rather sexual violence committed by men against women. This means that at a very basic level, there will be difficulties in using it to address (i) men and boys as sellers of sex and/or victims within prostitution and (ii) the distinctions between adults, young people and children in prostitution and their experience of violence in commercialised sexual exchanges. Second, an important development in Kelly's work was eschewing the dominance of legal definitions of sexual violence and including in her definition some of the more 'blurry' activities, such as harassment, obscene phone calls and the like. This chapter focuses on what is most commonly understood and known as prostitution – the direct exchange of sex for money. What is excluded from the discussion are the 'blurry' activities in which a sexual service is provided but where there is no physical contact (e.g. webcams, telephone sex lines and so on).

## Victimisation in prostitution: the problems of naming and measuring

The past two decades has seen a reawakening of criminological, sociological and anthropological research (and feminist campaigning) interest in prostitution (Phoenix 2009; Campbell and O'Neill 2006; Kinnell 2010; Sanders 200; Munro and della Guista 2008). Most of that research can be described as critical scholarship that focuses on policy development, innovation, reform and implementation. Notwithstanding this, there has also been a steady flow of localised and small-scale ethnographic and survey research examining the conditions of existence for individuals in prostitution. Together, the findings of that research tell a fairly consistent, if contradictory, tale in which involvement in prostitution is seen as being both a strategy for achieving economic and financial stability and security (or merely economic survival) and a form of victimisation in that, for many, involvement in prostitution has exposed them to a range of violent and criminal forms of behaviour such as rape, assault, sexual assault, robbery, intimidation, violence and so on (Phoenix 2001, 2002 and 2009; O'Neill 2001).[1] The literature is littered with accounts of exploitation and intimidation, of violent physical assaults, of sexual assaults and rape, of harassment by community vigilantes or by policing 'purges', of street robbery (for those working from the streets), of clients refusing to pay, of the force of necessity and poverty driving women's choices, of the coercive and corrosive effect of drug and alcohol dependency, of housing problems and homelessness, of backgrounds marked by domestic abuse, child abuse (physical, sexual and emotional) and mental health problems and so on. Research also confirms that street work is more dangerous than indoor work – especially if indoor workers are able to work together (Sanders 2008; McKeganey and Barnard 1996; Church *et al.* 2001; Day and Ward 1999; Kinnell 2006, 2010; Campbell and O'Neill 2006). The risks and realities of violence are not evenly distributed across all types and forms of prostituting activities or for all constituencies of sex workers (Kinnell 2010). Women and girls working the street tend to be most at risk from a broad range of violences. Those individuals whose lives are marked by increased levels of social and economic stability and security (i.e. escort workers, indoor workers) tend to experience less violence generally and a narrower range of violences.

Recognition of the high levels of (sexual) victimisation[2] in prostitution raises a series of difficult methodological and epistemological questions. There is no question that victimisation – sexual or otherwise – punctuates the lives of women in prostitution. What remains, however, are two points of discussion: (i) the extent of that victimisation and whether it is ever possible to measure and (ii) how to make sense of it. In examining some of these questions, this section makes the case that the concept of a continuum of sexual violence does not *readily* lend itself to generating new insights into the lives of women involved in prostitution. The concept was developed in relation to Kelly's stated aim of giving a 'voice' to women whose experiences had not figured in public, academic and policy debates (i.e. those who were outwith criminal justice or health and welfare agencies) and with the express purpose of addressing one of the key research questions, that is the 'long-term impact of sexual violence'. In order to accomplish these twin aims, Kelly's research population were 'women' and her object of inquiry was both the experience of sexual violence and the way those experiences came to be meaningful. Although seemingly obvious, it is worth noting that Kelly's object of inquiry was constituted as being *in the context of everyday, ordinary life* and not in relation to a specific set of activities, events or social relationships, much less in relation to a diverse social institution. In this way, the concept of a continuum was developed *because* the data demonstrated links between the way women experience a broad range of behaviours in everyday life (from unwanted sex, to harassment, to rape) and the impact this had on their everyday life. Her interview sample was relatively small (n=60) and was what might be termed 'opportunistic' in that she visited a range of women's groups with leaflets and tear-off strips. The interviewees, by and large white British women, were a more or less homogeneous sample in that they were women attending a women's group of one variety or another.

In relation to prostitution, however, there are profound difficulties in even beginning to specify the prevalence or impact of sexual victimisation perpetrated against individuals in the prostitution. This is not 'just' a problem of (self)disclosure, as Kelly (1988) noted. Nor is it 'merely' a problem of quantification. The problem is basic and fundamental. As discussed in the introduction to this chapter, prostitution is a social institution – and a highly diverse one. Women working in prostitution can work in complete isolation from welfare, statutory or voluntary agencies, as in the case of women working from their own homes and using the Internet as a point of contact with clients. Alternatively, they may be working from the streets in which case they could be known to other working women and a range of agencies tasked with working with them. Some of these women are able to secure for themselves very stable lives and very high incomes. Others are involved as a form of economical survivalism. In this respect, often the only thing that women in prostitution have in common is that they are involved in the commercial exchange of sex for money. At the risk of oversimplification, it may be that the contexts and experiences of women working from different venues and in different ways are so diverse as to render any analytical grouping of them together meaningless – even, or especially, for the purpose of understanding sexual violence.

Research in prostitution has the added difficulties associated with identifying and gaining access to unknown, hidden or indeed 'vulnerable' and marginalised research participants (O'Connell Davidson and Layder 1994). Often UK data produced about prostitution (qualitative or quantitative) are, in reality, data produced about research participants (i) who, in stark contrast to Kelly's research population, are accessed through outreach, criminal justice or other welfare agencies; (ii) for whom prostitution has become the type of problem that means that they are compelled, or inclined, to seek help; (iii) or who may be part of pro- or anti-campaigning groups and thereby frame their experiences by particular sets of a priori assumptions. Inferences or extrapolations from data collected about the experiences of these individuals in prostitution will not necessarily be meaningful across the full range of all individuals involved in prostitution(s), including those who have never accessed services or campaigning groups. By their very nature, outreach services or other voluntary or statutory welfare services often work with only a very small sector of prostitution such as street work, escort or parlours. It may well be that recent attempts to quantify sexual violence in prostitution have an inherent tendency to *overestimate* the extent and prevalence of sexual violence if only because there is an over-representation of individuals who are accessed through welfare or criminal justice agencies and who work in less stable and more risky environs. In order to make any methodologically robust, meaningful statements (or to produce 'evidence') about the extent, range and prevalence of violence, it is vital that the general population, from which the sample is derived, can be described. This is simply not possible with research in prostitution and has led to what Wagenaar (2010) refers to as the 'fallacy of unwarranted generalisations'. Wagenaar (2010) argues that prostitution research is marked by a tendency to make large quantitative generalisations from small scale qualitative research. Take for instance a frequently quoted statistic: 'more than half of UK prostitutes have been raped and/or seriously sexually assaulted' (Eaves 2008). This statistic was drawn from an earlier Home Office publication.

Another area in which there is a growing body of literature concerns violence experienced by women involved in street prostitution (Barnard and Hart, 2000; Lowman, 2000; Miller and Schwartz, 1995; Pyett and Warr, 1999; Williamson and Foleron, 2001; McKeganey and Barnard, 1996). Barnard and Hart, (2000) found that it was the location of prostitution, whether indoors or street, rather than any other factor that was significantly associated with incidence of violence. In their survey including 115 street prostitutes in Leeds and Glasgow, they found that 81 per cent had experienced client violence, with 47 per cent having been slapped, punched or kicked, 37 per cent having been robbed by clients, 28 per cent having suffered attempted rape, and 22 per cent having been raped. May *et al.* (1999) reported similarly that over three-quarters of the 67 women involved in prostitution in their study had been subjected by clients to physical, sexual or other forms of violence. In a survey of 193 women involved in prostitution conducted in London, Ward *et al.* (1999) found that 68 per cent of those involved in street prostitution had experienced physical assault and all had a mortality rate twelve times higher than expected for London. Moreover, the majority of street prostitutes have had multiple experiences of violence, not only from their clients but also from passers-by abusing them both verbally and physically (McKeganey and Barnard, 1996; Campbell *et al.*, 1996).

(Hester and Westmarland 2004: 81)

The estimated number of women involved in prostitution at any one time in the UK is between 40,000–80,000 (Phoenix and Sanders 2010). The combined sample referred to above is 375, i.e. between 1% and 0.5% of the estimated total population of sex workers. The point here is that there is very little that can be known with any degree of certainty or robustness where it comes to the question of the wide-ranging nature or prevalence of victimisation against women in prostitution. It is almost impossible to characterise, describe or measure in any meaningful way the totality of social *contexts* that women in prostitution inhabit. Studies that purport to measure victimisation in prostitution start with the taken-for-granted assumption that the experience of selling sex for money overrides other or wider social, political, economic and ideological conditions. They also tend to start with the bracketing-off of the way in which the systems of regulating prostitution may (or may not) shape women's vulnerability to victimisation. For these studies also tend to start from the assumption that the common experience of selling sex for money is *analytically more relevant and important* than the diversity of contexts making up the institution of prostitution or the manner in which it is regulated and prostitute-women's lives governed. Against this, Kelly's concept of a continuum of sexual violence is limited in helping to understand the issue of sexual victimisation in prostitution, if only because it was never developed to understand experience and impact *in relation to a specific social institution, much less such a highly complex, highly regulated, quasi-legitimate and diverse one as prostitution.*

## Applying the concept of a continuum of sexual violence to prostitution

This section asks whether and in what ways the logic underpinning Kelly's concept of a continuum of sexual violence maps onto women's experiences of (sexual) victimisation in prostitution. I make the case that it does not. This is primarily because, first, Kelly's concept of sex is ahistorical and asocial and, second, using the concept of a continuum of sexual violence produces profound theoretical closures that pertain to the way in which women in prostitution are regulated by government and by economic inequalities.

To remind the reader, Kelly's definition of sexual violence is 'physical, visual, verbal or sexual acts' that are experienced as a 'threat, invasion or assault' and act to limit, constrain or otherwise harm women's sexual autonomy. Framing this definition is a particular construction of sexuality. Kelly was keen to displace the then naturalistic constructions of sexuality as being biologically determined and being highly gendered (that is to say, men's sexuality as being predominantly active, women's as being passive). Drawing on feminist theories of patriarchy, Kelly substituted a construction of 'sexuality' and 'sex' as being the primary locus of men's social control over women within patriarchal societies (i.e. societies structured by gendered relations of power). In this analysis, 'sexuality' and 'sex' are treated as the activities and behaviour that we most commonly associate with the terms, or to use Kelly's words 'intimate relations'. Kelly presents a vision of heterosexual sex and sexuality that in essence is shaped by social relations of gendered inequality. In so doing she implicitly draws a distinction between sexual behaviours that are *ipso facto* 'inappropriate' (those in which sex is used as a mechanism of control and power) and those that are 'appropriate' (those where sex is not a mechanism of control, but is somehow 'authentic' in experience). The dividing line between the two is whether the woman consented. The difficulty in Kelly's construction of sexual violence (as a sociological phenomenon) is that she uses a profoundly asocial notion of consent. For Kelly, consent is rooted in the concept of free will, that is to say it is based on the simplistic notion that the individual had no or limited choice. These assumptions then facilitated an analytical approach in which she could group inappropriate, violent sexual behaviours along with behaviours like unwanted sex, obscene telephone calls and unwelcome sexual visual imagery, for what they share is that they are unwarranted, unchosen sexual encounters. What is neglected in this analysis, however, are two things: (i) the way in which sociocultural and normative frameworks shape, blend, blur or otherwise impact upon which behaviours are seen as appropriate and which are not – within societies, across time and across societies – and (ii) the way in which wider social forces act upon and limit choices. The next part of this chapter unpicks the implications of this.

## Late modern sex: sex-as-leisure, sex-as-pleasure

How sex is experienced by individuals and how it is regulated has, in the past 50 years, dramatically changed across most Western industrial societies. With the advent of moderately safe and reliable contraception, 'sex' in late modernity has become unhooked from the traditional constraints and controls of biology, family and to a lesser extent religion. As a set of embodied experiences, it has also been moved beyond traditional relationships and particularly from courtship rituals and marriage. Normative ideologies of gendered sex have also changed. Contemporary public discourses on sex focus on 'good' sex and how to have it, how much sex is too much and how many partners are too few or too many. Satellite television stations provide an endless series of programmes dedicated to helping the viewer enjoy their sex life just as confessional television programmes have become increasingly sexual in their tone. Sex has become so visible in late-modern cultures that it has prompted some to speculate about the democratisation of sex, or the pornographication of culture (Attwood 2006). The argument runs like this: contemporary, late modern cultures are increasingly preoccupied with sexual values, practices and identities, are marked by more permissive sexual attitudes, new forms of sexual experiences and expressions and have witnessed a shift or 'breakdown' of the rules, regulations and rituals that have operated to exclude that which once was considered 'obscene' from the everyday (Attwood 2006). There has been also an extension of sexual consumerism in which sexual products (and services) are increasingly available to a wider and wider range of consumers (McNair 2002). Combined with this process of sexual liberalisation there has also been a significant shift in the links between sex and consumption. So, for instance, Giddens (1992), Plummer (2003) and Bauman (1998, 2003) have all noted in varying ways the degree to which sex saturates consumer cultures and particularly the media. Researchers in the area of prostitution picked up on this expansion of 'sex-as-leisure' and 'sex-as-pleasure' and sought to understand what it signifies about the organisation of social life as well as the organisation of prostitution. So, for instance, Bernstein (2001: 84) noted that one of the features of late-modern societies is the reconfiguration of erotic life 'from a relational model of sex to a recreational model of sex' in which pursuit of sexual intimacy and 'fun' is not hindered by the expansion of a marketplace for sex but is facilitated by it – or rather by the ways that the erotic in the new sexual marketplace is not infused with ambiguity or hypocrisy of intimate emotional relationships (see also Prasad 1999).

What this means in practice is that sex and how it is experienced has changed significantly since Kelly's earlier work. The wide availability and acceptability of pornography reshapes what is considered 'beyond the pale' or inappropriate, just as the extension of sexual consumerism also reshapes what is considered degrading, obscene or, indeed, unwarranted and unchosen. While I would not want to take this argument to a logical extreme, these significant sociocultural changes do call into the question the possibility of analysing 'the sexual' and 'sex behaviours' separately from the highly complex and layered normative field that make up 'sex'. More than anything else, they call into question the utility of forms of analysis of complex, wide-ranging sexual behaviours that draw a single line between those which are 'wanted' and those which are not. This is especially the case in prostitution or other forms of what might now be called 'sexual consumerism'.

Leaving aside these sociocultural issues, Kelly's concept of a continuum was also based on the way in which she combined the issue of consent (or lack thereof) in sexual behaviours and the loss of individual control over sexual autonomy. Street prostitution highlights some of the profound difficulties of defining sexual violence in such a way. The backgrounds of the women who get involved in street prostitution are depressingly familiar. At least five decades of empirical research confirms that they come from backgrounds punctuated by sexual and physical abuse within families or by partners, have grown up in social care and have been raped or sexually assaulted prior to their involvement in prostitution (Phoenix 2001, O'Neill 2001). For many individuals across Europe, involvement in street prostitution is driven, for the most part, by financial necessity. One of the striking features of empirical research is the way in which women will recount tales in which they struggled to secure an economically stable future for themselves and their dependants. The literature is replete with quotations from women who talk about being 'forced', 'compelled' or 'having no other choice' but to go into prostitution (see especially Phoenix 2001: ch. 4). Such narratives fit nicely within Kelly's formulation of a continuum of sexual violence. However, and this is the point, to map prostitution onto a continuum of sexual violence (or to explain street working women's experiences as part of the continuum of sexual violence) requires (i) the transposition of women's *economic conditions and their individual economic motivations* into a condition of sexual victimisation and (ii) a conception of consent which denies the way in which wider social circumstances act to limit individuals' choices. What gets lost in that transposition is how a number of wider, non-sexual albeit gendered, processes shape and constrain women's autonomy – sexual or otherwise.

## The limits to sexual violence

Perhaps one of the more pronounced limitations of applying the concept of a continuum of sexual violence to prostitution is in specifying the boundaries of the concept, i.e. between sexual violence and other forms of violence and/or victimisation that women experience. Kelly's concept was a conscious attempt to blur what were the then taken-for-granted boundaries between different types of acts that may have an impact on women's sexual autonomy. For her, there was no limit to the concept of a continuum of sexual violence as long as the behaviour in question was sexual. In her discussion of the limits or boundaries of the concept, Kelly (1988: 40) includes sex (that is to say, behaviours which result in (intended or actual) ejaculation) *and* 'words describing women's bodies and sexuality', 'images portraying women as inferior' and pornography. In that these behaviours operate to reduce a woman's autonomy, they are constituted by Kelly as being part of the continuum of sexual violence.

In the context of prostitution, however, the question arises as to whether all forms of victimisation that sex workers experience are, indeed, sexualised or constituted as sexual victimisation. One of the defining features of prostitution is that it is a job shaped by 'the sexual'. Research has demonstrated time and again how a woman's status as 'sex worker', 'prostitute' or 'prostituted-woman' operates as a master status (Becker 1969). Her status as mother, wife, lover, sister, worker, resident and so on are eclipsed and overwritten by her prostituting activities and her prostitute identity (Phoenix 2001, 2009; Melrose 2009; Scoular 2009; O'Neill 2008; O'Connell Davidson 1998, 2006). At the level of lived realities, this means that for many women in prostitution, particularly those who work and live in the UK or other countries that regulate prostitution predominantly through criminal justice, there is little distinction between their lives *in* prostitution and their lives *outside* prostitution (see especially Phoenix 2001). This subjective experience is mirrored in the regulatory regime within the UK and other countries in that many women in prostitution now find that the totality of their lives and relationships are open to scrutiny by state and non-governmental organisations working with them to 'exit' them from prostitution (Phoenix 2009). This is seen most clearly in relation to young people who are in prostitution (or, to use the most contemporary discursive term, 'the sexual exploitation of young people'). The guidance which shaped how sexually exploited young people are dealt with (*Safeguarding Children in Prostitution*, DoH/HO 2000) drew a formal line of distinction between those young people who are sexually exploited and those who voluntarily return to prostitution. For the latter category, appropriate intervention may well be criminalisation. For the former category, appropriate intervention will never be criminalisation and will always be provided within a child protection framework. At heart, the line of distinction inheres around whether the young person is classified as a victim or an offender. With that, the agencies have been forced to focus on establishing the degree to which a young person is voluntarily engaged in prostitution, i.e. whether (or not) s/he is being coerced into exchanging sex for money. In order to make this assessment, the totality of a young person's life is examined, including family, school, work and social relationships. At the levels of subjective identity, policing and intervention, many young people's and women's social experiences implode on and are organised around their prostituting activities. Put simply: for many women in prostitution (and the agencies working with them), there is no life defined as being outside 'the sexual'.

Within this context, it is difficult to use Kelly's concept of a continuum of sexual violence to understand the different types of victimisation and violent experiences that women in prostitution have. At the risk of stating the obvious, if there is no life defined as being outside 'the sexual', then all forms of victimisation and violence are, within Kelly's formulation, sexual. *All* unwanted invasions and threats that happen during the course of a woman's involvement in prostitution will be part of the continuum of sexual violence. This would include behaviour that has no sexual content, such as being robbed or physically assaulted by a punter, being harassed by the community or the police, or being exploited by a partner in order to fund his drug habit. This is not an esoteric debate. If the violence and victimisation that any woman experiences while being involved in prostitution, in any of its manifestations, is analytically categorised as (i) sexual violence and (ii) thereby similar to rape, sexual assault and sexual harassment, then the specificity of that victimisation is lost. What is foreclosed within such a conceptual framework is the recognition of the specific conditions of existence for women in prostitution, and the articulation between these and formal, political responses, i.e. the regulation and policing of prostitution. Using Kelly's concept of a continuum of sexual violence results in an inability to recognise, analyse and explain how formal regulatory systems do, or do not, leave women vulnerable to the types of economic and physical victimisation described above. Important dimensions of the lived experiences of many women in prostitution get lost – such as, in the UK, the way that community safety policies pitch the safety of one group of women against the safety of another (cf. Melrose 2009), or how policies which seek to criminalise punters (especially now with strict liability) undermine women's attempts to protect themselves, or policies which criminalise indoor working (bawdy houses, brothels) undermine women's attempts to organise themselves and work in ways that generate safety (Phoenix 2009; Scoular and O'Neill 2007; Sanders 2009). Applying the concept of a continuum of sexual violence to prostitution means that there is no space left to recognise and understand what makes women in prostitution vulnerable to the various forms of victimisation described in the literature. It also obscures the differences between the experiences, impact and meaning of a prostitute woman being battered or raped at home or being robbed or raped by a client.

**The dangers of a teleological explanation**

It is perhaps unsurprising that important distinctions between economic and social conditions of existence, between economic and sexual victimisation and between governmental responses to the victimisation of women and the victimisation of sex workers are obscured by Kelly's concept of a continuum of sexual violence. Kelly analytically privileged gender over all other forms of social differentiation and inequality (that is, economic, ethnic, age, sexuality, disability and so on) by using a functionalist logic in which the disparate forms of harms, abuse, intrusion, coercion, threat and violence in the realm of the sexual are understood *in relation to the function* they serve in maintaining relationships of gendered inequality. The continuum 'functions' as a mechanism of social control. Kelly was not describing *sexual* violence or describing sexual *violence* but rather a means to a specific social end – the control of women by men. At the risk of repetition, sexual violence exists *because* it functions to control women. This form of teleological and essentialist feminist theorising was thoroughly critiqued over two decades ago and for that reason I will refer readers to that literature (Nicholson 1989; Jaggar and Bordo 1989; Harding 1986, 1987; Butler 1993, 2004, 2006). Suffice to say, however, teleological argument and analysis of this type jar with contemporary sociological and criminological audiences, particularly because of the manner in which they tend to conceal the historical, ideological, political, economic specificity of any social phenomena.

My call to maintain analytical specificity is not 'just' about producing good knowledge. It is also about the politics of prostitution and policy reformation. In the UK, the past decade has borne witness to the gradual acceptance, at governmental level, of what is at heart an ideological position in regards to prostitution. This position has been developed as a logical extension of the lack of specificity in characterising, describing and analysing 'the problem' of prostitution. Instead, the vulnerability of women in prostitution to victimisation has been conflated with their status as victims and the drive of policy has been to abolish prostitution on the grounds that it is sexual violence against women. This is an historical departure from the 'traditional' negative regulationism marking British policies on prostitution. Prior to the massive reforms in the past decade, prostitution was seen as a matter of private morality except in as much as it offends or is 'injurious' to 'decent citizens'. Constituting prostitution as a matter of private morality has meant that women have not been criminalised or regulated for being involved in the commercial exchange of sex for money, per se, but rather for the manner in which they do it. The policy landscape now is very different. In May 2000, the Department of Health and Home Office jointly issued guidance (*Safeguarding Children Involved in Prostitution*) that recommended dealing with those under the age of 18 years old and involved in the commercial exchange of sex for money as victims of child abuse, in the first instance. By 2002, this guidance was formalised in the Department of Health's published *National Plan for Safeguarding Children from Commercial Sexual Exploitation*. By the end of 2004, the organisation of local services had shifted. In most large cities, new services were developed for young people and worked to a different agenda, with different sources of funding and in different ways than services working with adults. Barnardo's took a pioneering role in developing services for children with their flagship project, Sexual Exploitation of Children of the Streets (SECOS) in Middlesbrough. The impact was that sexual health and drugs outreach services became cautious of working with young people if only because they could no longer guarantee anonymity and confidentiality, or indeed a non-judgemental approach. By redefining young people's involvement in prostitution as child sexual abuse, harm minimisation outreach services became subject to the statutory powers (and responsibilities) of child protection legislation and the statutory agencies tasked with protecting children. The ultimate effect was that these services withdrew provision for anyone under the age of 18. This was made possible by the simple discursive shift that constituted young people as *victims* of child abuse, exploitation and coercion. The guidance on young people inaugurated a process that has continued since – the ever more finely tuned demarcation of types of victims (and not-victims) involved in prostitution for whom fundamentally different interventions are seen as appropriate, justified and, indeed, necessary (see also Phoenix 2002a, 2002b, 2006).

So, in December 2001, the Home Office, through the Crime Reduction Partnerships, spent £850,000 funding 11 pilot projects 'to reduce the number of young people and women involved in prostitution, reduce crime and disorder associated with street-based prostitution and find out which interventions helped women to exit prostitution' (Home Office 2004: v). The results of that research were published in a document entitled *Tackling Street Prostitution: towards a holistic approach*. In the same year, the Home Office also published its first consultation about prostitution in the form of *Paying the Price* (HO 2004b) and subsequently published its recommendations in a document entitled *A Coordinated Strategy on Prostitution* (HO 2006). The approach adopted was called 'enforcement plus support' in which welfare support is offered *alongside* criminal justice interventions. In this way, so the logic goes, women are given all the help they need to exit from prostitution – but they also become legitimate and appropriate subjects of (increasingly) punitive criminal justice responses should they 'choose' to return to prostitution (Phoenix 2006, 2008a and 2008b; Scoular and O'Neill 2007). In this 'coordinated', 'strategic' approach, a more central role is played by criminal justice agencies in relation to policing (especially street-based) prostitution. Police and court disposals become the major point of referral to welfare agencies to help women with debt counselling, drug and alcohol problems, housing and so on. Put simply, welfare is being delivered to this population of women through criminal justice – the point being that should such welfare be refused, or should women not comply with the programmes, traditional criminal justice punishments are seen as warranted and justified.

Arguably the guidance on young people and the adoption of a new strategy on prostitution form only part of the 'quiet revolution' in prostitution policy. The concern about sexual exploitation of children ushered in a raft of new legislation. The Sexual Offences Act (2003) and the Protection of Children and Prevention of Sexual Offences (Scotland) Act 2005 criminalised *any* adult involvement in the commercial sexual exploitation of children and young people by inter alia making it illegal to purchase sex from a young person (i.e. anyone under the age of 18) or to facilitate or encourage the sexual exploitation of a young person. In a related move, the Asylum and Immigration (Treatment of Claimants, etc.) Act 2004 and the Scottish Criminal Justice (Scotland) Act 2004 brought in a further set of measures that have criminalised the trafficking of women and children for the purposes of commercial sexual exploitation. In 2006 the Home Office published its consultation on human trafficking: the result of which established the UK Human Trafficking Centre in Sheffield. By March 2007, the Home Office published the *UK National Action Plan on Tackling Human Trafficking*. Taken together, these form a comprehensive set of measures which operate to criminalise the movement of women and children for the purposes of prostitution. The final set of Acts has moved the 'agenda' for regulating prostitution *in the name of protecting women against victimisation* even further. In Scotland the Prostitution (Public Places) Act 2007 criminalises soliciting for prostitution in a public place (known as 'kerb-crawling'). Since then, in the Criminal Justice and Immigration Bill (2008) Labour sought to criminalise the purchase of sex altogether and to create a new court disposal (a 'prostitution rehabilitation order') that would compel women to leave prostitution. Although the prostitution-related provisions were ultimately defeated, similar measures were re-introduced with the Policing and Crime Act 2010 in which Engagement and Support Orders (which compel women in prostitution to seek help), Closure Orders and a strict liability offence of purchasing sex from an individual who is exploited have been introduced. During the same time period there have been other policy changes worthy of note. The Criminal Justice and Policing Act (2001) extended police powers of arrest in kerb-crawling. The Crime and Disorder Act (1998) introduced antisocial behaviour orders which some local authorities and police constabularies have taken up to use against prostitute women.

The words of Harriet Harman, then Deputy Leader of the Labour Party, in her Labour Party conference speech in 2009 neatly summarise the discursive shift that made possible this raft of new policy measures. Ms Harman was unequivocal: 'Prostitution is not work – it's exploitation of women by men' (http://www.labour.org.uk/harriet-harman-speech-conference). The irony to note here is this: in the name of protection against exploitation and violence a series of measures have been introduced whose effect is an intensification of regulation not of women in prostitution, per se, but of those women with few, if any, social resources to make different sorts of choice (Phoenix 2008a, 2008b).

The point of this section has been to highlight one of the consequences on the lives of actual women of not maintaining analytical specificity in relation to women's involvement in prostitution. The 'war over meanings' that often accompanies feminist interventions regarding prostitution is not a dry academic debate. It feeds into and out of policy debates and shifts. My final criticism, therefore, of Kelly's concept of a continuum of sexual violence is that it is a concept founded upon the discursive conflation of *victimisation* and *victimhood*, that is to say, Kelly's concept fails to draw a line of demarcation between the incidents occurring in individuals' lives (i.e. their experiences of victimisation) and the social contexts and identities of those individuals who are victimised (i.e. their status as 'victims' and the objective effects such status incurs). It may be the case that one enduring impact of feminist scholarship about sexual violence, of which Kelly's text was only one part, was that it generated the political drive for government to address gendered sexual victimisation. But without analytical specificity, or an understanding of the wider economic, political and ideological conditions shaping women's choices, political interventions are based on overly simplistic binary distinctions between 'victims' of prostitution and 'voluntary sex workers'. The final sting in the tail then is that this form of teleological, essentialising analysis may well have provided the discursive (and ideological) conditions that ushered in policy reforms which, paradoxically, make women in prostitution more (not less) vulnerable to victimisation.

## Conclusion

What conclusions can be drawn from this discussion? The concept of a continuum of sexual violence is highly problematic. In the context of prostitution, it conflates the economic, the sexual and the violent in such a way as to obscure any depth of understanding of the *specific* experiences of women *in prostitution*. The second and broader conclusion is that when examining sex and sexual violence (or victimisation) in an economic context (i.e. prostitution) there is an absolute need to maintain analytical specificity if a fully social understanding is to be achieved. There can be little doubt that gendered social control and gendered violence are experienced by women in prostitution in profoundly different ways than other women – the point of analysis is not to flatten those differences in the service of a political campaign. Instead, it is to understand gendered violence and the social, economic, political and ideological conditions that make them possible in order to identify possible points of meaningful (and not punitive) intervention. Therefore a final conclusion that can be drawn is that in theorising sexual violence there is a paramount need to contextualise and build theories which are capable of both recognising and denying the lived realities. To put it another way and in the context of prostitution: the violence is real. The harm is real. None of what has been said negates the fact that violence in prostitution is a problem. The known scale of it is disturbing and *should* be shocking. The human cost to its victims is probably unquantifiable. The gendered nature of it is unquestionable. But to categorise it as something else (i.e. 'just' another manifestation of male violence against women) is an indication of our lack of sociological and criminological imagination. Instead, we need an analysis that both recognises and denies these facts. We need to recognise the historical, social, economic, ideological and political conditions that give rise to the vulnerabilities experienced by women in prostitution and shape the official responses to it while simultaneously denying the inevitability of it in contemporary societies.

## Further reading

For general reading on prostitution Sanders, T., O'Neill. M. and Pitcher, J. (2009) *Prostitution: sex work, policy and politics*. London: Sage provides a good introductory level book which covers a range of different issues. Over the past 15 years, there have been a number of high quality research monographs published on people's experiences of prostitution. They are:

O'Connell Davidson, J. (1988) *Prostitution, Power and Freedom*. Michigan: University of Michigan Press.
O'Neill, M. (2001) *Prostitution and Feminism*. Oxford: Wiley Blackwell.
Phoenix, J. (2001) *Making Sense of Prostitution*. London: Palgrave.
Sanders, T. (2005) *Sex Work: A Risky Business*. Cullompton: Willan Publishing.
Sanders, T. (2009) *Paying for Pleasure: Men Who Buy Sex*. Cullompton: Willan Publishing.

There is a growing literature on the sexual exploitation of children.

Melrose, M., Barrett, D. and Brodie, I. (1999) *One Way Street? Retrospectives on Childhood Prostitution*. London: The Children Society provides a good introduction.
For more contemporary research, please see Pearce, J.J., Williams, M. and Galvin, C. (2002) *It's Someone Taking a Part of You*. London: National Children's Bureau.
Pearce, J. J. (2009) *Young People and Sexual Exploitation*. London: Routledge.

For commentaries and discussion about legal reform and policy please see:

Kinnell, H. (2010) *Violence and Sex Work*. Cullompton: Willan Publishing.
Matthews, R. (2008) *Prostitution, Politics and Policy*. London: Taylor and Francis.
Phoenix, J. (ed) (2010) *Regulating Sex for Sale: Prostitution Policy Reform in the UK*. Bristol: Policy Press.
Self, H. (2003) *Prostitution, Women and the Misuse of Law: the Fallen Daughters of Eve*. London: Frank Cass.

Hardy, K., Sanders, T. and Kingston, S. (eds) (2010) *New Sociologies of Sex Work*. London: Ashgate.
Munro, V. and della Giusta, M. (eds) (2008) *Demanding Sex: Critical Reflections on the Regulations of Prostitution*. London: Ashgate.
Bernstein, E. (2007) *Temporarily Yours: Intimacy, Authenticity and the Commerce of Sex*. Chicago: University of Chicago Press.
Weitzer, R. (2010) *Sex for Sale: Prostitution, Pornography and the Sex Industry*. London: Taylor and Francis.

## Notes

1 The tale told in recent studies is not fundamentally dissimilar to the narratives told in research about involvement in prostitution for the previous two centuries (see also Phoenix 2001 and 2009). Involvement in prostitution is dominated by women, women whose lives are marked by poverty, homelessness, alcohol and drug problems, complex social and personal welfare difficulties and so on. It is largely men who purchase sex. Those women and young people whose lives are less socially and economically secure tend to get involved in the more marginalised and dangerous forms of prostitution, such as street work.

2 At this stage in the discussion, it is helpful to adopt the term 'sexual victimisation' as opposed to sexual violence. The term 'victimisation' is used in order to draw a conceptual break between the behaviours that are being discussed (i.e. rape, sexual assault, assault, harassment and so on) and how they are analytically understood. To do this does not deny the very real and visceral experiences of victimisation, but it does facilitate the questioning of how these experiences are made sense of by criminologists and sociologists and, more, it permits a deeper critical understanding of the concept of sexual violence.

## References

Attwood, F. (2006) 'Sexed up: theorising the sexualisation of culture', *Sexualities*, 9(1): 77–94.
Bauman, Z. (1998) *Work, Consumerism and the New Poor*. Milton Keynes: The Open University Press.
Bauman, Z. (2003) *Liquid Love: On the Frailty of Human Bonds*. Cambridge: Polity Press.
Becker, H. (1969) *Outsiders: Studies in the Sociology of Deviance*. London: Macmillan.
Bernstein, E. (2001) 'The meaning of the purchase: desire, demand and the commerce of sex', *Ethnography*, 2(3): 389–420.
Butler, J. (1993) *Bodies That Matter: The Discursive Limits to Sex*. London: Routledge.
Butler, J. (2004) *Undoing Gender*. London: Routledge.
Butler, J. (2006) *Gender Trouble*. London: Routledge.
Campbell, R. and O'Neill, M. (2006) *Sex Work Now*. Cullompton: Willan Publishing.
Church, S., Henderson, M. Barnard, M. and G. Hart (2001) 'Violence by clients towards female prostitutes in different work settings: questionnaire survey', *BMJ*, 322: 524.
Day, S. and Ward, H. (2001) 'Violence towards female prostitutes', *BMJ*, 323: 7306.
Department of Children and Family Services (2009) *Safeguarding Children and Young People from Sexual Exploitation*. London: The Stationery Office.
Department of Health/Home Office (2000) *Safeguarding Children in Prostitution*. London: The Stationery Office.
Eaves (2008) Eaves Information Sheet – *Prostitution, Eaves4Women*. London. Available

at: http://www.eaves4women.co.uk/Documents/Factsheets/Prostitution%20fact sheet.pdf

Giddens, A. (1992) *The Transformation of Intimacy: Sexuality, Love and Eroticism in Modern Societies*. Cambridge: Polity Press.

Harding, S. (1986) 'The instability of the analytical categories of feminist theory', *Signs*, 11(4).

Harding, S. (ed.) (1987) *Feminism and Methodology*. Bloomington, Indiana: Indiana University Press.

Hester, M. and Westmarland, N. (2004) *Tackling Street Prostitution: Towards an Holistic Approach?* London: HMSO.

Home Office (2004b) *Paying the Price*. London: The Stationery Office.

Home Office (2006) *A Coordinated Strategy on Prostitution*. London: The Stationery Office.

Jaggar, A. and Bordo, S. (eds) (1989) *Gender/Body/Knowledge: Feminist Reconstructions of Being and Knowing*. New York: Rutgers University Press.

Kelly, L. (1987, 2002) 'The continuum of sexual violence', reprinted in K. Plummer (2002) *Sexualities: Some Elements For an Account of the Social Organization of Sexualities*. London: Taylor and Francis.

Kelly, L. (1988) *Surviving Sexual Violence*. Cambridge: Polity Press.

Kinnell, H. (2006) 'Murder made easy: the final solution to prostitution', in R. Campbell and M. O'Neill, *Sex Work Now*. Cullompton: Willan Publishing.

Kinnell, H. (2010) *Violence and Sex Work in Britain*. Cullompton: Willan Publishing.

McKeganey, N. and Barnard, M. (1996) *Sex Work on the Streets: Prostitutes and Their Clients*. Milton Keynes: The Open University Press.

McNair, B. (2002) *Striptease Culture: Sex, Media and the Democratization of Desire*. London and New York: Routledge.

Melrose, M. (2009) 'Out on the streets and out of control: drug using sex workers and prostitution policy', in J. Phoenix (ed.) *Regulating Sex for Sale*. Bristol: Policy Press.

Munro, V. and M. della Giusta (eds) (2008) *Demanding Sex: Critical Reflections on the Regulation of Prostitution*. Aldershot: Ashgate

Nicholson, L. (ed.) (1989) *Feminism/Postmodernism*. London: Routledge.

O'Connell Davidson, J. (1998) *Prostitution, Power and Freedom*. Oxford: Polity.

O'Connell Davidson, J. (2006) 'Will the real sex slave please stand up?', *Feminist Review*, 83, 4–22.

O'Connell Davidson, J. and Layder, D. (1994) *Methods, Sex and Madness*. London: Routledge.

O'Neill, M. (2001) *Prostitution and Feminism*. Cambridge: Polity Press.

O'Neill, M. (2008) 'Sex, violence and work services to sex workers and public policy reform', in G. Letherby, P. Birch, M. Cain and K. Williams (eds) *Sex and Crime*. Cullompton: Willan Publishing.

Phoenix, J. (2001) *Making Sense of Prostitution*. London: Palgrave.

Phoenix, J. (2002a) 'In the name of protection: youth prostitution policy reforms in England and Wales', *Critical Social Policy*, 22(2): 353–75.

Phoenix, J. (2002b) 'Youth prostitution policy reform: new discourse, same old story', in P. Carlen (ed.) *Women and Punishment: the struggle for justice*. Cullompton, Devon: Willan Publishing.

Phoenix, J. (2006) 'Regulating prostitution; controlling women's lives', in F. Heidensohn (ed.) *Gender and Justice: New Concepts and Approaches*. Cullompton: Willan Publishing, pp. 76–95.

Phoenix, J. (2008a) 'Be helped or else! Economic exploitation, male violence and prostitution policy in the UK', in F. Munro and M. della Giusta, (eds) *Demanding Sex: Critical Reflections on the Regulation of Prostitution*. London: Ashgate.

Phoenix, J. (2008b) 'Reinventing the wheel: contemporary contours of prostitution regulation', in G. Letherby, J. Williams, P. Birch and M. Cain (eds) *Sex as Crime*. Cullompton: Willan Publishing, pp. 27–46.

Phoenix, J. (2009) *Regulating Sex for Sale: Prostitution Policy Reform in England and Wales*. Bristol: Policy Press.

Phoenix, J. and Sanders, T. (2010) 'Prostitution policies in the UK', presented to ESF Exploratory Workshop *Exploring and Comparing Prostitution Regimes in Europe*, 15–17 September, Birkbeck, University of London.

Plummer, K. (2003) 'Introduction, representing sexualities in the media', *Sexualities* 6 (3–4): 275–6.

Prasad, Monica (1999) 'The morality of market exchange: love, money and contractual justice', *Sociological Perspectives*, 42(2): 181–215.

Sanders, T. (2008) *Paying for Pleasure: Men Who Buy Sex*. Cullompton: Willan Publishing.

Sanders. T. and Scoular, J. (eds) (2010) *Regulating Sex/Work: From Crime Control to Neo-liberal Regulation*. London: Wiley Blackwell.

Scoular, J. (2009) *The Subject of Prostitution: Sex/work, Law and Social Theory*. London: Glasshouse Press.

Scoular, J and O'Neill, M. (2007) 'Regulating prostitution: social inclusion, responsibilisation and the politics of prostitution reform', *British Journal of Criminology*, 47(5) 764–78.

Wagenaar, H. (2010) 'Discussion and comments' presented to ESF Exploratory Workshop *Exploring and Comparing Prostitution Regimes in Europe*, 15–17 September, Birkbeck, University of London.

# Chapter 11

# Practitioner commentary: treating the perpetrators of sexual violence – an applied response

*Ruth E. Mann*

**Meet Ruth Mann**

Dr Ruth Mann is a Chartered Forensic Psychologist employed by the National Offender Management Service (NOMS) – an agency of the Ministry of Justice. Ruth has responsibility for the treatment of convicted sexual offenders serving sentences in custody or the community, including programme design and evaluation, staff training, and operational policy. Ruth has been involved in the treatment of sexual offending for over 20 years and has published and presented widely on this topic. Her particular research interests include the identification of evidence-based treatment targets and methods, the role of cognition in sexual offending, the validation of assessment methodologies, and the relationship between psychological, social and biological factors in sexual offending.

**Introduction**

This chapter provides a commentary on the theory chapters in the Handbook, exploring their relevance to policy and practice in the treatment of those convicted for sexual violence. In order to evaluate the contribution of some of the ideas expressed I have particularly considered them in the light of two issues which currently occupy the minds of those who are responsible for the management and treatment of perpetrators. First, to what extent do the ideas presented in the theory chapters enable practitioners to be clearer about the overlap and differences between punishment, rehabilitation and correctional quackery? There have been some powerful debates in the recent literature over the punitive nature of interventions for offenders (e.g. Glaser 2010;

Prescott and Levenson 2010; Ward 2010). For example, Glaser (2010) proposed that treatment programmes for offenders are unethical according to traditional codes of ethics, and that they more correctly should be described as forming part of an offender's punishment. Gendreau *et al.* (2009) have also criticised much of current practice with offenders for drawing on intuitive models of how we want offenders to be different rather than adhering firmly to evidence-based practice, terming the tendency to work from intuition as 'correctional quackery'. Recently, debate in the sex offender treatment field has intensified about the extent to which typical treatment practices best meet the descriptions of punishment, rehabilitation, or correctional quackery (e.g. Mann *et al.* 2010b).

It is hardly contentious to suggest that, where evidence exists, policy and practice in the management and treatment of perpetrators of sexual violence should be evidence-based. That is, interventions should be designed in accordance with the findings of evaluation studies of rehabilitation with offenders. Meta-analyses of interventions with offenders have identified a number of key principles associated with greater effectiveness in terms of reduced reoffending (e.g. Andrews and Bonta 2006), although with sexual offenders in particular, evaluations have generally found only modest impact on reoffending (e.g. Lösel and Schmucker 2005), suggesting that there is considerable room for improvement in our understanding of 'What works?' with sexual offenders. Where sufficient evidence does not exist, then theory-based policy is permissible. Interventions could be designed and implemented based on theoretical 'models of change' (specifications for how and why the programme ought to work), although such endeavours should be considered experimental and so would only be ethical if accompanied by robust research and evaluation. Particularly when evidence does not exist, policy-makers and those in applied practice need to be highly cognisant of the dangers of correctional quackery, which could also be termed instinct-based policy, where interventions are delivered without regard to the evidence base and without respecting the need for an evidence base. Those who succumb to correctional quackery explicitly or implicitly reject the scientific approach and overemphasise approaches that 'feel right'. Such interventions are frequently ineffective or even harmful (Gendreau *et al.* 2009).

The second, and related, question is to what extent do the ideas presented in this section of the Handbook develop our knowledge in relation to the risk, need and responsivity principles of offender rehabilitation? Developed by Andrews and Bonta (2006), the Risk-Need-Responsivity (RNR) principles have an established evidence base, and have been specifically demonstrated to hold in relation to the rehabilitation of those convicted of sexual offending (Hanson *et al.* 2009). The principles essentially state that rehabilitation programmes should: (a) target higher risk offenders and should be proportionate to the risk of the participants; (b) target the factors known to raise risk of reoffending – typically labelled as 'dynamic risk factors' or 'criminogenic needs'; and (c) use methods to which offenders are most likely to respond. Broadly, the methods of offender rehabilitation interventions should be cognitive-behavioural, and more specifically, interventions should be flexible enough that they can be personalised to each participant's individual characteristics, cultural world and learning style.

Considering the chapters in Part Two of this book, several themes emerge of interest to those who work with perpetrators.

## Individual v. societal responsibility for offending

One theme running through the chapters, not always explicitly stated, is that of responsibility for offending. Traditionally (Salter 1988) and to this day (McGrath et al. 2010) treatment programmes for sexual offenders have greatly emphasised the treatment goal of 'taking responsibility' for offending. An offender is usually considered to have taken responsibility for his offending if he gives an account of his offending in a way that matches the official records, and if he additionally attributes his offending to stable internal factors, rather than external or unstable factors which are typically categorised as excuses. So, to give a crude example, an offender who explains his offending by reference to his sexually deviant interests would be more likely to be regarded as taking responsibility for his offending than one who refers to alcohol and stress as contributing factors. While this has been the accepted approach to working with violent perpetrators for many years, more recently it has been observed that the evidence base for this practice is actually weak if not non-existent, and that there may be dangers in placing too much emphasis on the need for internal attributions of cause (Maruna and Mann 2006). Consequently, there has been a call for empirically established dynamic risk factors for offending, such as sexual interests and intimacy deficits, to receive the greatest emphasis in any intervention programme (Mann et al. 2010).

In two of the chapters in this section (Phoenix and Jones) there is an implicit argument that responsibility for sexual violence lies at the broad societal level. It is argued that sexual violence performs a function for society and that it is the male-dominated society that 'benefits' from it. In some contrast, Vetere's and Brown's chapters point more to individual responsibility for sexual violence. In the Introduction to this part of the book, it is commented that 'being able to challenge [distancing of responsibility for violence] in such a way that the perpetrator recognises their responsibility for their behaviour is central to the success of such clinical work'. However, Vetere's chapter describes an approach to intervention that, in line with other recent thinking on sexual violence, actually concentrates more on what has been termed active responsibility – taking responsibility for the future – than on passive responsibility – where the perpetrator is required to make detailed statements of his full responsibility for his violence. Vetere's practice in asking 'future questions' and exploring family members' aspirations are excellent examples of inspiring and encouraging active responsibility for change.

## Assessing individual motivations from offence behaviours

Brown's chapter in this volume focuses in particular on whether there can be said to be a continuum of sexual violence, aiming to develop Kelly's 1988 conceptualisation of sexual violence into an argument which holds greater explanatory and predictive power. Brown's analysis addresses both victim and perpetrator experiences of sexual violence (seen, for example, in Table 7.1). The chapter is particularly concerned with distinguishing different types of sexual violence against adult women (the sexual abuse of children is not included in the analysis) examining whether qualitative distinctions can be made between sexually violent behaviours and whether particular offender pathologies may be associated with different behaviours. Although the chapter also acknowledges the need to answer the 'why?' questions about sexual violence, its main focus is on the definition and categorisation of such violence, arguing that it is more psychologically significant to categorise violent acts in terms of observed behaviours than in terms of internal processes. Brown deals with five categories of sexual violence: sexual harassment, domestic violence, stalking, rape, and sexual murder; noting in particular that there are some overlaps between stalking and domestic violence, and that some behaviours could occur in more than one category (e.g. the use of a weapon can occur in both rape and sexual murder). Some behaviours occur so frequently across all categories (for example, threats of violence) that they can be considered to be core components of sexual violence generally, while other less frequent behaviours are more specific to particular categories – the modus operandi for that category – and the most low-frequency behaviours could be seen as the signatures of particular offenders. Brown discusses some published analyses of the behaviours associated with different types of violence which have identified common themes (for instance, movement of the body in sexual murder) and then subtypes of behaviour enabling that offence type to be divided into clusters (for instance, the four clusters associated with sexual murder were labelled rape, fury, perversion and predator; Kocsis *et al*. 2002). As this last example shows, one benefit of such attempts to cluster offence behaviours is the potential for linking observable behaviours to motivations and thus intervention approaches. The behaviours associated with intimacy-seeking might demand a different rehabilitative focus than the behaviours associated with revenge.

In the literature and in current practice with those who have sexually offended, it is already agreed that interventions need to be flexible enough to respond to individual criminogenic needs. Identification of such needs usually takes place through a multimodal approach including particularly offender self-report (both unsystematically through interview and systematically through psychometric testing) and analysis of observable behaviours. The latter, however, usually follows an idiographic approach and there is definitely room for a more evidence-based approach. The idea that analysis of offending behaviours using multidimensional scaling could assist in classifying offenders' criminogenic needs is appealing. In this chapter, Brown describes only a few such studies and they are described non-critically so from this review it is not possible to draw a confident conclusion about the potential for developing assessments based on such studies. However, there is clearly a promising line of enquiry emerging here which could usefully assist those who assess perpetrators of sexual violence.

## The likely effect of social acceptance of sexual violence on programme effectiveness

Jones argues that rape cannot be understood if it is divorced from its sociological context. That is, rape is a worldwide, extremely widespread, phenomenon, completely underestimated from the number of rapes for which convictions are achieved. In fact, the normalcy of rape, and the likelihood of escaping conviction, mean that the convicted rapist is probably highly unrepresentative of the average perpetrator of sexual violence.

Two arguments in particular are featured in this chapter. The first is that a rape is very unlikely to result in a criminal conviction. Thus, for a man, to rape a woman is 'a low-risk activity'. The second argument is that rape is found worldwide, in all cultures and societies, and particularly is so associated with times of war that it clearly forms one of the weapons of war. Drawing on the evidence base for both these arguments, the author concludes that 'rape [is] an everyday event rather than an out-of-the-ordinary violation' (p. 194). The solution to the problem of rape must originate from society rather than from within individual rapists.

Such an argument makes for interesting reflection given that most jurisdictions mainly attempt to respond to the problem of sexual offending through rehabilitative programmes for individual offenders. These programmes are based on psychological theories of offending, and so concentrate on attempting to change attitudes, teaching new skills, and enabling offenders to find pro-social ways to meet their sexual and intimacy needs. Evaluations of psychological programmes for offenders show mixed results but, in general, modern programmes seem to achieve small but robust reductions in offending rates (e.g. Lösel and Schmucker 2005; Hanson *et al.* 2009). However, the scrutiny and discussion of the effectiveness of such programmes is intense, and when the programmes fail to have large effects on recidivism, or when individuals reoffend despite having participated in an intervention, the blame is laid either at the door of the individual offender ('he failed to respond to the programme') or of the programme itself ('the programme was not effective'). Taking a sociological perspective, however, it might be worth asking if any programme operating from a purely psychological perspective could be expected to have more than a small effect, given the argument that rape must serve certain functions for society. Can it be possible to convince a rape perpetrator that his attitudes are faulty, or that his victim is not responsible for his behaviour, when such beliefs that justify rape are shared by numerous others across history and across cultures? Is it even ethical to operate a programme which is based on the notion that those who sexually offend do so because of individual pathology, when in fact the evidence is that 'sexual violence is embedded in social systems' (p. 195)?

Jones's chapter acknowledges both that social attitudes are hard to shift and that, if rape serves a function for society, there may be a lack of will to change social attitudes that accept sexual violence. In her conclusion, Jones states that 'to engage in meaningful research into sexual violence, we need to understand the connections between the micro-dynamics (why individual men rape) and the macro patterns (why rape is a global phenomenon)' (p. 197). If this is a necessity for meaningful research, it is also true for meaningful intervention. While many convicted men respond positively to rehabilitation programmes focused on sexual offending, it is also the case that many offenders are resistant to the idea of undertaking such programmes (Mann 2009) and that their resistance is often linked to the perception that the psychological perspective of such programmes labels and pathologises them. Perhaps a more honest approach would be to assist these men to examine and reject attitudes that condone sexual violence, while acknowledging that on the sociological evidence they are not in fact deviant or abnormal. It may be a tricky path to tread, to depathologise those who rape without condoning or excusing their harmful behaviour, but it may ultimately be a better way to engage and change sexual violence perpetrators.

## Conclusions

In conclusion, these chapters are a valuable reminder that interventions designed to reduce sexual offending should acknowledge and reflect both sociological and psychological explanations for sexual violence. Interventions that take a purely psychological approach have a modest impact on reoffending but these chapters offer an explanation for why the individualist psychological approach may limit their impact and provide several ideas for improving the effectiveness of services for offenders. As argued at the outset of this commentary, it is essential that the policies and practices that are intended to combat sexual violence are evidence-based. Academics can offer valuable independent critiques of the scientific basis for practitioners' endeavours, and provide new information and new perspectives on the evidence base to assist policy-makers and practitioners continually to improve the standards of applied practice. Academics and those in applied settings must recognise their mutual dependence in achieving the goal of reducing sexual violence.

## References

Andrews, D.A. and Bonta, J. (2006) *The Psychology of Criminal Conduct*. 4th edition. Cincinnati, OH: Anderson.

Gendreau, P., Smith, P. and Theriault, Y.L. (2009) 'Chaos theory and correctional treatment: Common sense, correctional quackery and the law of fartcatchers', *Journal of Contemporary Criminal Justice*, 25: 384–96.

Glaser, B. (2010) 'Sex offender programmes: New technology coping with old ethics', *Journal of Sexual Aggression*, 16: 261–74.

Hanson, R.K., Bourgon, G., Helmus, L. and Hodgson, S. (2009) *A meta-analysis of the effectiveness of treatment for sexual offenders: Risk, need and responsivity*. Corrections Research User Report: 2009–10. Public Safety Canada.

Kocsis, R.N., Cooksey, R.W. and Irwin, H.J. (2002) 'Psychological profiling of sexual murders; an empirical model', *International Journal of Offender Therapy and Comparative Criminology*, 46: 532–54.

Lösel, F., and Schmucker, M. (2005) 'The effectiveness of treatment for sexual offenders: A comprehensive meta-analysis', *Journal of Experimental Criminology*, 1:

117–46.

McGrath, R.J., Cumming, G.F., Burchard, B.L., Zeoli, S. and Ellerby, L. (2010) *Current Practices and Trends in Sexual Abuser Management: The Safer Society 2009*. North American Survey. Brandon, VT: Safer Society Press.

Mann, R.E. (2009) 'Getting the context right for sex offender treatment', in D. Prescott (ed.) *Building Motivation for Change in Sexual Offenders*. Brandon, VT: Safer Society Press.

Mann, R.E., Hanson, R.K. and Thornton, D. (2010) 'Assessing risk for sexual recidivism: Some proposals on the nature of psychologically meaningful risk factors', *Sexual Abuse: A Journal of Research and Treatment*, 22: 172–90.

Mann, R.E., Ware, J. and Barnett, G. (2010b, October) *Rethinking treatment targets for sexual offenders*. Symposium presented at the Annual Conference of the Association for the Treatment of Sexual Abusers, Phoenix, Arizona, USA.

Maruna, S. and Mann, R.E. (2006) 'A fundamental attribution error? Rethinking cognitive distortions', *Legal and Criminological Psychology*, 11: 155–77.

Prescott, D.S. and Levenson, J.S. (2010) 'Sex offender treatment is not punishment', *Journal of Sexual Aggression*, 16, 275–85.

Salter, A.C. (1988) *Treating Child Sex Offenders and Victims: A practical guide*. London: Sage Publications.

Ward, T. (2010) 'Punishment or therapy? The ethics of sexual offending treatment', *Journal of Sexual Aggression*, 16: 286–95.

**Part Three**

# Acts of Sexual Violence

# Introduction

*Sandra Walklate and Jennifer Brown*

## Introduction

In this section of the book we have invited authors to focus their concerns on particular acts of sexual violence, what we know about the nature of those acts and the impacts that they have. We also invited authors, where appropriate, to consider the policy responses to the particular acts with which they are concerned and to reflect upon the efficacy of those responses. As is the case elsewhere in this book, the value of understanding acts of sexual violence as part of a continuum also features in the analyses presented here. The particular acts of sexual violence covered include: rape, domestic violence, murder, child abuse and Internet offending where it has a sexual dynamic. Thus what we have here is a review of the nature and extent of sexual violence that covers some traditional territory (rape) and some newer territory (sexual crime associated with the Internet). However, as we shall see, there are some common threads that bind our understanding of these acts together. What follows is a brief overview of each of the contributions and then some observations on the common threads between them.

Jan Jordan (in Chapter 12) provides a stimulating and illuminating insight into the persistence of rape as a social and policy problem. She situates her analysis within what might be considered to be a 'post-feminist' world in which 'we have done rape'. In the UK for example, the combined effects of the Sexual Offences Act 2003 and the commitment by the Coalition Government to put Rape Crisis funding on a secure basis as well as provide funding for the extension of their services might suggest that the feminist case in relation to rape has been not only made and proven but also accepted. Yet there is equally contradictory evidence of such, as Lovett and Kelly's (2009) comparative analysis of attrition rates for cases of rape across a number of jurisdictions demonstrates. (The ambivalent evidence on this issue is explored in more detail in the conclusion.) Moreover, as Brown *et al.* (2010) have suggested, while there has been some change in public attitudes towards rape, especially in it being seen as the woman's 'own fault', other more prejudicial views persist among a significant minority of the population. In the face of these contradictory forces, Jordan encourages us to think critically about both the extent to which the issues that surround rape have or have not changed and why. For her the key dynamic in understanding the contemporary situation lies within the politics and processes of silencing.

Jordan suggests to us that women themselves silence their experiences of rape, the police response adds to this, followed by the courts and the trial process, compounded by formal and informal supports, the media, researchers and academics. The cumulative effects of the dynamics of silencing, whether intentional or unintentional, result in women failing to acknowledge what has happened to them. In particular, the grey areas of rape (notably when the victim knows the offender) are minimised by the media and criminal justice professionals and not accommodated in law. Such 'silent collusion' with what counts as 'real rape' mutes women's experiences and their voices. This is added to by the research process and associated ethical requirements which place additional limits on what people are 'permitted' to talk about and how this is conveyed in academic writings. Jordan keenly reminds us to constantly look, not to the tip of the iceberg (the post-feminist world) but to what is supporting that world beneath the waterline. She leaves us with a clear question: whose interests does the post-feminist vision of the world serve? Certainly not the women on whose testimony the analysis in her chapter is derived from.

In a similar vein Nicole Westmarland (in Chapter 13) maps the nature and extent of domestic violence (primarily in the UK) and traces the changing policy context in responding to domestic violence. As with rape, the introduction of multi agency risk assessment conferences (MARACs) for cases of domestic violence, independent domestic violence advisers (IDVAs) and specialist domestic violence courts (all discussed by Westmarland) have been heralded as marking a sea change in understanding and responding to violence against women. Moreover, while these can be viewed as major steps forward in joining up policy responses in this arena, domestic violence remains a hard problem to solve. For example, the embrace of risk assessment for victims 'at risk' of domestic violence illustrates similar contradictions to those observed by Jordan for women who have been raped. In particular the focus on the 'at risk' victim, and the 'one size fits all' risk assessment tools adopted (see Robinson and Rowlands 2009), reflects a tendency to silence the victims' voice in that process, both male and female victims. Moreover, Westmarland also charts for us the development of programmes for perpetrators of domestic violence (these programmes are also taken up by Stephanie Kewley in Chapter 17) where she points to the shortage of places on such programmes as well as difficulties concerning what 'success' on such a programme might mean. As Mooney (2007: 159) has asked: 'How can violence be both a public anathema and [still be] a private common place?' (Our addition.) This is indeed a good question and one that is also implied by Anette Ballinger's discussion of sexual murder in Chapter 14.

As Ballinger acknowledges, the statistics on murder point to a huge disparity between the sexes. Coleman and Osborne (2010: 13) report that: 'In 2008/09, around three in four female victims (76%) knew the main or only suspect at the time of the offence, the same proportion as the previous year.

However, a greater proportion of these female victims (69%) were killed by their partner, ex-partner or lover in 2008/09 compared with 2007/08 (50%).' So, not only is there a sexual disparity in relation to murder, this disparity does not seem to be changing. Moreover it is a statistic that is repeated internationally (see inter alia, Wilson and Daly 1998). Connecting with Chapter 10 by Jo Phoenix, Ballinger explores this phenomenon through two particular case studies. Both involved the murder of sex workers whose vulnerability is also evidenced in Jo Phoenix's discussion of prostitution(s). The first case study is of Peter Sutcliffe from the early 1980s. The second is that of Steve Wright, whose crime took place in the new millennium. In both cases Ballinger explores their similarities and differences in how the activities of both of these men were constructed and responded to. One key difference is that the ordinariness of Peter Sutcliffe seemed to fool the police in the 1980s but the acknowledged ordinariness of serial killers was pronounced in the search for Steve Wright. However, on the other hand, the woman-blaming explanations that were drawn upon to understand the behaviour of both men remained depressingly the same. These men had problems because of a bad wife or mother! Of course, Ballinger argues that this kind of response to the murderous acts of both of these men only makes sense if they are situated within a deeply mysogynistic culture; a culture that can take different forms but is, for example, being perpetuated by the 'freedom' of the Internet. (See also David Shannon's Chapter 16). Ballinger's chapter begins to offer part of an answer to the question posed by Mooney (2007) insofar as she puts squarely on the table the problem of masculinity that gives voice to some men while silencing others and certainly silences women, sometimes fatally.

The politics around whose voices are heard and listened to is given an added dimension by Stephanie Petrie in Chapter 15. She considers the complex interplay between violence, sex and the child. She takes as her starting point a critical understanding of what we understand by the concept of the child and childhood. Suggesting that the use of both terms has implied both a uniform and a unifying understanding of childhood that denies children their agency and competency, Petrie argues that, as a result, the adult concern about children and sex silences the sexuality of children and produces policies that fail to recognise their competencies. The ebbs and flows of policies between prevention and protection of child sexual abuse produced as a result of those cases that 'slip through the net' fail to recognise the child, the normalisation of violence in their lives (from war to their experience of state institutions as well as within their family circle) and unify understandings of the offender. Little of which takes into account children and young people's own voices. David Shannon, on the other hand, offers us a unique empirical insight from a study of young people's experiences of online sexual solicitation in which the voices of these young people can certainly be heard.

Shannon addresses the question of what kinds of sexually abusive behaviours children are exposed to on the Internet and what choices do children themselves make when exposed to contact that they feel uncomfortable with. From the empirical data that he produces, it is evident that the process of being exposed to online sexual solicitation is neither a simple nor a straightforward one with a key moment in the contact process being the shift from the chat room to MSN email contact. It is at this juncture that the content of the contact changes, changing once again when contact moves from online to offline. He introduces the notion of a 'pyramid of sexually abusive online contact'; the shape of which comprises a number of variables including the vulnerability/complicity of the child and the amount of manipulation required by the adult to gain access to the child. Most children most of the time 'block' online contacts when the content of that contact changes. This, it must be remembered, is in a context in which most children/ young people, most of the time, are still more at risk from sexually abusive behaviour from people who are close to them. By implication Shannon not only draws our attention to the extent of knowledge that children and young people have about managing their online lives, but also makes a strong case for appreciating the extent to which the concept of a continuum is equally useful in understanding the processes involved within a particular kind of sexual activity for all the participants. More implicit than explicit in Shannon's work is the predominance of males using the Internet for the purpose of making contact with young people. So, resonating with other chapters in this section, the question of men and their relationship with masculinity raises its head as a cause for concern. This issue is at the heart of Stephanie Kewley's practitioner's commentary on what might be done in the face of the types of sexual violence presented in this part of the book.

Kewley, writing from the perspective of a probation officer, following Jordan, makes a sound case for the centring of victims' experiences as being the focal point for practice interventions. In the light of understanding these experiences she argues that there should be a deeper analysis of treatment needs, that the distancing behaviour of men from their use of violence needs to be challenged, and that there is a clear case for inclusive bridging programmes that refocus men's relationship with their gender identity before they are accepted onto treatment programmes. Doing this might better ensure that they are encouraged to accept their behaviour, take responsibility for it, and to learn that there are other acceptable ways of responding to situations they find challenging. Without this kind of response the implication might be that policy responses and practitioners alike remain silent on men's relationship with the use of violence.

Taken together these chapters encourage us to think about a number of issues: whose voices get listened to and why in the research process (Jordan, Petrie and Shannon), the efficacy of policy responses (Jordan, Westmarland and Petrie) and the challenges of masculinity (Ballinger, Shannon and Kewley). Readers may well find other thematics in the material presented here. However, one that is dominant and worthy of further comment is the politics of silencing.

## The politics of silencing

In 2004 the English edition of Thomas Mathieson's *Silently Silenced: Essays on the Creation of Acquiescence in Modern Society* was published. While this book does not address questions of sexual violence (that was not its purpose), what it eloquently draws attention to is the myriad ways in which silencing works. Silencing mechanisms clearly operate by force. For Mathieson this means the force at the state's disposal. For many women this is the physical and psychological force deployed by men, usually those men close to them, to make them acquiesce in their treatment of them. In the contributions in this section of the Handbook we can see the evidence of this in the work of Jordan and Ballinger. However, as Mathieson demonstrates, that silencing also works effectively in very silent ways, hence silently silenced; through individualisation, normalisation, co-option, superficial endorsement, and displacement of responsibility. We can see each of these strategies evident in the chapters presented here.

The continued prevalence of beliefs about why rape and sexual murder happen (blame the victim) and to whom (the deserving victim) preserves mechanisms of *individualisation* found in ideological processes that frame experiences and our understandings of them. The chapters by Jordan and Ballinger tell us a story that has changed little at a fundamental level despite the *superficial endorsement* of policies, policy-makers and practitioners for alternative ways of thinking about these events. Of course, such processes of individualisation encourage the self-silencing that Jordan discusses as well as the distancing strategies employed by men to deny their violence to women highlighted by Kewley. The latter also hints at *displacement of responsibility*; especially as an individual strategy, though displacement of responsibility can also be identified as a collective or institutional process, as Petrie alludes to, in how the problem of 'child abuse' and children's exposure to violence is frequently discussed as though this occurred in a vacuum isolated from wider societal endorsement of violence (in war, etc.).

Feminists have long been sensitive to the dangers of *co-option* (of their concerns being used for other political purposes) in relation to policies and responses to sexual violence (see for example Matthews 1994; Walklate 2008). However, the rise of political and policy responses to sexual violence does not mean that this danger has diminished. Co-option can take a number of guises. For example, from Westmarland's Chapter 13 we might observe the targeting of women 'at risk' in settings of domestic violence by mechanisms that assess their 'risk factors' as one potential area for such co-option. Such a strategy, that suggests a linear and uniform understanding of domestic violence, not only silences problematic men, but *normalises* the experience of domestic violence for all those who might be subject to it. The failure of practitioner responses to develop programmes that are inclusive of all men known to be violent towards women (as observed by Kewley) fails to challenge the implied pathological nature of such violence, thereby adding to the silencing process that normalises it. Taken together, the silencing of voices (whether women's, children's or those of men who experience violence at the hands of women) effectively, and unintentionally, supports policies that on the one hand may seem to be addressing the problem of sexual violence while simultaneously doing little to change it. Hence a politics of silencing, in which some voices are rendered more silent than others, policies offer a superficial endorsement to change, but the gendered nature of the processes under scrutiny remains the same.

## Conclusion

The chapters presented here serve to remind us that the gendered nature of sexual violence persists despite the claims made that we are now in a post-feminist world. So, as Mooney (2007) observed, contemporarily there might be 'public anathema' with regard to sexual violence but it is still a 'private common place'. The reasons for this are complex but are clearly as stitched into cultural norms and values as they are embedded within institutional and policy understandings of the nature and extent of the problem. However, as Mooney herself suggests, the values whereby men's violence to women is sustained in the face of public imperatives otherwise 'exist throughout the width and breadth of popular culture' (Mooney 2007: 169). Consider, for example, the vicarious pleasure gained by some young males in witnessing violence on a 'good night out' (Winlow and Hall 2006). The cultural value attached to violence, especially for men, is profound. But so are the economic imperatives that afford the opportunity and the sustenance for the development and engagement with policies. As many countries enter an era of austerity, it will be interesting to see whether or not the alignment that has been made between feminist concerns about sexual violence and political decisions that have fuelled some of the policy responses discussed in these chapters will remain. In any event, voices still need to be heard to ensure that the nature and extent of sexual violence documented here in a range of guises continues to be rendered problematic.

## References

Brown, J., Horvath, M., Kelly, L. and Westmarland, N. (2010) *Has Anything Changed?* London: Government Equalities Office.

Coleman, K. and Osborne, S. (2010) 'Homicide', in K. Smith and J. Flatley (eds) *Homicides, Firearm Offences and Intimate Violence 2008/09 – Supplementary Volume 2 to Crime in England and Wales 2008/09*. London: Home Office.

Lovett, J. and Kelly, L. (2009) *Different Systems: Similar Outcomes*. London Metropolitan University: CWASU.

Mathieson, T. (2004) *Silently Silenced*. London: Waterside Press.

Matthews, N. (1994) *Confronting Rape*. London: Routledge.

Mooney, J. (2007) 'Shadow values, shadow figures: real violence', *Critical Criminology*, 15: 159–70.

Robinson, A. and Rowlands, J. (2009) 'Assessing and managing risk among different victims of domestic abuse: limits of a generic model of risk assessment', *Security Journal*, 22(3): 190–204,

Walklate, S. (2008) 'What is to be done about violence against women?', *British Journal of Criminology*, 48(1): 39–54.

Winlow, S. and Hall, S. (2006) *Violent Night*. London: Berg.

Wilson, M. and Daly, M. (1998) 'Sexual rivalry and sexual conflict: recurring themes in fatal conflicts', *Theoretical Criminology*, 2: 291–310.

# Chapter 12

# Silencing rape, silencing women

*Jan Jordan*

**Meet Jan Jordan**

Jan Jordan is an Associate Professor in Criminology at Victoria University of Wellington, New Zealand; a feminist; and a passionate advocate for victims of rape and sexual assault. One of her research aims has been to assist women in telling their own stories, with her first book being a series of narratives from women working in the sex industry. She has been actively involved in researching sexual violence for nearly 20 years, with much of her focus being on women's experiences of reporting rape to the police. More recently she has been exploring issues of victimisation and survival, particularly in the context of making sense of the experiences of an amazing group of women who were all attacked by the same serial rapist. As well as teaching criminology classes Jan is a regular contributor to police training courses on sexual assault investigations, and in both contexts aims to challenge conventional thinking and promote greater understanding of the complex dynamics involved in violence against women, and the reasons why we need to do all we can to prevent its occurrence.

**Introduction**

> Rape has long been considered a crime so unspeakable, so shameful to its victims, that they are rendered mute and cloaked in protective anonymity... The victims of rape must carry their memories with them for the rest of their lives. They must not also carry the burden of silence and shame.
>
> (Raine 1998: 6)

Understanding the crime of rape is both defiantly simple and surprisingly complex. One person, predominantly male, asserts their will over another person, typically female, to sexually violate their body. The simplicity of the physical act obscures recognition of the myriad ways it impacts on those victimised, while also ignoring the complex dynamics giving rise to its occurrence. In the crime of rape a woman's body is invaded and possessed – she is for that moment enslaved to the will of a man. His act of rape smudges her temporarily out of existence. He mutes her voice then afterwards insists on her silence. He may not need to verbalise this decree since his actions are buttressed by solid traditions supporting the privileging of men's lives and voices. In colluding with the rapist, society silences the victim.

Today, a decade into the twenty-first century, we know more about the prevalence of rape and the complex dynamics giving rise to its occurrence than any previous generation. The reforms of the past 40 years have facilitated an environment within which sexual victimisation research is funded and conducted, inquiries and commissions undertaken, and survivors' narratives published. It is easy to be lulled into a post-feminist haze of complacency that we have 'done' rape and the way is clear for victims to speak and be heard. This chapter seeks to interrogate the silence that, despite such reforms, still surrounds rape.

It begins with the historical silencing of women's voices before outlining feminist challenges to patriarchal control. Reforms and changes made in recent years are reviewed before asking why these have not had greater impact, and why such a loud and resounding silence continues to surround the crime of rape. Six key silencing agents are identified:

(i) the self;
(ii) police responses;
(iii) court and trial processes;
(iv) formal and informal supports;
(v) researchers and academics;
(vi) the media.

Each is examined in order to illustrate the processes that ultimately collude to undermine and mute the voices of victims of rape.

## Silencing in history

Silencing is a hallmark of oppression, and there is 'an association between the degree to which a society silences its women and the prevalence of rape' (Taslitz 1999: 19). Within the context of patriarchy a long history exists of the silencing of women's voices. Violence against women was an invisible backdrop, accepted and endured as a consequence of what it meant to be born female. In earlier periods of European history, women who were perceived as a threat to male control risked being labelled as spell-cackling witches and were sadistically tortured and/or burned to death (Daly 1979; Garland 2003; Hester 1992). Alternatively, their ability to speak, as well as that of any woman perceived as a gossip or nuisance, could be painfully restricted through application of the torture device known as the scold's bridle, an effective means of silencing not only them but all those who witnessed or heard about this event and feared for their own safety (Boose 1991; Faith 1993). Even folk tales and fairy stories underscore the importance of a woman being silent while warning of the perils of speech, with such inferences evident even in modern adaptations. In the Disney movie version of *The Little Mermaid*, for example, the good woman has to give up the power of speech to win her man while the woman with a voice is a witch and a liar. 'Ariel, the muted beauty, is thus the Good Woman. The Sea Witch, the woman with voice, is the Lying Woman, cold and deadly.' (Taslitz 1999: 21)

Historically and cross-culturally the overt use of physical and sexual violence has functioned as a key mechanism for perpetuating patriarchal control (Brownmiller 1975; Easteal 1998; Faith 1993; Griffin 1971; Jordan 2004; Kelly 1988; Stanko 1985; Tong 1984; Walklate 1995). Women experiencing violence often had few legal channels available to them, particularly when victimised by their husbands. As long as the latter used sticks or rods no thicker than their thumbs, their abuse of their wives could be justified as chastisement (Lentz 1999). Thus the physical beating of wives was at times not only condoned but legitimated as a necessary form of admonishment for keeping the lesser sex under control (Dobash and Dobash 1992; Faith 1993; Pollock 1995; Sutch 1973). While the most extreme and horrific forms of wife-beating might result in offenders appearing in court, the latter were portrayed as so barbarous and brutish that the behaviour was driven underground, becoming silenced and unspeakable (Hunt 1992).

The act of rape has been a real and often effective means of asserting control over women, particularly in the context of the power relations within intimate partnerships. As Brownmiller (1975) pointed out, the earliest forms of male/female bonding occurred in the context of one man staking his claim to another through sexually acquiring her body – in the act of raping her, she became his. Over time this practice became sanitised through women's bodies being exchanged on payment of either a bride price or dowry. What the woman said or wished was of no consequence; since she was a piece of property owned by a man, if she was raped it was her father or her husband who were recognised in law as the rightful victim (Brownmiller 1975). The woman's voice was nowhere to be heard. Since men were the only legitimate viewers and observers, and the male gaze predominated, the male's words predominated also.

Denying the truth of women's words served as a muting device. Most women could not speak of their pain and nor could they name and shame the cause of their suffering. The rape of virgins, however, carried different expectations. In this context the victim was expected to be so upset that she would immediately report it (Burgess 1999), a stipulation dating from the thirteenth century when the authority for Anglo-Saxon times, Henry of Bracton, decreed that the procedure following the rape of a virgin should be as follows:

> She must go at once and while the deed is newly done, with the hue and cry, to the neighbouring townships and show the injury done to her to men of good repute, the blood and her clothing stained with blood and her torn garments.
>
> (quoted in Burgess 1999: 9)

The expectation that genuine (and innocent) victims would immediately report the rape extends to the present day with evidence suggesting police officers often interpret delayed reporting as a possible indicator of a false complaint (Brown *et al.* 2007; Jordan 2004; Stewart *et al.* 1996). Such an interpretation ignores the ways women have been taught to mute their voice and remain silent, and also fails to understand the impact of centuries of suspicion surrounding the words of a woman. The impossible bind this places a raped woman in becomes obvious:

> She is ordinarily expected to be mute, yet she is expected to and must speak promptly and loudly, and in anguish, if there is a 'real' rape ... She will be judged by the cultural themes of silence and voice, not by the natural psychological reactions to rape or an informed understanding of its causes and circumstances.
>
> (Taslitz 1999: 4)

Men's voices and actions generally prevailed until progressively challenged during the first and second waves of feminism. Once the ugly underbelly of patriarchy was exposed it was hoped its injustices would be challenged in favour of a human-rights-based approach to social equality. Understandably, anger over the crime of rape was particularly pronounced in early feminist circles.

## The feminist challenge

The 1970s was characterised by social and political movements on multiple fronts challenging the status quo and, within the context of the women's movement in particular, was accompanied by consciousness-raising and increased truth-speaking regarding violence against women and children (Dann 1985; Gavey 2005; Jones 2004; Jordan 2004; Pollock 1995). Many women were galvanised into campaigns resisting men's violence and promoting self-defence (Bart and O'Brien 1985; Medea and Thompson 1974; Searles and Berger 1987). When police and crime prevention advice suggested females stay off the streets to reduce their risk of being raped, women pointed out the risks within the home, while some, such as Golda Meir, argued instead for curfews on men to keep the streets safe for women (Meyer 1974). Optimism ran high that patriarchy would soon be dead and all gender-based inequalities eradicated. There have been many victories, such that the world now is often viewed as a very different place from those raw and raucous early days of feminist protest and outrage. The social, economic and political position of many women has improved, often masking the marginalisation and exploitation characterising other women's lives. Increased recognition of human rights has led to greater international condemnation of violence against women, with most nations declaring themselves as signatories to such charters as the United Nations Convention on the Elimination of All Forms of Discrimination Against Women.

Reflecting such advances, the authors of a book published in 1999 opened it with the following observation:

During the 1980s and 1990s there has been a sea change in the recognition of male violence against women and children, not only in Britain, but in many other parts of the world.

(Gregory and Lees 1999: 1)

This comment reflects the hard work by feminist activists whose efforts to reform the justice system resulted in significant changes being made enabling greater recognition of, and improved responses to, allegations of sexual violence (Donat and D'Emilio 1992; Jones 2004; Kitzinger 2009; Pollock 1995). This is evident legally, for example, in the ways many countries have extended their definitions of rape to recognise the varied forms this can take, no longer limiting this to forced penile–vaginal intercourse. This has been achieved in different ways internationally. In England and Wales, for example, the Sexual Offences Act 2003 broadened the definition of rape to include oral penetration (Temkin and Krahé 2008; Walklate 2008), while New Zealand legislation earlier sought to resolve the inclusion dilemma by creating an umbrella category of 'sexual violation' that included both rape and 'unlawful sexual connection', the latter including all orifices and means of penetration (Sullivan 1986).

Also significant in terms of legal reform has been the criminalisation of rape occurring in the context of marriage. This occurred in American states from the late 1970s onwards (although marital rape was not recognised as a crime in all states until 1993 (Ferro *et al.* 2008)), in New Zealand in 1986 (Jordan 2004; Sullivan 1986); and in 1991 in Australia (Heath 1998), as well as England and Wales (Kennedy 1992; Kitzinger 2009). The fact that it is only in the past 20 years or so that spousal immunity to charges of rape was abolished provides a stark reminder of how robust the tentacles of patriarchy are, as well as how much we still need to wrestle with. Today this is still apparent in the relatively few incidents of rape in marriage reported compared with what we now know regarding its prevalence (Bennice and Resick 2003; Ferro *et al.* 2008). For example, 7.7 per cent of a large, randomised national sample of women in the United States had experienced forced vaginal, oral or anal sex perpetrated by a spouse or partner during their lifetime (Tjaden and Thoennes 2000), yet it is widely accepted that the barriers for wives reporting rape are even greater than for women victimised in other contexts, resulting in few such cases ever coming to police attention (Bennice and Resick 2003; Bergen 2006).

Progress has also been made in improving the environments within which victim/survivors of rape are forensically examined. For instance, in the 1980s in New Zealand, it was not unusual for women who had been raped to be medically examined by male doctors in police cells (Young 1983). Today the majority of those who have been raped are examined by specially trained women doctors in a medical setting, with most also able to have a support person present if desired (Jordan 2001). Internationally a range of models have developed aiming to treat victims with respect for their individual rights and dignity, including sexual assault referral centres (SARCs) in the United Kingdom and many European countries and the use of sexual assault nurse examiners (SANEs) in the US (Lovett *et al.* 2004; Kelly 2005). At the NGO level, feminist groups have pressured for state funding of counselling and support agencies for victims/survivors, and worked hard to provide continuity of services in the face of often meagre or erratic resourcing (Jones 2004).

Overall there have been many significant gains in law, policing, medicine and research. From this perspective we can celebrate progress in challenging the extent of patriarchal control and exposing the realities of violence against women. We know so much more now about rape, and have identified 'best' and 'promising' practices in relation to how to respond to its occurrence. As well as increased recognition of their needs within the criminal justice and social service sectors, there are also growing numbers of books containing narratives from rape victims/survivors (for example, Brison 2002; Easteal 1994; Jordan 2008; Raine 1998; Sebold 1999). Yet while the successes deserve to be applauded, by no means are they sufficient to suppress the need for ongoing campaigning and consciousness-raising. Four decades of feminism may have improved the services available for many victims/survivors but have made little dent in rape's occurrence or the attitudes surrounding it. Despite the insights gained and advances made, there are many ways in which rape is still shrouded in silence.

Indicators include a continuing reluctance on the part of victims/survivors to disclose generally or report sexual violence to the police, linked to the pervasiveness of rape myths within society that continue to blame and shame the victims of rape (Bohner *et al.* 2009; Du Mont *et al.* 2003; Myhill and Allen 2002; Temkin and Krahé 2008). Recent studies of public attitudes reveal a strongly judgemental stance towards victims if they were wearing sexy clothing or were drunk at the time of the rape (Amnesty International 2005). Similarly, mock juror trials also show many still display a willingness to forgive the rapist while blaming the victim (Finch and Munro 2006; Munro and Kelly 2009). Victims who do report still risk being disbelieved by the police, and continuing high attrition rates result in a minority of complainants receiving validation from the criminal justice system (Kelly *et al.* 2005; Temkin and Krahé 2008; Triggs *et al.* 2009; Walklate 2008). It is little wonder that many women refrain from speaking or feel silenced when they do.

To speak of silence denotes a passive state of being, a perception that obscures the acts of silencing that produce this state. One of the first arenas in which this occurs is in the contexts of rapists' efforts to control victims. One way they maintain their position of privilege is by undermining the voice, the very perceptions, of those whom they wish to keep powerless: 'No, you weren't raped!', 'I could tell you wanted it', 'You said no but meant yes.' When I undertook research with women who had all survived being attacked by the same serial rapist (Jordan 2008), many recounted the impact of the first words he said to them – 'Shut up!' Any attempts by them to speak triggered the same response – 'Shut up!' The removal of their voice was reinforced by his tying gags over the women's mouths – he wanted them silent, his ability to do what he came there to do depended on their silence. To him, they were objects with no voice, no humanity.

The rapist is not the only one who stifles victims/survivors' voices. Our society incorporates a wide range of individuals and institutions that either intentionally or unconsciously may operate in ways that inhibit the abilities of victims/survivors to speak and/or be heard. The next section of this chapter examines the dynamics associated with the six key silencing agents identified earlier.

## (i) The self

Rape is a fundamental attack on the self, and an attempt to silence the self. Susan Brison, who survived a near-fatal rape and attempted murder in the south of France, later described:

> the difficulty of regaining one's voice, one's subjectivity, after one has been reduced to silence, to the status of an object, or, worse, made into someone else's speech, an instrument of another's agency.
>
> (Brison 2002: 55)

Awareness has grown in recent years regarding the difficulties rape victims/ survivors experience naming and defining what has happened to them as rape, with one of the first to explore this phenomenon being Mary Koss. In a conference paper presented in 1980, she and Cheryl Oros made the distinction between 'acknowledged' and 'unacknowledged' rape victims to draw attention to how many women were unable to acknowledge that they had been raped (Koss and Oros 1980). Two key factors associated with women being unacknowledged rape victims involved issues regarding the victim–perpetrator relationship and the offender's use of violence. Specifically, women were more likely not to acknowledge themselves as victims of rape when they knew the offender, had been romantically involved with him, and had a prior sexual relationship with him. Unacknowledged rape victims were also more likely than acknowledged rape victims to receive fewer threats of bodily harm and experience less offender violence. The authors concluded that the differences between these two groups arose more from these situational factors than from attitudinal factors associated with the internal belief systems of the women, given that there was virtually no difference in adherence to rape-supportive beliefs between acknowledged and unacknowledged rape victims (Koss and Oros 1980).

Greater understanding of women's struggles to define themselves as rape victims later emerged from Liz Kelly's research showing how few women are able or willing to label their experiences of forced sex as rape (Kelly 1988). Their reluctance reflects in part a confusion regarding the nature of rape, and the predominance of 'real rape' stereotypes (Brown and Horvath 2009; Estrich 1987; Fisher *et al.* 2003; Jordan 2004; Kelly 2002; Lea *et al.* 2003; O'Keeffe *et al.* 2009; Temkin and Krahé 2008). The continuum of sexual violence Kelly posited demonstrated clearly how the legal polarities of rape and consensual sex fail to reflect the grey and complex dynamics surrounding many women's experiences of intercourse, and the extent to which elements of pressure and coercion feature prominently in their relationships and sexual encounters. This has been more recently explored and further validated in Nicola Gavey's work questioning the extent to which experiences closer to, or equating with, rape are frequently accepted by women as 'just sex' (Gavey 2005). Both her and Liz Kelly's research demonstrate that, in contrast to prevailing myths suggesting that women are constantly crying rape, they more typically minimise their experiences of coercive sex and refrain from labelling the men in their lives as abusers and rapists (Gavey 2005; Kelly 1988).

The complexities of the continuum of women's experiences are not easily accommodated within the rigid distinctions of the law. Police officers evaluating allegations of rape typically display limited awareness of the structural and contextual variables surrounding its occurrence, operating instead with high and often unrealistic expectations of women's abilities to say 'no' and men's willingness to hear and respect their wishes. What I have heard many police officers articulate is their belief that complaints of rape frequently follow episodes of what they term 'regretful sex', implying women are willing participants until they wake or sober up next morning and recall the reasons why they should have said no. The apparent police commitment to this concept minimises, even ignores, the various ways men might coerce women or use alcohol and drugs to secure their compliance. It is little surprise that high numbers of victims refrain from labelling their experiences as rape and mute themselves in its aftermath.

Sceptics might ask: how do we know that so many women silence themselves? The short answer is that we may not be able to say how many, since we are trying to measure something resisting knowledge of its own existence, but we know many do. We are given clues on several fronts. One is in the way that so many victims decide to speak out many years after having been raped or abused. In Koss's later Sexual Experiences Study, for example, 42 per cent of those participating had told no one about what had happened until the safety of an anonymous questionnaire enabled them to do so (Koss *et al* 1987). Many of the women could not, or would not, label what had happened to them as rape, yet when researchers analysed their descriptions of what happened during the incident, it was clear that many had in fact been subjected to behaviours conforming with legal definitions of rape.

A second indicator is that research evidence consistently shows that a minority of women who have been raped report such occurrences to the police. This is evident in the discrepancy between the findings of victimisation studies compared with police statistics on reported rapes. Research conducted in the United Kingdom (Painter 1991) indicated that one in four women would experience rape or attempted rape during their lifetime, with over 90 per cent telling no one at the time. Other research has estimated a lifetime probability of 50 per cent for rape victimisation, suggesting that as many as one in every two females will experience at least one incident of rape in her lifetime (Sheffield 1994, cited in Ferro *et al*. 2008). While more recent studies suggest an increased willingness to tell someone what has happened (for example Myhill and Allen 2002; Walby and Allen 2004), that person is more likely to be a friend or family member than a police officer. Furthermore, despite alleged improvements within policing and a spate of legislative reforms, recent British Crime Survey results indicate that less than half of those who are raped break the silence and tell anyone at all (Kelly *et al* 2005;

Myhill and Allen 2002; Walby and Allen 2004).

A further factor indicating self-silencing behaviour comes from counsellors and agency workers who report that significant numbers of those approaching them in need of support are victims of historical rapes, incidents that their clients describe as events they wished to bury and deny but which keep interfering with their lives (Burgess and Hazelwood 1999; Gordon and Riger 1991; Ventegodt *et al.* 2005). These individuals may self-silence for many years, with shame being one key factor often associated with victims/survivors feeling unworthy of recognition. As Judith Herman has so aptly described, in the crime of rape:

> [t]he perpetrator seeks to establish his dominance not only by terrorizing the victim but also, often most effectively, by shaming her. Crimes of dominance have a ritualized element designed to isolate the victim and to degrade her in the eyes of others.
>
> (Herman 2005: 572–573)

However, just as the self can silence recognition of the experience of rape, even for many years, so also can the self speak of rape, with some survivors consciously acknowledging in their accounts the difficult decision they had to make to break their silence. Relevant here also are the cultural expectations that may influence victims initially to seek to smooth over ruptures and restore social relationships, minimising their pain and the harm suffered in the process. While a woman may decide it is necessary to mute her voice in the immediate aftermath of rape, as she heals she may regain her voice and speak out – only to find her speech regarded with suspicion and any inconsistencies highlighted as 'evidence' of her falsehood. In the unlikely event of the case reaching court,

> Defence counsel draws on themes of breached silence to craft a courtroom story of the lying woman, thus by definition revising the rape narrative to one of consensual sex.
>
> (Taslitz 1999: 25)

Similar inferences have been made in response to adults disclosing their experiences of childhood sexual abuse, with one of the most extreme forms of self-silencing – repression – attracting high levels of sceptical and even vitriolic criticism. Not only has this resulted in the discrediting of victims/survivors, it has also been accompanied by an undermining of the credibility of the therapists treating them, some of whom have been accused of creating and implanting 'false memories' (Herman and Harvey 1993; Porter *et al.* 1999). Disempowering and devaluing the therapists emerges as a means of muting them as well as their clients.

So far this discussion has considered the role of the self as the silencing agent, rather than considering to what extent the self is being silenced by others. While external silencing agents will shortly be examined, discussion concerning the role of the self would be incomplete if it failed to mention that the decision to speak out can be a recurring dilemma for victims/survivors of rape rather than a one-off choice. The reactions of those around them to their disclosures can have significant impacts on whether or not they continue to speak, and in which contexts. This issue was explored in a qualitative study where eight women were taken as a subsample from a larger study and interviewed to ascertain why they had initially disclosed rape then silenced themselves (Ahrens 2006). Key factors associated with the decision to become silent again involved negative reactions from professionals or from family friends, leading to the women sometimes feeling uncertain whether what they had experienced was rape, as well as feeling either that disclosure was ineffective or that other people's responses caused them to blame themselves for the rape. Even with such a small sample, the length of time the women chose to remain silent following a negative response to their initial disclosure of rape ranged from nine months to 19 years (Ahrens 2006).

It is easy to assume that speaking out about rape is a healthier and automatically more positive option than staying silent. Predictions based on immunology research, for instance, suggest that long periods of inhibiting emotional expression can be injurious to both psychological and physical health (Pennebaker 1988, 1989, cited in Ahrens 2006). For some victims/ survivors of rape, however, the choice to remain silent is based on their attempts to avoid the negative reactions they fear will follow disclosure (Ahrens 2006). Given the adverse impacts negative reactions can have on victim/survivor well-being (Campbell et al. 1999; Campbell et al. 2001; Golding et al. 1989; Filipas and Ullman 2001; Littleton et al. 2006; Ullman and Filipas 2001; Ullman et al. 2006), in this sense the decision to remain silent may at times constitute a measure of self-preservation.

From this perspective it is possible to view the unacknowledged rape victim as more unacknowledging than unacknowledged. While the latter has connotations of victims being locked in a fixed state, shifting the language to the active voice enables recognition of victim agency. Decisions around disclosure, even disclosing to oneself, may shift with time in response to changes in internal and external factors. Just as the self can silence, so can it dare to speak. It is also possible that the ability to survive rape may be enhanced by disclosure, should those being disclosed to respond with empathy and sensitivity (Littleton et al. 2006). The next sections of this chapter summarise how the responses of others can also contribute to the silencing of victims' voices.

## (ii) The police

The ways in which formal agencies respond to disclosures of rape hold both the potential for validation and the risk of disempowerment. This has been well researched with respect to police responses to women's allegations of rape victimisation. Many studies have demonstrated the benefits derived from a positive police response, particularly for victim/survivor well-being as well as for community safety when such allegations result in an offender being held accountable (Gregory and Lees 1999; Jordan 2001; Kingi and Jordan 2009; McMillan and Thomas 2009). The opposite impacts, however, have also been demonstrated; namely that when disclosures are met with negative unaffirming responses, these may enhance the initial harm experienced by the victim/survivor while leaving offender behaviour unchecked (Campbell *et al.* 2001b; Gregory and Lees 1999; Jordan 2004; Madigan and Gamble 1991; McMillan and Thomas 2009). Not being able to hear or validate a disclosure of rape can result from conscious and intentional responses, such as by blaming victims for 'getting themselves raped'. It can also occur unintentionally through responses arising from ignorance, where the persons receiving the information lack understanding of how to respond appropriately and supportively.

The first way in which the police may be associated with the silencing of rape victims' voices is indirectly, when fears about how they will respond can be a key factor inhibiting victims from reporting rape (Du Mont *et al.* 2003; Bachman 1993; Burt and Katz 1985; Epstein and Langenbahn 1994; Freckelton 1998; Gartner and Macmillan 1995; Koss *et al.* 1987; LeDoux and Hazelwood 1999; Myhill and Allen 2002; Spohn and Horney 1992; Temkin and Krahé 2008). While in recent years many police organisations have sought to improve their responses, we should not assume that the barriers to disclosure have been removed. The reasons for victims/survivors deciding not to report remain complex, with rape myths still pervasive in their ability to affect how victims, perpetrators, criminal justice system workers and the public view and respond to rape (Bohner *et al.* 2009; Lovett and Horvath 2009; Munro and Kelly 2009; Stanko and Williams 2009; Temkin and Krahé 2008). A frequently accepted estimate suggests that only one in ten rapes are reported to the police, with some studies finding a reporting rate of only 5 per cent (Koss *et al.* 1987). Rape has been identified as the most under-reported crime, with the factors affecting reporting including the victim–offender relationship, extent of visible injuries, and fear of how others, including police, might react (Gilmore and Pittman 1993; Kelly 2002; Myhill and Allen 2002; Sable *et al.* 2006).

When asked to identify factors affecting their willingness to report, commonly mentioned by victims/survivors is their fear that the police will not believe them (Fisher *et al.* 2003; Jordan 2001, 2004; Kelly *et al.* 2005; Stern 2010). This fear is not ungrounded, given the high levels of police scepticism identified in the 1970s and 1980s (Gregory and Lees 1999; Jordan 2004; Young 1983). Such attitudes were visibly apparent in the shocking documentary screened in England in 1983 showing a detective interrogating a woman as she made a complaint of rape (Adler 1987; Gregory and Lees 1999; Smith 1989). While screened with the intention of highlighting skilled police interviewing techniques, the brutal interrogation caused such a public outcry that the police department involved subsequently spent many years trying to 'live this incident down' (Gregory and Lees 1999: 4). Since then a range of measures have been introduced aimed at improving police responses. These have included specialist training for detectives undertaking adult sexual assault investigations as well as improvements to the physical environments in which victims are interviewed and examined.

It is frequently assumed that changes in legislation and policy will automatically result in changes in practice and improved experiences for victims. More recent research with rape complainants offers some reassurance that the worst excesses are less likely to occur. For instance, a recent New Zealand study based on interviews with 36 victims/survivors who had reported an incident of sexual violence to the police found that more than two-thirds (68 per cent) retrospectively said they were 'satisfied' or 'very satisfied' with the way the police had dealt with them (Kingi and Jordan 2009). A minority of respondents in this study referred to experiencing the police as cold and insensitive or disbelieving. However, other evidence suggests continuing high levels of scepticism with police having the capacity to silence victims by disbelieving their accounts of rape. In an environmental scan of agencies and key informants that respond to victims/survivors of sexual violence, nearly one third of respondents (29 per cent) identified the fear of not being believed as a significant factor discouraging victims/survivors from reporting to the police (Mossman *et al.* 2009). Concerns regarding not being believed or taken seriously were expressed particularly in relation to the following groups: sex workers; people with mental health issues; people who had made a previous sexual violation complaint; male victims/survivors; and women raped by their partners (Mossman *et al.* 2009). While community service providers were concerned that genuine cases risked being wrongly labelled as 'false' complaints, some police respondents alluded to false complaints being extremely common, with one stating: 'I would guess from 16 months on crime squad that about 60–70 percent of reported sex violation cases are false complaints' (quoted in Mossman *et al.* 2009: 95). Other research also confirms continuing police adherence to beliefs in excessively high numbers of false complaints (Gregory and Lees 1999; Kelly *et al.* 2005), and, as O'Keeffe *et al.* have recently asserted: '[I]t still seems to be the case that disbelief is the default position' (O'Keeffe *et al.* 2009: 252). These studies indicate the difficulties and challenges posed in relation to achieving significant attitude change within police organisations, in ways parallel to what Krahé and Temkin have asserted regarding the limited success likely to derive from law reform measures when the attitudes of those within the system remain largely unchanged (Krahé and Temkin 2009).

The police may also silence victims unintentionally through responding in ways experienced as invalidating by complainants. This can occur, for example, in contexts where police may decide to cease investigation of a case because they consider there is insufficient evidence to proceed. Commentators have observed that the way the adversarial justice system operates effectively places a responsibility on the police to anticipate likely case outcomes should the complaint proceed to trial, with views about convincing cases based on stereotypes (Brown *et al.* 2007; Munro and Kelly 2009). Unless such decisions are communicated in a supportive and validating way, complainants in cases where police determine there is insufficient evidence to proceed can experience such decision-making as a form of silencing.

The ways in which complainants are interviewed can also function to silence, even partially. Some commentators have argued that assigning male police to interview women rape complainants immediately places barriers interrupting full and frank disclosure (Goodstein and Lutze 1992; Pike 1992). The assumption that victims of sexual violence would be more appropriately dealt with by female officers has seen some police departments specifically deploying women in such roles (Brown *et al.* 1993; Goodstein and Lutze 1992; Martin 1997; Pike 1992). Research on the significance of gender suggests the issue is not straightforward – while some victims may express a preference for being interviewed by policewomen, many maintain that the most important attributes in an interviewer are such qualities as a caring professionalism; qualities neither the male nor female gender have a monopoly over (Brown and Heidensohn 2000; Heidensohn 1992; Jordan 2002). In fact, to survive within a highly masculinist culture, some policewomen can display a distinct lack of empathy towards victims whom they judge as 'getting themselves raped' and be harsher in attitude than some of their male colleagues (Jordan 2002, 2004; Martin 1997; Toner 1982). Furthermore, female detectives in a study I conducted described how even when complainants found male detectives supportive and professional, some were not able to disclose the most personal and potentially shaming aspects of the rape to them, reserving these for when experienced women officers subsequently reinterviewed them (Jordan 2009).

Complainants may also feel silenced by police when they are met with attitudes suggesting officers blame victims or perceive them as partially responsible for the rape. This can lead to some complainants attempting to conceal aspects of their own behaviour that they fear being judged about. One context in which this may arise is in relation to the volume of alcohol consumed by the complainant. Awareness of the prevalence of victim-blaming attitudes around female intoxication can influence complainants to report having consumed significantly less than they actually had on the night in question (Jordan 2004). The result can be a silencing spiral, whereby their omission and silence about factors seen as contributory result in increased levels of police scepticism regarding their allegation of rape, which in turn can lead to their withdrawing the complaint and opting to stay silent.

The above examples and situations illustrate how the manner in which police officers perceive and respond to women alleging rape can contribute to the silencing of women's voices. Important to acknowledge also is the extent to which some victims/survivors will resist attempts to silence them and remain steadfast in their determination to keep speaking their truth. As gatekeepers to the criminal justice system, the police play a pivotal role in determining which cases are investigated and likely to proceed further to eventual trial in a court of law (Gilmore and Pittman 1993; Gregory and Lees 1999; Jordan 2004; Kerstetter and van Winkle 1990). Should a case be referred to trial, the way the adversarial justice system operates can be experienced by some as a silencing mechanism, as will be examined in the next section.

## (iii) The courts

Referring to the treatment of rape complainants within the court system as a 'second rape' has become a depressingly recurrent theme in international research (Adler 1987; Doyle and Barbato 1999; Koss 2000; Madigan and Gamble 1991; Martin and Powell 1994; Orth 2002). The victim becomes a witness within the adversarial justice system that operates in many parts of the world including North America, England, South Africa, Australia and New

Zealand. In the 1970s the trial process came under rigorous criticism for the ways in which victims could be interrogated regarding their previous sexual history, a process designed to induce shame, besmirch their morality and undermine their credibility as legitimate victims (Heenan 2002–03; Temkin and Krahé 2008; McDonald 1994; Scutt 1998; Young 1983). A major aspiration within legal reform initiatives has been to limit the extent to which the victim's previous sexual history can be disclosed in court, with many formal barriers to such disclosure now existing. In practice, however, defence lawyers have responded by becoming increasingly adept at using inferences to raise question marks within jurors' minds regarding victim morality and credibility (Doyle and Barbato 1999; Jordan 2008; Scutt 1998; Temkin 2000; Temkin and Krahé 2008). This underscores the sentiment expressed by even some key players within the criminal justice system that the success of reforms will always be compromised in an adversarial system that by its very nature enlists both sides as contestants within the battleground of the courtroom. In their recent review of the justice gap in sexual assault cases, Temkin and Krahé cite the case of a Queen's Counsel in England who specialised in defending rape cases for many years until his conscience no longer allowed him to participate in what he termed 'a very unfair contest' (quoted in Temkin and Krahé 2008: 129). When police and prosecutors were asked in another study if they would recommend that a close friend or family member report a rape to police, most said they would (88 per cent of police and 85 per cent of Crown Prosecutors). However, when asked if they would recommend them taking this case through the court system, their responses dropped considerably to 59 per cent of police and 39 per cent of prosecutors (Mossman *et al.* 2009). In the trial arena, many knew that who wins does not always equate with a just and fair outcome.

In New Zealand one of the most dramatic recent cases to highlight the ways in which this system favours the defendant's rights over the complainant's occurred in an historic rape case involving a woman named Louise Nicholas (Nicholas 2007; Rowe 2009). She initially alleged having been raped as a teenager by three police officers in the 1980s, describing several repeat occurrences of police turning up on her doorstep with alcohol, looking for 'sex', in the small city in which she lived. Early attempts to hold these men accountable for raping her failed, partly through the perjury of a senior police 'mate', and the betrayal she experienced rendered Louise silent for many years (Kitchin 2007; Taylor 2007). When the case finally reached trial, she was portrayed as a 'police groupie' and a slut (*New Zealand Herald* 2007), while there was a resounding silence in the courtroom regarding the backgrounds of the accused. When all three men were acquitted, media coverage showed only the one who was currently a serving police officer walking away celebrating his freedom (*Dominion Post* 2007). It was months before the truth could be publicly revealed that the other men had been unable to leave the court with him because they were travelling in a prison van back to the prison in which they were currently serving custodial sentences for a similar-sounding pack rape of another woman. While such information was kept from the jury in case it was prejudicial to the defendants, no such discretion restricted the defence from portraying the complainant in as damning a way as possible.

The gross injustice of this case, along with several similar scenarios involving other women, led to the Prime Minister at the time, Helen Clark, ordering a Commission of Inquiry into Police Conduct with the aim of not only facilitating investigation of these particular cases but also assessing more generally police culture and the investigation of sexual assault offences (Bazley 2007). The Commission's findings included identifying what Liz Kelly has termed 'a culture of scepticism' (Kelly *et al*. 2005) within the New Zealand police, with recommendations including the need for greater police training around adult sexual assault investigations and the adoption of a Code of Conduct to guide police officer behaviour (Bazley 2007; Rowe 2009).

This case provides a window into silencing on several levels. These include the initial self-silencing by the victim, followed by her later initial disclosure being silenced for many years by the responses of police personnel. When it was later revealed how many people in this community, and police station, knew of how sexually violent some officers were, accusations were made that a conspiracy of silence existed (O'Connor 2006). The police force's reluctance to identify and punish offenders from within its ranks parallels the Catholic Church's reluctance to hold abusing priests responsible for their wrongdoing, with fears regarding the tarnishing of institutional reputations translating in effect to collusion with the perpetrators and the continued silencing of their victims. The eventual trial of the three men in 2006, by which time two of the accused had left the police, was accompanied by the silencing of factors seen as potentially prejudicial to their fair trial. No such restraint was imposed on testimony and insinuations detrimental to perceptions of the victim's character as a witness. A positive effect from the publicity accorded this trial, however, was its leverage in lifting the veil of silence surrounding the inequities of the existing system and the manner in which it mobilised many New Zealanders to agitate for reforms in this area. Since then a government Task Force into Sexual Violence has been held and research commissioned to review current responses and hopefully inform new developments (Kingi and Jordan 2009; Mossman *et al*. 2009; Triggs *et al*. 2009).

Today the question remains: to what extent do victims of rape continue to feel silenced within the court process? Complainants still report finding it difficult to give their account fully and to feel heard within a system that appears more oriented to ensuring it is the accused who 'gets their day in court'. They are required to give their evidence in response to questions, meaning that background details are often omitted that would help to contextualise the circumstances surrounding the rape (McDonald 1997; Temkin and Krahé 2008; Young 1998). Aspects of the trial process that many complainants continue to find difficult include having to face the defendant in the courtroom and being subjected to cross-examination by the defence. While women attacked by stranger rapists can often consider it empowering to face the man who raped them in court (Jordan 2008), women raped by men they know may find it more difficult to confront the perpetrator again. Having to see him in court, and be seen by him, can be traumatic, rendering some women silent in their fear. Knowing this, defence counsel will sometimes manipulate the situation to shut down the complainant's testimony. One way they may do this is by deliberately standing in a direct eyeline between the complainant and the defendant while cross-examining her, making it impossible for her not to see the offender and feel intimidated (Kingi and Jordan 2009). As Matoesian's analysis of courtroom talk demonstrated, the complainant is dominated and disqualified through the questioning, accusing and blaming that are endemic within trial processes (Matoesian 1993). In order to see the offender who raped them convicted, complainants need to not only withstand attempts to discredit their testimony and character but also display what Wendy Larcombe has described as 'discursive competence, resistance and, indeed, verbal fortitude' (Larcombe 2002: 146).

It is of little surprise that of the very few cases that progress to trial, even fewer result in the offender being convicted. Internationally there have been high levels of concern raised in recent years over the excessively high attrition rates in rape cases (Johnson *et al.* 2008; Kelly *et al.* 2005; Stern 2010; Temkin and Krahé 2008; Triggs *et al.* 2009). Much publicity has been given to what has even been termed the 'attrition rate crisis' in the UK, where analysis of a large data-set conducted for the Home Office indicated that the conviction rate for reported rape cases had been declining, reaching an all-time low of 5.6 per cent in 2002 (Kelly *et al.* 2005). A recent New Zealand analysis of adult sexual violation also showed that only 13 per cent of reported cases resulted in conviction (Triggs *et al.* 2009). The attrition process itself becomes a form of systemic silencing. At every stage of the disclosure process there is the potential for those hearing the victim to discredit the victim and in that discrediting to silence the voice of rape victimisation (Taslitz 1999).

While attention is often drawn to the many law reform measures introduced in recent years, the extent to which these have resulted in significantly improved experiences for rape complainants in court seems limited. Recent research involving interviews with judges and barristers identified a range of problems they perceived as linked to low conviction rates in rape cases, some of which persisted after being identified by barristers almost a decade earlier (Temkin 2000; Temkin and Krahé 2008). These issues included incompetence by police officers and prosecutors and 'bad behaviour' by defence counsel, as well as the rape myths and stereotypes held by many jury members (Temkin and Krahé 2008: 141). To this list Temkin and Krahé also added the problematic attitudes of some judges, evident in their interpretation and application of the law and functioning in ways that limit the effectiveness of reform measures.

Further limitations inhibiting law reform success are also evident. For instance, while details regarding a complainant's previous sexual history may not be permissible in court, crafty defence lawyers are skilled at finding ways to insinuate and smear jurors' perceptions of victims (Heenan 2002–03; Kingi and Jordan 2009; Temkin 2000; Temkin and Krahé 2008). Similarly, the understandable reluctance of victims to report rape is presented in ways that insinuate that a delayed complaint should be interpreted as a false complaint (Doyle and Barbato 1999; Temkin 2000). By the end of a trial, some victims have expressed a hatred and contempt for the defence lawyer equal to, if not stronger than, the feelings they hold for their actual rapist (Jordan 2008). Complainants in cases resulting in the defendant's acquittal may feel even more strongly muted by this experience, a fact I was reminded of as I was finishing this chapter. A woman who had endured years of sexual violence from a professional person of high credibility telephoned me, gutted at this man's acquittal by a jury, and described how this verdict said only too clearly to her, 'Get back in your box, woman.' Recent qualitative research conducted with rape complainants revealed that while there were mixed views regarding their experiences of policing, all were united in their condemnation of court processes, describing these as 'degrading' and 'traumatic' (Kingi and Jordan 2009: 95). Thus, although the injustices of the court system for rape complainants have been widely identified and condemned, and various initiatives introduced in an attempt to improve victims/survivors' experiences, the process continues to remain fraught, and women's voices continue to be silenced.

It is not only within the justice system that victims of rape can feel silenced. The police and courts operate within the context of a society shaped by patriarchy and still characterised by high levels of victim-blaming and rape-supportive beliefs. The next section raises concerns regarding how even those supposedly focused on victim/survivor well-being may inadvertently contribute to their silencing.

## (iv) Formal and informal supports

Counselling and supporting victims/survivors of rape and sexual assault is demanding work, necessitating high skill levels as well as in-depth understanding of the complex dynamics involved. Many victims attribute much of their ability to survive to the support received, often emphasising the importance of being able to speak and be heard (Ahrens 2006; Campbell 2002; Kingi and Jordan 2009). Both formal and informal support systems have been recognised in this regard, with victims/survivors varying in the extent to which they depend on and value the roles of counsellors and rape advocates or family and friends. Feeling heard and believed by others is important, with supporters often being valued primarily for their abilities to listen and validate rather than for the proffering of good advice (Kingi and Jordan 2009).

While the capacity to hear and validate another person's recounting of possibly the most traumatic events they have ever experienced is clearly significant, so also are the impacts resulting from negative or inappropriate responses to that recounting. Victims/survivors have described a range of ways in which some have felt invalidated and unheard by those they turned to for support (Campbell and Raja 1999; Campbell et al. 2001b; Jordan 2008; Kingi and Jordan 2009). One way this can happen is when counsellors operate within a preferred modality that may sit uncomfortably with a particular victim/survivor. For example, a woman attacked by a stranger home-invasion rapist described how the counsellor she saw insisted she pretend to be an angel floating over her life and describe what she saw; something too mystical and alien for this very practical woman to accomplish (Jordan 2008). Another baulked at a counsellor's insistence that she pretend the rapist was sitting opposite her and start talking to him; ironically a stipulation over how she should speak that effectively silenced her from disclosing further (Jordan 2008).

A second way that can result in some victims/survivors feeling silenced is when those supporting them insist on treating them as either victims *or* survivors, rather than appreciating that they hold both identities within them. This is evident when, for example, an individual is viewed as passive, vulnerable and lacking all agency, and responded to accordingly. The ways they find to help themselves manage and survive an attack are overlooked and negated, and their recovery may be presented as necessitating dependence on, and protection by, others. In such a scenario their identity as a victim is reinforced in ways that silence their capacity for autonomy and survival.

A similar, reverse process can operate when surviving is emphasised in ways that trivialise women's experiences of victimisation. This has occurred, for example, in contexts where family members may prematurely pressure victims to return to work and continue their lives as if nothing has happened, or act in ways that makes it difficult to even acknowledge the rape occurred (Jordan 2008). Either way, a part of them is silenced.

Individual counsellors and support agencies operate within a wider social and political context that also impacts on victims/survivors. When the blanket of silence smothering rape was shaken by the women's movement in the 1970s, this enabled greater recognition of the extent of men's violence against women and children. The challenges and campaigns that followed were not universally supported, however, and since then an angry backlash has sought to undermine the credibility of feminists and advocates working against violence (Faludi 1991; French 1992; Gavey and Gow 2001). By the 1990s the speaking out that characterised the 1970s was under attack from an array of mechanisms seeking to nail the blanket back in place and re-silence victims. One insidious weapon involves assaults on the credibility of those who have been victimised, achieved at times by a duplicitous playing of the victim card against victims. Thus while moves to professionalise services appear well intentioned, these typically result in a privileging of the voices of professionals in ways that silence and pathologise victims, rendering them susceptible to diagnosis, medicalisation and treatment for their mental 'illness' (Breckenridge 1999).

Such processes have been cemented even further into place this century, a recent example evident in New Zealand where in the last year the state has moved to reduce the capacity for support agencies to counsel rape victims in favour of reliance on professional psychologists (Binning 2010; Collins 2010). The ability to access funded support is now tagged to a mental health diagnosis having been made, placing the stigma of mental illness on victims of rape in ways that may detrimentally affect their future lives in a multitude of ways. Pathologising the victim also aids and abets the perpetrators of rape, enabling defence lawyers to launch further attacks on a complainant's credibility. Once again, the state colludes with perpetrators and victims are rendered mute.

If even those trained to provide support can mute victims, how much more so those around them, family and friends, who are not only untrained but also struggling to manage their own feelings following the rape of a loved one. Victims/survivors have spoken of how their parents in particular may act from their own guilt and pain, or from their ignorance regarding how to respond appropriately (Jordan 2008). Some assume a position of silence and shrink from naming or acknowledging the 'rape'. Susan Brison describes how lonely she felt following her rape attack in a foreign country when those around her kept acting and speaking as if no rape had occurred. While her mother did at least send her a card featuring the 'bluebird of happiness' to keep her cheerful, most family members and friends refrained from contacting her during her recovery in hospital. As she experienced it:

> These are all caring, decent people who would have sent wishes for a speedy recovery if I'd had, say, an appendectomy. Their early lack of response was so striking that I wondered whether it was the result of self-protective denial, a reluctance to mention something so unspeakable, or a symptom of our society's widespread emotional illiteracy that prevents people from conveying any feeling that can't be expressed in a Hallmark card.

> In the case of rape, the intersection of multiple taboos – against talking openly about trauma, about violence, about sex – causes conversational gridlock, paralyzing the would-be supporter. We lack the vocabulary for expressing appropriate concern, and we have no social conventions to ease the awkwardness.
>
> (Brison 2002: 12)

In a different context another woman recounted how a family member from overseas was due to visit her parents just a few days after she was raped. How to manage this situation became a perplexing family issue, resolved at the time by her mother insisting no mention should be made of the rape during what was intended to be a happy family reunion (Jordan 2008). Such a level of silencing and denial was almost more than her daughter could bear, even while knowing that her mother meant well and was trying to do the best for everybody.

Ultimately, the silence and lack of response from those surrounding the victim/survivor confirm that she has experienced the unspeakable. One arena within which victims/survivors are encouraged to talk is in the research context, although this setting can have its own silencing mechanisms, as the next section will explore.

## (v) How researchers and academics silence

Research conducted with victims/survivors of rape is often credited with helping them to voice their experiences and presented as a beneficial and sometimes empowering experience (Campbell 2002; Gordon and Riger 1991; Jordan 2008; Stanko 1997). Such a positive outcome is to some extent dependent on the motivation and style of the researcher as well as on the methodological approach taken. General victimisation studies, such as the British Crime Survey, have been criticised at times for the ways questions about sexual assault have been handled (Kelly *et al.* 2005; Radford 1987; Walby and Myhill 2001), resulting in increasingly sophisticated approaches being undertaken in an effort to improve response rates (Mayhew and Reilly 2007; Myhill and Allen 2002; Walby and Myhill 2001). What is apparent is that many victims of rape and sexual assault will stay silent about these incidents when participating in such research, with the result being that their experiences and perspectives are then excluded from consideration in the analysis. If and when they do open up to a researcher, or even drop lead lines, the latter may be uncomfortable with the topic and ignore such leads or divert the interview to 'safer' areas of investigation. The ability to speak freely and fully about a crime that has for so long been muted is still a difficult endeavour, for both speaker and listener, particularly given the reluctance or inability of many of those experiencing it even to acknowledge or define it as a crime.

Most feminist researchers have shown a distinct preference for qualitative interviewing, particularly favouring approaches that facilitate respondents being able to articulate narratives in their own words (Campbell *et al.* 2009; Jordan 2001, 2004, 2008; Kelly 1988; Reinharz 1992; Stanko 1990). Even within such qualitative contexts, however, researchers can still silence participants by their questions and responses. For example, researchers who are uncomfortable with the subject matter may find it difficult to broach sensitive topics and, even unconsciously, 'censor' what is able to be discussed. Others may intentionally curtail participants' ability to talk about what they most want to talk about in favour of discussing what they, the researchers, assume to be of interest or significance. Another way in which silencing may occur is when ethics committees, acting as the gatekeepers protecting research subjects, have insisted researchers agree not to ask participants about the rape itself on the assumption that this may be traumatising. In practice such an insistence can effectively silence participants from speaking about the things they most want and need to be able to voice. In my experience, I had my anxieties firmly confronted when, one after another, participants in a research study began voluntarily disclosing details regarding how they had experienced the actual attack itself. What some said was that this was the only time they had felt free to tell the whole story, and had not been concerned about how such telling might impact on the listener (Jordan 2008). In such circumstances insisting that they 'shut up' in order not to contravene perceived, external ethical anxieties seemed inappropriate, and could have been felt as yet another form of silencing echoing their experience with the rapist.

Feminist interviewing practices lend themselves particularly to creating a research environment within which participants may feel able to break their silence regarding a rape incident itself, or aspects associated with it. This is because, as other rape researchers have noted, 'feminist interviewing attunes to the emotionality of women's lived experiences' (Campbell *et al.* 2010). The ability to listen and validate, and to refrain from objectifying participants, is an important aspect of feminist methodologies (Campbell *et al.* 2009; Fonow and Cook 1991; Hollway and Jefferson 2000). There is a danger that those researching traumatic experiences such as rape and child sexual abuse may cling to notions of researcher objectivity as a means of insulating or immunising themselves from the contagion of emotion (Ellis 1996).

Acknowledging the impacts of researching rape, and using the emotions generated as further material for reflection and analysis, stands in direct contrast to positivist exhortations to eliminate researcher subjectivities. Studies conducted in the US by teams led by Rebecca Campbell demonstrate the importance of recognising the emotional realities accompanying rape research for both interviewees and interviewers. In relation to interviewees, Campbell *et al.* (2010) studied narrative data from 92 rape survivors to explore how they were affected by participating in research interviews. They found that the overwhelming majority experienced the interview positively, with the *burden of surviving rape* eased by having someone willing to listen and fully hear their story (Campbell *et al.* 2010: 76). This finding echoes that of other feminist researchers (e.g. Jordan 2008; Kelly 1988; Stanko 1990), reinforcing the power of being gifted a context within which the speaking of the unspeakable is encouraged. This sentiment was reinforced by Susan Brison, who, while introducing her own survivor narrative, observed how:

> the trauma survivor must find empathic listeners in order to carry on. Piecing together a shattered self requires a process of remembering and working through in which speech and affect converge in a trauma narrative...how saying something about the memory does something to it.
>
> (Brison: x–xi)

Interviewers may also experience a need to find 'empathic listeners' as they grapple with the complex emotional reactions triggered through participating in research on sexual violence. Campbell's 'research on the researchers' highlighted the ways in which exposure to the realities of rape generated powerful emotional responses, similar to the secondary or vicarious victimisation acknowledged as affecting those close to trauma victims (Campbell 2002). Recognising the value of emotional responses in shaping the research process itself, as well as informing analysis and interpretation, helps in validating the very experiencing of such emotions while also suggesting a potential need for the availability of support for interviewers (Ellis 1996). Denying the existence and value of emotional responses, or dismissing them as compromising and dangerous, serves to silence a significant dimension increasingly acknowledged by researchers of trauma and violence (Campbell 2002; Ellis 1996; Jordan 2008; Kelly 1988; Liebling and Stanko 2001).

A tangential but related issue involves recognising how the silencing of rape researchers can operate as a parallel process to the silencing of rape victims. This can be experienced in the difficulties associated with having studies on sexual violence funded and prioritised, as well as in the struggles to find publishers for rape research. The confusing of rape and sex extends into rape, like sex, being viewed as a taboo area for public discussion, a source of discomfort inviting suppression. Many a dinner party conversation has ground to a poignant silence when, asked what I research, I've replied 'rape', while my hosts have no doubt wished I had been able to reply, 'rose cultivation' or 'endangered trout conservation'. Attempts to silence researchers on rape may occur when they are subjected to attack for being feminist and therefore not objective – a refrain harking back to the male gods of positivism and their 'owning' of the truth. Interviewers may be expected to silence their own emotional responses to what they are hearing, and respond as neutrally as possible. Further assaults on their 'objectivity' are made should a researcher disclose her own victimisation experiences, meaning that instead many will self-silence rather than risk the refutation of their research on these grounds.

The ability to have rape research findings presented in the media is another area fraught with difficulty, and is the last silencing agent we will now consider.

## (vi) The media

All of the silencing agents discussed are exposed to and affected by media representations of sexual violence, with the various forms of media being widely recognised as 'a key arena in which rape is defined' (Kitzinger 2009: 74). What is evident is how selectively reported the crime of rape is, and the potential this holds for distorting awareness and understanding of rape (Boyle 2005; Lees 1995). The media's search for newsworthiness dictates that certain kinds of rape stories are more likely to receive journalists' attention than others, which will remain silenced and invisible. This results in a privileging of rape stories involving extreme forms of violence, stranger attacks and serial rape. The most typical and prevalent rapes – those committed against women by their partners, husbands and boyfriends – are the least likely to receive media attention (Howe 1998; Meyers 1997). Newspapers justify this on the basis that they are fed crime stories by the police, and while there is some truth in this, in practice a self-fulfilling spiral is the end product. The police assess reported rapes against the 'real rape' stereotype and see only those conforming as newsworthy, meaning newspapers publish accounts of these and reinforce views that these are the only 'real rapes', and so it goes on. Such a process conveys a powerful message to victims of other kinds of rape, impacting on the extent to which they feel able to divulge it as well as on how those they disclose to respond.

Concern regarding media treatment of rape has also been voiced in recent years over the disproportionate attention given to accounts of 'false complaints' (Gavey and Gow 2001; Kitzinger 2009). This tendency reflects centuries-old attitudes portraying women and children as vexatious liars (Jordan 2004; Lees 1997; Taslitz 1999). Such an emphasis has dangerous consequences. In suggesting that false complaints are numerous, the emphasis is placed on women's lack of veracity in ways that continue to obscure and silence the realities of rape. This reinforces historical stereotypes of lying women, influencing everyone (including potential jurors) and also serving as a warning to victims of rape that speaking out carries the risk of being disbelieved. As a consequence, both individual victims as well as the wider truths around rape are silenced.

Before concluding this section it is important to note also the positives associated with changing media depictions of rape, for the news is not all bad. Growing media awareness of rape has helped to bring into public discourse behaviours and experiences that were previously seen as 'unspeakable'. While early recognition of rape in the 1970s was often reflected in sensationalist and overtly sexist depictions, these have largely been replaced by increased recognition of rape as a serious issue (Soothill and Walby 1991; Kitzinger 2009). There have been occasions where media coverage has been instrumental in helping to achieve legal and criminal justice reforms. For example, outrage following the televised screening of the 1983 documentary in the United Kingdom showing police interrogating a rape victim stimulated national debate and inquiries, with similar responses and government actions evident in New Zealand in the wake of media exposure regarding police officers who rape. (See Kitzinger 2009 for further examples.) It is also important to recognise the ways in which exposing previously hidden realities in the media helps to create a climate within which victims may feel encouraged to speak out, as well as equipping them at times with the tools and language needed to facilitate disclosure (Kitzinger 2009).

A complex and multifaceted relationship therefore exists between the media and rape. While positive changes have occurred in their reporting and representation, nevertheless the potential remains for them to still play a significant silencing role in relation to rape. This is achieved in part through what they focus on (for example, false allegations, stranger attacks) as well as through an incident-specific focus that fails to engage in wider critiques of the societal attitudes that support and perpetuate rape (Howe 1998; Kitzinger 2009; Meyers 1997; Young 1998). This ultimately means they may be unwitting colluders in the continuing denial of the realities not only of rape, but of all the many forms of violence and oppression of women that silently scream to be seen and heard.

## The silencing continues

So far the primary aim of this chapter has been to explore and examine ways in which, despite the silence of rape being broken, the silencing of rape still continues. In each of the areas canvassed it is evident that progress has been made and advances in knowledge and understanding achieved, yet so much more remains to be done.

It is evident, for example, that women still struggle to name their experiences as rape, and to define themselves as victims. More than 20 years after Liz Kelly developed the continuum of sexual violence, it is apparent that unwanted sexual behaviour continues to be a prevalent feature in heterosexual relationships with notions of male sexual entitlement impacting on women (Gavey 2005; Patton and Mannison 1998). Despite reforms, and some improvements in police responsiveness, there is still often a reluctance to report rape and involve the police, with many continuing to fear being blamed or disbelieved, and barriers to reporting rape identified as prevalent 30 years ago still influential in contemporary settings (Sable et al. 2006). Legal reforms seem even less impactful in improving victims/survivors' experiences, with trial processes continuing to feel like a 'second rape'. Such negative experiences, combined with dismal prospects of cases resulting in offenders being convicted, not only silence these particular victims but operate in ways that mute others from coming forward. While intimate partner violence is attracting greater recognition, incidents of marital and partner rape are less openly acknowledged, with sexual violence continuing to be the silent and less visible component within 'family' and 'domestic' violence (Kelly and Regan 2001). None of the above should be surprising given how entrenched and embedded rape myths and victim-blaming attitudes have proven to be, and how resistant they are to substantial change (Amnesty International 2005; Brown and Horvath 2009; Lovett and Horvath 2009; Temkin and Krahé 2008).

An implicit assumption underlying much of this chapter has been that breaking the silence is a positive eventuality, something to encourage and promote. This is a reasonable assumption given what we already know regarding the dangers of repression and the terrors associated with 'unspeakability'. A word of caution is needed, however, in order to allow space for recognising the agency and autonomy of victims/survivors and respecting their decision-making regarding when and how to speak. There are times when opting for silence may be a sensible, understandable choice, essential for their safety and self-preservation.

Further discussion is also needed concerning what comes next after breaking the silence. What language do we use to give voice to these realities? How to speak of rape poses immense challenges given the diversity and complexity of the range of experiences subsumed beneath this small four-lettered word, as well as the variety of ways in which rape can impact on victims. Some complainants feel so ashamed they cannot bear to continue talking to the police, since:

> These are things we don't talk about, language you don't use, certainly not with a stranger – talking about my vagina, my body – I could barely find words for what they wanted, needed, me to tell them about.
>
> (quoted in McMillan and Thomas 2009: 272)

Before resolving the difficulties of deciding how to speak of rape, those victimised by rape need some sense of themselves as able and entitled to speak and give voice, but what is 'voice'? Feminist sociologist Shulamit Reinharz describes 'voice' as:

> having the ability, the means, and the right to express oneself, one's mind, and one's will. If an individual does not have these abilities, means, or rights, he or she is silent.
>
> (Reinharz 1994: 180)

Furthermore, is it responsible to encourage speaking out when there is no guarantee of the capacity of others to listen? What does it mean if we allow ourselves to truly hear the voices of those who have been raped? How do we assure them that they have been heard, believed? This raises issues regarding the importance of empathy and validation in the individual listener as well as prompting questions regarding the responsibilities associated with bearing witness to the atrocity of rape. Declaring ourselves willing to listen and know about rape carries a responsibility to respond in ways not only affirming to the individual victim/survivor but also that challenge the gendered and structural inequalities that give rise to rape. The silence of rape needs to be broken by all of us, not just its latest victims.

## Conclusion

This chapter speaks of that which may no longer be unspeakable but is still too often unspoken. In considering the ways in which women's voices around rape may still be silenced, attention was focused on the key 'muting' agents involved. There have been positive advances since feminists exposed many of the realities regarding violence against women and began challenging the most oppressive forms of gender inequality. Unsurprisingly, such exposure was not welcomed by those directly wielding, or even benefiting from, such power and control. As the silence around rape began to be broken, attempts were made to silence those doing the speaking, and the past few decades have seen recurring cycles occurring of 'speak the truth/silence the truth'.

To speak of the silence surrounding rape evokes both promise and despair – despair that a decade into the twenty-first century such silence is still so evident alongside the reassurance that this is no longer an absolute silence, that in some contexts at least the crime of rape can be named. There is power in the act of naming for 'to speak and to be heard is to have power over one's life. To be silenced is to have that power denied' (Ahrens 2006: 263). Given that, as many feminists have observed (e.g. Brownmiller 1975; MacKinnon 1987), rape functions as a tool of oppression, a means for keeping women subordinate, the inevitable question is: 'How, then, can we expect women to break the silence about the very experience used to reinforce powerlessness?' (Ahrens 2006: 263). That women do speak out, fight back and resist attests to the capacity for individual agency and survival, and is ultimately empowering in demonstrating that 'the body-self can be rewritten, that it is not doomed to perpetuate and replicate existing power structures' (Cahill 2001: 205).

Anger that women should presume to speak ran high in some quarters, as a mid-1990s US example chillingly reveals. In 1995 an email listing 75 reasons 'why women (bitches) should not have freedom of speech' was sent by four Cornell University freshmen to 20 friends, then circulated so widely that it crashed at least three campus email systems. Among the reasons on the list were the following:

11. If my dick's in her mouth, she can't talk anyway.
38. If she can't speak, she can't cry rape.
47. Nothing should come out of a woman's mouth, SWALLOW BITCH.

(quoted in Raine 1998: 216)

When the university administrators investigated this incident, they faced strong opposition on two fronts – from women's groups outraged when no action was taken against the students; and from advocates of free speech outraged that there was even an investigation. The students concerned, as well as responding that it was only a joke, also stated in their defence that every saying had been obtained from such sources as song lyrics, comedians' acts, television shows and T-shirt slogans – these were not only their views, but the sentiments and stereotypes of the society they (and we) live in. The message emanating from its patriarchal core is clear: 'The only good woman is a silent woman.'

It is no surprise that feminist critiques and analyses met with strong resistance. The backlash against feminism speaks not only in the ugly voice of overt violence but also in more insidious ways, such as by undermining the credibility of all those seeking greater recognition of, and support for, those victimised by rape and sexual assault. While the victims risk depiction as outright liars or sufferers of its more benevolent form, 'false memory syndrome' (Herman and Harvey 1993; Porter *et al.* 1999), those advocating on their behalf can also face attempts to silence them. In the case of agencies supporting victims of rape and child sexual abuse, for instance, this can be manifest in low levels, or even withdrawal of, funding. Thus while the rhetoric of victims' rights receives government attention, manifest in charters and policies receiving positive media acclaim, financial support for agencies supporting victims continues to be a major area of struggle and neglect (Humphreys 2010). Fostering state dependency and competition between agencies for scarce resources can work both to exert control and silence critique and protest.

Resistance to change has also been a feature within criminal justice system agencies. While the rhetoric of reform may be voiced, in practice it is hard to release the tenacious grip of traditionally conservative and masculinist attitudes.

> Law is naturally conservative; it relies on precedent and background assumptions, and seeks interpretations consistent with those assumptions. Legal change is, accordingly, generally incremental. It is just enough reform to look good to large segments of the public, to preserve the system from collapse, and to make everyone feel proud, but not enough reform as to wreak radical change...Patriarchal rape tales will not give up the ghost easily.
>
> (Taslitz 1999: 42)

Internationally inquiries and commissions come and go, their findings repeatedly documenting how dire the situation is and advocating the urgent need for reform, before lapsing back into the silence of apathy and collusion. Government funding for such inquiries to be conducted may be hard won, but is typically granted and broadcast amidst a fanfare of pledges and promises signalling a commitment to change. Less well publicised is the eventual lack of follow-through to funding and implementing the recommendations deemed necessary for real change to occur. In this way the rhetoric of change is upheld while underlying structures and realities remain largely intact, demonstrating what Liz Kelly has identified as 'the paradoxical way in which feminist knowledge both informs reform processes and is simultaneously disavowed' (Kelly 2008: 271–2).

While feminist campaigns have seen some advances made, their impacts have not been universally experienced. Greater attention needs to be given to those groups at greater risk of being silenced; those whose particular vulnerabilities are interpreted as further undermining their credibility and legitimacy as victims. These include indigenous and ethnic minorities, sex workers, lesbians, women with disabilities, and those with histories of repeat victimisation.

Centuries of silencing of women's voices is not easily broken, and just as the speaking out needs to continue, we can also expect to see attempts to silence continuing also. A particularly insidious silencing device is the refrain that asserts women and men now live equally in a post-feminist world characterised by gender symmetry surrounding violence. Listen hard, for from the silence surrounding rape sneers a voice: 'Ha! Patriarchy is not yet dead!'

## Further reading

For an early and insightful analysis of the historical silencing of rape victims, there is no better starting point than Susan Brownmiller's book, *Against Our Will: Men, Women and Rape* (1975). Inspiring accounts of how individual women find the courage to speak and to survive include: Susan Brison, *Aftermath: Violence and the Remaking of the Self* (2002); Jan Jordan, *Serial Survivors: Women's Narratives of Surviving Rape* (2008); Nancy Venable Raine, *After Silence: Rape & My Journey Back* (1998): and Alice Sebold's memoir, *Lucky* (1999). To understand more fully the reasons why women may self-silence, read Liz Kelly's book *Surviving Sexual Violence* (1988) and also Nicola Gavey's analysis in *Just Sex? The Cultural Scaffolding of Rape* (2005). Good coverage of how stereotypical attitudes towards sexual violence continue to affect victims' experiences of the criminal justice system can be found in *Sexual Assault and the Justice Gap: A Question of Attitude* (Jennifer Temkin and Barbara Krahé (2008)), while a range of useful, contemporary analyses can be found in Miranda Horvath and Jennifer Brown (eds) *Rape: Challenging Contemporary Thinking* (2009).

## References

Adler, Z. (1987) *Rape on Trial*. London: Routledge and Kegan Paul.

Ahrens, C.E. (2006) 'Being silenced: The impact of negative social reactions on the disclosure of rape', *American Journal of Community Psychology*, 38: 263–74.

Amnesty International (2005) *Sexual Assault Research: Summary Report*. Prepared by ICM for Amnesty International UK, London.

Bachman, R. (1993) 'Predicting the reporting of rape victimizations: Have rape reforms made a difference?' *Criminal Justice and Behavior*, 20(3): 254–70.

Bart, P.B., and O'Brien, P. (1985) *Stopping Rape: Successful Survival Strategies*. New York: Pergamon.

Bazley, Dame M. (2007) *Report of the Commission of Inquiry into Police Conduct, Volume 1*. Wellington: Commission of Inquiry into Police Conduct.

Bennice, J.A. and Resick, P.A. (2003) 'Marital rape: History, research, and practice', *Trauma, Violence, and Abuse*, 4(3): 228–46.

Bergen, R.K. (2006) 'Marital rape: New research and directions', VAWNET Applied Research Forum, National Online Resource Center on Violence Against Women (accessed 8 July 2010).

Binning, E. (2010) 'Sexual abuse survivors to challenge ACC changes', *New Zealand*

*Herald*, 3 May: 6.

Bohner, G., Eyssel, F., Pina, A., Siebler, F. and Viki, G.T. (2009) 'Rape myth acceptance: Cognitive, affective and behavioural effects of beliefs that blame the victim and exonerate the perpetrator', in M. Horvath and J. Brown (eds) *Rape: Challenging Contemporary Thinking*. Cullompton: Willan Publishing.

Boose, L.E. (1991) 'Scolding brides and bridling scolds: Taming the woman's unruly member', *Shakespeare Quarterly*, 42(2): 179–213.

Boyle, K. (2005) *Media and Violence*. London: Sage Publications.

Breckenridge, J. (1999) 'Subjugation and silences: The role of the professions in silencing victims of sexual and domestic violence', in J. Breckenridge and L. Laing (eds) (1999) *Challenging Silence: Innovative Responses to Sexual and Domestic Violence*. Sydney: Allen and Unwin.

Brison, S. (2002) *Aftermath: Violence and the Remaking of the Self*. Princeton, NJ: Princeton University Press.

Brown, J. and Horvath, M. (2009) 'Do you believe her and is it real rape?', in M. Horvath and J. Brown (eds) *Rape: Challenging Contemporary Thinking*. Cullompton: Willan Publishing.

Brown, J., Maidment, A. and Bull, R. (1993) 'Appropriate skill-task matching or gender bias in deployment of male and female police officers?', *Policing and Society*, 3: 121–36.

Brown, J.M., Hamilton, C. and O'Neill, D. (2007) 'Characteristics associated with rape attrition and the role played by scepticism or legal rationality by investigators and prosecutors', *Psychology, Crime and Law*, 13(4): 355–70.

Brown, J. and Heidensohn, F. (2000) *Gender and Policing: Comparative Perspectives*. Basingstoke: Macmillan.

Brownmiller, S. (1975) *Against Our Will: Men, Women and Rape*. Harmondsworth: Penguin.

Burgess, A.W. (1999) 'Public beliefs and attitudes towards rape', in R. R.Hazlewood and A.W. Burgess (eds) *Practical Aspects of Rape Investigation: A Multidisciplinary Approach* (2nd edition). Boca Raton: CRC Press.

Burgess, A.W. and Holmstrom, L.L. (1979) *Rape Crisis and Recovery*. Bowie, MD: Robert J. Brady.

Burgess, A.W. and Hazelwood, R.R. (1999) 'The victim's perspective', in R.R. Hazelwood and A.W. Burgess (eds) *Practical Aspects of Rape Investigation: A Multidisciplinary Approach* (2nd edition). Boca Raton: CRC Press.

Burt, M.R. and Katz, B.L. (1985) 'Rape, robbery, and burglary: Responses to actual and feared victimization, with special focus on women and the elderly', *Victimology: An International Journal*, 10: 325–58.

Cahill, A.J. (2001) *Rethinking Rape*. Ithaca: Cornell University Press.

Caignon, D. and Groves, G. (1987) *Her Wits About Her: Self-defense success stories by women*. New York: Harper and Row.

Campbell, R. (2002) *Emotionally Involved: The Impact of Researching Rape*. New York: Routledge.

Campbell, R. and Raja, S. (1999) 'Secondary victimization of rape victims: Insights from mental health professionals who treat survivors of violence', *Violence and Victims*, 14(3): 261–75.

Campbell, R., Sefl, T., Barnes, H.E., Ahrens, C.E., Wasco, S.M., and Zaragoza-Diesfeld, Y. (1999) 'Community services for rape survivors: Enhancing psychological well-being or increasing trauma?', *Journal of Consulting and Clinical Psychology*, 67: 847–58.

Campbell, R., Adams, A.E., Wasco, S.M., Ahrens, C.E. and Sefl, T. (2009) 'Training interviewers for research on sexual violence: A qualitative study of rape survivors' recommendations for interview practice', *Violence Against Women*, 15(5): 595–617.

Campbell, R., Adams, A.E., Wasco, S.M., Ahrens, C.E. and Sefl, T. (2010) '"What has it been like for you to talk with me today?" The impact of participating in interview research on rape survivors', *Violence Against Women*, 16(1): 60–83.

Campbell, R., Ahrens, C., Wasco, S., Sefl, T. and Barnes, H. (2001a) 'Social reactions to rape victims: Healing and hurtful effects on psychological and physical health outcomes', *Violence and Victims*, 16: 287–302.

Campbell, R., Wasco, S., Ahrens, C., Sefl, T. and Barnes, H. (2001b) 'Preventing the "second rape": Rape survivors' experiences with community service providers', *Journal of Interpersonal Violence*, 16: 1239–59.

Collins, S. (2010) 'Denied help for sexual abuse, dead days later', *New Zealand Herald*, 27 April: 4.

Daly, M. (1979) *Gyn/Ecology: The Metaethics of Radical Feminism*. London: Women's Press.

Dann, C. (1985) *Up From Under: Women and Liberation in New Zealand 1970–1985*. Wellington: Allen and Unwin/Port Nicholson Press.

Dobash, R.E. and Dobash, R.P. (1992) *Women, Violence and Social Change*. London: Routledge.

*Dominion Post* (2007) 'All acquitted but two are already in jail for rape', *The Dominion Post*, 2 March. Edition 2, page 1.

Donat, P. and D'Emilio, J. (1992) 'A feminist redefinition of rape and sexual assault: Historical foundations and change', *Journal of Social Issues*, 48(1): 9–22.

Doyle, S. and Barbato, C. (1999) 'Justice delayed is justice denied: The experiences of women in court as victims of sexual assault', in J. Breckenridge and L. Laing (eds) *Challenging Silence: Innovative Responses to Sexual and Domestic Violence*. Sydney: Allen and Unwin.

Du Mont, J., Miller, K. and Myhr, T.L. (2003) 'The role of "real rape" and "real victim" stereotypes in the police reporting practices of sexually assaulted women', *Violence Against Women*, 9(4): 466–86.

Easteal, P. (1994) *Voices of the Survivors*. Melbourne: Spinifex Press.

Easteal, P. (1998) 'Rape in marriage: Has the licence lapsed?', in P. Easteal (ed.) *Balancing the Scales: Rape, Law Reform and Australian Culture*. Leichhardt, Sydney: The Federation Press.

Ellis, J.M. (1996) 'Close to home: the experience of researching child sexual abuse', in M. Hester, L. Kelly and J. Radford (eds) *Women, Violence and Male Power*. Buckingham: Open University Press.

Epstein, J. and Langenbahn, S. (1994) *The Criminal Justice and Community Response to Rape*. Issues and Practices in Criminal Justice series, National Institute of Justice. Washington: US Department of Justice.

Estrich, S. (1987) *Real Rape*. Cambridge, Massachusetts: Harvard University Press.

Faith, K. (1993) *Unruly Women: The Politics of Confinement and Resistance*. Vancouver: Press Gang Publishers.

Faludi, S. (1991) *Backlash: The Undeclared War Against Women*. London: Chatto and Windus.

Ferro, C., Cermele, J. and Saltzman, A. (2008) 'Current perceptions of marital rape: Some good and not-so-good news', *Journal of Interpersonal Violence*, 23(6): 764–79.

Filipas, H.H. and Ullman, S.E. (2001) 'Social reactions to sexual assault victims from various support sources', *Violence and Victims*, 16(6): 673–92.

Finch, E. and Munro, V.E. (2006) 'Breaking boundaries: Sexual consent in the jury room', *Legal Studies*, 26(3): 303–20.

Fisher, B.S., Daigle, L.E., Cullen, F.T. and Turner, M.G. (2003) 'Reporting sexual victimization to the police and others: Results from a national-level study of college women', *Criminal Justice and Behavior*, 30(1): 6–38.

Fonow, M.M. and Cook, J.A. (1991) *Beyond Methodology: Feminist Scholarship as Lived*

*Research*. Bloomington: Indiana University Press.

Freckelton, I. (1998) 'Sexual offence prosecutions: A barrister's perspective', in P. Easteal (ed) *Balancing the Scales: Rape, Law Reform and Australian Culture*. Leichhardt, Sydney: The Federation Press.

French, M. (1992) *The War Against Women*. London: Hamish Hamilton.

Garland, A. (2003) 'The great witch hunt: The persecution of witches in England, 1550–1660', *Auckland University Law Review*, 9(4): 1152–80.

Gartner, R. and Macmillan, R. (1995) 'The effect of victim-offender relationship on reporting crimes of violence against women', *Canadian Journal of Criminology*, 37(3): 393–429.

Gavey, N. (2005) *Just Sex? The Cultural Scaffolding of Rape*. Hove: Routledge.

Gavey, N. and Gow, V. (2001). ' "Cry Wolf", cried the wolf: Constructing the issue of false rape allegations in New Zealand media texts', *Feminism and Psychology*, 11(3): 341–60.

Gilmore, K. and Pittman, L. (1993) *To Report or Not To Report: A Study of Victim/Survivors of Sexual Assault and Their Experience of Making an Initial Report to the Police*. Melbourne: Centre Against Sexual Assault (CASA House) and Royal Women's Hospital.

Golding, J., Stein, J., Siegel, J., Burnam, M. and Sorenson, S. (1988) 'Sexual assault history and use of health and mental health services', *American Journal of Community Psychology*, 16(5): 625–43.

Goodstein, L. and Lutze, F. (1992) 'Rape and criminal justice system responses', in Imogene Moyer (ed.) *The Changing Roles of Women in the Criminal Justice System: Offenders, Victims, and Professionals* (2nd edn). Illinois: Waveland Press.

Gordon, M.T. and Riger, S. (1991) *The Female Fear: The Social Cost of Rape*. Urbana: University of Illinois Press.

Gregory, J. and Lees, S. (1999) *Policing Sexual Assault*. London: Routledge.

Griffin, S. (1971) 'Rape: The all-American crime', *Ramparts*, September: 26–35.

Heath, Mary (1998) 'Disputed truths: Australian reform of the sexual conduct elements of common law rape', in P. Easteal (ed.) *Balancing the Scales: Rape, Law Reform and Australian Culture*. Leichhardt, Sydney: The Federation Press.

Heenan, M. (2002–03) 'Reconstituting the "relevance" of women's sexual histories in rape trials', *Women Against Violence*, 13: 4–17.

Heidensohn, F. (1992) *Women in Control? The Role of Women in Law Enforcement*. Oxford: Clarendon.

Herman, J. (2005) 'Justice from the victim's perspective', *Violence Against Women*, 11(5): 571–602.

Herman, J.L. and Harvey, M. (1993) 'The false memory debate: Social science or social backlash?', *Just Us*, May/June: 5–8.

Hester, M. (1992) *Lewd Women and Wicked Witches: A Study of the Dynamics of Male Domination*. London: Routledge.

Hollway, W. and Jefferson, T. (2000) *Doing Qualitative Research Differently: Free association, narrative and the interview method*. London: Sage Publications.

Howe, A. (1998) 'Notes from a "war" zone: Reporting domestic/family/home/epidemic (men's) violence', in A. Howe (ed.) *Sexed Crime in the News*. Sydney: The Federation Press.

Humphreys, L. (2010) 'Support agencies "near collapse".' *Taranaki Daily News*, 4 May: 4.

Hunt, M. (1992) 'Wife beating, domesticity and women's independence in eighteenth-century London', *Gender and History*, 4(1): 10–33.

Johnson, H., Ollus, N. and Sami, N. (2008) *Violence Against Women: An International Perspective*. New York: Springer.

Jones, H. (2004) 'Opportunities and obstacles: The Rape Crisis Federation in the UK',

*Journal of Interdisciplinary Gender Studies*, 8: 55–69.

Jordan, J. (2001) 'Worlds apart? Women, rape and the reporting process', *British Journal of Criminology*, 41(4): 679–706.

Jordan, J. (2002) 'Will any woman do?: Police, gender and rape victims', *Policing: An International Journal of Police Strategies and Management*, 25(2): 319–44.

Jordan, J. (2004) *The Word of a Woman? Police, Rape and Belief*. Houndmills, Basingstoke: Palgrave Macmillan.

Jordan, J. (2008) *Serial Survivors: Women's Narratives of Surviving Rape*. Sydney: The Federation Press.

Jordan, J. (2009) 'Serial survivors: A multi-victim case study'. Paper presented at the Australasian Council of Women and Policing Conference, Perth. http://www.auspol-women.asn.au/conferences/Papers%2009/Jan%20Jordan.pdf

Kelly, L. (1988) *Surviving Sexual Violence*. Cambridge: Polity Press.

Kelly, L. (2002) *A Research Review on the Reporting, Investigation and Prosecution of Rape Cases*. London: Her Majesty's Crown Prosecution Service Inspectorate.

Kelly, L. (2005) *Promising Practices Addressing Sexual Violence*. Expert paper prepared for an expert group organized by the UN Division for the Advancement of Women, 17–20 May Vienna, Austria.

Kelly, L. (2008) 'Contradictions and paradoxes: International patterns of, and responses to, reported rape cases', in G. Letherby, K. Williams, P. Birch and M. Cain (eds) *Sex as Crime?* Cullompton: Willan Publishing.

Kelly, L., Lovett, J. and Regan, L. (2005) *A Gap or a Chasm? Attrition in Reported Rape Cases*. Home Office Research Study 293. London: Home Office Research, Development and Statistics Directorate.

Kelly, L. and Regan, L. (2001) *Rape: The Forgotten Issue? A European Attrition and Networking Study*. London: Child and Woman Abuse Studies Unit.

Kennedy, H. (1992) *Eve Was Framed: Women and British Justice*. London: Vintage.

Kerstetter, W.A. and van Winkle, B. (1990) 'Who decides?: A study of the complainant's decision to prosecute in rape cases', *Criminal Justice and Behavior*, 17(3): 268–83.

Kingi, V. and Jordan, J. (with Moeke-Maxwell, T. and Fairbairn-Dunlop, P.) (2009) *Responding to Sexual Violence: Pathways to Recovery*. Wellington: Ministry of Women's Affairs.

Kitchin, P. (2007) 'Straight from the detective's nose', *The Dominion Post*, 11 August: 5.

Kitzinger, J. (2009). 'Rape in the media', in M. Horvath and J. Brown (eds). *Rape: Challenging Contemporary Thinking*. Cullompton: Willan Publishing.

Koss, M.P. (2000) 'Blame, shame, and community: Justice responses to violence against women', *American Psychologist*, 55: 1332–43.

Koss, M.P. and Oros, C.J. (1980) 'The "unacknowledged" rape victim.' Paper presented at the Annual Convention of the American Psychological Association, Montreal.

Koss, M.P., Gidycz, C.A. and Wisniewski, N. (1987) 'The scope of rape: Incidence and prevalence of sexual aggression in a national sample of higher education students', *Journal of Consulting and Clinical Psychology*, 55: 162–70.

Krahé, B. and Temkin, J. (2009) 'Addressing the attitude problem in rape trials: Some proposals and methodological considerations', in M. Horvath and J. Brown (eds). *Rape: Challenging Contemporary Thinking*. Cullompton: Willan Publishing.

Larcombe, W. (2002) 'The "ideal" victim v successful rape complainant: Not what you might expect', *Feminist Legal Studies*, 10: 131–48.

Lea, S., Lanvers, U. and Shaw, S. (2003) 'Attrition in rape cases: developing a profile and identifying relevant factors', *British Journal of Criminology*, 43: 583–99.

LeDoux, J.C. and Hazelwood, R.R. (1999) 'Police attitudes and beliefs concerning rape', in R.R. Hazelwood and A.W. Burgess (eds) *Practical Aspects of Rape Investigation: A*

283

*Multidisciplinary Approach* (2nd edn). Boca Raton: CRC Press.

Lees, S. (1995) 'Media reporting of rape: the 1993 British "date rape" controversy', in D. Kidd Hewitt and R. Osborne (eds) *Crime and the Media: The Postmodern Spectacle*. London: Pluto.

Lees, S. (1997) *Ruling Passions: Sexual Violence, Reputation and The Law*. Buckingham: Open University Press.

Lentz, S.A. (1999) 'Revisiting the rule of thumb', *Women and Criminal Justice*, 10(2): 9–27.

Liebling, A. and Stanko, B. (2001) 'Allegiance and ambivalence: Some dilemmas in researching disorder and violence', *British Journal of Criminology*, 41(3): 421–30.

Littleton, H.L., Axsom, D., Radecki Breitkopf, C. and Berenson, A.B. (2006) 'Rape acknowledgment and post assault experiences: How acknowledgment status relates to disclosure, coping, worldview, and reactions received from others', *Violence and Victims*, 21: 765–82.

Lovett, J. and Horvath, M. (2009) 'Alcohol and drugs in rape and sexual assault', in M. Horvath and J. Brown (eds) *Rape: Challenging Contemporary Thinking*. Cullompton: Willan Publishing.

Lovett, J., Regan, L. and Kelly, L. (2004) *Sexual Assault Referral Centres: Developing good practice and maximising potentials*. Home Office Research Study 285. London: Home Office Research, Development and Statistics Directorate.

MacKinnon, C. (1987) *Feminism Unmodified: Discourses on Life and Law*. Boston, Massachusetts: Harvard University Press.

Madigan, L. and Gamble, N. (1991) *The Second Rape: Society's continued betrayal of the victim*. New York: Lexington Books.

Martin. P. Y. (1997) 'Gender, accounts and rape processing work', *Social Problems*, 44(4): 464–82.

Martin, P. and Powell, R. (1994) 'Accounting for the "second assault": Legal organizations framing of rape victims', *Law and Social Inquiry*, 19: 853–90.

Matoesian, G.M. (1993) *Reproducing Rape: Domination through Talk in the Courtroom*. Cambridge: Polity Press.

Mayhew, P. and Reilly, J. (2007) *New Zealand Crime and Safety Survey 2006: Key Findings*. Wellington: Ministry of Justice.

McDonald, E. (1994) 'Gender bias and the law of evidence: The link between sexuality and credibility', *Victoria University of Wellington Law Review*, 24(2): 175–88.

McDonald, E. (1997) '"Real rape" in New Zealand: Women complainants' experience of the court process', *Yearbook of New Zealand Jurisprudence*, 1(1): 59–80.

McMillan, L. and Thomas, M. (2009) 'Police interviews of rape victims: Tensions and contradictions', in M. Horvath and J. Brown (eds) *Rape: Challenging Contemporary Thinking*. Cullompton: Willan Publishing.

Medea, A. and Thompson, K. (1974) *Against Rape*. New York: Farrar, Straus and Giroux.

Meyer, M. (1974) 'Rape: the victim's point of view', *Police Law Quarterly*, 3(3): 38–44.

Meyers, M. (1997) *News Coverage of Violence Against Women: Engendering Blame*. Thousand Oaks: Sage.

Mossman, E., MacGibbon, L., Kingi, V. and Jordan, J. (2009) *Responding to Sexual Violence: Environmental Scan of New Zealand Agencies*. Wellington: Ministry of Women's Affairs.

Munro, V.E. and Kelly, L. (2009) 'A vicious cycle? Attrition and conviction patterns in contemporary rape cases in England and Wales', in M. Horvath and J. Brown (eds). *Rape: Challenging Contemporary Thinking*. Cullompton: Willan Publishing.

Myhill, A. and Allen, J. (2002) *Rape and Sexual Assault of Women: Findings from the British Crime Survey*. London: Home Office.

*New Zealand Herald* (2007) 'Police sex case: "Why would I lie about this, why would I make this up?"', *New Zealand Herald*, 4 March.

Nicholas, L. (2007) *Louise Nicholas: My Story*. Auckland: Random House.

O'Connor, T. (2006) 'Rape trial's menacing shadow', *The Nelson Mail*, 4 April: 11.

O'Keeffe, S., Brown, J. and Lyons, E. (2009) 'Seeking proof or truth: Naturalistic decision-making by police officers when considering rape allegations', in M. Horvath and J. Brown (eds) *Rape: Challenging Contemporary Thinking*. Cullompton: Willan Publishing.

Orth, U. (2002) 'Secondary victimization of crime victims by criminal proceedings', *Social Justice Research*, 15(4): 313–25.

Painter, K. (1991) *Wife Rape, Marriage and the Law*. Manchester: University of Manchester, Department of Social Policy.

Patton, W. and Mannison, M. (1998) 'Beyond learning to endure: women's acknowledgement of coercive sexuality', *Women's Studies International Forum*, 21(1): 31–40.

Pike, D.L. (1992) 'Women in police academy training: Some aspects of organizational response', in I. Moyer (ed.) *The Changing Roles of Women in the Criminal Justice System: Offenders, Victims, and Professionals* (2nd edn). Illinois: Waveland Press.

Pollock, J. (1995) 'Gender, justice and social control: a historical perspective', in A.V. Merlo and J.M. Pollock (eds) *Women, Law, and Social Control*. Boston: Allyn and Bacon.

Porter, S., Yuille, J.C. and Lehman, D.R. (1999) 'The nature of real, implanted, and fabricated memories for emotional childhood events: Implications for the recovered memory debate', *Law and Human Behavior*, 23(5): 517–37.

Radford, J. (1987) 'Policing male violence: policing women', in J. Hamner and S. Saunders (eds) *Women, Policing and Social Control*. London: Macmillan.

Raine, N.V. (1998) *After Silence: Rape and My Journey Back*. New York: Three Rivers Press.

Reinharz, S. (1992) *Feminist Methods in Social Research*. New York: Oxford University Press.

Reinharz, S. (1994) 'Toward an ethnography of "voice" and "silence",' in E. Trickett and R. Watts (eds) *Human Diversity: Perspectives On People In Context*. San Francisco, CA: Jossey-Bass, Inc.

Rowe, M. (2009) 'Notes on a scandal: The official enquiry into deviance and corruption in the New Zealand Police', *The Australian and New Zealand Journal of Criminology*, 42(1): 123–58.

Sable, M.R., Danis, F., Mauzy, D.L. and Gallagher, S.K. (2006) 'Barriers to reporting sexual assault for women and men: perspectives of college students', *Journal of American College Health*, 55(3): 157–62.

Scutt, J. (1998) 'Character, credit, context: Women's lives and judicial "reality"', in P. Easteal (ed.) *Balancing the Scales: Rape, Law Reform and Australian Culture*. Leichhardt, Sydney: The Federation Press.

Searles, P. and Berger, R.J. (1987) 'The feminist self-defense movement: A case study', *Gender and Society*, 1(1): 61–84.

Sebold, A. (1999) *Lucky*. Boston: Little, Brown and Company.

Smith, L. (1989) *Concerns About Rape*. London: HMSO.

Soothill, K. and Walby, S. (1991) *Sex Crime in the News*. London: Routledge.

Spohn, C. and Horney, J. (1992) *Rape Law Reform: A Grassroots Revolution and its Impact*. New York: Plenum.

Stanko, E.A. (1985) *Intimate Intrusions: Women's Experiences of Men's Violence*. London: Routledge and Kegan Paul.

Stanko, E. (1990) *Everyday Violence: How Women and Men Experience Sexual and Physical Danger*. London: Pandora.

Stanko, E.A. (1997) '"I second that emotion": Reflections on feminism, emotionality and research on sexual violence', in M.D. Schwartz (ed.) *Researching Sexual Violence Against Women: Methodological and Personal Perspectives*. Thousand Oaks, California: Sage.

Stanko, B. and Williams, E. (2009) 'Reviewing rape and rape allegations in London: What are the vulnerabilities of the victims who report to the police?', in M. Horvath and J. Brown (eds) *Rape: Challenging Contemporary Thinking*. Cullompton: Willan Publishing.

Stern, Baroness V. (2010) *Stern Review of Rape Reporting in England and Wales*. London: Home Office.

Stewart, M.W., Dobbin, S.A. and Gatowski, S.I. (1996) '"Real rapes" and "real victims": The shared reliance on common cultural definitions of rape', *Feminist Legal Studies*, 4: 159–77.

Sullivan, G. (1986) *Rape Crisis Handbook: Counselling for Sexual Abuse*. Wellington: Wellington Rape Crisis Centre.

Sutch, W.B. (1973) *Women with a Cause*. Wellington: New Zealand University Press.

Taslitz, A.E. (1999) *Rape and the Culture of the Courtroom*. New York: New York University Press.

Taylor, P. (2007) 'The Louise Nicholas saga – Out of the shadows', *New Zealand Herald*, 11 August.

Temkin, J. (2000) 'Prosecuting and defending rape: Perspectives from the Bar', *Journal of Law and Society*, 27(2): 219–48.

Temkin, J. and Krahé, B. (2008) *Sexual Assault and the Justice Gap: A Question of Attitude*. Oxford: Hart Publishing.

Tjaden, P. and Thoennes, N. (2000) *Full Report of the Prevalence, Incidence, and Consequences of Violence Against Women: Findings From the National Violence Against Women Survey*. Research Report. Washington, DC, and Atlanta, GA: US Department of Justice, National Institute of Justice, and US Department of Health and Human Services, Centers for Disease Control and Prevention.

Toner, B. (1982) *The Facts of Rape*. London: Arrow Books.

Tong, R. (1984) *Women, Sex and the Law*. Savage, Maryland: Rowman and Littlefield.

Triggs S., Mossman S.E., Jordan J., Kingi V. (2009). *Responding to Sexual Violence: Attrition in the New Zealand Criminal Justice System*. Wellington: Ministry of Women's Affairs.

Ullman, S.E. and Filipas, H.H. (2001) 'Correlates of formal and informal support seeking in sexual assault victims', *Journal of Interpersonal Violence*, 16(10): 1028–47.

Ullman, S.E., Filipas, H.H., Townsend, S.M. and Starzynski, L.L. (2006) 'The role of victim–offender relationship in women's sexual assault experiences', *Journal of Interpersonal Violence*, 21(6): 798–819.

Ventegodt, S., Kandel, I., Neikrug, S. and Merrick, J. (2005) 'Clinical holistic medicine: Holistic treatment of rape and incest trauma', *The Scientific World Journal*, 5: 288–97.

Walby, S. and Allen, J. (2004) *Domestic Violence, Sexual Assault and Stalking: Findings from the British Crime Survey*. London: Home Office Research Study 276.

Walby, S. and Myhill, A. (2001) 'New survey methodologies in researching violence against women', *British Journal of Criminology*, 41: 502–22.

Walklate, S. (1995) *Gender and Crime: An Introduction*. London: Prentice Hall.

Walklate, S. (2008) 'What is to be done about violence against women? Gender, violence, cosmopolitanism and the law', *British Journal of Criminology*, 48: 39–54.

Young, A. (1998) 'Violence as seduction: Enduring genres of rape', in A. Howe (ed.) *Sexed Crime in the News*. Sydney: The Federation Press.

Young, W. (1983) *Rape Study: A Discussion of Law and Practice. Volume I*. Wellington: Institute of Criminology and Department of Justice.

## Chapter 13

# Co-ordinating responses to domestic violence

*Nicole Westmarland*

**Meet Nicole Westmarland**

Nicole is a senior lecturer in Criminology at Durham University. Most of her work has focused on male violence against women, including domestic violence, rape, forced marriage and prostitution. Between 2003 and 2009 she was chair of Rape Crisis (England and Wales) – the national network of Rape Crisis Centres. She continues to be a trustee of her local group: Tyneside Rape Crisis. It is important to her to continue involvement in the grass-roots women's movement, which is central to the direction of her academic work. Nicole has completed two studies on domestic violence perpetrators and it is this area of work that she will be focusing on over the next three years. With Professor Liz Kelly, she will be managing an ESRC funded study investigating the effectiveness of domestic violence perpetrator programmes, in order to answer the question 'What do perpetrator programmes add to co-ordinated community reponses to domestic violence?'

**Introduction**

Domestic violence is an international problem which affects large numbers of women and a smaller, but still considerable, number of men as victim survivors. Although it is often seen solely as a criminal justice matter, its impacts are deep and wide ranging. For example, it can have extensive consequences for the health of victim survivors (e.g. Doyal 1995; Department of Health 2000) and long-lasting effects on children. The cost to the public purse of domestic violence is substantial (Stanko *et al.* 1997; Walby 2004; Westmarland *et al.* 2005).

This chapter starts by considering definitional issues, the nature and extent of domestic violence, a description of how domestic violence fits within Kelly's continuum of sexual violence, and an overview of domestic violence perpetrators. The policy context is then described, through an analysis of six key shifts that have taken place in relation to domestic violence since the publication of Kelly's 1988 *Surviving Sexual Violence*. These key shifts are:

1. the shift to multi-agency working and information sharing from confidentiality and single-agency responses;
2. the recognition of the incidence, prevalence and costs of domestic violence;
3. the expansion of services and development of new interventions;
4. shifting priorities – started with repeat victimisation (volume) then risk (seriousness) – now both;
5. recognition of the importance of prevention work; and
6. the widening policy agenda.

### Defining domestic violence

In *Surviving Sexual Violence*, Kelly (1988) takes a feminist approach to domestic violence, placing it within the context of a patriarchal society whereby men's power over women leads them to assume a right of sexual access to women and justifies some level of force and coercion. She highlights that the term 'domestic violence' was not in use until the mid 1970s. Since then, the definition of domestic violence has changed, and the term now has a wider meaning than ever before. Changes over time have included: a widening of the boundaries used to classify behaviours as 'domestic violence'; a recognition of violence within same-sex relationships; the inclusion of so-called 'honour'-based violence; and the extending of the definition of relationships in which domestic violence can take place (predominantly an expansion from ex/partner to ex/partner and other family members). Some, predominantly local authorities, now prefer to use the term 'domestic abuse', in recognition that many of the behaviours listed within definitions do not involve physical violence.

In practice, the terms 'domestic violence' and 'domestic abuse' are generally used interchangeably to mean the same thing. In the early 2000s, most domestic violence definitions (including that of the Home Office) referred to violence within intimate relationships only (Hester and Westmarland 2005). However, most now include violence against other family members, including so-called 'honour' violence. For example, Women's Aid defines domestic violence as:

> ...physical, sexual, psychological or financial violence that takes place within an intimate or family-type relationship and that forms a pattern of coercive and controlling behaviour. This can include forced marriage and so-called 'honour crimes'. Domestic violence may include a range of abusive behaviours, not all of which are in themselves inherently 'violent'.
>
> (Women's Aid 2010: website)

Within the criminal justice framework, there is no single crime termed 'domestic violence'. Instead, perpetrators are arrested for a range of criminal offences that can also be committed within a non domestic violence context. The most common offences that domestic violence perpetrators are arrested for include: criminal damage, common assault, actual bodily harm, harassment, threat to kill and theft (Westmarland and Hester 2006; Hester *et al.* 2008). In other words, a perpetrator might be arrested, charged and convicted for criminal damage within a domestic violence context, but it would be 'criminal damage' and not 'domestic violence' that they would have on their criminal record and for which they would be sentenced.

In 2003 the government considered but ultimately decided against introducing a specific offence of 'domestic violence', or to include it as an aggravating factor when sentencing. They argued that in order to ensure that violence and abuse within the home are treated as seriously as crimes outside of the home, both forms of offence should be treated the same within the criminal justice system:

> The Government believes that a separate offence of domestic violence would not necessarily help victims. There is a full range of charging options already. To reduce that range – common assault through to grievous bodily harm, and rape – diminishes the offence.
>
> (HM Government 2003: 29)

While this approach does make some theoretical sense, it encounters problems in practice. A range of studies have noted that perpetrators reported to the police for domestic violence are very unlikely to be convicted and punished for their offence. In a study in the Northumbria Police area, it was found that only four out of 869 domestic violence incidents resulted in the suspect being convicted and given a custodial sentence (this equates to 0.4 per cent of incidents – less than one in 200) (Hester *et al.* 2003; Hester 2006). In a study in Bristol, only seven out of 784 domestic violence incidents resulted in the suspect being convicted and given a custodial sentence (this equates to 0.9 per cent of incidents – less than one in a hundred) (Westmarland and Hester 2006). Critics of these figures point out that not all of these incidents are 'crimes', and therefore many could never result in a conviction regardless of the effectiveness of the investigation and prosecution (for example, the Crown Prosecution Service publish higher conviction rates based on recorded crimes, not incidents; see for example Crown Prosecution Service Management Information Branch 2007). However, herein lies one of two crucial problems which relate to definitional issues in this area: despite a range of campaigns proclaiming that 'domestic violence is a crime', this is not strictly true. Instead, it would be more accurate (though admittedly not as eye-catching) to say 'only some forms of domestic violence are crimes'. When commonly used operational definitions of domestic violence are considered, such as those listed above, it is clear that there are behaviours covered by the definition that are not criminal offences. This is more the case for some forms of financial and psychological abuse than for physical and sexual violence. Behaviours such as 'name calling' and 'continuously putting the victim down' are common forms of domestic violence, covered within the Women's Aid definition of domestic violence, but would be difficult if not impossible to fit within the criminal justice framework. Kelly (1988) found that some of the women in her study did not define their experience as 'domestic violence', sometimes using alternative terms such as 'fighting'.

The second key problem in relation to definitional issues is the cumulative nature of domestic violence in contrast to the 'single incident' focus of the criminal justice framework:

> Domestic violence involves patterns of violent and abusive behaviour over time rather than individual acts. However, the criminal justice system is primarily concerned with specific incidents and it can therefore be difficult to apply criminal justice approaches in relation to domestic violence.
>
> (Hester and Westmarland 2006: 35)

The criminal justice framework therefore fails also to account for the 'pattern of coercive and controlling behaviour' that is contained within many definitions of domestic violence. Therefore, the lived experiences of domestic violence victim survivors are arguably close to definitions of domestic violence, but they continue to be some distance from how domestic violence is defined within the criminal justice framework.

## Domestic violence and Kelly's continuum of sexual violence

Kelly (1988) applies the notion of a continuum to domestic violence in terms of frequency, severity, and the form/s of violence and abuse experienced. In terms of frequency, she found that over half (53 per cent) of the women in her sample had experienced domestic violence. She acknowledges that this is higher than other studies had found, and explains that some of her participants had been interviewed specifically because they had disclosed that they were a survivor of domestic violence, thereby increasing the prevalence rate within her sample. She also notes that the frequency of domestic violence within a relationship varies, which can be viewed as another continuum. In terms of a continuum of severity, Kelly notes that murder lies at the most extreme end, along with attempted suicide. Indeed, a substantial proportion of the women she interviewed had either attempted or contemplated suicide. The form/s of violence and abuse experienced are described as being a variable combination of the threat of violence, emotional violence, forced sex and physical assault. Among the women in Kelly's sample, the threat of violence was found to be the most common, with 100 per cent of those disclosing domestic violence being threatened with violence on at least one occasion.

The critique above of the 'single incident', and arguably narrow, definition of domestic violence within the criminal justice framework fits with the experiences described by the women in Kelly's study. Kelly highlighted there were multiple experiences of a range of violent and abusive behaviours disclosed within her interviews. Ultimately, she argued, it is essential to hold on to the complexity of women's experiences. This chimes closely with the Swedish Women's Peace reforms in 1988, whereby a new offence of 'gross violation of a woman's integrity' was created. This new law enables more emphasis to be given to repeated incidents, and has been linked to higher reporting and conviction rates (Lindström 2005).

## Nature and extent of domestic violence

It is very difficult to determine how much domestic violence occurs, as figures are dependent upon which definition is used and how the violence and abuse is measured. Official crime statistics (cases reported to the police) and self-report figures (through the British Crime Survey) are discussed below.

### Official crime statistics

Official crime statistics are the most likely of the two aforementioned measures to underestimate domestic abuse. This is because the definition of domestic violence used is narrowed by the criminal justice framework (as discussed above) and because a large proportion of domestic violence incidents are not reported to the police (Gracia 2004; Hester and Westmarland 2005). Unlike many other forms of crime, official crime statistics for incidents of domestic violence reported to the police are difficult to find. This is because it is not a single crime, and is therefore reliant upon police officers 'flagging' a case as domestic violence. This, in turn, relies upon police officers recognising an incident as being within a domestic violence context. Even with this potential undercounting, it is clear that domestic violence constitutes a large volume of reported crimes. In 2007–08, in England and Wales, there were 686,000 domestic violence incidents reported to the police (Thompson 2010). A proportion of these incidents results in homicide. Official Home Office homicide statistics for England and Wales (taken from Coleman and Osborne 2010) show that in 2008–09, 53 per cent (n=102) of female homicide victims were killed by their partner or ex-partner. This compares with 7 per cent (n=32) of male homicide victims. This means that an average of two women per week are killed by a partner or ex-partner – a statistic that has remained stable over time. As a cumulative figure this makes for even more difficult reading – in the USA between 1976 and 1996 a total of 31,260 women were killed by an intimate partner (US Department of Justice 1998).

### Self-report studies

Self-report studies ask men and women directly about their experiences of domestic violence rather than relying on police reports. Typically, such studies show much higher rates of domestic violence than are shown in official statistics. In England and Wales the governmental self-report crime study is the British Crime Survey. Domestic violence and other forms of interpersonal violence are measured through a special intimate partner violence module which is periodically added on to the main 'sweep' of the survey. The most recent sweep of the intimate partner violence module was conducted in 2008–09 and covers emotional, financial and physical abuse by partners and/or family members. It also includes all sexual violence and stalking (not limited to partners and/or family members). The questions are given as a 'self-completion' module, which means that the person answering the questions does not need to verbally disclose their answers to an interviewer (this method was introduced in 2001 following criticisms of early versions of the British Crime Survey). It asks adults aged between 16 and 59 (this limited age range remains a common criticism of the survey) about whether they have experienced certain violent and abusive behaviours either within the past 12 months or since the age of 16.

The findings show that more than one in four women (28 per cent) and around one in six men (16 per cent) disclose experiencing at least one form of domestic abuse since the age of 16 (Roe 2009). It is estimated that this equates to around 4.5 million female and 2.6 million male victims (Roe 2009). The data also show that women are more likely than men to be repeat victims, to have experienced injuries as a result of the abuse, to have experienced abuse more than 20 times in the past 12 months and to have experienced domestic abuse for six years or more (Roe 2009).

## Domestic violence perpetrators

The term 'domestic violence perpetrator' can conjure up a picture of an outwardly aggressive, violent man who instils fear into those around him. In fact, the reality is often very different and many of the perpetrator's friends, family and colleagues would never suspect that they use violence towards their partner. In 2004, Dobash et al. compared the backgrounds of 424 men who had murdered other men with 106 men who had murdered an intimate partner. They were particularly interested in the relative conventionality of each of the groups, and found that in many ways the men who had murdered an intimate partner were actually more 'ordinary' or 'conventional' than the men who had murdered other men (Dobash et al. 2004). Hester et al. (2006) developed a typology of domestic violence perpetrators who were reported to the police. One of the groups of perpetrators, the 'dedicated repeat domestic violence' group, was especially likely to appear non-violent or even 'placid' to their friends or to agencies they came into contact with. One of the men, for example, repeatedly punched and kicked his pregnant girlfriend and smashed a glass over her head. He explained in his research interview:

> ...I said to my friend, I says, would you say I was a violent person? [He looked] shocked straight away, because like, in the situations we were in, I would be the one that would try and diffuse it, say to someone, look, things aren't that bad, you know, then try and diffuse the situation...I says well tell that to my fiancée.
>
> (interview with 'Grant', cited in Hester et al. 2006: 6)

Similarly, 'Brendan', who hospitalised his wife, told of his friends' reactions to finding out he was a domestic violence perpetrator:

> They find it funny that I'm doing this [perpetrator programme]. Even my

doctor says I'm a very placid person.

(interview with 'Brendan', cited in Hester *et al*. 2006: 6)

The most frequent response to domestic violence perpetrators who are seeking to change their behaviour is assessment for suitability onto a domestic violence perpetrator programme. These tend to take a feminist-inspired, cognitive behavioural approach and consist of weekly group work sessions which aim to educate men about gender equality within relationships and how to eliminate their use of violent, abusive and controlling behaviour. For example, the aims of the Probation Service's Integrated Domestic Abuse Programme (IDAP) are: to:

- provide known victims and current partners of men undertaking IDAP with information to inform safety planning;
- help men undertaking IDAP understand why they use violence and abuse against partners and ex partners, and the effects of this behaviour on their partners, children, others and themselves;
- encourage men to take responsibility for their violence in their relationships;
- motivate men to take specific positive steps to change their behaviours in their relationships;
- encourage men to learn how to use non-controlling behaviour strategies in their relationships in order to prevent future violence and abuse.

Such programmes are now widespread within the criminal justice field (through prison and probation for court-mandated perpetrators) but there are very few community programmes (for non-court-mandated perpetrators). Fewer than one in ten local authorities (n=37) in Britain has a voluntary sector domestic violence perpetrator programme (Coy *et al*. 2009). Of those that do exist, over half (n=19) are located in just three regions – in London, the north-east and the north-west (Coy *et al*. 2009). Although the criminal justice programmes are more widespread, even they are not able to keep up with the number of offenders sentenced for domestic violence related offences – there are not enough places on programmes for all offenders and waiting lists can be long (Bullock *et al*. 2010).

It is argued that the stilted development of community domestic violence perpetrator programmes in the UK is, in part, due to a lack of evidence in terms of whether programmes 'work' (Westmarland *et al*. 2010). There has been a lack of clarity about what 'works' means in this context, with many of the early studies using only police reports of physical violence, and/or only using convicted offenders. The largest UK study was undertaken by Dobash *et al* (2000) in Scotland, who compared two groups of men convicted for domestic violence related offences. The first group were sentenced to attend a domestic violence perpetrator programme, and the second received an alternative criminal justice sentence. They found that those attending the perpetrator programme were less likely to be using violence in a relationship after 12 months than those receiving alternative sentences. In the US, Gondolf (2002) included both court- and non-court-mandated men in his multi-site evaluation of 600 men who had attended well-established perpetrator programmes. He compared those who completed the programme with those who dropped out of the programme in the early stages. Gondolf found that men who completed the programme were far more likely to stop using violence than men who dropped out, and that the majority of men who completed the programme were no longer using violence within a relationship at the four-year follow-up point.

Narrow understandings of 'success' are also argued to have contributed to the stilted development. When a range of different stakeholders (men on programmes, female ex/partners, practitioners, funders/commissioners) are asked what success means from their perspective, it is clear that success is wider than the cessation of physical violence. Westmarland *et al.* (2010) argue that when these different stakeholders are asked about what success means to them, their responses, and thus the notion of the 'success', can be broken down into six key criteria (which apply whether the partners stay together or decide to separate):

1. an improved relationship between men on programmes and their partners/ex-partners which is underpinned by respect and effective communication;
2. for partners/ex-partners to have an expanded 'space for action' which empowers through restoring their voice and ability to make choices, while improving their well-being;
3. safety and freedom from violence and abuse for women and children;
4. safe, positive and shared parenting;
5. enhanced awareness of self and others for men on programmes, including an understanding of the impact that domestic violence had on their partner and children;
6. for children, safer, healthier childhoods in which they feel heard and cared about.

## The policy context

When Kelly was writing *Surviving Sexual Violence* in the 1980s, there was no central government leadership on domestic violence. This has changed significantly, and there are now a range of policy documents and nationally led interventions, including specialist domestic violence courts, independent domestic violence advisers/advocates, and the Violence Against Women and Girls Strategy. There has also been a range of new legislation, including the 2004 Domestic Violence, Crime and Victims Act and the 1997 Protection from Harassment Act. These are part of key shifts that have occurred over the 20 years since the publication of *Surviving Sexual Violence*. These shifts, which are detailed in depth in the following, have impacted upon current societal and governmental approaches to domestic violence.

**Shift from confidentiality and single-agency responses to multi-agency working and information sharing**

In the early and mid 1980s there was very little information sharing between agencies, particularly between the statutory and voluntary sectors. This began to change in the late 1980s when the first experimental multi-agency projects were established in response to widespread criticism about the adequacy of services for domestic violence victims (Hague 2000). In the 1990s domestic violence forums began to be rolled out across many parts of the country. These forums placed an emphasis upon partnership working, a strategy inspired by the co-ordinated community responses developed in the USA. A model known as the 'Duluth approach' was and continues to be particularly influential. Its name is taken from the first city in Minnesota to establish a co-ordinated community response to domestic violence (see Shepard and Pence 1999). By the turn of the new century it was widely acknowledged in the UK that a multi-agency approach to tackling domestic violence was the way forward (Hague 2000; Humphreys *et al.* 2001), with at least 200 local domestic violence fora in existence (Hague 2000). Similar multi-agency approaches were also beginning to take form in relation to some other crimes, as required under the 1998 Crime and Disorder Act, which required some organisations to form partnerships to tackle crime and disorder.

In 2004, the Home Office issued guidance stressing the importance of safe sharing of personal data in domestic violence cases (Douglas *et al.* 2004). This guidance was issued because of confusion from professionals about what they could and could not share and under which circumstances (Douglas *et al.* 2004). It also followed a number of high-profile cases where information had not been shared – most notably the Soham murders of Holly Wells and Jessica Chapman[1] – but also a number of domestic violence cases. For example:

> In 1999, Mark Goddard was convicted of the murder of his wife Patricia after he stabbed her four times in the chest and abdomen. Patricia's post-mortem examination revealed 38 areas of previous injury and two areas of deep bruising to her scalp. In the five months before her death, her employer and six different agencies were aware of her problems and the abuse she was suffering including health, housing and police services. These agencies had never informed anyone else about their concerns. We cannot know if Patricia's life could have been saved but we do know that a far more comprehensive risk assessment could have been carried out if information had been disclosed to other agencies.
>
> (Douglas *et al.* 2004: Box 3)

The Home Office guidance also listed a range of benefits of responsible information-sharing. It aimed to help domestic violence victims and their children by enabling:

- timely action to be taken to protect clients and children from further abuse;
- comprehensive risk identification and safety planning based on a full account of the facts and circumstances of each client's situation;

- the right sort and combination of advice, support and advocacy to be offered at the right time based on a full and accurate account of the client's needs and history, including other service contact and use;
- clients to avoid the added distress of having to repeat details of their history of experience of domestic violence and other circumstances each time they encounter a different service.

(Douglas *et al.* 2004)

Since then, multi-agency working has become even more entrenched and is now a staple element of responses to domestic violence (see for example the new interventions described below).

## The recognition of the incidence, prevalence and costs of domestic violence

Earlier in the chapter there was a discussion about the different ways of measuring domestic violence. This variety of measures has contributed to a necessary acknowledgement that domestic violence is more widespread than previously thought. Male violence against women is now acknowledged by the United Nations to be of pandemic proportions (United Nations 2006). This recognition that domestic violence is not limited to a minority of 'problem' households has meant that a wide range of professionals have had to accept that domestic violence impacts on their work. Police officers, GPs, health visitors, housing officers, midwives, solicitors and social workers are among the professions that have been required to acknowledge their role in responding to domestic violence (see for example Department of Health 2005; Stanley *et al.* 2009). This has led to a significant increase in the number of professionals involved in domestic violence cases, and an expectation that a wider range of professionals will have the required knowledge and experience needed. Although feminists had certainly already uncovered the high prevalence of domestic violence and other forms of male violence against women (e.g. Hanmer and Saunders 1984), the fact that the government's own crime surveys started to show the same meant that the issue could no longer be ignored or dismissed as feminist exaggeration and/or scaremongering.

In the late 1990s and early 2000s, acceptance of the incidence and prevalence allowed for the calculation of the financial costs of domestic violence. In a small-scale study, Stanko *et al.* (1997) calculated the cost of domestic violence to be £90 for every household in one London Borough. Using British Crime Survey data, Walby (2004) was able to calculate this at a national level. The figures were shocking, and are still regularly cited at policy-makers' and managers' conferences and meetings today. Walby estimated the cost of domestic violence to public services (Criminal Justice System, health care, social services, housing) to be £3.1 billion per annum. The loss to the economy was estimated at £2.7 billion, with an additional £17 billion in human and emotional costs (pain and suffering that is not counted in the cost of services).

## The expansion of services and development of new interventions

Alongside the recognition of the ubiquitous nature of domestic violence there has been an expansion of services and new interventions. Soon after New Labour came into power in 1997, they launched the Crime Reduction Programme, a large-scale research and evaluation programme aimed at understanding what interventions best reduced different types of crime in the most cost-effective manner. One strand of the Crime Reduction Programme was called the Violence Against Women Initiative. This strand was launched in 2000, and aimed to discover which approaches were most effective at tackling domestic violence, rape and sexual assault (see Hester and Westmarland 2005). The Crime Reduction Programme suffered from a range of problems, including the difficulty of assessing the cost-effectiveness of interventions aimed at reducing crimes that are difficult to measure, such as domestic violence and prostitution. However, the lessons learned through the Violence Against Women Initiative have been built upon in subsequent initiatives and evaluations. These include the following.

### Multi-agency risk assessment conferences (MARACs)

MARACs aim to: 'bring local statutory and voluntary agencies together to protect those women at highest risk from repeat victimisation' (HM Government 2009: 17). First developed in South Wales in 2003, MARACs first came onto the national policy agenda in England and Wales in 2006. Soon after, the Home Office (2008) was arguing that they were the 'cornerstone' of their approach to high-risk victims, following nearly two million pounds' investment in domestic violence interventions including MARACs the previous year. By 2009 there were 225 MARACs across England and Wales (Home Office 2009). In summary, MARACs are said to offer benefits such as: increased, ongoing communication; risk assessment; advocacy; the translation of policy into action; and greater accountability for perpetrators (Robinson and Tregidga 2007).

Evaluations of MARACs show some very positive findings regarding their ability to increase the safety of the highest-risk domestic violence victims. The original South Wales MARAC reduced violence as recorded by reported police incidents and self-report interviews with victim survivors (Robinson 2004). Longitudinal research shows that over four in ten victims reported no further violence one year after the MARAC (Robinson and Tregidga 2007). The ability to share information between agencies has been identified as one of the main benefits of a MARAC. As Robinson and Tregidga (2007: 1132–3) explain:

> The communication of information within the meetings serves to fill the gaps in the knowledge of particular cases. Each agency can provide a different and thus crucial perspective. Their differing perspectives enable the jigsaw of individual situations to be pieced together and, therefore, provide a more accurate assessment of risks faced by the women in question.

However, process evaluations have revealed difficulties with MARACs. These difficulties include: the absence of some key agencies, especially health (Howarth *et al.* 2009; Coy and Kelly 2010), poor understandings of the gendered dynamics of domestic violence (Coy and Kelly 2010), an overreliance on independent domestic violence advisers (IDVAs) in terms of knowledge and follow-up actions (Coy and Kelly 2010; Robinson 2009), and concerns about an increased throughput leading to too many cases, inappropriate risk thresholds and the premature closing of cases (Coy *et al.* 2009). These are all issues which could, arguably, be altered and lead to improved MARACs. However, a further critical concern is based deeper at the roots of what a MARAC is about. This is the 'disregard of victim-survivor consent and respect for their privacy rights' (Coy and Kelly 2010: 109), whereby victim survivors may not even know that their case is being discussed at a MARAC or that professionals are sharing personal information about them and their children. This means that something told in apparent confidence to one professional may then be shared with many more at a MARAC if the victim is assessed as being high risk. This is the opposite of the empowerment model that feminists have argued for many years should be placed at the centre of any domestic violence interventions.

### Independent domestic violence advisers (IDVAs)

IDVAs are 'trained specialists providing independent advocacy and support to high-risk victims' (HM Government 2009: 7). The first hundred were trained in 2005/06 and by 2009 there were over 700 across England and Wales (HM Government 2009). The previous government had promised further investment (over £5 million) into IDVAs and MARACs in 2010/11; however, at the time of writing it is unclear whether these interventions will be prioritised by the coalition government.

IDVAs are designed to provide support to ensure a co-ordinated community response to domestic violence. For example, their role within a MARAC is a central one. However, serious concerns have been levelled at the policy of funding IDVAs (and their sister independent sexual violence advisers – ISVAs). First, it can be argued that they simply duplicate existing voluntary sector services, meaning that IDVAs are receiving funding in place of long-standing women's sector organisations that have arguably been doing the work of an IDVA for many years or even decades (since the 1970s in some cases). The term 'advocacy' is wide ranging and is often used to mean different things (Kelly and Humphreys 2000), since it draws upon both the legal context and rights-based approaches (Hester and Westmarland 2005). Many have highlighted that although advocacy is a relatively new concept, it is not a new practice, since aspects of it have always been integral to services within the women's movement (Coy and Kelly 2010). Likewise, Robinson (2009) points out that 'the label is newer than the type of work' (p. 11), meaning that while 'IDVAs' and 'advocacy' have not always been the terms used, the forms of support they offer have long been available. One of the interviewees in Coy and Kelly's (2010) study of IDVAs in London reported that the only difference between their IDVAs and other workers was whether they had been on a particular training course. One aspect that separates the

IDVA role from existing responses to domestic violence may be their focus on only those cases that are assessed as high risk. Coy and Kelly (2010) cite many interviewees in their study who were of this opinion. However, this in itself has raised concerns that IDVAs, alongside MARACs, have meant that the government's core response was not to domestic violence per se, but only to *high-risk* domestic violence victims. As one of the IDVA managers interviewed in Coy and Kelly (2010) highlights:

> Funding for advice workers, no one's interested in funding for that really. All the money's in high risk. Which is kind of counter-productive…We'll wait for them to get high risk and then we can work with you.
>
> (IDVA manager, cited in Coy and Kelly 2010: 32)

A second key concern levelled at IDVAs is their very name. As the 'I' in IDVA stands for 'independent', there is arguably an assumption made that they will be located within the voluntary and community specialist domestic violence sector. However, this is not always the case, and IDVAs are frequently located within other organisations, including the police. In a national evaluation of IDVAs, Robinson (2009) found that 'independence' has been acknowledged as one of the key ingredients of an effective IDVA service. Accordingly, the evaluation concluded that IDVAs should be managed by specialist domestic violence projects. Where this was the case, IDVAs were able to prioritise victim safety and provide essential 'institutional advocacy' within a co-ordinated community response whereby they were able to inform and change practice within multi-agency partnerships.

### Specialist domestic violence courts (SDVCs)

SDVCs are multi-agency approaches to domestic violence which aim to identify and risk assess domestic violence cases and provide additional support for victims in order to bring more offenders to justice (HMCS, HO and CJS 2008). By the end of 2009, there were 127 specialist domestic violence courts (SDVCs) in England and Wales (HM Government 2009). Rather than being a physically separate building, the term SDVC refers to a 'whole system' approach – typically one court within a standard magistrates' court will be allocated all domestic violence cases on a given day and there will be specially trained magistrates and support workers in attendance. There is now a range of studies which confirm that a key benefit of a SDVC is to increase the likelihood of consistent decision-making and appropriate sentencing following conviction (Westmarland 2009). Additional benefits that have been identified are improvements in a range of areas, including court and support services for victims, advocacy and information sharing, and victim participation and satisfaction (leading to increased public confidence in the criminal justice system) (Cook *et al.* 2004).

### Shifting priorities – started with repeat victimisation (volume) then risk (seriousness) – now both

In the 1990s, when policy-makers first began to take domestic violence seriously, attention was placed on the high levels of 'repeat victimisation'. Repeat victimisation began as a policing term in recognition that a small number of people are exposed to an inordinate amount of criminal offences, where 'the same person or place suffers from more than one incident over a specified period of time' (Bridgeman and Hobbs 1997). Domestic violence, by definition being a pattern of incidents over time against the same victim/s, is a prime example of an offence with a high level of repeat victimisation. As most governments' crime and disorder agendas are to reduce crime, tackling offenders who commit high volumes can make a big difference to official crime statistics. In 1995/96 the Home Office designated the reduction of repeat victimisation as a policing performance indicator, meaning that additional focus was given to domestic violence.

Farrell *et al.* (1993) conducted one of the first British studies into repeat victimisation of domestic violence reported to the police. They found that there exists a 'heightened risk period' whereby a household with a domestic violence incident reported to the police has an 80 per cent chance of another domestic violence incident within one year. In the shorter term, after an initial incident, 35 per cent reported a second incident to the police within five weeks. After a second, 45 per cent reported a third incident within a further five week time period. In Sherman's (1992) US study on domestic violence, cases of this nature were labelled the 'chronic cases'.

Hanmer *et al.* (1999) published a key study entitled *Arresting Evidence*, in which they evaluated an innovative new approach to repeat victimisation introduced by West Yorkshire police. This approach consisted of a three-tiered graded response to domestic violence incidents reported to the police. The responses placed an equal focus on the victim and the offender, and the response levels were of increasing intensity. It was found that the new approach both reduced repeat victimisation (the proportion of incidents that were one-off increased from 66 per cent to 85 per cent) and increased the time intervals between incidents (the time between attendances increased to over one year for 50 per cent of men).

Over time, it became clear that the victims who were frequently known to the police were not necessarily those who were at the highest risk of domestic homicide. For example, the highest-risk victims may be those who are most scared of contacting the police, or they may have rung the police once but, having received a poor response, decided it was not safe or worthwhile making further contact.

The notion of assessing a person and assigning them a category of risk is a relatively recent innovation and relates to the risk of homicide or serious harm from which recovery can be expected to be difficult or impossible (Howarth *et al.* 2009). However, in a review of 13 domestic violence murders, Thornton (n.d.) found that seven had no prior domestic violence incidents reported to the police. Of those that had had police involvement and been risk assessed, none had been assessed as high risk using the DASH risk assessment[2] (of the six assessed, one was assessed as medium and five as standard). In addition, one study found there to be no correlation between police risk assessment level and arrest, with incidents rated as 'high risk' not significantly more likely to result in arrest than those rated as lower risk (Hester and Westmarland 2006). This means that questions must be asked about the effectiveness and usefulness of risk assessing discrete incidents rather than the overall pattern of behaviour (Hester and Westmarland 2006).

## Recognition of the importance of prevention work

The response to domestic violence internationally has been to situate the victim and any children at the heart of interventions so as to ensure their safety (Westmarland and Hester 2006). This focus is also acknowledged in the HM Government Violence Against Women and Girls Strategy, which outlines plans to include work on prevention and states that:

> Traditionally, effort has been concentrated on providing support services once women have been victimised. But it is just as important to focus on proactive interventions to prevent violence as reactive services for those who need help after the event.
>
> (HM Government 2009: 20)

However, since the end of a relationship does not necessarily signal an end to the perpetration of domestic violence, this means that a focus solely on the victim and children cannot in itself reduce domestic violence substantially over time (Westmarland and Hester 2006). Domestic abusers may go on to reoffend against new partners (Hester and Westmarland 2006) or continue to abuse the original partner and children in other ways, for example through child contact arrangements (Hester and Radford 1996; Radford and Hester 2006). In a longitudinal study of domestic violence perpetrators reported to the police, exactly half the perpetrators (50 per cent) were reported again on at least one occasion during the three-year follow-up period (Hester and Westmarland 2006). Nearly one in five (18 per cent) of the perpetrators who reoffended did so against a different partner from the one they originally offended against (Hester and Westmarland 2006). Some women's support projects report providing support to a series of different women over time who have all accessed support in relation to the same perpetrator (Westmarland and Hester 2006).

Despite acknowledgement that to end violence against women requires investment in primary prevention (to prevent violence from happening in the first place) and secondary prevention (to prevent violence from continuing or increasing once identified) work, such investment has not yet surfaced. As budgets are again rolled back as part of the present international financial crisis, it is likely to be some time before the investment that is needed can be fully implemented. Until then, any prevention work will remain piecemeal, and it continues to be difficult to imagine a world free from violence against women.

**The widening policy agenda**

Rather than standing alone, domestic violence now fits as one area of a policy response to violence against women. This was not the case throughout the 1990s and much of the 2000s. Kelly and Regan (2001) refer to the 1990s as the 'decade of domestic violence', by which they mean that domestic violence took precedence over other forms of violence against women, and issues such as rape and other forms of sexual abuse were sidelined. Feminists have long argued that there are overlaps between forms of violence against women and that a gender-based analysis is key to understanding and tackling such violences. This is clearly inherent within Kelly's aforementioned continuum of abuse.

The encompassing of domestic violence within a wider framework of violence against women has been a long task, and one which Kelly (as chair of the End Violence Against Women Initiative) has been central to. In fact, after many years lobbying government to develop an integrated violence against women strategy, Kelly and Lovett in 2005, in reference with women's groups, developed their own outline of what should be included in a national violence against women strategy. They proposed that a national strategy should include: a long-term commitment to prevention; clear goals and priorities; the co-ordination of interventions for different forms of violence and abuse; and an evaluation of the impact of these interventions on the prevalence and seriousness of abuse. The lack of an integrated strategy was also highlighted in a number of submissions to the United Nations Committee on the Elimination of all forms of Discrimination Against Women (CEDAW) (see for example submissions by Sen and Kelly 2007; the Women's National Commission 2008; and Women's Resource Centre 2008). Subsequently, the UK was specifically questioned on their lack of such a strategy during their examination by the Committee in 2008, despite their protestations that such a strategy existed in 'all but name' (United Nations 2008: 9).

It was not until late 2009 that the government launched its integrated violence against women policy entitled *Together We Can End Violence Against Women and Girls* (HM Government 2009). Here, the government accepted that:

> A number of initiatives over the last decade have made a real difference, but many of these have focused only on specific offences. These distinctions can create artificial barriers. For example many women suffer both domestic and sexual abuse in the same relationship. Although the Government has published a number of separate plans in recent years for dealing with different problems, so far these have not been brought together in one place.
>
> (HM Government 2009: 4)

This recognition of the importance of looking across different forms of violence against women in designing effective responses had already been taking place on the ground in some policy documents. A good example of this can be found within the national police guidance for investigating domestic violence cases (NPIA 2008). Here is listed a range of 'potential associated investigations' which includes: harassment, child abuse, honour-based violence, prostitution, missing persons and vulnerable adult abuse. They also highlight that the police may be called to incidents that are 'not overtly domestic abuse' (NPIA 2008: 18) where they include street disturbances and public order matters such as breach of the peace, antisocial behaviour, neighbourhood disputes, nuisance calls, animal abuse, criminal damage and assaults. They advise: 'Whatever the type of incident, it is essential that the domestic abuse element is properly identified, including risk, and the necessary processes and support services put into place' (NPIA 2008: 18). This level of understanding and leadership constitutes an important positive shift in responding to domestic violence and is one that differs significantly from the position of the late 1980s.

## Conclusions

Domestic violence is said to have moved from the margins to the centre, in which central and local government in the UK now view and respond to domestic violence in a way that would have been unthinkable in the 1970s and 1980s (Hague 2006). This increased attention has given rise to a massive expansion of research, policy and practice documents. In 1988, Kelly wrote:

> If I had begun this research project in 1987 the thought of reviewing the existing literature on sexual violence would have produced mild hysteria. Since the 1970s there has been a 'knowledge explosion'...
>
> (p. 43)

The violence against women knowledge explosion has kept on erupting, and now even reviewing one sub-area of the study of violence against women (for example child contact, perpetrator programmes, health impacts) is enough to produce moderate hysteria! This knowledge explosion is ultimately a positive step. Although it makes it difficult for researchers to be confident that they have conducted a full and thorough literature review (especially given the expansion of the Internet and the ease of access of organisational 'grey' literature), there is now more knowledge available than ever before. This upwards trajectory will undoubtedly continue into the future. What is needed at this juncture are several very large-scale, multi-country studies to synthesise and consolidate existing knowledge and test hypotheses on a large scale.

The recognition that no single agency can provide a full response to domestic violence, since domestic violence cuts across so many different agencies, has been important (Hague 2006). The recognition was necessary to instigate the shifts discussed above, for example the need for information sharing and acknowledgement of the ubiquitous nature of violence against women. Given these shifts, it might be concluded that the situation for domestic violence victims is better in 2010 than it was in 1988. However, this is not necessarily the case. While there have certainly been some major steps forward, for example joining up policy on different forms of violence against women, there remain some significant limitations. The main limitations are the continued lack of primary and secondary prevention work and, linked to this, a continued lack of focus on domestic violence perpetrators. Therefore, although there are now some improved services for victim survivors of domestic violence since Kelly wrote *Surviving Sexual Violence* in 1988, it remains the case that we are still a long way away from actually ending domestic violence.

## Further reading

For a general overview of domestic violence, including policy and practice responses, a good starting point is *Domestic Violence – Action for Change*, by Gill Hague and Ellen Malos (2005, third edition). In terms of offenders, Dobash *et al.*'s 2004 study of men convicted of murder is a fascinating article. To help visualise the lack of specialist services on the ground in relation to domestic violence, see Coy *et al.*'s (2009) *Map of Gaps*. For a USA perspective, but with many of the examples used also being relevant in the UK, *Coercive Control* (2009) by Evan Stark provides joined up thinking on a lot of debates on domestic violence.

Hague, G. and Malos, E. (2005) *Domestic Violence: Action for Change* (3rd edn.). Cheltenham: New Clarion Press.
Stark, E. (2009) *Coercive Control: How Men Entrap Women in Personal Life*. New York: OUP USA.

## Notes

1 In 2002 Holly Wells and Jessica Chapman, both aged ten, were murdered by Ian Huntly in Soham, Cambridgeshire. In 2003 the Bichard Enquiry was tasked with investigating alleged failings in relation to the storage and sharing of police intelligence. The police were heavily criticised within the Bichard Report and a number of recommendations were made.
2 The Domestic Abuse, Stalking and Harassment and Honour Based Violence (DASH) Risk Identification, Assessment and Management Model is the Association of Chief Police Officers (ACPO) accredited model (see www.dashriskchecklist.co.uk for further information)

## References

Bridgeman, C. and Hobbs, L. (1997) *Preventing Repeat Victimisation: the police officer's guide*. London: Home Office.
Bullock, K., Sarre, S., Tarling, R. and Wilkinson, M. (2010) T*he delivery of domestic abuse programmes – an implementation study of the delivery of domestic abuse programmes in probation areas and Her Majesty's Prison Service*, Ministry of Justice Research Series 15/10. London: Ministry of Justice.
Coleman, K. and Osborne, S. (2010) 'Homicide', in K. Smith and J. Flatley (eds) *Homicides, Firearm Offences and Intimate Violence 2008/09 – Supplementary volume 2 to crime in England and Wales 2008/09*. London: Home Office.
Cook, D., Burton, M., Robinson, A. and Vallely, C. (2004) *Evaluation of Specialist Domestic Violence Courts/Fast Track Systems*. London: Crown Prosecution Service and Department for Constitutional Affairs.
Coy, M., Kelly, L. and Foord, J. (2009) *Map of Gaps 2 – The Postcode Lottery of Violence*

*Against Women Support Services in Britain.* London: End Violence Against Women Coalition and Equality and Human Rights Commission.

Coy, M. and Kelly, L. (2010) I*slands in the Stream: An evaluation of four Independent Domestic Violence Advocacy Schemes in London.* London: Trust for London/Henry Smith Charity.

Crown Prosecution Service Management Information Branch (2007) Domestic violence monitoring snapshot, available at: http://www.cps.gov.uk/publications/prosecution/domestic/snapshot_2006_12.html

Department of Health (2000) *Domestic Violence – A resource manual for health care professionals.* London: Department of Health.

Department of Health (2005) *Responding to Domestic Abuse: A Handbook for health professionals.* London: Department of Health.

Dobash, R.E., Dobash, R.P., Cavanagh, K. and Lewis, R. (2000) *Changing Violent Men.* London: Sage Publications.

Dobash, R.E., Dobash, R.P., Cavanagh, K. and Lewis, R. (2004) 'Not an ordinary killer – Just an ordinary guy: When men murder an intimate woman partner', *Violence Against Women*, 1(6): 577–605.

Douglas, N., Lilley, S.J., Kooper, L. and Diamond, A. (2004) *Safety and Justice: sharing personal information in the context of domestic violence – an overview*, Home Office Development and Practice Report. London: Home Office.

Doyal, L. (1995) *What Makes Women Sick – Gender and the political economy of health.* London: Macmillan Press.

Farrell, G., Clarke, K. and Pease, K. (1993) 'Arming the toothless tiger: Court injunctions, family protection orders and domestic violence', *Justice of the Peace*, 6 February: 88–90.

Gondolf, E.W. (2002) *Batterer Intervention Systems: Issues, outcomes and recommendations.* California: Sage.

Gracia, E. (2004) 'Unreported cases of domestic violence against women: towards an epidemiology of social silence, tolerance, and inhibition', *Journal of Epidemiology and Community Health*, 58: 536–7.

Hague, G. (2000) *Reducing domestic violence…What works? Multi-agency fora*, Crime Reduction Research Series No. 4. London: Home Office.

Hague, G. (2006) Guest editors' introduction, *Violence Against Women*, 12: 531–42.

Hanmer, J., Griffiths, S. and Jerwood, D. (1999) *Arresting evidence: Domestic violence and repeat victimization*, Policing and Reducing Crime Unit Paper 104. London: Home Office.

Hanmer, J. and Saunders, H. (1984) *Well Founded Fear: Community study of violence to women.* London: HarperCollins Publishers Ltd.

Hester, M. (2006) 'Making it through the Criminal Justice System: Attrition and domestic violence', *Social Policy and Society*, 5: 79–90.

Hester, M., Hanmer, J., Coulson, S., Morahan, M. and Razak, A. (2003) *Domestic Violence – making it through the Criminal Justice System.* Sunderland: University of Sunderland and Northern Rock Foundation.

Hester, M. and Radford, L. (1996) *Domestic Violence and Child Contact Arrangements in England and Denmark.* Bristol: The Policy Press.

Hester, M. and Westmarland, N. (2005) *Tackling Domestic Violence – effective interventions and approaches.* London: Home Office.

Hester, M. and Westmarland, N. (2006) 'Domestic violence perpetrators', *Criminal Justice Matters*, 66(1): 34–5.

Hester, M., Westmarland, N., Gangoli, G., Wilkinson, M., O'Kelly, C. *et al.* (2006) *Domestic Violence Perpetrators: Identifying Needs to Inform Early Intervention.* Bristol: University of Bristol and Home Office.

Hester, M., Westmarland, N., Pearce, J. and Williamson, E. (2008) *Early evaluation of the Domestic Violence, Crime and Victims Act 2004*, Ministry of Justice Research Series 14/08. London: Ministry of Justice.

HM Government (2003) *Safety and Justice: The Government's Proposals on Domestic Violence*. London: HM Government.

HM Government (2009) *Together We Can End Violencec Against Women and Girls – a strategy*. London: HM Government.

HMCS, HO and CJS (2008) *Justice with Safety: Specialist domestic violence courts review 2007–08*. London: HMCS, HO and CJS.

Home Office (2008) *Saving Lives. Reducing Harm. Protecting the Public: An action plan for tackling violence 2008–11*. London: Home Office.

Home Office (2009) *An Action Plan for Tackling Violence 2008–11 – One year on*. London: Home Office.

Howarth, E., Stimpson, L., Barran, D. and Robinson, A. (2009) *Safety in Numbers: A multisite evaluation of Independent Domestic Violence Advisor Services*. London: The Henry Smith Charity.

Humphreys, C., Hague, G., Hester, M. and Mullender, A. (2001) *Domestic Violence Good Practice Indicators*, Centre for Study of Safety and Well-Being. Warwickshire: University of Warwick.

Kelly, L. (1988) *Surviving Sexual Violence*. Minnesota: University of Minnesota Press.

Kelly, L. and Humphreys, C. (2000) *Outreach and Advocacy Approaches in Reducing Domestic Violence: what works?* London: Home Office.

Kelly, L. and Lovett, J. (2005) *What a Waste. The case for an integrated violence against women strategy*. London: DTI.

Kelly, L. and Regan, L. (2001) *Rape: The Forgotten Issue? A European research and networking project*. University of North London: Child and Woman Abuse Studies Unit.

Lindström, P. (2005) 'Violence against women in Scandinavia: A description and evaluation of two new laws aiming to protect women', *Journal of Scandinavian Studies in Criminology and Crime Prevention*, 5: 220–35.

NPIA (2008) *Investigating Domestic Abuse*. Bramshill: National Policing Improvement Agency.

Radford, L. and Hester, M. (2006) *Mothering through Domestic Violence*. London: Jessica Kingsley.

Robinson, A. (2004) *Domestic Violence MARACs for Very High-risk Victims in Cardiff, Wales: A process and outcome evaluation*. Cardiff: Cardiff University.

Robinson, A.L. (2009) *Independent Domestic Violence Advisors: A process evaluation*. Cardiff: Cardiff University.

Robinson, A.L. and Tregidga, J. (2007) 'The perceptions of high-risk victims of domestic violence to a coordinated community response in Cardiff, Wales', *Violence Against Women*, 13: 1130–48.

Roe, S. (2009) Intimate violence: 2007/08 British Crime Survey, in D. Povey (ed.) *Homicides, Firearm Offences and Intimate Violence 2007/08* (3rd edn), Home Office Statistical Bulletin 02/09. London: Home Office.

Sen, P. and Kelly, L. (2007) *CEDAW Thematic Shadow Report on Violence against Women in the UK*, retrieved from http://www2.ohchr.org/english/bodies/cedaw/docs/ngos/UKThematicReportVAW41.pdf

Shepard, M.F. and Pence, E. (1999) *Coordinating Community Responses to Domestic Violence: Lessons from Duluth and beyond*. London: Sage.

Sherman, L. (1992) *Policing Domestic Violence: Experiments and Dilemmas*. New York: Macmillan.

Stanko, E., Crisp, D., Hale, C. and Lucraft, H. (1997) *Counting the Costs: estimating the impact of domestic violence in the London borough of Hackney*. Swindon: Crime Concern.

Stanley, N., Miller, P., Richardson Foster, H. and Thomson, G. (2009) *Children and Families Experiencing Domestic Violence: Police and children's social services' responses*. London: NSPCC.

Thompson, G. (2010) Domestic violence statistics, standard note: SN/SG/950. London: House of Commons Library.

Thornton. S. (nd) *Does prior history of domestic violence predict domestic murder or other serious assaults?* Powerpoint presentation available at www.crim.cam.ac.uk/news/ebp/documents/pdh.ppt

United Nations (2006) *In-depth Study on All Forms of Violence Against Women, Report of the Secretary-General*. New York: United Nations General Assembly.

United Nations (2008) *Committee on the Elimination of Discrimination against Women, Forty-first session, Summary record of the 843rd meeting*, retrieved from http://daccess-dds-ny.un.org/doc/UNDOC/GEN/N08/417/32/PDF/N0841732.pdf?OpenElement

US Department of Justice (1998) *Violence by intimates: Analysis of data on crimes by current or former spouses, boyfriends, and girlfriends*, March.

Walby, S. (2004) *The Cost of Domestic Violence*. London: Women and Equality Unit.

Westmarland, N. (2009) *Sunderland Specialist Domestic Violence Court – First Year Evaluation*. Durham: Durham University.

Westmarland, N. and Hester, M. (2006) *Time for Change*. Bristol: University of Bristol.

Westmarland, N., Hester, M. and Carrozza, A. (2005) *Domestic Abuse in Bristol. Findings from a 24-hour snapshot*. Bristol: University of Bristol.

Westmarland, N., Kelly, L. and Chalder-Mills, J. (2010) *What Counts as Success?* London: Respect.

Women's National Commission (2008) *Submission to the United Nations' Committee on the Convention on the Elimination of all forms of Discrimination against Women*, retrieved from http://www2.ohchr.org/english/bodies/cedaw/docs/ngos/WNC_UK41.pdf

Women's Resource Centre (2008) *The State of the Women's NGO Sector – Shadow Report submitted to the United Nations Committee on the Elimination of Discrimination against Women (CEDAW) in response to the United Kingdom's 6th Periodic Report*, retrieved from http://www2.ohchr.org/english/bodies/cedaw/docs/ngos/WRCUK41.pdf

Women's Aid website, www.womensaid.org.uk, accessed 21 February 2010.

# Chapter 14

# Destroying women: sexual murder and feminism

*Anette Ballinger*

## Meet Anette Ballinger

Anette Ballinger is a lecturer in Criminology at Keele University. She is the author of the award-winning book *Dead Woman Walking: Executed Women in England & Wales 1900–1955* (Ashgate: 2000) (Hart Socio-Legal Prize 2001), and has written several book chapters and journal articles on the subject of gender and punishment in modern history. More recently her research interests have also included contemporary issues – particularly in relation to state responses to violence against women. She is currently working on a book entitled *Capitalising on Punishment: Gender, Truth and State Power*, to be published by Ashgate.

## Introduction

An account of sexual murder which does not address gender is not merely incomplete, but systematically misleading.

(Cameron and Frazer 1987: 1)

Femicide ... is not some inexplicable phenomenon or the domain only of the mysterious deviant. On the contrary, femicide is an extreme expression of patriarchal 'force'. It, like that other form of sexual violence, rape ..., is a social expression of sexual politics, an institutionalized and ritual enactment of male domination, and a form of terror that functions to maintain the power of the patriarchal order.

(Caputi 1992: 204–5)

One of the most fundamental and enduring achievements of second-wave feminism has been its success in creating new discourses and hence a new language within which violence against women in both the public and private sphere can be understood. Thus, contemporary taken-for-granted terms such as sexual harassment and domestic violence did not enter discourse until the 1970s, when second-wave feminists named such experiences, thereby ensuring that from then onwards, they would no longer be 'unspeakable', but instead become firmly placed on the public agenda.

However, as Liz Kelly has noted, 'the unnamed should not be mistaken for the non-existent' (1988: 141). Hence, while the term 'sexual violence' did not exist until feminists named it as such in the 1970s, and the distinct category, 'sexual murder', did not come into being until the mid to late nineteenth century, when the newly established 'experts' from professions such as psychiatry, psychology and medicine identified it, the existence of these forms of *behaviour* has been evident throughout history. The creation of new discourses such as sexual violence and sexual murder thus brought with them the possibility of identifying 'a tradition', within which abusers and killers of the past, present and future could, and can, be discussed, analysed and understood in ways which were not possible prior to the mid nineteenth century (Cameron and Frazer 1987: 22).

Liz Kelly's book *Surviving Sexual Violence* played an important role in the creation of these new discourses, by identifying and naming specific forms of sexual violence which had hitherto been endured in silence by a substantial section of the female population, despite being part of their everyday lived experiences. For example, Kelly was at the forefront of establishing key terms such as 'survivor' to denote 'the extent to which women are able to reconstruct their lives so that the experience of sexual violence does not have an overwhelming and continuing negative impact on their life' (1988: 163). She also developed the term ' "continuum" to describe both the extent and range of sexual violence' recorded in her research (1988: 74). In this way, Kelly played a key role in creating a new language within which sexual violence against women could be discussed. Moreover, she emphasised that her use of the term 'continuum' should not 'be interpreted as a statement about the relative seriousness of different forms of sexual violence…[because] the degree of impact cannot be simplistically inferred from the form of sexual violence women experience or its place within a continuum…*with the important exception of sexual violence which results in death*' (1988: 76, my emphasis). It is this most extreme form of sexual violence – sexual murder – which is the focus of this chapter. More specifically, through two case studies, that of Peter Sutcliffe, who was found guilty of murdering 13 women in 1981, and Steve Wright, who was convicted of killing five women in 2007, a number of key themes relevant to sexual murder will be explored through a pioneering body of feminist literature published during the same period as Kelly's *Surviving Sexual Violence*.

## A question of definition

The term 'sexual murder' potentially includes a wide variety of deadly violence. If sexual murder is defined as all murders which are in some way linked to a sexual motive, then paedophiles who kill children fall within this category. So do the mass rape and murder of women by enemy soldiers

309

frequently associated with genocide (Maguire 1998). Serial killers who engage in homosexual necrophilia with their victims, such as Dennis Nilsen, clearly belong within this category (Masters 1986). Indeed, the more common forms of murders associated with domestic violence may also include a sexual motive. McNeill (1996), for example, has made a connection between so-called 'honour killings', in which husbands kill their unfaithful wives (and in some cases their lovers too) in defence of their honour in non-European cultures, and men in the UK who utilise the infidelity of their wives or girlfriends as both an excuse and defence for killing them.[1]

The issue of women as perpetrators of sexual murder is periodically debated, most commonly in the wake of an individual (and very rare) high-profile case being uncovered. Such cases typically involve the woman in the role of an accomplice while her male partner is regarded as the main initiator and instigator. While examples of the 'female serial killer' operating alone have been identified intermittently throughout history,[2] there is little or no evidence to suggest that such women killed to satisfy their sexual desire.[3] Even when women take on the role of accomplice in what have been identified as sexual murders, their motives appear more ambivalent, due to their existing relationship with the main male perpetrator of such crimes. One example of such ambivalence can be seen in the case of Myra Hindley, who was found guilty of being Ian Brady's accomplice in five cases of child murder during the 1960s (Cameron and Frazer 1987: 24). Thompson and Richard, in their study of women's role in serial killing teams, note that there was 'no evidence to suggest that Hindley would have committed murder or participated in any serious criminal activity if she had not been in a relationship with Brady ... Hindley's role in the murders was solely based upon her relationship with Brady' (2009: 270).[4]

Thus, while this chapter does not seek to deny women's involvement in sexual murder, it nonetheless maintains that there is no '"gender equivalence" in sexual violence' (Bourke 2009: ix). Apart from the massive statistical imbalance between the men and women involved in such crimes – for example, 'men commit 86% of domestic murders' (Morrison 2008: 22) – the motivations, levels of emotional involvement and indeed physical participation are simply not comparable. This lack of 'gender equivalence' can be understood as being linked to women's subordinate position within a heteropatriarchal social order:

> Patriarchy defines reality in masculine terms and women's worth is identified in relation to her male counterpart – she derives her social status from her relationship with men. When women internalise this ideology, they see their social status as contingent upon their maintenance of relationships with men.
>
> (Thompson and Richard 2009: 273)

Thus, within the context of the male/female sexual murder dyad, women's involvement in such crimes is frequently linked to misguided attempts to maintain their relationship with their partners. With regard to Hindley, for example, Thompson and Richard argue that 'she worried Brady would lose interest in her and seemed willing to do anything to maintain the relationship' (2009: 270). This is not to imply that Hindley, and other women in similar positions, were not willing participants. On the contrary, overemphasising women as irrational, overemotional and victimised beings 'rather than responsible agents' 'reinforces their inequality, and lack of full citizenship, and hence stands in direct conflict with the feminist struggle for gender equality' (Ballinger 2008: 50; Morrissey 2003: 25). As Morrissey notes, 'many portrayals of women who kill depict them as so profoundly victimised that it is difficult to regard them as ever having engaged in an intentional act in their lives' (2003: 25). Thus, it is important to avoid overgeneralising women's oppression, and instead take into account the 'multiple determinants' utilised by individuals to 'act upon themselves and order their own lives in numerous and variable ways' (McNay 1992: 65). Within this context, the analysis adopted here aims to acknowledge 'the reality of power without presenting woman as eternal victim and insists on the agency of the oppressed without denying the reality of oppression' (Connell 1987: 149). In other words, while acknowledging female agency within the constraints of heteropatriarchy, the sheer statistical disparity between women and men involved in violent crime and sexual murder should also be recognised. For example, men commit 90 per cent of all violent crime in the UK (*Guardian Weekend* 10 December 2005) while 'nine out of ten women prisoners have been convicted of non-violent offences' (*Guardian* 3 May 2006). With specific regard to sexual violence, it is estimated that 50,000 rapes occur annually in Britain (*New Statesman* 18 June 2007), and in the London area alone, gang rapes rose by a third between 2001 and 2002 (*Guardian Weekend* 5 June 2004).[5]

With regard to specific types of sexual murder, for example the killing of sex workers, at least 60 such women were murdered in the UK between 1992 and 2002, and 'many more are missing' (*Guardian* 16 September 2002). Indeed, such statistics are mirrored internationally, for example in Canada, where just one man, Robert Pickton, was suspected of having killed 60 prostitutes over two decades, although he eventually stood trial for 'only' 27 of these murders (*Guardian* 5 August 2005). Moreover:

> Women who sell sex in the UK have standardised mortality rates six times higher than the general population, the highest for any group of women; they are 18 times more likely to be murdered…54% of women in the sex industry have suffered violence and 34% have been raped.
>
> (Smith 2008)

Once again, the lack of 'gender equivalence' hardly needs stating. Rather, it is statistics such as these which ensure that no further justification is necessary for concentrating on the subject of sexual murder committed by men against women in the remainder of this chapter. More specifically, these statistics also justify a particular focus on murders involving sex workers.

As with violence towards women in general, violence towards prostitute women in particular also has a long history, as exemplified by the case of Jack the Ripper, who killed five prostitutes in 1888, and the Peter Sutcliffe case which concluded in 1981 when he was convicted of murdering 13 women and injuring another seven. In the aftermath of the Sutcliffe case, a number of authors developed feminist analyses of the gendered nature of sexual murder. Thus, apart from Kelly's book *Surviving Sexual Violence*, other important works were also published during the period 1987–1992, which sought to theorise sexual violence and murder. It is to these works this chapter now turns.

## Killing for pleasure

The fact that sexual killers are without exception male has attracted no sustained discussion that we are aware of. Some writers manage to leave it out completely, while others, implicitly recognising it, nevertheless treat it as totally natural and unproblematic. For a feminist, of course, it is neither of those things. It is a fact about our culture that cries out for explanation.

(Cameron and Frazer 1987: 30)

Cameron and Frazer opened their book *The Lust to Kill* by stating, 'we regard ourselves as seeking out not objective truth, but rather an alternative interpretation of the world' (1987: xi). True to their word, they went on to produce a sophisticated, and arguably underrated, analysis of sexual murder which placed gender at the forefront of their thesis when they maintained that, far from being an aberration, sexual violence is characterised by its normality, albeit at the extreme end on the continuum of 'ordinary' masculinity.

Similarly, Caputi introduced her book *The Age of Sex Crime*, published a year later, by promising 'to provide a political analysis and demythicization of this most extreme form of patriarchal violence' (1988: Preface). Together with Smith's *Misogynies* (1989) and Radford and Russell's edited collection *Femicide* (1992), these books provided a powerful challenge to traditional, androcentric accounts of violence against women – built on feminist theory, method and epistemology.

Caputi identified the persona of Jack the Ripper as instigating the *type* of killer closely associated with sexual murder (1988: 12). In between killing and mutilating five women in the Whitechapel district of London in 1888, he is assumed to be the author of letters sent to the Metropolitan police which allowed him to be characterised as a man of 'irony and wit...a stylish and likeable rogue...rather than the repulsive and lethal misogynist his actions reveal him to be' (Caputi 1988: 21). He has subsequently been described as 'the hero of horrors in Victorian times' (Caputi 1988: 50), thereby illustrating an important discourse within androcentric and misogynistic culture – the murderer as hero – signifying the admiration and celebration frequently surrounding serial killers in both the UK and USA (Caputi 1988: 50–62; Cameron 1992: 186–7).

Smith added another important strand to the history of sexual murder when she identified the film *Psycho* as the first to market 'female fear as a commodity':

In 1960, the shower scene in Hitchcock's *Psycho*...shocked audiences who had never seen anything like it on their cinema screens; today such scenes are ten a penny. Terror, torture, rape, mutilation and murder are handed out to actresses by respectable directors as routinely as tickets to passengers on a bus. No longer the stock in trade only of pornographers and video-nasty producers, they can be purchased any day at a cinema near you.

(1989: 16)

The move from the porn industry to mainstream cinema of the sexualisation of violence had begun, with the consequence that acts of sexual violence had also been moved 'from the sphere of solitary, unadmitted fantasy into the domain of shared experience':

The viewer is no longer alone, those acts which he may have imagined privately, perhaps with a degree of shame, have also been visualised by the screenwriter, the director, the special effects man, and the hundreds of other people involved in the making of a film. And here, sitting in the seats that stretch in front and behind, are dozens of other men who have, like him, paid money to see them.

(Smith 1989: 18)

Smith had thus identified the historical context to the massive expansion of the sex industry which has taken place during recent decades and which, in turn, has brought with it a corresponding increase in the sexualisation of popular culture (Smith 2008; Walter 2010). By implication, she had therefore also provided historical context for the association between sex and violence which, supported by the porn industry, has entered a hitherto unprecedented symbiotic relationship during recent decades (Walter 2010: 102–18).

Radford and Russell termed their edited collection *Femicide* 'an anthology on the politics of woman killing' (1992: xiii). The collection focuses on six important themes within misogynist killing: the history of femicide; the private sphere as a more dangerous place for women than the public sphere; an understanding of femicide as crossing the boundaries of 'race, class and culture', hence, it cannot be confined to any one group or nation; media representations of femicide; the criminal justice system's response to femicide; and the way in which feminist activism plays a crucial role in organising challenges to this crime (1992: xi–xii).

Radford stated that 'one purpose of this anthology has been to name femicide and to identify it as an urgent issue for feminists and others concerned with violence against women' (1992: 351). It did much more than that, demonstrating that this crime is 'as old as patriarchy itself' (1992: 25); that far from being 'unusual and isolated incidents, [femicides are] a recurring expression of male sexual violence'; that woman-blaming explanations for this crime are used so frequently 'that they have become a credible part of mainstream discourse, even encoded in law'; that the state has failed and continues to fail to protect women from femicide; and that media representations of the perpetrators of this crime as psychopaths or 'mad

313

beasts' (1992: 352) 'masks the sexual politics of femicide'(1992: 4).

Thus, taken together, apart from placing the crime of sexual murder within its historical context, and exposing the 'transgressive hero' status of its proponents within a misogynistic culture, these authors had identified a number of other key themes relevant to this subject, including the normalisation and acceptance of sexual violence against women generally and prostitute women in particular; the emphasis on explanations of sexual murder which focus on the pathology of individual offenders to the detriment of the wider culture of masculinity and phallocentricity; and the prevalence of woman-blaming explanations involving significant women in the life of the offender such as mother, wife or the victim herself.

In contrast to the commonsensical comparisons made between Jack the Ripper and the so-called Yorkshire Ripper in true crime literature and the media, these early works presented a feminist challenge to populist representations of sex killers which made a major contribution to gender analyses, as will become apparent in the following section, where the relevance of these key themes is illustrated through the case study of Peter Sutcliffe.

### 'Normal' men, 'normal' violence: early feminist analysis of sexual murder

> The murderer is different from other human beings only in degree and not in kind.
>
> (Cameron and Frazer 1987: 64)

> Is this violence really aberrant, or is it somehow in tune with the workings of our society?
>
> (Cameron and Frazer 1987: 32)

A key aspect of early feminist analysis of sexual murderers was the challenge to mythical stereotypes of the 'sex-beast' or 'psychopath' who is pathologically driven to commit exceptionally violent and gruesome murders; or, alternatively, 'the loner', likely to live with an elderly relative, as suggested by police during the hunt for the Yorkshire Ripper (Smith 2008). The firmly (but wrongly) held belief that the sexual murderer is recognisable from the outside, showing visible signs of his wickedness, and hence stands out as a result of his *difference* to other men, has repeatedly proved to be inaccurate. In relation to the Sutcliffe case, for example, Smith commented:

> One of the chief ironies of the whole Yorkshire Ripper case is that the police spent millions of pounds fruitlessly searching for an outsider when the culprit was just an ordinary bloke, a local man who shared their background and attitudes to a remarkable degree.
>
> (1989: 124)

Similarly, Bland observed:

Sutcliffe, rather than being the loner of the Ripper myth, was a man who was regularly immersed in a normal male culture of drinking, prostitution and violence.

(1992: 251)

Caputi too noted that 'the actual man, Sutcliffe, clashed utterly with the image of the Ripper that had been so pervasively and unforgettably projected' (1988: 44). Instead, it was 'his very ordinariness' which fooled police nine times (Bland 1992: 250). Thus, feminist theorists were able to demonstrate that 'the enormously powerful popular stereotype' of serial killers and/or sexual murderers as 'monsters' or beasts who have nothing in common with 'ordinary' men plays an important role in the maintenance of the heteropatriarchal social order, because it serves to draw attention away from the gendered aspect of such crimes, and instead 'obscures the phenomenon it appears to be explaining' by ignoring the fact that the 'beast' is inevitably *male* (Cameron and Frazer 1987: 35, original emphasis).

Not only did Sutcliffe turn out to represent all the key aspects of 'normal' manhood by being 'a married man living in a semi-detached house in a good suburb' and in full-time employment (Smith 1989: 188), he also engaged in culturally normalised levels of violence against women regularly – another theme identified by feminists in their analysis of sexual murder. Contemporary statistics such as those cited in the introduction, demonstrate this normalisation of violence against women. This was as true three decades ago as it is today. For example, 12,505 attacks on women were reported in London in 1981. Taking under-reporting into account, the actual number of attacks suffered by women annually in the capital alone was estimated at 50,000 (Smith in Bland 1992: 251). As noted earlier, such statistics increase up to 18 times where prostitute women are concerned. Once again, the Sutcliffe case exemplifies the validity of these statistics since, long before he began killing women, he appears to have considered them fair game for casual, apparently unproblematic violent assaults, as can be seen from his friend Trevor Birdsall's recollection of one such attack:

He had a sock and I think there was a small brick or stone in it...I think [he said] he hit her on the head...But Peter never showed any hostility to prostitutes and there was nothing unusual in his attitude towards them.

(Bland 1992: 251)

In short, engaging in casual violence against sex workers did not make him 'the monster the police sought. It actually made him an admirable exponent of social values.' As such, 'far from "deviating from the norm", Sutcliffe was an exaggeration of it' (Bland 1992: 252). So normal in fact were both his attitude towards women, and engagement in violence against them, that they were openly shared by various sections of the male population. For example, the police officers working on the case 'made the same distinction between "respectable" women and prostitutes' as Sutcliffe did, encapsulated by the infamous statement by Assistant Police Chief Constable, Jim Hobson:

He has made it clear that he hates prostitutes. Many people do. We, as a police force, will continue to arrest prostitutes. But the Ripper is now killing innocent girls. That indicates your mental state and that you are in urgent need of medical attention. You have made your point. Give yourself up before another innocent woman dies.

(Caputi 1988: 93–4)

As Caputi notes, 'from such official statements we learn that it is normal to hate prostitutes. The killer is even assured of solidarity in this emotion.' Only when he starts killing non-prostitutes is his behaviour regarded as problematic. Furthermore, the murderer's motives and actions are matter-of-factly aligned 'to larger social interests as well as police goals' (1988: 94), again emphasising the existence of shared values between a sex killer and the wider non-criminal male population.

Further evidence of the shared 'moral standards' between a notorious serial killer and 'normal' men is demonstrated by a male journalist who wrote in 1981:

It is the main grief work for the families of Jack's non-professional victims to try to understand how their girls came under this man's hands. By having the same killer as the prostitutes, their daughters have somehow been tainted.

(Martin in Caputi 1988: 94–5)

A final example of the prevalence of misogynistic attitudes within the entire male population demonstrates not only the acceptance, indeed approval, of violence against prostitutes, but also one of the themes identified by feminists - the sexual murderer as a 'hero' to be admired and celebrated. When the police attempted to play a tape sent to them – supposedly from the 'Ripper' – over the Leeds United football ground's loudspeakers, 'it was drowned out with chants from fans of You'll never catch the Ripper. 12 nil! 12 nil!' (Bland 1992: 239).[6]

In order to explain this fratriarchy[7] between Peter Sutcliffe – a sexual serial killer who terrorised women for several years – and 'ordinary' men, including the police officers working on his case, feminist theorists increasingly paid attention to the wider culture of masculinity within their theoretical framework. In the following section I elaborate upon this framework.[8]

## Theorising sexual murder

While the focus of this chapter so far has been on authors who specifically analysed the subject of sexual murder, a number of other authors were producing wider forms of gender analyses during the period 1987–1992 which were to become extremely influential for decades to come. Among these were Connell's *Gender and Power* (1987) and Smart's *Feminism and the Power of Law* (1989). By fusing the work of these authors with the analysis provided by the authors already under discussion, a gendered analysis emerges which challenges populist representations of individual sexual murderers as 'monsters' or 'beasts', and instead provides a wider context which takes heteropatriarchy and phallocentrism into account.

In her examination of law and masculinity Smart wrote that they are both 'constituted in discourse and there are significant overlaps in these'. Consequently, 'law is not a free-floating entity, it is grounded in patriarchy...':

> This is not a simple reductive statement akin to 'all law is man-made', rather it is intended to draw upon an understanding of how the constitution of law and the constitution of masculinity may overlap and share mutual resonances.
>
> (1989: 86)

Smart elaborates her analysis by applying the concept of phallocentrism, a term utilised to denote the way in which 'the political-legal-cultural structure of modern societies is based on *masculine imaginary*' (Hudson 2002: 34, original emphasis):

> The term 'phallocentrism' invokes the unconscious and raises profound questions on the part that the psyche and subjectivity play in reproducing patriarchal relations. Phallocentrism attempts to give some insight into how patriarchy is part of women's (as well as men's) unconscious, rather than a superficial system imposed from outside and kept in place by social institutions, threats or force. It attempts to address the problem of the construction of gendered identities and subjectivities.
>
> (Smart 1995: 78)

Meanwhile, in his definition of the concept 'hegemonic masculinity' as the dominant cultural form of masculinity, Connell noted that 'despite the varieties of gendered performances available to social actors, in western society masculinity has a hegemonic quality that cuts across other social structures', and as such, hegemonic masculinity 'exerts its influence on all men in a society':

> At its core, hegemonic masculinity is based upon the legitimation of gender definitions that require the subordination of women to men and the subordination of non-hegemonic masculinities (for example, 'sissies' or 'punks') to the dominant form. For men, these definitions shape larger gender performances by enforcing a set of acceptable scripts through which they can establish and 'prove' their masculinity. Men constantly face the need to reinforce their masculine status as it is constantly policed by their peers.
>
> (Connell in Mullins 2006: 9)

Within the context of Smart's identification of 'phallocentrism' and 'overlap' between the law and masculinity, and Connell's identification of 'hegemonic masculinity' as the dominant form of behaviour to which men are under pressure to adhere, the fratriarchy between sexual murderers such as Peter

Sutcliffe and 'ordinary' men can now be explained. For example, in relation to the rape trial, Smart notes that 'from the judge to the convicted rapist there is a common understanding' about female sexuality (Smart 1989: 31). Put another way, regardless of which side of the law the men in the courtroom stand on, they all share the site of hegemonic masculinity, and from this site, 'women's bodies are sexualised terrain' (Smart 1989: 38).

In applying this theoretical framework not only to individual men who engage in sexual murder, but also to police officers (as one aspect of Smart's concept of law) working on the Sutcliffe case, and the wider male public including football fans, they can all be understood as sharing – albeit in various degrees – the same ideological and cultural terrain – that of hegemonic masculinity. In turn, this helps to explain why football fans were able to celebrate the Ripper's 'victory', as well as why police officers made the same distinction between 'innocent' victims and those of 'loose morals' as Sutcliffe himself did:

> How on earth, given their own attitudes on women and female sexuality, did the police expect to be able to recognise the killer if they came face to face with him? If, as they believed, the man was disgusted by prostitutes – well, so were they. If he expressed disapproval of married women going to pubs without their husbands, or said he couldn't stand women who drank too much, or remarked that women who went out alone late at night were no better than whores, would they really think something was wrong about this one and arrest him? Or would they dismiss him as an average bloke, the kind who can be found leaning on the bar in the local pub – not to mention the police pub – any night of the week?
>
> (Smith 1989: 128)

In sum, when theorising sexual murder, the inclusion of Smart's 'overlap' between law and masculinity, and the application of Connell's concept of 'hegemonic masculinity', exposes – indeed underlines – the normality and acceptance of male violence and misogyny. In turn, this reveals a wider context 'which society tries to avoid thinking about' – that 'brutal killings such as Sutcliffe's' are merely one aspect of a widespread misogyny and culture 'which encourages and supports a male sexuality based on violence and aggression towards women' (Bland 1992: 252).

### Asking for it: woman-blaming explanations of sexual murder

> Not content with sins of omission in failing to ask why sex-killers are men, many writers go one step further and attempt to erase men altogether. Inevitably then, they focus on women: what do women do to get themselves murdered? How do we provoke the lust to kill?
>
> (Cameron and Frazer 1987: 31)

The feminist claim that the crimes of sexual killers cannot be considered aberrant, but instead represent an extension of 'normal' masculinity, hence such murderers bear a remarkable resemblance to the 'ordinary bloke', has not been embraced by phallocentric 'expert' knowledge. In this section I therefore elaborate upon the theme of woman-blaming explanations – the ways in which either the murder victims themselves, or other women closely associated with the sexual murderer, are held responsible for these crimes within a culture where misogyny is taken as a given.

Woman-blaming explanations are not only proposed as part of the commonsensical framework frequently adopted within the genre of 'true-crime', they also feature as standard fare within legal expert knowledge. Thus, there are echoes of Smart's overlap between law and masculinity in Bland's analysis of the Sutcliffe case when she explores the various woman-blaming explanations put forward for his crimes during his trial:

> For the prosecution, Sutcliffe was responsible for his actions in the sense of having *rationally* responded to the behaviour of certain women. These were: a prostitute who 'cheated' him of £5, his wife Sonia and...his mother. The fact that these women had acted to precipitate his behaviour, however, effectively *removed* his responsibility. For the defence, Sutcliffe was not responsible for his actions because he was acting under the delusion of experiencing a 'divine mission.' To the psychiatrists, this mission was 'understandable' in terms of the behaviour of certain women (again the cheating 'prostitute,' Sonia and his mother). In effect, these women were pointed to as the precipitators if not the cause of the Ripper's actions.
>
> (Bland 1992: 245, original emphasis)

Here Bland not only supported Smart's overlap between law and masculinity – it mattered not whether legal experts spoke on behalf of the defence or prosecution, they were united around the hegemonic belief that the women around Sutcliffe were at the root of his murderous behaviour – she also identified an additional overlap, that between law and psychiatry. Thus, within a phallocentric culture where hegemonic masculinity is the dominant form of masculinity to which men are expected to lend their support, it made perfect sense to medical experts that Sutcliffe considered himself to be on a mission to 'clean the streets' of prostitutes:[9]

> ...in the case of Sutcliffe, as in many other cases of male violence against women, the language of law and psychiatry met in a common 'understanding' of Sutcliffe's acts, in terms of *female precipitation*.
>
> (Bland 1992: 244, original emphasis)

This common understanding is illustrated first, by medical evidence on behalf of the prosecution in relation to the incident of the 'cheating prostitute' which stated that it was a '"perfectly sensible reason for harbouring a grudge against prostitutes"...providing "a perfectly common-sense motive..."' and second, by the legal opinion that this was 'a classic case of provocation'. Killing prostitutes therefore:

was a reaction which...was not altogether surprising, the reaction of a man who had been fleeced and humiliated...the sort of loss of control which you don't have to be mad for a moment to suffer.

(Sir Michael Havers in Bland 1992: 246)

In short, legal and medical experts as well as Sutcliffe himself '– supported by the media and the police – all shared a common morality that killing prostitutes "made sense"' (Bland 1992: 246). This was particularly true in relation to the 'cheating prostitute' who had 'humiliated' him by short-changing him by five pounds, thus propelling him into killing 13 women and attacking another seven. As Bland notes, by that logic, 'the "provocation" of a shopkeeper short-changing a man' should prompt him to hate and kill all shopkeepers (1992: 246).

These various experts also agreed that Sutcliffe's wife Sonia was a 'key precipitator in the killings' (Bland 1992: 246). This was due to her 'difficult' and 'highly-strung' personality, the symptoms of which included an insistence on the removal of outdoor footwear when entering the house and turning the TV off before serving dinner – behaviour patterns which ensured Sutcliffe was regarded as a 'henpecked' husband (Bland 1992: 247). This woman-blaming interpretation of Sonia's behaviour confirms Kennedy's observation that 'nagging is seen as the female equivalent to violence', hence violent male retaliation in response to it is understandable within phallocentric law, indicating that 'the willingness to recognise the male experience is a reflection of the male nature of our courts' (1993: 206, 205).

Finally, the stereotypical mother-hating explanation of sexual murder was also evident in this case, as when his mother's 'clinginess' and over-reliance on her son were identified as being partly responsible for his murderous acts. As Caputi notes, this explanation fails to 'wonder why little girls – overwhelmingly the actual victims of abuse by fathers and father figures – do not grow up to enact wholesale slaughters against men' (1988: 86). Thus, far from explaining what makes sexual killers commit murder, such woman-blaming explanations reflect the wider culture within which this reasoning makes sense and seems plausible. 'If they did not, they would make no sense, either to the murderer or to those he seeks to convince' (Cameron and Frazer 1992: 365). A case in point, the discourse of the dominating/demanding mother as an explanation for sexual murder only 'entered popular awareness in the 1950s and 1960s' (*ibid.*: 364) via films such as *Psycho*. Since then it has been increasingly applied, regardless of whether it bears any resemblance to reality.[10]

It is therefore not surprising that sexual murderers like Sutcliffe employ such clichéd explanations of their crimes, since they, like the rest of the population, have learned to utilise them 'to justify their behaviour and "negotiate a non-deviant identity" for themselves' (Cameron and Frazer 1992: 365). That these victim-blaming explanations take the particular form of holding the women responsible who are closely associated with the sexual murderer – including his victims – is no coincidence, for this is a crime 'rooted in a system of male supremacy in the same way that lynching is based in white supremacy' (Caputi in Cluff *et al.* 1997: 293). As such, they serve to detract from the wider sexual politics of a culture within which expressions of sexual violence have become normalised and 'the sexual criminal has become the epitome of masculinity, embodying the ideal of a patriarchal structure' which is inherently misogynistic (Cluff *et al*. 1997: 300).

It is also an explanation which excludes the agency of sexual murderers. However, as noted earlier in relation to women involved in sexual murder, *both* human agency *and* wider social factors within a heteropatriarchal culture are crucial components within analysis. This is because human beings *act*:

> Human behaviour...is not determined by laws analogous to those of physics. It is not deterministically 'caused'. It needs to be explained...by interpretation of what it means and elucidation of the beliefs or understandings that make it possible and intelligible.
>
> (Cameron and Frazer 1992: 368)

Thus, the arguments made so far have focused on a number of key themes regarding sexual murder identified in early feminist writing, including the history and normalisation of the sexualisation of violence which led to the recognition that the behaviour of men who engage in sexual murder is not an aberration from normal masculinity, but an exaggeration of it; hence the chapter has also highlighted the way in which sexual killers frequently share the same terrain of hegemonic masculinity with 'ordinary' men – including those who staff the criminal justice system and the media. In turn, these insights have led to a substantial feminist critique of woman-blaming explanations of serial murder, as well as of expert knowledge more broadly, by arguing that such explanations reflect – and only make sense within – an already deeply misogynistic culture. Focusing on the case of Steve Wright, who was found guilty of murdering five sex workers in 2008, I now explore what – if anything – has changed, in relation to these themes, since this pioneering feminist work was produced.

### 'Misogyny is the theory, paying for sex the practice':[11] Ipswich 2006

> Thirty years after the Yorkshire Ripper murders, it seems there is still no shortage of men who hate women.
>
> (Smith 2008)

Twenty-seven years after the conviction of Peter Sutcliffe, Steve Wright was found guilty of the murders of five women whose remains were found within the Ipswich area in the autumn of 2006. All had worked as prostitutes to finance their drug dependency, and it was in this capacity that Wright had met the women. He was arrested only weeks after the bodies of the victims were found, suggesting an improvement in police efficiency compared with the bungled investigation of Peter Sutcliffe, who had been interviewed nine times by police before being arrested. Nor did investigating officers in the Ipswich case engage in crude distinctions or comparisons between sex workers and 'respectable' women. Indeed, when media headlines announced that 'five "prostitutes" had been murdered', there was public outrage, suggesting a change in attitude towards women working in the sex industry (Smith 2008).

In relation to the key themes discussed above, however, there is little or no indication of such positive change. Thus, just as Sutcliffe had turned out to be 'an ordinary bloke', so Wright was described 'as quiet and unassuming, inhabiting a world that...revolved around his local pub and golf course. He was "a good bloke", and the police were as surprised as anyone when his DNA led straight to him' (Smith 2008). This was reiterated by his former friend who described Wright as a 'nice, lovely guy...We drink together, play golf together, go on holiday together. It's unbelievable – I've known him for years' (Harrison and Wilson 2008: 199).

Descriptions such as these demonstrate the durability and continuing relevance of the insistence by early feminists that, far from deviating from normal masculinity, the sexual killer is an exaggeration of it. Indeed, the impact of this argument has secured its absorption into mainstream discourse as illustrated by forensic psychologist David Canter's observation that men who commit violence against sex workers 'are not an unusual sample of the population...[but] can include senior army officers, businessmen, doctors, pillars of the community'. Similarly, Britton, another psychologist, notes 'that the majority of men who murder prostitutes are ordinary and mundane...' (cited in O'Kane 2002).

The enlightened opinions of these experts have, however, failed to make an impact upon woman-blaming explanations of such crimes. Wright's murderous acts have been blamed on his mother, who left the family when he was a child, supposedly leaving him 'in perpetual search of a mother figure' (Cochrane 2008). Little attention was paid to the wider context of his father's exaggerated masculinity which meant 'that the marriage was violent and that Wright was afraid of [him]' (Smith 2008). His crimes were also blamed on his partner who 'emerges as an older partner no longer interested in sex, and who is therefore presented as a reason why Wright chooses to buy sex from younger women' (Harrison and Wilson 2008: 253).

Far from being confined to the Wright case, such woman-blaming explanations for extreme forms of male violence are as common in the twenty-first century as they were during the twentieth century, as exemplified in the cases of Mark Dixie and Levi Bellfield. Dixie, who was found guilty of five sex offences and the rape and murder of Anne Bowman, had been abandoned by his mother 'outside a care home when he was 12'. Bellfield, convicted of the murders of Marsha McDonnell, Amélie Delagrange and Millie Dowler as well as the attempted murder of Kate Sneedy, and a suspect in 20 other unsolved crimes against women, 'including five rapes', had a mother who was 'a "strong-willed matriarch"', and her 'close relationship with him...contributed to his psychiatric problems' (Cochrane 2008).

Such examples illustrate how woman-blaming explanations for male violence continue to serve an important function in the twenty-first century, by distracting attention away from, and mystifying, the inherently misogynistic personalities and attitudes of its perpetrators. Wright, for example, had a long history of domestic violence against his ex-wife, including banging 'her head against a wall as punishment for folding some sheets' incorrectly, suggesting that his violent father may have had considerably more influence over his future criminality than his absent mother. Bellfield believed that 'girls who dyed their hair blonde were "impure sluts", who "deserved to be messed around with."' That misogyny was taken as a given within the culture in which these sexual killers operated is illustrated by the fact that, 'without fear of redress or chastisement', Bellfield could boast to his friends 'he had shaved himself from top to toe to ensure he didn't leave any DNA behind at the crime scene' (Cochrane in 2008). Rather than indicating a reduction in misogynistic attitudes in the twenty-first century, such statements would appear to be on the same continuum as the chanting by football fans in the 1970s, outlined above.

That such woman-blaming explanations continue to flourish suggests the fratriarchy between sex killers and 'ordinary' men is alive and well, and that criminal and non-criminal men still stand on the same terrain of hegemonic masculinity within a wider culture of misogyny. This claim is supported by both general observations relating to the law and the criminal justice system as well as individual cases processed through that system.[12] For example, that same culture bears witness to the fact that 'only 5.3% of rape cases ends in a conviction or that one in five women are abused in childhood ... [which] mostly ... goes unpunished' (Cochrane 2009).

How are we to account for this stubborn persistence of male fratriarchy and cultural misogyny a decade into the twenty-first century, despite the fact that 'women have undoubtedly benefited from greater economic, civil and political freedom' since the 1970s, when Peter Sutcliffe was at large? (McNay 2004: 171). In an attempt to explain this persistence I shall conclude by returning to one of the themes identified by early feminist theorists – the normalisation of violence against women.

## Conclusion

> The world has caught up with me and surpassed me. Ninety years ago I was a freak ... now I'm an amateur.
>
>  (fictional Ripper in *Time after Time*, cited in Caputi 1988: 29)

In 1988 Liz Kelly wrote:

> The increasing entry of women into the public sphere of work and the revival of feminist campaigning for sexual equality has undoubtedly been accompanied by an increased public sexualisation of women throughout the mass media. Several feminist researchers have suggested that increasing demands from women for greater autonomy and equality will increase sexual violence in the short-term as men attempt to reassert their dominance.
>
> (1988: 30)

While even Kelly may have underestimated the massive intensification in the sexualisation of mainstream culture, and with it a huge expansion of the sex industry in the twenty-first century, her words were nonetheless apt and prophetic, because a key discourse within this intensification and expansion has been the portrayal of 'the sexual act in violent terms' – reflected at its most basic level in the language utilised to describe it – 'as a matter of banging, drilling, ramming, pounding and thrashing' (Morrison 2008). Similarly, albeit in reverse order, the 'portrayal of violence is now often laced with either explicit sex or sexual innuendo, making aggression seem an intrinsic part of the erotic experience' (Cluff *et al.* 1997: 301).

These developments have not only confirmed but also cemented the normalisation of violence against women identified by early feminist writers. Arguably, the biggest change which has taken place since the 1970s is the colossal expansion in information technology – particularly the arrival of the Internet, which has rendered campaigns and protests against pornographic images in the public sphere almost meaningless, since the entire range from soft to hard-core porn can now be delivered directly 'to everyone's desk' (Walter 2010: 102). Put simply, the Internet has enabled a massive expansion in, and normalisation of, the porn industry which in turn has, arguably, made the biggest single contribution to the increasing sexualisation of popular culture and wider social relationships. That sexualisation is both inspired and informed by porn and can be understood as operating on a continuum around women's bodies from pubic waxes, bondage-inspired clothing and footwear, surgically enhanced breasts and lips through to extreme forms of sexual violence:

> Through the mainstreaming of pornography and the new acceptability of the sex industry, through the modishness of lap and pole-dancing, through the sexualisation of young girls, many young women are being surrounded by a culture in which they are all body and only body.
>
> (Walter 2010: 125)

In turn, this 'pornification of our culture' is tolerated, indeed celebrated, because it is being sold back to us as evidence that full equality between men and women has finally been reached (Walter 2010: 117). Women have become 'liberated' to the point where they now have the freedom to explore 'their bodies more' and 'to concentrate on their sexual allure' (Walter 2010: 103, 108).

The particular form this liberation has taken can, however, equally be understood to reinforce existing inequalities within heteropatriarchy, because what is being sexualised is the power relationship within which women are subordinate, objectified and dehumanised. In short, the specific form this hypersexualisation takes reinforces the dominant heteropatriarchal social order by eroticising male power and female subordination. Tracing the history of porn, Power supports this argument when she observes that silent pornographic films made between 1905 and 1930 'abound in sweet expressions and moments of shared affection', which in the twenty-first century have been replaced 'by a combination of artificial and destructive antagonisms between men and women'. Hence, in modern porn films, 'it is rare to see a woman smile, or laugh'. What is being sold back to us is 'the worst of our aspirations: domination, competition, greed and brutality' (Power 2009: 53, 55, 56).

The argument that the growing acceptability of porn into mainstream culture contributes to increasing levels of objectification, brutalisation and dehumanisation of women is supported by both male consumers of porn and female sex workers. One male respondent in Walter's research reported:

> It had a huge effect on my behaviour with women. I was unable to think of women except as potential pornography. I looked at them in a purely sexual way...I had no idea how to interact with women as people.
>
> (cited in Walter 2010: 110–11)

Meanwhile, Angela, a sex worker, observed that:

> What was extreme five years ago is commonplace now. I get enquiries about being tied up, being gagged, they want to tie you up, they want threesomes...Basically you've consented to being raped...for money.
>
> (cited in Walter 2010: 61)

As noted above, humans have agency, hence my aim is not to present a causal effect between porn and sexual violence. However, as also noted, agency takes place within a wider sociocultural context, hence, the specific choices humans make are not random or meaningless, but spring from a culture within which they make *sense*. If that culture predominantly portrays sex as synonymous with the subordination of women, a sexual dynamic is created 'in which the putting-down of women, and ultimately, the brutalisation of women, is what sex is taken to be' (cited in Power 2009: 47). Within this context:

> Sexual murder is not a piece of abnormal sexual behaviour determined by innate drives, but a cultural category with a social significance. Sex killers are not responding unthinkingly or involuntarily, to stimulus, they are adopting a role which exists in the culture, as recognizable and intelligible to us...
>
> (Cameron and Frazer 1992: 379)

In turn, taking these wider cultural factors and power relations into account helps to explain why there has been no change to 'the risk associated with prostitution', whose women continue to 'make up the largest single group of unsolved murders in Britain' with a third of prostitute killers never caught (O'Kane 2002). More broadly, they might also help to explain the continuing existence of male fratriarchy, as illustrated for example – (among a plethora of examples one could have chosen) – by an agony uncle writing for *Zoo* magazine, who considered it acceptable to advise a jilted male reader to 'cut your ex's face, and then no one will want her' (*The Guardian* 2010). Such examples serve to remind us that:

> The rise of a hypersexual culture is not proof that we have reached full equality, rather, it has reflected and exaggerated the deeper imbalances of power in our society.
>
> (Walter 2010: 8)

Thus, not only has Kelly's 1988 observation that sexual equality may be accompanied by 'an increased public sexualisation of women' been confirmed beyond expectations, her prediction that women's wider 'equality will increase sexual violence ... as men attempt to reassert their dominance' has also been confirmed – for example by Smith, who in 2007 wrote about the sex industry:

> What this huge industry offers isn't just sex but an opportunity to exercise power over women, which is why it flourishes both in traditional cultures and ones like our own where some men feel a corrosive level of discontent about the growing equality of the sexes.
>
> (*The Guardian* 13 April 2007)

In turn, this raises wider questions, not only about how the state polices the sex industry, but also about how it protects sex workers.[13] At the time of writing, yet another sexual murderer, Stephen Griffiths, has been charged with killing three women who sold sex on the streets of Bradford. They thus belonged to a group who continue to make up one of the most vulnerable sections of the population, for 'while only one in four sex workers are on the streets, they make up three-quarters of the victims' (*Independent on Sunday* 30 May 2010). These statistics reinforce Britton's point that sex killers do not single out prostitutes as victims for complex psychological reasons – '*they kill because prostitutes are easy to kill*' (*The Guardian* 16 September 2002, my emphasis). Yet, while sex workers are increasingly understood as victims who need support to enable them to leave prostitution, for example through 'exit strategies', the 2009 Policing and Crime Act can nevertheless be understood as having increased their vulnerability by forcing street workers into poorly lit, less populated areas (*The Independent* 30 May 2010). Wilson writes with respect to the Ipswich murders:

> What these ... murders reveal is that those who want to kill and kill again can only do this when the social structure in which they operate allows them to do so by placing value on one group or groups to the detriment of others.
>
> (2007: 294)

More broadly, when discussing all the prostitute women who have been murdered during the past four decades, including Sutcliffe's victims, he rejects victim-blaming explanations which focus on prostitutes 'getting killed as a consequence of putting themselves in harm's way', and instead focuses on the failure of the police to keep vulnerable groups of women safe:

> The police ... collectively failed to police appropriately; collectively failed to deliver a service to one group within the community; and collectively failed to give to these women the protection of the state.
>
> (2007: 96)

Wilson's observations chime with key aspects of the analysis put forward in this chapter, particularly the need to shift the focus from individual murderers to the wider socio-economic/cultural structures within which both victims and perpetrators exist. Only when such wider structures are addressed will it be possible to challenge the dominant heteropatriarchal social order which sustains the male fratriarchy that has allowed violence against women to become normalised. Only then will it be possible to address the most serious fallout from that normalisation of violence – sexual murder.

## Acknowledgements

Many thanks to Jennifer Brown and Sandra Walklate for their encouragement and helpful comments, and to Joe Sim, Steve Tombs and Dave Whyte for their support.

## Further reading

For further reading on the topic of hegemonic masculinity and its relationship to the state, please see: Connell, R.W. (1994) 'The state, gender and sexual politics: theory and appraisal', in H.L. Radtke and H.J. Stam *Power/Gender*. London: Sage; Franzway, S., Court, D. and Connell, R.W. (1989) *Staking A Claim*. Polity Press. This book also contains a section on the subject of sexual violence.

For further elaboration on the phallocentric nature of law, please see: Smart, C. (1989) *Feminism and the Power of Law*. London: Sage; Smart, C. (1995) *Law, Crime and Sexuality*. London: Sage. For a detailed and thoughtful account of the Peter Sutcliffe case please see: Burn, G. (1984) *Somebody's Husband, Somebody's Son: The story of the Yorkshire Ripper*. London: Pan Books. For an elaboration on the subject of serial killers and their victims – particularly prostitute women – please see: Wilson, D. (2007) *Serial Killers*. Winchester: Waterside Press.

## Notes

1 See for example, the case of Richard Holtby in *The Guardian*, 21 June 2006.
2 Exemplified by Mary Ann Cotton, who was suspected of having killed 22 members of her family in the latter part of the nineteenth century (Adam, H.L. (1911) *Women and Crime*. London: T.Werner Laurie).
3 One notable exception is that of Karla Faye Tucker, executed in Texas in 1998 (Herberle 1999: 1108).
4 Carol Ann Lee's book *One of Our Own* (2010) presents a more forceful approach to the issues of Hindley's agency.
5 In terms of domestic violence, national statistics consistently indicate 'that on average, two women are killed a week "by a current or former partner" which "constitutes 42% of all female victims of homicide." Additionally, the Council of Europe found "that domestic violence is the biggest cause of death and disability for all women under the age of 44"' (*Guardian* 19 April 2006; Edwards 1989; Boyle 2005 in Ballinger 2009: 21). Moreover, 'approximately 80% of all domestic abuse victims are women, and "around one in three women who arrive at inner-city accident and emergency hospital departments have suffered domestic abuse"' (*Guardian* 20 June 2007 in Ballinger 2009: 21). Furthermore, domestic violence accounts for a quarter 'of all violent crime' (Itzin 2000: 357) and only 37 per cent of men would reject the possibility of using violence against their partner (Mooney 2000: 38).

Thus, despite numerous attempts to demonstrate that women are guilty of domestic abuse on a par with men, this is easily disproved by statistics alone – there simply is no research data available to date which demonstrates equivalence in the number of men who have lost their lives or been seriously injured as a result of a violent attack by their female partners.

6  When the Ripper killed again the chanting changed to 'Ripper 13, police 0!' (cited in Bland 1992: 240).

7  Remy applies the concept of fratriarchy to men who 'attempt to preserve something of the atmosphere of the stag night well into middle age. Some...simply never really grow up, and remain psychologically trapped in the fratriarchal men's hut for the rest of their lives. In rebellion against female values, particularly those associated with the mother...the fratriarchal fraternity...usually has a markedly delinquent character, including a penchant for gratuitous violence' (Remy 1990: 45).

8  For an elaboration of police culture, particularly the 'cult of masculinity' within this profession at the time of the Sutcliffe investigation, see Smith, D.J. and Gray, J. (1983) *Police and People in London*. London: Policy Studies Institute, especially pp. 91–97.

9  This phrase is borrowed from Ward Jouve's book *The Street-Cleaner* (1986) London: Marion Boyars).

10 This is exemplified in the case of Albert DeSilvo, the Boston Strangler who, despite harbouring consuming rage 'against his drunken, brutalizing father...nevertheless had his crimes rationalised through the pathological mother-son relationship' (Caputi 1988: 66).

11 Smith in *The Independent*, 13 April 2007.

12 See, for example, the case of Richard Holtby, who was cleared of murder after having strangled his ex-partner Suzy Healey, who had threatened 'to go out with someone else', and who consequently was considered to have 'been subjected to a "low degree" of provocation' by the trial judge, hence, was convicted of manslaughter (*The Guardian*, 21 June 2006).

13 Indeed, the recent inquiry concerning the Metropolitan Police's investigation of the Worboys case raises serious questions about the state's failure to protect all women from sexual violence. Worboys remained at large – raping and sexually assaulting 'at least 85 victims' – after police officers failed to follow up various lines of inquiry, thus missing 'crucial investigative opportunities' and 'committing serious errors of judgements.' The IPPC concluded its report by upholding 'complaints against five Met officers' (*The Guardian*, 20 January 2010).

## References

Ballinger, A. (2008) 'Reconceptualising social control: a case-study in gender, punishment and murder', in H. Johnston (ed.) *Punishment and Control in Historical Perspective*. Basingstoke: Palgrave.

Ballinger, A. (2009) 'Gender, power and the state: same as it ever was?', in R. Coleman, J. Sim, S. Tombs and D. Whyte (eds) *State, Power, Crime*. London: Sage.

Bindel, J. in *The Guardian*, 5 August 2005.

Bland, L. (1984/1992) 'The case of the Yorkshire Ripper: mad, bad, beast, or male?', in J. Radford and D.E.H. Russell (eds) (1992) *Femicide: The Politics of Woman Killing*. Buckingham: Open University Press.

Bourke, J. (2009) 'Foreword', in R.J. Herberle and V. Grace, V (eds) *Theorizing Sexual Violence*. London: Routledge.

Cameron, D. (1992) '"That's Entertainment?: Jack the Ripper and the selling of sexual violence', in J. Radford and D.E.H. Russell (eds) *Femicide: The Politics of Woman Killing*. Buckingham: Open University Press.

Cameron, D. and Frazer, E. (1987) *The Lust to Kill*. Oxford: Polity.

Cameron, D. and Frazer, E. (1992) 'On the question of pornography and sexual violence: Moving beyond cause and effect', in C. Itzin (ed.) *Pornography*. Oxford: Oxford University Press.

Caputi, J. (1988) *The Age of Sex Crime*. London: The Women's Press.

Caputi, J. (1992) 'Advertising femicide: Lethal violence against women in pornography and gorenography', in J. Radford and D.E.H. Russell (eds) *Femicide: The Politics of Woman Killing*. Buckingham: Open University Press.

Cluff, J., Hunter, A. and Hinch, R. (1997) 'Feminist perspectives on serial murder: a critical analysis', in *Homicide Studies*, 1: 291–308.

Cochrane, K. (2008) 'How could it happen again?' *The Guardian*, 27 February 2008.

Connell, R.W. (1987) *Gender and Power*. Cambridge: Polity Press.

Davies, N. (1993) *Murder on Ward Four*. London: Chatto and Windus.

Edwards, S. (1989) *Policing Domestic Violence*. London: Sage.

*Guardian* 16 September 2002; 5 June 2004; 5 August 2005; 10 December 2005; 19 April 2006; 3 May 2006; 13 April 2007; 20 June 2007; 22 February 2008; 27 February 2008; 2 August 2008; 20 January 2010; 7 May 2010.

Harrison, P. and Wilson, D. (2008) *Hunting Evil*. London: Sphere.

Herberle, R. (1999) 'Disciplining gender; or, are women getting away with murder?', *Signs* 26: 4.

Hudson, B. (2002) 'Gender issues in penal policy and penal theory', in P. Carlen (ed.) *Women and Punishment*. Cullompton: Willan Publishing.

*Independent* 13 April 2007; 30 May 2010.

Itzin, C. (1992) *Pornography*. Oxford: Oxford University Press.

Itzin, C. (2000) 'Gendering domestic violence: the influence of feminism on policy and practice', in J. Hanmer and C. Itzin with S. Quaid and D. Wigglesworth (eds) *Home Truths about Domestic Violence*. London: Routledge.

Kelly, L. (1988) *Surviving Sexual Violence*. Oxford: Polity.

Kennedy, H. (1993) *Eve Was Framed*. London: Vintage Books.

Lee, C.A. (2010) *One of Our Own*. Edinburgh: Mainstream Publishing.

Maguire, S. (1998) 'Dispatches from the front line', in D. Cameron and J. Scanlon (eds) (2010) *The Trouble and Strife Reader*. London: Bloomsbury.

Masters, B. (1986) *Killing for Company*. London: Coronet Books.

McNay, L. (1992) *Foucault and Feminism*. Cambridge: Polity.

McNay, L. (2004) 'Situated intersubjectivity', in B. Marshall and A. Witz (eds) *Engendering the Social: Feminist Encounters with Sociological Theory*. Maidenhead: Open University Press.

McNeill, S. (1996) 'Getting away with murder?', in *Trouble and Strife*, 33, Summer.

Mooney, J. (2000) 'Revealing the hidden figure of domestic violence' in J. Hamner and C. Itzin. (eds) *Home Truths about Domestic Violence*. Routledge: London.

Morrison, B. (2008) *The Guardian*, 2 August 2008.

Morrissey, B. (2003) *When Women Kill*. London: Routledge.

Mullins, C. (2006) *Holding your Square: Masculinities, Streetlife, Violence*. Cullompton: Willan Publishing.

*New Statesman* 18 June 2007.

O'Kane, M. (2008) in *The Guardian*, 16 September 2002.

Power, N. (2009) *One Dimensional Woman*. Ropley: Zero Books.

Radford, J. and Russell, D.E.H. (eds) (1992) *Femicide: The Politics of Woman Killing*. Buckingham: Open University Press.

Remy, J. (1990) 'Patriarchy and fratriarchy as forms of androcracy', in J. Hearn and D.

Morgan (eds) *Men, Masculinities and Social Theory*. London: Unwin Hyman.

Smart, C. (1989) *Feminism and the Power of Law*. London: Routledge.

Smart, C. (1995) *Law, Crime and Sexuality*. London: Sage.

Smith, D.J. and Gray, J. (1983) *Police and People in London*. London: Policy Studies Institute.

Smith, J. (1989) *Misogynies*. London: Faber and Faber.

Smith, J. (2008) 'The same old story?', in *The Guardian*, 22 February.

Thompson, J. and Richard, S. (2009) 'Women's role in serial killing teams: reconstructing a radical feminist perspective', in *Critical Criminology*, 17: 261–75.

Walter, N. (2010) *Living Dolls*. London: Virago.

Wilson, D. (2007) *Serial Killers: Hunting Britons and their Victims 1960–2006*. Winchester: Waterside Press.

# Chapter 15

# Violence, sex and the child

*Stephanie Petrie*

## Meet Stephanie Petrie

Stephanie Petrie is currently an Honorary Senior Research Fellow at the University of Liverpool after a long career as a social worker and manager of social services in statutory and third sector organisations in the north and Midlands. Much of this work was concerned with children and women who had experienced violence and abuse, usually from those known to them. Sometimes the way in which state organisations and professionals responded or failed to respond was also abusive. During her professional life Stephanie used a range of methods developed to create opportunities for children, young people and adults to have a meaningful and realistic say in what happened to them in professional and legal decision-making processes. As an academic she has transferred these methods to research with which she has been involved to help young participants to be better able to share the actuality of their world as they experience it. With others she has been involved in studies about teenage pregnancy and young parenting; girls' educational achievement in a seaside town; children's day care; lone parents and welfare reform and child abuse. A professional commitment to respect for persons and their competencies is grounded in formative personal experiences including being the daughter of an immigrant, a survivor of male violence in the home and harassment in the workplace, and a lone parent.

## Introduction

> ...our choice of terminology may function like a self-fulfilling prophesy: what we name may become what we see.
>
> (Crittenden 2008: 10)

Exposing children to violence and sex may seem to be unequivocally abusive as there is substantial evidence to show that child sexual abuse can have lifelong adverse consequences (Wilson 2010; Walsh *et al*. 2010). In the new millennium media and public attention in complex affluent societies such as the UK has focused upon scandal after scandal involving the prolonged sexual abuse of children. A few examples highlight the extreme and horrific nature of these crimes. In Austria Josef Fritzl kept his daughter imprisoned for 24 years and fathered seven children by her (BBC News 2009); in Germany Wolfgang Priklopil kidnapped 10-year-old Natascha Kampusch and held her captive for eight and a half years (Mail Online 2010); and in England two sisters were made pregnant by their father a total of 18 times over a 25-year period (BBC News 2010a). The horror evoked by cases such as these has been eclipsed in the media by the emerging details of the extent of child sexual abuses by Roman Catholic priests in many parts of the world (*New York Times* 2010). It has been argued that the continuing denial by some senior clergy in the Church was rooted in a 'victim'-blaming attitude (Taylor 2010).

Abuse of children, however manifested, can best be understood as a continuum. Kelly (1988) identifies two ways of understanding sexual violence as a continuum: first, continuum as a generic framework, and in this sense it is possible to consider the commonalities underlying the involvement of children in sexual activity and violence in many societies. Second, Kelly also suggests that the concept of continuum makes possible the documentation and naming of a range of abusive acts while 'acknowledging there are no clearly defined and discrete analytic categories' (1988: 76) into which they can be placed. From this perspective I will consider specific actions and situations to explore why some adult/child sexual interactions are considered abusive yet others are disregarded. As violence, sex and even 'child' are socially constructed terms and sometimes socially specific phenomena, identifying harm is not always clear-cut. For example the Pitcairn Islands, a British protectorate and isolated community in the Pacific, was the site of a major police investigation by Britain and New Zealand in 2000. Sexual intercourse between adult men and prepubescent girls was apparently socially sanctioned and had been the norm for many decades. Some women in the community were clear they had been raped against their will when they were children but others argued their society was being judged by different cultural standards and that the sexual behaviours in question were not abusive – just different (Marks 2009).

Consequently this chapter seeks to explore the complexities and contradictions in cultural and social attitudes towards 'children' and 'childhood', sex and sexual behaviours and violence. The construction of 'child abuse' and how this has been defined in UK policies and legislation designed to protect children and young people will then be examined. In conclusion the implications for the lives of children will be critically considered. It will be argued that contradictory constructions of 'child' and 'childhood' embedded in international conventions, UK policies, legislation and practices do not protect children and young people and may further harm them.

### What is a child, what is childhood?

Two broad strands can be identified when conceptualising 'child' and 'childhood' – the first arises primarily from many decades of developmental psychology and the second is a more recent emerging paradigm, the 'new' sociology of childhood.

### Nature v. nurture: born bad or made bad?

Much research attention has been paid in complex affluent societies to child development in order to identify the conditions that promote optimal maturation and, of perhaps greater concern, to understand why some children become 'problem' adults. Contributions made by Lorenz, Bowlby, Ainsworth and Piaget (see Mitchell and Ziegler 2007) have been particularly important in revealing the relationship between biological preparedness for maturation, learning stimulated by the environment and the emotional relationship between a child and their primary caregiver. The only theorist, however, who addressed children's sexuality to any extent was Freud (Mitchell and Ziegler 2007).

Although he worked primarily with adults Freud's theories seek to explain the development of personality from birth through psychosexual stages. Each developmental stage of a child's personality revolves around a significant erogenous zone – oral; anal; phallic; latency and, from the onset of puberty, genital. Freud's major contribution to our thinking about childhood is that adult personality is affected by psychosexual development and determines the sort of person we become. These theories were controversial during Freud's lifetime and remain contested, but constructs such as 'ego'; 'subconscious'; 'defence mechanism'; 'Oedipal complex' and so forth have entered everyday language and understanding and have been influential. Notwithstanding the lack of positivist research evidence for Freud's theories many of his ideas have become truisms even if crudely understood.

Positivism has been the dominant research paradigm for several centuries and rests on a number of principles. The most important can be summarised as a belief in an objective reality that can be uncovered by systematic collection of verifiable empirical data in order to test out hypotheses derived from theory. Positivism relies heavily on statistical analysis to demonstrate causal links and generalisability. Freud's theories, however, grew out of his clinical work with adults and children and he did not use positivist methods to 'prove' his theories. From his work he grew to understand 'reality' as having several layers and the 'unconscious' mind as a powerful driver affecting individual personality and behaviour. The 'unconscious' was often revealed in dreams and other symbolic manifestations and Freud developed ways of interpreting these in order to uncover the hidden and powerful personality determinants. Even today with the sophisticated neurological investigative techniques that are now available it is not possible to 'prove' the existence of the 'id', 'ego' or 'super-ego' personality elements theorised by Freud. They cannot be identified through examinations of brain activity or structure. Monitoring of hormonal levels and other bio-chemical changes in children and young people has not revealed evidence of the psychosexual stages of development.

Nevertheless Freud's theories have such resonance that they have become accepted as universal 'truths' and incorporated into everyday wisdom. For example, explanations for pathological and dangerous behaviour are commonly sought in early experiences especially involving sexual abuse and exposure to violence. It has been suggested, for example, that Mary Bell, who murdered four-year-old Martin Brown and three-year-old Brian Howe in 1968 when she was 11, had been severely and multiply abused, including sexually, in her early childhood (Sereny 1998). Sereny argues that her abusive experiences caused psychological damage and were causal factors in the abuse and murder by her of two younger children. Similar arguments have been made in relation to Thompson and Venables, who murdered James Bulger in 1993 (BBC 2001) and the Edlington brothers, who murderously assaulted two peers in 2009 (Walker and Wainwright 2010).

Attachment theory (Bowlby 1951), is another key developmental conceptualisation concerned with childhood. Bowlby was influenced by Freud's theories and regarded infants' need for emotional connection with the caregiver as a basic and inherent drive. Attachment theory links abusive experiences and deprivations in early years to problematic behaviours in late childhood and teenage years and adult personality impairments and mental health. Bowlby's influential monograph (1951) drew on empirical studies with war orphans and 'juvenile delinquents'. He argued that depriving infants of maternal care during the first three years of childhood led to behavioural and personality problems including 'juvenile delinquency' and adult mental ill health. A major critique of attachment theory, however, was that the focus on the mother/child relationship excluded fathers and presupposed a particular family form. Attachment theory was used to justify social policies in the US and UK in the 1950s and 1960s aimed at preventing mothers entering the workforce.

Like Freudian theory discussed earlier, however, attachment theory is well known but poorly understood. Bowlby and colleagues such as Mary Ainsworth (Ainsworth *et al.* 1978), who explored childhood in other ethnic and cultural settings, continued to develop attachment theory for many decades and recognised that it was the quality and consistency of the caring relationship that was important, not the gender or number of primary caregivers:

> What has stood the test of time has been the proposition that the qualities of parent-child relationships constitute a central aspect of parenting, [and] that the development of social relationships occupies a crucial role in personality growth.
>
> (Rutter cited in Howe *et al.* 1999: 10)

Indeed seeking to explain and understand the relationship between the individual and society has been a feature of most secular or religious grand theories and propositions in Western societies from the 'Age of Enlightenment' in the eighteenth century onwards. In the twentieth century primary socialisation theories, drawing on developmental psychology, gained ground in complex, affluent societies influenced by functional sociologists such as Talcott Parsons (Parsons and Bales 1956).

Primary socialisation conceptualises childhood as the social space where children are acculturated into the mores and expectations of the society in which they live – in essence adult culture is transmitted to children through social institutions such as the family, the school and so on. Notwithstanding the diminution of the centrality of functionalism following the emergence of the postmodern discourse in the late twentieth century (see Giddens 1991), primary socialisation theory, underpinned by developmental psychology, is still highly influential in relation to debates and policies about the 'family' in particular, especially when considering deviance. It has been argued that some children can be socialised into a dysfunctional subset of the dominant social culture, and primary socialisation theory has been used to explain both violence and criminality (Hoffman *et al.* 1995; Oetting *et al.* 1998).

Current debates, however, suggest an ecological understanding of child development is the most accurate. That is, the biological mechanisms necessary for maturation are inherent but capacities vary from child to child. Crucially, however, environmental factors can affect a child's development positively or negatively, whatever their innate capacities. Indeed the latest studies show that abusive experiences in early childhood affect brain chemistry to such a degree that damage to neurological structures and neurological activity is caused. Cognitive impairment and low impulse control may result, although whether or not this is lifelong, or whether the brain can re-adapt and, if so, the conditions necessary for this, are unknown (DiPietro 2000; Crittenden 2008). There remains a tendency, however, to regard genetic inheritance and childhood experiences as binary opposites in attempts to identify key factors in dysfunctional adult behaviour. In other words children are either born bad or made bad. Nevertheless the focus on the relationship between the adult and child and recognition given to the child's contribution towards developing and maintaining that relationship within attachment theory suggests a shift in perspective. Sutton (1994) defines attachment as 'the constellation of feelings and behaviours demonstrated by babies towards their parents and other caregivers' (1994: 41). These are the ways in which infants seek to meet their needs by gaining attention and nurture from the caregiver thus demonstrating that even babies have agency. The 'new' sociology of childhood develops this thesis using a different theoretical approach.

### The 'new' sociology of childhood: 'becoming' adult or 'being' a child?

Of course the biological maturation of children into adulthood is a cultural universal as childhoods are generationally limited. Children become adults but the point at which this change takes place varies historically and between societies notwithstanding the common experiences of physiological and psychological maturation. Aries (1973) argued that although younger members of the human species clearly existed in the Middle Ages they were not granted a special or distinctive social status – children were not separated from work, sex, childbirth, death, or capital punishment. Drawing on the diary of the court physician of Louis XIII of France in the early seventeenth century he describes:

> ... the liberties which people took with children, by the coarseness of the jokes they made, and by the indecency of gestures made in public, which shocked nobody and which were regarded as perfectly natural ... 'he laughed uproariously when his nanny waggled his cock with her fingers.'
>
> (Aries 1973: 98)

Once children were weaned they participated in society according to their abilities in ways similar to adults. Only gradually did political and economic institutions respond to the notion that children's needs were different, as demonstrated for example by the rise of universal schooling in the late nineteenth century in countries such as the UK. Consequently in the past two centuries transition points between childhood and adulthood were often marked by social rituals. In the nineteenth century in Western cultures girls were allowed to wear their hair pinned up and boys to wear long, instead of short, trousers as signifiers of the transition from childhood to adulthood. Until the mid twentieth century the twenty-first birthday was important as the point at which a young person living at home was given the 'key of the door'. These rituals have largely disappeared leaving a socially ambiguous space between childhood and adulthood that is difficult for young people and adults to negotiate.

In order to better understand the nature of 'childhood' and the social space occupied by children the 'new' sociology of childhood challenges the primary socialisation thesis based on a rigid understanding of child development:

> ...developmental psychology and socialisation theory emphasised the 'changing' (i.e. unstable) state of 'the child' en route to the stable status of adult. The child was regarded as 'becoming' rather than 'being'...this description of 'the child' as 'passive' bore little or no resemblance to the everyday lives and actions of children.
>
> (James and James 2004: 27)

Although children are united by a set of common maturational experiences childhood is fragmented by the diversities of children's everyday lives. Therefore there is not one 'childhood' but many 'childhoods'. The two central propositions of the 'new' sociology are that childhood is a social construction and children have agency as social actors. Gender, class, ethnicity, culture and the societies lived in will affect a child's early experiences yet children are not passive individuals but interact with their environment in ways that affect their lives.

This is not to deny that children are powerless in relation to economic resources and excluded from meaningful participation in social processes and institutions (Franklin 2002). Children, however, do have agency and competencies from birth. Optimal development requires opportunities for babies, young and older children to engage with adults in ways that respect and promote their competencies. For example, according to the Pikler/Gerber childcare practices (Petrie and Owen 2005) an adult should interrupt the play of a small child with the same respect given to a peer reading a newspaper. The bodily integrity of babies and toddlers should be respected and they should not be picked up without warning, especially from behind. There are small but significant ways through which adults can demonstrate respect for children's competencies by creating choice. Gerber points out that parents who discourage thumb sucking but tolerate a dummy are actually exercising parental power. The thumb belongs to a child who can choose when to self-soothe, the dummy is in adult control and is given when the adult wants the child to be quiet.

Respect for children is not a characteristic of complex affluent societies. It has been argued that children are perceived as 'non-adults' rather than young citizens (Qvortrup 2004). The term 'child' is often used as a universal, as in the title of this chapter, 'the child'. Are adults homogenised in the same way? Do we refer to 'the adult'? Of course not, we differentiate between different adult cultures and conditions (James and James 2004). Terms associated with children are often used as terms of abuse for adults (Franklin 2002), such as when cognitive confusion in older people is called a 'second childhood', demeaning both children and older people. Adults are told to stop 'being childish' as a criticism of behaviour and low-status adults, such as female administrative staff, are sometimes called 'girls'. How adults understand and engage with children shapes their experiences of being a child. How children respond to adults affects their behaviour in turn towards children. Adults wish to control the behaviour of children, children seek to follow their own desires and wishes consequently the '"study of children's lives…is essentially the study of child–adult relations"' (Mayall 2002, cited in James and James 2004, : 21) '…Indeed all of these perspectives make "childhood", 'children" and 'the child" very slippery concepts indeed!' (*ibid.*: 22).

## Sex and the child

If concepts of 'children' and 'childhood' are slippery then the addition of sex compounds the problem.

### *The innocence of childhood*

Archard argues that the contemporary concept of childhood is asexual – a good childhood being equated with sexual innocence. 'The sexual abuse of children is horrific precisely because it robs children of an innocence that is rightfully theirs' (2004: 49). This can be seen in the recent review of research regarding the sexualisation of young people commissioned by the UK government (Papadopoulos 2010). The findings of the report are based on studies of children and young people undertaken by adults and key adult informants, with no involvement by children or young people themselves. It is argued that children are being sexualised prematurely and that this leads to relationship violence between peers and makes them vulnerable to sexual abuse by adults. All 36 recommendations focus on programmes aimed at children and young people designed to change their behaviour or control the images and messages they receive from the media. In fact concern about the adverse impact of technology on the sexual behaviour of young people is not new. In a talk entitled 'Some Difficulties in Dealing with Girls' given in 1916 by the Reverend Cree, Honorary Secretary of the Church Penitentiary Society, to a conference of Rescue Societies, it was reported as follows:

> Now the difficulties which we experience with girls at the present time are not those difficulties which we experienced when I first took up this work some years ago. The home life is entirely different. The picture

palace has made a difference in even small towns and girls have no idea of discipline or obeying anybody...They have fallen into sin and are beginning to feel the earthly punishment of sin, they do not know what sin is at all.

(Barnardo's Archive, D239/J4/6/1)

There have of course always been consequences for young people from unprotected or unwanted sex. One of the consequences of sex is pregnancy and this remains a contemporary concern as the UK, along with the USA, has the highest rates of teen pregnancy among comparable countries (OECD 2009). This correlates, however, with high rates of child poverty rather than the sexualisation of young people (UNICEF 2007, CPAG 2009).

Whilst there is adult anxiety about children and sex it is adult silence about the sexuality of children that is most striking:

The concept of the 'desired' sexual life events in childhood and adolescence has received little attention from researchers...By contrast the topic of 'unwanted' sexual life events experienced by children and adolescents has been the subject of intense investigation.

(Browne 1995: 210)

Sexual development is the one developmental domain not considered in the UK child development checklists (Sheridan *et al.* 2001), current 'child in need (sec. 17, Children Act (CA) 1989)' assessment schedules (DoH, DfEE, HO 2000) or government guidance (DoH 2000) used by professionals charged with supporting and protecting children in the community. Health, education, emotional and behavioural development, identity, family and social relationships, social presentation and self-care skills are all considered to be dimensions of a child's developmental needs (DoH, DfEE, HO 2000) but sex is only mentioned in passing in relation to sex education for older children. Guidance for professionals regarding sexual activity and children is presented in a pathological not developmental context. The current inter-agency child protection guidelines, for example, pay attention to extreme examples of sexual activity such as female genital mutilation, forced marriage and sexual exploitation (DCSF 2010). The agency or competencies of young people, who are, after all, experts in their own lives, are unrecognised. Yet without their insights and problem-solving capacities interventions are unlikely to be effective.

Young people are very aware of the negative images of sex with which they are presented and don't find such a viewpoint helpful:

...in sex education and stuff...they talk about the worries more, but if they talked about the good side of it and not just the bad, we wouldn't be sort of not scared but worried...we've just got all these negatives cos we've never done it – we don't know positives.

(Year 8 young men, Bell *et al.* 2004: 32)

Young people want sex education that explores the emotional aspects of sex, such as how to begin and end sexual relationships and how to deal with the embarrassment of losing an erection rather than simply how to put a condom on a polystyrene penis (Bell *et al.* 2004). Sex education in Britain is usually aimed at secondary school students, unlike Sweden, for example, where sex education begins at eight years old. As Archard (2004) points out, powerful adults in contemporary affluent societies fear that giving children knowledge about sex will push them into sexual activity. Knowledge is power and gives children and young people choice. Without knowledge their agency is curtailed and their choices restricted.

Adults' retrospective experience of childhood is in any case likely to differ enormously from the actuality of contemporary childhood. The lived lives of children and young people cannot be understood without their involvement and participation, yet young people frequently feel silenced and judged unfairly:

> Teenagers are wrong. We're criminals apparently. We don't have an opinion because if we argue back with the police we're under sixteen so we don't have a right to say anything. We have to say it in a statement if the police have arrested us...which just gets ignored anyway because we are under sixteen.
>
> (School R, Year 11, Petrie *et al.* 2006: 27)

Considering sex, children and young people in isolation from all of the other environmental factors to which they are exposed reflects adult preoccupations rather than the actualities of children's lives.

## Child sexual abuse: a new phenomenon or an old story by another name?

Systematic attempts to rescue children from the sex industry were evident as early as the eighteenth century. Child Rescue Societies had been well aware of this trade in young girls for some time. For example, in the archive of the Thomas Coram Foundation for Children the common fate of foundlings is described as follows:

> ...if permitted to live, either turn them into the streets to beg or steal, or hire them out to loose persons.
>
> (Thomas Bernard, London, 1799, cited in Pugh 2007: 28)

Almost a century later little had changed:

> May 1872, K.D., No.797

> Parents living, brought to the Refuge by her mother for safety as her father...was for turning the girl out onto the streets...[father] has consented to K's emigration.
>
> (Barnardo's Archive, D239 J2/1/1)

In 1885 W.T. Stead, Deputy Editor of the *Pall Mall Gazette*, famously exposed child prostitution by buying a 13-year-old girl from her mother.

Sexual activity, including penetration, between men and young women in their family was termed incest and was also well known to childcare charities in the early twentieth century:

> The case was placed on the Auxiliary Boarding Out list in 1932 ... There was a previous child F who was admitted at the age of one year and eleven months at which time L was only 3 mths old. The mother from an early age was brought up by a relative owing to the death of the maternal grandmother. When she was 12 years of age she returned to live with the maternal grandfather who was then 44 years of age and for the next five and a quarter years this man had incestuous relations with her. The girl's father is the putative father of both children.
>
> (Barnardo's Archive, C2/5/6)

The sexual abuse of children in out-of-family care, a current concern, was evident in earlier periods too:

> The above child stated that the foster-mother's son exposed himself to her on three occasions. She was very frank in her statement and said she was terrified of him ... S begged to be removed from Mrs P's care. She said she was very fond of 'grandma' (as she calls foster-mother) but hates Uncle H. From the child's statement I do not think actual intercourse took place, but I have arranged for the child to be medically examined immediately – WB, 30.8.1938.

> The child was brought to me by Mrs B on the 31.8.1938 re interference by a man. The girl seemed quite sure the man only touched her vulva with his hand and as the girl greatly objected to an examination I considered it advisable not to make an examination – Dr F. (Barnardo's Archive, C2/5/6)

The child was placed with another foster mother immediately. The trust the girl had in the Lady Visitor to tell, the willingness of the Visitor to believe, the respect the doctor had for the child's body and the speed with which the situation was dealt with compare very well with more recent allegations of sexual abuse such as those involving Victoria Climbié[1] (Johnson and Petrie 2004).

Although incidents similar to those described above were known it was not an area of child welfare that attracted research or predictive and preventive theorising. Efforts were directed towards removing children from environments that were considered morally as well as environmentally unhealthy. Children who had been involved in sexual activity were commonly considered to be morally damaged and without vigilant attention would slide once more into 'a vicious and immoral life' (Infant Care Committee 1916, Barnardo's Archive D239/J4/6/1). From the 1970s onwards, however, a sea change occurred in the way in which sexual activity between adults and children was understood, driven in part by the narratives of the survivors of child sexual abuse and feminist theorising (Woodiwiss 2009). Definitions of child sexual abuse were proposed that conceptualised the child as 'victim' rather than co-conspirator. One definition of child sexual abuse is 'the involvement of dependent developmentally immature children and adolescents in sexual activities they do not fully comprehend, are unable to give informed consent, that violates the social taboos of family roles and which aim at the gratification of sexual demands and wishes of the abuser' (Furniss 1991: 4). Broadly speaking this definition remains the same and underpins current health and welfare practices (Wilson *et al.* 2008). There are many social constructs within this definition, however, such as 'dependent', 'development', 'immaturity', 'sexual activities', 'informed', 'consent,' 'social taboos', 'family roles', 'gratification' and so on that vary historically and culturally over time and from society to society.

Determining what is abusive and what the consequences may be are judgements that are influenced by the values and perspectives of the adults involved. Crittenden describes the emotional responses child sexual abuse triggers in adults in a paper she gave to a professional audience:

> I was describing as compassionately as possible, the developmental pathway of a typical incestuous sexual abuser... But when he became a young father and I described how he dressed, bathed and comforted his preschool-aged daughter, the 'temperature' of the audience suddenly shot up. People got agitated... 'He's grooming her!' 'That's sexual abuse!'... We strip a complex and painful situation of its complexity, reducing it to a simple, albeit unrealistic, dichotomy. Why? Because it makes our job easier.
>
> (Crittenden 2008: 10)

One manifestation of a discourse that constructs children primarily as 'victims' and child sexual abuse as a one-dimensional experience is the way in which attention focused on the single male 'perpetrator' as the dangerous 'Other' from the 1970s onwards in the UK and USA. Indeed it is the individual 'perpetrator' in complex affluent societies that generates the greatest concern despite the fact that the sexual abuse of children during wars and civil unrest is widespread and systematic (UN General Assembly 2009). Focusing on identifying 'perpetrators' in this way neither reveals the common characteristics of abusive events and experiences nor assists in documenting and naming the range of abusive acts (Kelly 1988).

### Violence and children

Child sexual abuse and its consequences are multifaceted. Differentiating child sexual abuse from other forms of abuse oversimplifies a complex issue. It is important to examine all the narratives of violence to which young people are exposed in order to recognise the continuum of abuse. A few examples highlight the incompatibility between the actuality of the lives of some children and young people and the dominant discourses of 'child' and 'childhood'.

### Who are 'victims'; who are 'perpetrators'?

From the 1970s onwards research focused on the individual adult male as 'perpetrator' of child sexual abuse, as early evidence suggested they were male and 'victims' mainly female (Finkelhor 1986; Furniss 1991). Theorising centred on whether causality was single- or multifactorial. As with child development theories, however, current debates suggest an ecological approach is the most useful framework within which to understand child sexual abuse. That is, recognising there are multiple pathways to abusive behaviours associated with multiple triggers and buffers that either facilitate or block the abusive act (Elliott and Beech 2009). Early theories tended to presuppose a dichotomy between 'victim' and 'perpetrator' and to categorise abuse by distinct descriptors such as physical, emotional or sexual:

> However, victims of child maltreatment are unlikely to be subject to only one type of abuse. For example sexual abuse and physical abuse are usually accompanied by emotional abuse, which includes verbal assaults, threats of sexual or physical abuse, close confinement... withholding food and other aversive treatment. Within each type of maltreatment, there is a continuum of severity ranging from mild to life-threatening.
> (Browne and Hamilton-Giachritis 2007: 49, 50)

In the past decade growing awareness of boys as 'victims' and women, children and young people as 'perpetrators' has challenged the construction of 'victim' and 'perpetrator' as a gendered binary opposite.

Children can simultaneously be abused and abuse, as with the Edlington brothers, aged 10 and 11, who attacked and sexually assaulted two peers, aged 9 and 11, leaving one for dead (Walker and Wainwright 2010). Women criminalised as 'perpetrators' raise further questions about what is considered to be sexually abusive. In 2004 controversy raged in Australia about the sentencing of a 37-year-old female PE teacher for her sexual relationship with a male student three months short of his sixteenth birthday. Despite the insistence of the young man he was not a 'victim' and that sex had been consensual, public outrage meant her suspended sentence was reviewed and changed to six months in prison. Public opinion and media attention arose because three months earlier a male teacher had been given a custodial sentence of two years and three months for a sexual relationship with a 14-year-old female student who described feeling threatened and coerced. Nevertheless the judiciary were accused of gender bias as the two situations were perceived by public opinion to be comparable (Angelides 2008).

More recently in Wales a 28-year-old mother of four children was given an 18-month prison sentence for sexual activity with a 13-year-old boy. Sexual activity included kissing and fondling and sending him texts inviting him to sleep with her (BBC News 2010b). While there may well have been a breach of trust in the above situations it is arguable that the judicial and public response had less to do with harms caused to the young person than with the dominant discourse of sexuality (Leonard 1997) and social constructions of 'child' and 'childhood'. Indeed the young men in question may well have suffered greater harm by their participation in legal proceedings that labelled them as 'victim', which is not the social script usually offered to young men who have had their first sexual experience with an older woman.

## 'Normalised' violence against children

War and civil unrest are endemic in the human condition and increased affluence and complexity in societies have simply made the technologies of war more sophisticated and increased the likelihood of large numbers of non-combatants suffering death or injury, as in the recent war in Iraq. There is substantial evidence that rape and sexual violence against girls is common during conflicts and a suspicion that assaults against boys are under-reported:

> Such violations are often perpetrated in a rule of law vacuum as a result of conflict, and there often exists a prevailing culture of impunity for such crimes...Sexual violence appears to be especially prevalent in and around refugee camps and settlements for internally displaced populations.
>
> (UN General Assembly 2009: 5)

The West seems little concerned about the violence affecting children and young people caused by their military actions. Furthermore it can be argued that the pervasive discourse of the 'War on Terror' shares characteristics with the demonisation of Jews in Hitler's Germany, and that it stereotypes and dehumanises Muslim children and young people as well as adults in the UK. The 'War on Terror' suggests that violence is the best and only way to counter violence. Children and young people in countries such as the UK and USA live in a society where violence is normalised and even valorised. The instant nature of communication media ensures that they view the death and destruction of others, through war, famine or natural disasters all over the world, on an almost daily basis.

State institutions also legitimate violence towards children. The UK has one of the lowest ages of criminal responsibility – 10 years (12 in Scotland) – in Europe, with the highest rates of penal custody associated with high rates of peer abuse and suicide (Goldson 2002). The tension between welfare and punishment has characterised juvenile justice policies, legislation and practices for the past 40 years (Goldson and Muncie 2006). Even though current policies and practices are somewhat contradictory and veer between punitive and restorative justice, those engaged in 'criminal' behaviour are constructed primarily as 'offenders' not 'children' (Frost and Parton 2009). The conditions for young asylum seeking children in Yarl's Wood Immigration Centre have been criticised in formal inspections since 2005 and the latest report continues to raise concerns (Travis 2010). The centre is run by a private security company, Serco, and the report by the Chief Inspector of Prisons, Anne Owers, following her inspection in November 2009, details the use of force against children on two occasions in the preceding year. On many other occasions children witnessed force being used against adult asylum seekers held there. In the six months preceding the inspection 420 children had been detained for short or longer periods. Often traumatised by the events experienced and witnessed in their countries of origin these children are held in a facility with all the security features of a prison (Burnett 2009).

Corporal punishment is another example of violence children and young people sometimes experience in UK familial settings and until recently in schools. It's a good example of how swiftly social attitudes towards the parent/ child relationship change. Fifty years ago parents and teachers routinely used corporal punishment to control children's behaviour. Indeed those who did not were considered lax. Although smacking is not yet criminalised in the UK as in some Scandinavian and other European countries, it is forbidden in schools and can be investigated as child abuse (Lyon *et al.* 2003). When corporal punishment is used to control behaviour, violence is simply normalised. The message conveyed is only what not to do rather than what is better to do and so offers no alternatives. Since adults tend to smack when they are stressed the model shown is that the way to deal with frustration is through violence.

The UK is one of the countries that have used the 'Mosquito' device extensively. The device emits a high-pitched noise that can only be heard by young people under the age of 25 due to age-related hearing changes in adults. It is purchased by public authorities and located in public areas, where young people congregate. The noise is said to be unpleasant but not physically harmful, but is indiscriminate. Babies in prams, toddlers, those with restricted mobility or learning impairments are all affected and cannot move out of range unaided. Young people targeted have not committed an offence yet it is considered legitimate to subject them to an unpleasant experience and curtail their social and physical space. The manufacturer's website quotes the Home Secretary saying the device was 'very helpful' in dispersing groups of young people in answer to a question in the House of Commons on 8 February 2010. A call for a ban was rejected (Compound Securities 2010). Shami Chakrabarti, Director of Liberty, asks, 'What sort of society uses a low level sonic weapon against its children?' (Liberty 2010). In the context of these contradictions and changing landscape of child abuse what are the implications for children and young people in the UK?

## Protecting children and young people

The changing social constructions of 'child' and 'childhoods', sex and sexual behaviour and violence are observable in the ebb and flow between protection and prevention in policies and legislation in the UK. These changes owe more to changing social attitudes and political agendas than to the sufferings of children.

### Policies and legislation

The current legal framework in the UK for protecting children and young people from abuse remains the Children Act (CA) 1989. Although there have been four administrations in the UK since devolution in 1999 – England,

Northern Ireland, Scotland and Wales – policies and legislation designed to protect children remain the same or have developed in similar ways. It is not necessary in any administration to convict someone of a criminal offence in order to prove a child has suffered 'significant harm' (sec. 31(2) and (9)) and take statutory action to protect them. The CA 1989 provides a single legal framework for all court proceedings affecting children and young people other than adoption and juvenile justice. Thus child protection and divorce hearings use the same courts and access the same orders with the same burden of proof.

The underpinning philosophy of the Act is that 'the child's welfare shall be the court's paramount consideration (Part I, 1(1))'. Although the CA 1989 falls short of the standards of the United Nations Convention on the Rights of the Child (UNCRC) 1989 (ratified by the UK in 1991), for the first time in law children and young people have been given the right to have their wishes and feelings taken into consideration in any court hearing concerning their upbringing. There is a caveat, however, which is 'in light of their age and understanding' (Part I, 1, 3(a)) and, as with child development measures discussed earlier, legal definitions of 'child' are linked to chronological age and determine whether or not they are regarded as capable of forming a view about matters that concern them. For example, it has been legal for young women to have sex once they are 16 years old since the nineteenth century. For gay men, however, consensual sex between those aged 21 or over was only decriminalised in 1967 and reduced from 21 to 18 years in 1981. It was as recently as 2000 that gay young men gained equal rights with young women for consensual sex. For more than 30 years young men were not considered mature enough to make decisions about their own sexuality.

Since the early 1980s these changing social constructions of 'child', 'childhood' and 'abuse' have been influenced by developments in forensic child protection, inquiries into child deaths from abuse and political and public opinion. These factors heightened professional sensitivity to child abuse and its consequences. From the public inquiry into the death of seven-year-old Maria Colwell in 1974 through the subsequent decade 27 inquiries into child death from abuse were held, contributing to a 'child rescue' professional culture (Corby 2000). Interventions by professionals to safeguard children from child sexual abuse increased but a change in professional behaviour followed the Cleveland affair in 1987. A hundred and twenty-one children were removed from their families on legal orders in spring and summer of that year because of suspected child sexual abuse. The resulting public inquiry generated public and political unease with the level of state intervention in family life (Campbell 1988). Simultaneously evidence was emerging about widespread, organised and serious abuse involving physical, sexual and emotional harm in state institutions that had, in some instances, been endemic for several decades (Frost and Parton 2009). There was a loss of confidence in the state as a protector of children in families and as a corporate parent. Coupled with the consequences of child poverty, which had tripled during the Thatcher/Major Conservative governments from the late 1970s onwards (Burden *et al.* 2000), and the election of New Labour in 1997, the child protection pendulum was pushed back towards an emphasis on prevention and away from protection.

Research commissioned by government (DoH 1995) was also highly influential as this showed that for the majority of families involved in formal child protection investigations no action was taken but neither were any supportive services offered. Maintaining a child protection system heavily biased towards formal processes and legal intervention was obviously costly. The guidance issued in 2000 (DoH, DfEE, HO) was to deal with all these concerns by directing state social workers to reduce 'social exclusion' by refocusing their work to support children and their families in the community. Protecting children from abuse was to be approached from an ecological rather than forensic perspective. Simultaneously the universal philosophy of health, education and welfare services provided by the Welfare State was being superseded by a 'market' model monitored through an increasingly complex array of performance indicators. I have argued elsewhere that the impact of 'markets' in welfare has constructed children as commodities to be exchanged between purchasers and providers for the lowest cost and for the shortest time (Petrie 2010). A long-term stable relationship with an experienced professional virtually disappeared as many child protection services became short-staffed or staffed by newly qualified or short-term agency staff. What has become increasingly evident is that without a consistent overview of a child's health and development and the establishment of a trustful relationship, as the child S had with the Barnardo's Lady Visitor in 1938, the sufferings of children can easily be overlooked.

Despite the increasing political importance of child protection policies and practices, flagship assessment tools (DoH, DfEE, HO 2000) and major policy programmes such as *Every Child Matters* (DfES 2005) child deaths from multiple abusive experiences continue. There have been systemic failures in child protection services in a number of local authorities in the UK, including Doncaster, Birmingham, Cornwall and the London borough of Haringey, where children known to professionals have died. In Haringey Victoria Climbié (Laming 2003) and Baby Peter[2] (Haringey Local Safeguarding Children Board 2009) were seen by many professionals from many agencies in their short lives but remained invisible. Victoria was the responsibility of four social services departments, three housing authorities, two hospitals, two police child protection teams and one independent-sector agency, all of whom had responsibility for her in the 11 months she spent in England. Baby Peter was seen 60 times by health and social care workers in eight months. The recruitment and training of children's services social workers has now become a major agenda for government in the UK (Social Work Reform Board 2010) but there are more fundamental fractures in adult/child relations in the UK than professional malaise alone.

## Implications

Frosh (2002) defines abuse as the destructive manifestation of adults' power over children. Returning to the examples outlined at the beginning of this paper, not only is this evident but the invisibility of the children and young people abused by adults is also clear. The 'perpetrators' were not the wandering sociopaths of urban legend. All were located in communities and were known to neighbours and colleagues. In some cases the abuse was known. Wolfgang Priklopil's colleague met the captive Natascha on more than one occasion, and abuses by Roman Catholic priests were confessed to their superiors who protected them and covered up their crimes. A deep-rooted disregard for children and young people in complex affluent societies is revealed by these examples and is especially evident in the UK. Three recent international studies of comparable countries show that children and young people in the UK, along with their peers in the USA, fare worse in most areas of 'well-being' than children and young people in other countries. Well-being is also a constructed term but is defined by the Child Poverty Action Group as: 'the many different factors which affect children's lives: including material conditions; housing and neighbourhoods; how children feel and do at school; their health; exposure to dangerous risks; and the quality of family and classmate relationships children develop' (CPAG 2009: 2). Why do children and young people in the UK fare so badly? Policies and legislation promote their welfare, services are heavily monitored and inspected and, in comparison with other countries, are better resourced as the UK invests £90,000 per child from birth compared with the OECD average of £80,000 (OECD 2009).

On the one hand 'childhood' has been given an almost iconic status. At a time of concern about environmental disasters of global proportions children have become the symbolic, as well as generational, future (Atmore 1998) and adults construct 'childhood' as a social space free from loss, pain, separation and unhappiness of any kind. This construction does not match the actualities of the lives of large numbers of children. As outlined earlier, children and young people caught up in the juvenile justice or immigration systems are silenced. A child or young person who is simultaneously 'victim' and 'perpetrator' is not viewed holistically but falls into the category of being 'born bad'. Since 'desired' sexual experiences of children and young people are little understood their sexuality is viewed primarily in pathological and often apocalyptic terms. They are not believed if they say they do not feel 'victimised' by sexual experiences and are not believed if they say a respected figure has sexually abused them. Adult/child relations in contemporary societies are often characterised by contradictions and incompatibilities. These are particularly evident when issues relating to violence and sex emerge. More than two million children under 15 years worldwide are living with AIDS and nine out of ten of these live in sub-Saharan Africa. According to the international AIDS charity Avert (2009), access to sexual health advice, condoms and treatments for mothers and their children is minimal. Some children are infected through sexual abuse, including rape, and involvement in the sex industry.

The philosophies underpinning international conventions such as the United Nations Convention on the Rights of the Child 1989 and UK domestic legislation discussed earlier support the rights of children and young people to express their views about matters that concern them and have them taken into account. But child development models that are largely constructed in age/stage terms are embedded in policies and legislation. Some children within these age-constructed definitions of 'child' lose their status as children for socially constructed reasons. When is a 'child' not a 'child'? When their construction as the 'Other' eliminates their identity as 'child' – as in the case of young 'perpetrators' of abuse, 'criminal' activity, asylum seekers or those living in resource-poor countries. When is 'abuse' not 'abuse'? When systemic violence by adults towards children and young people takes place in penal institutions, immigration centres or in war-torn countries. Being a 'child' in the twenty-first century in many countries, including affluent as well as resource-poor countries, can be unsafe despite the rhetoric in international and domestic legislation and policies. Without the active contribution of children and young people in all matters that concern them the actualities of their lives will go unrecognised and the avoidable abuse of children and young people will continue.

## Further reading

Familial violence and sexual abuse against children have been dominant targets for state intervention in family life in the UK for many decades although legislation and policies have regularly shifted in emphasis in response to sociopolitical pressures. Corby (2006, 3rd edn) gives a useful historical analysis of the changing child abuse perspectives in the UK. Child protection services, however, are currently under scrutiny once more. The 'Monro Review of Child Protection' has produced three reports that critique the deficiencies in the current systems and propose alternative approaches:

*Part One: A Systems Analysis (Sept. 2010)*
*http://www.education.gov.uk/munroreview/downloads/TheMunroReviewofChildProtection-Part%20one.pdf*

*Part Two: Interim Report: The Child's Journey (Feb. 2011)*
*http://www.education.gov.uk/publications/standard/publicationDetail/Page1/DFE-00010-2011*

*Final Report: A Child Centred System (May 2011)*
*http://www.education.gov.uk/childrenandyoungpeople/strategy/laupdates/a0077242/munro-review-final-report*

Whether these recommendations are to be adopted or not remains unclear in light of the proposed sea change in UK health and welfare services and eligibility. From a psychological perspective Crittenden (2008) draws on many decades of family therapy practice and research to offer an understanding of child abuse in complex affluent societies such as the USA and the UK.

As far as the perspectives, experiences and opinions of children and young people are concerned UK legislation now requires a children's commissioner in all four countries. Commissioners are tasked with promoting the rights and establishing the views of their young citizens:

**England**
http://www.childrenscommissioner.gov.uk/
**Scotland**
http://www.sccyp.org.uk/
**Wales**
http://www.childcom.org.uk/
**Northern Ireland**
http://www.niccy.org/

Franklin [2002] (2005) gives an overview of children's rights not only in the UK but also in European and Pacific Rim countries and in relation to global issues. For current insights into the violence and exploitation facing children and young people worldwide the United Nations Children's Fund (UNICEF) website is a useful source: http://www.unicef.org/.

Archard [2004](2009), however, offers a note of caution and provides a critical commentary on the 'rights' agenda, reflecting on the theoretical approaches to childhood, the ethical contradictions embedded in the notion of the rights of the young and the complexities of relationship between children, their families and the state.

## Notes

1 Victoria Climbié was a seven-year-old child from West Africa who had been sent by her parents to live with her great-aunt Marie-Thérèse Kouao to get a better education. They lived initially in France and for less than a year in London, England. In those months Victoria was neglected and physically and sexually abused by Kouao and her lover Carl Manning. She was referred to many health and welfare agencies but died in 2000 after spending the winter bound and left in a bin bag in an unheated bathroom. She had 128 separate injuries to her body. Her death led to the Laming Inquiry (2003) and subsequent Children Act 2004.

2 Peter Connelly was 17 months old and living in Haringey, London, England when he died in August 2007 after suffering more than 50 injuries, including a broken back, at the hands of his mother and her boyfriend. His death led to further inquiries, a national review of children's social care resulted and the Director of Haringey Children's Services, Sharon Shoesmith, was removed from her post.

## References

Ainsworth, M.D., Blehar, M.C., Waters, E. and Wall, S. (1978) *Patterns of Attachment.* New Jersey: Erlbaum.

Angelides, S. (2008) 'Sexual offences against "children" and the question of judicial gender bias', *Australian Feminist Studies*, 23(57): 359–73.

Archard, D. (2004) *Children. Rights and Childhood.* Abingdon: Routledge.

Aries, P. (1973) *Centuries of Childhood.* Harmondsworth: Penguin.

Atmore, C. (1998) 'Towards 2000: Child sexual abuse and the media', in A. Howe (ed.) *Sexed Crime in the News.* Sydney: Federation Press, pp. 124–44.

Avert (2009) *Children, HIV and AIDS,* available at http://www.avert.org/children.htm (accessed 30 July 2010).

Barnardo's Archive (Accessed March 2010) for access, application must be made to Barnado's Head Office.

BBC News (2001) 'Bulger statement in full', available at http://news.bbc.co.uk/1/hi/uk/1402798.stm (accessed 31 July 2010).

BBC News (2009) 'Profile Josef Fritzl', available at http://news.bbc.co.uk/1/hi/7371959.stm (accessed 17 March 2010).

BBC News (2010a) 'Apology for daughters raped by Sheffield man', available at http://news.bbc.co.uk/1/hi/england/south_yorkshire/8559750.stm (accessed 10 March 2010).

BBC News (2010b) 'Bridgend woman who seduced teen jailed for 18 months', available at http://news.bbc.co.uk/1/hi/wales/8589178.stm (accessed 30 March 2010).

Bell, J., Clisby, S., Craig, G., Measor, L., Petrie, S. and Stanley, N. (2004) *Living on the edge: sexual behaviour and young parenthood in seaside and rural areas*. Hull: University of Hull/ Working Papers in Social Sciences and Policy.

Bowlby, J. (1951) *Maternal Care and Mental Health*. Geneva: World Health Organisation.

Browne, K. (1995) 'Child sexual abuse', in J. Archer (ed.) *Male Violence*. London: Routledge, pp. 210–30.

Browne, K. and Hamilton-Giachritis, C. (2007) 'Child abuse: defining, understanding and intervening', in K. Wilson and A. James (eds) *The Child Protection Handbook* (3rd edn). Edinburgh: Ballière Tindall, pp. 49–68.

Burden, T., Cooper, C., Petrie, S. (2000) *'Modernising' Social Policy: Unravelling New Labour's Welfare Reforms*. Aldershot: Ashgate.

Burnett, J. (2009) 'Free the Yarl's Wood child detainees', *The Guardian*, 10 December 2009, available at http://www.guardian.co.uk/commentisfree/libertycentral/2009/dec/10/child-detainees-yarls-wood (accessed 30 March 2010).

Campbell, B. (1988) *Unofficial Secrets*. London: Virago.

Child Poverty Action Group (CPAG) (2009) *Child Wellbeing and Child Poverty: Where the UK stands in the European table*. London: CPAG.

Compound Securities (2010) 'Home of the Mosquito', available at http://www.compoundsecurity.co.uk/ (accessed 2 April 2010).

Corby, B. (2000) *Child Abuse* (2nd edn). Buckingham, Philadelphia: Open University Press.

Crittenden, P.M. (2008) *Raising Parents. Attachment, parenting and child safety*. Portland, Oregon: Willan Publishing.

Department for Children, Schools and Families (DCSF) (2010) *Working Together to Safeguard Children*. Nottingham: HM Government.

Department for Education and Skills (DfES) (2005) *Every Child Matters: Aims and Outcomes*, available at http://www.everychildmatters.gov.uk/aims/ (accessed 27 January 2010).

Department of Health (DoH) (2000) *Assessing Children in Need and Their Families: practice guidance*. London: The Stationery Office.

Department of Health (DoH) (1995) *Child Protection. Messages from Research*. London: HMSO.

Department of Health, Department for Education and Employment, Home Office, (DoH, DfEE, HO) (2000) *Framework for the Assessment of Children in Need and Their Families*. London: The Stationery Office.

DiPietro, J.A. (2000) 'Baby and the brain: advances in child development', *Annual Review of Public Health*, 21: 455–71.

Elliott, I.A. and Beech, A.R. (2009) 'Understanding online child pornography use: Applying sexual offense theory to internet offenders', *Aggression and Violent Behavior*, 14(3): 180–93.

Finkelhor, D. (1986) *A Sourcebook on Child Sexual Abuse*. Newbury Park, CA: Sage.

Franklin, B. (2002) 'Children's rights and media wrongs', in B. Franklin (ed.) (2002) *The New Handbook of Children's Rights: comparative policy and practice*. London: Routledge, pp. 15–42.

Frosh, S. (2002) 'Characteristics of sexual abusers', in K.Wilson and A.James (eds) *The Child Protection Handbook*. London: Balliere Tindall, pp. 71–88.

Frost, N. and Parton, N. (2009) *Understanding Children's Social Care*. London: Sage.

Furniss, T. (1991) *The Multi-professional Handbook of Child Sexual Abuse*. London: Routledge.

Giddens, A. (1991) *Modernity and Self Identity. Self and Society in the Late Modern Age*. Cambridge: Polity Press.

Goldson, B. (2002) *Vulnerable Inside: Children in Secure and Penal Settings*. London: Children's Society.

Goldson, B. and Muncie, J. (2006) *Youth Crime and Justice*. London: Sage.

Haringey Local Safeguarding Children's Board (LSCB) (2009) *Baby Peter Serious Case Review*, available at http://www.haringeylscb.org/index/news/babypeter_scr.htm (accessed 2 April 2010).

Hoffman, J., Ireland, T., and Widom, C. (1995) 'Traditional socialization theories of violence. A critical examination', in J. Archer (ed.) *Male Violence*. London: Routledge, pp. 289–303.

Howe, D., Brandon, M., Hinings, D. and Schofield, G. (1999) *Attachment Theory, Child Maltreatment and Family Support: A Practice and Assessment Model*. Basingstoke: Macmillan.

James, A. and James, A. (2004) *Constructing Childhood, Theory, Policy and Social Practice*. Houndmills, Basingstoke: Palgrave Macmillan.

Johnson, S. and Petrie, S. (2004) 'Child protection and risk-management: The death of Victoria Climbié', *Journal of Social Policy*, 33(2): 179–202.

Kelly, L. (1988) *Surviving Sexual Violence*. Cambridge: Polity Press.

Laming Report (2003) *The Victoria Climbié Inquiry: report of an inquiry by Lord Laming*, Cmnd. 5730. London: The Stationery Office.

Leonard, P. (1997) *Postmodern Welfare – Reconstructing an Emancipatory Project*. London: Sage.

Liberty (2010) 'Help us stamp out the Mosquito', available at http://www.liberty-human-rights.org.uk/issues/young-peoples-rights/stamp-out-the-mosquito.shtml (accessed 3 April 2010).

Lyon, C., Cobley, C., Petrie, S. and Reid, C. (2003) *Child Abuse* (3rd edn). Bristol: Family Law/Jordans.

Mail Online (2010) 'Natascha Kampusch: He put me inside the cellar for eight-and-a-half years, preserved alive like an Egyptian Pharaoh', available at http://www.dailymail.co.uk/news/worldnews/article-1245899 (accessed 17 March 2010).

Marks, K. (2009) *Lost Paradise: From Mutiny On The Bounty To A Modern-Day Legacy of Sexual Mayhem, The Dark Secrets of Pitcairn Island Revealed*. New York: Free Press, Simon & Schuster.

Mitchell, P. and Ziegler, F. (2007) *Fundamentals of Development: the psychology of childhood*. Hove: Sussex: Psychology Press.

*New York Times* (2010) 'Abuse scandals ripple across Europe', available at http://www.nytimes.com/2010/03/25/world/europe/25church.html?src=me (accessed 28 March 2010).

Oetting, E.R. and Donnermeyer, J.F. (1998) 'Primary socialization theory: the etiology of drug use and deviance', *Substance Use and Misuse*, March, 33(4): 995–1026.

Organisation for Economic Co-operation and Development (OECD) (2009) *Doing Better for Children*. Paris: OECD.

Papadopoulos, L. (2010) *Sexualisation of Young People Review*, available at http://www.homeoffice.gov.uk/about-us/news/sexualisation-young-people.html (accessed 2 March 2010).

Parsons, T. and Bales, R. (2002 [1956]) *Family Socialization and Interaction Process*. London: Routledge.

Petrie, S. (2010) 'The "commodification" of "children in need" in welfare markets: Implications for managers', *Social Work and Social Sciences Review*, 14: 9–26.

Petrie, S., Hughes, G. and Bennett, K. (2006) *A Report for Blackpool Council on the Educational Achievement of Young Women at Key Stage 4*. Liverpool: University of Liverpool Working Paper.

Petrie, S. and Owen, S. (eds) (2005) *Authentic Relationships in Group Care for Infants and Toddlers – Resources for Infant Educarers (RIE). Principles into Practices*. London and Philadelphia: Jessica Kingsley Publishers.

Pugh, G. (2007) *London's Forgotten Children*. Briscombe Port, Stroud: Tempus.

Qvortrup, J. (2004) 'Editorial: The waiting child', *Childhood*, 11(3): 267–73.

Sereny, G. (1998) *Cries Unheard. The Story of Mary Bell*. Basingstoke: Macmillan.

Sheridan, M.D. revised and updated by Marian Frost and Dr Ajay Sharma (2001) *From Birth to Five Years, Children's Developmental Progress*. London: Routledge.

Social Work Reform Board (2010) 'The Government's implementation plan for social work reform', available at http://www.dcsf.gov.uk/swrb/ (accessed 2 April 2010).

Sutton, C. (1994) *Social Work, Community Work and Psychology*. Leicester: British Psychological Society.

Taylor, L. (2010) 'Suffer the little children', *New Humanist*, 125(1): 16–19.

Thomas, T. (2009) 'Sociology of childhood', in T. Maynard and N. Thomas (eds) (2009) *An Introduction to Early Childhood Studies* (2nd edn). Los Angeles, London: Sage, pp. 33–46.

Travis, A. (2010) 'Yarl's Wood detains baby for 100 days, damning report reveals', *The Guardian*, 24 March 2010, avaliable at http://www.guardian.co.uk/uk/2010/mar/24/yarls-wood-children-baby-report (accessed 30 March 2010).

United Nation Children's Fund (UNICEF) (2007) *Child Poverty in Perspective: An overview of child well-being in rich countries*. Florence: Innocenti Research Centre.

United Nations General Assembly (2009) *Report of the Special Representative of the Secretary-General for Children and Armed Conflict*. New York: UN.

Walsh, K., Fortier, M. and DiLillo, D. (2010) 'Adult coping with childhood sexual abuse: A theoretical and empirical review', *Aggression and Violent Behavior*, 15: 1–13.

Walker, P. and Wainwright, M. (2010) 'Edlington brothers jailed for torture of two boys', *The Guardian*, 22 January, available at http://www.guardian.co.uk/uk/2010/jan/22/edlington-brothers-jailed-torture-boys (accessed 30 March 2010).

Wilson, D.R. (2010) 'Health consequences of childhood sexual abuse', *Perspectives in Psychiatric Care*, 46(1): 56–64.

Wilson, K., Ruch, G., Lymbery, M. and Cooper, A. (2008) *Social Work. An introduction to Contemporary Practice*. Harlow: Pearson Education.

Woodiwiss, J. (2009) *Contesting Stories of Childhood Sexual Abuse*. Basingstoke: Hampshire: Palgrave Macmillan.

# Chapter 16

# Under their parents' noses – the online sexual solicitation of young people

*David Shannon*

## Meet David Shannon

David has been working as a researcher at the Swedish National Council for Crime Prevention for four years. Prior to taking up his current position, he worked as Director of Studies for the undergraduate and postgraduate programmes at Stockholm University's Department of Criminology, where he was also involved in researching different aspects of youth crime. Since moving to the National Council, David's research focus has become more varied, and besides researching sexual offences against children, he has also participated in projects focused on discrimination in the criminal justice system and violence in schools. His work continues to involve researching and writing about youth crime, responses to youth crime and youth victimisation more generally.

## Introduction

> It's a bit comical really because my parents were watching TV in the same room. I'm not sure how old the guy was, but at least twenty. I sent a couple of pictures of my face (nothing sexual) and he started writing things like how he wished I was there so he could fuck me in the arse and the mouth, and other similar 'dirty talk'. It wasn't exactly a turn on, especially with my parents in the same room.
>
> (girl aged 13)

The quotation presented above is a description provided by a teenage girl of an online sexual contact she had with an adult at the age of 13. The reason for choosing to begin the chapter with this particular quotation is that it provides a very good illustration of the way in which the Internet has brought the possibility of sexual contacts with adults into children's homes in a very new way. This is not the kind of thing you would expect a man in his twenties to be saying to a 13-year-old sitting in the same room as her parents – but the Internet makes it possible.

Attempts by adults to develop relationships with children for the purposes of sexual exploitation and abuse are of course nothing new (e.g. Martens 1989; McAlinden 2006). However, with the rapid expansion in Internet use among young people from the mid to late 1990s, an awareness gradually developed among practitioners, researchers and policy-makers that this new medium provided a new and for the most part completely unmonitored arena for contacts between adults and children. The anonymity provided by Internet communications was recognised as creating favourable conditions for adults wishing to develop manipulative relationships with young people (e.g. Stanley 2001), and our knowledge of the ways in which adults are using the Internet for the purpose of sexually exploiting and abusing children has been slowly growing ever since.

Research on the online sexual solicitation of children remains relatively limited, but it is continuously expanding. Research has focused on questions of the prevalence of online solicitation (e.g. Finkelhor *et al.* 2000; Wolak *et al.* 2006; Brå 2007), on risk factors for exposure to online sexual contacts (e.g. Mitchell *et al.* 2001), on the modus operandi of adults who use the Internet to establish sexual contacts with children (e.g. Gallagher *et al.* 2006; Alvin Malesky Jr. 2007), on the content of online sexual contacts (e.g. O'Connell 2003; O'Connell *et al.* 2004), and on the methods employed by adults to persuade children to meet them offline for the purposes of sexual exploitation and abuse (e.g. Wolak *et al.* 2004a; Shannon 2008).

Central findings to date show that children experience online sexual contacts both from adults and from other young people. They also show that exposure to such contacts appears to be less widespread among younger children, but becomes increasingly common as children approach and enter their teenage years. Girls are exposed to online sexual solicitation to a much greater extent than boys, and boys and men are responsible for the vast majority of the online contacts described in the literature (e.g. Finkelhor *et al.* 2000; Wolak *et al.* 2006; Brå 2007). Besides sex and age, risk factors for exposure to online sexual contacts include often visiting chat sites, and using the Internet to communicate with people one does not already know offline (e.g. Mitchell *et al.* 2001). Researchers have also identified factors that appear to be correlated with the likelihood that young people will develop close friendships or romantic relationships with people they have met online, including poor communication between the child and his or her parents, high levels of intrafamilial conflict, problems in other areas, such as at school, and involvement in crime (Wolak *et al.* 2003). The research also shows that adults intent on sexually abusing young people employ a range of strategies to establish and develop contacts with potential victims, and that such contacts can be established in order to commit both online and offline sexual offences (e.g. O'Connell 2003; Shannon 2008).

The existing research thus contains descriptions of a wide range of different aspects of online sexual contacts (see for example Choo 2009 for a recent summary), but it is still rare to find a compact, comprehensive overview of the range of different types of sexually abusive and exploitative contacts to which children are being exposed on the Internet. On the basis of four complementary data sets collected by the Swedish National Council for Crime Prevention, the current chapter will attempt to provide a descriptive overview of precisely this kind, examining a range of different types of sexually abusive Internet contacts and providing examples of both different forms of *online* sexual abuse and also of a number of different strategies employed by adults to persuade children to meet them for the purposes of committing *offline* sexual offences.

The data are drawn from the following sources:

- an online questionnaire survey conducted among 1,000 15 to 17-year-olds;
- a representative national pencil and paper survey of youths in their final year of compulsory education (aged 15); and
- two data sets based on police reports and transcripts of police interviews with young victims of sexual offences.

The next section describes these data sets in brief and outlines how they are used for the purposes of the remainder of the chapter. The presentation then moves on to illustrate various different types of online sexual contacts that children are exposed to, primarily on the basis of young people's own descriptions of incidents that they themselves have experienced. Online strategies employed for the purpose of creating opportunities for offline sexual offences are then described, and the chapter concludes with a brief discussion of the question of the likely prevalence of sexually abusive online contacts, and by positing a model of the relative frequency of different types of online sexual abuse.

## The data

Of the four data sets employed in this chapter, two were collected specifically to illuminate the nature of online sexual contacts with children in connection with a piece of research that the Swedish National Council for Crime Prevention was instructed to carry out by the Swedish government. The first of these, an online questionnaire survey of young people aged 15 to 17, provided a particularly rich source of insights into the nature of the online sexual contacts experienced by young people. The sample makes no claims to be representative, since once the questionnaire had been developed,[1] the data collection process was subcontracted to an established survey company, who then sent an invitation to participate in the survey to youths in the relevant age range who were (self-selected) members of a large online survey panel. The survey was conducted in the autumn of 2006 and remained open until approximately 1,000 respondents had completed the questionnaire. The data were then analysed by the author at the National Council for Crime Prevention.

Among other things, the online survey gave the respondents the opportunity, under conditions of complete anonymity, to describe in their own words contacts of a sexual nature that they had had with persons they 'knew or believed' to be at least five years older than themselves prior to their 15th birthdays (15 being the age of sexual consent in Sweden). Twenty-one per cent of the respondents (35 per cent of the females, seven per cent of the males) reported an online sexual contact of this kind before the age of 15. The online survey participants' descriptions of contacts they had themselves experienced are employed in this chapter as the principal basis for illustrating the different types of sexual contacts to which young people are exposed online. In cases where respondents had experienced more than one such contact prior to their 15th birthdays, they were asked to describe the incident involving the *oldest* person by whom they had been contacted.

The second data set comprises police offence reports and police interviews with victims of suspected sexual offences against persons under 18 years of age where the perpetrator and the victim had been in contact with one another online.[2] The relevant offence reports were identified by means of an electronic search of the offence report databases of 14 of Sweden's 21 police authorities, including those covering the country's three metropolitan areas. The search was necessary because at the time of the study, Internet-related sexual offences were not recorded by the Swedish police in a way that made it possible to distinguish them from other offences. The search process identifies relevant incidents by means of a computerised search of what are termed the 'offence descriptions' contained in each offence report. These are in effect a summary of the circumstances surrounding the reported incident written in the recording officer's own words.

The search noted the identity of reports where the offence description contained any of a number of pre-specified search terms indicating that the reported incident might have involved an Internet contact. These were then examined, and irrelevant cases excluded, producing a material comprising 315 offence reports. In cases where the offence report contained information indicating that an *offline* sexual offence had been, or may have been, committed against the victim, documentation from the police investigation into the offence, including police interviews with the victims, was requested from the relevant police authorities.[3]

In the current context, these data are employed primarily to describe the strategies used by sex offenders to arrange offline meetings with children. At the same time it should be noted that the descriptions of exclusively online contacts found in the police data matched very well with the descriptions collected in the web survey, although the police data contained more examples of the more serious types of incidents and of offences involving repeated contacts over relatively long periods of time. Another important difference is that the descriptions in the offence reports were written by police officers and simply do not have the same ring of authenticity as those provided by the young respondents in the online survey, and as will become clear, many of the web survey descriptions also provide insights into how the shorter contacts developed, and how the youths dealt with them. Information of this kind is not always available in the police offence reports, where the focus was primarily directed at describing the factors of interest in assessing whether or not a 'crime' had taken place.

The final two data sets, which were not collected specifically in order to examine the nature of sexually abusive or exploitative online contacts, are employed as a means of placing the findings from the first two data sets in a broader context. The third data set, which focuses on the prevalence of online sexual contacts between adults and children in Sweden, comes from a nationally representative school sample of 15-year-olds. Here the National Council has been able to exploit a recurrent self-report survey on involvement in crime and exposure to victimisation (e.g. Svensson and Ring 2007; Brå 2010), and added an item to the questionnaire used in the 2008 wave of data collection which corresponds to the question posed in the online survey.[4]

The fourth data set comprises a systematic sample of the reported offences registered by the Swedish police in 2008 under the crime codes for rape against persons under 18 years of age. The sample comprises 25 per cent of the reported offences against females, and 50 per cent of those against males. The data set once again draws information from both offence reports and police interviews with the young victims of these crimes. These data were collected in order to produce an overview of the nature of the rape offences against children currently coming to the attention of the Swedish justice system. Here the material is employed to provide an indication of the proportion of reported suspected rape offences against young people that originated in an online contact between the perpetrator and the victim.

## Different types of online sexual contacts

Analyses of the web survey descriptions and the police data respectively showed that the online contacts could be organised on the basis of a number of different elements which occurred repeatedly in both data sets. Sometimes one of these elements occurred in isolation in the context of a given contact, at other times contacts involved two or more elements. The focus is here directed first and foremost at describing the different elements themselves and to this end the contacts have been organised into five (non-mutually exclusive) categories. The question of the relationship between these five categories of contacts, and of whether they can or should be viewed as different parts of a continuum, or as different 'stages' in a general grooming process, is addressed towards the end of the chapter in connection with the presentation of a descriptive model of sexually abusive online contacts.

The five categories of contacts are as follows:

- contacts involving sexual questions and 'dirty talk';
- contacts involving sexual images;
- contacts involving web cameras;
- contacts that are extended to mobile phones;
- contacts involving attempts to arrange offline meetings.

Within these categories of contacts, the data show quite substantial variations in the specific content of the contacts in individual cases. These include variations in for example how the contact was developed and in the type of language used by the adults concerned, and it would not be possible in the context of a single chapter to provide both a concise overview of different categories of online contacts and a more detailed examination of the level of variation within each category. The web survey descriptions employed to illustrate the different types of contact have therefore been chosen on the one hand with the objective of providing a broad sense of the nature of a given category in relation to the other categories exemplified in the text, and on the other with the intention of exemplifying various other aspects of the online contacts described in the data sets. These relate to among other things where the contacts were established, how they were developed and also indications of possible vulnerabilities on the part of the young people who had experienced them. These aspects are not in themselves specific to any given category, but rather appear in the data in connection with all of the categories of contacts illustrated below.

The web survey respondents were asked the age of the person they had been in contact with, and this information, along with the age of the respondent at the time of the contact, is presented in connection with each description.[5] The descriptions quoted have in certain cases been shortened somewhat, and the names of specific Internet communities have been removed and replaced with 'community' or 'chat room', but otherwise they have simply been translated from Swedish to English.

### Sexual questions and 'dirty talk'

The quotation presented at the beginning of this chapter represents one example of the first type of contact. The two quotes below present additional examples.

> It was a 46-year-old man who made sexual remarks and asked if I wanted to see his penis. He also asked if we could meet.
>
> (boy aged 14; man aged over 35)

> He started by asking about things like: where do you live, how old are you, how's it going in school, how many friends have you got, what are things like at home...then when we'd chatted for 30 minutes he starts asking if I was a virgin, if I was single, how I wanted it and then if we could meet and so on...I blocked him of course.
>
> (girl aged 14; man aged over 35)

This last example illustrates the way in which the adult often takes a little time to develop a relationship of trust with the child before moving on to introduce the sexual content into their communication. At the same time, however, the quote clearly indicates that it is the adult who is managing the content of the online conversation, and at the same time acquiring information about the child which may prove helpful in deciding upon a strategy to further his apparent sexual intent, fishing for indications of possible vulnerability. One recurrent theme in both the literature (e.g. Mitchell *et al.* 2001; Alvin Malesky Jr. 2007) and our own data is that many of the children who find themselves getting into serious difficulties online have characteristics that make them particularly vulnerable to this kind of contact. The next quote shows one of the ways in which such vulnerabilities may be exploited.

### Sexual images

> Two different men chatted with me on a community and got me to give them my MSN address. I didn't have many friends, and low self-esteem. They were nice to me and after a while they started asking me to send pictures. I sent a few photos. We chatted more, and they both started asking for a bit more revealing...naked pictures...I hesitated, but then I thought they're so nice, so why not, I'm never going to meet them. So I took some more pictures and sent them. After a while I realised what I'd done was wrong and I blocked them both and stopped using that address.
>
> (girl aged 13; men aged over 35)

In this quote, which describes how a girl was persuaded to send sexual images to two adults, we see once again that the adults first take the time to develop a relationship of trust, in this case by 'being nice' to the child. And they then get her to do what they want gradually, by stages – first ordinary pictures, then naked pictures.

The above description is also interesting for a number of other reasons. First, it shows how the Internet provides opportunities for people interested in sexual images of children to get children themselves to contribute to the enormous and ever growing number of child exploitation and abuse images circulating on the Internet. It also illustrates where the contact begins and how it develops in the online environment. The girl in this case meets the men on the chat site of an online community, and the communication is then transferred to MSN Messenger, an example of what is known as an instant messaging application. These applications allow you to chat over the Internet, and to send pictures and film clips, and also to use a web camera for video conversations. And they allow you to do these things in private, without being seen by anyone else online, which you cannot do if you are communicating with someone in a public chat room. In both the web survey and the police data, the most common scenario described was for the initial contact to have taken place in the public chat room of one of several popular internet communities, and for the two people involved to agree to move over to MSN Messenger, where their communication became private. And it was usually only after the contact had been shifted over to MSN Messenger that the adults started to introduce the sexual elements into the communication.

Both the web survey and the police material also contained examples of cases where it was the adult who had sent sexual images to the child. In the police material, these included sexual images that were purportedly of the adult him- or (very rarely) herself, photographs of young children in sexual poses, and pornographic film clips where either the adult himself or others, including children, were depicted engaging in a variety of sex acts. The web survey data, however, only contained descriptions of the first type of images, as in the following short example.

I thought he was about the same age as me, then one evening he sent me pictures of himself and his intimate parts. I blocked him and took him off my list!

(girl under 12; man aged 18–24)

This last quote also illustrates another central, and this time more positive, theme from the web survey descriptions, which is that many, and perhaps the majority, of children seem to learn very quickly how to end unwanted contacts as soon as something happens that they don't feel comfortable with. 'Blocking' a person in the way described by the girl in the quotation means that you no longer actively have to reject contacts from a person trying to reach you via an instant messaging application because any messages they subsequently try to send you will be filtered out by the application itself. Someone who really wants to reach you can get around this of course, but blocking people in this way makes things more difficult for them. In our material, with a few exceptions, this kind of 'blocking' activity appeared to be sufficient as a means of avoiding further contacts from the individuals concerned.

### Contacts involving web cameras

The material included two principal categories of contacts involving web cameras. The first of these involved men attempting to persuade children to take off their clothes and/or to engage in sexual acts in front of their web cameras.

> ...I didn't think of it as a particularly bad experience, it was more that I got irritated at the guy. He wanted me to photograph myself with the web cam in string panties, which I did, out of curiosity as much as anything. Never had much self-confidence, especially not about my body, ...and I suppose I hoped I'd get a few compliments. Anyway, he wasn't satisfied with the picture I sent, he wanted me to stand up in it...I got stressed then because I knew mum and dad were downstairs...It didn't feel all that bad, a bit degrading because the picture wasn't good enough and I'd really tried to make it good...I took him off my MSN-list and that was the end of it.
>
> (girl aged 13; man, age unknown)

Once again, many of these webcam contacts effectively involved adults attempting to persuade children to participate in the production of child exploitation images. The police data included a number of much more serious incidents than that described above, however, where girls aged 10 to 13 had been given money to pose naked on several occasions over a number of months. The police data also included cases where the adult had first persuaded the child to pose partially nude, and had then saved these pictures and used them to blackmail the child. For the most part the children were blackmailed into sending even more revealing pictures or into participating in cybersex, but there were also cases where blackmail had been used to try to coerce the child into agreeing to an offline meeting.

The other main category of webcam contacts involved men manipulating children into opening their webcam windows and then exposing themselves to these children in various ways.

> It wasn't actually that he wanted me to do anything, but he contacted me on MSN, and turned on his webcam pointed at his sex organ where he was sitting and masturbating. Then he wrote a load of dirty things to me. I shut everything down as quickly as I could of course, and then I blocked him. But it was very unpleasant all the same.
>
> (girl aged 13; man, aged 25–35)

A number of descriptions were about incidents where adults had both exposed themselves and attempted to get the child to do the same.

> He asked me to show my breasts in the webcam and to have camsex with him, and he wanted to give me a dildo for my birthday...and he sat and had a wank for me in front of his webcam, etc.
>
> (girl aged 13; man over 35)

And as the following quotes show, the descriptions occasionally gave an indication that adults had been able to exploit the respondents' own curiosity and willingness to participate in online sex.

> We chatted for a while, then we started to talk sex. In the end we used webcams to see each other. I was totally up for it.
>
> (boy aged 14; man aged 25–35)

> He was nice, and showed me a picture of himself...then we discussed sex and he asked if I knew what cybersex was. Um, yeah...then he taught me.
>
> (girl aged 14; man aged 18–24)

### Extending contacts to mobile phones

The following two descriptions are examples of cases where the adult had succeeded in extending the contact offline by obtaining the child's mobile phone number:

> I chatted with him for a bit, then we swapped mobile phone numbers, and he sent a few texts asking friendly questions, then it got a lot dirtier.
>
> (girl aged under 12; man over 35)

> He started talking about totally ordinary things, then he asked for my MSN, and I gave it to him. Then he wrote a load of nasty questions, and wrote that he was doing sexual things to me. So I blocked him. But somehow he got hold of my number and called me and said he was going to stick his sex-organ into me and, well, loads of things like that.
>
> (girl aged 13; man aged 25–35)

Here it is worth noting that in those cases in the police data where children had actually met sex offenders offline, extending the contacts to the child's mobile phone was almost without exception the first stage in the process of moving the relationship from the online to the offline environment. Research has also noted that this represents a very significant step (e.g. O'Connell 2004). Once the adult has the child's phone number he[6] has gained access to him or her 24/7 and irrespective of whether or not the child chooses to spend time online. The police data included several examples of contacts where children had been sexually harassed by phone (for example in the form of sexually abusive texts and/or pornographic MMS messages) for upwards of a year before the contact had been reported to the police.

In some cases the children had provided their phone numbers themselves; in other cases, they had given out their names, and the adults had been able to obtain their mobile phone numbers using various kinds of online directory enquiry services, as in the following example.

> He was nice at first, got my MSN, started saying weird things, started pestering me, said that I had to answer his questions or he'd come round my house, and then he sent me all my personal details that he'd got from hitta.se (or somewhere similar) although I didn't know you could do that back then, and I got very scared.
>
> (girl aged 14; man aged 18–24)

### Attempts to arrange offline meetings

The web survey respondents reported that the adult with whom they had been in contact online had attempted to extend the contact to the offline environment, for example to phone contacts or by trying to arrange to meet the respondent, in just over 20 per cent of cases. The descriptions from the web survey that described adults having tried to arrange offline meetings showed that the adults had sometimes been very clear about the fact that they wanted to have sex with the respondent, as in cases for example where the child had been offered payment for sex, or where the adults made their sexual interest obvious in other ways, as in the two examples presented below.

> A man in his fifties wanted me to perform sexual services and meet him and get money for it. Then I asked if he didn't care about my age and he said the younger the better.
>
> (girl aged 12; man over 35)

> It was a man who wanted to have sex with me, and he wanted to pay for me to travel to meet him, said he really fancied me...
>
> (girl aged 12; man over 35)

In other cases, it was more a question of the adults saying that they wanted to meet as friends, to maybe watch a film or video, or do something fun together.

> He started talking to me about my interests and he said he was 15, then

after a week it came out that he was at least 25. He wanted to meet and do something fun, but my parents had scared me off stuff like that, so I gave up talking to him. But after a while I got a dirty mail where he said he'd met another boy.

(boy aged 13; man aged 25–35)

A small number of the web survey descriptions showed that the respondent had either met, or been on his or her way to meet, the adult offline. None of these descriptions described sexual offences having taken place at any of these meetings, however, and online contacts leading to offline sex offences are therefore described below on the basis of the police data.

## Online strategies leading to offline sex offences

The search of the police report databases identified a total of 69 reports relating to offline sex offences committed by perpetrators who had met the victims online. Of these, almost one-fifth occurred between perpetrators and victims of roughly the same age (an age difference of at most five years). All the victims in these cases were female, the majority aged between 15 and 17 and the perpetrators were males aged between 15 and 22. The victims had come into contact with the perpetrators, or with friends of the perpetrators, online and had then met them, often together with friends both of their own and of the perpetrator, to do something together on the evening that the offence took place. At some point during the evening, the perpetrator had then sexually assaulted the victim. In some cases the assault had gone no further than unwanted sexual touching, but in many cases the victim had been raped, sometimes saying that she had been too drunk to resist or that she had been asleep at the time of the assault. The offence almost always occurred on the first occasion that the victim met the perpetrator offline.

The analysis of the remaining offline sex offences in the police data identified three strategies that had been employed by adults to persuade the victims of these offences to meet them offline. These are referred to here as 'Friendship and romance (or just sex)', 'Promises of modelling work', and 'Offers of payment for sexual services'.

### Friendship and romance (or just sex)

The largest group of offline offence reports (n=29) related to cases where the perpetrators had for the most part developed friendships with the victims, first online and then also by means of mobile phone contacts. In some cases the child had fallen in love with the perpetrator. The victims were for the most part under 15 years of age, and the youngest victim was aged 11 at the time of the offence. All victims with one exception were female. The age of the perpetrators (all male) ranged between 17 (one case) and 44 years.

In approximately one-third of these cases the perpetrator was at least 20 years older than the victim, and it was relatively common in this particular group of offences for the perpetrators to have lied about their age. It was rare for them to have claimed to be the same age as the victims, but a 34-year-old had claimed to be 26, for example, and a 37-year-old claimed online to be 25, only to then 'confess' that he was in fact 28 when he eventually met the victim (a 13-year-old girl). Some perpetrators had also sent very misleading images of themselves to the victims in the course of their online contacts.

The length of the Internet contacts varied greatly. In approximately one-third of cases the online contact had continued for over six months (and for up to over two years) prior to the commission of the offline offence. Many of these longer online contacts involved children who described having problems at school, with bullying for example, or at home, and having felt a need to talk to someone. Initially the perpetrators had been very understanding and were often described by the children as 'kind' and 'considerate', or similar. The contacts were sometimes very intensive, at least for short periods, with telephone contacts and long chat conversations several times a day. The victims' parents were nonetheless mostly either completely unaware that their children were in touch with the perpetrators, or had no idea where these contacts were heading.

Virtually all of the offences resulting from these longer-term contacts had been committed in the perpetrators' homes, and the victims had often travelled to another town to meet them. Sometimes the children knew they would be having sex with the man before going to the offline meeting. In other cases, however, they had been raped or forced to engage in other sexual acts and described having been shocked at the men's behaviour. Some of the victims said that they had been in touch with the man for so long that they felt they really knew him, but when they finally met him offline he was a completely different person.

In cases where the online contact preceding the offline meeting had been shorter than six months, it was usually much shorter. In these cases, the perpetrator and victim had typically been in touch online and by mobile phone for less than a month (and in two cases for less than a week) before deciding to meet offline. As a rule, the material in these cases also included indications that the children were experiencing sometimes quite serious problems in other areas of their lives – such as long-term exposure to bullying, serious problems at home, and contacts with the child-psychiatric sector and the social services. Two of the victims had been placed in compulsory care institutions.

In some of the cases in this category of offence reports the police interview material shows that the victims did not feel any great emotional attachment to the perpetrator. Instead the perpetrator was able to exploit the fact that the child was herself open to the idea of meeting an older man for sex. Among these victims there were also a few who did not want the offences to be reported to the police since they did not feel the perpetrators had done anything wrong. Two of the victims (both aged under 15) stated, for example, that they had already met men aged between 20 and 35 for sex. They also stated that they often talked to people on the Internet and talked sex with the majority of them. One of these girls described how she had also had phone sex with a number of men she had met online.

Even in those cases where the victim had been coerced into offline sex, the child did not always break off the contact as a result. In several cases, the child had continued the contact with the perpetrator subsequent to the assault, and some of the children had met the perpetrators again and had been subjected to additional sexual assaults.

### Promises of modelling work

Seven of the offence reports related to cases where the victims had been lured to an offline meeting with an offer of some kind of modelling job. All these victims were females aged between 13 and 17 years. The perpetrators (all male) were aged between 23 and 62. In one case the victim had answered an Internet advert for a modelling job, but the girls had otherwise been contacted on communities or by email by men who had seen a picture that the girls had themselves published online, either on an Internet community or on a home page of their own.

In the initial stages of the contact, the perpetrators had first been very flattering about the girls' photographs, and had then moved on to convincing descriptions of their experiences from the modelling industry, where they claimed for the most part to work as professional photographers. These Internet contacts continued for anything from a few days to up to two months prior to the victims meeting the men offline. With a single exception, the perpetrators had promised the victims that the modelling assignment would not involve them being photographed nude.

As a rule, the perpetrators continued in their role as photographers at least in the initial stages of the offline meetings. In a typical case, the victim would first be photographed with her clothes on, and would then be asked to undress. The perpetrator would begin to sexually assault the victim by means of unwanted sexual touching, which he might explain as being necessary to correct the girl's poses. In the majority of cases, the sexual assault did not go any further than this sexual touching, often because the victim succeeded in getting away from the perpetrator. In two cases, however, the victims had been raped.

### Offers of payment for sexual services

Nine of the police reports relating to offline offences involved men who had offered the victims money for sex. The victims in these cases comprised males and females aged between 14 and 17. The perpetrators (all male) were aged between 25 and 49. The Internet contacts between victim and perpetrator had on occasion been very short, but the majority had continued for between one month and up to three to four months prior to the offline meeting. Five of the victims had travelled to another town to meet the perpetrator, and in five cases the victim had met the perpetrator for sex on two or more occasions.

In over half of the cases, the victims had been forced to engage in sexual acts that they did not wish to perform, and which they had not agreed to in advance. It was also often the case that the victim and perpetrator had agreed prior to the meeting that the perpetrator would use a condom. In virtually all cases, however, the victims were then either persuaded or coerced into having unprotected sex with the perpetrators.

## A common part of everyday life online?

Having exemplified different types of online sexual contacts, and having described a number of strategies employed to persuade potential victims to attend offline meetings, two central questions remain to be addressed. The first of these, that of the prevalence of online sexual contacts, is examined in the next section. The second question is that of the relative frequency of different types of contacts. This is approached, a little speculatively, in the subsequent section by means of an attempt to bring the findings from the different data sets together in a simple model emphasising a number of central aspects of the online sexual solicitation phenomenon.

### The prevalence of online sexual contacts

The web survey questions that elicited the descriptions of online sexual contacts presented earlier first asked the youths whether they had ever had an Internet contact with a person they knew or believed to be at least five years older than themselves that they would describe as sexual. A follow-up question was then asked to elicit whether they had experienced an Internet contact of this kind before their 15th birthdays. As was noted towards the beginning of the chapter, 35 per cent of the female respondents and seven per cent of the males reported having experienced such a contact. Since we have no information about the representativeness of the web survey sample, however, we cannot use these figures as a basis for statements about the likely prevalence of contacts of this kind.

Having since had an opportunity to pose a very similar question to a representative sample of 15-year-olds at school, however, we can speak to this issue with somewhat more suitable data. At the end of 2008, 13 per cent of the school sample (21 per cent of girls and a little under six per cent of boys) stated that, *over the course of the preceding 12 months*, they had experienced an online contact that they would describe as sexual with a person they knew or believed to be at least five years older than themselves. As would be expected, experience of such contacts was much more common among those who reported that they often chatted online with people they didn't already know offline. Among the girls who reported often chatting online with people they didn't know, fully 45 per cent reported having experienced a sexual contact with someone at least five years older than themselves. Among the boys who often chatted with people they didn't know, the corresponding figure was slightly over 12 per cent. The corresponding figures among the girls and boys who stated that they never or only rarely chatted online with people they didn't know were ten per cent and just over two per cent respectively.

We cannot of course be sure how many of the contacts reported in the school survey may in fact have been from other young people, rather than from adults, but there is nothing in our data to suggest that online sexual contacts from adults constitute a marginal or small-scale phenomenon. In fact several of the answers provided by youths in the online survey suggest rather the opposite, that contacts of this kind have become a more or less unremarkable part of everyday life for many young people online.

It happens almost every day that old men add you on MSN and want to start talking about sex and send on the webcam when they're having a wank and send pictures of their sex organs.

(girl)

Everyone with different fetishes hits on you if you log in as a girl. If you log in as a boy you get loads of comments from old men. They even offer you money for sex. Try it yourself!

(boy)

Thus the data indicate that exposure to online sexual contacts of various kinds is nothing unusual for many young people today. To further contextualise the question of the significance of the Internet for the prevalence of *offline* sexual offences against children, we might also ask: What proportion of offline sexual offences against children appear to originate in Internet contacts?

The fourth data set collected by the Swedish National Council for Crime Prevention makes it possible to provide a partial answer to this question, at least with regard to the most serious sexual offences that are brought to the attention of the criminal justice system. As was noted earlier, this data set comprises a systematic sample of 25 per cent of all sexual offences recorded by the Swedish police in 2008 under the crime codes for rape against females under the age of 18, and 50 per cent of those against males.

On the basis once again of the information contained in offence reports and interviews with the victims, it was possible to establish the nature of the relationship between perpetrator and victim in 83 per cent of the 456 cases in the sample. Of these cases, just over eight per cent involved registered suspected rape offences against young people who had first come into contact with the perpetrator online.

None of the cases identified related to victims under the age of 12. Among the female victims, online contacts accounted for a somewhat larger proportion of the recorded offences against 12–14-year-olds (15 per cent) than of those against 15–17-year-olds (8 per cent). The numbers of recorded offences against male victims are so small as to make the presentation of percentages potentially misleading (there were only 21 cases involving 12–17-year-old male victims in the entire sample). Of these, there was a single recorded suspected rape resulting from an online contact among the 12–14-year-old male victims, and a further single case among the 15–17-year-olds.

To put these figures into a broader perspective, we can note that current/ former boy/girlfriends and family members together accounted for 29 per cent (12–14-year-old victims) and 19 per cent (15–17-year-old victims) of perpetrators; and persons completely unknown to the victim, or whom the victim had met for the first time at most a few hours prior to the offence (with no prior online contact having taken place), accounted for 19 per cent (12–14-year-olds) and 35 per cent (15–17-year-olds) of perpetrators respectively. Taken together, these figures suggest that Internet contacts may well be playing a significant role in relation to the number of offline sex offences being committed, but that young people are on the whole still much more at risk from people close to them or whom they meet in the course of their social activities in a range of offline environments.

It is also important to note that the perpetrators in a substantial minority of the cases resulting from online contacts in this fourth data set were not very much older than the victims. The perpetrator was at least five years older than the victim in approximately two-thirds of the Internet-related cases involving 12–14-year-old victims, and in just under half of the cases involving 15–17-year-old victims.

### The pyramid of sexually abusive online contacts

As a means of attempting to put the different pieces of the picture together, it may be useful to conceptualise sexually abusive online contacts in terms of a pyramid, as in Figure 16.1 below.

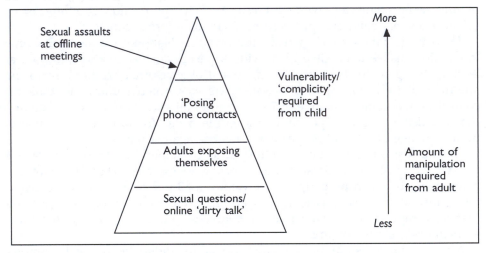

**Figure 16.1** The pyramid of sexually abusive online contacts

At the base of the pyramid we have a very large number of online sexual contacts that are currently being directed at young people.

Our data suggest that the majority of these contacts are probably blocked fairly quickly by the young people concerned, and are thus relatively 'unsuccessful' from the perspective of the would-be abuser. The question of whether contacts are likely to be successful from the abuser's point of view would seem in part to depend on what it is that the offender wants from the young person concerned. And it would also seem to depend on whether the abuser comes into contact with a child who is in some way vulnerable to the specific approach he (or she) has chosen to use.

The prevalence of different types of Internet-related sexual offences is probably also related to the amount of manipulation required from the abuser to get the young person to do what he wants. So it's probably *relatively* easy for an adult to manipulate children to give out their MSN addresses and then open up their webcam window so that the adult can expose himself. On the other hand, it is probably more difficult to persuade children to give out their phone numbers, to pose naked or engage in cybersex, or to agree to an offline meeting. Given the probable number of attempted online contacts, then, the proportion that result in *offline* sex offences is likely to be relatively small. At the same time, the findings from our final data set indicate that online contacts lead to a far from insignificant proportion of the more serious offline sexual offences that are coming to the attention of the police, particularly in relation to victims aged 12–14.

It might be tempting to see the different levels of the pyramid in terms of a continuum through which perpetrators move in order to arrive at the ultimate goal of an offline meeting; as different 'stages', if you will, in a grooming process focused on creating opportunities for the *offline* sexual exploitation or abuse of children. Our data strongly suggest, however, that the reality is rather more complicated. Many online perpetrators simply do not appear to be interested in offline contacts. As is the case with offline 'exhibitionists' (Sugarman *et al.* 1994; Rabinowitz-Greenberg *et al.* 2002), for example, some online exhibitionists may well also be inclined towards establishing other more 'hands-on' forms of contact with potential victims, while others are not. Similarly, collectors of sexually exploitative or abusive images of children may or may not be intent upon having sex with children offline (e.g. Craig *et al.* 2008). Our data contained examples of adults who had first persuaded children to send sexual images of themselves, and who had then persuaded these same children to meet them offline, and both our own data, and previous research (e.g. Gallagher *et al.* 2006), contain examples of individuals having used images sent by children to attempt to blackmail these children to meet them offline. Further, the use of both (child-) pornography and 'dirty talk' are widely acknowledged in the research literature as means of desensitising potential victims in the context of the grooming process (e.g. Krone 2004; McAlinden 2006). At the same time, however, our own data nonetheless indicate that for many perpetrators, the sexually abusive online contact may itself be the 'goal' rather than a 'means' to some other end.

More or less irrespective of the specific goal of a given perpetrator, the data sets collected by the National Council suggest a victim selection process that is as follows. The Internet provides potential sex offenders with access to a more or less unlimited number of young people. Of these young people, some are more vulnerable to contacts of this kind than others as a result of such factors as varying levels of knowledge and experience of the Internet and also a number of different background, psychological and social characteristics. The more children a perpetrator attempts to contact, the higher the probability that he will come into contact with a child who is vulnerable to precisely the type of strategy that he has chosen to use. As far as the perpetrator is concerned, we may assume that it makes little difference which of the children he contacts react positively to his approaches. Instead he exploits the fact that certain children have characteristics that will lead them to 'self-select' as victims. In this sense, the online sexual solicitation of children by adults is very reminiscent of other cybercrime phenomena, such as 'phishing', for example, or begging letters sent by email in the form of spam.

## Concluding remarks

Clearly the Internet has changed the way we live our lives, and this is perhaps particularly true for young people. Young people use the Internet to meet new people, they use the Internet to maintain friendships with people they like, they use it to fall in love, and they have very real boyfriends and girlfriends whom they have never met offline. The social world of many young people today spans the Internet and what we often still refer to as the 'real world' with no clear dividing line between the two, and what happens to young people online is thus just as much a part of their 'real world' or 'real life' as what happens offline.

The literature on children's use of the Internet has been careful to point out that it has the potential to play a very positive role in child development. In the area of relationships, for example, the Internet has been described as providing previously unknown opportunities for children to learn about sexual issues that may be difficult to discuss with parents or teachers, or with anyone else for that matter, in the context of more traditional social environments (e.g. Calder 2004). The Internet serves as a forum for counselling services, for information about sexually transmitted diseases and safe sex, as well as for information and advice for young people feeling insecure about their sexuality.

At the same time, however, there are many potential pitfalls and dangers associated with the Internet. These include the supply of distorted and at times extremely misleading information, the easy accessibility of violent images and pornography, and the opportunities provided by the Internet for new forms of bullying and sexual harassment and abuse. The presence on the Internet of adults who are actively seeking contact with young people in order to sexually exploit and abuse them naturally also falls within this category.

To safeguard the positive potential of the Internet, it is important that we do all we can to minimise the risks that young people face online. Parents need to be aware of these risks, as do teachers and other professional groups that work with children, and since young people cannot and should not be constantly monitored by adults, these groups also need to be equipped with a knowledge of what is needed to empower children to themselves deal with the risks associated with Internet use.

Unfortunately, we are today still in a situation where young people often know much more about the Internet than the adults who should ideally be able to mentor them. Hopefully this will gradually begin to change as today's 'Internet generation' matures into the parents, teachers and childcare professionals of tomorrow. There are nonetheless important challenges that even this much more Internet-savvy generation of adults will continue to face, since, as we know, the Internet is a highly changeable environment. It is therefore essential that we continuously monitor the nature of the dangers that confront young people online, that we stay abreast of developments in this rapidly changing environment, and that we work to ensure that minimising the risks faced by young people online is made as important a priority as that of minimising the dangers faced by children in offline environments.

## Further reading

The website of the Crimes Against Children Research Center is a very useful starting point for further reading on online sexual violence against children (http://www.unh.edu/ccrc/internet-crimes/). Amongst other things the site offers access to papers written on the basis of the data collected in three large research projects: The National Juvenile Online Victimization Study (of which there are now three waves), the Youth Internet Safety Survey (also three waves) and the Survey of Internet Mental Health Issues (a large-scale survey of mental health professionals' assessments of their clients' problematic Internet experiences). Kim-Kwang Raymond Choo's (2009) literature review of *Online Child Grooming* provides a wide-ranging insight into the diversity of topics covered by research in this area, while Sonia Livingstone's (2009) *Children and the Internet* (Oxford: Polity Press) presents a very thought-provoking account both of the ways in which children's lives have been changed by the advent of widespread Internet use and of the everyday online practices and experiences of young people themselves.

## Notes

1 Many of the formulations employed in the questionnaire were inspired by the telephone survey instrument developed at the Crimes Against Children Research Center in New Hampshire for use in the first Youth Internet Safety Survey (Finkelhor *et al*. 2000).
2 The data collection approach was once again inspired by work conducted at the Crimes Against Children Research Center, this time in the National Juvenile Online Victimization Study (Wolak *et al*. 2004b).
3 The offences included in the study were reported between 1 January 2004 and 26 September 2006. The material can be broken down into different types of contacts as follows. 1) Cases where perpetrator and victim had only been in contact online (n=179); 2) Cases where perpetrator and victim had been in contact both online and offline (e.g. by phone), but where the material provides no sure indication of a sexual offence having taken place at an offline meeting (n=45); 3) Cases where an adult perpetrator who already knew the child offline had used the Internet to develop the existing relationship for sexual purposes (n=22); 4) Cases where the perpetrator and the victim came into contact with one another online, and where the perpetrator had subsequently committed a sexual offence against the victim at an offline meeting (n=69). A more detailed presentation of the police data can be found in Shannon 2008.
4 The survey is conducted among a representative sample of youth in their final year of secondary education (aged 15). The sample is drawn systematically from a list of all Swedish schools with year nine classes, ordered by school size. The 2008 survey was completed by a total of 6,893 students, which represents a response rate of 80% of the original sample (Brå 2010).
5 The nature of Internet communications means of course that it is never easy to know how old someone is if your only contact with them has been online, and thus the participants' responses as to the age of the person contacting them will in many instances constitute a 'best guess'.
6 Males were responsible for the vast majority of the contacts described by both the web survey respondents and by those who reported incidents to the police. Both data sets did, however, also contain a small number of examples of contacts which the respondent or victim stated had been initiated by an adult female. None of the *offline* sex offences had been committed by females, however.

371

# References

Alvin Malesky Jr., L. (2007) 'Predatory online behavior: Modus operandi of convicted sex offenders in identifying potential victims and contacting minors over the internet', *Journal of Child Sexual Abuse*, 16: 23–31.

Brå (2007) *The online sexual solicitation of children by adults in Sweden*. English summary of Brå-report No. 2007: 11. Stockholm: Swedish National Council for Crime Prevention.

Brå (2010) *Brott bland ungdomar i årskurs nio.* (Crime among youths in year nine. Results from the Swedish School Survey on Crime 1995–2008). Report 2010: 6. Stockholm: Swedish National Council for Crime Prevention.

Calder, M. (2004) 'The Internet: potential, problems and pathways to hands-on sexual offending', in M. Calder (ed.) *Child Sexual Abuse and the Internet: Tackling the new frontier*. Lyme Regis: Russell House Publishing.

Choo, K.R. (2009) *Online Child Grooming: A literature review on the misuse of social networking sites for grooming children for sexual offences*. Canberra: Australian Institute of Criminology.

Craig, L.A., Browne, K.D. and Beech, A.R. (2008) *Assessing Risk in Sex Offenders. A practitioner's guide*. Chichester: John Wiley and Sons.

Finkelhor, D., Mitchell, K.J. and Wolak, J. (2000) *Online Victimization: A report on the nation's youth*. Alexandria: National Center for Missing and Exploited Children.

Gallagher, B., Fraser, C., Christmann, K. and Hodgson, B. (2006) *International and Internet Child Sexual Abuse and Exploitation*. Huddersfield: University of Huddersfield, Centre for Applied Childhood Studies.

Krone, T. (2004) A typology of online child pornography offending. *Trends and Issues in Crime and Criminal Justice* no. 279. Canberra: Australian Institute of Criminology.

Marcum, C.D. (2007) 'Interpreting the intentions of internet predators: An examination of online predatory behaviour', *Journal of Child Sexual Abuse*, 16: 99–114.

Martens, P. (1989) *Sexualbrott mot barn. Presentation och diskussion av några centrala teman inom forskningsområdet.* (Sexual offences against children. Presentation and discussion of central research themes), Brå-report 1989: 1. Stockholm: Fritzes.

McAlinden, A-M. (2006) '"Setting 'em up": Personal, familial and institutional grooming in the sexual abuse of children', *Social and Legal Studies*, 15: 339–62.

Mitchell K., Finkelhor, D. and Wolak, J. (2001) 'Risk factors and impact of the online sexual solicitation of youth', *Journal of the American Medical Association*, 285, 1–4.

O'Connell, R. (2003) *A Typology of Child Cybersexploitation and Online Grooming Practices*. Preston: University of Central Lancashire, Cybersex Research Unit.

O'Connell, R. (2004) 'From fixed to mobile Internet: The morphing of criminal activity online', in M. Calder (ed.) *Child Sexual Abuse and the Internet: Tackling the new frontier*. Lyme Regis: Russell House Publishing.

O'Connell, R., Price, J. and Barrow, C. (2004) *Cyber Stalking, Abusive Cyber Sex and Online Grooming. A programme of education for teenagers*. Preston: University of Central Lancashire, Cybersex Research Unit.

Rabinowitz-Greenberg, S.R., Firestone, P., Bradford, J.M. and Greenberg, D.M. (2002) 'Prediction of recidivism in exhibitionists: Psychological, phallometric, and offence factors', *Sexual Abuse: A Journal of Research and Treatment*, 14, 329–47.

Shannon, D. (2008) 'Online sexual grooming in Sweden – Online and offline sex offences against children as described in Swedish police data', *Journal of Scandinavian Studies in Criminology and Crime Prevention*, 9: 160–180.

Stanley, J. (2001) Child abuse and the internet. *Child Abuse Prevention Issues*, No. 15. Melbourne: Australian Institute of Family Studies.

Sugarman, P., Dumughn, C., Saad, K., Hinder, S. and Bluglass, R. (1994) 'Dangerousness in exhibitionists', *Journal of Forensic Psychiatry*, 5: 287–96.

Svensson, R. and Ring, J. (2007) 'Trends in self-reported youth crime and victimisation in Sweden, 1995–2005', *Journal of Scandinavian Studies in Criminology and Crime Prevention*, 8, 153–177.

Wolak, J., Finkelhor, D. and Mitchell, K.J. (2004a) 'Internet-initiated sex crimes against minors: Implications for prevention based on findings from a national study', *Journal of Adolescent Health*, 35(5): 424–33.

Wolak, J., Mitchell, K.J. and Finkelhor, D. (2003) *Internet Sex Crimes Against Minors: The response of law enforcement*. Alexandria, VA: National Center for Missing and Exploited Children.

Wolak, J., Mitchell, K. and Finkelhor, D. (2004b) *National juvenile online victimization study (N-Jov): Methodology report*. New Hampshire: Crimes against Children Research Center, University of New Hampshire.

Wolak, J., Mitchell, K. and Finkelhor, D. (2006) *Online Victimization of Youth: Five years later*. Alexandria: National Center for Missing and Exploited Children.

# Chapter 17

# Practitioner commentary: working with sexual violence

*Stephanie Kewley*

## Meet Stephanie Kewley

Stephanie is currently a Programme Manager for the National Probation Service. For the past eight years she has worked as a treatment practitioner in both custodial and community settings, delivering a range of offending behaviour programmes to offenders. Much of her practice has focused on work with perpetrators of sexual violence. Stephanie is also a part-time PhD student with the University of Birmingham. Her thesis explores how religiosity and religious affiliation assist sexual offenders engaged in the process of desistance.

## Introduction

The prevalence of sexual violence is of global concern. Indeed the World Health Organisation identifies sexual violence as a major public health problem (Violence Against Women 2009). The damaging effects of sexual violence against women are well documented, from emotional and psychological effects to physical injuries and death (Harvey *et al.* 2007).

This chapter presents a practitioner's perspective of working with sexually violent offenders and *Surviving Sexual Violence* by Liz Kelly (1989) provides a central focus for exploring sexual violence within the National Probation Service of England and Wales (NPS). The chapter summarises the breadth of sexual violence, briefly discussing the effectiveness and limitations of interventions used by the NPS when working with an offending population. Commentary considers how Kelly's continuum and definition of sexual violence is addressed within the Criminal Justice System (CJS), in particular the unhelpful labelling and underdeveloped assessment process for men convicted of sexual violence against an intimate partner. The chapter concludes with a number of proposals.

## The scope of sexual violence and the CJS

Kelly (1989) defines sexual violence as physical, visual, verbal or sexual acts that threaten or hurt, degrade or take away a woman/girl's ability to control intimate contact. Kelly records the enormity of the incidence rates experienced by 60 women interviewed for her study. Women were sampled in the main from social service or crisis centres: 78 per cent experienced three forms of sexual violence at some point in their life; 50 per cent experienced rape; 70 per cent discussed sexual assaults, from being touched indecently by a stranger to forced sexual acts with a partner; 50 per cent had been abused by a family member; and 53 per cent had experienced domestic violence. One hundred per cent of the sample had felt the threat of violence from either a stranger or a known male at some point in their life. The threat of violence experienced by all of these women is alarming and of concern.

In her study, sexual harassment was the most common form of abuse taking place at the workplace or in the street (Kelly 1989). The women described this as 'intrusive and involved assumptions of intimacy that women felt were inappropriate and/or involved men treating women as sexual objects' (p. 103). Ninety-three per cent experienced harassment as a 'normal experience which occurred on an everyday basis' (p. 81). Sexual harassment, obscene calls and pressure to have sex were the most regular experiences. Kelly could not include these statistics in her overall data analysis as the women reported too many incidents and could not recall individual events accurately.

Perpetrators in her study were neither exclusively known partners nor strangers; indeed Kelly's definition of sexual violence does not distinguish the relationship status of the perpetrator with the victim. The relationship status within her definition is immaterial. However, the issue of the sexual perpetrator and the victim's relationship does appear to be pertinent within the wider societal view of sexual violence. Attitudes supporting abuse dominate the media, and myths surrounding rape, for example, are cultivated that hold victims responsible for the abuse of their partner. Myths support the idea that rape is deserved and even enjoyed, the seriousness of abuse is minimised, and victims are doubted and questioned as to why they stay in a relationship if it is so bad (Carlyle 2008).

Evidence suggests that the likelihood of sexual assault is greater for a woman when she is in an intimate or dating relationship, and is perpetrated more commonly by her partner than by a stranger (Abbey et al. 2006). Yet the media generate contrary stories of stranger-perpetrated sexual crimes, fuelling myths and moral panic, publishing stories of women and children vulnerable to a subclass of sexual deviants who will never reform (Ducat et al. 2009), men lurking behind bushes or outside school gates. Not only do such myths aim to cause widespread fear (Quinn et al. 2004) and denigrate individuals (West 2000), they are used to demonise a very small percentage of the male population and minimise the actions of others. Of concern is that such minimisation allows the wider population of men (and women) to disassociate themselves from sexual violence. This disassociation suppresses the voice of victims and fosters a silence, as documented in an earlier commentary by Jan Jordan (see Chapter 12). A continuum of sexual violence should be viewed as one spectrum, yet society generates an unhelpful offending hierarchy whereby the more severe cases of sexual violence are heard (although not often enough), and the regular and routine sexualisation of and violence against women is silenced. Buying into this hierarchy fosters disassociation and allows many perpetrators of partner abuse not to consider their abuse as sexual. Yet there are common and interesting similarities between those men who offend against partners and those who offend against adult women who are strangers that cannot be ignored.

Such similarities are evident through comparison of different types of offenders. Consider the generally violent/antisocial type of domestic violent perpetrator; he carries out his acts of abuse in a generalised way, is not restricted to intimate abuse, is more likely to misuse substances and have generally antisocial attitudes towards women (*CDVP Theory Manual* 2005). Similarly, there is a view that the adult stranger rapist fundamentally expresses hostility and anger towards women generally, has the need to exert and gain power and control over her, and likely uses alcohol as a primary strategy to justify his actions (Craig *et al.* 2008). Rees and Rivett (2005) considered four subtypes of domestic violence perpetrator: antisocial; narcissistic; less antisocial; and borderline emotionally dependent. These can be paralleled to sex offenders who perpetrate abuse against adult women and who present with poor attachment styles, hold antisocial attitudes, are narcissistic and can be personality disordered (Beech *et al.* 2009). Furthermore, both groups present with inadequate relationship skills and poor intimacy levels (Beech *et al.* 2009; *CDVP Theory Manual* 2005). Finally, although there are limited studies in relation to men who rape their partners (Finkelhor and Yllö 1987; Groth *et al.* 1977), of the studies available, perpetrators are defined as having similar profiles to those who rape strangers or women in non-intimate relations. And yet, society stereotypes and stigmatises one group of offenders as sexual deviants (Quinn *et al.* 2004) but waters down the stereotype and labelling of offenders who are domestically abusive, despite their many shared offending behaviours.

Kelly's (1989) small sample alone cannot be generalised to all women. Indeed, research into sexual violence is problematic due to the complex range of definitions used, differing abusive behaviours studied and incompatible methodological approaches (Kelly *et al.* 2005). One significant survey that begins to deal with the issue of representation and generalisation is the British Crime Survey (BCS). In 2008–2009, of the 46,000 participants, three per cent of women aged 16 to 59 reported having experienced either actual or attempted sexual assault in the past 12 months. Police-recorded crime data for the same period registered 40,787 incidents of rape, sexual assault and sexual activity with children and 10,701 incidences of 'other' sexual offences (Crime in England and Wales 2008/2009, 2009). The BCS and police-recorded crime data, however, only record offences legally defined; these are much narrower definitions than Kelly's. Furthermore prevalence, not incidence, is recorded and although intimate violence is recorded as the most common type of violence, it is not defined as sexual violence. This omission accounts for a recorded 226,000 incidents. Other findings support the BCS editors' view that incidence and prevalence of sexual violence against women by men is under-reported and therefore potentially underestimated (Bogner *et al.* 2007; Butler and Welch 2009; Taylor and Gassner 2009; Walby and Allen 2004).

## Provision within the NPS

No single agency or policy in isolation can deal with the issue of sexual violence (Levenson and D'Amora 2007). In fact, sociopolitical belief systems are so embedded and ingrained that broader cultural, national and societal approaches towards gender need to be challenged (Hearn and Whitehead 2006). Relying on CJS organisations to resolve the issue causes concern for some radical feminists, who argue that the law is in itself oppressive towards women and merely reflects the wider societal problems regarding gender (DeKeseredy and Dragiewicz 2007). Only one per cent of Kelly's (1989) women interviewed reported their assaults to the police and more alarmingly only a maximum of five men were charged. The difficulty in securing successful prosecution of sexual violence is commonly noted (Kelly *et al.* 2005; Rumney 2009), with many rape cases failing to make it past the investigation stage (Brown *et al.* 2007). Myths in society and the media that support abusive behaviour around date rape or rape where the victim was intoxicated both decrease victims' confidence in reporting and compromise individuals' capacity to believe victims (Meyer 2010). Prosecuting cases of sexual violence becomes complex and fraught with issues such as the reliability of evidence from a traumatised victim recalling abuse from many previous years (Porter *et al.* 2003) or indeed victims withdrawing statements later (Robinson and Cook 2006). Given the small minority of offenders prosecuted, CJS agencies are therefore limited in the ways in which they can have an impact on reducing sexual violence within society (Robinson and Cook 2006).

The NPS's fundamental aim is to both protect the public and reduce reoffending, working predominantly with offenders who are convicted of a criminal offence and sentenced to either custodial or community sentences. Men convicted of a sexual assault can be mandated to attend and engage in an offending behaviour programme as part of their rehabilitation. Offending behaviour programmes are accredited interventions built upon theoretical foundations and empirical evidence. Such interventions are known to reduce reoffending (Maguire *et al.* 2010) although there are criticisms of their effectiveness too (Stanley 2009). Accredited programmes delivered by the NPS are based on the 'What Works' literature (Maguire *et al.* 2010), adopting a cognitive behavioural approach (CBT), which is known to have a positive effect, particularly when working with sexual offending behaviour (Lösel and Schmucker 2005).

Kelly's (1989) definition and continuum of sexual violence is all-inclusive and does not specify perpetrator relationship with the victim; however, within the NPS, two separate treatment pathways are available, one for those deemed sexual offenders and one labelled domestic violence perpetrators. For those labelled sexual offenders, each probation area delivers one of three accredited programmes: Northumbria Sex Offenders Group (NSOGP), Thames Valley Sex Offender Group (TV-SOGP) and the West Midlands (C-SOGP) (Mandeville-

Norden and Beech 2004). Each programme is designed to work with a wide range of sexual offences from assaults against intra- and/or extra-familial children and adults to non-contact offences such as indecent exposure or possession of illegal pornography. In recent evaluations offenders completing such programmes had significantly lower reconviction rates, when compared with offenders not completing treatment (Hanson *et al.* 2009; Hollis 2007). For domestic violence offenders two accredited programmes are delivered for low- to medium-risk offenders within the community: the Integrated Domestic Abuse Programme (IDAP) and the Community Domestic Violence Programme (CDVP). Current domestic violence programmes are restricted to offenders who perpetrate abuse to women within the context of an intimate relationship (*CDVP Theory Manual* 2005). The success of these programmes is less encouraging, and questions remain regarding the effectiveness of both CDVP and IDAP (Hollis 2007).

Prior to sentencing an assessment by a probation officer identifies a suitable programme for the offender. The pre-sentence report highlights the risk and needs of the offender and advises the court of sentencing options available. A range of eligibility and suitability criteria must be met before programme recommendations are made. For the sex offender group programme, the offender must be a male, over 21 years of age, and have committed a sexual offence. For the domestic violence programme, the offender must be a male and have been assessed as moderate to high risk on the Spousal Assault Risk Assessment (SARA). Both are required to have some level of motivation to address their offending behaviour. Whilst offenders may be eligible for group work, some may not be suitable in special circumstances, such as absolute denial, severe disruptive substance misuse, low-level IQ (although poor literacy would not exclude) and some diagnosed personality disorders such as psychopathy (Kennington *et al.* 2002).

Following sentencing, further treatment assessments are made. However, it is at this stage that detailed treatment assessments stop for men subject to domestic violence programmes. Along with continual risk of harm and risk of reconviction assessments, a Structured Assessment of Risk and Need (SARN) (*PC17/2007 – Assessment and Management of Sex Offenders* 2007; Webster *et al.* 2006) is completed for sexual offenders. The SARN framework uses four domains, allowing assessment of 16 dynamic risk factors. These include a sexual interest domain, distorted attitudes domain, socio-affective functioning domain and a self-management domain (Craig *et al.* 2008). SARN provides an assessment of stable dynamic risk factors that can be addressed during treatment along with those acute dynamic factors that project imminence of risk. The higher the deviancy, the more intensive treatment an offender requires. The tool is used dynamically throughout the offender's treatment, measuring any change in the offender's deviancy.

Agreeing treatment targets, such as through the SARN framework, enables collaboration between the probation officer, the programme facilitators (accredited staff members who deliver the programme to the group of offenders), and the offender himself. Individualised focus on the offender's need increases motivation and engagement; indeed a lack of congruence with programme material is thought to have an impact on attrition (Cadsky *et al.*

1996). Yet practitioners working with domestically violent men are not empirically guided to inform treatment in this way. An assessment of motivation and willingness to change is made with current assessments; however, individual treatment targets are not routinely agreed.

Theories that explain domestic abuse are multifaceted and an understanding of individuals' treatment needs is required. A pro-feminist theory underpins the intervention but other theoretical foundations support the programme too (e.g., nested ecological model; intergenerational transmission; psychological; early trauma; borderline personality and attachment disorders; drug and alcohol abuse (Corvo *et al.* 2008)).

Contrary to the moderate success experienced with sex offender programmes, domestic violence programmes fare less favourably, attracting harsh criticism (Stanley 2009). High levels of attrition on domestic violence programmes is neither a recent nor localised phenomenon (Bowen and Gilchrist 2006). Alarmingly, dropouts pose an even greater risk than those starting a programme (Mahon *et al.* 2009). Understanding why attrition occurs so specifically for this group of men is of great importance.

## Concluding comments

The high incidence rates of sexual violence experienced by women, regardless of their relationship to the perpetrators, is a societal responsibility (Carlyle *et al.* 2008). The NPS, although not solely responsible, can play a significant part in addressing this issue. In order to begin to prepare offenders and assist practitioners to deliver effective and responsive treatment, the following proposals are made.

Pre-treatment screening to analyse offender types and treatment needs is essential (Mahon *et al.* 2009); as evidenced in this chapter, this is current practice for sexual offenders. However, current practices for those assessing men who offend against an intimate partner, even if the offence is overtly sexual, are limited to risk and not treatment needs analysis. Although risk assessment is vital, they are indeed ineffective in assessing treatment need. One must question whether this could be compounding high attrition experienced on such programmes. The first proposal is that a universal sexual abuse treatment needs analysis be developed. This would draw upon what is already known about men who offend against adult female victims, enabling intervention practitioners and perpetrators to locate specific deficits requiring attention during treatment.

The second proposal requests further examination of the similarities in treatment needs of men convicted of sexual offences against women who are strangers and of those in intimate relationships. If a shared treatment need is identified, offenders could begin to consider together the issues of sexual violence across the continuum, without an offending hierarchy. From a practitioner's perspective, men on domestic violence programmes tend to distance themselves from sexual abuse, whilst being willing to consider violent behaviour; few take responsibility for sexual abuse. Similarly, men referred to sex offender programmes for offences against adult females are treated through an intervention primarily designed for child sex offenders (Allam *et al.* 2006). They spend time distancing themselves from sexual deviancy towards children. West Midlands Probation piloted a separate group for offenders against adult women and found that these men had a greater sense of responsibility than offenders in mixed groups.

Third, it is proposed that an induction or bridging programme prior to men engaging in the offence-specific programme should be explored. Preparatory programmes are known to enhance offenders' self-esteem and allay fears around attending a programme (Marshall and Burton 2010). A bridge programme would look to aid attrition by motivating men to engage before they start the treatment, aid treatment needs identification, and act to refocus the gender identity of men to encourage and empower masculinity. Early stages of domestic violence programmes are spent working with resistance and conflict; educational messages about sexual violence become lost in therapeutic battles. Interventions could be offered to all men who are sexually violent to adult women regardless of their relationships.

Perhaps controversial is the idea that the attitudes and behaviours of men found guilty of sexual violence should be considered no different from those of men not prosecuted. To do the opposite potentially allows men not brought before criminal proceedings to distance and disassociate themselves from sexual violence. An inclusive approach enables men to become familiarised with language and behaviours outside of legal terminology and begin to recognise the disturbing normality of sexual violence within their society and their own behaviours (Kelly 1989). Currently the NPS is limited to working with statutory offenders yet research shows that mixing groups of statutory and non-statutory cases has a positive effect on attrition (Rees and Rivett 2005). This final proposal calls for further analysis of the effects of mixed groups.

Taking theoretical models and concepts from the academic world into the real world brings implementation and design challenges to practitioners (Bourgon *et al.* 2009). Incorrect and inappropriate targeting of offenders leads to higher dropout rates, more so for high-risk men (Palmer *et al.* 2009). An understanding of Kelly's continuum of sexual violence assists us to reframe how we work with men who perpetrate abuse to women, regardless of the relationship with the victim. We must not be limited or drawn into the stereotyped images of sexual offenders portrayed in the media but widen our appreciation. We must not lose sight of the fact that the experiences of victims of rape and domestic violence are not dissimilar. One victim reflects that, 'I don't think you stand much chance really, you're no safer whether you're in the house or out of it' (Kelly 1989: 98).

## References

Abbey, A., Parkhill, M., BeShears, R., Clinton-Sherrod, A. and Zawacki, T. (2006) 'Cross-sectional predictors of sexual assault perpetration in a community sample of single African American and Caucasian men', *Aggressive Behavior*, 32(1): 54–67.

Allam, J., Middleton, D. and Browne, K. (2006) 'Different clients, different needs? Practice issues in community-based treatment for sex offenders', *Criminal Behaviour and Mental Health*, 7(1): 69–84.

Beech, A., Craig, L. and Browne, K. (2009) *Assessment and Treatment of Sex Offenders: a Handbook*: Wiley.

Bogner, D., Herlihy, J. and Brewin, C. (2007) 'Impact of sexual violence on disclosure during Home Office interviews', *The British Journal of Psychiatry*, 191(1): 75.

Bourgon, G., Bonta, J., Rugge, T., Scott, T. and Yessine, A. (2009) 'Translating "What Works" into sustainable everyday practice: Program Design, Implementation and Evaluation'. Available at http://dsp-psd.pwgs.c.gc.ca/collections/collection_2010/2p-ps/PS3-1-2009-5-eng.pdf

Bowen, E. and Gilchrist, E. (2006) 'Predicting dropout of court-mandated treatment in a British sample of domestic violence offenders', *Psychology, Crime and Law*, 12(5): 573–87.

Brown, J., Hamilton, C. and O'Neill, D. (2007) 'Characteristics associated with rape attrition and the role played by scepticism or legal rationality by investigators and prosecutors', *Psychology, Crime and Law*, 13(4): 355–70.

Butler, B. and Welch, J. (2009) 'Drug-facilitated sexual assault', *Canadian Medical Association Journal*, 180(5): 493.

Cadsky, O., Hanson, R., Crawford, M. and Lalonde, C. (1996) 'Attrition from a male batterer treatment program: Client-treatment congruence and lifestyle instability', *Violence and Victims*, 11(1): 51–64.

Carlyle, K., Slater, M. and Chakroff, J. (2008) 'Newspaper coverage of intimate partner violence: Skewing representations of risk', *Journal of Communication*, 58(1): 168–86.

*CDVP Theory Manual* (2005).

Corvo, K., Dutton, D. and Chen, W. (2008) 'Toward evidence-based practice with domestic violence perpetrators', *Journal of Aggression, Maltreatment and Trauma*, 16(2): 111–30.

Craig, L., Browne, K. and Beech, A. (2008) *Assessing Risk in Sex Offenders: A Practitioner's Guide*: John Wiley and Sons Inc.

Crime in England and Wales 2008/2009 (2009) *Findings from the British Crime Survey and police recorded crime*, 1(11/09). Retrieved from http://rds.homeoffice.gov.uk/rds/pdfs09/hosb1109vol1.pdf

DeKeseredy, W. and Dragiewicz, M. (2007) 'Understanding the complexities of feminist perspectives on woman abuse: A commentary on Donald G. Dutton's Rethinking Domestic Violence', *Violence Against Women*, 13(8): 874.

Ducat, L., Thomas, S. and Blood, W. (2009) 'Sensationalising sex offenders and sexual recidivism: Impact of the Serious Sex Offender Monitoring Act 2005 on media reportage', *Australian Psychologist*, 44(3): 156–65.

Finkelhor, D. and Yllö, K. (1987) *License to Rape: Sexual abuse of wives*. New York: Free Press

Groth, A., Burgess, W. and Holmstrom, L. (1977) 'Rape: Power, anger, and sexuality', *American Journal of Psychiatry*, 134(11): 1239.

Hanson, R.K., Bourgon, G., Helmus, L. and Hodgson, S. (2009) 'A meta-analysis of the effectiveness of treatment for sexual offenders: risk, need, and responsivity'. Retrieved from http://ocipep-bpiepc.qc.ca/res/cor/rep/fl/2009-01-trt-so-eng.pdf

Harvey, A., Garcia-Moreno, C. and Butchart, A. (2007) 'Primary prevention of intimate-partner violence and sexual violence: Background paper for WHO expert meeting May 2–3, 2007', World Health Organization.

Hearn, J. and Whitehead, A. (2006) 'Collateral damage: Men's "domestic" violence to women seen through men's relations with men', *Probation Journal*, 53(1): 38.

Hollis, V. (2007) *Reconviction Analysis of Interim Accredited Programmes Software (IAPS) Data*. London, UK: Research Development Statistics, National Offender Management Service.

Kelly, L. (1989) *Surviving Sexual Violence*. Cambridge: Polity Press.

Kelly, L., Lovett, J. and Regan, L. (2005) *A Gap or a Chasm?: Attrition in Reported Rape Cases*. Home Office Research Study 293. London: Home Office Research,

Development and Statistics Directorate.

Kennington, R., Dodds, M., McGregor, G. and Grubin, E. (2002) *Northumbria Sex Offender Programme: Theory Manual*. Northumbrian Probation Service.

Levenson, J. and D'Amora, D. (2007) 'Social policies designed to prevent sexual violence: The Emperor's new clothes?', *Criminal Justice Policy Review*, 18(2): 168.

Lösel, F. and Schmucker, M. (2005) 'The effectiveness of treatment for sexual offenders: A comprehensive meta-analysis', *Journal of Experimental Criminology*, 1(1): 117–46.

Maguire, M., Grubin, D., Lösel, F. and Raynor, P. (2010) '"What Works" and the Correctional Services Accreditation Panel: Taking stock from an inside perspective', *Criminology and Criminal Justice*, 10(1): 37.

Mahon, M., Devaney, J. and Lazenbatt, A. (2009) 'The role of theory in promoting social work values and its potential effect on outcomes in work with domestically violent men', *Irish Probation Journal*, 151.

Mandeville-Norden, R. and Beech, A. (2004) 'Community-based treatment of sex offenders', *Journal of Sexual Aggression*, 10(2): 193–214.

Marshall, W. and Burton, D. (2010) 'The importance of group processes in offender treatment', *Aggression and Violent Behavior*, 15(2): 141–49.

Meyer, A. (2010) 'Too drunk to say no', *Feminist Media Studies*, 10(1): 19–34.

Palmer, E., McGuire, J., Hatcher, R., Hounsome, J., Bilby, C. and Hollin, C. (2009) 'Allocation to offending behavior programs in the English and Welsh probation service', *Criminal Justice and Behavior*, 36(9): 909.

PC17/2007 – *Assessment and Management of Sex Offenders* (2007) Retrieved 3 July 2010 from http://www.probation.homeoffice.gov.uk/files/pdf/PC17%202007.pdf

Porter, S., Campbell, M., Birt, A. and Woodworth, M. (2003) '"He said, she said": A psychological perspective on historical memory evidence in the courtroom', *Canadian Psychology/Psychologie canadienne*, 44(3): 190–206.

Quinn, J., Forsyth, C. and Mullen-Quinn, C. (2004) 'Societal reaction to sex offenders: A review of the origins and results of the myths surrounding their crimes and treatment amenability', *Deviant Behavior*, 25(3): 215–32.

Rees, A. and Rivett, M. (2005) '"Let a hundred flowers bloom, let a hundred schools of thought contend": Towards a variety in programmes for perpetrators of domestic violence', *Probation Journal*, 52(3): 277.

Robinson, A. and Cook, D. (2006) 'Understanding victim retraction in cases of domestic violence: Specialist courts, government policy, and victim-centred justice', *Contemporary Justice Review*, 9(2): 189–213.

Rumney, P. (2009) 'Sexual assault and the justice gap: a question of attitude – by Jennifer Temkin and Barbara Krahé', *Legal Studies*, 29(4): 696–9.

Stanley, S. (2009) 'What Works in 2009: Progress or stagnation?', *Probation Journal*, 56(2): 153.

Taylor, S. and Gassner, L. (2009) 'Stemming the flow: challenges for policing adult sexual assault with regard to attrition rates and under-reporting of sexual offences', *Police Practice and Research*, 11(3): 240–55.

Violence Against Women (2009) *Fact Sheet No 239*. Retrieved 2 July 2010 from http://www.who.int/mediacentre/factsheets/fs239/en/

Walby, S. and Allen, J. (2004) *Domestic Violence, Sexual Assault and Stalking: Findings from the British Crime Survey*. Home Office Research, Development and Statistics Directorate, 276. London: Home Office.

Webster, S., Mann, R., Carter, A., Long, J., Milner, R., O Brien, M. *et al.* (2006) 'Inter-rater reliability of dynamic risk assessment with sexual offenders', *Psychology, Crime and Law*, 12(4): 439–52.

West, D. (2000) 'Paedophilia: plague or panic?', *Journal of Forensic Psychiatry and Psychology*, 11(3): 511–31.

**Part Four**

# Responding to Sexual Violence

# Introduction

*Jennifer Brown and Sandra Walklate*

## Introduction

The key foci of interventions in sexual violence are perpetrators and their victims. On the one hand sexual offending is somehow considered 'different' (Thomas 2005). Society still continues to demonise the offender, the media represent them as monsters and the sex offender is often the subject of bullying and harassment once incarcerated. Thomas further observes that professionals find offenders difficult to work with, and communities find it hard to permit released offenders to reintegrate. On the other hand, as Kelly (2008: 256) notes, sexual violence is distinctive because it 'violates personal intimate and psychological boundaries' of its victims. She charts the 'heady combination of activist protest, passionate polemic and more considered research and commentary [which] led Governments to embark on reforms of statutory and procedural responses to rape and sexual assault' (p. 253). The four chapters and practitioner commentary that make up this final section of the Handbook look at various aspects of responding to sexual violence. Helge Hoel and Duncan Lewis look at the work context especially from the perspective of lesbian, gay, bisexual and transsexual (LGBT) employees. Kate Cook lays out the different emphases adopted by public sector and voluntary organisational responders. Hazel Kemshall and Rebecca Campbell's chapters take a health perspective on sexual violence. Sheila Coates, director of the South Essex Rape and Incest Crisis Centre, presents views of women who are themselves casualties of the fallout of sexual violence, some victims, some mothers of victims.

There are a number of cross-cutting themes that underpin the contributions:

- shifting emphasis between victims/survivors and offenders;
- sexual violence as a health or a justice issue;
- identification and management of risk;
- extending the continuum of violence.

The questions posed by these chapters relate to the nature and purposes of interventions. Are they designed to eliminate sexual violence, support its victims, punish or treat those guilty of offending? There is both optimism and pessimism expressed about the project of protecting the vulnerable and preventing sexual violence. The authors describe a number of interventions which have enjoyed variable success so the picture is not as bleak as Ward (1995) suggests, i.e. that negative attitudes reinforced by pervasive social forces of self-perpetuating rape myths lead to unavoidable adverse outcomes for the victims of sexual violence.

### Shifting emphasis between victims/survivors and offenders

Interventions are designed to prevent, reduce or ameliorate some harm (Brown and Horvath 2009). In the case of sexual violence the focus tends to be on provision of services to mitigate the adverse consequences of the trauma experienced by its victims or predicting and diverting those who perpetrate it. Thus Becki Campbell in Chapter 21 describes the situation in the United States where victim survivors of sexual violence are often taken to emergency departments. Once there, lack of training, delays in treatment and failures to inform patients about sexually transmitted infections or pregnancy lead to further feelings of violation. As well as conducting invasive medical examinations, Campbell reports that medical professionals may also ask invasive personal questions sufficient for survivors to label this a second rape. As a form of secondary victimisation, one of Campbell's own studies showed that victims of non-stranger rapes not only received lesser levels of medical services but also encountered more secondary victimisation and suffered higher levels of post-traumatic stress compared with those seeking no help at all. In addition demographics played a role in how much information the victim was given about sexually transmitted infections and risks of pregnancy. In Chapter 20 Hazel Kemshall draws attention to Kelly's proposition that the relationship between the victim and her abuser is immaterial from the point of view of assessing harm. But Campbell's research shows that it does matter not only who the offender is but also who the victim is and the relationship between them. Where a victim knows her attacker, is young or from an ethnic minority, she is more likely to have her case rejected by law enforcement. Stanko and Williams (2009) found a similar picture emerged from analysis of Metropolitan Police data. Helge Hoel and Duncan Lewis also suggest in Chapter 18 that it is important to be aware of who the victim is and they argue that lesbian, gay, bisexual or transsexual employees are in a special position regarding sexual harassment and bullying at work precisely because of the nature of possible prior victimisations. They discuss the cultural norms and practices of work that can make this an unsafe environment in a way that is analogous to dangerous domestic situations. They propose that what is acted out in the workplace is a spillover from the world outside so that prejudice and discriminating behaviours are enmeshed in group norms and practices at work.

Sheila Coates in Chapter 22 very firmly forces our attention to the harm experienced by the victims of sexual violence. The quotations from participants to a focus group to discuss their experiences of sexual violence are stark and raw. They make difficult reading and it is distressing to hear the poor professional response which, as a consequence, makes it less likely that the victim will seek the police's help on another occasion. However, when professionals are engaged and in touch, the support victims receive is greatly appreciated. The under-reporting of rapes weakens the connection between crime, punishment and restitution, both for individuals and society at large (Allen 2007). Thus successful investigative interactions are likely to reinforce victims/survivors' perceptions of the greater probability of achieving a conviction and so encourage greater likelihood of reporting. Low conviction rates are likely to be an inhibitory reporting factor (Stern 2010). Littleton *et al.* (2008) point out that not reporting may elevate a victim/survivor's risk of experiencing further victimisation and result in maladaptive coping. Fisher *et al.* (2003) present other consequences of not reporting sexual victimisation:

- Victims/survivors may not have access to assistance services;
- It precludes gathering of intelligence and possible suspect identification for police;
- Estimates of rates of sexual victimisations are likely to be inaccurate.

Kate Cook in Chapter 19 highlights notions of the 'abnormal' sex offender and society's wish to find rapists strange even if they accept they are not necessarily strangers. If offenders are 'odd' says Cook, and equally their choices about with whom (children, casual acquaintances) and how (violently) to have sex, then the heterosexual majority do not feel threatened in the way they might if acknowledging that oppressive sex is experienced in the mundane routines of social life. Giner-Sorolla and Russell (2009) proposes that, as well as threats to the integrity of the person, rape presents threats to community cohesion and cultural values. Much of Petrie and McGregor's chapters (this volume) show how law is slanted towards preserving men's sexual autonomy at the expense of women's and that sexual norms operate to maintain the status quo.

Interventions aimed at looking at the interrelationship between perpetrator and victim such as restorative justice options, discussed by Kemshall in Chapter 20, have excited strong reactions. Cossins (2008) worries that restorative justice conferences mean that offences are downgraded in some way by being taken out of the criminal justice system, suggesting offences are taken less seriously and outcomes are too lenient. Campbell's Chapter 21 reports that low levels of law enforcement effort is associated with higher levels of PTSD in victims/survivors. Felson and Paré (2007) show that victim–offender relationship does play a role in satisfaction with perceived quality of the police investigation. They found from their American data that victims were more dissatisfied when the offender is someone they know rather than a stranger. Victims whose partners assault them are especially dissatisfied with police response. Felson and Paré (p. 216) conclude that their findings indicate not a blanket criticism of police but that dissatisfaction is directed at non-stranger attacks. The issue of perceived leniency towards the alleged aggressor was a factor in the dissatisfaction as a result of both police enquiries and court proceedings, so Coussins may have a point. Daly's (2008) response is as an advocate of restorative justice conferencing in some cases. Her analyses found that court victims spent more time waiting for a final disposition (range one to 28 months, median six) than conference victims (range one to 11, median three). Of 226 court cases she analysed, 115 (51 per cent) were proved of a sexual offence (three convicted at trial); eight of a non-sexual offence (three were acquitted at trial); and 100 dismissed or withdrawn. In comparison, of 118 conferences, 111 (94 per cent) were proved. Daly asks the question: if you were a victim, which avenue would you prefer – an early admission to offending or a delayed (or no) admission?

Given that research continues to demonstrate that prosecution and conviction rates for sexual offences are depressingly low and that criminal justice system procedures are distressing and traumatising for victims/ survivors (Clark 2010), understanding what victims/survivors see as justice and consider as fair is essential to developing procedures to meet their needs. Clark analysed the narratives of 22 victims/survivors of sexual assault, and identified information, validation, voice and control as their key needs. Campbell and Kemshall's chapters particularly show how the criminal justice system continues to fall short of addressing these needs for the victims of sexual violence, and alternative approaches may fare better. Coates's collation of what women want with respect to the criminal justice's response lists female police officers, mandatory training to increase their awareness about the impact of rape, specialist services for the hard to reach such as Asian women, and specialist support services.

### Sexual violence as a health or a justice issue

Kate Cook reminds us that, for women, rape is not difficult to define in terms of their lived experience, but it is very difficult to prove. For men the difficulty is in defining that what they do is sexually violating as penetration is part of normal sex. Kemshall in Chapter 20 continues the theme of earlier analysis by Petrie whereby sex offenders are demonised and society's construction prefers the anonymous rapist or invisible stranger paedophile to the more likely intimate or familial abuser. Criminal justice creates the role of victim seeking remedy through law. Both Campbell and Cook show how the law fails either to protect or indeed successfully prosecute sexually violent perpetrators. Campbell relays the US attrition rates for every 100 rape cases reported to the police – only seven achieve a guilty verdict in court. Cook describes a similar verdict rate in England and Wales and highlights the emotional fallout of the 'lost' 10,000 cases that do not even reach court.

In the face of the criminal justice system's failure to either reduce incidence of sexual violence or prosecute offenders, Kemshall articulates a preventative public health approach while Campbell describes the curative Sexual Assault Nurse Examiner (SANE) programme. Kemshall shows how criminal justice focuses on surveillance, intensive measures of control and restriction through containment. The problem is that relatively few offenders are in fact imprisoned. Ministry of Justice statistics for 2007/8 reveal that 31,178 men and 838 women were arrested for sexual offences (Ministry of Justice 2010). Of these 18 per cent of men and 10 per cent of women received some form of custodial sentence with about half actually going to prison. Thus the victim and the public are unlikely then to be protected from perpetrators of sexual violence by their being in custody. Kemshall makes the case for switching attention from preventative custody solutions to preventative interventions. Thus she identifies the need to intervene and prevent sexually abusive behaviour in children. Farr *et al.* (2004) indicate that while the precise numbers of sexual offences committed by adolescents is unknown, research from the USA suggests that approximately one in five rapes and up to half of child molestations are perpetrated by adolescents. From their comparison of adolescent sex offenders and a normative control the former exhibited higher levels of callous sexual attitudes towards females. Interestingly, the sex offending adolescents had a less well developed sense of their own masculinity. Whittaker *et al.* (2006) found that adolescent sex offenders scored lower on a sexual knowledge questionnaire compared with a non-offending comparison group. These findings suggest that working with adolescents to understand sexual functioning, developing appropriate empathic skills and positive sense of masculinity by enhancing social skills of perspective taking may be beneficial in preventative efforts. Polaschek (2010) remains less than sanguine at the efficacy of programmes aimed at intervening with violent men as most are re-convicted of a further offence but Kemshall reiterates the importance of increasing public awareness about such programmes and the need to continue public funding of them.

Networking and social connectiveness are shown to be important for both those being targeted and those doing the targeting for sexual violence. Kemshall describes the 'Good Lives Model' which was a reaction against the rather pessimistic 'nothing works' position. The underlying principle is that offenders are human beings and seek satisfaction in certain areas of life that is important to their well-being (McMurran 2010). The trouble is that offenders seek satisfaction in highly problematic areas. Kemshall argues that this approach attempts to reintegrate offenders into leading better (good) lives. However, the model appears less successful in situations where there are looser networks and weaker social ties. Hoel and Lewis also point out that weak networking linkage outside the workplace adds to the vulnerabilities of LGBT workers and heightens their risk of being targeted for workplace bullying.

Kemshall's shift of emphasis to supporting victims is marked by a shift of philosophy where there is a stark difference between the medico-legal practice and the lived experience of victims. Interestingly, when Rebecca Campbell describes the SANE project she states that its philosophy is to help the victim as patient first and foremost. This programme was devised in collaboration with rape crisis and victim advocacy and is a 24-hour first response for the psychological, medical and forensic care of sexual assault victims/survivors. Most are located in emergency departments although there are some that are community based. The aim is to minimise trauma and maximise the probability of reliable forensic evidence collection. There are now some 500 such programmes in America and Canada. Campbell evaluates why they spread: their relative advantages are easily apparent and compatible with nursing practice; it is a standardised intervention model and has a codified training; there are observable benefits to survivors; the medically collected forensic evidence is more thorough and accurate. Campbell notes that not only is there more positive feedback from victims who have used the SANE programmes but they experience greater post-assault infection care and there is a greater number of reported cases to law enforcement agencies. Patients using SANE are not obliged to report to the police, but if they decide to do so then the forensic evidence collected by staff can be released. So an intervention designed to rename the victim as a patient actually increases the likelihood of her reporting to the police and the quality of the forensic evidence collected increases chances of securing a conviction.

## Identification and management of risk

Risk is also a theme that interlaces the chapters. Hoel and Lewis talk about the risks associated with being targeted in the workplace. Elsewhere in this volume risk factors associated with being the victim of domestic violence are discussed (see for example Chapter 7 by Brown). Walby and Myhill (2000) identified some key factors associated with the likelihood of suffering domestic violence. These were a history of previous assault, actual or potential separation from the violent partner, being unemployed and economically dependent on the partner, poverty and social exclusion, being younger. The Metropolitan Police Service has a checklist assessment to monitor escalation in reports of domestic violence which includes some of these factors (Richards 2003). Kemshall observes that one failure can hazard the credibility of such approaches. A recent failure, that of the death of Arsema Dawit (IPCC 2010), is a tragic case in point. Miss Dawit reported an assault and threats to kill her made by her ex-boyfriend in April 2008. Notwithstanding her age – she was 15 – previous injuries, and separating from her boyfriend, there was insufficient police response. Miss Dawit was murdered by her boyfriend in June 2008. The IPCC concluded there had been a series of omissions, misunderstandings and assumptions such that the information given to them about the assaults and threats was insufficiently acted upon. Regan and Kelly (2008) analysed seven cases of murder following histories of domestic violence and concluded that the risk markers would not have highlighted danger signals in these particular cases and that more qualitative factors should feature in risk assessment tools.

Kemshall's discussion about managing risks takes the focus to communities which become a potential source of vigilance and monitoring. However, she notes that risks are not equally distributed in communities, with some having a disproportionate share. What might be conceived as community involvement in sharing responsibility for managing risks may on the one hand be experienced as 'dumping' whereby overloaded and under-resourced and hard to reach groups feel abandoned. On the other hand more affluent communities may exhibit 'nimbyism' (not in my back yard) faced with the prospect of hostels or halfway houses and their attendant adverse effect on property values (McGuickin and Brown 2001).

Risk assessment is a critical tool for decision-makers such as sentence adjudicators, parole boards and probation officers, who primarily focus on whether an intervention has decreased the risk of offending, and influences placement of offenders in the community or their retention in custody (Serran *et al.* 2010). Kewley in her practitioner commentary (Part Three of this Handbook) alludes to the work of the probation service in both protecting the public and reducing reoffending. She describes two offender behaviour programmes dealing with sex offending and domestic violence although she questions this bifurcation as, clearly, there is a good deal of overlap between behaviours (cf. Chapter 7 by Brown, this volume).

**Extending the continuum of violence**

All the contributors to this section discuss ideas in relation to Kelly's continuum of violence. Rebecca Campbell argues that Kelly's definition of sexual violence is couched in the language of the survivors and speaks of invasion, hurt, being degraded and lacking control. She believes that the continuum can be mirrored in help-seeking behaviours. She describes the sense of physical and psychological invasion experienced by survivors during medical examinations. These feelings shade into the violation of the rape itself and survivors may suffer secondary victimisation at the hands of those who are supposed to be supporting them. Cook discusses the attrition process whereby cases fall out of the criminal justice process and says that simply pointing victims to report to the police to get justice is insufficient to resolve their victimisation. The continuum of sexual violence, she argues, broadens the definition beyond the fixed and narrow boundaries of legal definitions. The continuum is a useful analytic device to design responses to sexual violence starting with women's experiences. The SANE programme is an example of listening to women and drawing on the expertise of the voluntary sector to design interventions with care for the person at the heart.

Hoel and Lewis, contrary to Kelly's position, argue for a continuum of severity, from the relatively harmless acts to the rarer and more severe actions. They suggest that the severity of a bullying act in the workplace, or its long-term impact, radically redefines the relationship between the bully and the victim and even possibly the former's relationship with significant others within the organisation. They give by way of an example the forced outing of an LGBT employee, with the ordeal being exacerbated by a hostile or homophobic work environment.

**Conclusion**

The implications to be drawn from these chapters is that responding to sexual violence is not about focusing on either the offender or the victim, but that as their encounter locks them together, interventions should take a look at the relationship. Responses need to harness both justice and medical resources and ally public and voluntary sectors. Feminist activism may wish to eliminate sexual violence, so activating public awareness and education is a long-haul project, and maintenance of programmes that support victims and work with offenders in the medium term is a policy priority. The recommendations at the end of Coates's practitioner contribution are not dissimilar to those evident in other enquiries and reviews (e.g. Stern 2010). Two questions emerge from the analysis presented in the chapters: why is there such a postcode lottery in provision; and can services to victims of violence withstand the financial pressures of the economic downturn?

## References

Allen, W.D. (2007) 'The reporting and underreporting of rape', *Southern Economic Journal*, 73(3): 623–41.

Brown, J. and Horvath, M.A. (2009) 'Is it real rape and do you believe her?', in M.A. Horvath and J.M. Brown (eds) *Rape: Challenging Contemporary Thinking*. Cullompton: Willan Publishing.

Clark, H. (2010) 'What is the justice system willing to offer? Understanding sexual assault victim/survivor criminal justice needs', *Family Matters*, 85: 28–37.

Cossins, A. (2008) 'Restorative justice and child sex offences: the theory and the practice', *British Journal of Criminology*, 34(3): 359–78.

Daly, K. (2008) 'Setting the record straight and a call for radical change: A reply to Annie Cossins on "Restorative Justice and Child Sex Offences"', *British Journal of Criminology*, 48: 557–66.

Farr, C., Brown, J.M., Beckett, R. (2004) 'Ability to empathise and masculinity levels: comparing male adolescent sex offenders with a normative sample of non offending adolescents', *Psychology Crime and Law*, 10: 155–67.

Felson, B.B. and Paré, P.-P. (207) 'Does the criminal justice system treat domestic violence and sexual assault offenders differently?', *Justice Quarterly* (September), 24: 435–59.

Fisher, B.S., Daigle, L.E., Cullen, F.T. and Turner, M.G. (2003) 'Reporting sexual victimisation to the police and others', *Criminal Justice and Behavior*, 30(1): 6–38.

Giner-Sorolla, R. and Russell, P. (2009) 'Anger, disgust and sexual crime', in M.A. Horvath and J.M. Brown (eds) *Rape: Challenging Contemporary Thinking*, pp. 46–73. Cullompton: Willan Publishing.

Independent Police Complaints Commission (2010) Police contact between 30 April 2008 and 2 June 2008 with Arsema Dawit and her family. London: The Commission.

Kelly, L. (2008) 'Contradictions and paradoxes; international patterns of, and responses to, reported rape case', in G. Letherby, K. Williams, P. Birch and C. Cain (eds) *Sex as Crime?*, pp. 253–79. Cullompton: Willan Publishing.

Littleton, H., Breitkopf, C.R. and Berenson, A. (2008) 'Beyond campus; unacknowledged rape among low-income women', *Violence Against Women*, 14: 269–86.

McGuickin, G.K. and Brown, J.M. (2001) 'Managing risk from sex offenders living in communities: comparing police, press and public perceptions', *Risk Management*, 3: 47–60.

McMurren, M. (2010) 'Theories of change', in J.M. Brown and E.A. Campbell (eds) *Cambridge Handbook of Forensic Psychology*, pp. 118–25. Cambridge: CUP.

Ministry of Justice (2010) Statistics on women in the criminal justice system 2008/9, available http://www.justice.gov.uk/publications/docs/women-criminal-justice-system-2008-09.pdf (accessed 30 October 2010).

Polaschek, D. (2010) 'Rehabilitating violent offenders', in J.M. Brown and E.A. Campbell (eds) *Cambridge Handbook of Forensic Psychology*, pp. 441–52. Cambridge: CUP.

Regan, L. and Kelly, L. (2008) 'If only we'd known; an exploratory study of 7 intimate partner homicides', *SAFE, The Domestic Assault Quarterly*, 27, Autumn: 4–7.

Richards, L. (2003) MPS Risk Assessment model for domestic violence Appendix III, available at http://www.met.police.uk/csu/pdfs/AppendixIII.pdf (accessed 30 October 2010).

Serran, G.A., Marshall, W.L., Marshall, L.E. and O'Brien, M.D. (2010) 'Sexual offender assessment', in M. Horvath and J. Brown (eds) *Rape: Challenging Contemporary Thinking*, pp. 299–306. Cullompton: Willan Publishing.

Stanko, B. and Williams, E. (2009) 'Reviewing rape and rape allegations in London; what are the vulnerabilities of the victims who report to the police?', pp. 207–28. In M. Horvath and J. Brown (eds) *Rape: challenging contemporary thinking*. Cullompton: Willan Publishing.

Stern, Vivien (2010) *The Stern Review*. London: Government Equalities Office.

Thomas, T. (2005) *Sex Crime: Sex Offending and Society* (2nd edn) Cullompton: Willan Publishing.

Walby, S. and Myhill, A. (2000) 'Assessing and managing the risk of domestic violence', in J. Taylor-Browne (ed.) *Reducing Domestic Violence*. London: Home Office.

Ward, C.A. (1995) *Attitudes towards Rape: Feminist and Social Psychological Perspectives*. London: Sage.

Whittaker, M.K., Brown, J.M. and Beckett, R. (2006) 'Sexual knowledge and empathy: a comparison of adolescent child molesters and non-offending adolescents', *Journal of Sexual Aggression*, 12: 143–54.

## Chapter 18

# Bullying, harassment and sexual orientation in the workplace

*Helge Hoel and Duncan Lewis*

### Meet Helge Hoel and Duncan Lewis

Helge Hoel is Senior Lecturer in Organisational Psychology at Manchester Business School at the University of Manchester. He carried out the first nationwide survey of workplace bullying in Great Britain in 2000 and subsequently the first evaluation study examining the effectiveness of organisational anti-bullying interventions. He has written and contributed to a number of books, articles and reports in the area of bullying, violence and harassment. Recently, he has embarked on an inter-disciplinary path, contributing to a broadening of the bullying research agenda into the areas of sociology, law and industrial relations. He is currently Principal Investigator of a ground-breaking study of Lesbians, Gay and Bisexuals' (LBGs) experience of discrimination, bullying and harassment (with Duncan Lewis), sponsored by the Economic and Social Research Council (ESRC).

Professor Duncan Lewis is Professor of Management at Plymouth School of Management and was previously Acas Professor at the Glamorgan Business School near Cardiff. Duncan has spent over a decade researching workplace bullying and was part of a team located at Cardiff University exploring ill-treatment at work with special reference to race and ethnicity which was funded by the ESRC, Acas and the former Commission for Race Equality (CRE). Duncan is working alongside Helge on the new ESRC funded research project which will undertake the UK's first nationally representative study of bullying, harassment and discrimination at work amongst lesbian, gay and bisexual employees. This major UK study is backed by the UK's Equality and Human Rights Commission and supported by Acas, Stonewall and the Chartered Institute for Personnel Development.

### Introduction

The issue of workplace bullying has received considerable and growing attention in recent years (Aquino and Thau 2009; Di Martino *et al*. 2003).

Although already referred to as the research topic of the 1990s (Hoel *et al.* 1999), more than 80 per cent of empirical studies about the issue have actually been published since 2000 (Nielsen *et al.* in 2009). In terms of its consequences, bullying and harassment is associated with reduced job satisfaction and a number of mental and physical health problems (Einarsen and Mikkelsen 2003). Unsurprisingly, such experiences also affect organisations by means of increased absenteeism and turnover, as well as reduced productivity, which manifest themselves in substantial organisational and societal costs (Giga *et al.* 2008a). However, one issue which has received little or no attention within the literature is the experience of lesbian, gay and bisexual employees (LGB). This lack of attention exists despite the fact that Stonewall (2007), the gay rights lobbying group, suggests that nearly one in five lesbians and gay men had experienced bullying due to their sexual orientation, with 13 per cent of the population reporting that they had witnessed verbal bullying in the workplace, and nearly four per cent having reported witnessing physical or violent anti-gay bullying. This chapter aims to address this gap in knowledge. Moreover, responding to the overall approach of the book we will explore the particular nature of violent interactions as experienced by lesbians, gay men and bisexuals in the workplace.

In terms of the structure of the chapter, and having provided some background information, we examine various dimensions of the concept of workplace bullying and its effects on people at work. This is followed by a more in-depth investigation of the LGBs' experience of bullying and harassment and its impact. In order to throw light on these experiences, theoretical perspectives which may account for their presence will be explored, emphasising in a separate section how the sexuality of recipients might impinge upon the nature of their experience. In a final section we discuss how organisations might respond to and possibly mitigate the problem.

## Background

Reviews of the literature of the wider field of bullying and harassment (Aquino and Thau 2009; Einarsen *et al.* 2011; Hoel *et al.* 1999) suggest that an often confusing array of concepts and terms is employed to account for these phenomena, despite the fact that there seemingly exists very considerable conceptual overlap between them (Einarsen *et al.* 2011; Hershcovis, in press). Research carried out by the European Foundation for the Improvement of Living and Working Conditions (Di Martino *et al.* 2003) identified some new trends in international research and practice on the issues of violence and harassment taking place: first, there appears to be a shift in focus from physical to psychological violence despite the fact that levels of exposure to physical violence are still high and possibly on a par with psychological violence; second, considerable attention is being paid to repeated negative and unwanted acts, many of which are relatively common in the workplace; and third, there seems to be an expansion of the notion of an employer's duty of care to incorporate the concepts of dignity and respect of workers to sit alongside employer responsibility for employee safety and health. This reflects a greater societal concern with issues surrounding human rights and mirrors the 2004 expansion of the scope of anti-discrimination regulations within the European Union (the Treaty of Amsterdam). As such the new inclusion of disability, age and religion mirrors, in principle, US regulation of 'protected groups' with one important exception, sexuality. US employers are still free to discriminate on the grounds of sexuality, where the legal principle of 'employment at will' still applies (Lewis *et al.* in press). Workplace dignity is already reflected in a move by many employers to replace their policies on bullying and harassment with an all-encompassing so-called 'dignity at work policy'. This is often portrayed as a positive move by employers, seemingly replacing a focus on something inherently negative with something more positive and upbeat. However, the term 'dignity at work' is more conceptually controversial than the term bullying because, as Bolton (2007) pointed out, its origins lie in dignified or decent work rather than personal undignified interactions. Thus, such a move is not without its problems, an issue we will return to later.

As has often been pointed out by research into violence in the workplace, women appear to be more vulnerable to violence than men (Chappel and Di Martino 2006). However, with exposure rates and relative risk of being the target of violence reflecting labour market segregation and different labour market contexts, with women over-represented in high-risk occupations and occupying different roles and positions compared with men (e.g. Di Martino *et al.* 2003), it is argued that the experience of violence, harassment and bullying should be seen as gendered (Ackers 1990; Simpson and Cohen 2004). In other words, women are over-represented in work with high reported levels of violence, e.g. teaching, health care and social work. Furthermore, women occupy to a greater degree than men low-pay and low-status jobs (Di Martino *et al.* 2003), with fewer women filling supervisory and managerial positions. However, women currently account for more than 50 per cent of the working population, a figure which is unlikely to be reduced given the new opportunity for flexible working arrangements pursued by many employers.

From what we know so far, minority groups defined in terms of race/ ethnicity, disability or sexuality appear to be over-represented among targets of violence, bullying and harassment, although the evidence is limited and results are not always consistent (Fevre *et al.* 2008; Giga *et al.* 2008a; Lewis and Gunn 2007). This lack of knowledge about the experience of minority workers seems in part to reflect their social standing and echoes a lack of advocacy (Di Martino *et al.* 2003). Thus, to some extent, to become the focus of research and political attention requires the backing of strong support networks and the ability to create sufficient interest among researchers and other interested parties to steer necessary resources in the direction of systematic scientific exploration. As argued above, little or no attention has been paid to the experience of violence, bullying and harassment by lesbians, gay men and bisexuals (LGBs), a disparity which we will address. Thus, we intend to explore the experience of this under-researched group, particularly focusing on acts and behaviour targeting their sexuality and how sexuality is exploited in scenarios of bullying and harassment.

## Workplace bullying: conceptual delineation, evidence and consequences

As indicated above disagreement still exists regarding how to define workplace bullying (Lewis 2006). Nevertheless, there appears to be a growing agreement internationally about how to understand the phenomenon and its defining characteristics. This conceptual convergence is accounted for by factors such as greater awareness and public debate about the issues, spreading of common terms at international meetings and in publications, the introduction of new legislation addressing the issue, ground-breaking decisions by the courts and the proliferation of collective agreement targeting the problem (Di Martino *et al*. 2003).

Bullying is concerned with exposure to negative, unwanted acts or behaviour on a continuum from common and relatively harmless acts to rare and very severe actions. The behaviour can be direct and indirect, with shouting an example of the former and gossiping the latter. Similarly, bullying acts may be active or passive, with humiliation and criticism representing active acts, while ignoring or excluding an employee indicates passive bullying behaviour. In the same way, some acts might concern or be directed at the way work is being carried out, sometimes referred to as work-related bullying, while other behaviour might refer directly to the persons at the receiving end, in other words, person-related bullying (Einarsen *et al*. 2011). However, it is often argued that the central defining characteristic of bullying is persistency of exposure, with the experience being repeated and often patterned. It follows logically that longevity or duration also plays a core role, with most bullying scenarios lasting for a very considerable time, measured in terms of months and years rather than weeks (Einarsen *et al*. 2011). Despite the focus on persistency, there still appears to be an agreement that one-off acts or more isolated incidents might constitute bullying in some cases. Such situations are generally associated with the severity of the act or their long-term impact which radically redefines the relationship between the protagonists and possibly the target's relationship with significant others within the organisation. A poignant example of such a one-off event would be the outing of an LGB employees, or in other words, making the target's sexuality public, against their will, as a one-off act with the ordeal possibly exacerbated by a hostile or homophobic work environment.

Another core characteristic of bullying is the imbalance of power between target and perpetrator, a disparity which might be present at the outset or emergence of the conflict and crystallise itself through the ongoing bullying process (Einarsen *et al*. 2011). In this respect it is important to emphasise that power imbalance might simply be a reflection of the hierarchical position of those involved. Alternatively, it might result from power drawn from alternative sources, sometimes referred to as referent power (French and Raven 1959), including such things as experience, knowledge or access to social support and internal networks (Hoel *et al*. 1999). Thus, having access to intimate knowledge about a person, for example concerning their sexuality or sexual practices, possibly obtained within the confines of a friendship or even a relationship, could be used as a powerful weapon against an opponent during an escalated conflict. The escalating nature and dynamics of the process should also be emphasised, which suggests that it is not always clear from the outset who might end up in an inferior position, when an escalated personalised conflict becomes a case of bullying and victimisation (Einarsen *et al.* 2011). With reference to Kelly's continuum of violence one could suggest that either party in the escalating phases of a conflict could make use of violent acts to various degrees of severity in order to counteract or defeat their opponent. Moreover, if at one point in the process one of the parties is able to establish superior relational power over their opponent, the nature of the process will change from mutual aggression to bullying. At this stage one may argue that the violent acts performed by the bully or perpetrator may take on different meaning in the eyes of the target, with even violent acts rated as low level by observers having the potential to be perceived as severe by the recipient.

Whilst the intent of the perpetrator is commonly featured in discussions about the core characteristics of bullying, disagreement still exists on this issue. Not only is it important to make a distinction about intent in terms of the intention to cause harm as opposed to the intent of the act itself, it should also be noted that, whilst an act of bullying and indeed its harmful effects may be premeditated, it might not be the intent of the perpetrator to victimise the target. For example, a manager who is under severe pressure to meet organisational targets may put excessive demands on an individual employee over a period of time, without personally intending to harm the individual. Yet, the individual might feel bullied by their ordeal and suffer detrimental effects to their health and well-being. Still, and more importantly, as the only people who can verify the presence of intent are the perpetrators themselves, the issue of intent remains a hypothetical question and can only be inferred retrospectively (Einarsen *et al.* 2010; Hoel *et al.* 1999). Nevertheless, there is little doubt that perceived intent is of importance to the target as the perceived motivation for the behaviour will impact on its effects on the recipient. It has also been argued that the focus should be moved from intent to one of acceptability, with consideration of likely intent possibly affecting how an offence might be sanctioned by the organisation but irrelevant for the establishment of whether bullying has taken place or not. Thus, perpetrators' attempts to justify their behaviour by referring to tradition or culture should be rejected with reference to the 'reasonable person' legal standard (e.g. Prior and Fitzgerald 2003), particularly where there is reason to believe that the perpetrator is aware that the behaviour is unwelcome. Although potential victims might draw some comfort from this legal position, it raises a problem where bullying of LGBs is rooted in widespread societal homophobia where the man (and woman) in the street might not object to the behaviour.

When examining the characteristics of bullying, a distinction should also be made between subjective and objective bullying. Subjective bullying refers to the individual's perception of events, while objective refers to incidents or processes verified or confirmed by others (Brodsky 1976). Whilst the experience of bullying always remains in the 'eye of the beholder', and as such is a subjective experience, organisations would need more objective criteria to establish whether it has taken place or not when receiving a complaint of bullying. Unfortunately for recipients, many incidents take place without witnesses present which might militate against the opportunity for a fair hearing (Hoel and Einarsen 2011). Here we would limit ourselves to point out three factors which might be particularly relevant to the experience of LGBs. First, as the meaning of an individual event cannot fully be appreciated by others without prior knowledge of previous events involving the target and the protagonists, they might not appreciate the full meaning of an act or an event which is obvious to recipient and perpetrator. Thus one could envisage situations where knowledge of someone's sexuality could be exploited in this way. Second, where word stands against word, the organisation might come down on the side of the more powerful or those who fulfil key jobs, and who are therefore considered difficult to replace. This argument might be extended to include cultural dominance, including sexuality (Hearn and Parkin 2001) where perceived deviant sexuality might be a factor undermining social standing and even trustworthiness. Third, as a target's ordeal might affect their behaviour and emotions, and even their mental stability (Einarsen and Mikkelsen 2003), they are likely to cut a sad figure and as such cannot rely on sympathy for their cause (Hoel and Einarsen 2011) or articulate clearly what has happened to them.

It is suggested that around five to 20 per cent of employees, depending upon context and research methodology applied, suffer from bullying at any one time (Zapf et al. 2011). In terms of occupational context, Zapf et al. argue that international research suggests that public administration, education and social work are sectors where the frequency of bullying is reported to be particularly high. As previously argued, women appear to be more at risk of bullying than men. Research also suggests that there might be an interaction between sex and organisational status with women in managerial positions significantly more exposed to bullying than their male counterparts (Hoel et al. 2001). What has emerged by way of evidence also suggests a heightened risk of exposure for ethnic minorities (Giga et al. 2008a) and LGBs (Grainger and Fitzner 2006), although there appears to be considerable variation in experience between sub-groups (Hoel and Cooper 2000). This suggests that neither ethnicity nor sexuality should be seen as unifying concepts in terms of their constituents' experience. For example, in terms of ethnicity, Hoel and Cooper (2000) reported that whilst Asian respondents were over-represented among targets of bullying, African-Caribbeans, for their part, were no more at risk of bullying than white employees. It should also be mentioned that simply being in a minority position could act as an antecedent of bullying, for example, being a male nurse in a predominantly female environment has been seen to increase the risk of exposure to bullying (Eriksen and Einarsen (2004). Moreover, it is also important to acknowledge the issue of multiple or overlapping identities, and ask the question whether risk could be seen as additive or indeed interactive, with exposure to one exacerbating the effect of exposure to other risks (Lee 2002). Although research does not provide support for such hypotheses, it is plausible to suggest that individuals facing harassment tend to adapt to the situation which appears to protect them against experiencing additional, or additive, harm when exposed to other forms of harassment (Raver and Nishii 2010).

Looking at the overall picture for bullying and harassment within the EU area, it is acknowledged that exposure rates vary considerably (Zapf *et al.* 2011). Whilst discrepancy in numbers might reflect variation in the methodology applied (Di Martino *et al.* 2003), with the validity of some studies questionable, the difference in numbers might also mirror the attention given to the problem in various EU states, with some countries addressing it systematically while others seemingly turn a blind eye to the problem. Even worse, in some cases the state has actually introduced new legal measures to legitimise discriminatory practices. An example of this is a law passed by the Lithuanian Parliament in 2009 referred to as the 'Protection of Minors against the Detrimental Effect of Public Information'. According to Amnesty International, this law which mirrors the British Clause 28 (introduced by Margaret Thatcher and repealed in 2001), represents an 'institutionalisation of homophobia' (Amnesty International 2009), and its very existence is a blatant breach of EU regulation. Such regulatory political intervention may, therefore, be seen to legitimise bullying and violence against LGBs in a region which has a recent history of public violence towards gay and lesbian citizens.

Bullying manifests itself psychologically, physically and behaviourally. Thus, being exposed to bullying is associated with anxiety, depression and a series of psychosomatic symptoms as well as with cognitive effects such as loss of concentration (e.g. Leymann 1996). In severe cases the experience may also lead to symptoms resembling post-traumatic stress disorder (PTSD) (Einarsen and Mikkelsen 2003). Responding to their ordeal by means of aggressiveness, erratic behaviour, frequent mood swings and social withdrawal (e.g. Field 1996), and therefore effectively undermining any support they may have received previously from colleagues, would also lead to an increasing spiral of social isolation (Leymann 1996). It is assumed that individuals' pre-existing vulnerability will impact on the consequences of exposure (Hoel *et al.* 2004). In this respect, it is of course possible that LGBs as a group might be more vulnerable than their heterosexual counterparts due to possible previous negative experiences in and outside work and other problems surrounding their sexuality and sexual identity. Moreover, to the extent that LGBs might have weaker links to internal social networks, perceptions of exclusion and isolation might develop faster, to the detriment of their social standing and opportunities for a positive outcome to their case.

For the organisation, the consequences of bullying tend to manifest themselves in higher levels of absenteeism and turnover and a reduction in productivity (Giga *et al.* 2008a). Incorporating the costs involved in internal investigations, and adding the potential cost of litigation and those arising from damage to brand and public reputation, the total bill which organisations might face could indeed be very considerable (Hoel *et al.* 2010). As the effects appear to extend to bystanders and witnesses (Rayner *et al.* 2002), the seriousness of the problem is further emphasised.

### Sexual orientation, bullying and harassment

In assessing the existing evidence we need to draw attention to the fact that the validity of existing data is questionable. Thus, it is commonly agreed that research on sexual orientation often suffers from the application of weak methodologies with respect to sample and sampling procedures, and the measures and instruments applied (e.g. Croteau 1996; Griffith and Hebl 2002). In this respect most studies have relied on probability sampling, using various self-selection approaches such as snowballing. In addition white employees and the better educated are often over-represented within the samples, with implication for generalisation (Croteau 1996). On this matter, research on sexual minorities has much in common with other discrimination-based studies where interrelated shortcomings of access and cost explain the weaknesses of available datasets, and thus reliability of conclusions drawn. As far as LGB employees are concerned, this problem has been further exacerbated by potential concern with anonymity and confidentiality (Day and Schoenrade 1997), where fear of involuntarily disclosing one's sexuality might raise the bar further.

In terms of the magnitude of the problem, a recent large-scale survey by the Department of Trade and Industry into perceptions of fair treatment at work (Grainger and Fitzner 2006) revealed that 18 per cent of LGBs reported experiencing 'unfair treatment' at work, double the national average. Similarly, Stonewall (2007), suggests that nearly one in five lesbians and gay men had experienced bullying due to their sexual orientation, with 13 per cent of the population reporting that they had witnessed verbal bullying in the workplace, while nearly four per cent reported witnessing physical anti-gay bullying. Acas (2007) suggested that 22–48 per cent of LGB employees experience bullying/harassment while a study by TUC (2000) suggested that 44 per cent reported discrimination associated with their sexuality.

The most commonly reported behaviours associated with bullying and harassment were verbal abuse, jokes and pranks, homophobic remarks, threats of physical abuse and what is referred to as a 'homophobic culture' (Acas 2007), with many of the behaviours directly or indirectly playing on the sexuality of targets. Acas makes a distinction between three forms of discrimination: direct blatant, subtle unspoken homophobia and unfair treatment. Although blatant discrimination might be less common, informal or subtle discrimination appears to be widespread (Griffith and Hebl 2002). In this respect harassment and violent attacks might live side by side with common but less openly aggressive forms of discrimination in terms of undermining the credibility and respect of their recipients (Croteau 1996).

It is likely that the frequency and forms of discrimination, bullying and harassment of LGBs will vary with the local or employment sector context (Beale and Hoel, in press). Although evidence is sparse, the problems vary substantially between occupations, with for example hotel/restaurant and prison/police in the private and the public sector respectively associated with particularly high levels of complaints (Acas 2007). Research also indicates that whilst some experiences might be similar for lesbians and gay men other experiences may not. This highlights that we need to be careful in applying a 'one size fits all' explanation and should treat LGBs as separate constituencies with to some degree their own distinct experiences. Moreover, in some cases, the fact that individuals belong to a minority ethnic group or religion, or are labelled disabled, suggests a complex mix of multiple identities which could impact on their experience. As argued by one BME interviewee in a rare British study of LGB employees' experiences, it is 'like dealing with homophobic experience from a BME perspective' (Colgan *et al*. 2008: 47).

While we have already addressed how research reveals that discrimination, bullying and harassment affect its recipients, some studies also indicate that these forms of negative experience might have a particular detrimental effect on the mental health of LGBs (e.g. Cochran 2001; Ellison and Gunstone 2009). Despite methodological shortcomings, an in-depth review of the literature, supplied by a meta-analysis of studies looking into this issue, concluded that 'whenever significant differences in prevalence of disorders between LGBs and heterosexual groups were reported, LGBs had a higher prevalence than heterosexual groups' (Meyer 2003: 684). Within this general picture, some studies (e.g. Ellison and Gunstone 2009) have reported higher levels of mental health disorder for lesbians compared with gay men. By contrast, Meyer's meta analysis (2003) yielded no significant gender differences with the exception of 'substance use disorder', which appears to be of less significance for men than for women.

When assessing the findings on LGBs' mental health situation, Meyer (2003) argues that one needs to bear in mind that it was not until 1973 that homosexuality was removed from the American Psychiatric Association's *Diagnostic and Statistical Manual of Mental Disorders*. The stigma caused by this has negatively affected the ability to get a clear picture of the health situation of LGBs as advocate groups resented the idea of enhanced mental health problems among gay men and lesbians. However, with recent discussions moving in the direction of interpreting findings of any over-representation of mental health problems in terms of the breadth and magnitude of social stress experienced by these sections of the population, the attitude to such findings is changing (Cochran 2001). Hence, mental health problems are explained by reference to the various additional pressures or social stressors affecting LGBs and captured by the term 'minority stress' (Meyer 2003). Such stressors and their implications will be explored in more depth later. Here we will limit ourselves to emphasising that social stressors in terms of 'minority stress' are seen to exist independently of how these are perceived or appraised by the individual (Meyer 2003). As far as the UK is concerned, it may be argued that although attitudes to homosexuality and LGBs appear to be changing in a positive direction (NCSR 2010), homophobia is still widespread in society and affects in many ways the lives of lesbians and gay men (EHRC 2009).

Belonging to a socially stigmatised group may also bring about perceptions of shame and self-hatred or what has been referred to as internalised homophobia (Meyer 2003). In its extreme this might lead to suicide or ideas of or attempts at suicide among LGBs. Although evidence among the adult population is not clear, not least due to biases and shortcomings associated with sampling (Meyer 2003), the sort of feelings that can lead to suicide attempts appear to be particularly strong in young LGBs, particularly among boys (Meyer 2003), or those who are uncertain about their sexual identity and who might find it hard to come to terms with their sexuality (Imich *et al*. 2001).

The experience of 'minority stress' may also be associated with the process of self-disclosure and the degree of openness about one's sexuality.

Consequently, fear of bullying, violence and discrimination in and outside work might be important factors in explaining LGBs' decision to 'come out' or not, or more accurately, their level of personal disclosure of their sexuality at work (Day and Schoenrade 1997; Ward and Winstanley 2006). Disclosure has been described as a double-edged sword due to the potential risks and emotional costs involved with openness as well as the disadvantages of staying 'closeted' in terms of lost opportunities for integration with social networks and consequent reduced access to information (Griffith and Hebl 2002). In this respect, the task of concealment both inside and outside of work can place a psychological strain on individuals, leading to stress-related illness (Ragins 2008). Moreover, Day and Schoenrade (1997) reported that LGB employees who had chosen to disclose their identity at work were likely to suffer less role conflict, reduced role ambiguity compared with those who had not disclosed. However, findings of the outcomes of disclosure are contested, with some finding higher degrees of job satisfaction and organisational commitment and less work–home conflict for those revealing their sexuality (Day and Schoenrade 1997), while others also report that disclosure was associated with higher levels of anxiety (Griffith and Hebl 2002). It has also been argued that in some cases individuals had little choice and have been forced to self-categorise or 'out' themselves in order to be able to draw attention to their case and receive a fair hearing (Ward and Winstanley 2006).

Altogether, fear of failure, being ridiculed, ostracised or exposed to violence at work may ultimately impact on LGBs' career choices as they search for careers and places of work which they consider friendly or at least where they can feel safe. In the study by Colgan et al. (2008) referred to above, LGB respondents pointed to negative experiences in school as a possible barrier to continuing into further or higher education. Furthermore, although far from necessarily being seen as a safe environment, certain industries were considered more gay friendly, for example, retailing, local government and the IT sector, with public sector jobs generally seen as more likely to provide LGBs with equal opportunities than the private sector. By contrast, LGBs would avoid particular 'macho' occupations, such as engineering, where they feared they would become isolated. No doubt, such considerations might impact on the opportunity for self-actualisation and overall standard of living.

## Theoretical perspectives on bullying and harassment of LGBs and people with disabilities in the workplace

Research into workplace bullying was pioneered in Sweden by Heinz Leymann in the early 1980s (Leymann 1996). Since the beginning, discussion about the phenomenon's causes and antecedents has been a contentious issue, with Leymann gradually becoming an exponent of a view which denies any involvement of personality factors in scenarios of bullying, instead explaining bullying entirely in terms of environmental or situational factors. By contrast, popular or lay explanations of bullying, supported by accounts by articulate victim campaigners (e.g. Field 1996) often favour a focus on personality factors, although in the latter cases it is the personality traits of bullies which have been the centre of attention.

Research on the personality of targets of bullying has suggested that bullying is associated with higher levels of neuroticism (Zapf and Einarsen 2010) and anxiety (Coyne *et al*. 2000), and with lower self-esteem than non-victims (Einarsen *et al*. 1994). One study also reported that targets of bullying were more suspicious than those who had not been bullied. In a more recent study, Glasø *et al*. (2007) identified two subgroups of victims with one subgroup (nearly two-thirds of the victims) strongly resembling the personality profile of a non-victimised control group, while a smaller victim group (approximately one-third of victims) stood out from the control group in terms of being more neurotic and less agreeable, extrovert, conscientious and intelligent. This study appears to suggest that there is no such thing as a general target profile (Glasø *et al*. 2010). Moreover, due to shortcomings of methodology, with studies so far relying on cross-sectional samples, it is difficult to conclude to what extent personality is a risk factor in bullying or whether the particular personality profile identified in some victims may actually be the result of the bullying process, or what Leymann referred to as 'a normal response to an abnormal situation' (Leymann 1996).

Alternatively, bullying has been explained by reference to features of the situation, the so-called work environment hypothesis. As argued by Salin and Hoel (2011) various features of the work environment may impact on perpetrator behaviour as well as on targets' opportunity to retaliate or defend themselves. Typically, studies have identified factors directly associated with the organisation of work such as role conflict and with the style of leadership applied (Hauge *et al*. 2007). There is also evidence that bullying is linked to organisational change (Skogstad *et al*. (2007a)), with a change of management seen as a particular risk factor (Rayner *et al*. 2002). According to Hoel *et al*. (in press), as far as the perceptions of targets of bullying are concerned, bullying is most strongly associated with a style of leadership which applies punishment arbitrarily, seemingly unrelated to prior target behaviour and, thus unpredictable, making it difficult for targets to defend themselves. Another style associated with bullying is laissez-faire, a style of leadership indicating that managers abdicate their responsibility, typically failing to intervene when required or expected, including when someone is being bullied or victimised (Hoel *et al*., in press; Skogstad *et al*. 2007b).

Within the wider work environment perspectives, bullying can also be explained by reference to socialisation processes, in which employees gradually succumb to prevailing negative organisational norms and, by implication, ensure the reproduction of bullying and violence. Whilst this particularly applies to behavioural patterns of perpetrators, it might also impact on recipients, contributing to the establishment of a victim mentality. Evidence of this has emerged from studies in as different contexts as nursing (Randle 2003), the fire service (Archer 1999) and restaurant kitchens (Bloisi and Hoel 2008). Interestingly, in both the fire service and among chefs, sexualised harassment and violence are reported among frequently applied bullying behaviour. In some contexts and settings it is realised that what is acted out within the workplace is by and large a reflection and a spillover of violent behaviour external to the workplace. In other words, in terms of the experience of LGBs, social prejudices and heterosexist norms in the wider society are likely to fuel oppression and even mistreatment within the workplace. It should additionally be noted that in some cases bullying is also carried out deliberately as a measure of social control where other, preferable control methods might not suffice (Beale and Hoel, in press).

## Specific explanation of sexuality and bullying

Social identity theory and the seminal work of Tajfel (1978) can be a useful starting point to explore how LGBs might encounter bullying as a result of their sexuality. According to Tajfel (1978), internalised social identities associated with social groupings, such as being gay or heterosexual, define one's own self-concept and one's emotional significance in being a member of that social group. In an organisational setting how one retains an LGB identity while continuing to belong to other communities of the workplace presents a possible situation where bullying might occur. Bar-Tal (1998) reminds us that the very essence of group beliefs provides the foundation for their existence. It therefore follows that if that group denies or rejects the existence of gay people then bullying, harassment and discrimination are likely to be eventualities. There is of course a long tradition in groups of handing out mistreatment to perceived deviants by socially categorising them and exaggerating differences (Marques *et al.* 1998). This is because the unification of group beliefs requires the group to have a coherent sense of identity such as 'we are builders' or 'we are engineers'. Similarly, group beliefs are built upon shared confidence in their ideals which are seen as 'facts' that become central components of their belief systems (Bar Tal 1998). Prejudices and discriminatory behaviour become part of group norms and practices, such as telling of gay jokes or widespread adoption of sexualised innuendo that might be used to 'test out' and suppress minorities (Ward and Winstanley 2006).

The increasing globalisation of labour markets, and thus of organisational constituencies, is also a potential key source of bullying for sexual minorities, with prejudices and discriminatory beliefs of majority and minority constituents fertile breeding grounds for bullying. Gay employees must face the prejudices of not only majority groups but also other minority groupings. Religious doctrine for example is often used as a rationale to underpin homophobic behaviour ranging from the AIDS campaigns of the 1980s through to gay clergy in the twenty-first century. Dudley and Mulvey (2009) showed how religious fundamentalism was more likely to result in gay prejudice while those with an egalitarian upbringing produced an opposite result. In a US study of homophobic attitudes to AIDS among ethnic students, Long and Millsap (2008) found that ethnic minority groups had a much greater fear of AIDS, resulting in a more homophobic attitude, and this was greatest among men. Gay employees therefore face a double jeopardy of discrimination from both majority and minority groups. However, as Lewis (2003) noted, black and white attitudes to homosexuality and gay rights is a complex issue with many black US citizens disapproving of homosexuality but African Americans being more in favour of legislation outlawing discrimination against gays then white citizens, possibly reflecting their own struggle for civil rights.

Industry characteristics such as those associated with uniformed and 'blue light' services have a recent tradition of trying to eradicate discrimination and bullying of minorities (see for example Archer 1999; Giga *et al.* 2008b). However, cultural attitudes are deeply ingrained and it can sometime require years of policies, training and reinforcement to address such ingrained behaviours. It is only after decades of intervention that progress seems to be made against accepted norms as evidenced by the Stephen Lawrence Inquiry into the London Metropolitan Police Service (see Lewis and Gunn 2007) which found that the cultural norms of racism in the service had prevented a meaningful investigation into Stephen Lawrence's murder taking place. (See also the full Macpherson report 1999.) As Bar-Tal (1998) noted, similarity of beliefs has a significant effect upon discriminative behaviour where values and ideologies and goals can underpin beliefs. This long road of intervention can result in workplaces being categorised as 'safe' or 'unsafe' by minority groups. As suggested above, this might have implications for career choices and career moves with gay men and women frequently using word of mouth to indicate which workplaces are safe and which are not.

Invisible stigmas as first described by Goffman in 1963 can be widespread for a range of employees, including LGBs. The depth and spread of invisible stigmatisation in organisations is described by Ragins (2008), who explains how the invisibility of their situation leads individuals from stigmatised groups to conceal their identities in order to avoid prejudicial treatment and behaviours. For some LGBs the concealment of their sexual identity is not simply a work issue as their social lives can be a source of identification of their identity by their colleagues, for example being seen in a gay bar or at a Gay Pride event. Thus the pressure of thinking about 'who knows' and 'who does not know' could become an intolerable source of anxiety. In a work environment, such dilemmas can lead to feelings of vulnerability and be amplified by working or living in close-knit communities where everyone knows everyone else.

As bullying can be considered a form of breakdown in relationships, it is easy to understand how both voluntary or involuntary disclosure can put relationships under strain or even damage or end them. As Ragins (2008: 197) notes, 'Friends, family and co-workers may feel uncomfortable, threatened, or even repulsed by the newly revealed stigma. They may feel shocked, foolish, and betrayed by the realisation that their relationship may not be as close as they had imagined.' Of course there may also be positive outcomes for disclosure including a palpable sense of psychological relief and rediscovered energy at no longer having to conceal their identity (Woods 1994).

Heterosexism is a term which suggests that heterosexuality is the only acceptable or indeed legitimate sexual orientation (Simoni and Walters 2001 in Ragins and Wiethoff 2005) and according to Herek (1993: 89) is 'an ideological system that denies, denigrates, and stigmatises any non-heterosexual form of behaviour, identity, relationship, or community'. According to Ragins and Wiethoff (2005) it is prejudice in the form of heterosexism, rather than homophobia, with its focus on personal discomfort and fear, which most accurately captures the organisational experience of many LGBs. Waldo (1999) showed that the further an organisation's culture was towards heterosexism the less likely it was that employees would disclose their sexuality. This concealment strategy is often referred to as a 'spiral of silence', a concept first described by Noelle-Neumann in 1974 in research on public opinion. The 'spiral of silence' theory postulates that when people are not sure that they agree with the majority, they are reluctant to express opinions using the social environment as a reference point (Bowen and Blackmon 2003). For LGB employees who disclose within a dominant organisational culture of heterosexism, this could result in stigmatisation and labelling as deviant. Such a situation led Noelle-Neumann (1991) to argue that fear and the threat of isolation lead to a spiral of silence, particularly when the dilemma has a moral component or is attached to values or beliefs. Bowen and Blackmon (2003) note that the spiral of silence is particularly influential when ostracisation exists in a work group, for example, being shunned at meetings, not being invited to social events or being ignored during lunch breaks. Bullying research tells us that isolation and ostracism are possible outcomes of exposure to bullying (Leymann 1996). Similarly, the strain and concealment caused by being a victim of bullying while working alongside colleagues who are oblivious to what is occurring can be a major source of stress (Lewis 2004).

Woods (1994) identified three concealment strategies used by LGB employees at work, including using a counterfeiting strategy of passing themselves off as heterosexuals; evading the issue by censoring their identity and maintaining social distance; and finally adopting an integration strategy by openly disclosing their stigmatised identity. It is believed that some LGB employees use a range of disclosure versus non-disclosure strategies (Croteau 1996) thus supporting Goffman's (1963) assertion that each social situation and interaction requires a judgement to weigh the costs and benefits of disclosure versus non-disclosure. This is particularly difficult for invisible stigmas such as LGB because they are not necessarily perceived as stigmas. Furthermore, as Ragins (2008) notes, those with hidden stigmas that are undisclosed are not fully in control of the disclosure process. In terms of bullying, this allows for gossip and rumours to be spread which can permeate the organisation resulting in involuntary self-outing.

The more aggressive or even violent forms of bullying, direct discrimination and harassment might be directly related to homophobia. Homophobia is a direct and explicit hatred of gay men and lesbian women (Weinberg 1972) which Ragins and Wiethoff (2005) argued had no direct counterpart in racism or sexism. As previously noted, many homophobic beliefs are rooted in religious fundamentalism although Walters and Moore (2002) note that LGBs themselves can display internalised homophobic tendencies that need to be 'unlearned'.

Extreme forms of homophobia can manifest themselves as 'hate crime'. In a 2008 report on hate crime by LGB campaigning organisation Stonewall (Dick 2008), 20 per cent of lesbian and gay people surveyed had experienced a homophobic hate crime or hate incident within the past three years with three-quarters of survey participants deciding not to report their experience to police and the majority not reporting their hate crime experience to third parties of any kind. It is important to note that differences exist between 'hate incidents' and 'hate crimes'; hate incidents are described by the UK's Association of Chief Police Officers (ACPO) as 'any non-crime incident which is perceived by the victim or any other person, as being motivated by hostility or prejudice based on a person's sexual orientation', while a hate crime is defined by ACPO as 'any hate incident, which constitutes a criminal offence, perceived by the victim or any other person, as being motivated by prejudice or hate based on a person's sexual orientation (Dick 2009). The law in the UK at the time of writing allows for those who perpetrate racial and religiously motivated hate crime to be charged with aggravated harassment or assault but the same condition does not exist for homophobic hate crimes where perpetrators would be charged with the more general condition of assault. Hate crimes are unlikely to be enacted in the workplace but hate incidents are a much more realistic possibility. The hate crime associated with homophobia is normally associated with events outside of workplaces such as the reported activities of Westboro Baptist Church in the USA where funerals of HIV victims were picketed by church members bearing signs such as 'God Hates Fags' (Walters and Moore 2002) or the extreme violence displayed against LGBs as reported by Moran (2004) and Dick (2008). Dick (2008) showed that 17 per cent of victims of homophobic hate crimes had experienced physical assault with 12 per cent experiencing unwanted sexual contact.

Brenner et al. (2010) showed how gay and lesbian employees' openness about their sexuality (outness) had a direct bearing on an organisation. Their study showed how marginalisation, or what they term 'stigmatisation salience' heightens negative self-focus attention that subsequently minimises disclosure. The Brenner et al. study also showed that where organisations were willing to take action against heterosexism, employees were more likely to disclose their sexual orientation. This finding supports the notion that gay and lesbian employees are less likely to be negatively focused on being a member of a sexual minority when they feel more protected from organisational heterosexism. Evidence such as this could be effectively used by organisations as a policy response by being pro-LGB and challenging the conventions of heterosexism. By making it clear that the organisation will not tolerate bullying, discrimination or harassment of LGB employees, there is a greater likelihood that LGB staff will feel comfortable about disclosure of their identities which, from the evidence of researchers such as Woods (1994) and Day and Schoenrade (1997), produces more effective employees.

## Organisational responses to bullying and harassment of LGBs

We will argue that a successful response to bullying and harassment against LGB employees in the workplace would adopt a wider perspective, locating the problem within the overall work situation of LGBs. In doing so, it should be recognised that sexual orientation is a significant organisational issue that has risen in prominence through legislative and societal awareness. There are also the moral and ethical drivers of change towards a greater acceptance of sexual orientation diversity (Lansing and Cruser 2009). It also makes sound business logic to have strategic awareness of the economics of LGB behaviour. As Lansing and Cruser (2009) noted, the purchasing power of gay people in the USA was then twice that of as the combined spend of African Americans and Asians and gay people were much more likely to spend dollars on brands where there is a positive association with anti-discriminatory, pro-gay policies. This sort of evidence should be important to the organisational decision-makers, and might move the LGB agenda into the boardroom, not simply to be left on the desks of those deployed in human resources (HR) departments. This factor is reflected in initiatives such as the British LGB campaign group Stonewall's 'Diversity Equality Index', which measures standards of good practice among UK employers in the area of sexual orientation (Stonewall 2010).

Creating a workplace climate that allows for a more holistic appreciation of the contribution of LGB colleagues requires the development of policies and practices that embrace LGBs as an important component in the diversity agenda and not simply a fringe component. Thus, diversity in all its forms should not simply be associated with legal compliance but explained as a source of competitive advantage by ensuring diversity is incorporated into vision, mission, goals and objectives of the organisation. In smaller firms, this challenge falls to the senior executives and owners. In larger firms, it requires direct intervention by middle managers who are the voice of the organisation to subordinate and entry level employees (Lansing and Cruser 2009).

It is these middle managers in larger organisations who must be trained, monitored and evaluated to ensure that the policy is not seen as a remote diktat but an engendered set of principles to which the whole organisation subscribes. However, for this to happen, it is necessary for an audit of missing best practice to be undertaken otherwise how will employees and the managers identify what needs to be done? A central feature of this audit should be the relationship of the organisation to its external stakeholders. If an organisation is closely involved in partnership with others then it makes strategic sense to better understand their diversity agenda and their diversity practices. What might be the cost of losing the commercial value of a partnership by failing to adopt sound diversity practices of a partner or by losing one's own talent to a competitor because one's own practices are falling short?

Policy creation is of course only the beginning. Without effective monitoring of procedures and practices the policy is likely to be left rather powerless (Rayner and Lewis 2011). Additionally, any policies or processes will require regular review to ensure compliance with recognised best practice of agencies which in the UK would be the Equalities and Human Rights Commission (EHRC) or the Advisory, Conciliation and Arbitration Service (Acas). Policy-makers and reviewers would also need to be cognisant of emerging case law.

Additional interventions within organisations and employee representative groups might include appropriate forms of information transfer. For LGBs who are yet to disclose their identity it is necessary to provide a broad spectrum of information sources that could act as signposts to organisational networks and routes to self-organising support as outlined by Colgan and Ledwith (2000). Additionally, proactive and pro-LGB organisations could provide LGB mentoring through effective role models, but again this would need extremely sensitive handling for LGBs who are yet to disclose their identity. Mentoring of LGB colleagues by those who have disclosed their sexual orientation could produce significant personal and organisational benefits. Brenner *et al.* (2010) showed how gay employees who were open about their sexuality or had outed themselves were more helpful in their behaviours thus producing more effective organisational outcomes. It is posited that being 'out' perhaps allows gay employees to redirect their energies away from strategies aimed at preventing disclosure, or that they simply feel a more positive orientation to the organisation that employs them (Day and Schoenrade 1997). The stigmatisation salience referred to earlier therefore appears to have a direct bearing on psychological health as well as on organisational and personal performance. This has direct implications for organisational policies and management and workplace practices.

Equally important in an organisational context is the role of trade unions and employee representative groups. These can be a powerful force for good in the promotion of LGB rights but only if the trade unions or employee representative groups themselves recognise the potential tensions within the different diversity agendas. Based on the evidence of Lewis (2003) and Dudley and Mulvey (2009) there are clear lessons for both employee representative groups and HR officers in recognising that tensions do exist in the way LGBs are perceived by other minorities (Colgan and Ledwith 2000). Thus it might be too simplistic to expect an equal division of attention to the six equalities strands identified by diversity champions. It therefore makes sense to create an individual component element for promotion of LGB rights to counter any bias that might exist.

One of the most difficult challenges at an organisational level for both LGB employees and employers is the way complaints are reported and investigated. Bullying research demonstrates that there can be an unwillingness to report bullying incidents because of fears of the impact on careers and working relationships, or that no action will be taken or because line managers are the cause of the incidents (Rayner and Lewis 2010). These reasons are compoounded for LGB employees when their sexual identity is hidden or where they do not wish their colleagues to perceive them differently. Thus whilst bullying complaints per se need to be handled with a degree of sensitivity, bullying complaints of an LGB nature are even more complex. It is therefore essential that policies clearly state that bullying and harassment will not be tolerated, including on the grounds of sexual orientation, and that clear examples and definitions are used to explain this to all employees. This suggests that representatives of the LGB constituency should be consulted about policy content already at the development stage, incorporating what Colgan *et al.* (2008) refer to as 'everyday experience of LGBs'. Managers will need specific training on handling the confidential nature of bullying of LGBs, especially for those who have not disclosed their sexual identity. Ultimately, as confidence in the policy depends on how it is enforced and how complaints are dealt with by the organisation (Wright *et al.* 2006), failure to act, or in the case of LGBs, possibly downplaying the seriousness of homophobic incidents, would have repercussions for its use and for wider trust in management.

In line with senior management commitment and line management support, systems and processes should support informal dispute resolution where possible (Gibbons 2007) although where hate incidents or hate crimes exist then clearly a more formal route is needed. At an organisational level, informal solutions may well require the involvement of others such as mediators, counsellors, trade union representatives and employee assistance programme (EAP) specialists. It is critical that all those deployed in intervention strategies are clearly cognisant of equality regulations as they apply to sexual orientation so that interventions are applied sensitively. Similarly, it is essential that although seen as informal, such procedures are shown to be taken seriously, thus demonstrating organisational commitment to LGB equality. In the event that an employee has experienced bullying or harassment on the grounds of their sexuality and has to take time away from work, for example through stress caused by exposure to bullying, they must be provided with appropriate support to return to work, possibly with agreed adjustments to their role or potentially to their place of work. This will require sensitive management and the appointing of a supportive manager, mentor or colleague to assist them to get back to normal working life. Such a return to work could involve a period of home working where practicable but not at the expense of failing to address the inappropriate behaviours associated with bullying. We are certainly not advocating the isolation of an LGB employee from their colleagues; rather we suggest that flexible working from home might suit the gradual return to work necessary after an incident of bullying and harassment. Ultimately, the key to a longer-term solution is a culture change that sees zero tolerance of discrimination on grounds of sexual orientation, as with any other form of discrimination. In terms of homophobia, an effective strategy to deal with it is knowing or being friends with LGBs, which is a more effective predictor of attitude change than either demographic characteristics or parental attitudes (Walters and Moore 2002).

## Note

The chapter was written before the 2010 Equality Act came into power and readers ought to be cognisant of that.

## Further reading

For a comprehensive overview of the issue of bullying and harassment in the workplace we recommend the edited book by Einarsen, S., Hoel, H., Zapf, D. and Cooper, C.L (2011) *Bullying and Harassment in the Workplace. Developments in Theory, Research and Practice*. London/Atlanta, GA: CRC Press. Brodsky, C.M. (1976) *The Harassed Worker*. Toronto: Lexington Books, D.C. Heath and Co., remains a 'must read' for those interested in harassment.

For an overview of the problem of violence and harassment within EU states, including legal responses to the problem, we point to the European Agency of Safety and Health at Work report (2011) downloadable from http://osha.europa.eu/en/

publications/reports/violence-harassment-TERO09010ENC

A challenging but interesting book is Hearn, J. and Parkin, W. (2001) *Gender, Sexuality and Violence in Organizations: the Unspoken Forces of Organization Violations*. London: Sage. The following reports also provide additional reading on sexual orientation inside and outside the workplace:

EHRC (2009) *Beyond Tolerance: Making sexual orientation a public matter*. Manchester: Equality and Human Rights Commission.

Stonewall (2007) *Living Together: British attitudes to lesbians and gay people*. London: Stonewall.

Acas (2007) *Sexual Orientation and Religion or Belief Discrimination in the Workplace*. London: Advisory, Conciliation and Arbitration Service (Acas).

## References

Acas (2007) *Sexual orientation and religion or belief discrimination in the workplace*. Research paper 01/07. London: Acas.

Acker, J. (1990) 'Hierarchies, jobs, bodies: A theory of gendered organizations', in J. Lorber and S. Farrell (eds) *The Social Construction of Gender*. London: Sage Publications.

Amnesty International (2009) Available at http://www.amnesty.org.uk/news_details. asp?NewsID=18264, posted 18 June 2009.

Aquino, K. and Thau, S. (2009) 'Workplace victimization: Aggression from the target's perspective', *Annual Review of Psychology*, 60: 717–41.

Archer, D. (1999) 'Exploring "bullying" culture in the para-military organisation', *International Journal of Manpower*, 20(1/2): 94–105.

Bar-Tal, D. (1998) 'Group beliefs as an expression of social identity', in W. Worchel, J.F. Morales, D. Paez J.C. and Deschamps (eds) *Social Identity: International Perspectives*. London: Sage Publications.

Beale, D. and Hoel, H. (in press) 'Workplace bullying and British employers: exploring questions of cost, policy, context and control', *Work, Employment and Society*.

Bloisi, W. and Hoel, H. (2008) 'The expectation of abusive work practices and bullying among chefs: a review of the literature', *International Journal of Hospitality Management*, 27: 649–56.

Bolton, S.C. (2007) *Dimensions of Dignity*. London: Elsevier Butterworth-Heinemann.

Bowen, F. and Blackmon, K. (2003) 'Spirals of silence: The dynamic effects of diversity on organizational voice', *Journal of Management Studies*, 40(6): 1393–417.

Brenner, B.R., Lyons, H.Z. and Fassinger, R.E. (2010) 'Can heterosexism harm organizations? Predicting the perceived organizational citizenship behaviors of gay and lesbian employee', *The Career Development Quarterly*, 58: 321–35.

Brodsky, C. M. (1976) *The Harassed Worker*. Toronto: Lexington Books, D.C. Heath and Co.

Chappel, D. and Di Martino, V. (2006) *Violence at Work* (3rd edn). Geneva: International Labour Office.

Cochran, S.D. (2001) 'Emerging issues in research in lesbians' and gay men's mental health: Does sexual orientation really matter?', *American Psychologist*, 56: 931–47.

Colgan, F. and Ledwith, S. (2000) 'Diversity, identities and strategies of women trade union activists', *Gender, Work and Organization*, 7(4): 242–57.

Colgan, F., Creegan, C., McKearney, A. and Wright, T. (2008) *Lesbian, Gay and Bisexual Workers: Equality, diversity and inclusion on the workplace*. London: London Metropolitan University.

Coyne, I., Seigne, E. and Randall, P. (2000) 'Predicting workplace victim status from personality', *European Journal of Work and Organizational Psychology*, 9: 335–49.

Croteau, J. M. (1996) 'Research on the work experiences of lesbian, gay and bisexual people: An integrative review of methodology and findings', *Journal of Vocational Behavior*, 48: 195–209.

Day, N.E., and Schoenrade, P. (1997) 'Staying in the closet versus coming out: Relationships between communication about sexual orientation and work attitudes', *Personnel Psychology*, 50: 147–63.

Dick, S. (2008) 'Homophobic hate crime: The Gay British Crime Survey 2008'. London: Stonewall.

Dick, S. (2009) 'Homophobic hate crimes and hate incidents'. London: Equalities and Human Rights Commission.

Di Martino, V., Hoel, H. and Cooper, C.L. (2003) 'Preventing violence and harassment in the workplace.' European Foundation for the Improvement of Living and Working Conditions. Luxembourg: Office for Official Publications of the European Communities.

Dudley, M.G. and Mulvey, D. (2009) 'Differentiating among outgroups: Predictors of congruent and discordant prejudice', *North American Journal of Psychology*, 11(1): 143-56.

EHRC (2009) *Beyond Tolerance: Making sexual orientation a public matter*. Manchester: Equality and Human Rights Commission.

Einarsen, S., Hoel, H., Zapf, D. and Cooper, C.L. (2011) *Bullying and Harassment in the Workplace. Developments in theory, research and practice*. London/Atlanta, GA: CRC Press.

Einarsen, S. and Mikkelsen, E.G. (2003) 'Individual effects of exposure to bullying at work', in S. Einarsen, H. Hoel, D. Zapf and C.L Cooper (eds) *Bullying and Emotional Abuse in the Workplace: International Perspectives in Research and Practice*, pp. 127–44). London: Taylor and Francis.

Einarsen, S. Raknes, B.I. and Matthiesen, S.B. (1994) 'Bullying and harassment at work and their relationships to work environment quality: an explanatory study', *European Work and Organizational Psychologist*, 4: 381–401.

Ellison, G. and Gunstone, B. (2009) *Sexual Orientation Explored: A study of identity, attraction, behaviour and attitudes in 2009*. Manchester: Equality and Humans Rights Commission.

Eriksen, W. and Einarsen, S. (2004) 'Gender minority as a risk factor of exposure to bullying at work: The case of male assistant nurses', *European Journal of Work and Organizational Psychology*, 13: 473–92.

Fevre, R., Robinson, A., Jones T. and Lewis, D. (2008) *Disability: Work Fit For All*. London: Equalities and Human Rights Commission, Insight Report No. 1.

Field, T. (1996) *Bullying in Sight*. Wantage: Success Unlimited.

French, J. and Raven, B.H. (1959) 'The bases of social power', in D. Cartwright (ed.) *Studies of Social Power*, pp. 150–67. Ann Arbor, MI: Institute for Social Research.

Gibbons, M. (2007) 'Better dispute resolution: A review of employment dispute resolution in Great Britain'. London: Department for Trade and Industry.

Giga, S., Hoel, H. and Lewis, D. (2008a) *The Costs of Workplace Bullying*. London: Unite the union/Department for Business, Enterprise and Regulatory Reform.

Giga, S., Hoel, H. and Lewis, D. (2008b) 'A review of black and minority ethnic employee experiences of workplace bullying'. London: Unite the union/Department for Business, Enterprise and Regulatory Reform.

Glasø, L., Løkke, T. and Hoel, H. (2010) 'Bullying in the workplace', in C.L. Cooper and R. Burke (eds) *Risky Business: Psychological and behavioural costs of high risk behaviour in organizations*. London: Gower Publishing Ltd.

Glasø, L., Matthiesen, S.B., Nielsen M. B. and Einarsen, S. (2007) 'Do targets of bullying portray a general victim personality profile?', *Scandinavian Journal of Psychology*, 48,

313–9.

Goffman, E. (1963) *Stigma: Notes on the Management of Spoiled Identity*. Englewood Cliffs, NJ: Simon and Schuster.

Grainger, H. and Fitzner, G. (2006) *The first fair treatment at work survey*. Employment relations research series no. 63. London: DTI.

Griffith, K.H. and Hebl, M.R. (2002) 'The disclosure dilemma for gay men and lesbians: "Coming out"at work', *Journal of Applied Psychology*, 87: 1191–9.

Hauge, L J., Skogstad, A. and Einarsen, S. (2007) 'Relationships between stressful work environments and bullying: Results of a large representative study', *Work and Stress*, 21(3): 220–42.

Hearn, J. and Parkin, W. (2001) *Gender, Sexuality and Violence in Organizations: the Unspoken Forces of Organization Violations*. London: Sage.

Herek, G.M. (1993) 'The context of anti-gay violence: Notes on cultural and psychological heterosexism', in L.D. Farnets and D.C. Kimmel (eds) *Psychological Perspectives on Lesbian and Gay Male Experiences*, pp. 89–107). New York: Columbia University Press.

Hershcovis, S. (in press) ' "Incivility, social undermining, bullying...Oh My!": A call to reconcile constructs within workplace aggression research', *Journal of Organizational Behavior*.

Hoel, H. and Cooper, C.L. (2000) 'Destructive conflict and bullying at work'. Unpublished report, University of Manchester Institute of Science and Technology.

Hoel, H., Cooper, C.L and Faragher, B. (2001) 'Workplace bullying in Great Britain: The impact of occupational status', *European Journal of Work and Organizational Psychology*, 10: 443-61.

Hoel, H. and Einarsen, H. (2011) 'Investigating complaints of bullying and harassment', in S. Einarsen, H. Hoel, D. Zapf, and C.L. Cooper (eds) *Bullying and Harassment in the Workplace. Developments in theory, research and practice*, pp. 341–57 London/Atlanta: CRC Press.

Hoel, H., Einarsen, S., Sheehan, M. and Cooper, C.L. (2011) 'Organisational effects of bullying', in S. Einarsen, H. Hoel, H., D. Zapf, and C.L. Cooper (eds) *Bullying and Harassment in the Workplace. Developments in theory, research and practice*, pp. 129–47. London/Atlanta: CRC Press.

Hoel, H., Faragher, B. and Cooper, C.L. (2004) 'Bullying is detrimental to health, but all bullying behaviours are not necessarily equally damaging', *British Journal of Guidance and Counselling*, 32: 367–87.

Hoel, H., Glasø, L., Hetland, H., Cooper, C.L. and Einarsen, S. (in press) 'Leadership style as predictor of self-reported and observed workplace bullying', *British Journal of Management*.

Hoel, H., Rayner, C. and Cooper, C.L. (1999) 'Workplace bullying', in C.L. Cooper and I.T. Robertson (eds) *International Review of Industrial and Organizational Psychology*, 14: 195–230. Chichester: John Wiley and Sons.

Imich, A., Bayley, S. and Farley, K. (2001) 'Equalities and gay and lesbian young people: implications for educational psychologists', *Educational Psychology in Practice*, 17(4) 375–463.

Lansing, P. and Cruser, C. (2009) 'The moral responsibility of business to protect homosexuals from discrimination in the workplace', *Employee Relations Law Journal*, 35(1): 43–66.

Lee, D. (2002) 'Gendered workplace bullying in the restructured UK Civil Service', *Personnel Review*, 31: 205–27.

Lewis, G.B. (2003) 'Black and white differences in attitudes to homosexuality and gay rights', *Public Opinion Quarterly*, 67: 59–78.

Lewis, D. (2004) 'Bullying at work: the impact of shame among university and college lecturers', *British Journal of Guidance and Counselling*, 32(3): 281–300.

Lewis, D. (2006) *Workplace Bullying and Harassment: Building a Culture of Respect*, Acas Policy Discussion Papers, No. 4. London: Acas.

Lewis, D., Giga, S. and Hoel, H. (2011) 'Discrimination and bullying', in S. Einarsen, H. Hoel, D. Zapf, and C.L. Cooper (eds) *Bullying and Harassment in the Workplace. Developments in theory, research and practice*. London/Atlanta: CRC Press.

Lewis, D. and Gunn, R.W. (2007) 'Workplace bullying in the public sector: understanding the racial dimension', *Public Administration and International Quarterly*, 83(3): 641–65

Leymann, H. (1996) 'The content and development of mobbing at work', *European Journal of Work and Organizational Psychology*, 5: 165–84.

Long, W. and Millsap, C.A. (2008) 'Fear of AIDS and homophobia scales in an ethnic population of university students', *Journal of Social Psychology*, 148(5): 637–40.

Macpherson, William (1999) *The Stephen Lawrence Inquiry*. London: The Stationery Office.

Marques, J.M., Paez, D. and Abrams, D. (1998) 'Social identity and intragroup differentiation as subjective social control', in S. Worchel, J.F. Morales, D. Paez and and J.C. Deschamps (eds) *Social Identity: International Perspectives*. London: Sage Publications.

Meyer, I.H. (2003) 'Prejudice, social stress, and mental health in lesbian, gay and bisexual populations: Conceptual issues and research evidence', *Psychology Bulletin*, September, 129: 674–97.

Moran, L.J. (2004) 'The emotional dimensions of lesbian and gay demands for hate crime reform', *McGill Law Journal*, 49: 925–49.

NCSR (National Centre for Social Research) (2010) *British Social Trends*. London: NCSR.

Nielsen, M.B., Skogstad, A., Matthiesen, S.B., Glasø, L., Aasland, M.S. and Notelaers, G. (2009) 'Prevalence of workplace bullying in Norway: Comparison across time and estimation method', *European Journal of Work and Organizational Psychology* 18(1): 81–101.

Noelle-Neumann, E. (1974) 'The spiral of silence: a theory of public opinion', *Journal of Communication*, 24: 43–51.

Noelle-Neumann, E. (1991) 'The theory of public opinion: the concept of the spiral of silence', in J.A. Anderson (ed.) *Communication Yearbook*. Newbury Park, GA: Sage, pp. 256–87.

Prior, J.B. and Fitzgerald, L.F. (2003) 'Sexual harassment research in the United States', in S. Einarsen, H. Hoel, D. Zapf and C.L Cooper (eds) *Bullying and Emotional Abuse in the Workplace: International Perspectives in Research and Practice*, pp. 79–100). London: Taylor and Francis.

Ragins, B.R. (2008) 'Disclosure disconnects: Antecedents and consequences of disclosing invisble stigmas across life domains', *Academy of Management Review*, 33(1): 194–215.

Ragins, B.R. and Wiethoff, C. (2005) 'Understanding heterosexism at work: The straight problem', in B. Dipboye and A. Colella (eds) *Discrimination at Work: Psychological and Organizational Bases*. Mahwah, NJ: Lawrence Erlbaum Association.

Randle, J. (2003) 'Bullying in the nursing profession', *Journal of Advanced Nursing*, 43: 395–401.

Raver, J.L. and Nishii, L.H. (2010) 'Once, twice, or three times as harmful? Ethnic harassment, gender harassment, and generalized workplace harassment', *Journal of Applied Psychology*, 95: 236–54.

Rayner, C., Hoel, H. and Cooper, C.L. (2002) *Workplace Bullying: What we know, who is to blame and what can we do?* London: Taylor & Francis.

Rayner, C. and Lewis, D. (2011) 'Managing workplace bullying: the role of policies', in

S. Einarsen, H. Hoel, D. Zapf and C. Cooper (eds) *Bullying and Harassment in the Workplace. Developments in theory, research and practice.* London/Atlanta: CRC Press.

Salin, D. and Hoel, H.C. (2011) 'Organisational causes of workplace bullying', in S. Einarsen, H. Hoel, D. Zapf and Cary. L. Cooper (eds) *Bullying and Harassment in the Workplace. Developments in theory, research and practice.* London/Atlanta, GA: CRC Press.

Simoni, J.M and Walters, K.L (2001) 'Heterosexual identity and heterosexism: Recognizing privilege to reduce prejudice', *Journal of Homosexuality*, 3: 31–48.

Simpson, R. and Cohen, C. (2004) 'Dangerous work: The gendered nature of bullying in the context of higher education', *Gender, Work and Organization*, 11(2): 163–86.

Skogstad, A., Matthiesen, S.B. and Einarsen, S. (2007a) 'Organizational changes: a precursor of bullying at work?', *International Journal of Organizational Theory and Behavior*, 10: 58–94.

Skogstad, A., Einarsen, S., Torsheim, T., Aasland, M. and Hetland, H. (2007b) 'The destructiveness of laissez-faire leadership behaviour', *Journal of Occupational Health Psychology*, 12: 80–92.

Stonewall (2007) *Living Together: British attitudes to lesbians and gay people.* London: Stonewall.

Stonewall (2011) Britain's Top 100 Employers for lesbian, gay men and bisexual staff (http://www.stonewall.org.uk/atwork/4763.asp), accessed 11 June 2011.

Tajfel, H. (1978) 'Social categorization, social identity and social comparison', in H. Tajfel (ed.) *Differentiation between Social Groups: Studies in the social psychology of intergroup relations.* London: Academic Press.

TUC (2000) *Straight Up! Why the law should protect lesbian and gay workers.* London: Trades Union Congress.

Waldo, C.R. (1999) 'Working in a majority context: A structural model of heterosexism as minority stress in the workplace', *Journal of Counseling Psychology*, 40: 218–32.

Walters, A.S. and Moore, L.J. (2002) 'Attention all shoppers, queer customers in aisle two: Investigating lesbian and gay discrimination in the marketplace', *Consumption, Markets and Culture*, 5(4) 285–303.

Ward, J. and Winstanley, D. (2006) 'Walking the watch: the UK fire service and its impact on sexual minorities in the workplace', *Gender, Work and Organisation*, 13: 193–219.

Weinberg, G. (1972) *Society and the Healthy Homosexual.* New York: St. Martin's Press.

Wong, N. (2005) 'National survey shows gay-specific marketing practices may influence brand loyalty and purchase decisions of gays, lesbians and bisexuals', *Harris Interactive*, 5 April available at http://sev.prnewswire.com

Woods, J. D. (1994) *The Corporate Closet: The professional lives of gay men in America.* New York: Free Press.

Wright, T., Colgan, F., Creegan, C. and McKarney, A. (2006) 'Lesbian, gay and bisexual workers: equality, diversity and inclusion in the workplace', *Equal Opportunities International*, 25: 456–70.

Zapf, D. and Einarsen, S. (2011) 'Individual antecedents of bullying: Victims and perpetrators', in S. Einarsen, H. Hoel, D. Zapf and Cary, L. Cooper (eds) *Bullying and Harassment in the Workplace. Developments in theory, research and practice.* London/ Atlanta, GA: CRC Press.

Zapf, D., Escartin, J., Einarsen, S., Hoel, H. and Vartia, M. (2011) 'Empirical findings on prevalence and risk groups of bullying in the workplace', *Harassment in the Workplace. Development in Theory, Research and Practice*, pp. 75–105. London/Atlanta, GA: CRC Press.

# Chapter 19

# Public sector and voluntary sector responses: supporting survivors

*Kate Cook*

## Meet Kate Cook

Kate Cook is a feminist and a teacher, activist and writer. She has been involved in the struggle against rape since 1990, when she joined Manchester Rape Crisis as a volunteer collective member. Since then she has worked in campaigning groups (Justice for Women, Campaign to End Rape and Truth About Rape Campaign) and has completed a degree and PhD in law, all inspired by that original involvement with rape crisis. Kate is now deeply honoured to be a patron of Manchester Rape Crisis and teaches about the law on rape to students studying law at Manchester Metropolitan University. She is also a member of the group Safety4Sisters (North-west), which she writes about here.

## Introduction

Rape is a crime against women. Rape is a deadly insult against you as a person. Rape is the deprivation of sexual self-determination. Rape is a man's fantasy, a woman's nightmare. Rape is all the hatred, contempt, and oppression of women in this society concentrated in one act.

(Medea and Thompson 1974: 11)

Rape is unique as it is an inherently lawful activity made illegal because of lack of consent.

(Stern Review 2010: 7)

This chapter examines the state of official and non-official responses to rape in England and Wales and begins with two strikingly different views on rape. The language of the first quotation, from Medea and Thompson, is a woman-centred definition of rape from 1974 and is based on women's lived experience. Contrast this approach with the remark below it, which a 'lawyer' reportedly made to Baroness Vivien Stern's review of rape published in March 2010. Right at the outset, the executive summary of this review considers a legal nicety worth commenting upon, in favour of women's experience. The argument the lawyer makes is that sexual intercourse is legal unless consent is withdrawn, when it becomes a crime. This phallocentric view favours the male version of sexuality as penile penetration and is starkly at odds with the woman-centred approach. For women, rape is not difficult to define, but it is proving difficult to convince public authorities of this.

The chapter explores these variations in meaning and links them to differing aims, within public and voluntary responses. It suggests that the topic of 'domestic abuse' has received more attention than 'rape' typically does. The focus on rape here is a deliberate attempt to redraw this bias, whilst also allowing for a reconsideration of the value of the concept of the continuum of sexual violence in the field of responses. The chapter aims to compare public and voluntary responses and, in doing so, is bound to draw some rather sweeping generalisations simply in order to allow space for a range of discussion. It is worth saying, at the outset, that within these general trends there are also exceptions. There are, for example, women who are very angry with responses from the women's voluntary sector, perhaps because the service was not open when they wanted to use it. Equally, there are women who feel that individuals within the statutory agencies have provided them with a first-class service. In general, however, as Sara Payne's recent review of rape victim experience (2009) shows, the public sector is lagging behind the women's voluntary sector in terms of women's levels of satisfaction.

In looking forward, the chapter considers some of the threats faced by the women's voluntary sector as well as examining the suggestions raised by the Stern Review. Having examined these differences the chapter concludes that it is vital that the women's voluntary sector continues to try to find ways of creating responses based on women's experience, rather than being led by public sector response models.

## Rape and domestic violence responses

Although the ideas from Kelly's continuum have undoubtedly had an impact in British policy and practice, it can be seen that responses to violence against women tend to be split into two strands. One of these considers 'rape', while the other concentrates on 'domestic violence' or, to use the currently favoured term, 'domestic abuse'. Keeping these two separate tends to undermine a central truth of the continuum, that all violence against women is interlinked.

The women's voluntary sector is dominated by the women's refuge movement, with the (far poorer and geographically less evenly spread) rape crisis movement having a lesser public status (Jones and Cook 2008). Where government attempts to respond to 'violence against women' (for example in the recent *Together We Can End Violence Against Women And Girls: A Strategy* document, published 2009) the result has tended to be that rape is sidelined, while domestic abuse is given centre stage. On the face of it, then, the argument that these forms of violence are strongly interconnected has failed to make a strong impact. As Kelly noted, the connections within the continuum created a challenge for women's services (1988: 236–38) but also for other responses to sexual violence.

Public responses now appear to pay attention to the connections between rape, domestic abuse, sexual harassment, stalking and other forms of sexual violence. Under New Labour there have been many attempts to improve laws and services for abused women. To work in practice, these need to consider the linkages between fear, truthfulness and violation and also between poverty, immigration status and violation. In practice though, service provision still tends to blame women for being weak or unconvincing victims, rather than consider the effects and reality of their victimisation. There is still a tendency to think of sexual violence last, after considering a range of woman-blaming explanations first. Women remain aware of these issues and abusers play on this knowledge, to increase their leverage over women. Consider these comments from survivors of familial abuse:

> V: I was not able to say anything because he said, 'If you tell anyone they won't believe you, even the police will not believe you – they listen to their citizens not to you, they will arrest you for complaining and deport you'.
> A: He told me several times that he had told everyone I was mad...no one would listen to me. If I contacted the police, they could consider me mad and arrest me.
>
> (participants quoted in: Anitha 2008: 42.)

Powerlessness is only increased by women's knowledge of the failures of public service responses to violence. The gap between the rhetoric of care for victims and the reality of service response remains problematic. In contrast, rape crisis and the other services which women run tend to focus on whatever forms of violence they are able to respond to. Each group, within their own local environment, may provide specialist services to different groups of women and may be more or less able to work along an inclusive, continuum-led definition of sexual violence. This means that rape crisis and others are capable of understanding and listening, but that their stretched resources impact severely on whom they are able to respond to, and in what settings. Rape crisis tends to be painfully aware of these failings:

> Because we are so busy trying to keep the services going we don't look at older women, we don't look at disabled women. We try to be proactive, we have a healthy lesbian and bi group going in the agency but we have done no proactive work around disability...I hold my head in shame about some of this.
>
> (worker from the Cornwall centre quoted in Jones and Cook 2008: 44)

Whatever their current capacity, these groups have tended to be strongly influenced by the idea of a continuum of sexual violence. Their central philosophy is to believe what women tell them and to be part of a movement which aims to end rape. The Cornwall-based Women's Rape and Sexual Abuse Centre, for example, combines rape crisis work with work on domestic abuse, including work with men who are perpetrators (*ibid.*: 24–6). The wish to retain the divide between domestic abuse and rape is still something led by the public sector, for reasons which are explored below.

## What do we want to achieve?

Before trying to evaluate responses from the public and private sector any further, it is worth considering what these constitute. This discussion outlines the contrasting aims of public and private responses before examining which services make up these key responses. Feminist activist responses to rape are part of a movement which wants to change the world. This movement views rape as a socially constructed tool used to protect and further male interests (Jones and Cook 2008 ch. 1; Brownmiller 1999) and hopes to be part of change which will eventually eliminate rape. Hence one of the leading English lobbying groups on rape in recent years is the Campaign to End Rape. The name of the campaign is, in itself, a challenge to patriarchal norms and assumptions that rape is unavoidable. This idea remains so dominant that Andrea Dworkin spoke of wanting to achieve just one day off, in which there would be no rape (speech from 1983, printed in Buchwald *et al.* 1993). However, the feminist anti-rape movement still believes that the world can be transformed so that all days become rape-free.

In contrast to this aim of transformation, the focus of public sector responses tends to be on regulation through the criminal justice system. Public response to rape can be characterised as being driven by the following aims: justice; to lessen victim dissatisfaction; and to dampen feminist claims of unfairness. All of these can be illustrated by the Stern Review's wish to move away from the conviction rate debate, regarding rape (Stern 2010: 42–6). The focus on a weak conviction rate is said to be a poor strategy, as it discourages reporting. In fact, the focus on low conviction rates and high attrition also provides a focus for victim dissatisfaction and for feminist activism. Consequently, the Stern report prefers to use a different measure of success. The figure usually quoted is the percentage of reported cases which achieve a conviction (usually stated to be around 6 per cent: *ibid.*). The review prefers to focus on the cases which get as far as trial, of which 58 per cent result in a conviction. This, the Baroness concludes, is a much more useful statistic. The feminist anti-rape movement is bound to disagree and the reasons for this are explored next.

The high attrition and low conviction rate for rape has been a major feminist anti-rape campaigning tool for around 15 years now. Perhaps the first person to write about this was the late Sue Lees, in the first edition of her volume *Carnal Knowledge: Rape on Trial* (1996), where she broke down the numbers of cases achieving various key stages in the criminal justice process. This showed that each year the initial number of reported cases was gradually worn away by the action of disbelief and inefficiency within the criminal justice system, so that the number reaching court was only a small proportion of those initially recorded as crimes. Little has changed here. Recent figures published by the Crown Prosecution Service (CPS 2009) suggest that there is still considerable case wastage between police recording and referral to prosecutors. The same publication shows that the CPS only lays charges in around 40 per cent of the cases referred to them for a decision (*ibid*.: 34–41). The number of recorded cases of 'rape of a female' for 2008–9 is 12,165 (Home Office 2009a: 31). The figure for 'rape of a male' is 968 (*ibid*.). CPS figures for that year show that 2,018 convictions for rape (or lesser offences) were achieved (CPS 2009: 35). This represents 16.6 per cent and is calculated differently from the more widely publicised and lower conviction rates which focus on convictions for rape, ignoring offences downgraded during the criminal justice process.[1]

Of the 3,495 cases that the CPS reports prosecuting (*ibid*.), 57.7 per cent did achieve a conviction and this is the figure on which the Stern Review suggests we should concentrate. Indeed, it is clear that this is a powerful figure for women to know, when their case gets as far as Crown Court.[2] However, an aim of feminist campaigning has always been to highlight that there are problems across the range of criminal justice responses to rape and it is clear that this remains valid today. Cases which are dropped before court become invisible, if the focus is only on the 58 per cent success rate achieved at trial. Women such as this participant in Sara Payne's research become disenfranchised.

> Mine didn't get to court; my emotions are all over the place...the police were crap. They sent me a letter to tell me the case was not going to court. ...If somebody had talked to me and explained to me why this wasn't going to court...it would have been so much better...that letter made me feel so small and demeaned.
>
> (Payne 2009: 19)

The figures discussed above are summarised in Table 19.1 to make it clear that the Stern recommendation would involve acknowledging the loss of only 1,477 cases from the system, which did not result in a conviction. The 9,638 cases lost earlier in the process, as a result of complainant withdrawal or police or CPS failure to proceed, are simply written out of public notice.

**Table 19.1** Summary of figures quoted above

| | | |
|---|---|---|
| Number of recorded rapes 2008–9 | 13,133 | |
| Number which the CPS prosecuted | 3,495 | Attrition 9,638 |
| Number of convictions | 2,018 | Attrition 1,477 |
| | | Total 11,115 |

A gap evidently remains between the agenda of public response and the feminist activists' wish to end rape. Following concerted efforts from feminists, there have been shifts in the public perception of women who experience violence. Where the rape claim is taken seriously, public policy now sees these women as 'victims of crime'. However, the group allowed within that label remains limited. A liberal democracy perceives its primary role in relation to such victims as being to prosecute wrongdoers and ultimately protect victims (including other innocents who are not yet victimised by this wrongdoer). The government directs victims towards the police, in order to achieve justice (as though this will resolve their victimisation). Public responses then come initially from the police, from hospitals and medical staff, where they become involved in a particular case, and in some instances, from social or care workers. Farther down the line, victims can encounter public support services (led by Victim Support, the Witness Service, and sexual assault referral centres) and these are also linked in to the criminal justice system. Women may also have contact with specialist workers called 'independent sexual violence advisers' (ISVAs).

Victim Support is a charitable organisation (www.victimsupport.org.uk) which accesses victims via police records of crime and also provides support within the court system, via the Witness Service. It is a quasi-official body which makes claim to independence, but clearly works alongside the Home Office, police, court service, and others within the system. So, whilst Victim Support is a part of the 'voluntary sector' in its use of volunteers, it is viewed as a public sector response, for the purposes of this discussion.

Sexual assault referral centres (or SARCS) have been the government's preferred model for support for victims of rape and sexual assault. They operate alongside the police, providing a range of support (which varies in different locations: Payne 2009: 13) alongside forensic examination facilities. In police force areas where there is a SARC (29, at the time of writing: www.homeoffice.gov.uk/crime-victims/reducing-crime/sexual-offences/sexual-assault-referral-centres) victims who report sexual offences are referred to the centre by the police themselves.

ISVAs are a relatively new idea, and are workers who are funded by the Home Office, but placed within SARCs, in police stations or in rape crisis centres, to work with women on a one-to-one basis. This role begins to blur the boundaries between rape crisis and public responses to rape. The women's voluntary sector views the creation of this role as a useful step in terms of public responses. The sector is also concerned that the 'independence' of these workers is not properly guaranteed, and this hampers their work in the field. The Stern Review provides some description of the ISVA role and concludes that this is an important and welcome specialism, which should receive ongoing public funding (Stern 2010: ch. 4). Altogether, these are currently the core public responses for women who experience rape.

The key problem with public responses, which Sara Payne has recently identified, is inconsistency (2009: 17, previously highlighted by EVAW in their 'Map of Gaps' http://www.endviolenceagainstwomen.org.uk/pages/resources. html, accessed 18 June 2010). Around the country, and even within particular areas, cases are treated differently, according to the local police, SARC, ISVA or Victim Support policies or priorities. As the 'Map of Gaps' illustrates, the same charge of inconsistency can be laid at the door of the women's voluntary sector. The problem here tends to be one of funding and resources, rather than policy.

The voluntary sector responses which provide a different model are focused within the rape crisis and women's refuge movement, as discussed above. These groups grew from entirely different roots from the public organisations and have no primary allegiance to criminal justice as a response to sexual violence. In addition, there is a range of other independent groups which operate within the voluntary sector, providing important services to survivors of violence. A notable exclusion from the general description just given is the magnificent Southall Black Sisters (SBS). This is a long-established women's group in London, which provides a range of local services to black women. The group also has a national and international lobbying profile and has been instrumental in some key changes and campaigns (www.southallblacksisters. org.uk). Another leader in its field is Survivors' UK, which works with male survivors of child sexual abuse and rape (www.survivorsuk.org). This discussion returns to the topic of male rape later on, in reviewing some current challenges faced by the voluntary women's sector.

The Rape Crisis movement grew from the Women's Liberation movement in America, which grew across the United States in the 1960s. Consciousness-raising has been described as the 'method' of this movement (MacKinnon 1989: ch. 6), the same method employed within the continuum itself.

## Which rapes?

This section of the discussion considers the role of consciousness-raising in defining 'rape' and contrasts this with public definitions. As the opening quotation illustrated, this feminist consciousness-raising model defines rape as it is described by women. The definition is constantly changing and expanding to encompass the range of women's experiences.

Both the rape crisis support model and the concept of the continuum use a consciousness-raising approach and are capable of allowing rape definitions to adapt. In contrast, the public sector definition of rape is relatively fixed and is largely derived from the legal context. It is true to say that public responses now understand using 'rape' as a basket term, which includes a range of differing violent acts. Nevertheless, the public conception of 'rape' is narrower than the women's sector definition, in a number of ways. The following discussion will highlight these problems of scope and demonstrate that these lead to a false sense of a common terminology. When a feminist within rape crisis says 'rape' she means something far wider than a colleague in the police or the medical or legal professions is likely to appreciate. To illustrate, I recall talking with a friend, some years ago now, who was distressed at the police response to her report of rape. She had been told that this was not 'rape' and felt that her experience was being dismissed or diminished for some unaccountable reason. In fact the police had not meant to be disbelieving or unsupportive. The officer in question was commenting that the offence committed was sexual assault, not rape, in the eyes of the law. My friend and this officer were not using the terminology in the same way.

A modern feminist definition of 'rape' might be: sexualised violence which constitutes a range of possible acts and is perpetrated by men and boys upon women and girls. Rape is a mechanism for the exploitation of power difference

423

and the sum of the acts of rape maintain and reinforce the patriarchy which can also be characterised as being racist, ageist, able-ist, heterosexist, and beauty-ist. Rape is very commonly perpetrated by men and boys acting within patriarchal stereotypes. Women and girls are also sometimes able to access forms of patriarchal power and thus they can be capable of performing these acts of rape, though they do so far less often.

This definition tries to do justice to the knowledge which feminism has gained from women's experiences. It acknowledges a patriarchal cause and reason for rape's dominance, whilst acknowledging the range of other forms of difference which are reinforced and used within rape. The definition is unpicked further below, with some comparison with the public view of rape.

The feminist definition here begins with a 'range of possible acts', deliberately failing to name or detail these, since women's experience teaches that the list is never closed. It is clear that when Kelly developed the continuum model in 1988, she already knew that rape was made up of a range of linked acts. Some women experienced one or more of these on one occasion. Others were subjected to repeated and diverse attacks, over periods of years. To this extent, public responses have done some catching up, in the intermediate years. These acts of 'rape' are now defined within sections 1–4 of the Sexual Offences Act 2003. Section 1 covers the legal offence of rape and the act here is penile penetration of the vagina, anus, or mouth. Section 2 covers other acts of penetration with body parts or objects, where the penetration is of the vagina or anus. Section 3 relates to what the law terms 'sexual assault' and covers a wide range of other forms of sexual touching, which presumably covers other sexual penetration of the mouth, since this is excluded from section 2. Finally, section 4 covers being forced to do sexual acts to another, against one's will. This might include being forced to masturbate an attacker or their accomplice.

The law now covers a range of acts which can be recognised as a fair attempt to detail the acts that a continuum of rape would describe. At least to this extent the law has been influenced by survivor-led calls for change. Public services (linked to law) should now be capable of understanding the range of acts which survivors perceive to be rape as some form of sexual offence though survivors can still find that the terms they use differ from those of the police and others.

Early British feminist work on rape revealed that inflexibility in language resulted in complaints about non-supportive responses from public agencies (Ginsburg and Lerner 1989). Certainly SARCs, ISVAs and police officers now have the capacity to change to this degree. That said, one key problem for the law remains the drive to identify individual acts to charge as specific offences (under sections 1–4, for example). A woman might tell of being raped on a number of occasions; sometimes with objects, sometimes while being hit or bound, other times being made to perform acts on others. The law responds with a list of charges, under the Sexual Offences Act, but perhaps also under other legal provisions. In total, this list may not sound very much like the experience which the survivor has detailed. She may continue to view this as a mismatch. This is far more marked when the course of abuse went on over a number of weeks, or years. These 'specimen' charges rarely do justice to women's experience. This drive from the criminal law, to reduce an ongoing campaign of sexual violence to a list of specific offences, can create a sense of not being understood, which makes it harder for public responses to appear supportive. The continuum model would suggest that it might be more productive to conceptualise violence against women as a blanket offence and to think in terms of periods of abuse, rather than single moments within that time frame.[3]

Kelly's concept of the continuum also allows for further investigation into the nature of rape, examining the contexts in which these acts of rape occur and the range of possible rapists. These aspects may remain harder for public agencies to respond adequately to. Much of what is now known about rapists was already there, in *Surviving Sexual Violence*. Kelly's original research discussed women's differing experiences of rape and made the links that established the idea of a continuum in the first place. Perpetrators can be strangers, acquaintances, dates, friends, friends of friends, family members, husbands and partners, ex-husbands and ex-partners, boyfriends who are gang members, carers, religious leaders, care workers, teachers, coaches, bosses, colleagues, taxi drivers, bus drivers and indeed, the proverbial man on the Clapham omnibus. This last chap, in case you haven't come across him before, is much beloved of the law. He has been used as a model for the 'reasonable man' for many years now and is supposed to represent a standard, objective, sensible man.[4] Herein lies a problem then: in translating the continuum into services, the public sector struggles with the notion of the 'reasonable man' as rapist. To put it another way, the myth of the loner rapist may have been diluted, but rapists are still not perceived to be normal men.

Research from Kelly (1988), Lees (1996), Brownmiller (1975), Russell (1982) and many others has now made it clear that women's experience teaches that the men who rape are just men, nothing more. However, acknowledging this breadth of perpetrators remains a tough challenge for public responses. The police and other agencies are naturally keen to be able to identify the men who rape, with a view to isolating them in prison and creating a safer society. This is a central function of a criminal justice response. If all men truly are potential rapists (as Brownmiller originally asserted) then this task becomes more fraught.

This tension can be examined with reference to the public sector preference for dealing with domestic abuse over rape. The men who commit domestic abuse are less of a challenge to public understandings. They can be seen to be acting outside of the norm when they have hit a woman partner, and so can be separated from the 'normal man' simply by becoming a violent partner. Other men and heterosexual women, who have vested interests in keeping a safe distance from involvement in this label, can know that they (or their men) are not violent partners. Inclusion within the group of violent partners becomes a self-fulfilling abnormality. Footballer Paul Gascoigne was seen to become an abnormal man when he was accused of wife-beating. His hero status was revoked. Men who abuse can be identified and their actions distinguished from the norm; this makes a public response manageable.

By contrast, the label of 'rapist' is far more complex. When a man is accused of rape, he is perceived as having committed an act which all heterosexual men (want to) perpetrate. His act of penetrative sex is understood as simply sex (as illustrated by the comment from the Stern Review, used at the beginning of this chapter). If he is shown to have acted outside of the normal range of sexual behaviour, then his status may change. For example, he can be appreciated as an abnormal man if he has sex with children, or with too many partners, or perhaps in too odd or violent a manner. In such a case, his oddness singles him out from the norm, and the application of the label 'rapist' does not threaten the heterosexual majority. However, if he has simply had intercourse with a woman who says it was rape, how does the majority keep its distance from the label? When Craig Charles,[5] Mick Hucknall,[6] and Kobe Bryant[7] were accused of rape they did not become abnormal men in the public consciousness. The rapist label does not attach easily and when these complaints went away, so too did any need to re-evaluate the status of these men. Feminism can accept that the man on the Clapham omnibus is a rapist, if women say so. The rest of society struggles with this knowledge and still wants to find that men who rape are 'strange', even if they are not 'strangers'.

Meanwhile, more has been learnt in the past 20 years about the contexts in which rape occurs. Feminist anti-rape theory encompasses rape in marriage and relationships, the rape of children, rape in children's homes, in schools, churches, dentists' offices, and in swimming clubs. Rape in the sex industry is on the public agenda, as it was in Kelly's first outline of the continuum. Activists now focus on rape in the lives of trafficked women, asylum seekers, and other migrant women, including domestic servants, and 'mail-order' brides. Cults, groups and other organisations which exist to perpetrate the sadistic and ritualistic rape of women and girls are also taken seriously within feminist practice. Situations where women are co-opted into abusing roles by men, and where women abuse in isolation, can also be included in this model.

Women in rape crisis work with women who are in prison, in hospital, and in other institutional settings. Lesbians, disabled women, ethnic minority women, and the elderly can also experience types of rape fuelled by homophobia, racism, able-ism, and/or ageism. Contrary to academic stereotypes of anti-rape feminism as white and middle-class, women working in the field fight hard to create services which consider the issues raised by multiple oppressions and to work with and within minority groups. Women are targets for rape in war, in civil war, and in other forms of sectarian dispute. All of these are within the ambit of rape crisis work. Rape crisis workers around the world know these contexts and can support women who visit or call them. A consciousness-raising-led continuum means that survivors' knowledge can be adapted into existing frameworks' practice and policy. None of this can be said with any confidence in relation to public sector responses.

Victoria, a lesbian from Sierra Leone, was forced to marry a man who was 'rough' with her and she was threatened with circumcision (complete excision of her genitalia) to 'cure' her lesbianism. Eventually she fled her husband and country, trying to get to America. She landed in London and was then kept in the UK where her asylum claim was not taken seriously, as she would not name her lesbian lover. She was then moved around the country:

They don't care how people live. They abolished slavery but it is the same treatment we are having, you have no choice where you go, you are put in different houses and they don't care what those houses are like as long as they can say that refugees have shelter, somewhere to sleep. ...In one house water was pouring in when it rained. When the council came and checked the house they said it was not fit for anyone to live in.

(WAST 2008: 32)

Victoria's situation was not understood by the law and the total failure of public responses to this survivor made her feel afraid and alone. Her life began to feel more hopeful when she met the women's group WAST (Women Asylum Seekers Together) and began to find friendship and strength from this woman-led response (www.wast.org.uk, accessed 18 June 2010).

Feminist services work with women regarding their related experiences of violence, and other acts on the continuum are examined as part of a feminist response to rape. Women may also want to talk about being followed, wolf-whistled, the sense of being stalked, being touched on public transport, or other incidents which may not appear relevant within a statutory context, but which are important within a woman's life. These 'little rapes', as Medea and Thompson once characterised them, are still seen as simply 'the way things are' within mainstream responses (1974: 29–55). Working with women who are poor, have immigration or other legal problems, speak a language other than English, cannot find somewhere to live, need an abortion – all of these are part of the task, for WAST, Rape Crisis groups, SBS and others.

Women who are in contact with public services tend to experience a sense of being measured against a model of rape which is not of their choosing. This disjunction leads to the well-known sense of dissatisfaction many survivors report. Sara Payne's recent review of rape victim experiences (2009) is just one of the latest in a line of research that stretches back to early works in the US (Russell 1982) and here (Hall 1985, and the Campaign to End Rape (CER) study of 2010, currently being analysed www.cer.truthaboutrape.co.uk, accessed 18 June 2010). Payne concludes strongly that the 'majority' of women she met had been failed by public responses (2009: 8). She says that the most common problem is lack of belief (2009: 11). In Payne's version, this is a society-wide problem and not something specific about the police, the judiciary, or other professions. Yet public opinion surveys show that a large proportion of the public does not believe that women are to blame for rape (85 per cent strongly disagree with the assertion that if a woman is raped it is usually her own fault: *Attitudes to Rape* 2010, quoted in Baird and Campbell 2010: 20). It is not at all clear that this would be true of a sample of police officers. Simple issues of dignity can also prove too challenging for public services. As one survivor put it:

There really should be females all the way through. It's simple things like, a male liaison officer returned my clothes...there he was, holding up my underwear, ticking it off. It was awful.

(Payne 2009: 16)

The public response perpetrates another 'little rape' against a survivor in simple and stupid mistakes such as this.

## Continuum-based responses

Central differences in philosophy, aims, definitions and the willingness to create women's space, mean that public responses lag behind the women's voluntary sector. Despite Liz Kelly's personal willingness to advise the public sector, it continues to work outside of continuum-led responses, most of the time. One clear way to see this is in the focus of multi-agency forums, usually led by local authorities. These groups bring together workers from the mainstream of responses to (usually) domestic abuse with workers from the women's refuge movement. Commonly the local rape crisis groups struggle to get a seat at these public sector dominated groups and all of those present often find these to be frustrating and limited meetings (the roles of multi-agency work in relation to rape crisis are discussed further in Jones and Cook 2008: ch. 3).

Within feminist practice and in academia, the continuum continues to be viewed as a powerful tool. It is useful because it places blame firmly with abusers, without limiting or identifying which men might be involved. The continuum also helps feminists, as supporters, teachers, campaigners and authors, to make sense of women's complex histories of abuse. It allows for links to be made and maintained between theory and practice. As it is built on survivors' testimony, the continuum can expand and change to incorporate new knowledge from survivors.

In a number of contexts, the public responses to rape are not likely to be sufficiently survivor-led to react adequately to the complex reality of women's lives. Thus these agencies will continue to provide services which do not rate highly in terms of survivor satisfaction and which do not meet the needs of all women. American author Beth Richie has argued that these questions of exclusion can be resolved by focusing service design around the most excluded groups (Richie 1996). In this way, the women who seem the most 'difficult' can become worthy of central attention. In addition, services that are created for the most excluded groups are actually more accessible to all. For example, if a service considers that visually impaired women are excluded, and concentrates on producing literature in a variety of formats, everyone who has reading limitations can also benefit, alongside the target group.

In using Richie's model, the first step is to identify which women are not being included. In relation to services for women experiencing sexual violence, it could be argued that the following are some of the most excluded groups:

- sex workers;
- asylum seekers;
- trafficked women and girls;
- adult survivors of childhood abuses;
- women in prison and other institutions;
- elderly women;

- women with physical/sensory or learning disabilities;
- women with mental ill health.

Combining a continuum-led response, which assumes linked events and gets its knowledge from women's lived experience, with Richie's suggestion for service design can lead to real changes in provision.

Safety4Sisters (S4S) is a Manchester-based coalition of workers from the women's voluntary sector, but also from the public sector and higher education, who have come together to tackle problems around responses to some of these groups. S4S aims:

> to be a forum for any interested individual or service provider, to discuss experiences and problems on the ground in supporting women with no recourse, and who essentially have a commitment to finding ways and exploring new ideas to improve and secure support and protection/safety for women with no recourse.
>
> (S4S 2010, unpublished)

This forum defines 'women with no recourse' as:

1) Women on visas;
2) Failed asylum seekers who have been made destitute;
3) Women who have been trafficked;
4) Women not able to access housing benefits due to Habitual Residence Rule (European women); and
5) Women with no immigration status.

> (*ibid.*)

The women that Safety4Sisters focuses on are challenging in a political sense for the public sector. They make up part of the class of 'immigrants' and they are seen as risky groups for politicians to support. It could be argued then that it is not surprising that in this area it has proven possible to create a women-led forum. The group recognises these sisters are vulnerable to homelessness, exploitation, further rapes and abuses, and to deportation. Drawing from the experiences of the asylum seekers in WAST, this forum tries to use the continuum and Richie's approach to service provision to position these excluded women at the centre of the field of vision.

The Safety4Sisters agenda is set by the women's voluntary sector. Meetings are open to workers from the public sector, they are not women-only and the group meets at offices belonging to Manchester City Council. The meetings of this forum are inspiring and invigorating and explore ways of improving service provision for women with multiple mainstream exclusions. The forum allows women within the public sector, who come from a philosophy of belief in and who subscribe to the continuum, to work with women from the voluntary sector, on terms defined by the voluntary sector. Within this group, for example, there are women now employed by the council, but who have previously worked within women's services. They are able to take part without feeling co-opted by a mainstream agenda, which probably also makes it easier for them to return to their day jobs. In other words, this is a place where women (and meetings invariably are just women, despite an open policy) can come together without the public sector restrictions of definition, aim and scepticism.

S4S as a model is interesting and worthy of further exploration. It may, in time, be copied elsewhere. That said it remains an unfunded venture, limited by the pressures of time, money, and woman-power. These limitations are common across the women's voluntary sector and they impact on service provision and lobbying power. If the earlier contention that the public agenda aims to dampen feminist claims of unfairness is accepted, it becomes clear that it is actually in the public interest to keep women's groups in this position. The real change which the feminist anti-rape movement aims for is likely to be too incisive for public support. Women's groups which struggle for survival are not a threat to the status quo, or to the status of the man on the Clapham omnibus. Rape will continue whilst the public sector responds quietly and the women's sector struggles for survival.

Recent funding initiatives from government show how this works in practice. In January 2010, for example, the government announced an £860,000 'combined fund to support victims of sexual violence' (press release dated 27 January, www.justice.gov.uk/news/newsrelease270110b.htm, accessed 18 June 2010). This fund allowed voluntary groups to apply for one-year funding, provided they could submit a funding bid within a one-month window. Such funding allows some rape crisis groups to continue to provide services and it is an improvement on the previous dearth of central funding for this area of work. It can be argued then that this is an example of a strong government response to women's claims for support. Indeed, many women within rape crisis may well support such an argument. However, it is also apparent that any small voluntary group which is limited to uncertain one-year funding will continue to exist in a state of marginal confidence, at best. Within many of these organisations funding applications can only be completed where women stop providing services for the time it takes to complete the forms, as there is no administrative support or back-up. Planning for the future then becomes a matter of considering provision on a hand-to-mouth basis, which makes it very difficult to embark on new or innovative modes of support or lobbying to end rape. Women's Resource Centre research in 2008 studied 35 rape crisis centres and reported 134,000 contacts with users over a 12-month period (WRC 2008: 7). These same centres, however, had a combined waiting list for face-to-face services of 5.3 years. To have the status from which to effect real change, the women's sector needs far more funding that is also far more certain. Yet it is apparently not in the interests of the public sector to provide this.

In this way, then, the public sector can make it harder for continuum-led service provision to effect real change. The public sector is also prone to throwing other difficulties into the path of these groups. Funding may, for example, be limited, unless groups can show that they also provide services to male survivors. In local areas there can also be demand for access to groups by transwomen, who wish to become part of the rape crisis or other organisation.

From a feminist anti-rape perspective, both male survivors and transmen and women need to find the space to create their own continuum-based knowledge through survivor-led testimony. The experience of being raped as a man is palpably different from that of a woman or indeed of a transwoman or transman. Male survivors might experience doubt as to their masculinity, while female survivors are more likely to feel confirmation of their status as a (weak and yet provocative) woman.

> They bound my mouth so that I could not shout and pulled off my sari and then I understood what was going to happen. After the third man raped me I passed out...I want to forget what happened at that time but I can't forget, it always comes to my mind. People here always tell me it is not your fault. ...If I go back to my country people will tell my son that his Mum was raped... It is a matter of shame in my country.
>
> (Naima, in WAST 2008: 40-41)

Naima's experience cannot be replicated within male rape or transrape. Her experiences are bound up with the social construction of what it means to be female within a patriarchy. A male rape victim or trans victim might also wish to keep their experience of rape from their children, but for different reasons. In order to create support or space for these groups other theories of rape need to be developed further. This is not within the remit of these already stretched women's voluntary sector organisations.

A gender-neutral service demand is also a denial of the truth of the continuum. Within a feminist consciousness-raising-led model, rape is a gendered event. The wish to incorporate men can be seen as a misunderstanding as to how far society has come down the road to equality, or in the struggle to end the patriarchy. Some people clearly believe that equal service provision constitutes equality. Yet, as this discussion has demonstrated, the experiences remain different, within the (still functioning) patriarchy. Meanwhile for governments, police services, and councils, the wish for equality of service provision might have more to do with diluting feminist demands.

All of this remains important for society as a whole. Proper service provision that believes, listens to and supports survivors can potentially impact on health bills, social security costs and legal aid bills (Walby 2004). Women who receive support that allows them to make sense of their experiences can go on to live in as free a sense as any woman can. Eventually, an end to rape could even create women's freedom and autonomy in a meaningful sense. Catharine MacKinnon says of the women's movement that:

> It was a movement that knew that when material conditions preclude 99 percent of your options, it is not meaningful to call the remaining 1 percent – what you are doing – your choice.
>
> (MacKinnon 2005: 259–60)

She develops her description of this movement further:

> Any woman who was violated was our priority. It was a deeply collectivist movement. In this movement, when we said 'women, we,' it

had content. It didn't mean that we all had to be the same in order to be part of this common condition. That, in fact, was the genius, one of the unique contributions, of this movement: it premised unity as much on diversity as on commonality. It did not assume that commonality meant sameness.

(*ibid*. 261)

Working from women's lived experiences allows for sense to be made from diversity and from sameness. In both of these extracts, MacKinnon uses the past tense as she is constructing an argument about the dominance of liberalism. This can be compared with the suggestion here, that it is not in the public interest to support women's groups. MacKinnon concludes that liberalism cannot conceive of 'sexual misogyny' and consequently it rests upon assumptions of sexual inequality. To effect real change she suggests that there is a need for a 'sex-based hope' (*ibid*.: 268), perhaps thinking of writings by other feminists, such as Robin West, on 'female hedonism'. West argues that critical method should be measured against the ability to deliver 'happiness, joy and pleasure' (West 1987: 180) to women.

When we try to squeeze descriptions of our lives into the parameters laid out for us, the results are often not just distorted, but profoundly anomalous. We are trying too hard to assimilate, in our theory as well as in our professional and personal lives.

(*ibid*. 180–1)

If women's services simply try to fit their service provision into the mainstream offerings as to agenda and philosophy then the results are gravely limited. The Safety4Sisters model can claim some success as it clearly creates a space where women's views can be heard on a different level. Any agenda can focus on lessening women's suffering and (one day) increasing our pleasure, when it incorporates continuum-led ideas.

However, to effect real change, we need to add more service provision based on a continuum-led model. For example, Britain currently lacks a child abuse movement which understands the continuum and looks for answers which empower, rather than patronise, children. Anti-porn movements face liberal criticism, which MacKinnon and Dworkin faced (MacKinnon 1993). But a continuum-led anti-porn movement could begin to build another area of pleasure not pain.

## Conclusions

Public responses to rape can be characterised as being liberal and equality driven, dominated by criminal justice responses, and interested in keeping survivors and feminist activists quiet. In contrast, the women's voluntary sector tries hard to use the continuum and to be led by women's experience. This means believing women, providing women's space, and supporting a wish to end rape as defined by women ourselves. The women's sector can encompass a range of experiences which last for days, or weeks, or longer. The concept of 'conduct over time' is not problematic within this agenda. Women's services can focus on those most excluded, although they are hampered by a lack of resources.

Rape crisis centres tend to remain relatively powerless within local multi-agency hierarchies. The good news is that there has been some change over the past two years, and no more rape crisis centres have closed (documented in Jones and Cook 2008). New centres have been created in Bristol, Leeds and Trafford in Greater Manchester; and a new service for Suffolk is currently in the pipeline. Just as at the beginning of the movement, these new centres have not been created centrally, but came out of women's determination to provide services.

When the women's sector sets the agenda, it can afford to consider the complex realities of sexual violence in women's lives. It can also work with women who support the same aims, in national and local government. In reality, this division between public responses and those from the women's sector is becoming a little less absolute than previously. The women's sector still needs to remain clear that it has its own agenda and that it needs to be brave enough to continue to work outside the mainstream until the latter adopts a feminist philosophy – which is surely not yet.

The development of further women's sector led forums could be a step forward in creating a more dynamic agenda. However, under the 2010 coalition government, it is likely that these organisations will need to be created without funding, or central support. Within academia there is real space for feminist evaluation of women's service models to be used to build an even greater evidence base to convince the public sector of the value of women's survivor-led provision.

### Further reading

This chapter discusses the feminist model of rape crisis work and readers can learn more about that, and its struggle to respond to the public agenda, in *Rape Crisis: Responding to Sexual Violence* (Helen Jones and Kate Cook 2008). The philosophy underpinning this comes from a women's liberation movement which began in the USA and Susan Brownmiller's account of the beginnings of that movement also does much to illustrate those ideas (*In Our Time: Memoir of a Revolution*, 2000, Aurum Press Ltd). A little older, but nonetheless informative, Nancy Matthews' study of American rape crisis is *Confronting Rape: The Feminist Anti-Rape Movement and the State*, Routledge, 1994.

Since this chapter was written, the coalition government has shown itself to be more interested in the topic of sexual violence than was at first feared. Their *Call to End Violence Against Women and Girls* is now newly published and is worth reading (available at http://www.homeoffice.gov.uk/crime/violence-against-women-girls/). The choice of title alone suggests a vision which is at least aiming for real change.

## Notes

1 These figures can only be indicative, given that the cases recorded as crimes in 2008–09 are not always going to get to trial in that same year. To allow for such built-in problems it is more usual to look at trends in recorded crime statistics, rather than at the detail of any particular year. The trend in rape conviction rates, measured against convictions for rape only, has been declining for many years, having stood at 35 per cent in 1974. The most up-to-date figure available shows a conviction rate of 7.6 per cent. (Home Office 2009a; Ministry of Justice 2008: Annex A; Cook 2005).

2 It is, however, interesting to note that the 57.7 per cent success rate is the lowest quoted, among the range of types of violence against women prosecution quoted in the CPS report.

3 It is acknowledged that there are likely to be arguments against this, from a civil liberties approach, and that this chapter is not the place to explore this suggestion further.

4 In recent years he gets called the 'reasonable person' in some attempt to allow for gender neutrality; however, this attempt leads to an entirely new discussion which is not pertinent here.

5 Actor and comedian Craig Charles was accused of rape by his ex-girlfriend in 1994. The trial did not result in a conviction (http://news.bbc.co.uk/1/hi/uk_politics/3055859.stm, accessed 18 June 2010).

6 Lead singer with Simply Red, Manchester pop band. He was accused of rape in 2000 but the police dropped the investigation (http://www.telegraph.co.uk/news/uknews/1375942/Simply-Red-star-cleared-after-arrest-for-rape.html, accessed 18 June 2010.)

7 US baseball player Kobe Bryant was accused of rape in 2004. The criminal case fell apart after the police made a number of errors in handling the charges, which resulted in the complainant being unwilling to proceed (http://nbcsports.msnbc.com/id/5861379/, accessed 18.June 2010).

## References

Anitha, S. *et al.* (2008) *Forgotten Women: Domestic Violence, Poverty and South Asian Women with No Recourse to Public Funds*. Manchester: Saheli.

Baird, V. and Campbell, A. (2010) *Interim Government Response to the Stern Review*. London: Home Office.

Brownmiller, S. (1975) *Against Our Will: Men, Women and Rape*. New York: Fawcett Columbine (1993 edn).

Brownmiller, S. (1999) *In Our Time: Memoir of a Revolution*. New York: Random House.

Buchwald, E. *et al.* (1993) *Transforming a Rape Culture*. Minneapolis: Milkweed.

Cook, K. (2005) *Rape, the end of the story: a study of rape appeal cases* (unpublished Phd thesis: Manchester Metropolitan University).

Crown Prosecution Service (2009) *Violence Against Women Crime Report 2008–2009*. London: CPS.

Ginsberg, E. and Lerner, S. (1989) *Sexual Violence Against Women: A Guide to the Criminal Law*. London: Rights of Women.

Hall, R. (1985) *Ask Any Woman: A London Inquiry into Rape and Sexual Assault*. Bristol: Falling Wall Press.

Home Office (2009a) *Crime in England and Wales 2008–2009*. London: Home Office.

Home Office (2009b) *Together We Can End Violence Against Women And Girls: A Strategy*.

London: Home Office.

Jones, H. and Cook, K. (2008) *Rape Crisis: Responding to Sexual Violence*. Lyme Regis: Russell House Publishing Ltd.

Kelly, L. (1988) *Surviving Sexual Violence*. Minneapolis: University of Minnesota Press.

Lees, S. (1996) *Carnal Knowledge: Rape on Trial*. London: Hamish Hamilton.

MacKinnon, C. (1989) *Towards a Feminist Theory of the State*. Cambridge, Mass.: Harvard University Press.

MacKinnon, C. (1993) *Only Words*. Cambridge, Mass: Harvard University Press.

MacKinnon, C. (2005) *Women's Lives: Men's Laws*. Cambridge, Mass: Harvard University Press.

Medea, A. and Thompson, K. (1974) *Against Rape: A Survival Manual for Women: How to avoid entrapment and how to cope with rape physically and emotionally*. New York: Farrar, Straus and Giroux.

Ministry of Justice (2008) *Criminal Statistics, England and Wales 2008*. London: Ministry of Justice.

Payne, S. (2009) *Rape Victim Experience Review*. London: Home Office.

Richie, B. (1996) 'Young women and the backlash', keynote address at the *International conference on Violence, Abuse and Women's Citizenship*, Brighton, November 1996 (unpublished).

Russell, D. (1982) 'The prevalence and incidence of forcible rape and attempted rape of females', *Victimology*, 7: 81–93.

Safety4Sisters (2010) *Aims and Definitions*. Safety4Sisters (unpublished).

Stern, V. (2010) *The Stern Review: A Report by Baroness Vivien Stern CBE of an independent review into how rape complaints are handled by authorities in England and Wales*. London: Home Office.

Walby, S. (2004) *The Cost of Domestic Violence*. London: Women and Equality Unit.

West, R. (1987) 'The difference in women's hedonic lives', in D. Kelly Weisberg (ed.) (1996) *Applications of Feminist Legal Theory to Women's Lives: Sex, Violence, Work, and Reproduction*. Philadelphia: Temple University Press, pp. 162–83.

Women Asylum Seekers Together (WAST) (2008) *Am I Safe Yet? Stories of women seeking asylum in Britain*. Manchester: WAST.

Women's Resource Centre and Rape Crisis (England and Wales) (2008) *The Crisis in Rape Crisis*. London: Women's Resource Centre.

## Web resources

Campaign to End Rape: www.cer.truthaboutrape.co.uk
End Violence Against Women: www.endviolenceagainstwomen.org.uk
Home Office: www.homeoffice.gov.uk
Ministry of Justice: www.justice.gov.uk
Rape Crisis: www.rapecrisis.org.uk
Southall Black Sisters: www.southallblacksisters.org.uk
Survivors UK: www.survivorsuk.org
Victim Support: www.victimsupport.org.uk
WAST: www.wast.org.uk
Women's Resource Centre: www.wrc.org.uk

# Chapter 20

# Public sector and voluntary sector responses: dealing with sex offenders

*Hazel Kemshall*

## Meet Hazel Kemshall

Hazel Kemshall is currently Professor of Community and Criminal Justice at De Montfort University and a board member for the Staffordshire and West Midlands Probation Trust, an appointment she particularly values having spent her early career as a probation officer in that area. Her current Chair was the first in Criminal Justice at De Montfort, and the inclusion of 'Community' in the title is particularly important as it reflects both departmental and personal commitment to issues of community justice. All her career has been spent either working with or researching high-risk offenders. She has been privileged to be involved in the development of multi-agency public protection arrangements across the UK, and evaluations of alternative responses such as public awareness campaigns and environmental management such as Stop It Now! and the Derwent Initiative. She is particularly keen to see greater practical success in engaging the public in policy responses to the management of sex offenders, and in projects directly concerned with the community management of sex offenders such as Leisurewatch or Circles of Support. Such initiatives can reduce vigilantism and erode the unhelpful stereotype of the public as irrational, punitive and 'media dupes'.

## Introduction

This chapter considers public health responses to sexual offending, and places these within broader reintegrative and restorative justice paradigms. In addition to reviewing key public health responses, particularly those delivered by the voluntary sector such as public awareness campaigns and preventative work with offenders, the chapter also considers the additional value that broader reintegrative approaches can bring to the effective community management of sexual offenders.

Sex offenders have become the offenders we 'love to hate', characterised as 'monsters in our midst' (Thomas 2005). There is substantial public anxiety about sex offenders (Thomas 2004, 2005) and considerable media fuelling of community fears (Piper and Stronnach 2008; Silverman and Wilson 2002). Such media coverage holds the 'spectre of the mobile and anonymous sex offender' as particularly demonic (Hebenton and Thomas 1996: 429). This has been exacerbated by the construction of the 'predatory paedophile', the spectre of an invisible stranger in our midst preying on vulnerable children, often linked to the fear of child homicide (Wilczynski and Sinclair 1999). In large part, this has been a media-constructed moral panic playing on 'stranger-danger' (Kitzinger 1999), in contrast to the research evidence that most women and children are abused in their own homes, extended families or by offenders they know (Gallagher 2009); and that grooming behaviours are extensive (Wortley and Smallbone 2006). These media and public misperceptions have also found their way into policy, with criminal justice policy in particular focusing on the reduction of 'stranger-danger' through increased legislation and restrictive conditions targeting sex offenders (see Kemshall 2008: ch. 1 for a full review). Such policy and legislative responses also reflect, to a degree, political anxieties around individual high-profile cases and public perceptions of risk management failures (for example the infamous case of Sydney Cooke, see Kemshall 2003, 2008). Throughout the 1990s and into the 2000s this meshing of media and political anxieties on sex offenders, particularly paedophiles, resulted in a criminal justice policy approach characterised by surveillance, intensive measures of control and restriction, preventative sentencing, and containment, labelled 'community protection' by Connelly and Williamson (2000). Whilst the UK has not adopted this USA model totally, it is characterised by what Pratt (2000a, b) has called the 'retributive fallacy'. In brief, this is the contention that penal policies based on retributive sentencing are mistaken as they result in higher prison populations and fail to provide effective crime management. 'Public protection' becomes a politicised justification for retribution (Kemshall 2003, 2008; Pratt 2000a, b).

In effect, public protection acts as something of a 'veneer' for increasingly retributive and emotive sentencing, particularly for sex offenders (Thomas 2004). This can result in burgeoning prison populations, increasingly intrusive and costly community measures that become difficult to maintain in the long term, and the constant spectre that one risk management failure can threaten the credibility of the entire risk management system of sex offenders (Kemshall 2008; Nash 2006).

To date responses to sex offending across the Anglophone countries have tended to be dominated by statutory criminal justice policy, with the UK and USA leading such developments (see Kemshall 2008 for a full review). This chapter takes a different perspective by focusing on public health and voluntary sector responses to sexual offending, with a particular emphasis on public awareness campaigns, environmental risk management and community engagement in the management of sex offenders. Criminal justice policy has tended to focus on seriousness of harm, with attempts to grade harms and seriousness either by legislating that particular offences will receive mandatory life sentences or be considered for indeterminate public protection sentences (Kemshall 2008); or through risk assessment tools and procedures that identify offenders who present a 'significant risk of serious harm to the public' (Ministry of Justice 2009). This policy focus has been on offenders and their risk factors, rather than on the subjective experience of victims (see Kemshall 2008 for a full review). However, drawing on the experiences of victims, Kelly has argued that how victims perceive and experience sexual violence is important (1988, 2002). Based on this research Kelly has argued for a 'continuum' as an analytic device through which to understand the range of victim experiences of sexual violence and the range of offences actually committed. This is not, however, a continuum of seriousness, rather it is a continuum of felt experience with a range of attendant impacts on the victims (Kelly 2002), and covers a range of offence behaviours without implying any necessary progression towards more serious acts. The notion of a continuum provides a number of helpful things: a refocus on the victim experience (discussed elsewhere in this volume); a reminder of the range of sexual offending and that public policy responses need to engage with them all; a reminder that not all sex offenders are monsters (nor indeed is our experience of them always as 'monstrous'; and that media and political responses to sex offenders tend to ignore both the wide range of offences and victim experiences by over-focusing on 'stranger-danger' paedophilia (Kitzinger 2004). In the context of the present chapter, 'continuum' is an interesting device for 'testing' the fitness for purpose of public health and voluntary sector responses to sex offenders. For example:

- To what extent can such policy alternatives respond to a range of offenders, offence types and victim experiences?
- To what extent do they facilitate a refocusing away from 'the monstrous stranger-danger' to the sex offender who is daily in our midst?
- To what extent do they enable victims (actual and potential) to respond to sex offending in a meaningful and effective way?

Whilst the chapter does not claim to offer a comparison of criminal justice policies to public health and voluntary alternatives (see McAlinden 2010 for such a comparison), these questions do indicate some possible future criteria upon which such a comparison could be made.

### An alternative paradigm: Public health and voluntary responses to sex offending

Alternative responses to the largely retributive sentencing of the criminal justice system have largely been initiated and located within the third sector and public health responses to child sexual offending, most notably within faith-based communities or survivor groups (Kemshall and Wood 2007; Kemshall 2008: chs 4 and 5). In brief, these responses largely reject the punishment paradigm, and characterise sexual offending as a public health issue. Survivor groups in particular have been critical in foregrounding the range of victim experiences of both women and children (Kelly 1998; Tabachnick and Dawson 1999), and the importance of earlier intervention to prevent repetitive serious harm (www.stopitnow.org.uk accessed 16 February 16 2010).

### The public health approach

The characterisation of sexual and violent offending as a public health problem is most easily attributable to the work of Richard Laws (1996, 2000). In brief, Laws argues that traditional, reactive responses to such offending located predominantly in the criminal justice system have not proved to be effective in reducing the incidence of sexual or violent offending, and that perversely such approaches inflate public fears and rejection, particularly of sex offenders (2000: 30). The public health approach is characterised as preventive and 'forward-looking'. The 'public health approach' (PHA) has gained ground as a novel and potentially more effective method of dealing with child sexual abuse, and to a lesser extent adult sexual abuse and violent offending.

The PHA is located at three levels: the primary, secondary and tertiary:

- *the primary level*: at which the goal is prevention of sexually deviant behaviour before it starts, for example the identification and prevention of sexually deviant behaviour in children, and the long-term prevention of adults engaging in sexual abuse;
- *the secondary level*: at which the goal is the prevention of first-time offenders from progressing, or the opportunistic and 'specific offence' offender from becoming a generalist;
- *the tertiary level*: at which the goal is effective work with persistent and more serious offenders. Specific goals are usually effective treatment programmes and relapse prevention.

(see Laws 2000: 31)

Laws argues that as an alternative to (largely ineffective) incarceration, increased efforts should be targeted at levels 1 and 2. This requires increased attention to 'prevention goals' of which the following are seen as the most important:

- *Public awareness and responsibility*: This involves informing the public of 'the magnitude and characteristics of sexual offending', including how sex offenders groom, but more importantly that sex offenders are part of the community. The emphasis is upon adult responsibility for responding to sex offending, particularly against children.
- *Public education*: This involves challenging the myth that all sex offenders are demons and incapable of change, and an emphasis upon treatment programmes that work. The message that something can be done and that treatment is worth investing in is a key one.

These prevention goals are supported by direct targeting of sex offenders, to encourage both active and potential sex offenders/abusers to come forward for treatment. The emphasis is upon the prevention of those beginning to engage in abuse or thinking about it, and relapse prevention for those with established behaviours. Harm reduction and risk minimisation are seen as key components of such a strategy. As such, public health approaches offer a reasonable fit with Kelly's continuum model in so far as they target a range of victim experiences, seek to address a range of sexual offences, and enable victims and potential victims to respond to sexual offending in a positive way, for example by providing information to spot and address grooming behaviours (Kemshall 2008; the Derwent Initiative (TDI) 2007).

However, there are important limits to PHA. Within the UK for example, a key strand has been public awareness and education campaigns, pursued primarily by 'Stop It Now!', and the Lucy Faithfull Foundation (for a full review see Kemshall 2008: 78). Within the UK and Ireland, Stop It Now! has pursued three aspects of work:

- public awareness, public education and media campaigning;
- treatment and counselling for sexual offenders;
- a helpline targeted at adult abusers and those at risk of abusing; family and friends of abusers; parents of young people who are engaging in sexually inappropriate behaviours.

(www.stopitnow.org.uk accessed 16 February 2010)

However, in all three areas of work there are difficulties in the practical delivery of work, and in operating along the continuum identified by Kelly. In addition, PHA responses have largely focused on child sexual abuse, with some limited concern with sexual offending against adults. The next section will review these difficulties in some detail.

### Limits and difficulties with PHA responses to sexual offending

Stop It Now! (and similar organisations) attempts to build public awareness and community responsibility for sex offenders by influencing public debate and government policy on sex offenders, for example through lobbying, media campaigns, and direct communication with local communities. The latter has been the subject of a more recent initiative under the Home Office Child Sex Offender Review (CSOR) and involved a pilot of a public awareness campaign by the Lucy Faithfull Foundation with the conclusion that such campaigns have to be intensive, long-term and part of a broader awareness strategy (Collins 2009). However, there was some resistance to the message and the pilot events were not well attended, illustrating that the public find this a taboo and 'emotionally aversive' topic for discussion (Sanderson 2005). In the Lucy Faithfull pilots 'hard-to-reach' groups and ethnic minorities also proved challenging to engage.

In their earlier evaluation of Stop It Now! dissemination and public awareness campaigns Kemshall *et al.* argued for a strategy of working:

through targeted partnerships where the partner agency can carry the message into key user and key audience groups. This avoids 'wasting' the message, enables strong follow up and evaluation within more tightly bounded groups and enables a clearer cost-benefit analysis to be applied to dissemination.

(Kemshall *et al.* 2004: 12)

In addition, the authors concluded that communication needs to be:

> considered as a strategic issue within which cost-benefit is considered rather than viewing communication as a matter of pragmatism or opportunism.
>
> (Kemshall *et al.* 2004: 13)

However, public health campaigns are fraught with difficulty (Alaszewski 2006), not least that messages are prone to distortion by the media and can result in panics rather than rational discussions or debate (see Barnett and Breakwell 2003 on BSE; Boseley 2002 on the MMR vaccine debate). This has been particularly acute in child sexual abuse (Kitzinger 2004), an 'emotionally aversive' topic exacerbated by cultural taboos (Sanderson 2005). A key flaw of such public awareness campaigns is to underestimate the range and weight of intervening factors between the message and the receiver of the message. Social actors are not mere 'media dupes', but actively interpret, filter, select and rationalise such messages militating against a simple 'hypodermic' model of information giving and receiving (Kitzinger 2004; Hughes *et al.* 2006). Based on a range of health prevention studies, the Health Belief Model (Glanz *et al.* 2002: 52; see also Rosenstock *et al.* 1994) outlines the 'modifying factors' that can inhibit individual perceptions turning into actions. For example, the cognitive schema against which information is perceived and processed; whether the message can alter the cost–benefit analysis that individuals have; whether an individual believes they are 'at risk'; the costs to the individual of modifying (or not) their behaviour; and the individual's ability and self-efficacy to take actions (see for example Alder 1997 on sexual behaviour; Denscombe 2001 on smoking; Miller and Kitzinger 1998 on AIDS; Eisen and Zellman 1986 on medication compliance; Thirlaway and Hegg 2005 on alcohol and cancer). Public awareness campaigns on sexual violence show similar results, with campaigns on dating violence prevention showing low impact (Cornelius *et al.* 2009), with the cognitive schema of potential victims (that they do not think they are likely to be targeted or to be 'at risk') impacting on their reception and processing of key advice. Research shows that the prevalence and acceptability of 'rape myths', for example that victims are to blame, can result not only in some victims not reporting rape or to potential victims having an illusory perception of safety, but also in offenders and potential offenders rationalising sexual violence (see Bohner *et al.* 2009 for a full discussion). In addition, the power of such cognitive schema, particularly when institutionalised into criminal justice practices, can result in less impact for public and professionally targeted awareness campaigns about the nature of rape.

This wide-ranging body of research literature on public awareness/ information campaigns suggests that to be successful you have to:

- maximise the relevance of the message to the audience (Foubert and McEwen 1998);
- maximise audience perception of susceptibility to the risk (Bohner *et al.* 2009);

- give a clear message re benefits (Boseley 2002);
- promote self-efficacy and key actions that can be taken by the individual (TDI 2007; Kemshall 2008).

Building responsibility and engagement is also problematic. Communities and publics may resent 'being made responsible' for risks which they consider are the responsibility of paid professionals (e.g. police and probation); and involuntary risks are particularly resented (Slovic 2000). Increasing the awareness of professionals and parents about child sexual abuse is laudable although the extent to which it is reducing child sexual abuse is more difficult to discern (Kemshall *et al.* 2004). PHA displaces responsibility for risk management onto communities, treating them as a potential source of vigilance, monitoring, support and control – the community is seen as a resource for risk management (Kemshall and Wood 2007, 2008). However, risks and the resources to manage them are inequitably distributed (Johnston 2000) and some communities literally struggle to manage the risks within their midst. As Kitzinger puts it, 'some communities already felt under siege', particularly on under-resourced and under-policed housing estates (2004: 151). These perceptions were heightened by housing inequalities, poor local services and the release of prisoners into strained communities, coupled with perceptions that professionals could not provide sufficient protection. In this climate the public may conclude that it is having risks foisted upon it, with a differential impact upon various communities, and that 'involvement' is an official term for 'dumping'.

As early as 2001, the 'Report on the Expert Panel on Sex Offending in Scotland' (also known as the Cosgrove Report), argued for the involvement of the public in determining the development of effective community management strategies for sex offenders. Cosgrove expressed it thus:

> The final strand in this approach to community safety is the need to empower and involve local people in making their communities safer places to live. In the past, action by communities has not always been constructive or safe. It is therefore important that the management of sex offenders commands public confidence and that communities are encouraged to become involved in a constructive fashion.
>
> (p. 12)

However, engaging communities in a 'constructive fashion' has not always found policy support in the UK, particularly in England. The Home Office Child Sex Offender Review (CSOR) (Home Office 2007) attempted to broaden policy responses to sex offenders. The review focused on current practice with sex offenders, including work abroad, and its recommendations aimed to:

> provide greater child protection. This may be achieved through reducing re-offending by known offenders, preventing initial offending, and identifying where offences are taking place by increasing people's confidence to report them.
>
> (Home Office 2007: 5)

In essence, the report attempted to straddle two strands of thinking in the effective management of sex offenders – a strengthening of statutory responses and increased restrictive conditions; and a public awareness/education response rooted in the public health approach. The latter reflected the considerable influence of the children's charities such as Barnado's, NSPCC, and Stop It Now! Their influence is represented in the following comment within the Home Office report:

> During the review, those involved in protecting children stressed the importance of public involvement in enhancing child protection. We need to give the public the means to fulfil this role, and we need to achieve a culture change whereby the relationship between the police and the public is more open, with information being shared in both directions.
>
> (Home Office 2007: 9)

The review acknowledged that targeted public awareness and education of parents, particularly around grooming behaviours, and helping the public to accept and recognise that most sexual offenders are known to the victims, were important but difficult messages to achieve. In essence, this view attempted to counter the media presentation of all sexual offenders as 'predatory monsters' and to some extent better reflected Kelly's continuum of sexual offending.

To this end, action 1 of the review recommended a public awareness programme in partnership with 'non-governmental organisations', and in 2008–09 a pilot involving the Lucy Faithfull Foundation/Stop It Now! was carried out (as discussed in brief above). To support this, and to enhance public confidence in the police and greater dialogue between the two, action 2 of CSOR proposed 'increased awareness of how sex offenders are managed in the community' (p. 28). The report proposed easily accessible public information, especially about the statutory multi-agency public protection arrangements (MAPPA). The latter was not to involve public disclosure about individual cases (although MAPPA do have the power to disclose to third parties where risk and case management justify it), but was intended to 'reassure the public that protection arrangements are in place, and to ensure a transparent system operates in which the public is fully aware of the true level of risk' (Home Office 2007: 9). The MAPPA guidance 2009, however, gave little emphasis to communication with the public, providing six lines of coverage in section 25.7 (p. 220) stating:

> Two challenges facing MAPPA are how to effectively manage public expectations and how to handle media interest. The national MAPPA Communication Strategy requires each RA to produce and implement a media strategy and an annual communication plan. SMBs should make good use of the MAPPA leaflet, 'Keeping Our Communities Safe', to promote the work of MAPPA in its local area.
>
> (Ministry of Justice 2009: 220; and Home Office 2008 for the leaflet)

Whilst the guidance urged Strategic Management Boards to develop a 'wider strategy of communication and education of the public' (p. 220), to date this has been largely carried out by annual reports, with limited public accessibility, and with little accountability or transparency to victims or their relatives (as reviewed by BBC Radio Four, *File on Four*, 7 July 2009). The MAPPA leaflet comprises two pages providing a brief overview of MAPPA key functions, and it is difficult to see how this could be considered as a core feature of a public awareness and education strategy with local communities. There is no consideration of hard-to-reach groups, communication strategies to encompass diversity, or how to convey difficult messages about risk to the public. In this sense, official government policy has remained 'at odds' with public health approaches, and to some extent adapts such responses to a predominant community protection paradigm (see Kemshall 2008 for a full discussion).

The public awareness campaign by the Lucy Faithfull Foundation '*Educate 2 Protect*' experienced low take-up from ethnic minorities and 'socially disadvantaged' groups despite targeting areas of social deprivation and targeting ethnic populations through relevant print, radio and TV media (Collins 2009). In addition, translation issues especially of key terms, coupled with resistance to a taboo subject and the discussion of 'overtly sexual' subjects made engagement difficult (for example one inner city area had 106 different languages and dialects), and female participants were unwilling to discuss sexual matters with a male facilitator. Previous research by the NSPCC (2007) found resistance to reporting child sexual abuse in Asian communities, with a fear that such reporting brought shame onto the family concerned (research supported by Gilligan and Akhtar 2005). This translated into resistance to the Lucy Faithfull public awareness campaign (Collins 2009). The Lucy Faithfull evaluation concluded that recruitment and credibility of staff is critical, as well as the format and content of material.

### Treatment and counselling for sex offenders

Treatment should also capture the range of sexual offending outlined by Kelly's continuum. To some extent, this also presumes early, treatment-based responses rather than an over-reliance on punitive and restrictive measures. However, a lack of treatment programmes for sex offenders who actively request treatment has been seen as problematic (for example sex offenders can refer themselves via the Stop It Now! helpline but cannot always be matched to treatment, see Kemshall *et al.* 2004). A particular difficulty has been the provision of residential treatment units, dogged by adverse community reaction and opposition, and the lack of community based treatment programmes offering intensive structured programmes and relapse prevention. The latter are almost exclusively offered by probation or prisons under a 'punishment paradigm' in response to offending, and very little is offered as a preventative measure. In effect, these probation or prison-based treatment programmes are largely located at the tertiary level of intervention and targeted at either serious of persistent offenders, making Kelly's continuum largely redundant in practical terms. Such programmes are also characterised by a cognitive behavioural approach, focusing on changing 'distorted thinking' and remoralising the risky subject (Kemshall 2002). Whilst there is considerable evidence of effectiveness (Brown 2005), cognitive behavioural therapy has been criticised for its simplistic approach to sexual offending (Laws and Marshall 2003); lack of attention to the power dynamic in the commission of offences (Worrall 1997); and the over-emphasis upon confrontational techniques (Sheath 1990; Vivian-Byrne 2004). CBT has been refined in more recent years with greater attention to social factors, pro-social modelling and the role of the therapist, and treatment integrity (Dowden and Andrews 2004; Mann 2004; Marshall et al. 2003). However, CBT is still largely characterised by control and a correctional agenda (Kemshall 2002). More recent research evidence and policy developments have attempted to develop more integrative approaches (see Kemshall 2008 for a full review), for example through the use of resettlement and accommodation strategies to ensure stability and continuity of monitoring and interventions for offenders (NPS 2004: 6; Chartered Institute of Housing Scotland 2005). Increased attention to 'needs' has also been promulgated, with a recognition that where legitimate, the satisfaction of needs can increase not only motivation and compliance, but also the effectiveness of parallel interventions (see discussion on the 'Good Lives Model' below).

A key element in the Stop It Now! prevention and treatment of sexual offending is the helpline. The helpline has national coverage and seeks to provide information and advice for adults who are concerned about their own behaviour or the behaviour of someone they know. The targeted population for the helpline is:

- adult abusers and those at risk of abusing;
- family and friends of abusers;
- parents of young people who are engaging in sexually inappropriate behaviours.

The goal of reaching those concerned about their own behaviour has been a core and novel feature of the helpline, and an evaluation by Eldridge et al. (2006) found that the largest number of calls between June 2002 and May 2006 were from abusers or potential abusers, with 1,804 calls from 674 different callers representing 45 per cent of calls. The Helpline aims to challenge and change attitudes, with an emphasis on raising awareness and supporting people to take appropriate action. With an overall focus on reducing the number of victims of abuse, the issue of child protection remains the foremost concern of the helpline team. Thus confidentiality has limits, since helpline operators will notify the relevant authorities if they feel an identifiable child is at risk. These limits of confidentiality are clearly communicated to callers when they contact the helpline, and form part of the helpline protocols (Kemshall et al. 2004).

Whilst the helpline does not provide long-term counselling, a limited number of cases are selected for face-to-face treatment. Such treatment is severely limited by lack of resources and Stop It Now! actively campaigns for additional services for sexual abusers. However, preventative work remains hampered by a lack of treatment services, and by the absence of treatment

445

programmes outside of the criminal justice system. This makes direct work with offenders at Laws' primary and secondary levels of prevention difficult.

### Additional PHA responses: environmental and opportunity management approaches

In addition to early treatment, prevention strategies and public awareness campaigns, environmental and opportunity management approaches have also been an important strand in PHA responses. A prime example of this approach is the focus on the identification and management of sex offenders' grooming behaviours, for example through Leisurewatch, a branded product by the Derwent Initiative (www.derwentinitiative.org.uk accessed 16 February 2010). The project works to protect leisure sites (such as community centres, leisure halls and swimming pools) by training staff to recognise grooming behaviours and teaching staff how to challenge and manage them.

Leisurewatch encourages Criminal Records Bureau (CRB) checks on staff, provides training in Leisurewatch techniques (e.g. how to spot and act on grooming behaviours) for at least 80 per cent of frontline staff, establishes protocols with local police, and issues posters, information leaflets and a Leisurewatch manual. Continuity and stability of on-site Leisurewatch is facilitated by top-up visits, retraining if the 80 per cent rule is broken, a 'mystery visit' to ensure compliance, and tracking of any referrals to the police to evaluate outcomes. The overall aim is to make those leisure facilities used regularly by children safer, and to enable staff in those facilities to manage customers with protection in mind. It is of course possible that staff will also be offenders, and TDI accept this position on the basis that their training will make colleagues more vigilant (a position that has resulted in one successful prosecution). TDI are currently extending this work to parents' workshops, aimed at helping parents to challenge inappropriate behaviour in their own families, but also extending the notion of community responsibility and vigilance. The strategy is an interesting mix of public awareness campaigning, environmental and crime opportunity management (literally by managing crime away through increased vigilance), and targeting key staff for practical training (some 4,000 staff had been trained at time of writing; see Kemshall 2008: 98–99 for a full review).

Whilst the impact of the training has not yet been subject to independent evaluation, internal evaluations by TDI based on the feedback ratings of trainees have been positive, with results indicating that the training gives confidence, enabling staff (and thereby members of the public) to challenge inappropriate behaviours not only in the Leisurewatch sites but in other public places. Interestingly the evaluation forms administered post training indicate that knowledge and awareness rises, and 20 per cent of participants disclose that they or a close family member have been affected by sexual offending (see www.http://www.tdi.org.uk/Leisurewatch.htm accessed 13 May 2010; TDI 2007; and personal communication from Chief Executive TDI with the author). However, these claims need to be subject to longer-term, independent evaluation. Broader evaluation of impact is embryonic but developing, with

TDI tracking the response of police, probation and MAPPA to any referrals made, and the subsequent outcomes (for example parole recalls, prosecutions, successful convictions). This database also has the potential to track patterns of offending, identifying the modus operandi of individual offenders, and the particular locations used by sex offenders.

This approach is important in that it can respond to a range of sexual behaviours in a range of settings, thus operating (albeit not explicitly) with a notion of continuum, and all sexually inappropriate behaviour is taken seriously. One key aspect of the approach is its very focus on the mundane and sexually inappropriate behaviours embedded in daily life, for example in swimming pools, shopping malls, gyms, etc.; as well as with serious sexual offending (TDI 2007; Kemshall 2008). In addition, TDI attempts to actively engage local communities as 'participants in, rather than as passive recipients of, public protection' (TDI 2007: 7). Such engagement may itself reduce the dominant retributive response to sex offenders, and aid their safe, long-term reintegration into the community.

Environmental and opportunity management responses have the potential to respond to a range of offence and offender types, and to engage communities and victims proactively in risk management. Unlike broader public awareness campaigns the approach attempts to 'skill up' members of the public to identify and respond positively and effectively to grooming behaviours across a range of settings, and to exercise a constructive vigilance about sexually inappropriate behaviours. In this sense it represents a practical expression of Kelly's continuum concerns (1988, 2002).

## Reintegrative approaches

Reintegration of sex offenders into both society and 'good lives' has been the focus of more recent practice innovations. Reintegrative responses stem from a growing disillusion with the community protection paradigm and are rooted in restorative justice (McAlinden 2005; for a full discussion see Kemshall 2008). The most notable examples are Circles of Support and Accountability (COSA); and the 'Good Lives Model' (GLM) of intervention with sex offenders. Both examples promote reintegration rather than pure punishment, on the grounds of increased effectiveness and longer-term positive outcomes. Each will be considered in turn.

### Circles of Support and Accountability (COSA)

Circles of Support and Accountability (COSA) grew out of negative public reaction to the release of a sex offender into the community, and perceptions that formal supervisory mechanisms could neither successfully reintegrate sex offenders nor guarantee public safety (Wilson 2007; Wilson and Picheca 2005; Wilson *et al*. 2005, 2007). COSA has its roots in faith-based communities agreeing to form circles of support and accountability around a sexual offender, offering on the one hand contact and support, and on the other monitoring and vigilance. The approach takes a broadly restorative and re-integrative approach to sexual offending, and seeks to improve community

447

safety through the successful reintegration of sex offenders into the community (Wilson *et al.* 2007; for a detailed description of COSA see Correctional Service of Canada 2002; Wilson and Picheca 2005). This model has been adopted in the USA, UK, Netherlands, South Africa and Bermuda. Volunteers are largely from faith-based communities with a proportion having previous experience of corrections and motivated by a sense of altruism (Wilson *et al.* 2007). As Wilson succinctly puts it: 'Volunteers act as concerned friends or surrogate family members for the core members but with support and accountability set prominently in their minds' (2007: 37).

COSA have been evaluated in Canada and the UK with positive results. The Canadian Circles have taken particularly high-risk offenders (as determined by validated risk assessment tools), and the evaluations have striven to match COSA subjects with similar offence types and risk levels not in the Circle, i.e. a 'matched sample' in so far as ethical constraints allow, or with similarly profiled offenders using actuarial risk score predictions. The original pilot achieved a decrease in sexual offending of 70 per cent 'in comparison with either matched control subjects or actuarial projections' (Wilson 2007: 37; Wilson *et al.* 2007), with the UK pilot achieving similar reconviction results in its early stages, although numbers in this evaluation were small, totalling just 16, thus drawing general conclusions is difficult (Quaker Peace and Social Justice 2005, 2008; Bates *et al.* 2007). In addition, the UK evaluation also considered the identification of and response to recidivist behaviours (e.g. 'grooming') as well as actual reconviction rates, thus matching on pure recidivism rates is somewhat difficult as parole recalls were also considered.

The Canadian COSA has taken particularly high-risk offenders, but has achieved notable success with sexual recidivism of COSA offenders 70 per cent lower than offenders in a matched sample. In the three instances of sexual recidivism the reoffences were of less severity when matched to risk score predictions, thus achieving a harm reduction function (Wilson *et al.* 2007).

In addition, in a review to inform Scottish criminal justice policy, Kirkwood and Richley state:

> Survey data also indicated that the Circles improved core members' emotional well-being, helped them to integrate into society, and that core members believed the Circle reduced their chances of reoffending. Regarding community perceptions, a small survey of general members of the community found that 68% of respondents would feel safer if a sex offender in their local area was in a Circle than if he was not.
>
> (2008: 237)

COSA is also well received by professionals, with police and probation services valuing the contribution of Circles to the community risk management of sex offenders (Quaker Peace and Social Justice 2005, 2008), confirmed by Armstrong *et al.*'s survey of key stakeholders in England (2008). In brief:

> Circles bring an added dimension in terms of the support and supervision of offenders, as they can help the core members develop positive social relationships and engage in constructive activities that

may reduce re-offending more than traditional treatment approaches. They also highlighted the role that Circles can play in helping core members to integrate into society and that the involvement of the community may help to change simplistic media representations of sexual offenders.

(Kirkwood and Richley 2008: 238)

Armstrong *et al.* (2008) in a review for the Scottish Justice Department found no evidence of negative impact on volunteers, and there is potential for positive benefits, particularly in actively engaging communities in the community management of sex offenders, and in reducing public anxiety and fear.

In the Canadian context Wilson *et al.* (2007) found that 63 per cent of volunteers became aware of COSA through friends or family, and that 40 per cent had previous experience of corrections, with 28 per cent learning about COSA through their faith-based community. Volunteers are characterised by an interest in helping this client group and by a sense of altruism, and of course self-select towards this type of activity. Most have employment or volunteering histories in work with marginal groups. In this sense, they may not be typical of the wider community's views of sex offenders, more usually characterised by negativity and hostility (Silverman and Wilson 2002). A body of concerned volunteers does not necessarily constitute community engagement.

Whilst COSA has the laudable aim of community engagement and enabling the community to take responsibility for a community issue (Bates *et al.* 2007: 39; Wilson 2007), the extent of this community engagement is questionable. Wilson *et al.* (2002) acknowledge that transferability to larger, more anonymised, communities has been difficult and that 'larger communities appear to be at a distinct disadvantage when it comes to hands-on, community based risk management' (p. 379). This resonates with other evidence on the problems of transferability of restorative justice approaches from communitarian societies to those with weaker ties and looser networks (McAlinden 2005). However, COSA has certainly been effective in reducing public/community anxiety, vigilantism and hostility to sex offenders (Bates *et al.* 2007; Wilson 2007; Wilson *et al.* 2000; Wilson *et al.* 2007). The impact in the UK context is, however, limited. COSA has been largely co-opted to work alongside statutory services, particularly MAPPA, with professionals heavily involved in volunteer selection and training, and in COSA steering groups (Kemshall 2008). Thus COSA is tending to operate at the tertiary level of sexual crime prevention, although it does have the capacity to operate at the secondary.

### Good Lives Model

The Good Lives Model stems in large part from the work of Ward and Marshall 2004 (see also Ward and Maruna 2007), and is rooted in a critique of the dominant cognitive behavioural treatment model, and perceived limits to the risk–needs–responsivity paradigm. McCulloch and Kelly characterise GLM as proposing:

a more holistic and constructive way of conceptualising and engaging with offenders, focusing less on individual offender deficits and more on the personal, inter-personal and social contexts required to enable offenders to live a 'good life'.

(2007: 15)

GLM is essentially a strengths-based approach which 'focuses on promoting individuals' important personal goals, while reducing and managing their risk for future offending' (Whitehead *et al.* 2007: 579). In brief:

It takes seriously offenders' personal preferences and values – that is, the things that matter most to them in the world. It draws upon these primary goods to motivate individuals to live better lives; and ... therapists seek to provide offenders with the competencies (internal conditions) and opportunities (external conditions) to implement treatment plans based on these primary goods.

(Whitehead *et al.* 2007: 580)

In brief, GLM works with the offender to reframe approach goals and the means to achieve them positively and legitimately, and assists the offender in reconstructing a new identity that can action personal goals legally (Whitehead *et al.* 2007). For example, a sex offender may pursue relatedness and social/physical intimacy through inappropriate sexual relations with children (Ward and Stewart 2003). GLM will focus on positive and pro-social approach goals to achieve these 'primary goods' of intimacy legitimately and emphasise avoidance goals to prevent harm. GLM emphasises engagement and motivation as key processes of change, restorative approaches emphasise social inclusion and reintegration as key mechanisms for the prevention of offending, including sexual offending.

However, GLM has been critiqued on a number of grounds, not least that it is culturally and context specific, developed from work with indigenous peoples in Canada and Australia, and as such lacks transferability to other societies. McAlinden (2005) for example has argued that restorative approaches, including 'Good Lives', are more difficult to operate successfully in societies with looser networks and weaker social bonds. Social exclusion remains a significant barrier to living the 'Good Life', and offenders find it difficult to form and sustain strong normative bonds (McNeill 2006). Daly (2000) has also outlined the significant difficulties in pursuing restorative justice in 'unequal and diverse societies'. She also argues that 'strong stories of repair and goodwill are uncommon' (2002: 55). Cook (2006), in an extensive empirical study of restorative justice in Australia and America, found that achieving the ideals of restorative justice was 'more elusive than anticipated'. Indeed 'dynamics around gender, race and class reinforce social privilege and disadvantage' (2006: 107).

It has to be combined with a risk management approach but a therapeutic focus on needs may obscure attention to risks, and workers can find these tensions hard to manage (Kemshall 2008). The model also has limited efficacy with psychopaths who display limited empathy and remorse (Whitehead *et al.*

2007; Hemphill and Hart 2002). In addition, it is difficult to establish in a multimodal approach the impact achieved by GLM over and above more traditional risk management methods. Finally, comparison of GLM and more traditional risk management strategies is still lacking (see Bonta and Andrews 2003 for a full review).

Despite their roots in restorative justice, reintegrative approaches have tended to focus on offenders and the effective community management of their risk factors, with rather limited attention to the subjective experiences of victims (see Newell 2007 for example on restorative work with violent prisoners; and Wilson *et al.* 2002 on restorative approaches to sex offenders). However, the reintegrative focus does aim to erode the 'monstrous' framing of sex offenders and demonstrates that many sex offenders can be safely managed in the community. In this sense it is an important antidote to dominant criminal justice concerns with high-risk sex offenders, 'dangerous offenders' and 'serious harm'.

## Conclusion

As argued above, Kelly's 'continuum' (1998, 2002) is an interesting device for 'testing' the fitness for purpose of public health and voluntary sector responses to sex offenders. In essence, three questions were posed:

- To what extent can such policy alternatives respond to a range of offenders, offence types and victim experiences?
- To what extent do they facilitate a refocusing away from 'the monstrous Stranger-Danger' to the sex offender who is daily in our midst?
- To what extent do they enable victims (actual and potential) to respond to sex offending in a meaningful and effective way?

To differing degrees public health and voluntary sector responses to sex offenders do capture a range of offenders and offence types, particularly those with an emphasis upon early interventions and preventative strategies. To a lesser extent victim experiences are recognised and validated; survivor experiences for example have been critical in the development of Stop It Now!, and TDI/Leisurewatch recognises that the dividing line between offender and public and between offender and victim can be slim. All have facilitated a refocusing away from 'the monstrous Stranger-Danger', although public awareness campaigns and public engagement have been limited with differing grades of success. The specific targeting of groups and the focus on 'skilling up' appears to be more successful than broad public awareness campaigning (TDI 2007; Kemshall 2008). Knowing what to look for and how to respond appears to enable actual and potential victims to respond to sex offending in a meaningful and positive way in contrast to public education campaigns which can be resisted or misinterpreted.

However, the quality of evidence on the effectiveness of public health and reintegrative approaches is variable (see McAlinden 2010 for an overview of some current critiques, pp. 142–4). Some studies (e.g. Wilson *et al.* 2007) have striven to meet the standards of a matched sample, but evaluations tend to be limited by small numbers, difficulties in accurate matching of samples (for example of sex offenders in a Circle and those not) and lack of generalisability. For example, some projects and evaluations are context specific, located in the particular contexts of prisons, domestic violence interventions, or targeted at particular offence types, with limited transferability to other offenders and offence types. Daly (2006) for example has presented empirical evidence of the effectiveness of restorative approaches in the realm of 'intimate gendered violence' but recognises that transferability to other forms of violence cannot be assumed. The research base would benefit from larger-scale comparative evaluations, across settings and offence types, and across longer timescales to determine accurate recidivism rates. However, early evaluations indicate that such alternatives are worthy of further initiatives and evaluations.

In addition, all approaches under the broad banner of public health and reintegration have limits and difficulties in their practical deployment. Whilst they potentially have greater benefits to offer than traditional correctional and punitive approaches, constructing direct comparisons of these two approaches remains difficult, not least because public health responses have been co-opted by the dominant punitive paradigm (for example by MAPPA, or through the Child Sex Offender Review). This in itself has served to focus attention on offenders rather than victims, albeit within an overall goal of public safety and protection. The Public Health Approach has, however, rebalanced policy responses to sex offenders by focusing attention on a broad range of sexual offending, demonstrating that sex offenders can be safely managed in the community, and that exclusionary management techniques are self-defeating. PHA also values early and preventative interventions in contrast to the reactive and punitive responses of the criminal justice system. In addition, all the PHA responses value public engagement, with differing degrees of practical success. This in itself has played an important role in collapsing the gulf between communities and sex offenders, and in making the 'monstrous' manageable. PHA responses have demonstrated that the public are not necessarily irrational vigilantes, or mere 'media dupes', but are capable of rational and reasoned responses to child sexual abuse if appropriately informed. Whilst considerable barriers to engagement still exist, these alternative responses highlight how we might proceed and why we should try.

## Acknowledgements

Thanks are extended to Jason Wood and Gill Mackenzie who co-worked on two of the projects cited here. The views expressed in this chapter are the author's.

## Further reading

For a thorough and readable introduction to restorative justice approaches to work with high-risk sex offenders see McAlinden, A. (2010) 'Restorative justice and the reintegration of high risk sex offenders', in K. Harrison, (ed.) *Managing High Risk Sex Offenders in the Community: Risk Management, treatment and social responsibility.* Cullompton: Willan Publishing. For an introduction to public health approaches to sex offenders see Kemshall, H. (2008) *Understanding the Community Management of High Risk Offenders.* Maidenhead: McGraw-Hill/OUP, pp: 73–8, 94–102. For media framing of sex offending risks see Kitzinger, J. (2004) *Framing Abuse: Media Influence and Public Understanding of Sexual Violence Against Children.* London: Pluto Press.

The initial Home Office *Child Sex Offender Review* (2007) can be found at: http://webarchive.nationalarchives.gov.uk/20100413151441/http:/www.homeoffice.gov. uk/documents/CSOR/ (accessed 4 March 2011).

Helpful websites are: Stop It Now! http://www.stopitnow.org; The Derwent Initiative at http://www.tdi.org.uk/; Circles of Support and Accountability at http://www.circles-uk.org.uk/

## References

Alaszewski, A. (2006) 'Health and risk', in P. Taylor-Gooby and Jens Zinn (eds) *Risk in Social Science.* Oxford: Oxford University Press, pp. 160-179.

Alder, M.W. (1997) 'Sexual health; a health of the nation failure', *British Medical Journal*, 314, pp. 1743–6.

Armstrong, S., Chistyakova, Y., Mackenzie, S. and Malloch, M. (2008) *Circles of Support & Accountability: Consideration of the feasibility of pilots in Scotland.* The Scottish Centre for Crime and Justice Research. Downloaded from www.sccjr.ac.uk/files/ea609cb 5b161853a9a6edefe64436420.pdf (accessed 16 February 2010).

Barnett, J. and Breakwell, G.M. (2003) 'The social amplification of risk and the hazard sequence: the October 1995 oral contraceptive pill scare', *Health, Risk and Society*, 5: 301–13.

Bates, A., Saunders, R. and Wilson, C. (2007) 'Doing something about it: A follow-up study of sex offenders participating in Thames Valley circles of support and accountability', *British Journal of Community Justice*, 5: 19–42.

BBC (2009) Radio 4, *File on Four*, 7 July. www.bbc.co.uk/iplayer/episode/b00lgj3h/ File_on_4_07_07_2009/ (accessed 16 February 2010).

Bohner, G., Eyssel, F., Pina, A., Siebler, F. and Tendayi, Viki, G. (2009) 'Rape myth acceptance: cognitive, affective and behavioural effects of beliefs that blame the victim and exonerate the perpetrator', in: M. Horvarth and J. Brown (eds) *Rape: Challenging Contemporary Thinking.* Cullompton: Willan Publishing.

Bonta, J. and Andrews, D.A. (2003) 'A commentary on Ward and Stewart's model of human needs', *Psychology, Crime and Law*, 9: 215–8.

Boseley, S. (2002) ' "Multi-jabs pose no risk to babies', say US researchers', *The Guardian*, Tuesday 8 January, p. 9.

Brown, S. (2005) *Treating Sex Offenders: An Introduction to Sex Offender Treatment Programmes.* Cullompton: Willan Publishing.

Chartered Institute of Housing Scotland (2005) *Toward a National Accommodation Strategy for Sex Offenders.* A report commissioned by the CIH Scotland from R. Atkinson, J. Flint and S. Blandy. Edinburgh: CIH Scotland.

Collins, S. (2009) *Keeping the Public in Public Protection.* Lucy Faithfull Foundation.

Connelly, C. and Williamson, S. (2000) *A Review of the Research Literature on Serious Violent and Sexual Offenders.* Edinburgh: The Scottish Executive Central Research Unit.

Cook, K.J. (2006) 'Doing difference and accountability in restorative justice conferences', *Theoretical Criminology*, 10(1): 107–24.

Cornelius, T.L., Sullivan, K.T. and Wyngarden, N. (2009) 'Participation in prevention programs for dating violence: Beliefs about relationship violence and intention to participate', *Journal of Interpersonal Violence*, 24(6): 1057–78.

Correctional Service of Canada (2002) *Circles of Support and Accountability: A guide to training potential volunteers, Training manual 2002*. Ottawa.

Cosgrove, Lady (1999) *Reducing the Risk: improving the response to sex offending. Report of the expert panel on sex offending*. Edinburgh: Scottish Executive.

Daly, K. (2000) 'Restorative justice in diverse and unequal societies', in: M. Israel, A.J. Goldsmith and A. Goldsmith (eds) *Criminal Justice in Diverse Communities*. Federation Press.

Daly, K. (2002) 'Restorative justice: the real story', *Punishment and Society*, 4(1): 55–79.

Daly, K. (2006) 'Restorative justice and sexual assault: an archival study of court and conference cases', *British Journal of Criminology*, 48(4): 557–66.

Denscombe, M. (2001) 'Uncertain identities: the value of smoking for young adults in late modernity', *British Journal of Sociology*, 52: 157–77.

Dowden, C. and Andrews, D.A. (2004) 'The importance of staff practice in delivering effective correctional practice', *International Journal of Offender Therapy and Comparative Criminology* 48(2): 203–14.

Eisen, M. and Zellman, G.L. (1986) 'The role of health belief attitudes, sex education and demographics in predicting adolescents' sexuality knowledge', *Health Education Quarterly*, 13: 9–22.

Eldridge, H., Fuller, S., Findlater, D. and Palmer, T. (2006) *Stop It Now! Helpline Report*. Available at www.stopitnow.org (accessed 30 September 2007).

Foubert, J.D. and McEwen, M.K. (1998) 'An all-male rape prevention peer education program: decreasing fraternity men's behavioural intent to rape', *Journal of College Student Development*, 39: 548–56.

Gallagher, B. (2009) 'Child sexual abuse: informed or in fear?', *Criminal Justice Matters*, 77 (September): 6–7.

Gilligan, P. and Akhtar, S. (2005) 'Cultural barriers to the disclosure of child sexual abuse in Asian communities: what women say', *British Journal of Social Work*, 36(8): 1361–77.

Glanz, K., Rimer, B.K. and Lewis, F.M. (2002) *Health, Behaviour and Health Education. Theory, Research and Practice*. San Francisco: Wiley and Sons.

Hebenton, B. and Thomas, T. (1996) 'Tracking sex offenders', *Howard Journal of Criminal Justice*, 35(2): 97–112.

Hemphill, J.F. and Hart, S.D. (2002) 'Motivating the unmotivated: Psychopathy, treatment, and change', in: M. McMurran (ed.) *Motivating the Offender to Change: A guide to enhancing engagement in therapy*. Chichester: John Wiley and Sons, pp. 193–200.

Home Office (2007) *Child Sex Offender Review*. London: Home Office.

Home Office (2008) *Keeping Our Communities Safe*. London: Home Office.

Hughes, E., Kitzinger, J. and Murdoch, G. (2006) 'The media and risk', in P. Taylor-Gooby and J. Zinn (eds) *Risk in Social Science*. Oxford: Oxford University Press.

Johnston, L. (2000) *Policing Britain: Risk, Security and Governance*. London: Longman.

Kelly, L. (1988) *Surviving Sexual Violence*. London: Polity Press.

Kelly, L. (2002) 'The continuum of sexual violence', in K. Plummer (ed.) *Critical Concepts in Sociology*. London: Routledge, pp. 127–39. Reproduced from J. Holmes and M. Maynard (eds) (1987) *Women, Violence and Social Control*. London: Macmillan, pp. 46–60.

Kemshall, H. (2002) 'Effective practice in probation: an example of "advanced liberal responsibilisation"?', *The Howard Journal*, 41(1): 41–58.

Kemshall, H. (2003) *Understanding Risk in Criminal Justice*. Maidenhead: Open

University Press/McGraw-Hill.

Kemshall, H. (2008) *Understanding the Community Management of High Risk Offenders.* Maidenhead: Open University Press/McGraw-Hill.

Kemshall, H., Mackenzie, G. and Wood, J. (2004) *Stop It Now! UK and Ireland. An Evaluation.* Leicester: De Montfort University.

Kemshall, H. and Wood, J. (2007) 'Beyond public protection: an examination of community protection and public health approaches to high-risk offenders', *Criminology and Criminal Justice*, 7(3): 203–22.

Kemshall, H. and Wood, J. (2008) 'Risk management, accountability and partnerships in criminal justice', in B. Stout, J. Yates and B. Williams (eds) *Applied Criminology.* London: Sage Publications.

Kirkwood, S. and Richley, T. (2008) 'Circles of support and accountability: the case for their use in Scotland to assist in the community reintegration and risk management of sexual offenders', *SCOLAG Legal Journal*, 372 (October): 236–9.

Kitzinger, J. (1999) 'The ultimate neighbour from hell? Stranger danger and the media representation of paedophilia', in B. Franklin (ed.) *Social Policy, the Media and Misrepresentation.* London: Routledge, pp. 207–21.

Kitzinger, J. (2004) *Framing Abuse: Media Influence and Public Understanding of Sexual Violence Against Children.* London: Pluto Press.

Laws, R.D. (1996) 'Relapse prevention or harm reduction?', *Sexual Abuse: A Journal of Research and Treatment*, 8(3): 243–48.

Laws, R.D. (2000) 'Sexual offending as a public health problem: A North American perspective', *Journal of Sexual Aggression*, 5(1): 30–44.

Laws, D.R. and Marshall, W. (2003) 'A brief history of behavioural and cognitive behavioural approaches to sexual offenders. Part 1: early developments', *Sexual Abuse: A Journal of Research and Treatment* 15(2): 93–120.

Mann, R.E. (2004) 'Innovations in sex offender treatment', *Journal of Sexual Aggression*, 10(2): 141–52.

Marshall, W., Serran, G., Fernandez, Y., Mann, R. and Thornton, D. (2003) 'Therapist characteristics in the treatment of sexual offenders: tentative data on their relationship with indices of behaviour change', *Journal of Sexual Aggression*, 9(1): 25–30.

McAlinden, A. (2005) 'The use of "shame" with sexual offenders', *British Journal of Criminology*, 45(3): 373–94.

McAlinden, A. (2010) 'Restorative justice and the reintegration of high risk sex offenders', in K. Harrison, (ed.) *Managing High Risk Sex Offenders in the Community: Risk management, treatment and social responsibility.* Cullompton: Willan Publishing.

McCulloch, T. and Kelly, L. (2007) 'Working with sex offenders in context: Which way forward?', *Probation Journal*, 6(2): 197–218.

McNeill, F. (2006) 'A desistance paradigm for offender management', *Criminology and Criminal Justice*, 6(1): 39–62.

Miller, D. and Kitzinger, J. (1998) *The Circuit of Mass Communications: Media Strategies, Representations and Audience Reception in the AIDS crisis.* London: Sage.

Ministry of Justice (2009) *The MAPPA Guidance.* London: Ministry of Justice.

Nash, M. (2006) *Public Protection and the Criminal Justice Process.* Oxford: Oxford University Press.

National Probation Service (2004) *Sex Offender Strategy for the National Probation Service.* London: NPS.

Newell, T. (2007) 'Face to face with violence and its effects', *Probation Journal*, 54(3): 227–38.

NSPCC (2007) *Family 'Honour': Dilemma for British Asians Reporting Child Abuse.* Press release, 19 March, NSPCC.

Piper, H. and Stronnach, I. (2008) *Don't Touch! The Educational Story of a Panic*. London: Routledge.

Pratt, J. (2000a) 'The return of the wheelbarrow men or the arrival of postmodern penality?', *British Journal of Criminology*, 40: 127–45.

Pratt, J. (2000b) 'Emotive and ostentatious punishment: its decline and resurgence in modern society', *Punishment and Society*, 2(4): 127–45.

Quaker Peace and Social Justice (2005) *Circles of Support and Accountability in the Thames Valley: The First Three Years April 2002 to March 2005*. London: Quaker Peace and Social Justice. Downloaded from www.quaker.org.uk/shared_asp_files/uploaded files/82F718A7-9344-4A5C-A4A7-4B053FF22239_CirclesofSupport-first3yrs.pdf (accessed on 16 February 2010).

Quaker Peace and Social Justice (2008) *HTV Circles Six Years of Safer Communities: Six Year Report April 2002 to March 2008*. Downloaded from www.quaker.org.uk/shared_asp_files/GFSR.asp?NodeID=155465 (accessed on 16 February 2010).

Rosenstock, I.M., Strecher, V.J. and Becker, M.H. (1994) 'The health belief model and HIV risk behaviour change', in R.J. DiClemente and J.L. Peterson (eds) *Preventing AIDS: Theories and Methods of Behavioural Interventions*. New York: Plenum Press.

Sanderson, C. (2005) *The Seduction of Children: Empowering Parents and Teachers to Protect Children from Child Sexual Abuse*. London: Jessica Kingsley Publishers.

Sheath, M. (1990) 'Confrontative work with sex offenders: legitimised nonce bashing?', *Probation Journal*, 37(4): 159–62.

Silverman, J. and Wilson, D. (2002) *Innocence Betrayed: Paedophilia, the Media and Society*. Cambridge: Polity Press.

Slovic, P. (2000) *The Perception of Risk*. London: Earthscan.

Tabachnick, J. and Dawson, E. (1999) *Stop It Now! Vermont: Four Year Program Evaluation*. Available at www.stopitnow.org (accessed 2 February 2010).

TDI (the Derwent Initiative) (2007) *Tackling Sex Offending Together*. Newcastle upon Tyne: TDI.

Thirlaway, K.J. and Hegg, D.A. (2005) 'Interpreting risk messages: women's responses to a health story', *Health, Risk and Society*, 7: 107–21.

Thomas, T. (2004) 'Sex offender registers and monitoring', in H. Kemshall and G. McIvor (eds) *Managing Sex Offender Risk*. Research Highlights 46. London: Jessica Kingsley, pp. 225–48.

Thomas, T. (2005) *Sex Crime: Sex Offending and Society*. Cullompton: Willan Publishing.

Vivian-Byrne, S. (2004) 'Changing people's minds', *Journal of Sexual Aggression*, 10(2): 181–92.

Ward, T. and Marshall, W.L. (2004) 'Good lives, aetiology and the rehabilitation of sex offenders: a bridging theory', *Journal of Sexual Aggression*, 10(2): 153–70.

Ward, T. and Maruna, S. (2007) *Rehabilitation*. Key Ideas in Criminology Series. London: Routledge.

Ward, T. and Stewart, C. (2003) 'The treatment of sex offenders: risk management and good lives', *Professional Psychology: Research and Practice*, 34(4): 353–60.

Whitehead, P.R., Ward, T. and Collie, R.M. (2007) 'Time for a change: applying the good lives model of rehabilitation to a high-risk offender', *International Journal of Offender Therapy and Comparative Criminology*, 51(5): 578–98.

Wilczynski, A. and Sinclair, K. (1999) 'Moral tales: representations of child abuse in the quality and tabloid media', *Australian and New Zealand Journal of Criminology*, 32 (3) 262–83.

Wilson, R.J. (2007) 'Out in the open', *Community Care*, 19–25 April: 36–7.

Wilson, R., Huculak, B. and McWhinnie, A. (2002) 'Restorative justice innovations in Canada', *Behavioural Sciences and Law*, 20: 363–80.

Wilson, R. and Picheca, J. (2005) 'Circles of Support and Accountability: engaging the community in sex offender management', *ATSA Forum*, 15.

Wilson, R., Picheca, J. and Prinzo, M. (2005) *Circles of Support and Accountability: An evaluation of the pilot project in South Central Ontario.* Research Report R-168. Ottawa, ON: Correctional Service, Canada.

Wilson, R., Picheca, J. and Prinzo, M. (2007) 'Evaluating the effectiveness of professionally facilitated volunteerism in the community management of high risk sexual offenders: part two – a comparison of recidivism rates', *Howard Journal*, 46 (4) 327–37.

Wilson, R.J., Stewart, L., Stirpe, T., Barrett, M. and Cripps, J.E. (2000) 'Community based sexual offender management: combining parole supervision and treatment to reduce recidivism', *Canadian Journal of Criminology*, 42: 177–88.

Worrall, A. (1997) *Punishment in the Community: The Future of Criminal Justice.* London: Longman.

Wortley, R. and Smallbone, S. (2006) 'Applying situational principles to sexual offences against children', in R. Wortley and S. Smallbone (eds) *Situational Prevention of Child Sexual Abuse.* Monsey, NY: Criminal Justice Press, pp. 7–35.

For further information on the two pilots contact Stop It Now! on office@stopitnow.org.uk

## Chapter 21

# Changing the community response to rape: the promise of sexual assault nurse examiner (SANE) programmes

*Rebecca Campbell*

## Meet Rebecca Campbell

Rebecca Campbell is a Professor of Community Psychology and Program Evaluation at Michigan State University, USA. She has been involved in the anti-violence movement since she was 19 years old. In her sophomore year of college, she did an internship at a battered women's shelter and the experience changed her life. After that, she began training as a volunteer rape victim advocate in hospital emergency departments, a role she enjoyed for 15 years. Combining advocacy and research has always been a passion of Rebecca's, and her academic scholarship examines how the legal, medical and mental health systems respond to the needs of rape survivors. For the past seven years, Rebecca has been studying alternative community interventions for improving post-assault care for rape victims.

## Introduction

Sexual violence is a pervasive social problem: epidemiological data indicate that 17–25 per cent of women in the United States are raped in their adult lifetimes (Fisher *et al.* 2000; Koss *et al.* 1987; Tjaden and Thoennes 1998). Rape is one of the most severe of all traumas, causing multiple, long-term negative outcomes, such as post-traumatic stress disorder (PTSD), depression, substance abuse, suicidal ideation (and suicide) and chronic physical health problems (Koss *et al.* 2003). Rape victims have extensive post-assault needs and may turn to multiple social systems for assistance. Approximately 26–40 per cent of victims report the assault to the police and pursue prosecution through the criminal justice system, 27–40 per cent seek medical care and medical forensic examinations and 16–60 per cent obtain mental health services (Campbell 2008). When victims reach out for help, they place a great deal of trust in the legal, medical and mental health systems as they risk disbelief, blame and refusals of help. How these system interactions unfold can have profound implications for victims' recovery. If victims are able to receive the services they need, and are treated in an empathic, supportive manner, then social systems can help facilitate recovery. Conversely, if victims do not receive needed services and are treated insensitively, then system personnel can magnify victims' feelings of powerlessness, shame and guilt. Post-assault help-seeking can become a 'second rape', a secondary victimisation to the initial trauma (Campbell and Raja 1999; Campbell *et al.* 2001).

Kelly's (1988) concept of a 'continuum of sexual violence' revealed the wide range of sexual violations women endure, and consistent with that conceptualisation, it appears that the help-seeking process is itself sometimes a point on that continuum as well. To be clear, secondary victimisation is not the same as rape and their traumas are not equivalent. That said, when survivors describe their experiences with the legal and medical systems as something so fundamentally hurtful that it feels as if they are once again being violated, it suggests that help-seeking is sometimes on that continuum of violence. At a time of tremendous vulnerability and need, rape victims turn to their communities for help and risk further hurt. The trauma of rape extends far beyond the actual assault, and intervention strategies must address the difficulties rape survivors encounter when seeking community help. Although prevention efforts to eliminate rape are clearly needed, it is also important to consider how we can prevent further trauma among those already victimised. The purpose of this chapter is to review the extant research on rape victims' help-seeking experiences and examine promising new interventions that seek to create more consistently positive post-assault help-seeking experiences for all survivors.

### The community response to rape: helpful or hurtful?

When rape survivors seek community help after an assault, they are most likely to be directed to the medical system, specifically hospital accident and/or emergency departments (EDs) (Resnick *et al.* 2000). Although most victims are not physically injured to the point of needing emergency health care (Ledray 1996), survivors are sent to hospital anyway, primarily for forensic evidence collection (Martin 2005). The survivor's body is a crime scene and due to the invasive nature of sexual assault, a medical professional, rather than a crime scene technician, is needed to collect the evidence. The 'rape exam' or 'rape kit' usually involves plucking head and pubic hairs; collecting loose hairs by combing the head and pubis; swabbing the vagina, anus and/or mouth to collect semen, blood or saliva; and obtaining fingernail clippings and scrapings in the event the victim scratched the assailant. Blood samples may also be collected for DNA, toxicology and ethanol testing (Martin 2005).

For decades, both researchers and rape victim advocates have noted numerous problems with this hospital ED-based approach to post-assault care

(Campbell 2008; Campbell and Bybee 1997; Campbell and Martin 2001; Martin 2005). Many ED physicians are reluctant to perform the rape exam, which results in long wait times for survivors, who spend on average four to ten hours in the ED before they are examined (Littel 2001; Martin 2005). During this wait, victims are not allowed to eat, drink or urinate so as not to destroy physical evidence of the assault (Littel 2001; Taylor 2002). Most ED personnel lack training specifically in forensic evidence collection and, as a result, many rape kits collected by ED doctors are done incorrectly and/or incompletely. Even ED physicians with forensic training usually do not perform forensic exams frequently enough to maintain their proficiency (Littel 2001).

Forensic evidence collection is often the focus of hospital emergency department care, but rape survivors have other medical needs, such as information on the risk of sexually transmitted infections (STIs)/HIV and prophylaxis (preventive medications to treat any STIs that may have been contracted through the assault). The US Centers for Disease Control and Prevention (2002) and American Medical Association (1995) recommend that all sexual assault victims receive STI prophylaxis and HIV prophylaxis on a case-by-case basis after risk assessment. However, analyses of hospital records have shown that only 34 per cent of sexual assault patients are treated for STIs (Amey and Bishai 2002). Nevertheless, data from victims suggest much higher rates of STI prophylaxis: 57–69 per cent of sexual assault patients reported that they received antibiotics during their hospital emergency department care (Campbell 2005, 2006; Campbell *et al.* 2001; National Victims Center 1992). But not all victims are equally likely to receive STI-related medical services. Victims of non-stranger rape are significantly less likely to receive information on STIs/HIV or STI prophylaxis (Campbell and Bybee 1997; Campbell *et al.* 2001), even though knowing the assailant does not mitigate one's risk. In addition, one study found that Caucasian women were significantly more likely to get information on HIV than ethnic minority women (Campbell *et al.* 2001).

Post-assault pregnancy services are also inconsistently provided to rape victims. Only 40–49 per cent of victims receive information about the risk of pregnancy (Campbell *et al.* 2001; National Victims Center 1992). The AMA (1995) and the American College of Obstetricians and Gynecologists (1998) recommend emergency contraception for victims at risk of pregnancy, but only 21–43 per cent of sexual assault victims who need emergency contraception actually receive it (Amey and Bishai 2002; Campbell and Bybee 1997; Campbell 2005, 2006; Campbell *et al.* 2001). To date, no studies have found systematic differences in the provision of emergency contraception as a function of victim or assault characteristics, but hospitals affiliated with the Catholic church are significantly less likely to provide emergency contraception (Campbell and Bybee 1997; Smugar *et al.* 2000).

In the process of the forensic exam, STI services and pregnancy-related care, doctors and nurses ask victims many of the same kinds of questions as do legal personnel regarding their prior sexual history, sexual response during the assault, what they were wearing, and what they did to 'cause' the assault. For example, in instances of stranger rape, medical professionals may ask survivors if they had been out alone without 'proper accompaniment', whether they were dressed provocatively, or were engaged in other 'risk-taking' behaviours.

In situations of non-stranger rape, doctors and nurses often inquire whether survivors 'led on' the assailants (i.e., indicated that they did want sexual relations), sexually teased the assailants, or otherwise miscommunicated their intentions. Medical professionals may view these questions as necessary and appropriate, but rape survivors find them upsetting (Campbell and Raja 2005). It is important to keep in mind the broader context in which these questions are being asked. The rape exam is itself a highly invasive experience, including a lengthy vaginal and/or anal exam. To survivors, post-assault medical care can feel much like a second rape – a physical and emotional violation of their selves (Campbell et al. 2001).

Perhaps not surprisingly, experiences of secondary victimisation have a demonstrable negative impact on victims' mental health. Campbell (2005) found that as a result of their contact with emergency department doctors and nurses, most rape survivors stated that they felt bad about themselves (81 per cent), depressed (88 per cent), violated (94 per cent), distrustful of others (74 per cent), and reluctant to seek further help (80 per cent) (see also Campbell and Raja 2005). Only 5 per cent of victims in Ullman's (1996) study rated physicians as a helpful source of support, and negative responses from formal systems, including medical, significantly exacerbate victims' PTSD symptomatology (Filipas and Ullman 2001; Starzynski et al. 2005; Ullman and Filipas 2001a, b). Victims who do not receive basic medical services rate their experiences with the medical system as more hurtful, which has been associated with higher PTSD levels (Campbell and Raja 2005; Campbell et al. 2001). Specifically, non-stranger rape victims who received minimal medical services but encountered high secondary victimisation appear to be the most at risk: these women had significantly higher levels of PTSD symptoms than victims who did not seek medical services at all (Campbell et al. 1999).

If victims try to pursue criminal prosecution, their experiences with the legal system are not markedly better. In the United States, case attrition is staggering: for every 100 rape cases reported to law enforcement, on average 33 would be referred to prosecutors, 16 would be charged and moved into the court system, 12 would end in a successful conviction, and seven would end in a prison sentence (see Campbell 2008 for a review). Successful prosecution is not random: it is more likely for those from privileged backgrounds and those who experienced assaults that fit stereotypic notions of what constitutes rape (see Campbell 2008 for a review). Younger women, ethnic minority women and women of lower socio-economic status are more likely to have their cases rejected by the criminal justice system (Campbell et al. 2001; Frohmann 1997a, b; Spohn et al. 2001; Spears and Spohn 1997; cf. Frazier and Haney 1996). Cases of stranger rape (where the suspect was eventually identified) and those that occurred with the use of a weapon and/or resulted in physical injuries to victims are more likely to be prosecuted (Campbell et al. 2001; Frazier and Haney 1996; Kerstetter 1990; Martin and Powell 1994; Spohn et al. 2001; Spears and Spohn 1997). Alcohol and drug use by the victim significantly increases the likelihood that a case will be dropped (Campbell et al. 2001; Spears and Spohn 1997; Frohmann 1997 a,b; cf. Frazier and Haney 1996).

These data suggest that the odds of a case being prosecuted are not good, and the treatment victims receive from legal system personnel along the way is not much better. Across multiple samples, 43–52 per cent of victims who had contact with the legal system rated their experience as unhelpful and/or hurtful (Campbell *et al.* 2001; Golding *et al.* 1989; Filipas and Ullman 2001; Monroe *et al.* 2005; Ullman 1996). In qualitative focus group research, survivors described their contact with the legal system as a dehumanising experience of being interrogated, intimidated and blamed. Several women mentioned that they would not have reported if they had known what the experience would be like (Logan *et al.* 2005). Even victims who had the opportunity to go to trial describe the experience as frustrating, embarrassing and distressing, but they also took tremendous pride in their ability to exert some control in the process and tell what happened to them (Konradi 2007).

These experiences of secondary victimisation take a toll on victims' mental health. In self-report characterisations of their psychological health, rape survivors indicate that as a result of their contact with legal system personnel, they felt bad about themselves (87 per cent), depressed (71 per cent), violated (89 per cent), distrustful of others (53 per cent), and reluctant to seek further help (80 per cent) (Campbell 2005; Campbell and Raja 2005). The harm of secondary victimisation is also evident on objective measures of PTSD symptomatology. Ullman and colleagues have found that contact with formal help systems, including the police, is more likely to result in negative social reactions, which was associated with increased PTSD symptomatology (Filipas and Ullman 2001; Starzynski *et al.* 2005; Ullman and Filipas 2001a, b). In a series of studies dealing directly with victim–police contact, Campbell and colleagues found that low legal action (i.e., case did not progress/was dropped) was associated with increased PTSD symptomatology, and high secondary victimisation was also associated with increased PTSD (Campbell *et al.* 2001; Campbell and Raja 2005). In tests of complex interactions, Campbell *et al.* (1999) identified that it was the victims of non-stranger rape whose cases were not prosecuted and who were subjected to high levels of secondary victimisation who had the highest PTSD of all – worse than those who chose not to report to the legal system at all. Interestingly, when victims who did *not* report to the police were asked why they did not pursue prosecution, they specifically stated that they were worried about the risk of further harm and distress; their decision was a self-protective choice to guard their fragile emotional health (Patterson *et al.* 2009).

If some survivors are *more* distressed after post-assault contact with the medical and legal systems, and indeed many describe the experience as something that sustains and prolongs the rape, then it begs the question of whether secondary victimisation should be viewed as part of Kelly's continuum of sexual violence. Kelly (1988) offered the following definition of sexual violence:

Any physical, visual, verbal or sexual act that is experienced by the woman or girl at the time or later as a threat, invasion or assault that has the effect of hurting her or degrading her and/or takes away her ability to control intimate contact.

(p. 41)

The language of Kelly's definition is the very language survivors use in their accounts of medical and legal system contact: invasion, invasive, hurt, hurting, degrading, lack of control (Campbell 2002, 2008). The semantic overlap cannot be ignored. The trauma of secondary victimisation is not the same in scope or magnitude as the assault itself, but consistent with the idea of a continuum, is somewhere far too close to the rape itself. The opportunity for help and healing is missed and instead, like a high-pitched musical note held far, far too long, to the point of discomfort or pain, the sustaining trauma becomes another violation to endure. Whereas not all survivors characterise their post-assault help-seeking as such, many do and indeed all are to some extent at risk for such treatment.

## Changing the community response to rape: a SANE approach

Practitioners in the legal, medical and advocacy communities readily agreed that a new approach to post-assault care was needed, one that would attend to forensic legal issues as well as victims' psychological and medical needs (Martin 2005). In response, sexual assault nurse examiner (SANE) programmes were created in the 1970s by the nursing profession, in collaboration with rape crisis centres/victim advocacy organisations. These programmes were designed to circumvent problems with traditional hospital ED care by having specially trained nurses, rather than doctors, provide 24-hour, first-response psychological, medical and forensic care to sexual assault victims/survivors. SANE programmes are staffed by registered nurses or nurse practitioners who have completed a minimum of 40 hours of classroom training and 40–96 hours of clinical training, which includes instruction in evidence collection techniques, use of specialised equipment, injury detection methods, pregnancy and STI screening and treatment, chain-of-evidence requirements, expert testimony and sexual assault trauma response (Department of Justice 2006; Ledray 1999). Most SANE programmes are hospital-based (e.g., emergency departments) (75–90 per cent), but some are located in community settings (10–25 per cent) (e.g. clinics or rape crisis centres) (Campbell *et al.* 2005b; Logan *et al.* 2007). Nearly all programmes serve adolescents and adults, and approximately half serve paediatric victims/survivors as well (International Association of Forensic Nurses (IAFN) 2010a).

SANE programmes strive 'to minimize the physical and psychological trauma to the victim and maximize the probability of collection and preserving physical evidence for potential use in the legal system' (Young *et al.* 1992: 878). To address victims/survivors' psychological needs, SANEs focus on treating victims with dignity and respect to ensure that they are not retraumatised by the exam (Campbell *et al.* 2008). Many SANE programmes work with their local rape crisis centres so victim advocates can provide emotional support (Littel 2001; Taylor 2002). This delineation of roles is critical because rape victim advocates can offer victims/survivors confidentiality whereas SANEs may have to testify in court about their communications with survivors (Littel 2001). To attend to victims/survivors' physical health needs, SANEs treat victims' injuries, offer emergency contraception for those at risk of becoming pregnant, and provide prophylactic antibiotics to treat STIs that may have been contracted in the assault (Campbell *et al.* 2006; Ledray 1999).

For the forensic evidence collection itself, most SANE programmes utilise specialised equipment, such as a colposcope, which is a non-invasive, lighted magnifying instrument used for examining the anogenital area for the detection of microlacerations, bruises and other injuries (Voelker 1996). A camera is attached to the colposcope to document anogenital injuries (Lang 1999). Toluidine blue dye can also be used for trauma identification by enhancing the visualisation of microlacerations (Ledray 1999). The forensic evidence collected by the SANEs is typically sent to the state crime lab for analysis. If a case is prosecuted, SANEs may provide expert witness testimony (Campbell *et al.* 2007).

SANEs provide extensive post-assault services for rape victims/survivors, but truly comprehensive care involves the efforts of multiple service providers. Many SANE programmes today operate as part of multidisciplinary response teams (e.g. sexual assault response teams (SARTs) or co-ordinated community response initiatives (Littel 2001)). Recognising the importance of collaboration, some states require all SANE programmes that apply for state funding to have a multidisciplinary team to oversee the implementation (Littel 2001). Many SANE programmes continue to work closely with the members of the multidisciplinary team after implementation to review cases and verify that victims/survivors received comprehensive care (Littel 2001). Some SANE programmes also offer formalised multidisciplinary trainings on sexual assault that address strategies for working effectively with survivors, why injuries may or may not be present, and how forensic evidence can be used in law enforcement investigations and prosecution (Littel 2001; Stone *et al.* 2006).

SANE programmes have spread quite quickly since their inception in the 1970s and 1980s, to nearly 500 programmes currently in existence (IAFN 2010a). The vast majority of these programmes are located in the United States and Canada, but similar interventions exist in the United Kingdom, Europe, Australia, and New Zealand (IAFN 2010a). It is somewhat unusual for an intervention model to take root so quickly and in such large numbers, but Rogers' (2003) diffusion of innovation theory (DOI) can help explain why these programmes have been so transferable. DOI theory stipulates five conditions that facilitate the spread of novel practices, all of which are clearly evident in this short history of SANE programmes. The relative advantage of SANE programmes versus traditional ED care was readily apparent, and the intervention model was highly *compatible* with the values of nursing practice, not surprisingly because it was created by the nurses themselves. Although the intervention is very high in *complexity*, the formation of the International Association of Forensic Nurses in 1992 created a reasonably well-standardised intervention model with codified training and practice standards for SANE programmes. The investment in training required to become a forensic nurse was extensive, so *trialability* of the intervention was quite limited, but the *observable benefits* to rape survivors and community stakeholders were so immediate that these disadvantages hardly slowed the diffusion of the innovation. Recently, the US Department of Justice (2004, 2006) sanctioned this intervention model in its national protocol for sexual assault medical forensic examinations, which would also be expected to contribute to further growth of these programmes.

## The promise of SANE programmes: emerging data regarding their effectiveness

The widespread diffusion of SANE programmes has occurred despite *very* minimal evaluative research on their effectiveness (Campbell 2008). Nevertheless, emerging data suggest that these programmes have beneficial effects on victims' health care experiences and psychological well-being, and may also be instrumental in increasing legal prosecution rates. First, the medical forensic exam and evidence collection kit performed by SANEs is more thorough and accurate than what victims receive in traditional emergency department care. Ledray and Simmelink (1997) conducted an audit study of rape kits sent to the Minnesota Bureau of Criminal Apprehension. Twenty-seven kits conducted by SANEs were compared with 73 kits collected by physicians or non-SANEs with respect to completeness of specimens collected, documentation and maintenance of chain of custody. Overall, the SANE-collected kits were more thorough and had fewer errors than the non-SANE kits. A larger-scale study by Sievers *et al.* (2003) explicitly tested differences between SANE and non-SANE kits, and also found support for better evidence collection by SANEs. Specifically, this study compared 279 kits collected by SANEs and 236 by doctors/non-SANEs on ten quality control criteria, and found that in nine of these ten categories, the SANE-collected kits were significantly better. The kits collected by SANEs were significantly more likely than kits collected by physicians to include the proper sealing and labelling of specimen envelopes, the correct number of swabs and other evidence (pubic hairs and head hairs), the correct kind of blood tubes, a vaginal motility slide and a completed crime lab form. The Sievers *et al.* study provides the strongest evidence to date that SANEs collect forensic evidence correctly, and in fact, do so better than physicians. However, it is important to note that training and experience, not job title or professional degree, are the likely reasons behind these findings. Because SANEs have made it a professional priority to obtain extensive forensic training and practice, it is not surprising that current data suggest they are better forensic examiners than physicians and nurses who have not completed such training.

Forensic exams performed by SANE tend to be more technically accurate, but perhaps more importantly, *how* they are performed from the perspective of the survivors is qualitatively different. SANEs provide a full explanation of the process *before* the exam begins, and then continue to describe what they find throughout the exam, giving patients the opportunity to reinstate some control over their bodies by participating when appropriate (e.g. combing their own hair). In an evaluation of a midwestern US SANE programme, victims gave strong positive feedback about their exam experiences: all patients indicated that they were fully informed about the process, and the nurses took their needs and concerns seriously and allowed them to stop or pause the exam if needed (Campbell *et al.* 2008). This patient-centred care also seems to help victims' psychological well-being as survivors reported feeling supported, safe, respected, believed and well-cared-for by their SANE nurses (see also Ericksen *et al.* 2002).

As noted previously, the rape exam is more than forensic evidence collection, it is an opportunity to address survivors' health care needs as well. With respect to STI and emergency contraception care, national surveys of SANE programmes find service provision rates of 90 per cent or higher (Campbell *et al.* 2006; Ciancone *et al.* 2000). As with traditional emergency department medical care, SANE programmes affiliated with Catholic hospitals are significantly less likely to conduct pregnancy testing or offer emergency contraception (but do so at higher rates than non-SANE Catholic-affiliated emergency departments) (Campbell *et al.* 2006). In a quasi-experimental longitudinal study, Crandall and Helitzer (2003) compared medical service provision rates two years before to four years after the implementation of a hospital-based SANE programme, and found significant increases in STI prophylaxis care (89 per cent to 97 per cent) and emergency contraception (66 per cent to 87 per cent).

In addition to beneficial effects on victims' health, SANE programmes may be instrumental in increasing legal prosecution of reported cases. Multiple case studies suggest that SANE programmes increase prosecution, particularly plea bargains, because when confronted with the forensic evidence collected by the SANEs, assailants will plead guilty (often to a lesser charge) rather than face trial (see Campbell *et al.* 2005a for a review). Case study designs are often used in evaluations of new interventions (Rossi *et al.* 2004) and are useful for providing rich descriptive information about programmes and identifying outcomes (Yin 2009). However, it is difficult to determine whether the effects documented in case study research (e.g. increased prosecution) can be attributed to the focal intervention because this methodology does not include comparison groups or other methodological controls that permit causal inferences. To date, only three studies have rigorously evaluated whether SANE programmes increase prosecution.

With respect to research specifically on SANE interventions, Crandall and Helitzer (2003) used a quasi-experimental pre-post design to compare prosecution rates in a New Mexico jurisdiction two years before to three years after the implementation of a SANE programme. Their results indicated that significantly more victims/survivors treated in the SANE programme reported to the police than before the SANE programme was launched in this community (72 per cent versus 50 per cent) and significantly more victims/ survivors had evidence collection kits taken (88 per cent versus 30 per cent). Police filed more charges of sexual assault post-SANE as compared with pre-SANE (7.0 charges/perpetrator versus 5.4). The conviction rate for charged SANE cases was also significantly higher (69 per cent versus 57 per cent), resulting in longer average sentences (5.1 versus 1.2 years).

In a more recent and comprehensive study on this issue, Campbell and colleagues (2009) conducted a multi-study, mixed-methods evaluation of a US midwestern SANE programme. Overall, the purpose of this project was to examine whether adult sexual assault cases were more likely to be investigated and prosecuted after the implementation of a SANE programme within the focal county. In Study 1, they used a rigorous quasi-experimental design to determine whether there was a change in prosecution rates pre-SANE to post-SANE. The pre and post cases were equivalent on multiple criteria, except that the pre-SANE cases were examined by hospital emergency department personnel and the post-SANE cases were examined in the focal SANE programme. Using longitudinal multilevel ordinal regression modelling, Campbell and colleagues found that case progression through the criminal justice system significantly increased pre- to post-SANE: more cases reached the 'final' stages of prosecution (i.e. conviction at trial and/or guilty plea bargains) post-SANE. These findings suggest that the implementation of the county's SANE programme was instrumental in achieving higher adult sexual assault prosecution rates in this community.

To understand whether implementation of the SANE programme affected criminal justice system case processing, Campbell et al. also examined what factors predict case progression. What makes some cases more or less likely to move further through the system? Therefore, in Study 2, they tested a model that compared the predictive utility of victim characteristics (e.g. race, age), assault characteristics (e.g. victim–offender relationship) and forensic medical evidence (e.g. injury, DNA) in explaining case progression in the post-SANE era. In the hierarchical ordinal regression models, two victim characteristics were significant: survivors between the ages of 18 and 21 (i.e. younger women in the sample) were significantly more likely to have their cases move to higher case disposition outcomes; and alcohol use by the victim prior to assault significantly decreased the likelihood that the case would be prosecuted. Two assault characteristics were significant: penetration crimes (versus fondling crimes) and assaults in which the offender was an intimate partner/husband, ex-intimate partner/husband, dating partner, or family member (i.e. stronger relationship bonds between the victim and offender) were more likely to advance to higher disposition levels. After accounting for these victim and assault characteristics, medical forensic evidence could still predict significant variance in case outcomes. The more delay there was between the assault and when the survivor had the medical forensic exam, the less likely the case would progress through the system. Positive DNA evidence significantly increased the likelihood of case progression. With respect to specific findings in the medical forensic evidence exam, physical or anogenital redness was associated with increased likelihood of case progression.

The results of Studies 1 and 2 indicated that the SANE programme had been instrumental in increasing successful prosecution, but it is also important to understand how and why those changes occurred: what are the mediating mechanisms that contributed to these changes? To identify these mechanisms, Campbell et al. (2009) conducted in-depth qualitative interviews with law enforcement personnel and prosecutors regarding their perceptions of how the emergence of the SANE programme affected their work investigating and prosecuting adult sexual assault cases (Study 3). The findings of the study indicated that the SANE programme has been instrumental in the creation of more complete, fully corroborated cases. With the medical forensic evidence safely in the hands of the SANEs, law enforcement put more investigational effort into other aspects of the case. The training and ongoing consultation provided by SANEs often suggested investigational leads that law enforcement could pursue to further develop a case. As a result, the cases that were put forward to prosecutors reflect the collective efforts and expertise of law enforcement and the SANEs, and not surprisingly, the cases were stronger. Consequently, prosecutors were more inclined to move forward with charging cases, and over time, the prosecution rates did increase.

These qualitative findings were replicated and triangulated with quantitative data in Study 4. A quantitative content analysis of police reports revealed multiple significant mediated effects indicating that SANE involvement in a case was associated with increased law enforcement investigational effort, which in turn predicted case referral to prosecutors. Specifically, in cases in which the victim had a medical forensic exam, police collected more kinds of *other* evidence to support the case, which was associated with increased likelihood of case referral. In addition, in cases where SANE conducted a suspect exam (i.e. a forensic medical exam of the *suspect*'s body), police were also more likely to collect other evidence to support the case, and more likely to interview the suspect, both of which were associated with increased likelihood of case referral. In other words, evidence begets more evidence: the medical forensic evidence collected by SANEs may suggest specific leads that law enforcement can follow up on to obtain more evidence, and/or the efficiency of the SANE programme frees up law enforcement time to obtain other evidence. The additive effect of evidence from the SANEs plus the evidence collected by law enforcement created more complete documentation of the crime.

In Study 5, Campbell *et al.* (2009) conducted in-depth qualitative interviews with victims/survivors who received post-assault medical forensic exams in the focal SANE programme. The vast majority of survivors characterised their experiences at the SANE programme as positive, empowering and healing. The nurses and advocates worked together as a team to help survivors begin the process of reinstating control over their bodies and their lives. The programme links survivors to advocacy and support services at the rape crisis centre (with which this SANE is organisationally linked) so that they have the resources they need to focus on their own well-being and recovery. This attention to helping survivors heal indirectly affected their willingness to participate in legal prosecution. When survivors are not as traumatised, they are more willing and capable of participating in the prosecution process. In addition, survivors often had questions about the medical forensic exam and the process of criminal prosecution, and when SANE programme nurses and advocates provided patients with this information, it gave survivors more hope and confidence about their legal cases, which also indirectly contributed to increased victim participation.

However, positive experiences with the SANE programme did not guarantee that survivors would have similarly positive experiences with the legal system. The survivors interviewed in Study 5 had three distinct patterns of experiences with the criminal justice system. First, there were cases in which the victim wanted the case to be prosecuted, but criminal justice system personnel did not prosecute the case, which we termed *rejected cases* (n=7). These survivors described their experiences with the legal system as hurtful, disappointing, and disempowering. For example, a 21-year-old white woman who was assaulted by her ex-boyfriend, whom she had recently broken up with, described how she was hurt when the detectives treated her as if she was lying:

> They were just like non-reaction. No, 'how are you doing with this? Are you OK?'...they were just, kind of, they were victim-blaming. They were kind of looking at me like well, you had control of this situation. You should have did this or you should've done that. Well, that's not what happened. There are a lot of women who don't even report it, but you're gonna sit here and treat me like crap because you think that I'm lying?

Second, in some cases, the victims wanted the case dropped, but the criminal justice system personnel forwarded the case despite the victims' expressed desire to drop (termed *dragged cases*) (n=4). These survivors also characterised their contact with the legal system as frustrating, disempowering and hurtful. It appeared that law enforcement (and the forensic nurses) had serious concerns about potential lethality in these cases and therefore did not respect victims' wishes not to pursue prosecution. Finally, there were cases in which the criminal justice system's response matched the victims' wishes (termed *matched cases*) (n=9). These survivors had positive experiences with law enforcement, noting that the care and empathy they received from police helped them participate more fully in the investigation and prosecution process.

In the last study in this project, Study 6, the research team interviewed the forensic nurses in the focal SANE programme regarding their work with their patients and with local law enforcement. This SANE programme maintains a philosophy that patient care – not supporting law enforcement or building legal cases – is their primary goal. This SANE programme does not pressure their patients to report to law enforcement, and instead they emphasise that it is the survivors' choice and either way, the forensic nurses will be there to care for them. Therefore, it is entirely consistent with this SANE programme's practice that Campbell *et al.* (2009) did not find a direct link between SANE involvement and victim participation – there should not be. The forensic nurses' role is to provide care to their patients and, as it turns out, this can have an *indirect* benefit on victim participation in the criminal justice system. In SANEs' work with law enforcement, the evidence collected from victims and suspects, and all accompanying documentation, was made immediately and easily accessible to law enforcement so that it could be used to inform their investigation. In their ongoing case consultations with police, the forensic nurses provided information about medical forensic evidence in general, and injuries in particular, and encouraged law enforcement to conduct a thorough investigation of the case, regardless of the medical forensic evidence findings. These findings are consistent with the Study 3 and 4 results that SANE involvement in a case is associated with increased investigational effort.

This 12-year analysis of criminal justice system case outcomes revealed that more cases were moving through the system to higher levels of disposition (i.e., guilty pleas or guilty convictions) after the implementation of a SANE programme. The quasi-experimental design and supplemental data collection used in this project allowed Campbell and colleagues to conclude that these effects are reasonably attributable to the efforts of the SANE programme and not due to other changes over time in this community. The SANE programmes' work with law enforcement and their patients, though separate and philosophically distinct, is mutually reinforcing and provides instrumental resources for successful case prosecution.

## Conclusions

This chapter has highlighted the experiences of victims who sought help from formal social systems and the difficulties they encounter. But it is important to remember that many victims, indeed most, do not seek help from the legal, medical and mental health systems. When these survivors are asked why they do not, they say that they are concerned about whether they would even get help and that they are worried about being treated poorly (Patterson *et al.* 2009). Unfortunately, empirical research suggests this apprehension is probably warranted. At the same time, for some victims social system contact is beneficial and healing. The challenge then is to address the underlying problems in our social systems so that good care is more consistently provided to all victims, who have survived all kinds of assaults. Collaborative, multi-system innovations, such as SANE programmes, are changing the community response to rape. These interventions are not necessarily easy to implement as they require extensively trained medical personnel for their staffing, but the US Department of Justice (2004, 2006) has invested considerable financial resources in supporting training and technical assistance. Indeed, a primary long-term goal of the International Association of Forensic Nurses is enhancing the sustainability of existing SANE programmes and supporting their expansion to geographically diverse areas in the United States and in other countries (IAFN 2010b). Although there are few studies that provide empirical data to guide such expansion, it appears that SANE programmes are most successful when they are formed as part of a true multidisciplinary collaborative effort to improve community resources for survivors (Campbell *et al.* 2005). The reason why SANE programmes have the potential to change the community response to rape is their focus on the needs of survivors, first and foremost. That philosophy can be manifest in many types of community interventions, including, but by no means limited to, SANE programmes. The trauma associated with negative post-assault help-seeking can be prevented and our communities can be more effective in helping survivors heal from rape.

## Further reading

For a comprehensive review on the challenge rape survivors face when they contact the legal and medical systems, Patricia Yancey Martin's *Rape Work: Victims, Gender, and Emotions in Organization and Community Context* (2005) is an excellent resource. Amanda

Konradi's *Taking the Stand: Rape Survivors and the Prosecution of Rapists* (2007) provides
an in-depth look at rape victims' involvement with the American legal system. For
comprehensive how-to manuals for the creation of sexual assault nurse examiner
(SANE) programmes, see http://www.ojp.usdoj.gov/ovc/publications/infores/sane/sane
guide.pdf or http://www.ncjrs.gov/pdffiles1/ovw/206554.pdf. Another great resource for
practitioners working on the community response to sexual assault is the State of
Oregon Attorney General's Sexual Assault Task Force Manual, available by contacting
them at http://oregonsatf.org.

# References

American College of Obstetricians and Gynecologists (1998) 'Sexual assault' (ACOG
educational bulletin), *International Journal of Gynecology and Obstetrics*, 60: 297–304.

American Medical Association (1995) *Strategies for the Treatment and Prevention of Sexual
Assault*. Chicago, IL: Author.

Amey, A.L. and Bishai, D. (2002) 'Measuring the quality of medical care for women
who experience sexual assault with data from the National Hospital Ambulatory
Medical Care Survey', *Annals of Emergency Medicine*, 39: 631–8.

Campbell, R. (2008) 'The psychological impact of rape victims' experiences with the
legal, medical, and mental health systems', *American Psychologist*, 68: 702–17.

Campbell, R. (2006) 'Rape survivors' experiences with the legal and medical systems:
Do rape victim advocates make a difference?', *Violence Against Women*, 12: 1–16.

Campbell, R. (2005) 'What really happened? A validation study of rape survivors' help-
seeking experiences with the legal and medical systems', *Violence amd Victims*, 20:
55–68.

Campbell, R. (2002) *Emotionally Involved: The Impact of Researching Rape*. New York:
Routledge.

Campbell, R. and Bybee, D. (1997) 'Emergency medical services for rape victims:
Detecting the cracks in service delivery', *Women's Health*, 3: 75–101.

Campbell, R., Bybee, D., Ford, J.K., Patterson, D. and Ferrell, J. (2009) *A Systems Change
Analysis of SANE Programs: Identifying mediating mechanisms of criminal justice system
impact*. Washington, DC: National Institute of Justice.

Campbell, R., Long, S.M., Townsend, S.M., Kinnison, K.E., Pulley, E.M., Adames, S.B.
and Wasco, S.M. (2007) 'Sexual assault nurse examiners' (SANEs) experiences
providing expert witness court testimony', *Journal of Forensic Nursing*, 3: 7–14.

Campbell, R. and Martin, P.Y. (2001) 'Services for sexual assault survivors: The role of
rape crisis centers', in C. Renzetti, J. Edleson and R. Bergen (eds) *Sourcebook on
Violence Against Women* (pp. 227–41). Thousand Oaks, CA: Sage.

Campbell, R., Patterson, D., Adams, A.E., Diegel, R. and Coats, S. (2008) 'A
participatory evaluation project to measure SANE nursing practice and adult sexual
assault patients' psychological well-being', *Journal of Forensic Nursing*, 4: 19–28.

Campbell, R., Patterson, D. and Lichty, L.F. (2005) 'The effectiveness of sexual assault
nurse examiner (SANE) program: A review of psychological, medical, legal, and
community outcomes', *Trauma, Violence, & Abuse: A Review Journal*, 6: 313–29.

Campbell, R. and Raja, S. (2005) 'The sexual assault and secondary victimization of
female veterans: Help-seeking experiences in military and civilian social systems',
*Psychology of Women Quarterly*, 29: 97–106.

Campbell, R. and Raja, S. (1999) 'The secondary victimization of rape victims: Insights
from mental health professionals who treat survivors of violence', *Violence and
Victims*, 14: 261–75.

Campbell, R., Sefl, T., Barnes, H.E., Ahrens, C.E., Wasco, S.M. and Zaragoza-Diesfeld,

Y. (1999) 'Community services for rape survivors: Enhancing psychological well-being or increasing trauma?', *Journal of Consulting and Clinical Psychology*, 67: 847–58.

Campbell, R., Townsend, S.M., Long, S.M., Kinnison, K.E., Pulley, E.M., Adames, S.B. and Wasco, S.M. (2005b) 'Organizational characteristics of sexual assault nurse examiner programs: Results from the national survey of SANE programs', *Journal of Forensic Nursing*, 1: 57–64.

Campbell, R., Townsend, S.M., Long, S.M., Kinnison, K.E., Pulley, E.M., Adames, S.B. and Wasco, S.M. (2006) 'Responding to sexual assault victims' medical and emotional needs: A national study of the services provided by SANE programs', *Research in Nursing and Health*, 29: 384–98.

Campbell, R., Wasco, S.M., Ahrens, C.E., Sefl, T. and Barnes, H.E. (2001) 'Preventing the "second rape": Rape survivors' experiences with community service providers', *Journal of Interpersonal Violence*, 16: 1239–59.

Centers for Disease Control and Prevention (2002) 'Sexual assault and STDs – adults and adolescents', *Morbidity and Mortality Weekly Report*, 51 (RR-6): 69–71.

Ciancone, A., Wilson, C., Collette, R. and Gerson, L.W. (2000) 'Sexual Assault Nurse Examiner programs in the United States', *Annals of Emergency Medicine*, 35: 353–7.

Crandall, C. and Helitzer, D. (2003) *Impact evaluation of a Sexual Assault Nurse Examiner (SANE) program* (Document No. 203276). Washington DC: National Institute of Justice.

Department of Justice (2004) *A National Protocol for Sexual Assault Medical Forensic Examinations: Adults/adolescents*. Washington, DC: Author.

Department of Justice (2006) *National Training Standards for Sexual Assault Medical Forensic Examiners*. Washington, DC: Author.

Ericksen, J., Dudley, C., McIntosh, G., Ritch, L., Shumay, S. and Simpson, M. (2002). 'Client's experiences with a specialized sexual assault service', *Journal of Emergency Nursing*, 28: 86–90.

Filipas, H.H. and Ullman, S.E. (2001) 'Social reactions to sexual assault victims from various support sources', *Violence and Victims*, 16: 673–92.

Fisher, B.A., Cullen, F.T. and Turner, M.G. (2000) *The Sexual Victimization of College Women* (NCJ 182369). Washington, DC: US Department of Justice, Office of Justice Programs.

Frazier, P. and Haney, B. (1996) 'Sexual assault cases in the legal system: Police, prosecutor and victim perspectives', *Law and Human Behavior*, 20: 607–28.

Frohmann, L. (1997a) 'Discrediting victims' allegations of sexual assault: Prosecutorial accounts of case rejections', *Social Problems*, 38: 213–26.

Frohmann, L. (1997b) 'Complaint-filing interviews and the constitution of organizational structure: Understanding the limitations of rape reform', *Hastings Women's Law Journal*, 8: 365–99.

Golding, J.M., Siegel, J.M., Sorenson, S.B., Burnam, M.A. and Stein, J.A. (1989) 'Social support sources following sexual assault', *Journal of Community Psychology*, 17: 92–107.

International Association of Forensic Nurses (2010a) Database of the International Association of Forensic Nurses. Retrieved 21 June 2010 from http://www.forensic nurse.org.

International Association of Forensic Nurses (2010b) *The IAFN 2010–2012 Strategic Plan*. Arnold, MD: Author.

Kelly, L. (1988) *Surviving Sexual Violence*. Minneapolis: University of Minnesota Press.

Kerstetter, W. (1990) 'Gateway to justice: police and prosecutor response to sexual assault against women', *Journal of Criminal Law and Criminology*, 81: 267–313.

Konradi, A. (2007) *Taking the Stand: Rape Survivors and the Prosecution of Rapists*. Westport, CT: Praeger.

Koss, M.P., Bailey, J.A., Yuan, N.P., Herrera, V.M. and Lichter, E.L. (2003) 'Depression and PTSD in survivors of male violence: Research and training initiatives to facilitate recovery', *Psychology of Women Quarterly*, 27: 130–42.

Koss, M.P., Gidycz, C.A. and Wisniewski, N. (1987) 'The scope of rape: Incidence and prevalence of sexual aggression and victimization in a national sample of higher education students', *Journal of Consulting and Clinical Psychology*, 55: 162–170.

Lang, K. (1999) *Sexual Assault Nurse Examiner Resource Guide for Michigan Communities*. Okemos, MI: Michigan Coalition against Domestic and Sexual Violence.

Ledray, L.E. (1999) *Sexual Assault Nurse Examiner (SANE) Development and Operations Guide*. Washington DC: Office for Victims of Crime, US Department of Justice.

Ledray, L. (1996) 'The sexual assault resource service: A new model of care', *Minnesota Medicine*, 79: 43–5.

Ledray, L. and Simmelink, K. (1997) 'Efficacy of SANE evidence collection: A Minnesota study', *Journal of Emergency Nursing*, 23: 75–7.

Littel, K. (2001) 'Sexual assault nurse examiner programs: Improving the community response to sexual assault victims', *Office for Victims of Crime Bulletin*, 4: 1–19.

Logan, T., Cole, J. and Capillo, A. (2007) 'Sexual assault nurse examiner program characteristics, barriers, and lessons learned', *Journal of Forensic Nursing*, 3: 24–34.

Logan, T., Evans, L., Stevenson, E. and Jordan, C.E. (2005) 'Barriers to services for rural and urban survivors of rape', *Journal of Interpersonal Violence*, 20: 591–616.

Martin, P.Y. (2005) *Rape Work: Victims, Gender, and Emotions in Organization and Community Context*. New York: Routledge.

Martin, P.Y. and Powell, R.M. (1994) 'Accounting for the "second assault": Legal organizations' framing of rape victims', *Law and Social Inquiry*, 19: 853–90.

Monroe, L.M., Kinney, L.M., Weist, M.D., Dafeamekpor, D.S., Dantzler, J. and Reynolds, M.W. (2005) 'The experience of sexual assault: Findings from a statewide victim needs assessment', *Journal of Interpersonal Violence*, 20, 767–77.

National Victims Center (1992) *Rape in America: A Report to the Nation*. Arlington, VA: Author.

Patterson, D., Greeson, M.R. and Campbell, R. (2009) 'Protect thyself: Understanding rape survivors' decisions not to seek help from social systems', *Health and Social Work*, 34: 127–36.

Resnick, H.S., Holmes, M.M., Kilpatrick, D.G., Clum, G., Acierno, R., Best, C.L. and Saunders, B.E. (2000) 'Predictors of post-rape medical care in a national sample of women', *American Journal of Preventive Medicine*, 19: 214–9.

Rogers, E.M. (2003) *Diffusion of Innovations* (5th edn). New York: The Free Press.

Rossi, P.H., Lipsey, M.W. and Freeman, H.E. (2004) *Evaluation: A Systematic Approach* (7th edition). Thousand Oaks, CA: Sage.

Sievers, V., Murphy, S. and Miller, J. (2003) 'Sexual assault evidence collection more accurate when completed by sexual assault nurse examiners: Colorado's experience', *Journal of Emergency Nursing*, 29: 511–14.

Smugar, S.S., Spina, B.J. and Merz, J.F. (2000) 'Informed consent for emergency contraception: Variability in hospital care of rape victims', *American Journal of Public Health*, 90: 1372–6.

Spears, J. and Spohn, C. (1997) 'The effect of evidence factors and victim characteristics on prosecutors' charging decisions in sexual assault cases', *Justice Quarterly*, 14: 501–24.

Spohn, C., Beichner, D. and Davis-Frenzel, E. (2001) 'Prosecutorial justifications for sexual assault case rejection: Guarding the "gateway to justice"', *Social Problems*, 48: 206–35.

Starzynski, L.L., Ullman, S.E., Filipas, H.H. and Townsend, S.M. (2005) 'Correlates of women's sexual assault disclosure to informal and formal support sources', *Violence and Victims*, 20: 417–32.

Stone, W.E., Henson, V.H. and McLaren, J.A. (2006) 'Law enforcement perceptions of sexual assault nurses in Texas', *The Southwest Journal of Criminal Justice*, 3: 103–26.

Taylor, W.K. (2002) 'Collecting evidence for sexual assault: the role of the sexual assault nurse examiner (SANE)', *International Journal of Gynecology and Obstetrics*, 78: S91–S94.

Tjaden, P. and Thoennes, N. (1998) *Full Report of the Prevalence, Incidence, and Consequences of Violence Against Women: Findings From the National Violence Against Women Survey*. Washington, DC: National Institute of Justice.

Ullman, S.E. (1996) 'Do social reactions to sexual assault victims vary by support provider?', *Violence and Victims*, 11: 143–56.

Ullman, S.E. and Filipas, H.H. (2001a) 'Correlates of formal and informal support seeking in sexual assault victims', *Journal of Interpersonal Violence*, 16: 1028–47.

Ullman, S.E. and Filipas, H.H. (2001b) 'Predictors of PTSD symptom severity and social reactions in sexual assault victims', *Journal of Traumatic Stress*, 14: 369–89.

Voelker, R. (1996) 'Experts hope team approach will improve the quality of rape exams', *Journal of the American Medical Association*, 275: 973–4.

Yin, R.K. (2009) *Case Study Research: Design and Methods* (4th edn). Thousand Oaks, CA: Sage.

Young, W., Bracken, A., Goddard, M. and Matheson, S. (1992) 'Sexual assault: Review of a national model protocol for forensic and medical evaluation', *Obstetrics and Gynecology*, 80: 878–83.

# Chapter 22

# Practitioner commentary: response from South Essex Rape and Incest Crisis Centres (SERICC) Home Office Women's Focus Group

*Sheila Coates*

## Meet Sheila Coates

Sheila Coates, BA Women's Studies (Hons), MBE is the Director of South Essex Rape and Incest Crisis Centre (SERICC) and a member of the Policy and Strategy Group of Rape Crisis England and Wales (RCEW).

Sheila has 27 years of experience and knowledge of providing front-line services and strategic planning with regard to violence against women and girls services. She is a founder member of SERICC and co-founder of Thurrock Women's Aid; both charities are based in Essex and continue to provide effective services 27 years on from their inception.

Her role in formulating sexual violence policy and strategy on behalf of RCEW is well established and acknowledged by both Rape Crisis member organisations, ministers and officials in various government departments.

Prior to her current role, Sheila worked for a local refuge, undertaking 24-hour emergency call-out duty (1984–88) while also undertaking sexual violence counselling and organisational development work in a voluntary capacity for SERICC. She took up the lead role within SERICC in 1988 where she continued working as a qualified counsellor. In 1998 she successfully completed a women's studies degree at the University of East London.

In 2008 she was awarded an MBE for her work with women's issues and she was also presented with a Lifetime Achievement Award from her local authority, and a Black History Month Achievement Award from the local authority Black History Month celebrations.

She has also represented Rape Crisis England and Wales at the United Nations Commission on the Elimination of Discrimination against Women

(CEDAW) in 2008 and has chaired the Women's National Commission Sexual Violence group from 2008–2010.

## Introduction

It is vital that the formulation of women-centred strategy and policy hears and integrates the voices of victims/survivors and draws on the experience of frontline women centred service providers who acknowledge the continuum of violence in the lives of women and girls. All too often the focus of government and academia can be led by political positioning, gender-neutral theory or a misconception that policy initiatives will work in practice at a grass roots level; for example the Labour Government's continual heavy focus on developing a single-incident criminal justice response in the form of sexual assault referral centres (SARC) and independent sexual violence advisers (ISVA). These criminal justice single incident responses which are often badged as Co-ordinated Community Responses continue to be rolled out at the expense of the front-line specialist sexual violence women's sector and have created a hierarchy of 'victimhood' and need between women and girls who engage with the criminal justice system and those that don't.

South Essex Rape and Incest Crisis Centre (SERICC) opened as a registered charity in 1984. SERICC has provided sexual violence counselling on over 60,000 occasions and has a history of prioritising organisational activism in parallel with individual support and advocacy for women and girls who have experienced sexual violence at any time in their lives.

On 9 March 2009 the Home Office launched a cross-government consultation on Violence against Women and Girls in England. To inform this consultation the Home Office commissioned the Women's National Commission (WNC) to negotiate a number of focus groups in partnership with women's services with the aim of gathering the views of women and girls who have reported sexual violence to the police and of those who have chosen not to report.

The extracts that follow are taken directly from SERICC's service users' comments expressed at the SERICC Home Office focus group held in September 2009. The full focus group reports – *A Bitter Pill to Swallow* and *Still We Rise* (January 2010) – are available from the Women's National Commission website www.thewnc.org.uk

## The victims/survivors' voice and experience

- *Decisions to report*

  My dad abused all three of us. My middle sister got the worst of it; he used to kick the shit out of her, like a football. My mam was never in the house, she left us with him. He locked me in the house for 2 years, from when I was 11, until I was 13. He brought us over to my uncle's house to abuse us. But you get to a point where you think you're not going to destroy me. I tried to kill myself a couple of times when I was younger,

I've had no help to get over this. The kids' dad nearly destroyed me as well when I got into domestic violence, and I thought no, you're not going to destroy me this time sweetheart, no way. I've got 5 kids, I'm not being destroyed. It was women's services that helped me get through. I went to a women's refuge, then got support from SERICC.

I pray to god it doesn't, but if it happened to me again, I would never, ever report. If it happened to my family or any of my friends I would advise them not to report. I have suffered more as a result of reporting, I wish I had never reported. I would have tried to deal with it on my own.

After reporting I feel I don't live a lie anymore, I have lived a lie from when I was that high, with a brother that sexually abused me until I left home. Now that I have reported, I'm not living a lie. My partner would tell you that there was something not quite right in our family. One of us self harmed, I did everything for a quiet life. My sister just spent and spent. I have lost a lot because of this; I've lost my mum, my sister, my brother, all because I took it to court. But I would still do the same again. It's a problem when girls are reporting rape at 13, 14, 15, 16 but they're considered to have given consent, they're not taken seriously.

- **Postcode lottery of support**

  I just think it's a lottery depending on where you live. I was lucky, my doctor was very supportive, and he referred me to SERICC [South Essex Rape and Incest Crisis Centre]. SERICC were the ones who actually reported it to the police for me, with my permission. But my brother and sister have had no support, just 6 weeks of counselling. They have had nothing. It's a lottery depending on the service you go to, my doctor's surgery have been brilliant, so have SERICC, they have supported me, I wouldn't be who I am today without them. Whereas, my brother and sister and the other victims have had no support. Out of 5 victims, only one of us has had support, and that is because I live in this area and they live in another.

- **Police response**

  *Good and bad police experiences*

  I have had some good and bad experiences, I'm sorry if I cry I find it all quite emotional. I was sexually abused by two men from a baby until I was nearly 15 years old. My sister was abused as well, and she was the one who was brave enough to tell my mum. I didn't live with my mum when I was growing up, I lived with my nan, we didn't get on and I was quite a problem child, because of what I was experiencing. My mum turned me away. When my sister told her about what was happening, she believed my sister but she didn't believe me, she told me I was attention seeking. The police and social services were called. I didn't have to go to court, because my dad admitted what he had done to me and my sister. When the police came, they were really nice, we had to go for medical examinations, they were lovely. Social services were nice as well, but I felt that I was the one to blame, so I discontinued counselling. I wasn't getting any support from my mum, and my grandparents, who were like a mum and dad to me, passed away. But I didn't get any help. Later I tried to commit suicide, they wanted to put me in a mental health ward but I refused to go, and my doctor fought for me. I didn't get any help when I was raped again when I was 24. The police were quite good on this occasion but I was never offered any kind of help afterwards. It took the police 7–8 months to come and take a statement, then I made a complaint, and then I had to make a complaint about the fucking complaint! He was still walking the streets. If anybody touched my daughter, I wouldn't go to the police.

*Lack of confidence in the police – disparity of police responses*
If you could have some confidence that you would get the same treatment wherever you lived, then perhaps more people would come forward. It's only a week since my daughter was raped, and the disparity, even in the South East, I'm shocked at how different it can be. People who report to the police don't know what to expect, they are relying on them, they are relying on their integrity, and in our experience integrity is not there in many police forces in this country.

*Victim's feeling of isolation and being judged*
The person who went with my daughter when she reported her rape was made to leave the room. She was left on her own at one of the most vulnerable times in her life to deal with loads of questions. If somebody had been with her, perhaps they wouldn't have told her that nobody would believe her because she had been drinking, and asked whether she really wanted to be poked and prodded for hours on end. Perhaps they would have said, hang on, don't talk to her like that. There has to be some way of making sure the victim knows that what is happening to them is normal or not. Women need a specialist women's service to support them when they report. I and my daughter have never had any experience of this, until now, from getting support from rape crisis.

*Inappropriate police responses*
There is no prioritising of women's safety by the police. It was the rape trained response officer, a police woman, who knocked my daughter back after she'd been gang raped, she persuaded her not to give evidence, said she had been drinking so no one would believe her. And she was trained! It's only by going through the Haven and engaging with Sapphire that anything has happened, when the police found out we had gone to the Haven they were furious, tried to sabotage the whole thing. The detective investigating the case said he had spoken to their rape response officer and reminded her that she needs to put the victims needs first, which starts with believing the victim. Why does a rape response officer need to be told they should 'believe the victim'? We went to the police station the following day, and my daughter shrank back in her chair, and said, that's the officer who dealt with me. This stroppy little mare was dealing with a member of the public who was deeply distressed, psychotic or something, she was covered in blood. This officer just grabbed her, shoved her into a back room and came out

a few minutes later and she screamed, why do I always end up dealing with these people? In a waiting room full of members of the public. This woman obviously has a bad day every day.

*Minimising the seriousness of rape. Compulsory police training*
My daughter is a 5 foot 1, she's size 6, there's nothing of her. She got away from 3 men, I'll never know how she did it, she ran through a house, over a fence 8 foot high. She was in a terrible mess. The police did a cursory drive around; they knocked on two doors, and then said they were never going to find them. Their attitude is, it's a university town, if we worked on all of these things we would never stop working on suspected rape cases. My ex husband travelled to the place it happened – 3 days running around and knocked on every door. He has picked up witnesses, who saw my daughter screaming in the street, who saw the men driving off and picking her back up again, and dragging her back into the car. Other than that there wouldn't be a case because the police have done nothing. Every police force should have the same procedure and have compulsory training, it should be nationalised so that all women know what to expect from the police if they report rape.

*Positive police response*
The police where I was living in London were great, couldn't fault them. I reported in Hackney where my sister lives, 2 PCs came out and they thought it was just domestic violence, and I told them what happened and then they called someone else out from Waltham Forest where it happened. Two policemen came out and they stayed with me the whole time, I reported at 7pm, and they were supposed to finish their shift at 9pm and they stayed with me until 2am. They drove me to the Sapphire unit, they made sure I got in, the lady who met me at the unit was brilliant as well, she asked me some questions and then she drove me back to my sister's at 4am the next morning. Before I reported my rape I lived with my ex partner, I never reported because police just viewed it as a domestic, they said there was nothing they could do, they told me to sort it out yourself. Slowly things are changing; it used to be that they would just let them out in 2 hours and they would come back to get you. I was told 'no one would believe you'. You start to believe them.

My mum came with me, and the lady from Sapphire, who was lovely, she sat with my mum to make sure she was ok. Being able to have a shower, and nice toiletries, and they chat to you about your kids, it just makes it less of an ordeal. It should be available for everyone. I think it's the best thing that has happened for rape victims.

- **The marginalisation of victims'/survivors' needs**
  I worked in a prison; perpetrators are treated so well in prison. Human rights have gone mad; they are given more rights than the actual victim. I was sexually abused, I'm 36 now, and I'm still suffering from the effects. You get a few months put on the sex offenders register, for what? They get protection, who is giving us protection? In prison I used to work alongside these people, you see the grin on their faces, there is no rehabilitation. You see the same faces every time. My dad interfered with

me for years from 6 months old, my dad got 3 years, and he served 18 months. I've got a lifetime.

- *Dealing with court case*
  The police were great right up until the court case; then I felt like I was a villain and he was the victim. They asked my sister not to have screens round on the day we went to court. She is quite fiery; they said it would look better if she didn't have screens up. I said it's not a circus. My partner wasn't allowed in the court, it's a crown court anyone can go in. That's when I would fault the police, the trial. Up until then, they were great.

- *Sentencing*
  They need to review the sentencing. You go through years of abuse. You get 10 years for fraud. Are our lives worth less than money?

  A sentence should be a sentence; you shouldn't be allowed to get out on good behaviour, and given new identities. We need higher sentences.

- *Inadequate statutory responses*
  I asked for a security button and bars on the windows after he got out last year, but I was completely banned from going to London for about 4 months. My sister went to my house to pick up my post and it was smashed up. I asked for help so I could stay in my own home, they said if you don't move, your kids are gone. It's like I've done something wrong. They wonder why you don't report. It's not just the police, it's all of them, social services, housing, it's the whole response. I couldn't get any safe housing because I'd been raped.

- *Supportive response*
  I was lucky, I had support in the court from a women's service and they were lovely. I wasn't brought through the main entrance, I was brought in the side entrance which meant I didn't risk bumping into him or anyone connected to him, which was good. It was a closed court. I had a screen up, I said I'll give evidence but I want a screen. I went into the court first and then he was brought in, and then he left and then I was brought out. But my sister had to face him give evidence in front of him and he started taking the piss out of her. The judge warned him, and told his barrister to tell him to stop. She should have been given the option of a screen, she tried to kill him and then he tried to kill her and her daughter. He threatened to kill my two eldest boys as well, but this wasn't taken into account. It was just luck that he got 8 years, the judge put the maximum sentence on him; he is so dangerous. Armed police had to arrest him.

- *Screens in court*
  Screen or no screen you know they are there.

Women said they wanted the following, in particular, to change and improve services for women:

- **Male/female officers**

  There really could be females all the way through. It's simple things like, a male liaison officer returned my clothes, I don't particularly want them but he knocked on the door. There he was, holding up my underwear, ticking it off. It was awful. Females all the way through the system are desperately needed. Then again, some female officers can be right bitches towards you. Some male police officers can be great though. One of my officers was great. He told me he would get him and make sure he went down, and he did. Everybody has good and bad in them.

- **Mandatory police training**

  I want mandatory training for all law enforcement officers. So at least they have an inkling, if there is a rape they have some knowledge of how to go about it. They faff about, you are already depressed, you are already terrified. Mandatory training for all police; basic common sense. It doesn't take much. Everybody reacts differently, just because I'm not crying doesn't mean I'm not hurting. From what I've seen, these paedophiles, these rapists know more about the system than we do. Lawyers talk down to you, la de da, I'm not illiterate, I'm not stupid, I'm just stressed.

- **BME women's needs**

  In Asian communities, it's really shut away. There is this idea that you can deal with rape in the community. If you keep it inside the family, patterns repeat themselves. Asian doctors adhere to the view that children should keep quiet, parents know best. If we're going to work within communities we need to be sensitive, disbelief is common. There needs to be somewhere to go, like a refuge, specialist women's services. It's not safe leaving it with family members or reporting to the police, women end up committing suicide because they haven't got access to specialist women's services and BME women's services.

- **Effectiveness of the law**

  Many women are affected by the changes in the new laws – but in practice we haven't really seen any changes at all. The law is good enough, it's who is implementing that law.

- **Specialised women's services**

  There has to be help along the way, we need help immediately, from specialist women's services, not just a phone call in 6 months to say the case has got to court. There has to be more done for the women; and children too, because they are victims as well, but the court don't see it like that.

  I need closure, I wouldn't be able to report, I haven't got the courage or the strength. I just know I wouldn't. The person who abused me has got away with it, and he has got children, and I can't have children because of what happened to me. I just couldn't do it though, I couldn't sit there in court, with him staring at me, knowing what he did to me. Only one person in my life knows what happened to me, that is my husband. My family don't know. And there is no support for women like me. Except for from women's services. I'm not going to go anywhere else for help. And there are loads of women like me.

Six sessions of counselling is not enough. We need safe women-only services for women who've been abused; many women don't report to the police or won't ever go to health or other services. More women's services are needed so that these women can get help.

## Provision

All statutory services require a culture change where women and girls are not disbelieved or seen as to blame for violence perpetrated against them. Women are as concerned with how a service is delivered as with what is being delivered, and want to be treated with dignity and respect whomever they came into contact with. Existing legislation, strategies, policies and action plans developed to address different forms of violence against women and girls need to be effectively and consistently co-ordinated, implemented and monitored across the country. All services and partnerships should be required to prioritise the safety of women and girls at all stages of intervention, and to provide effective, co-ordinated and well-resourced approaches to ending violence against women and girls.

## Prevention

Prevention work needs to be undertaken on a societal, institutional, community and individual level that also addresses the multiple forms of inequality different groups of women experience because of their ethnicity, age, sexuality, disability, gender identity, religion or belief. Government needs to invest in a sustained national high-profile multimedia awareness campaign to educate the public on what constitutes violence against women and girls and the help available, to challenge perpetrators' attitudes to, and use of, violence and to reduce social tolerance of violence against women and girls. A co-ordinated response is needed between statutory and voluntary agencies so that all women who experience violence but who have no recourse to public funds have equal access to protection and can access safety, support and living expenses to minimise their dependence on their abusers.

Finally, any strategy on violence against women and girls needs to establish and implement a comprehensive legislative, policy and service framework to prevent violence against women and girls, and be underpinned by clear responsibilities, targets and review mechanisms, and sustainable resources for national and local specialist services for women and children experiencing violence and abuse.

**Key recommendations**

1.  Specialist police officers and prosecutors trained on all forms of violence against women should be available in every area, and systems also need to be introduced to enable anonymous third-party reporting in neighbourhoods and communities.

2.  Court services need to ensure consistent access to safety mechanisms and special measures to help women and girls give evidence in cases of violence and abuse. Women need to be regularly updated about the progress of their case, and cases of rape and sexual violence should be fast-tracked.

3.  Probation and prison officers in women's prisons need to be trained on violence against women and girls, to enable them to ask women about experiences of abuse on entry to the prison; to deliver discussion groups on violence prevention and the help available, and publicise services available on their release into the community.

4.  Women's services that are independent of statutory provision and that specialise in responding to violence against women need to be available in every area. These services need to be accessible for the most marginalised and vulnerable women, and provide timely, safe services that respond to complex and multiple needs, which focus on women's safety and empowerment without labelling or judging women or limiting the service to times of crisis or high risk.

5.  Statutory agencies, partnerships and service commissioners need to recognise the crucial role of specialist women's services and BME women's services in providing longer-term therapeutic and group support for women and girls, which in turn promotes women's self-esteem and empowerment as a means of preventing violence in the short and longer term.

6.  Health services (such as health visitors, GPs, practice nurses, A & E consultants, midwives, dentists, opticians, sexual health and psychiatric services), social services, community mental health and drug and alcohol rehabilitation services should be required to routinely ask about violence as part of existing procedures and be trained to respond effectively on disclosure, referring to specialist support services where necessary.

7.  Health professionals should be trained to identify girls at risk of female genital mutilation (FGM) and to respond sensitively and appropriately to women who have undergone FGM. Health services should employ professionals who can speak community languages to avoid the use of interpreters.

8.  GP surgeries need to play a greater role in identifying and responding to violence against women and girls, including the on-site provision of information and support for survivors provided by specialist women's services.

9.  The Department of Health should run a national public health campaign on identifying and preventing all forms of violence against women and girls.

10. Women and girls who experience child sexual abuse need access to

support as children and as adults, to aid their recovery and to minimise its devastating impact in later life. All professionals who work with children and young people should be trained in identifying and responding appropriately to violence against women and girls, particularly childhood sexual abuse.

11. Social services should adopt a believing stance on disclosure of violence and provide support to women in response. For those women who are mothers social services should focus on the mother's safety as a means of safeguarding and protecting children and young people from harm.

12. Publicity campaigns need to be accessible, to target specific communities and groups, and to address all forms of violence against women and girls. Specialist women's services should be involved in the development of campaign materials.

13. Statutory services (health, justice system, local government and local strategic partnerships) should address all forms of violence against women and girls through effective leadership, training, policy and performance standards, as part of their statutory duty to comply with public sector equality duties. Their work on the prevention of violence against women and girls should be measured in terms of increasing women's safety, empowerment, and access to specialist women's support services.

14. Men need to be engaged to speak out against violence against women and girls and to take an active part in the prevention of violence against women and girls.

15. Schools should be required to introduce a 'whole school' approach to preventing violence against women and girls which includes implementing policies to address violence, gender bullying and sexual harassment, and the compulsory teaching of violence against women prevention within a gender equality framework, from a very early age.

16. Every school should have a lead professional responsible for policy and training on violence against women and girls prevention, and disseminating information to others about training, guidance and services available.

### References

Women's National Commission (WNC) (January 2010) *A Bitter Pill to Swallow*. Report from the WNC Focus Groups to inform the Department of Health Taskforce on the Health Aspects of Violence against Women and Girls.

Women's National Commission (WNC) (January 2010) *Still We Rise*. Report from the WNC Focus Groups to inform the Cross-Government Consultation 'Together We Can End Violence against Women and Girls'.

### Web resources

South Essex Rape and Incest Crisis Centre: www.sericc.org.uk
Rape Crisis England and Wales: www.rapecrisis.org.uk
The Women's National Commission: www.wnc.org.uk

# Conclusion: taking stock – *plus ça change, plus c'est la même chose?*

*Sandra Walklate and Jennifer Brown*

## Introduction

This collection has contextualised and documented a vast array of theoretical and policy developments that, over the past 30 years or so, have contributed to the shifting contours of how we think about sexual violence and what interventions might be deemed appropriate when responding to sexual violence. Yet despite the powerful influence of second-wave feminism (Chesney-Lind 2006) and the formative work of Kelly (1988), used as the organising conceptual framework for the work presented in this collection, Stanko (2007) observes that she experiences more continuity with the past than change. Mooney (2007) asks in respect to domestic violence how it is that this can be such a public anathema but at the same time a private commonplace. Of course in this collection we have been concerned not just with domestic violence, but a wider range of sexual violences experienced not only by women but also by men, children and people of different ethnicities and sexualities. In the light of the focus of this book, then, Mooney's question is an even more pertinent one.

Commenting in particular on the search for more democratic interpersonal relationships, Giddens (1991) suggested that this search marked the beginnings of women becoming increasingly less complicit in the power of the penis. Indeed there is evidence for a decline in this complicity documented in the chapters here, especially in women's changing willingness to report crimes to the police observed by Sylvia Walby, Jo Armstrong and Sofia Strid. It is also found in the work of, inter alia, Piipsa (2004) and Lewis (2004). Indeed decline in complicity might also be a reflection of a decline in the acceptability of sexual violence more generally. Yet the dilemmas posed by Stanko and Mooney, of how to make sense of the simultaneous continuing presence of both a wide range of policy activity directed towards such violence and relatively unchanging experience of it, alongside some of the observations by our contributors, remains. In this concluding chapter we endeavour to offer a framework for understanding why this dilemma still exists and what, if at all, remains to be done about it. In order to do this we shall first of all summarise the paramount messages of the preceding chapters.

Dempsey (2007) usefully reminds us that in 1994 the United Nations required member states to show 'due diligence' in punishing acts of violence against women. Indeed this requirement, alongside European human rights legislation, has afforded the opportunity for such violence to be put on the agenda in a meaningful way in some countries. Kelly (2005) herself observes feminist activists were hugely influential in pushing women's issues into the UN human rights agenda. However, as the UN group INSTRAW (2005) recognised, the challenge was, and still is, to shift behaviour. Brown *et al.* (2010) refer to this problem as the 'implementation gap' and some appreciation of its continued presence can be found in the contributions to Part One of this book.

The persistence of sexual violence, as D'Cruze so cogently argues, posits a considerable challenge to the 'civilising process' that is taken by Elias (1994) to mark the emergence of modern societies. The historical legacy that D'Cruze draws our attention to, a legacy replete with silencing mechanisms that were/ are also strongly marked by social class, overlaid by a legal (McGregor) and cultural (Wynne-Davies) heritage, facilitates our understanding of why problems of what counts and is counted as sexual violence (see also Walby, Armstrong and Strid) remain. Here we are reminded that notions of the deserving victim, victim-blaming, and the power still to despoil a woman's 'moral' character, have deep roots indeed; roots that we still see bearing fruit in understandings of rape (Jones, Jordan), domestic violence (Westmarland) and prostitution (Phoenix). The need for 'required force' and an absence of consent in cases of rape, changes in the law notwithstanding, as McGregor points out, 'has not demanded enough of men's behaviour'. One is left asking the question, how far have we moved on from being 'thrown down' (D'Cruze) as the framework for understanding sanctioned as well as unauthorised sexual behaviour. An appreciation of the importance of historical context afforded by the chapters of D'Cruze and McGregor illustrates the intractability of sexual violence (including presumptions of who are the legitimate victims and offenders, an issue that is developed by Hoel and Duncan) despite evolving understandings of sexuality and sexual norms. These historical traces resonate down the centuries and remain with us today, referred to here as the 'implementation gap'. Walby *et al.* in this volume also discuss the 'justice gap'. The question of this 'gap' is the first thematic issue that we need to consider and we shall illustrate it with reference to responses to rape.

## The problems and possibilities of the 'implementation gap'

In a review conducted by Brown *et al.* (2010) to support Baroness Stern's investigation into rape in England and Wales (Stern 2010) they articulate three distinct phases of concern and reform with respect to sexual violence in the modern period, i.e. 1982–1998; 1999–2009; 2010 onwards. The first phase was marked by Roger Graef's documentary on Thames Valley Police about the oppressive interviewing of a rape victim (discussed in the chapter by Horvath and Yexley, who show how this was instrumental in leading to a programme of reform within policing and elsewhere). These reforms included improved police training such as sexual offence investigative trained officers (SOITs), changes in the law and introduction of sexual offences referral centres (SARCs). Harris and Grace (1999) examined the results of these innovations only to discover they had had relatively little impact. The second phase (1999–2009) also saw a flurry of activity that included the introduction of consolidating legislation, the Sexual Offences Act of 2003 that attempted some clarification around the question of consent. In addition, Her Majesty's Inspectorate of Constabulary (HMIC) and the Crown Prosecution Service (CPS) undertook a review of rape (HMIC/CPS 2002) again to find inconsistent rape recording practices, problems in police investigations, and failure to allocate special prosecutors to cases. A subsequent CPS review conducted in 2007 reported:

> The introduction of STO role, SARCs, WCUs and CPS rape co-ordinators, specialist lawyers and specialist case workers is, without doubt, leading to improvements in the CJS response to rape cases and a more professional approach to the treatment and care of victim-survivors. However 'intention' is not yet translating into fully effective practice on the ground, and several fundamental difficulties persist that are constraining the potential for more significant and sustained improvement.
>
> (p. 21)

A number of high-profile failures by the Metropolitan Police to investigate rape allegations properly, discussed in the introduction to this book, contributed to Harriet Harman, deputy leader of the Government of the day, commissioning the Stern Review (Stern 2010) and so marked a third phase of review and reform.

What then accounts for this cycle in which often a scandal triggers renewal of concern about sexual violence, and another round of commissioned reports that make much the same recommendations as those conducted previously? In his analysis of the problem, John Yates, then Association of Chief Police Officers (ACPO) lead on sexual crime, declared, 'We are policy-rich and implementation-poor' (*The Guardian*, 26 March 2009). This is a theme picked up by Baroness Stern in her review in which she observes that despite some improvement in practice and an improving prosecution rate, rape and sexual assault remain intensely problematic crimes.

So whilst there has been a great deal of problem description and analysis, as witnessed by a plethora of reports and policy innovation in the form of law reform and changes in practice, sexual violence remains under-reported, underinvestigated and underprosecuted, with patchy service provision in the form of SARCs or health care. Implementation failure is one of three suggested reasons why reforms fail (Lewis and Greene 1978). The other two reasons are programme overexpectation and conceptual failure, the latter occurring when a reform project is based on inaccurate or incomplete theory of causation. We can see evidence within this collection and elsewhere that responses to sexual violence fail on all three counts.

For example in understanding the policy implementation process, Rein (1983) argues that not only are there different constituencies calling for better co-ordination, their reasons for doing so vary, for example, efficiency, accessibility, advocacy, and/or participation. This variety and consequent lack of clarity about purpose (consider the continuing lack of common definition of domestic violence between the various agencies responding to it) contributes to what Lewis and Greene (1978) identify as reform overexpectation. In the absence of clarity, operationalising or prioritising change becomes confusing and unfocused. Rein (1983) adds that implementation requires practitioners to change their daily behaviour and Lewis and Greene (1978) also propose that implementation requires changes in the internal environment. The HMIC/CPS reviews referred to here, and the work of the IPCC into failed enquiries discussed in the Introduction, show that there is ample evidence for a mindset among criminal justice professionals that disbelieves women when they are reporting allegations of sexual violence under circumstances they – police and prosecutors – find unconvincing.

In a similar vein, Mike Shiner (2010) discusses the Metropolitan Police's reaction to the charge of institutional racism made by Lord Macpherson in his inquiry into their investigation of the murder of Stephen Lawrence. Shiner agrees with Savage (2003) that the British police service are especially adept at undermining, withstanding and inverting externally imposed change. Shiner argues that police officers were affronted by the charge which they took very personally. As a consequence they engaged in a series of denial or displacement strategies to avoid serious critical analysis of what Macpherson meant or how to remedy the problem of racism. Shiner suggests the police's institutional response to Macpherson's recommendations was to adapt, subvert or rebrand in order to try and offset the telling off they received. We might apply a similar analysis to the police's response to recommendations concerning sexual violence. Examination of the IPCC's findings in relation to failed investigations reveals examples of denial of women's allegations in preference to the accounts provided by male suspects. Recent publicity surrounding the behaviour of the Met's Sapphire officers (a unit dedicated to the investigation of sexual crime) shows some interference with women complainants' statements and a subversion of process. Shiner proposes that having such reactions in the face of criticism is realistic, which policy innovation should recognise and account for. In the case of racism, Shiner suggests that officers participate in restorative forums that confront them with the harmful consequences of their actions in a way which makes it difficult to negate. Perhaps such an innovation may be applied to policing sexual violence to overcome the continued no criming or taking no further action when allegations are made.

The HMIC/CPS litany of failed implementation also implies a conceptual failure, as suggested by Lewis and Greene. Helen Jones argues in her chapter, 'if existing theories of violence were too limited (and there is little doubt of that) and if the different expressions of sexual violence are connected (and there is little doubt about that) then what is needed is a connected approach that goes beyond current provisions.' If we add to this, the problems of attrition and conviction that are discussed in detail by Walby *et al.*, all lend support to Smart's (1989) observations on the power of phallocentrism and clearly suggest that the problems of both definition and understanding of sexual violence remain. This problem is considered from a number of different theoretical perspectives in Part Two of this book.

Whilst each of our contributors addresses the problem of definition differently, they all point to its contested nature. Vetere's work is appreciative of understanding the specificities of the context in which violence occurs for all those party to it. This stands somewhat in contrast to the socio-structural approach adopted by Jones. Yet all are agreed that lack of clarity on definitions compounds problems of measurement (see also Walby *et al.*) and contributes to what is considered normal and/or abnormal for both victims and perpetrators. This is a point made in different ways by Jones. She makes the case for extending our appreciation of sexual violence to include that perpetrated in times of conflict and war. Brown unpicks the normal/abnormal axis for our understandings of perpetrators and the associated demonisation of offenders (an issue which is also taken up later in the collection by Steph Petrie observing that vitriol is saved for the female sexual offender). Kemshall and Phoenix challenge some key assumptions about the relationship between sex and economics that also challenge what counts as normal. All in their different ways add to Kelly's (1988) concept of a continuum, either in breadth or depth and, by implication, point to its continuing conceptual power. For our contributors the 'everyday, routine, mundane (sexual) intrusions' (Kelly, Preface to this volume) have not fallen off their agendas. Nevertheless tensions do remain. Several of the Handbook authors are troubled by the definition of sexual violence offered by Kelly as it focuses on women and children as the targets of the violence and men as its perpetrators. There are elements that are sustainable, i.e. the notion of frequency as a characteristic of sexually violent behaviours and the harm rendered but we offer the following reworking of Kelly to encompass the extended range of sexual violence's purview taken by the present contributors. Sexual violence then is defined in terms of *the frequency (either high or low) with which any act having explicit or implicit sexual content comprising any actual or threatened behaviour, verbal or non-verbal aimed at an individual that (in)directly hurts, degrades, frightens or controls her/him at the time of the act or at any time in the future.*

It is possible to assess the contribution of each of the chapters to this volume in different ways but, arguably, taken together, they make the case for understanding the 'lived reality' of sexual violence not dissimilar to that made by both Kelly (1988) and Genn (1988). Whether exploring particular acts of sexual violence, or responses to such violence, appreciating the lived reality of both victims and perpetrators is perhaps central to making the shift in attitudes and behaviour commented on by INSTRAW, and a constituent element to the problem of implementation failure discussed above. The 'lived reality' of sexual violence that Kelly's work was so concerned to capture is also that which the criminal justice process still struggles with the most, as Kelly herself observes in the Preface to this volume. This is especially the case when the parties concerned are likely to be known to each other. That which takes place in private, its contested, intimate and potentially embarrassing sexual nature, alongside the perceived gender differentials in consequences, all contribute to difficulties in reporting, recording and successfully prosecuting such cases. Moreover, as Kelly comments in the Preface, if we take both gender and intersectionality on board then to speak out at all can create further problems, risks and dangers. The prime example here would be so-called 'honour' crimes. Indeed in a recent study by Weiss (2010: 304) she comments on the power of shame for both male and female victims that results in the fact that 'many victims tell no one about what happened, even their own family and friends, hindering a significant source of emotional support that can help with recovery after crime'. This is a finding that echoes the observations made by Jan Jordan in this collection on how victims can be differently silenced. In restating the case for an appreciation of the 'lived reality' of sexual violence our contributors also reassert the significance of Kelly's conceptual invention of the notion of a continuum of sexual violence. Yet the implementation focus still reflects a failure to grasp sexual violence in this way.

Kelly's continuum alerts us to the frequency of sexual violence's occurrence as common rather than rare and to the high levels of unreported incidences of such violence. Also key to this continuum is the idea that sexual violence arises out of the normal routines of everyday life, the purpose of which is to exert control, most often by men over women, but as this collection illustrates not exclusively, either by extremes of violence or by 'sexual innuendo' (see Chapters 8 and 18 by Jones and by Hoel and Lewis). The theoretical chapters in Part Two offer particular ways in which Kelly's conceptualisation may be used and extended to contextualise and connect with understandings of sexual violence more generally. Thus Jo Phoenix's analysis of sexual violence within prostitution challenges the concept of consent by introducing the notion of choice: the choice made to conduct an impersonal commercial transaction, i.e. selling sex. This kind of conceptual extension enables us to map the consequences of sexual violence in the light of the degree of control women may have and the choices they make, both of which may lead to a range of different outcomes. Choice is taken here to mean an internal state where the external expression of agreement (or not), verbal or non-verbal, may be congruent or incongruent with each other. Figure C.1 offers an illustration of this.

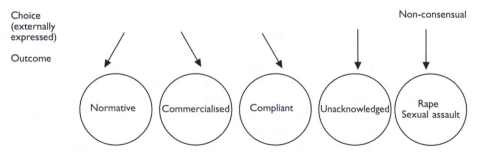

**Figure C.1** Different outcomes of sexual behaviours

The anchor points are the most straightforward and easily recognisable: mutually agreed sex and coerced sex under duress. It is the incongruent pairings that are the more problematic to interpret, for example a 15-year-old wanting sex cannot legally consent and thus the intercourse is unlawful; a sexually active woman who may not be inclined to have sex with her partner on the occasion of his returning home drunk but complies because of the possibility of other consequences is unlikely to define this as rape (Clarke *et al.* 2002). These different pathways can help to account for the large number of unreported sexual assaults from the unwanted and unacknowledged categories. They also point to the difficulties for prosecuting and investigating authorities in taking forward rape allegations in cases where there may be a degree of ambiguity about consent as a function of the combination of control and choice. Thus, taking on Phoenix's formulation of impersonalised commercial sex, this arises out of a choice women (or men) may make to engage in a commercially transacted sexual encounter, i.e. sex for money. So the decision to go into prostitution can be the result of intentional choice in which the sex is consensual but is clearly rather different from a mutually agreed romantic sexual encounter, or indeed sex as a consequence of trafficking. The absence of control and non-consensual sex leads more readily to the Estrich notion of 'real rape' (Estrich 1987) whilst the unwanted category maps onto the simple rape scenario that proves so problematic to police and prosecutors.

Thus more sophisticated and connected theorising, as called for by Kelly in the Preface, may create a stronger conceptual basis to develop policies and avoid implementation failure. This implies, as Helen Jones argues, redefining violence as a crime, extending what might be included in that redefinition (see for example the discussion of forced marriage and female genital mutilation by Walby *et al.*) and leads into an agenda for change that Sheila Coates's practitioner commentary eloquently asks for: mandatory training for all police officers; specialised services for victims of sexual violence; preventative strategies; co-ordination of responses; and sustained funding. If such pleadings are to successfully translate into policy, Rein (1983: 71) proposes incentivising those at the front line of implementation by sweetening reform with 'more funding and more comprehensive information'. This he argues is more likely to invoke support and co-operation from professionals than incur sabotage. Implementation viewed in this way becomes part of a policy practice continuum appropriately funded and focused in which the contending views of stakeholders are worked out at each stage. (This carries interesting implications on the need for a *continuum* in policy responses too.) However, as we have seen within this volume, many of our contributors have been concerned to document and comment on policy and practice responses to sexual violence, thus supporting the need to look for better means of implementation.

Horvath and Yexley, for example, document the extensive nature of policy and practical training changes that have been introduced in policing and McGregor notes the developments in relation to the law. Yet despite these interventions the silencing experienced by women, and some men, still persists. The observations of Jan Jordan and Sheila Coates are particularly powerful in this respect. However, if we look to policy responses outside of policing, Kate Cook on voluntary sector, Hazel Kemshall on criminal justice professional responses outwith policing, and Campbell on health professional responses, all point to the difficulties faced when such policy responses fail to appreciate the lived reality of violence. This is a lived reality that gives voice to some and not to others. Traditionally, those seen as legitimate victims are given a voice, a process that reflects all kinds of assumptions about who is more readily assigned victim status. As both Steph Petrie and David Shannon illustrate, the failure to appreciate the competencies of children in dealing with their experiences of exposure to sexual violence is a significant lacuna in all of the policy responses referred to here. Of course, for many professionals (and others), dealing with 'incidents' rather than 'processes', in a performance indicator driven culture, is not only easier, it is what is valued and what is rewarded. Leaving aside the way in which sexual violence is differently addressed dependent upon whether it is viewed as a criminal justice (Kemshall) issue or a health issue (Campbell), the importance of appreciating this wider policy context is commented on by Petrie, Horvath and Yexley, Kemshall and Westmarland. Thus it must be said that, whilst the police have been at the forefront concerning criticism in responding to sexual violence, they are not the only body to face the question of implementation failure.

To summarise, the breadth and depth of analysis offered by the contributors to this book conveys a number of messages: the influence of second-wave feminism as articulated by the intervention of Kelly; the persistent conceptual power of the deserving victim, victim-blaming, and associated processes of silencing; the recourse to violence primarily by men; and, despite a wealth of policy activity, the evidence that little progress seems to have been made in seriously changing behaviour. The question remains: why? In what follows we sketch out one way of making sense of the ambivalences that evidently remain towards sexual violence.

**Gender mainstreaming and gender violence**

One way of making sense of the issues presented in this book is to situate them within the broader context of gender mainstreaming. Given the importance of the role of international organisations like the United Nations and the European Community in endeavours to tackle gender inequalities (and that includes sexual violence) in their member organisations, this makes sense since it is through the conduit of gender mainstreaming that sexual violence has become a part of the agenda for these organisations. Indeed Walby (2009) argues that sexual violence is the fourth domain in which gender inequalities become institutionalised. Nancy Fraser (2009) posits that as a result of these activities, gender equality is now part of the social mainstream agenda but has yet to be realised in practice. Whilst Fraser (2009) is addressing a wide range of equality issues (unequal pay and so on), the gap between theory and practice that she comments on is very resonant of the observations made in the chapters of this book and the implementation process discussed above. However, in the light of the gap between theory and practice, her question is:

'is it possible that the cultural changes jump started by the second wave, salutary in themselves, have served to legitimate a structural transformation of capitalist society?' (*ibid.*: 99). As unpalatable as this question might appear to be, especially for those committed to the feminist movement, in asking it, we are forced to consider its implications as one way of making sense of the ambivalent relationship between what it is that is known about sexual violence and what it is that is done about such violence documented in this book.

In the context of debates around gender mainstreaming Walby (2005) reminds us that the terms themselves, gender equality and gender mainstreaming, represent a dualism. This dualism has embedded within it a number of policy possibilities in terms of process and outcome that reflect different models of equality: sameness, difference or transformation. These models of equality are familiar territory to feminist debate, but in the context of contemporary policy responses to sexual violence, it is possible to identify some of the tensions that gender mainstreaming and these different models of equality pose. At a fairly superficial level, but nonetheless significant, many public (and other) bodies have substituted the word gender for sex in such practices as how they survey their employees (asking such questions as what gender are you, followed by the options male or female!) as though this change in and of itself solves the gender inequality problem. At a deeper level, however, a change in terminology like this reflects an inability to grasp what the term gender actually means and thereby fails to recognise the possibilities of difference and transformation. Put simply it buys into 'one size fits all' policy responses. This is perhaps most usefully illustrated by the way in which risk and risk assessment practices (commented on in this volume by Kemshall and Westmarland) have spiralled up the policy agenda, not just for responding to offenders but also responding to 'at risk' victims.

Of course, as Robinson and Rowlands (2009: 191) suggest, risk assessment tools have their uses. They structure police response, aid resource allocation, and through information sharing raise awareness of safety issues for all concerned. However, the constraints imposed on these uses by the concept of risk itself need to be considered. As Robinson and Rowlands (2009) comment, risk assessment tools for 'at risk' victims implicitly reflect a normative heterosexism. This assumption includes and excludes all at the same time: a failure to recognise difference. In particular being identified 'at risk' has replaced an appreciation of cause and/or need understood in *context*. In other words not only does risk assessment erase individual experience situated within a particular socio-structural environment, it presumes all 'at risk' victims are the same. Thus the desire to prevent and extinguish interpersonal violence, especially partner violence, has proceeded to transpose *relationships*, which include, or once included, and may indeed continue to include, feelings like love and desire, into *risk factors* that can be measured and managed. (See also the discussion of risk assessment in Jennifer Brown's chapter in this book.) Such a transposition reflects the deeply embedded embrace of risk as a forensic concept (Douglas 1990) in which risk itself is understood as uniform and unifying (O'Malley 2006). Nowhere is this more the case than within the criminal justice process in which risk creep, and its material translation into risk assessment tools, serves to protect those charged with protecting us: the criminal justice professionals (see also Kemshall and Maguire 2001: 256).

Such risk creep also creates a degree of complacency as has been shown in recent cases investigated by the IPCC. In a recent case in Essex, IPCC Commissioner Len Jackson said:

> Our investigation found serious failings on the part of officers both individually and collectively in their response to allegations made by a highly vulnerable woman. Her serious allegations deserved a far more sympathetic, professional and determined response by Essex Police. A man has been imprisoned for a sexual assault, but it was only following the entreaties of the victim's family that a full criminal investigation was undertaken.
>
> We have substantiated a number of complaints made by the family including that the lack of positive action by officers was adversely influenced by the woman's mental health history. Police wrongly focused on the existence of a mental health condition, yet for instance failed to make arrangements for possible DNA evidence to be secured at the scene, despite the woman offering such evidence to the officers. I remain saddened for the victim and her family who have conducted themselves with great dignity throughout these protracted proceedings.
>
> The lack of help and support for this particular victim on two separate, traumatic occasions back in 2007 *did not stem from poor policies* – those policies, since updated, were in place. It stemmed from very poor policing and totally inadequate supervision. (emphasis added)

These words powerfully illustrate not only the problem of the implementation gap discussed above but also the problems that lie within presumptions of who and who is not 'at risk' and why. As an example it also adds some weight to the observations made by Walklate (2008: 48), who asked: 'who is imagined in the recourse to law as a response to violence against women?' She goes on to argue that,

> On the surface, it may appear that the needs of women as voiced by feminist campaigns have been so imagined. But have they? A deeper analysis might suggest that these imaginings have rather been the needs of the criminal justice process itself alongside those that inhabit this space.
>
> (Walklate 2008: 49)

In similar vein, by not only embracing risk assessment tools, but also demonstrating their deployment, it is possible for the criminal justice system and professionals to exhibit 'accountability' despite the shortcomings of that process. In this desire to demonstrate responsiveness and accountability, there is little space to accommodate the 'irrational life' of the individual; the kind of life that fails to fit with the expectations of the professional. The use of risk in this way integrates gender as a concern but fails to transform understandings of gender and thus simultaneously serves to deny difference and complex inequalities. It also reflects a tendency not to listen to women themselves and to appreciate the lived reality of their everyday lives (see also Miller and Meloy 2006).

To return to the question posed by Mooney for a moment that was quoted earlier; as she suggests, the values whereby men's violence to women is sustained in the face of public imperatives otherwise 'exist throughout the width and breadth of popular culture' (Mooney 2007: 169). For example, consider the vicarious pleasure gained by some young males in witnessing violence on a 'good night out' (Winlow and Hall 2006). Thus violence becomes 'folded into everyday life', an 'intertwining of the descent into the ordinary' in which 'ordinary people become scarred' (Das 2007); like when a woman living with violence judges that the risk of poverty and homelessness are worse than the violence she knows she will be subjected to (see also Genn 1988; Kirkwood 1993). This is her version of risk assessment and is not necessarily reflective of the violence of risk assessment tools or risk factors. This is the ordinary violence of everyday life. In fading out the voices of those who 'know otherwise', as Jordan in this volume suggests, this ordinariness of violence is rendered absent. So, to answer Mooney (2007), this is one way in which violence can be both public anathema and a private commonplace all at the same time. Thus unless we understand the 'lived reality' of, on the one hand, practitioners who are driven to take questions of gender and/or sexual violence seriously and, on the other hand, people's routine experiences of violence in their sociocultural context, we may forever be taking two steps forward and one step back and face the problems of the implementation gap. This last observation, however, leads us to consider processes that are arguably much deeper than the embrace of gender mainstreaming and an appreciation of its internal inconsistencies permits. This question raises the spectre of neo-liberalism and the relationship of second-wave feminism with it implied by Fraser's (2009) question.

## Feminism and the concession to neo-liberalism?

Fraser's (2009) question of the relationship between second-wave feminism and neo-liberalism is as uncomfortable as it is telling: is it possible that second-wave feminism has inadvertently contributed to the legitimation of neo-liberalism? As she observes, second-wave feminism coincided with the emergence of neo-liberalism and thrived under the conditions of privatisation, deregulation and imperatives for personal responsibility, and it is these conditions which, she suggests, facilitated the 'resignification' of feminist ideals. So, as neo-liberalism took a hold, the feminist challenge to the economy, in which women suffered from (mis)distribution, (mis)recognition and (mis)representation, became resignified as claims for justice centred on identity and difference. Neo-liberalism in its very essence can handle claims of difference and identity as simultaneously it struggles with claims rooted in class. In other words, under the conditions of neo-liberalism, feminist claims for recognition became separated from the feminist critique of capitalism. For example, the feminist challenge to the androcentric nature of the labour market, typified in the valorisation of waged work, has become revalorised as women entered the 'flexible' labour market and there emerged a 'new romance of female advancement and gender justice' (Fraser 2009: 110). Thus women at both the top and the bottom of the labour market are differently tied to the process of capitalist accumulation. The feminist desire to democratise state institutions to promote gender justice through citizen participation has become resignified as citizen empowerment in 'the big society' (in contemporary UK politics) in which the state is considered to be increasingly redundant. Finally, whilst second-wave feminism had an ambivalent relationship with debates around the nation state, this has been resignified in what Fraser (2009) refers to as the ngo-ification of feminist politics well represented at the UN and elsewhere where indeed the pressure towards gender mainstreaming, as observed earlier, has been evident. As a result, and it is worth quoting Fraser (2009: 113) at length on this:

> ... this capitalism [neo-liberalism] would much prefer to confront claims for recognition over claims for redistribution, as it builds a new regime of accumulation on the corner stone of women's wage labour and seeks to disembed markets from social regulation in order to operate all the more freely on a global scale.

Thus second-wave feminism has become an unhappy bedfellow of neo-liberalism similar to the way in which both those of the far right and feminists would like to ban pornography; an alliance produced from very different motivations. In the context of criminal justice policy, Fraser's observations add significantly to Garland's (2001) analysis of a 'culture of control'. The adaptation to failure of the criminal justice system to solve the problem of crime, alongside the emergence of performance indicators under the guise of new managerialism, informs the specific institutional setting in which many of the policy initiatives introduced in the UK need to be understood: a particular manifestation of neo-liberalism.

Fraser (2009) takes this opportunity to suggest that now is the time to reconnect feminism with systemic rather than individual subordination. However, her socio-historical analysis raises some interesting questions for the dilemmas that this edited collection foregrounds. Has the 'progress' that has been made in the recognition of sexual violence merely been a product of a particular historical epoch? Are the tensions that are observed around that 'progress' a reflection of the resignification of feminist concerns to match with the demands of neo-liberalism? Or, might some of the changes that have occurred during this epoch be deeper and longer-lasting? Has there been any real transformation? We have yet perhaps to find out.

### Conclusion: the future – a crisis or a double movement?

As suggested above, for Fraser the 2008–10 crisis of neo-liberalism affords feminism the opportunity to reconnect with the question of women's systemic subordination. However, the likely success of such a strategy may well depend upon whether or not there has been any real institutional transformation as a result of the 'affinity' with neo-liberalism. To test this out would require a deep excavation of the extent to which the 'risk-crazed governance' observed by Carlen (2008) has taken root or is merely an 'imaginary' that suppresses one form of knowledge in favour of another (see Walklate 2008 on responses to violence against women on this point). However, it may be that what is at stake here is also how we view the role of politics under neo-liberal capitalism. As Fox-Piven (2010: 111) observes:

> Neoliberalism is of course still capitalism, but it is a new kind of capitalism, powered by a new logic. … In other words, neoliberalism means that politics and the State have become more important instruments in the age-old capitalist project of class domination. … In sum, neoliberalism is a new *political* project to increase capitalist power and wealth. (our emphasis)

Whilst the extent to which this neo-liberal project has informed institutional pre-occupations globally (see for example O'Malley 2002) – as some of the contributions in this book illustrate – can be debated, it is nonetheless a moot point as to the extent to which politics will afford the space for the reconstitution of the feminist project along the lines suggested by Fraser. In the UK, Walklate's (2008) analysis implies that this is unlikely and as Jordan's chapter suggests, the struggle never ceases. As Polanyi (1957, 2001) argues, the retreat and advance of market capitalism shifts in the face of resistance to protect people and society from its worst excesses; and that includes the bankers! This is his concept of a double movement and it is a concept that may be of value in understanding the ever-present contradictory messages that surround debates and policy responses to sexual violence.

As austerity measures 'bite' differently in different economic contexts, it will be interesting to see what remains as important on national policy agendas and what slips down the hierarchy. In the UK, for example, it is already possible to see that there are some gains and losses. Rape Crisis, for example, have been assured a appropriate level of funding to extend their services by the current Home Secretary but the Women's National Commission is to be disbanded. At the same time police forces are facing significant funding shortfalls. What activities they are likely to reduce their involvement in as a result has yet to be evidenced, but responding to violence against women may well feature. On the other hand, the Minister for Justice has already made some telling interventions on both the expense of imprisonment and the appropriateness of its use. In this context it could be that the community alternatives proposed by the Corston Report on women, offending and vulnerability might be taken on board – not, of course, driven by the ethos of holism that featured so strongly in Corston, but driven by cost-effectiveness. This may be an unintended consequence of the present financial crisis, of that there is no doubt, and there will be others. However, transformation, as a model of equality, seems as remote now as when Elizabeth Wilson wrote her seminal book on violence against women published in 1983. The double movement of the capitalist process requires mechanisms for its continued viability and institutional policy responses form one of those mechanisms;

policy responses in which ensuring the wider engagement of the political community is crucial (Jessop 2002). However, these processes are never always one-sided. Institutions and individuals constantly interact with one another, always affording the social conditions for change. There have been improvements in levels of satisfaction with the police. There has been a recognition of the wider economic and social impact of sexual violence on society. We have markedly improved ways of assessing the nature and extent of sexual violence, who does what to whom, both nationally and internationally. We have suggested ways to close the implementation gap. As Liz Kelly observes in the Preface, the demand for more meaningful conceptual maps remains. Consequently the struggle for change and to change remains the same: *plus ça change, plus c'est la même chose*!

## References

Brown, J., Horvath, M., Kelly, L. and Westmarland, N. (2010) 'Connections and disconnections; assessing evidence, knowledge and practice in responses to rape'. http://www.equalities.gov.uk/search.aspx?terms=Brown+Horvath+kelly+Westmarland (accessed 13 November 2010).

Carlen, P. (2008) 'Imaginary penalities and risk-crazed governance', in P. Carlen (ed.) *Imaginary Penalities*. Cullompton: Willan Publishing.

Chesney-Lind, M. (2006) 'Patriarchy, crime and justice: feminist criminology in an era of backlash', *Feminist Criminology*, 1: 6–26.

Clarke, A., Moran-Ellis, J. and Sleney, J. (2002) *Attitudes to Date Rape and Relationship Rape: A Qualitative Study*. Sentencing Advisory Panel Research Report 2. Sentencing Advisory Panel.

Das, V. (2007) *Life and Words*. Berkeley: University of California Press.

Dempsey, M.M. (2007) 'Towards a feminist state: what does "effective" prosecution of domestic violence mean?', *The Modern Law Review*, 70(6): 908–35

Douglas, M. (1990) 'Risk as a forensic resource', *Daedalus*, 119(4): 1–16.

Elias, N. (1994) *The Civilising Process*. London: Blackwell.

Estrich, S. (1987) *Real Rape; How the Legal System Victimises Women who Say No*. Boston: Harvard University Press.

Fox-Piven, F. (2010) 'A response to Wacquant', *Theoretical Criminology*, 14(1): 111–16.

Fraser, N. (2009) 'Feminism, capitalism and the cunning of history', *New Left Review*, 56.

Garland, D. (2001) *The Culture of Control*. Oxford: Polity.

Giddens, A. (1991) *Modernity and Self Identity*. Oxford: Polity.

Genn, H. (1988) 'Multiple victimisation', in M. Maguire and J. Ponting (eds) *Victims of Crime: a New Deal?* Buckingham: Open University Press.

Harris, J. and Grace, S. (1999) *A Question of Evidence? Investigating and Prosecuting Rape in the 1990s*. London: Home Office.

HMCPSI (2007) *Without Consent*. London: HMCPSI.

HMCPSI and HMIC (2002) *A Report on the Joint Inspection into the Investigation and Prosecution of Cases involving Allegations of Rape*. London: HMCPSI and HMIC.

INSTRAW (2005) *The Review and Appraisal of the Beijing Platform for Action Critical Area D: Violence against Women*.

Jessop, B. (2002) *The Future of the Capitalist State*. Cambridge: Polity.

Kelly, L. (1988) *Surviving Sexual Violence*. Oxford: Polity.

Kelly, L. (2005) 'Inside Outsiders', *International Feminist Journal of Politics* 7(4): 471–95.

Kemshall, H. and Maguire, M. (2001) 'Public protection, partnership, and risk penality:

the multi-agency risk management of sexual and violent offenders', *Punishment and Society*, 3(2): 237–64.

Kirkwood, C. (1993) *Leaving Abusive Partners*. London: Sage.

Lewis, R. (2004) 'Making justice work: effective legal intervention for domestic violence', *British Journal of Criminology*, 44: 204–24.

Lewis, R. and Greene, J.R. (1978) 'Implementation evaluation; a future direction in project evaluation', *Journal of Criminal Justice*, 6: 167–76.

Miller, S.L. and Meloy, M.L. (2006) 'Women's use of force: voices of women arrested for domestic violence', *Violence Against Women*, 12: 89–115.

Mooney, J. (2007) 'Shadow values, shadow figures: real violence', *Critical Criminology*, 15: 159–70.

O'Malley, P. (2002) 'Globalising risk? Distinguishing styles of "neo-liberal" criminal justice in Australia and the USA', *Criminal Justice*, 2(2): 205–22.

O'Malley, P. (2006) 'Criminology and risk', in G. Mythen and S. Walklate (eds) *Beyond the Risk Society*. London: McGraw-Hill.

Piipsa, M. (2004) 'Violence against women as conveyed by surveys – the Finnish case', *Journal of Scandinavian Studies in Criminology and Crime Prevention*, 3: 172–93.

Polanyi, K. (1957/2001) *The Great Transformation*. Boston, Mass.: Beacon Press.

Rein, M. (1983) *From Policy to Practice*. London: Routledge.

Robinson, A. and Rowlands, J. (2009) 'Assessing and managing risk among different victims of domestic abuse: limits of a generic model of risk assessment', *Security Journal*, 22(3): 190–204.

Savage, S. (2003) 'Tackling tradition: reform and modernization of the British police', *Contemporary Politics*, 9: 171–84.

Shiner, M. (2010) 'Post Lawrence policing in England and Wales', *British Journal of Criminology*, 50: 935–53.

Smart, C. (1989) *Feminism and the Power of Law*. London: Routledge.

Stanko, E.A. (2007) 'From academia to policy making: changing police responses to violence against women', *Theoretical Criminology*, 11: 209–20.

Stern, V. (2010) The Stern Review http://www.equalities.gov.uk/PDF/Stern_Review_acc_FINAL.pdf (accessed 13 November 2010).

Walby, S. (2005) 'Gender mainstreaming: productive tensions in theory and practice', *Social Politics*, 12(3): 321–43, Fall.

Walby, S. (2009) *Globalization and Inequalities: Complexity and Contested Modernities*. London: Sage.

Walklate, S. (2008) 'What is to be done about violence against women?', *British Journal of Criminology*, 48(1): 39–54.

Weiss, K.G. (2010) 'Too ashamed to report: deconstructing the shame of sexual victimization', *Feminist Criminology*, 5(3): 286–310.

Winlow, S. and Hall, S. (2006) *Violent Night: Urban Leisure and Contemporary Culture*. London: Berg.

# Glossary of terms

**ACPO:** Association of Chief Police Officers, an umbrella organisation that comprises the membership of all chief police officers of the rank of Assistant Chief Constable, Deputy Chief Constable and Chief Constable of police forces throughout England and Wales.

**Attrition:** A contested term used to refer to the number of cases which 'fall out' of the criminal justice system at different stages in the process.

**CPS:** Crown Prosecution Service, being the organisation responsible for prosecuting cases in England and Wales.

**Culture of control:** A concept devised by Garland (2001) to capture the contemporary emphasis within UK and US criminal justice policy on a punitive response to offending behaviour and the wider processes that have been put in place to ensure that the responsibility for responding to and managing offending behaviour is widely dispersed between different organisations and wider society.

**Deserving victim:** This reflects the idea that some people are victims through no fault of their own and others are not; they have in some way or another contributed to what has happened to them and therefore 'deserve' the outcome. It is an idea that has its roots in the historical distinction between the 'deserving' and the 'undeserving' poor that informs much of the welfare system response in England and Wales.

**Gender mainstreaming:** A policy initiative designed to ensure that issues relating to gender feature in the development and implementation of policy not solely confined to sexual violence but covering all policy domains.

**Hegemonic masculinity:** Ideological and practical processes that endorse men as being the dominant sex in gender relations.

**Heteropatriarchy:** A term used not only to delineate the nature of male power but also to capture the heterosexual assumptions underpinning that power.

**HMIC:** Her Majesty's Inspectorate of Constabulary, the body having oversight of the police in England and Wales to ensure their efficiency and effectiveness.

**Homophobia:** A fear of homosexuality.

**IDVA:** Independent domestic violence adviser.

**Implementation gap:** The difference between the promise of policy and its actual practice.

**Incidence:** The number of events occurring in a specified time period.

**INSTRAW:** A United Nations unit whose full title is the International and Research Training Institute for the Advancement of Women.

**IPCC:** Independent Police Complaints Commission who investigate complaints against the police in England and Wales.

**Justice gap:** The difference between the number of people brought before the criminal justice system and the number of people receiving convictions as a result. Usually used in reference to cases of rape.

**LGB:** Lesbian, gay, bi-sexual.

**MARAC:** Multi-agency risk assessment conference.

**Neo-liberalism:** A term used to describe contemporary features of capitalism that value individualism and the free market.

**Paradox of power:** The assertion of power as a result of an individual's fear.

**Prevalence:** The number of events taking place over the course of an individual's lifetime.

**PTSD:** Post-traumatic stress disorder.

**Reasonable man:** A measure, usually used in the context of the law, to assess what might be considered to be appropriate or inappropriate behaviour, also sometimes referred to as the Clapham omnibus test.

**Reintegration:** Ways of thinking about managing offenders that ensures that they can be accepted back into their community.

**Risk assessment:** Ways of measuring the likelihood of things happening to people, usually linked to what has happened previously.

**SANE:** Sexual assault nurse examiner.

**SARC:** Sexual assault referral centre.

**SDVC:** Specialist domestic violence court.

**Sexual murder:** A term used most often in the context of serial killing, to highlight the underlying sexual motivation of the offender.

**Sexual violence:** Any physical or verbal act that is sexual in intent and content directed towards another person.

**Silencing:** A process whereby some voices are heard and others are not.

**SOIT:** Sexual offences investigative training applied to police officers.

**STO:** Specially trained (police) officer normally skilled to deal with sexual assault cases in particular.

**Survivor:** The term favoured by the feminist movement to capture the ways in which women routinely and actively resist the oppression they experience on a day-to-day basis. Historically put in opposition to the concept of victim though contemporarily there is greater awareness that the process of moving from being a victim to a survivor can be quite complex on an individual level that is not necessarily achieved by everyone. However, this is still an important term for political purposes.

**Victim blaming:** Assigning responsibility to the victim for events that have happened to them. Connected to notions of the deserving and undeserving victim.

**WCU:** Witness Care Unit associated with the care of vulnerable witnesses through the trial process.

# Index